GIF Animation Studio
Animating Your Web Site

GIF Animation Studio

Animating Your Web Site

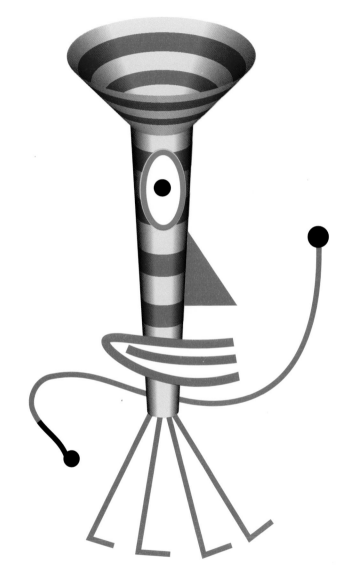

Richard Koman

Web Review Studio Series

GIF Animation Studio: Animating Your Web Site
Second Edition
By Richard Koman

Published by Songline Studios, Inc. and O'Reilly & Associates, Inc. 101 Morris Street, Sebastopol, CA 95472

Printing History: October 1996: First Edition
March 1997: Second Edition

Cover Illustration by John Hersey

Book Design by Bob Schmitt

Web Review and Web Review Studio are trademarks of Songline Studios, Inc.

Many of the designations used by manufacturers and sellers to distinguish their products are claimed as trademarks. Where Songline Studios, Inc. was aware of a trademark, the designations have been appropriately capitalized. Use of a term in this book should not be regarded as affecting the validity of any trademark or service mark.

Specific copyright notices, restrictions and license agreements for software included on the CD-ROM accompanying this book are included on that CD-ROM. All of the specification documents and programs described in this book and provided by vendors for inclusion on the CD-ROM are subject to change without notice.

While every precaution has been taken in the preparation of this book, the publishers take no responsibility for errors or omissions, or for damages resulting from the use of information in the book or the CD-ROM.

This book is printed on acid-free paper with 50% recycled content, 25% post-consumer waste. The publishers are committed to using paper with the highest recycled content available consistent with high quality.

ISBN: 1-56592-230-1

Contents

Preface

From June 1995 to May 1996, I was the managing editor of a Web site called *Web Review*. It was published by Songline Studios, an affiliate company of O'Reilly & Associates, formed as part of the sale of the Global Network Navigator Web site to America Online.

We conceived of it as an online magazine (probably much as Michael Kinsley considers *Slate),* complete with spread designs, page turning and the usual combination of tidbits, columns and features. Although it received critical acclaim — including positive notices in *The Wall Street Journal* and *The New York Times* (the *Journal* even ran a front-page story following up on a story we broke) — the hits and the advertising money didn't exactly pour in.

We tweaked the formula in a number of different ways, but one thing that seemed to resonate with our readers was a how-to column that Bob Schmitt and I wrote called *Web Innovator.* We tried to explain simply and easily how to create Web pages that used some of the more complex additions to HTML and other formats. I wrote several articles on frames and client-side imagemaps. Bob, *Web Review*'s art director, wrote a great piece on converting colors from RGB to hexadecimal (the system that HTML uses). I also wrote a piece on GIF animation.

That these pieces were well-received said much, I think, about how complicated the Web has become. Once upon a time, HTML was just a handful of tags, and you really could learn all you needed to know in an afternoon. That's no longer the case, what with frames, tables, hexadecimal colors, JavaScript, the Netscape plug-in syntax, Java ... to say nothing of Microsoft's HTML extensions.

We divined that there was a sophisticated audience out there — experienced Web publishers, not neophytes — who were having trouble staying abreast of all the changes. We called this the "Web innovator" audience — people doing cutting edge work on the Web and most in need of staying adept at Web authoring.

The response we got on this column convinced us to start this line of Web books, the Web Review Studio Series, as a means of exploring how Web publishers are creating the latest generation of the Web.

About this book

We originally conceived this book as a kind of survey of all the available animation technologies out there: not only GIF animation but also Java, Shockwave and the multitude of Netscape plug-ins. But as I started scouring the Web I discovered a lot of really good work happening in GIF animation. Much of that work is presented on these pages. Designers, I discovered, were taking to GIF animation, and the Web was starting to move as a result.

Shockwave and Java are great but they're overkill if you just want some straight forward animation. With GIF animation, no special authoring software is required. No programming skills are required. What is required is something more — the ability to make quality images, to

Web Review
http://webreview.com/

Global Network Navigator
http://gnn.com/

Slate
http://www.slate.com/

design a Web page where animated and static images work together. GIF animation can make your Web site move, but only you can decide whether or not it *should* move; and if so, *how* it should move.

Looking at some of these professionally created GIF-animated sites, it became clear that there was enough for a book focused on GIF animation. Not only a book that explained the technical details of how to create animations, but one that also showed off what designers were doing with GIF animation. I also knew that we would focus not just on the individual animations but how they were integrated into Web pages as well.

My hope is that this book will provide enough know-how and sense of what's possible so that more people will go out and make compelling animated sites. If we do that, GIF animation will be accepted as a standard part of the Web; if not, it will be discarded as a gimmick.

About the series

Other books in this Web "studio" series will continue the philosophy and structure of *GIF Animation Studio*. Each book will give you the tools and know-how you need, and look at compelling real-world examples of the technology in question. *Shockwave Studio* by Bob Schmitt January 1997) will open the source code of several especially interesting Shockwave movies and explain exactly how the creators did what they did.

Upcoming books will cover Java, JavaScript, Web design, sound, 3D and other technologies that continue to make Web designers' lives more complex.

Our audience

If you're familiar with O'Reilly & Associates' books, you know that this book and series are something of a departure for this company. While O'Reilly has numerous books dealing with the stuff behind the scenes (CGI, Perl, Java, etc.), these are the first books dealing with the creative side of the Web. We think these books can speak to both the folks who create Web sites for a living and those creating sites with no prospect of getting paid. But first and foremost the audience is creative professionals — the people who know design and graphics but don't know all the ins and outs of the myriad Web technologies available these days.

About the CD

A CD-ROM for Mac and Windows is included with this book. It includes freeware and shareware programs for authoring GIF animations and demo versions of other useful programs, such as Adobe Photoshop. More importantly, it includes the actual animation files we discuss in the book, so you can see exactly what they are without having to go out on the Web. The animations are copyrighted by the respective artists and you may not re-use them in any public way (including the Web) without the express consent of the copyright owner.

Web updates

The problem with books, of course, is that they're almost out of date as soon as they're printed. New software comes out; new products are released; new Web sites use the technology in ways not mentioned in the book. That will certainly be the case with GIF animation. I'll provide updates on new developments in the world of GIF animation on the *Web Review* site, *http://www.webreview.com/books/gif/index.html*.

Text conventions

Throughout the book, ***Bold italic*** is used to highlight menu commands. Plain *italic* is used for options within dialog boxes.

Important note

Because of all the HTML code on this CD, it is not compatible with Windows 3.x. Most of the material on the CD can be accessed from *http://webreview.com/books/ gif/software.html.*

Also, directory names are slightly different for Mac and Windows. Mac users will find sample files in a folder called Animations. On Windows, that folder is called Files. For the sake of simplicity, we'll refer to Macintosh names throughout the book.

Acknowledgments

A special tip o' the keyboard goes to Songline Studios art director Bob Schmitt for his work in designing and producing this book. Bob knows a lot about computer graphics and the Web and his input and experiments were invaluable.

Thanks also to Shawn Connally, my copy editor, and Sheryl Avruch, whose group at O'Reilly provided proofreading and quality control for the book. And thanks to Dale Dougherty and Tim O'Reilly for providing the guidance and support to make this series happen.

Finally, I'd like to thank my family, my wife Amy and son Nathan.

1
GIF Animation and the Web

The face of the Web is changing. Take a look around. It's a far cry from the text-and-graphics medium it was a year or so ago. Today, the Web is moving, making sounds, constantly grabbing your attention, raising the noise level. GIF animation is a part of that process.

On one hand, it's an exciting, attention-grabbing, multimedia world, full of entertainment and interactivity.

On the other hand, what many people see is a Web littered with huge blank spaces surrounding puzzle pieces. That's the mark of content that requires some Netscape plug-in you don't have. To which you might say, "Yuk! Never mind!"

Or you might click away, visiting a Netscape page that points you to another vendor's page, which directs you to the plug-in download page, where you download (in Windows) a self-extracting archive, which creates a setup program that you run to install the actual software. Unfortunately, the setup program asks you *where* you want to install the software (***Netscape\Program\Plug-ins*** is usually the right answer). And if you've done all that correctly, you still need to note the URL you were trying to view, quit and restart Netscape, and re-enter the URL.

Compared to *that* process, li'l ol' GIF animations start to look pretty nice. If you're using Netscape Navigator 2.0 or higher, or Microsoft Internet Explorer 3.0, GIF animations just *work*. GIF animation has clearly established itself as a core part of the Web language. You see them not just on experimental or amateur pages, but on the sites of the most button-down outfits in existence. The Dole '96 page. AT&T. Microsoft. c|net. MSNBC. Honda.

There are so many positives about GIF animations that I just have to make a list.

Users need no special software. As I just noted, all they need is a browser that supports GIF animation.

Standard file format. GIF is *the* graphics format for online images. Every Internet and online service application supports some version of the GIF standard, so it should be relatively easy for them to support the animation part of the standard. And since the animation is a GIF file, programs that don't support animation will still display a static image (usually the first frame but sometimes the last frame), not a question mark or a puzzle piece.

Ease of creation. At least on the Macintosh there are several good programs for creating animated GIFs. Creating simple animations is rather easy with programs like GIFBuilder and GIFmation, although it's more difficult with available Windows software.

No server configurations. You don't have to configure your server software (or, worse, ask your ISP or system administrator to do it for you) to serve a new data type, as you do with plug-ins.

Streaming technology. Users don't have to wait for the entire animation to download before they see something as they do with technologies like Macromedia Shockwave for Director. As soon as each frame is done, it displays. Even though that makes for a somewhat choppy animation effect on slower connections, it satisfies the user's demand to know that something is happening.

Easy on servers. Unlike server-push animation — in which a bunch of images are placed in a directory on a server and the server sends one to the user, waits for a signal that the first image has been received, then sends down the next one, and so on — a GIF animation delivers exactly one hit to the server. The browser takes care of everything else.

Of course GIF animation isn't the be-all and end-all. It does have limitations.

No sound.

No interactivity. Nothing lights up when you move your mouse around the image. You can't click in the animation to make something happen. Actually there is something in the GIF spec that lets you pause an animation until the user gives some input (presumably a click) but Netscape and Internet Explorer don't support that function.

Hard-disk crunching. This was a problem with earlier versions of Netscape. Netscape stored the GIF in your disk cache and every time it looped, it had to call it off the disk. This appears to be much less of a problem in Netscape 3.0 and Internet Explorer 3.0.

The GIF story

GIF animation is a real grassroots Net story. Netscape implemented support for GIF animation but didn't tell anyone. Individuals investigating the GIF standard who discovered that Netscape had implemented GIF animation and put the word out about how to create GIF animations.

Andrew Leonard told the story in a February 1996 column in *Web Review (http://webreview.com/96/02/09/ tech/edge/index.html)*. Here's an excerpt:

> Last December, a guy in New York discovers a hitherto unknown way to create animations for Web pages. He posts the news to a

couple of newsgroups in the comp.www.infosystems.* hierarchy. Some discussion ensues.

In mid-January, the discussion catches the attention of a trolling bystander who happens to be the chief technical officer of a well-regarded, San Francisco-based Web production house. He checks out the hack, decides it's a marked improvement over how his company has previously been handling animations, and alerts his colleagues with an in-house email message, giving it his seal of approval.

One of the recipients of the message is a Unix specialist who has been irritated that there is as of yet no Shockwave implementation for Unix — so he can't see all the cool Shockwave animations currently sprouting about the Net. He re-posts his boss' alert to a closed Shockwave mailing list, letting everyone there know that there is an alternative.

A subscriber to that mailing list copies the message over to a topic devoted to Netscape in the Web conference of the online service The Well. A number of Web developers regularly check this topic for the latest news, and one such developer decides to act. Within 24 hours, he's incorporated the animation technology on his own personal Web page.

And that's how the VRML logo on Jim Race's VRML page suddenly came to life two weeks ago — a stunning example of the Net at its best. No PR blitzes, no press releases, no orchestration of hype whatsoever required. Just the Net in all its circuitous, word-of-digital-mouth glory — a case study of grassroots action in the information age.

Royal Frazier is the man who got the animated ball rolling in December. But real credit for the GIF animation breakthrough belongs to Heiner Wolf, a German programmer at the University of Ulm.

In February of 1995, Wolf and some colleagues were experimenting with a project aimed at putting a model railroad on the Web. A key goal, says Wolf via email, was finding a way to animate the pages.

"[We wanted] some method to overwrite images on pages by newer ones. You can imagine my surprise when we looked into the GIF89a specification from CompuServe. It contained all we needed. Multiple images, difference images, and infinite image sequences. We just had to encode a sequence of GIF subimages on the fly."

> "And that's how the VRML logo on Jim Race's VRML page suddenly came to life two weeks ago — a stunning example of the Net at its best. No PR blitzes, no press releases, no orchestration of hype whatsoever required. Just the Net in all its circuitous, word-of-digital-mouth glory — a case study of grassroots action in the information age. "

But back then, no available browser supported the full GIF specification. So Wolf, a regular attender of Web-related conferences, decided to get the word out.

"I told my GIF story in '95 anytime someone asked about inline animation," he says.

Finally, Netscape bit. Scott Furman, a programmer responsible for imaging-related code, told Wolf that he would make sure Netscape Navigator supported the full range of possibilities for GIF89a.

Netscape did not decide, however, to make the news public. So despite Wolf's efforts, the greater Net community still remained in the GIF animation dark. Enter Royal Frazier.

One night in December, while playing around with the shareware program GIF Construction Set, Frazier (independently of Wolf) discovered the animation possibilities built into the GIF89a spec. And when he peered at his creation through the lenses of a few popular browsers, he found that only Netscape 2.0b3 ran the animation.

Lucky for the Web. Because although there's no shortage of animation action on the Web right now — Shockwave, of course; a new arrival, Sizzler from Totally Hip software, which allows "streaming animation"; and good old Java, continuing to plod its way along — there are some good reasons to embrace GIF animations.

First, in a single stroke, GIF89a animations transform the old way of doing low tech animations, "server push," into a moribund technology — roadkill on the info highway. Frazier argues that Web server administrators are bound to prefer GIF89a animations over server-push animations.

With a server-push animation, the server is constantly pushing out new images to the client — creating a steady stream of data going back and forth that sucks energy away from other concurrent processes such as FTP downloads. With a GIF89a animation, all the relevant information is downloaded to the client right at the beginning, forcing the client to do all the work. The speed of the animation is then determined by the size of its individual GIFs and how many horses the client processor has working.

Second, anybody can do it. You don't need a $1,000 Director program from Macromedia to create the animation, or have the years of experience in C++ programming necessary to hack a

"[We wanted] some method to overwrite images on pages by newer ones. You can imagine my surprise when we looked into the GIF89a specification from CompuServe. It contained all we needed. Multiple images, difference images, and infinite image sequences. We just had to encode a sequence of GIF subimages on the fly."

decent Java applet. Jim Race created his VRML logo animation (borrowing the GIFs from digital artist and all-around tech god Kevin Hughes) in half an hour.

Third, no special software or configuration is necessary to see a GIF89a animation. No plug-ins required. All you need is a recent version of Netscape. So Web crawlers can expect to see GIF animations springing up everywhere, without having to lift a finger.

As the Web races toward commercialization and high tech, proprietary software formats, it's refreshing to see that the core grassroots energy of the Net still thrives. We can only wonder what's next?

The facts about GIFs

Before we jump into creating animations, there are a few concepts it's helpful to understand.

What makes them animated? GIF animation is a lot like film, or cel, animation. In a real animation studio, images are painted on clear plastic sheets called cels. Some images are backgrounds for the scene; most of the cels are of characters moving. When the animation is filmed, cels are overlayed so that background layers show through.

You can think of GIF animation in similar terms. The file contains a number of frames that are layered on top of each other. In simple animations, each frame is a complete scene. In more sophisticated animations, the first frame provides the background and subsequent frames just provide the changing image. This is similar to the way cel animation works.

A GIF animation consists of a number of images and a "control block" that specifies the length of delay before the next frame is displayed, as well as other attributes like transparency, palettes and so on.

GIFs use palettes. Every GIF file contains a palette of the available colors for the image (or all of the images) in the file. The palette defines what colors will show up in the image. It's not quite as simple as that, though, because there's a *global palette,* sort of a default palette that all images will use unless otherwise noted, and *local palettes,* which are the palettes for each individual image.

GIFs are 8-bit or less. The absolute maximum number of colors in a palette is 256 (8-bit), although they can have fewer colors, which reduces file size.

What about Unisys?

GIF uses a compression scheme called LZW (standing for Lempel-Ziv-Welch), which is patented by Unisys. Although the GIF format was developed by CompuServe and everyone thought for years that it was completely public domain, Unisys let it be known about two years ago that they own the patent on the compression scheme and that they would collect royalties from software programs that use it. You don't have to worry about paying the royalty just for creating GIF files. Only software developers have to pay the royalty.

Browser weirdness

As with most Web technologies, GIF animators have to be concerned with how the various Web browsers handle GIF animation. As we said, Netscape was the first browser to support GIF animation, but that doesn't mean they did it right. In fact, as we'll see in this book, there are a number of problems with Netscape's implementation. Microsoft's support for GIF animation in Internet Explorer 3.0 is much better than Netscape's, but it's still not without problems.

A vast majority of Web users utilize one of these two browsers, but there are still the online services' browsers to worry about. The nice thing about GIF animation files is that they're still GIF files and every browser knows how to do something with them. Some browsers display the first frame and some the last frame.

This can be a problem if your first frame can't stand by itself. If you're building a name letter by letter, for instance, it won't look very good to have just the first letter displayed. If you keep this in mind, you can design around these limitations — by briefly displaying a complete image as the first frame, for instance.

But as GIF animation catches fire across the Web, this is increasingly a non-issue. America Online users will soon have access to both Internet Explorer and Netscape, and between Netscape, Internet Explorer and AOL users you're reaching just about everyone.

Tools

In the next several chapters we'll cover many of the leading programs for creating and modifying GIF animations. There are a number of other programs that have some GIF animation capability. Where possible we've tried to include copies of those programs on the accompanying CD. Here's a list of the programs to which we refer in this book.

Major programs

GIFBuilder. Macintosh only. Detailed in Chapter 2, GIFBuilder by Yves Piguet is the dominant Macintosh program for GIF animation. It's freeware that's easy and intuitive to use and boasts some super features like frame optimization.

PhotoImpact GIF Animator. Windows only. Described in Chapter 3, PhotoImpact GIF Animator is an excellent program for assembling GIF animations, optimizing files, and creating animation effects.

GIFmation. Macintosh only. This is commercial software, documented in Chapter 4, from BoxTop Software. It features a more visual interface than GIFBuilder and sophisticated palette handling options. We worked from a beta version of the software. A release version was not ready for inclusion on the CD, but you can download a demo version of GIFmation from BoxTop's Web site at *http://www.boxtopsoft.com.*

Adobe Photoshop. Mac and Windows. Photoshop is the standard graphics program, at least on the Macintosh.

It's something of a can opener, since it supports many different graphics file formats. It features very sophisticated color handling, image editing and special effects capabilities. We discuss Photoshop for managing palettes in Chapter 5 and explore the use of Photoshop filters for creating animations in Chapter 12. Tryout versions of Photoshop for Mac and Windows are included on the CD.

Kai's Power Tools 3.0. Mac and Windows. This is a package of plug-ins for Photoshop and compatible programs. In this book we deal mostly with KPT's Texture Explorer, which algorithmically generates textures. Demo versions of KPT 3.0 for Windows and Mac are included on the CD-ROM.

Other GIF programs

Also included on the CD are some other programs for creating GIF animations. We don't document these in the book but you may find them to be useful tools.

WebPainter. Macintosh only. WebPainter from Totally Hip Software is a general image-editing program that creates GIF animations as well as several other formats. It has a whole bunch of 2D painting tools and various animation features like onion skinning, multiple cel editing and foreground/background drawing cels. It also includes several pre-designed animations. WebPainter supports PICS, QuickTime and GIF.

GifGifGif. Mac and Windows. Published by Pedagoguery Software, GifGifGif is a specialized program for creating an animation of screen activity. GifGifGif records all your screen activity — typing, pulling down menus, dragging icons, etc. — and builds a GIF animation. It's a great application for software instruction and demonstration.

VideoCraft GIF Animator. Windows only. Andover Technology has added support for GIF animation to their VideoCraft digital video program and come up with a powerful offering. The program does morphs and other video effects and lets you use alpha channel masks for transparency.

Cel Assembler. Windows 95/NT only. A new program from Gamani Productions, Cel Assembler lets you preview all frames in a single window, preview animations in real time, optimize files, and manage palettes. For more information, see *http://www.gamani.com/tools/*.

Other software

In the "studio" section of the book (the part where we profile Web sites) you'll see references to several other programs. These are all commercial software products. We don't have demo versions of these programs on the CD but you may be interested in them for your own work.

DeBabelizer. Macintosh only. From Equilibrium Software, DeBabelizer Toolbox combines graphics processing, palette optimization and file translation in one program. It translates between over 70 bit-mapped graphics, animation and digital video formats, including DOS/Windows, Amiga, Sun, X Windows, Alias, Electric Image, SoftImage formats and others.

Several of the artists we profile say they used DeBabelizer to convert a QuickTime movie to a GIF file, for example. Equilibrium has created a free "Web version" of the product called DeBabelizer Lite Limited Edition for the Web. This version of the program lets you read and write BMP, GIF, PICT and TIFF files. This version doesn't support interlacing or transparency.

The free version of Debabelizer is available from *http://www.equilibrium.com/SoftwareDownload.html*. General information is available at *http://www. equilibrium.com/ProdInfo.html.*

Adobe After Effects. Macintosh only. Erik Josowitz used After Effects to composite the images for his animations for the *RECYCLED, RE-SEEN* exhibit (Chapter 9). After Effects is a tool for creating composites, 2D

animations and special effects. For more information see
http://www. adobe.com/prodindex/aftereffects/.

Elastic Reality. Macintosh, Windows NT and SGI
workstations. Peter Merholz used Elastic Reality in the
creation of his type animation for Voyager's site, described
in Chapter 10. Elastic Reality is a special effects system
combining warping and morphing technology with 2D and
3D animation, color correction, matte generation and
compositing tools. For more information see
http://www.avid.com/products/effects/er/index.html.

Adobe Illustrator. Macintosh (version 6.0), Windows
(version 4.1) and SGI workstations. A high-quality vector-
based drawing program, Illustrator is a great tool for
creating type effects and line art. Thomas Mueller used
Illustrator to set the type for the Jetscream animation
(Chapter 7). Illustrator 6.0 for the Mac rasterizes Illustrator
files (that is, it turns Illustrator's vector files into bitmap
files), which makes it easy to import them into Photoshop
and save them as GIF files. To make it even easier, Adobe
has released a GIF filter, so you can create GIF files directly
from Illustrator. The GIF filter is available from Adobe's site
at *http://www.adobe.com/prodindex/illustrator/main.html.*

The basics of GIF

In the next several chapters, we'll look at the technical
details of how to create GIF animations. Many of the
concepts are detailed in Chapter 2, *Getting Started with
GIFBuilder.* Even if you're using a PC, you should read
through the GIFBuilder chapter to gain an understanding of
how GIF animations work.

2

Getting Started with GIFBuilder

GIFBuilder 0.4
by Yves Piguet

Macintosh only.
Freeware.

On the CD:
Software/GIFBuilder

http:// iawww.
epfl.ch/ Staff/Yves.
Piguet/clip2gif-home/
GifBuilder.html

alk to most designers about GIF animation and they'll comment on how easy it was to create their first animation. That's because most of them used GIFBuilder, a freeware program for the Macintosh by Yves Piguet. Invariably they say something like "I just dragged my GIFs into GIFBuilder and — boom — it was done."

GIFBuilder is actually that simple, but it's also a lot more complex. Making animations that are as small as possible, that look good on both Windows and Macintosh, and that don't needlessly repeat bytes is slightly more complex than *drag-drop-you're done*.

Yves keeps working on the software, adding new features, removing bugs and so on. We've included the latest version (as of press time) of the software, version 0.4, on this book's CD. Since the 0.2 release that many people first used to create animations, Yves has added several new features including:

- The ability to import QuickTime movies, PICT files, and Adobe Premiere FilmStrip files.
- A frame optimization option that throws out parts of frames that have already been used.
- The ability to save individual frames as GIF files.

13

Raw materials

GIFBuilder 0.4 lets you import not only GIF files as individual frames, but also PICT, Photoshop 2.5 and 3.0, QuickTime movies, PICS files (created with Macromedia Director) and Adobe Premiere FilmStrip files. GIFBuilder also supports Photoshop 3.0 layers by importing each layer as a separate frame.

You can also convert QuickTime, PICS and FilmStrip files to GIF format without opening them by selecting *File/Convert* and choosing the file to convert. When you do this, current options are used, all frames are saved, and no file optimization (see *Optimizing your animation* later in this chapter) occurs.

First steps

Here's an incredibly simple animation used by illustrator John Hersey on his home page. This example shows the basics of creating an animation. There are only three frames to the whole animation, shown above.

The baby face belongs to John's son Cole, now $2\frac{1}{2}$ years old. "It's the perfect image for me because I feel like a kid most of the time anyway," says Hersey.

As you can see from the images above, the animation simply builds a series of concentric circles around the baby's face and loops forever.

When you start up GIFBuilder, the program opens a window called *Frames,* which is where all the animation work occurs, and a frame called *Animation,* which shows the image for each frame as you select it.

You import pictures simply by dragging them from your desktop (if your Mac supports drag-and-drop) to the Frames window. Or you can choose *File/Add Frame* to add frames one at a time. Drag-and-drop is standard in System 7.5 and makes life a lot easier when you're dealing with an animation of dozens of frames.

It's good practice to put all your images for an animation into their own folder and to name the files alphanumerically, which is how they are loaded as frames in GIFBuilder. Let's say the files are named *baby1.gif, baby2.gif* and *baby3.gif.* When we drag them over to GIFBuilder the images will already be in the correct order.

GIF Animation Studio

File Edit Options Animation Window							? ⬚

Frames	coolesignal.gif

3 frames	Length: 0.30 s	Size: 144x137	Loop: forever	1/3

Name	Size	Position	Disp.	Delay	Transp.
Frame 1	144x137	(0;0)	N	10	-
Frame 2	144x137	(0;0)	N	10	-
Frame 3	144x137	(0;0)	N	10	-

Figure 2-1. The Frames window is the primary interface. The Animation window displays the image for selected frames.

If you want to rearrange the order of images, simply select the filename and drag it to the desired position in the list.

Figure 2-1 shows what the Frames window looks like when we import John's three images.

If you just want to accept the default settings, select *File/Save* to write the new GIF file. Select a location for the file, click OK, and you're done.

The next step is to create the HTML that you'll put on your page. Select *Edit/Copy Image Tag.* This copies the IMG tag, with the correct HEIGHT and WIDTH tags, to the clipboard. You can then paste this line into your HTML editor, using the Macintosh Paste command (Command-V).

In the Frames window, you can flip through all of the possible options by double-clicking directly on the value for each frame. For example in Figure 2-1, all the frames display a dash under Transparency, which means none. Double-click on the dash to change it to the next possible setting. If you keep double-clicking you'll flip through all the possible settings for Transparency.

Figure 2-2. Set interframe delay by entering a number in the field or choose *as fast as possible*.

John Hersey's home page

http://www.hersey.com/

John Hersey, based in Marin County, CA, has created designs and illustrations for Swatch, *Wired,* Absolut, IBM, Apple, Adobe Systems, Microsoft, the *New York Times, LA Times, The Washington Post* and several national news magazines. He designed a Swatch watch (1996), *Wired's* Scenarios cover (1995), the Graphic Artists' Guild Pricing and Ethical Guidelines Handbook cover (1994), and a poster for the New Pop Exhibition at Museo Fortuny in Venice (1995). In addition, he's been profiled in *Communication Arts, Print, Step by Step, Portfolio* (Japan), and *The Face* (England) magazines. A digital portfolio is available on his constantly changing Web site.

Of course if you're not serving the GIF from the same directory as the HTML file, you may have to edit the HTML to reflect this.

Now just put the file on your server and you're serving the animation. There's no need to serve the component GIFs; all the images are contained in the new GIF file.

Changing the frame delay

The only change John made to these default settings was to change the interframe delay from the default of 10/100ths of a second to 20/100ths of a second.

To do this he selected Frame 1 in the Frames window and then selected **Options/Interframe Delay.** In the dialog box (Figure 2-2), he entered the number 20 and pressed OK. He did the same thing for Frame 2 and Frame 3.

The delay on Frame 1 gives a 20/100ths second delay between Frame 1 and Frame 2; the delay on Frame 2 puts a 20/100ths second delay between Frame 2 and Frame 3. But what about the delay on Frame 3? Since the animation loops, the delay on Frame 3 specifies the amount of time before Frame 1 reappears.

Since those are the only changes we're making, we can save the final GIF file. Just choose **File/Save As,** enter a filename (ideally ending with *.gif*) and click OK.

Changing the disposal method

This animation uses three full-frame images. The disposal method is *Unspecified,* which means that the entire frame will be replaced by the next frame. We'll discuss what the other disposal methods do later in this chapter. If you want to see the effects of changing the disposal method, select a frame and choose **Options/Disposal Method.** This brings up a pop-up menu with the four possible options: *Unspecified, Do Not Dispose, Restore to Background,* and *Restore to Previous.*

Understanding the Frames window

Let's look more closely at the Frames window. The Frames window provides a status report on the animation. A look at the top line of the Frames window tells you that the animation is three frames, it runs .3 seconds, the image size is 144 x 137, and it loops continuously.

Then there is information about each frame. The Frames window displays the following information about each image:

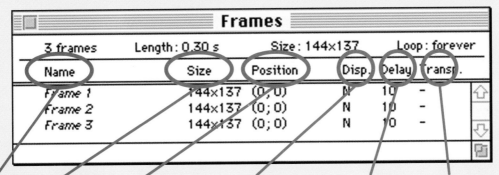

Frame name. The number of the frame in the animation.

Image size. The size of the image expressed as width by height. The unit is pixels. All frames don't necessarily have the same image size.

Position. The frame's position on an X,Y grid. In most animations, such as this one, all the frames are positioned at 0,0. In some animations, the first frame is used as a background and subsequent frames consist of smaller images containing only those pixels that are different from the original frame.

Disposal Method. This setting tells the GIF file what to do with previous frames. Should it get rid of each frame after it plays? Should it leave old frames? In standard animations, you'll use the *Unspecified* disposal method, which replaces each frame. In animations with transparency or optimized frames, you'll want to use other methods.

Delay. This refers to interframe delay — the amount of pause between frames. Delay is measured in 100ths of a second. The 10 you see here means that the delay is 10/100ths of a second.

Transparency. You can control the transparency of your animation by selecting the first pixel as the transparent color, or choosing white, black or none. In this example, none is selected.

Optimizing your animation

GIFBuilder 0.4 contains a fantastic feature that can dramatically reduce the size of your file. The command is **Options/Frame Optimization.** Just select this option before you write the file and chances are you'll see great savings in file size.

How much savings depends on the nature of the images. If you're repeating the same pixels in frame after frame, you could reduce file size by one-half or more, simply by choosing the frame optimization method.

Frame optimization works very well when you are simply adding more information to your first frame. Without frame optimization, you would have to isolate each part of the image in a separate frame and then position each frame by hand.

A good example of the power of frame optimization is a flashing lights animation Bob Schmitt and I put together for a tutorial on the *Web Review* Web site.

Figure 2-3 gives a decent representation of what happens in the animation. Basically we're creating a pattern of lights by lighting the two light bulbs on the end of an array and then lighting successive inner pairs of lights.

The first frame is the full array, with the two end bulbs lit. The second frame turns off the end lights and lights the next innermost lights. And so on until the last frame, when only the center bulb is lit.

Figure 2-4 shows the Frames window from GIFBuilder for this file, which weighs in at 14K. Every frame is the same size, 500 **x** 15, and is full-frame, positioned at 0,0. Note also that the disposal method is set to *Do Not Dispose.*

But take a look (Figure 2-5) at what happens when we

On the CD, in *Animations/ Samples/Chap2,* there are two files for the flashing lights animation — *blink1.gif* is not optimized; *blink2.gif* is optimized.

Check out the original article at *http://webreview.com/ 96/03/29/tag/index.html.*

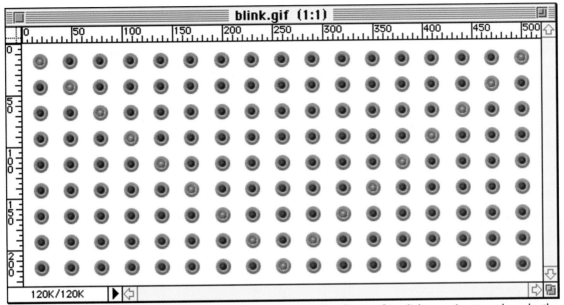

Figure 2-3. The individual images of the flashing lights animation. The effect is of two lights moving towards each other.

Frames					
9 frames	Length: 0.90 s	Size: 500x15		Loop: forever	
Name	Size	Position	Disp.	Delay	Transp.
Frame 1	500x15	(0; 0)	N	10	-
Frame 2	500x15	(0; 0)	N	10	-
Frame 3	500x15	(0; 0)	N	10	-
Frame 4	500x15	(0; 0)	N	10	-
Frame 5	500x15	(0; 0)	N	10	-
Frame 6	500x15	(0; 0)	N	10	-
Frame 7	500x15	(0; 0)	N	10	-
Frame 8	500x15	(0; 0)	N	10	-
Frame 9	500x15	(0; 0)	N	10	-

Figure 2-4. The Frames window for the unoptimized animation.

Frames					
9 frames	Length: 0.90 s	Size: 500x15		Loop: forever	
Name	Size	Position	Disp.	Delay	Transp.
Frame 1	500x15	(0; 0)	N	10	-
Frame 2	489x8	(5; 4)	N	10	-
Frame 3	429x8	(35; 4)	N	10	-
Frame 4	369x8	(65; 4)	N	10	-
Frame 5	308x8	(95; 4)	N	10	-
Frame 6	248x8	(125; 4)	N	10	-
Frame 7	188x8	(155; 4)	N	10	-
Frame 8	128x8	(185; 4)	N	10	-
Frame 9	68x8	(215; 4)	N	10	-

Figure 2-5. The Frames window for the optimized animation.

turn on frame optimization *(Options/Frame Optimization)* and save a new file.

All the settings for Frame 1 remain the same, but look at the rest of the frames. GIFBuilder has resized and repositioned all the subsequent frames so that they contain a rectangle with just the image that's changed from the previous frame.

Figure 2-6 shows Frame 1. It's full size, 500 x 15, and positioned at 0,0 — the top left corner.

In the second frame (Figure 2-7), GIFBuilder has trimmed the edges of the image away, so that just the lightbulbs remain. The image height has been reduced from 15 pixels to 8 and the width from 500 pixels to 489. Now take a look at the position for Frame 2 in the Frames window. The value is 5,4. That is, this image is positioned 5 pixels to the right (X axis) and 4 pixels down (Y axis). Those values are half of the size difference between frames.

The process continues with the next frame. In Frame 3 (Figure 2-8), we've trimmed away the entire far left and far right bulbs, since they're not needed anymore and we've trimmed the second lights down to the bulbs. The height of the image is still 8 pixels and that won't change in subsequent frames. The width, however, is now 429, a reduction of 60 pixels. And the position is now 35,4. We moved over 5 pixels in the second frame and now we're moving over 30 pixels (half the 60-pixel difference) for a total of 35.

The process continues that way, trimming about 60 pixels from the width of the graphic and moving the position over 30 pixels. Then we get to the last frame (Figure 2-9), in which only the center bulb is lit.

Although it took a while to explain what happened here, the work was all done by the program. And look at the results: Our 14K file is now only 6K!

If you check the file sizes on your Macintosh, you may see them all as 16K. The Mac Finder seems to round up file sizes in 16K increments. You can see the real file sizes by using Snitch and the Date & Size extensions. You can get these from:

ftp://mirror.apple.com/ mirrors/info-mac/cfg/ snitch-201.hqx

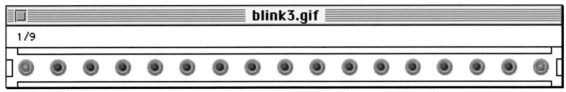

Figure 2-6. Frame 1 remains full size.

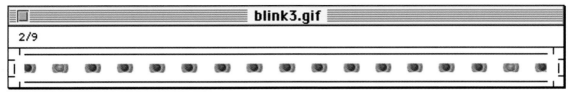

Figure 2-7. In Frame 2, the edges of the lights are no longer needed, so GIFBuilder removes them.

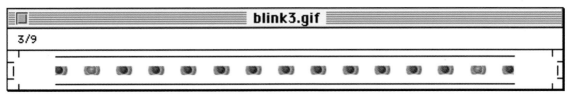

Figure 2-8. The optimization continues.

Figure 2-9. The final frame of the optimized animation.

Disposal methods

Next let's look at a somewhat mysterious option, the disposal method. This is set by highlighting one or all of the frames in the Frames window and choosing one of the options — *Do Not Dispose, Dispose to Background, Dispose to Previous* or *Unspecified*.

Picker problems

GIFBuilder uses Apple's standard HSL (hue-saturation-lightness) and RGB color pickers. Neither of these are terribly useful. The RGB color picker specifies colors in percentages, from 0 to 100%. But RGB is specified in values from 0 to 255 (there are 256 colors in 8 bits of data), so you can't simply plug in your true RGB numbers. Likewise Photoshop doesn't calculate HSL numbers (although it does HSB — hue-saturation-brightness — not the same thing). Essentially there's no precise way of selecting a color.

The workaround is to use white as the transparent color or to make sure the transparent color falls on the first pixel. If neither of those will work, you'll have to eyeball it.

The important thing to realize about disposal methods is that they are related to the transparency mode. That is, if your frames don't have transparency, you don't have to worry much about disposal methods. But if you are using transparency, then it's critical to set the right disposal mode.

What is disposal method? It is simply the answer to the question: What do you do with the previous frame? The choices are:

Unspecified. Use this option to replace one full-size, non-transparent frame with another.

Do Not Dispose. In this option, any pixels not covered up by the next frame continue to display. This is the setting used most often for optimized animations. In the flashing light animation, we wanted to keep the first frame displaying, so the subsequent optimized frames would just replace the part that we wanted to change. That's what *Do Not Dispose* does.

Restore to Background. The background color or background tile — rather than a previous frame — shows through transparent pixels. In the GIF specification, you can set a background color. In Netscape, it's the page's background color or background GIF that shows through.

Restore to Previous. Restores to the state of a previous, undisposed frame. Figures 2-10 and 2-11 show the effect of this option. Figure 2-10 shows the three component frames of the animation. The first frame is a full-frame image of the letter A. For the second frame, we took just the top half of the letter and applied a Gaussian blur in Photoshop. For the third frame we took just the bottom half of the letter and applied Photoshop's Ripple filter.

The first frame is set to *Do Not Dispose,* while the other two frames are set to *Restore to Previous.* Figure 2-11 shows the effect of these settings. The second frame displays the blurred top of the letter, while the bottom of the normal A from the first frame is displayed on the bottom. The third frame displays the rippled bottom of the A with the normal A from Frame 1 showing through the top.

The thing to remember about *Restore to Previous* is that it's not necessarily the first frame of the animation that will be restored, but the last frame set to *Unspecified* or *Do Not Dispose.*

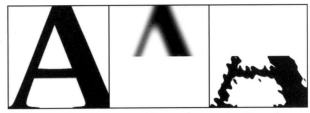

Figure 2-10. Three component frames for an animation using *Restore to Previous.*

And the most important fact is that Netscape doesn't correctly support *Restore to Previous.* It treats *Restore to Previous* as *Do Not Dispose,* so the last frame — not the last undisposed frame — shows through empty or transparent areas. Microsoft Internet Explorer 3.0 does handle *Restore to Previous* correctly.

Figure 2-11. Setting the first frame to *Do Not Dispose* and the subsequent frames to *Restore to Previous* produces the above images in Internet Explorer 3.0.

Transparency settings

Now let's look at transparency. The first thing to know is that although you can set transparency in a variety of programs — such as Adobe's GIF89a and BoxTop's PhotoGIF plug-ins for Photoshop — GIFBuilder discards these transparency settings. To make transparent animations, you must set transparency in GIFBuilder.

To do this, select one or all of your frames in the Frames window and choose **Options/Transparent Background.** This brings up another menu with the following options:

No. No transparency.

White. White pixels are transparent. (The RGB values for white are 255,255,255.)

Based on first pixel. The color of the "first pixel" of the animation — that is, the top left pixel, the one at coordinates 0,0 — is transparent. This is a handy option since often you'll have an image in the center and the four corners will be transparent.

Other. This option brings up a color picker so you can select a color for transparency.

Putting it all together

In the quest for the most efficient graphics, it makes sense to use transparency, optimization and disposal method together. Take a simple example: a spinning globe on a blue background.

Many designers will include the blue background as part of every frame and replace the entire image with each frame. But if you set the blue background to transparent *(Options/Transparency/Based on First Pixel)* and set disposal method to *Revert to Background,* you'll reduce the file size of each frame and improve the performance of the animation.

Since Web browsers use the background color of the page for the *Revert to Background,* you can set the background of the animation using the *BGCOLOR* tag. This has the advantage of divorcing the animation's background from the GIF file. If you decide you want a yellow background on your page, the animation's background changes automatically.

But *Revert to Background* isn't always the right answer. If you've optimized your animation, *Revert to Background* would only display each optimized image surrounded by

Background color is set with the BODY BGCOLOR tag. The color is specified with a hexadecimal value. The hex color system is explained in Chapter 5.

To tile an image in the background, use BODY BACKGROUND="tile.gif". You can't tile animations. If you try, Netscape won't display anything in the background, while Internet Explorer will display the first frame.

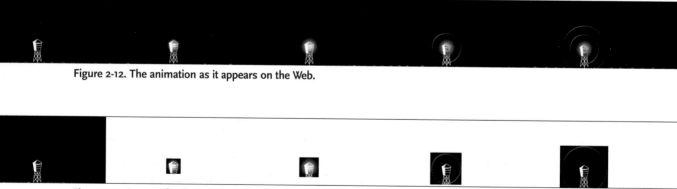

Figure 2-12. The animation as it appears on the Web.

Figure 2-13. Images for the tower animation after applying GIFBuilder's *Optimization* option.

GIF Animation Studio

SiteSpecific is a Web design and marketing agency in New York.

http://www.sitespecific.com

the background color. In this case, *Do Not Dispose* is the right choice.

Let's look at an example that puts all of these concepts together. Figure 2-14 shows a page from the SiteSpecific site.

Let's look at the tower animation in depth. SiteSpecific actually put this animation up as a full-frame animation without transparency or optimization. Optimizing the animation in GIFBuilder reduced file size from 20K to 16K. The full images are shown in Figure 2-12 and the optimized images are shown in Figure 2-13.

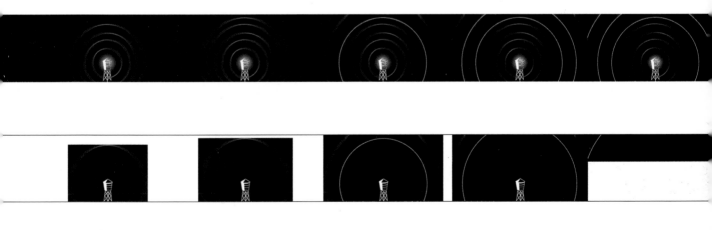

Figure 2-14. SiteSpecific's "latest" page combines several GIF animations to make a dynamic page. The earth, the tower, and the text are all separate animations. The page is at *http://www.sitespecific. com/Latest/*

Frames					
11 frames	Length: 1.75 s		Size: 350x168		Loop: forever
Name	Size	Position	Disp.	Delay	Transp.
Frame 1	350x168	(0; 0)	N	60	1
Frame 2	37x38	(156; 101)	N	5	1
Frame 3	49x49	(150; 95)	N	10	1
Frame 4	79x79	(134; 80)	N	15	1
Frame 5	123x108	(113; 60)	N	15	1
Frame 6	159x125	(95; 43)	N	15	1
Frame 7	202x145	(73; 23)	N	15	1
Frame 8	240x161	(54; 7)	N	15	1
Frame 9	306x168	(21; 0)	N	10	1
Frame 10	350x168	(0; 0)	N	10	1
Frame 11	350x66	(0; 0)	N	5	1

Figure 2-15. GIFBuilder's *Frames* window for the optimized animation.

With the animation optimized, the disposal method needs to be set to *Do Not Dispose,* so underlying images continue to display. The transparency setting is *Based on First Pixel.* It's certainly possible to leave transparency off (since it does little to affect file size). If the background color is also used in the image, leave transparency off. In this case, however, there are clean divisions between black and white and transparency works fine. Figure 2-15 shows the Frames window for the optimized, transparent animation.

Other options

This section specifies most of the other commands in GIFBuilder's *Options* menu.

Interlaced

This is a toggle switch to set whether the GIF will be interlaced or non-interlaced. Interlacing involves the progressive rendering of images, rather than waiting for the entire image to be downloaded before display. When interlacing is on, the first frame will display progressively, with the image divided into lines — some of which will display at first, while others display later. Interlacing can affect either the entire animation or a single image.

While interlacing is somewhat helpful for static GIF images, it doesn't help much with animations since each frame is on screen for a short amount of time.

Colors

This option selects the palette you will use for the file. Every GIF image has a palette, a list of up to 256 colors that can be used in the image. The issue with palettes is simply which colors should be used so the image will look as good as possible no matter which computer system it's being viewed on.

The options under the **_Color_** menu are shown in Figure 2-16.

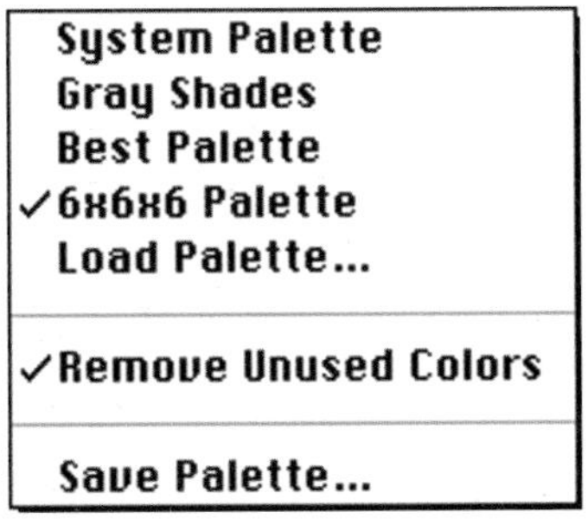

Before we get into the details here, let's just get this out front. Your best option is the *6x6x6 Palette,* otherwise known as the Netscape palette. This is the palette that Netscape uses in Windows. On the Mac, Netscape uses the Mac system palette. Thus if you confine yourself to the colors in the Netscape palette, you can't go wrong. Everyone in the world will see pretty much the same colors.

Figure 2-17 shows the Netscape palette. This 216-color palette is a subset of the Macintosh system palette, which is 256 colors (Figure 2-18). So it's not too much worse than designing with your system set to 8-bit color. But of course it is limiting — this palette contains virtually no grays and it also cuts out some of the darker reds and greens available on the Mac. So you may not be able to stick with the pure Netscape palette. In that case you should still keep the Netscape palette in mind, trying to deviate as little as possible to reduce dithering.

System Palette uses the standard 8-bit Macintosh system palette, shown in Figure 2-18.

Gray Shades uses 256 shades of gray, which are all that are required to show the full range of a grayscale image. Remember, though, that the Netscape palette contains very few grays, so a full-blown grayscale image won't look very good on Windows machines.

With **Best Palette,** GIFBuilder looks at the images and uses just the colors from the Mac system palette that you use in your image.

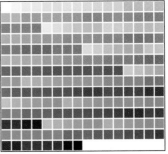

Figure 2-16. The Colors menu. Selecting *6x6x6 Palette* and *Remove Unused Colors* is usually your best option.

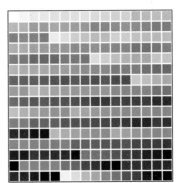

Figure 2-17. The 216-color Netscape palette.

Figure 2-18. The 256-color Mac System palette.

6x6x6 Palette. The Netscape palette, discussed above.

Load Palette lets you specify a palette file to use with the image. Use this option to load your custom palettes.

Remove Unused Colors. When this option is s elected, GIFBuilder removes unused colors from your palette, reducing file size.

Save Palette. Save the palette of your image.

Depth

You don't have to use all 8 bits if you don't need them. The *Depth* option lets you specify whether you want to limit the image to some number of bits less than 8. To do this select *System* or *Grayscale* palette from the *Colors* menu, then select *Bit Depth* from the *Depth* menu. For a black and white (not grayscale) image, select 1 bit.

It's probably better, however, to use the *6x6x6 Palette* and have GIFBuilder remove unused colors. The *6x6x6 Palette* requires the full 8 bits, so if you select that palette from the *Colors* menu you'll see the other bit depths grayed out.

Dithering

Dithering is a way to simulate intermediate color shades. It should be used with continuous-tone images. You should use the *6x6x6 Palette* with dithering so Windows doesn't try to dither the image a second time.

Image size

When *Minimum Size* is on, the size is calculated so that the animation's bottom right corner corresponds to the lowest righthand frame. Frames are always cropped to fit in the animation bounding box.

Background color

Regardless of what color you select in the background color option, Netscape and Internet Explorer display the background color or image you specify in your HTML

Bits	Colors
1	2
2	4
3	8
4	16
5	32
6	64
7	128
8	256

Reducing bit depth by 1 bit reduces the number of colors by half.

page. So this option doesn't affect the display of the GIF in Netscape, only in GIFBuilder itself (or any other program that properly implements the GIF spec).

The above-mentioned problem with the color pickers applies here as well.

Loop

In GIFBuilder, you can specify the number of times an animation loops — none, forever or any number you specify. In reality, Netscape doesn't recognize the fact that you've asked for five loops, or whatever. It only loops the animation or not. Internet Explorer 3.0, however, does recognize the number of loops you've specified.

One workaround to this problem is to build the looping right into the file by repeating the frame sequence a number of times. This of course increases the file size quite a bit and prolongs downloading.

Starting points

These settings are a good starting point for creating animations in GIFBuilder.

Color Palette: 6x6x6 (Netscape)

Interlacing: Off

Dithering: On for photographic images; Off for drawings with few colors

Image Size: Minimum Size

Background Color: Black

Looping: None or Forever

Transparency: Off

Disposal Method: Varies

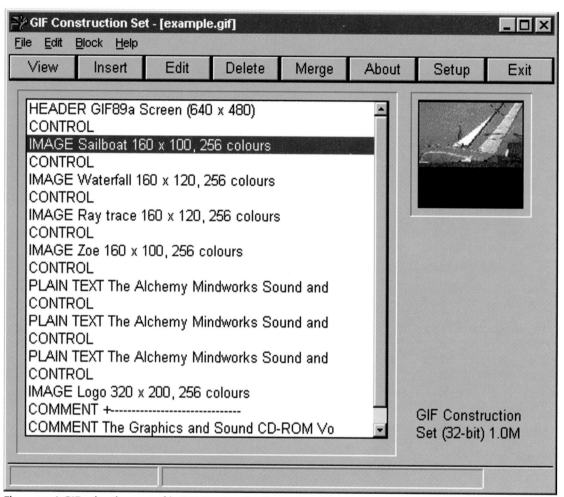

Figure 3-1. A GIF animation opened in GIF Construction Set.

3

Animating in Windows

GIF Construction Set is not included on the CD-ROM. It is available online from Alchemy Mindworks at *http://www.mindworkshop. com/alchemy/alchemy.html.*

Since the first edition of this book (published only a few months before this one!), Windows developers have jumped all over GIF animation. Back in September 1996, GIF Construction Set from Alchemy Mindworks was the only Windows program that let you create animated GIFs. As of this writing there were about half a dozen. And they're not just competing versions of the same basic program. Several of them offer very different and complementary capabilities.

In this chapter we'll discuss several of the best Window programs, all of which are included on the CD. Look for them in the *Programs/Software* folder. Appendix A has detailed installation information. (Windows 3.1 users, please note: The CD is not readable by Windows 3.1 computers.)

The programs we'll discuss in this chapter are:

- Photo Impact GIF Animator (Ulead Systems)
- Video Works GIF Animator (Andover Technology)
- WebPainter (Totally Hip)

If you skipped Chapter 2, I recommend you go back and at least skim it. Even though it discusses Mac software, it's worth reading to gain an understanding of the core GIF animation concepts.

PhotoImpact GIF Animator

PhotoImpact GIF Animator

30-day trial version
Windows 95/NT only $29.95

On the CD:
Programs/Software/Ulead
Ulead Systems Inc.
970 West 190th Street, Suite 520
Torrance, CA 90502
(310) 523-9393 x353 (Sales)
info@ulead.com
http://www.ulead.com

Ulead's GIF Animator 1.2 combines a very workable and attractive interface with strong special effects, compression and optimization. In fact I'd go so far as to say that no one trying to create animated GIFs on the PC should be without this program.

Key features of the program are:

- Super palette buildup.
- Special effects capabilities.
- Optimization.

Figure 3-1 shows the basic interface. At the bottom left, the *layer pane* consists of a list of frames in the animation. To the right, the *workspace* shows the contents of the selected frame. Above this is a toolbar for editing the attributes of each frame. And at the top is a standard application toolbar with button shortcuts for common operations.

When you start a new file, you'll see just one entry in the workspace, "Global information." When you select this line, the toolbar (shown in Figure 3-2) displays the global settings for the entire animation, including animation size, global palette, background color, and looping. In the

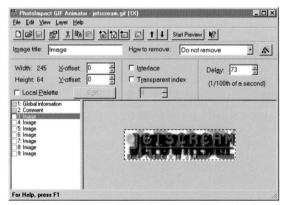

Figure 3-1. When you select a frame in PhotoImpact's layer pane, the frame image is displayed in the workspace area, while frame settings are displayed in a toolbar.

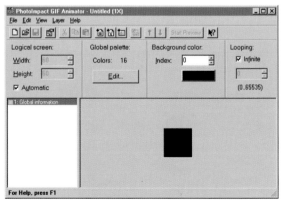

Figure 3-2. Global settings for a new animation are displayed in the toolbar when "Global information" is selected in the workspace.

toolbar, the *Logical Screen* area contains an *Automatic* checkbox. Checking this automatically sets the size of the animation to the size of the largest frame. If it's unchecked, you can enter a specific size in the width and height fields. Also notice that the global palette is set to 16 colors, the Windows system palette.

Building up a global palette

Let's look at what happens when you import the first image. The first file is a photo of a fish, which is composed mostly of blue hues. When you click on the *Add Images* button on the toolbar (or press the Insert key, or select the **Layers/Add Images** menu option), you'll see the *Build Up Global Palette From Image* dialog box shown in Figure 3-3. (If you don't get this dialog, make sure that *Show Preview Image Dialog Box* is checked in the *Image Layer* tab of the *Preferences* dialog.)

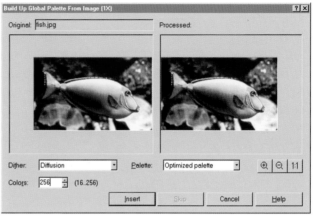

Figure 3-3. PhotoImpact GIF Animator can create a super palette as you add images to the animation.

On the left side of this dialog you see the original JPEG image. On the right side is the processed image. The various pop-up menus let you control dithering, palette and number of colors. Under *Dithering*, there are options for diffusion dithering, pattern dithering or no dithering. Always choose *diffusion.* The palette options are *optimized palette* (the best colors) or *safe palette* (the 216-color Netscape palette). Choose *optimized palette.*

The critical operation here is setting the number of colors to import into the palette. In choosing this number you'll have to balance such factors as the color ranges of the different images, the number of images and how many colors from subsequent images you'll be using. For instance, if you're creating a slide show out of photographs with very different color palettes, you'll want to limit the number of

Figure 3-4. Effect on quality of importing an image at 128 colors (left), 64 colors (center) and 32 colors (right).

colors you take from the first image, so that you'll have room to add colors from all your subsequent images.

In this example, we'll give the fish image enough colors for good quality but leave enough room in the palette for colors from other images. Change the number in the *Colors* area to 128. In Figure 3-3 you can see that the processed image is very close in quality to the original image. If you enlarge the images, you'll see that the processed image isn't actually as smooth as the original, but at normal magnification it's hard to see a difference. Actually, you can probably reduce the number of colors even more; at 100 colors the image is just starting to break up but is still acceptable. Figure 3-4 shows the results of processing the image with three different color settings.

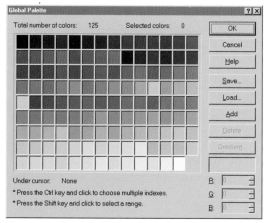

Figure 3-5. The global palette contains colors from the fish image.

When you've made your choices, click Insert and you'll return to the main window. Layer 2 holds the *fish.jpg* file we just imported. Highlighting that layer displays the image in the workspace and local attributes for the image in the toolbar above. Now click on the global information line to check the global settings again. You'll see that the global palette now has 125 colors. Click the *Edit* button to see the palette, shown in Figure 3-5.

Now we'd like to add our next image to the animation. But before we do that, let's go into the *Preferences* dialog and specify the number of colors to add from each subsequent image. Let's say that we only have three images for this animation. Since we used almost half of the available 256 colors for the first image, we want to limit the second and third image to 64 colors each. Here's the procedure:

- Select *File/Preferences* to open the dialog
- Click on the *General* tab
- Check the box that says "Automatically expand global palette if it has fewer than 256 colors"
- Enter the number 64 in the box labeled "Maximum number of colors to add for each new image."

Now let's try adding another, very different image. Figure 3-6 shows the *Color Remapping* dialog box that comes up when we import an image. This dialog doesn't have the option to specify the number of colors for the image. This is determined in the *Preferences* dialog, as discussed above.

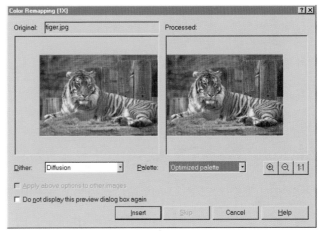

Figure 3-6. Inserting a new image brings up the *Color Remapping* dialog box.

Insert the image with its optimized palette and you'll see that the global palette now has 189 colors. Click the *Edit* button to view the new palette, and you'll see that we've made a super palette which contains colors from both the images – 125 from the fish image and 64 from the tiger.

You can keep adding images to the animation and as you do you'll continue to build a global palette. But when you hit 256 colors you won't be able to add any more colors to the palette. Images added after the palette has been filled will simply be mapped to the global palette. You can also save out your palettes as you import each image and load them later, which gives you a lot of control over the exact palettes you use.

Figure 3-7. The original frames of the Jetscream animation (top) are optimized within bounding boxes in GIFBuilder (center). PhotoImact GIF Animator's optimization includes just the changed pixels (bottom).

Optimization

In the last chapter, we discussed the concept of frame optimization. To recap, GIF animations don't need the entire image for every frame in the animation. You can set them to continue to display images from previous frames so subsequent frames only need to include the changed part of the image. The result is a substantially smaller file. GIFBuilder's Frame Optimization handles this automatically, but with a limitation: it defines the changed area within a rectangle.

PhotoImpact GIF Animator handles optimization much better. It actually calculates the exact pixels that have changed and includes only the changed pixels in the frame. For instance, take a look at the "Jetscream" animation from the PepsiMax site (see Chapter 7, *Combining Animations and Static Images*, for images and information about this site). Figure 3-7 shows the last two frames of the original animation and those frames optimized in GIFBuilder and PhotoImpact GIF Animator.

And the savings are substantial. The original 28K GIF is reduced to 25K in GIFBuilder but goes down to 21K with PhotoImpact's optimization scheme.

Special Effects

PhotoImpact also includes several special effects modules for creating scrolling banner animations, transition effects, rotating cube animations, and even color swapping animations. There isn't room to document these here, but you should find them fairly self-explanatory. The effects modules are:

- **Banner Effect.** Create rolling text animations, using any frame of your animation as the background.
- **Transition Effects.** Use built-in effects for smooth transitions from one image to another.
- **Color Animation**. Swap selected colors in an image.

- **Cube Effects.** Create a cool rotating cube effect with different images on the faces of the cube.

VideoCraft GIF Animator

VideoCraft GIF Animator from Andover Advanced Technology is a great example of how technology adapts to changing markets. Originally a morphing program for creating digital video, VideoCraft has been adapted to handle GIF animations. As such it is easily the most sophisticated video effects program capable of generating animated GIFs. In the future look for high-end effects programs like Adobe Premiere and Adobe AfterEffects to export to GIF as well.

Because support for GIF animation is an add-on, the interface for this program is quite different than most other GIF programs. As Figure 3-8 shows, the basic interface consists of a starting image and an ending image. You choose a transition effect, edit it to your preference, and then generate the animation file. Once you've created the animation you can open it in a standard GIF animation editor and fine-tune it.

Let's do a morph between two faces. In Figure 3-8 we have a starting image called oboe.jpg and an ending image called litlgrl.jpg. In the *Effects* area, the effect type is set to morph. Click on the *Edit* button or on the arrow between the image windows to bring up the Morph/Warp Editor, shown in Figure 3-9.

If you've done morphing before, you know that you have to indicate points that will be mapped from one image to another. The Morph/Warp Editor provides an easy interface for doing that. Click the top button to start creating points on the start image (oboe.jpg). As you click on the image to enter points, corresponding points will be created on the ending image.

VideoCraft GIF Animator

Windows only
30-day trial version
$30 to register

On the CD:
Programs/Software/Vidcraft/
Andover Advanced Technologies
532 Great Road
Acton, MA 01720, USA
(508) 635-5300
support@andatech.com
http://www.andatech.com

Figure 3-8. VideoCraft's *Project Editor* interface.

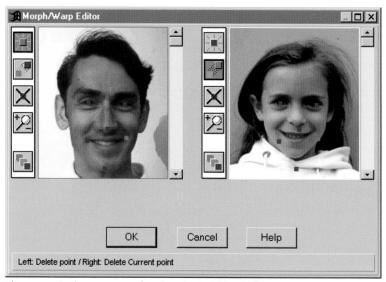

Figure 3-9. Setting up a morph animation in VideoCraft.

As you can see in Figure 3-9, the points don't exactly match up. For instance, inserting a point in the left corner of the man's mouth puts a corresponding point in the middle of the little girl's cheek. To move the points, select the second button, then click and drag the points into place. The third button deletes points and the fourth button magnifies the images. The bottom button lets you customize the colors used for different point types. When you've set the points, click *OK* to return to the *Project Editor* window.

The power of alpha channels

VideoCraft is fundamentally different than any other GIF animation program in that it supports masks and effects layers in alpha channels. If you're familiar with Adobe Photoshop or other high-end graphics programs, you're familiar with alpha channels. An alpha channel is a gray-scale image that masks the underlying image, much like a rubylith (or amberlith) overlay in the traditional graphics arts. The effect of an alpha channel depends on its contents.

In an alpha channel, black is opaque (the image is completely masked off), white is transparent (the image completely shows through) and grays are semi-transparent (the image shows through at varying levels of transparency depending on the shade of gray). Figure 3-10 shows the effect of masking an image with a simple alpha channel.

There are a lot of things you can do with alpha channels in VideoCraft. A simple example is to create a morph using masks of the starting and ending images to create a transparent GIF animation. After editing your morph points, click the *Options* button in the Project Editor. This brings up the dialog box you see in Figure 3-11. In the alpha mask area, select the file names for the starting image mask and the ending image mask and click *OK*. Now back in the Project Editor, select *GIF89a Animation* under *Output* and click on the Setup button. We'll discuss the *GIF Animation Setup* dialog in more depth shortly, but for now just check the *Transparent GIF* option. When you export the GIF file, the animation will be transparent where you masked off the background.

A more complex application of alpha channels is the use of effects layers. See that little box that says "123" down at the bottom of the Project Editor? That button lets you specify up to three layers of effects. If you've set an effect on layer 1, click the number 2 to generate a second effects layer and the number 3 for a third effects layer. Ed Lecuyer of Andatech notes: "You could animate the alpha channel with effects layers 1 and 2, then specify the animated alpha channel as a mask

Figure 3-10. An image is masked with an alpha channel to create a special effect. The image shows through the white part of the mask but is masked off by the black part of the mask.

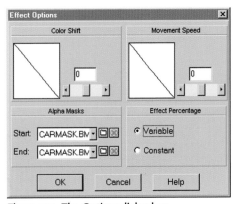

Figure 3-11. The *Options* dialog box.

in effect 3 over a static banner. Thus, the transparent area of the banner will be animated while the source image remains static!"

That's all a bit more complex than we have room for here, but the point is simple: VideoCraft's alpha channel support opens up a world of animation possibilities.

Exporting animations

When you're ready to create your animation, click on the movie camera icon to display the video panel. This panel lets you set the speed in frames per second, output option (GIF animation or separate GIF frames), and video quality (low, medium, or high). In addition, there's a *Setup* button that opens a dialog box (shown in Figure 3-12) for controlling the GIF file's global attributes.

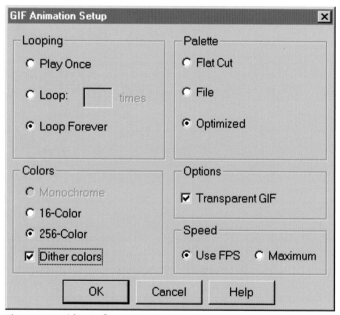

Figure 3-12. VideoCraft's *GIF Animation Setup* dialog box.

The GIF Animation Setup dialog lets you control looping, colors (you should choose 256 colors, dithered), palette, transparency, and speed. The palette options are:

- *Flat cut,* a standard 256-color palette with colors evenly distributed across the color spectrum. This option is definitely not recommended.

- *File,* which lets you load the palette of any GIF or BMP file. If you want to use the 216-color Netscape palette, choose this option and load the *Netscape.gif* file, which contains the Netscape palette.

- *Optimized* (the best 256 colors in the movie).

As discussed above, transparency is set by the alpha channel operations not by specifying a specific color as transparent. If you want your animation to use the alpha channel as a transparency mask, check the *Transparent GIF* option.

If you want the animation to play as fast as possible, check *Maximum* here. If you check *FPS* (frames per second), the speed is set by the FPS number you entered in the video panel.

Other effects

VideoCraft can do more than just morphing though. There are seven basic effect types and each of those have a large number of options. The effect types are:

- Colorize
- Morph
- Stylize
- Warp
- Distort
- Overlay
- Transition

For creating image-to-image transition effects, video special effects, morphing, and so on, VideoCraft GIF Animator is the best GIF animation tool we've seen. You'll want to hold on to a standard GIF editing package as well, so that you can go in and edit frames individually, apply frame optimization, and so on. Finally, remember that although high-end effects programs don't yet directly output GIF files, they do output AVI and QuickTime video, which can be imported into GIF editors.

WebPainter

Like VideoCraft, WebPainter from Totally Hip Software focuses on one aspect of animation but doesn't provide the same level of control over GIF files that straight GIF editors do. WebPainter shines as an animation package, with such features as onion-skinning, a registration point, separate background and cel layers, and built-in painting tools. WebPainter files are in a proprietary format; to work with GIF animations, you need to import and export them.

WebPainter

Windows 95/NT & Mac
30-day trial version
Full version $99.95

On the CD:
Programs/Software/WebPntr

Totally Hip Software Inc.
1224 Hamilton Street, Suite 301
Vancouver, BC
V6B 2S8 Canada
(604) 685-6525
info@totallyhip.com
http://www.totallyhip.com

Mac users will find the Mac version of the software on the CD in the *Software/WebPainter* folder.

Animating in WebPainter

Figure 3-13 shows the WebPainter interface with all of its many windows open. The important windows are the document window (labeled with the file name), the color tools window, the paint tools palette, and the cel strip. When you create a new document, you'll see the *Document Properties* dialog box, shown in Figure 3-14, which asks you to specify some general attributes of the animation.

In this dialog, you can specify whether your animation will use the 216-color Netscape palette or the Windows system palette (the color table option), the transparent color, the speed in frames per second, and the animation frame size. After entering your choices and clicking OK, a blank document window opens.

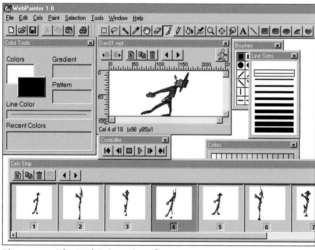

Figure 3-13. The WebPainter interface.

Using the paint tools, simply start drawing the first frame of your animation. WebPainter offers all of the usual painting and drawing tools, including pencil, paint brush, paint bucket, air brush, geometric shapes, etc. In the cel strip (activate it under the Tools menu if it's not already open), you'll see a single frame. To add more frames to your animation, click on the *New Cel* icon in the cel strip, or select **Cels/Add New Cel** to add several new frames.

To move to the next frame, click on its representation in the cel strip or click on the *Next Cel* button in the document window. Now here's a feature unique to WebPainter: Click on the *Onion-skin Previous* button in the document window and you'll see a shaded version of the

GIF Animation Studio

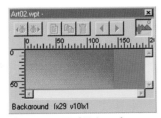

Document Properties ☒

Bit Depth: 8 Bits   Color Table: Custom Colors ▼

Transparent Color: [ ]   Frames per second: 15

Cel Size
Width: 100   Height: 100   Banner Sizes: 100 x 100 ▼

☐ Crop To Size

OK   Cancel

Figure 3-14. The *Document Properties* appears when you open a new document. Select *Paint/Document* to access it at any time.

image in the previous frame. This is a great tool for making sure that you're properly positioning incremental changes from frame to frame.

Another useful animation feature is the registration point. This is a point you can use to orient your cels; it doesn't appear when you export your animation. To set the reg point, select the tool from paint tool palette and click in the document window.

Following a technique used by traditional animators, WebPainter features separate background and cel layers. When animators at Disney or Warner Brothers create cartoons, they draw the background of a scene on its own

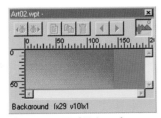

Figure 3-15. WebPainter lets you put the background image (left) and foreground animation (center) on separate layers.

layer and then lay over the cels for movements of the characters. (For a good description of the traditional animation process, check out Warner Bros! Animation 101 site at *http://www.wbanimation.com/cmp/ani_04if.htm*.)

In Web Painter, you can draw the background scene for your animation by clicking on the icon of the walking man in the main document window. This button toggles between the background layer and the cel layer. The background layer underlies all of the cel frames, while the cel frames contain just the foreground of the animation.

Figure 3-15 shows the separate background and cel layers of an animation, and what the animation looks like when the animations are put together. When outputting your GIF animation, you can choose to include or omit the background layer.

WebPainter works in a proprietary format, so you have to export your animation to GIF format. (WebPainter also exports individual GIF files, Sizzler sprites and AVI video files.) It's a bit difficult to control the properties of each individual frame in the *Export* dialog box (Figure 3-16) but all of the controls are there. One of the most important options in this dialog is *Changed Areas Only*, which performs the same function as the optimization command in PhotoImpact and GIFBuilder. One thing you won't find in this dialog box is the option for positioning a frame within the animation area. That's because WebPainter lets you position images directly in the document window.

The offset option you see here lets you crop every

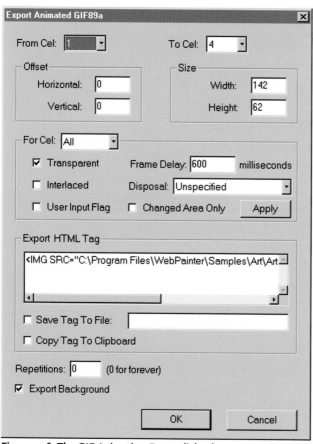

Figure 3-16. The GIF Animation *Export* dialog box.

frame in the animation file from the top left corner. It's a handy option if you tend to create multiple animation in one document. Just enter the coordinates for the point you want to be the top left corner. If you don't know the numbers, quit the export dialog, go back to the document window, and position the cursor at the point you want to crop. The X,Y coordinates for that point will be displayed in the document window's status bar.

Also notice the checkbox at the bottom labeled *Export Background*. If this is checked, your background layer will be included on each frame; if not, it won't be.

Still to be announced ...

The world of GIF animation is changing so quickly, there will no doubt be even more programs on the market before long. It's exciting to see so many different kinds of programs coming out for the Windows 95 platform, with so much more power than simply organizing static images into an animation file. Check the *GIF Animation Studio* Web site at *http://webreview.com/books/gif/* for the latest information on new tools.

4

Managing Palettes with GIFmation

GIFmation, another Mac-only program, offers a much more visual interface than GIFBuilder, something you see when you create your first animation. In this chapter, you'll learn how to use GIFmation to create animations and manage palettes.

Starting an animation

When you first create a new file, you see the dialog box shown in Figure 4-1. There are three areas to the dialog box:

Background Color. The *Background Color* section lets you set a background color for the file by moving RGB sliders. The color is previewed in the swatch to the right.

Palette. Every GIF animation must have a global palette, which can be used by all, one or several frames in the animation. By default, the *Global palette* checkbox is selected. Click on the *Palette Options* button to select the global palette to be used.

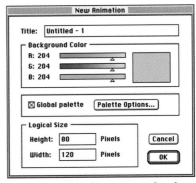

Figure 4-1. GIFmation's New Animation dialog box.

GIFmation

Macintosh only. $89
BoxTop Software, Inc.
302 Dr. Martin Luther
King, Jr. Drive
Starkville, MS 39759
1-800-257-6954 (ordering)
*http://www.
boxtopsoft.com.*

A release version of
GIFmation wasn't available
at press time, so we were
unable to include it on the
CD-ROM. A demo version
is expected to be available
from Boxtop's Web site.

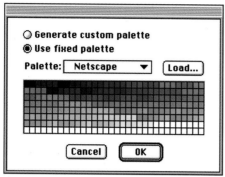

Figure 4-2. Specifying a global palette.

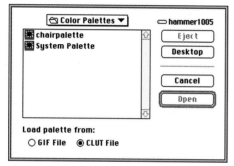

Figure 4-3. The Load palette dialog box.

Clicking on the *Palette Options* button brings up the dialog box shown in Figure 4-2.

The default setting is *Generate custom palette,* which is the same as Photoshop's adaptive palette (see Chapter 5). That is, the program creates the best possible palette based on the colors used in the image. *Use fixed palette* loads a pre-existing palette. The pop-up menu always lets you choose from the following palettes:

- Mac System Palette
- Grayscale
- Netscape Palette

Here we chose the Netscape palette (see the discussion in Chapter 5 if you're not sure why). If you want to use another palette, either one you've created in Photoshop or a palette from another image, click on the *Load* button. This brings up the dialog box shown in Figure 4-3. This box lets you select either a color palette file (known as a CLUT — for *color lookup table)* or another GIF file as the palette.

Logical Size. The *Logical Size* area (see Figure 4-1) sets the size of the animation itself, as opposed to the size of individual frames.

Once you've finally set all these global settings, your animation work space comes up, shown in Figure 4-4.

Importing images

Now we're ready to import some images into GIFmation. Select ***File/Import/Multiple*** and you'll see the dialog box shown in Figure 4-5.

Select files to import from the top list and click *Add* or *Add All* to add them to the list of files to be imported into the animation. In the version available when writing this book, there was no way to change the import order in this

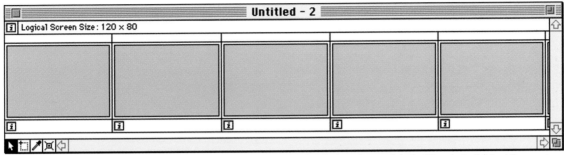

Figure 4-4. GIFmation's work space. Click the top *i* box to control global settings. Click the *i* box in individual frames to edit local settings.

dialog box; however, that's expected to change in the final version.

If your component images are GIFs, each image will be displayed in a frame in the animation strip, as shown in Figure 4-6.

Once you've loaded the frames, you can change the order by clicking in the bar above a frame and dragging it to your desired location. If you want to swap the positions of the first two frames, for instance, click in the bar above Frame 1 and drag it to the right. An arrow will appear as you pass over the left-hand edge of Frame 2. Keep going until an arrow appears above the right-hand edge; then release the mouse. Frame 1 and Frame 2 will switch positions.

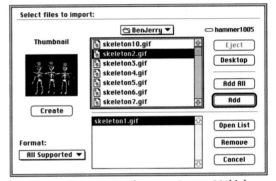

Figure 4-5. Import Multiple dialog box.

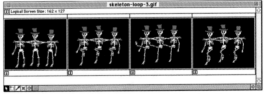

Figure 4-6. The dancing skeletons animation as displayed in GIFmation.

Importing full-color images

If you use full-color images, such as PICT or Photoshop's native format, you'll be asked to "quantize" the image. That is, the image needs to be converted from a full-color image with thousands or millions of colors to an indexed image with 256 colors or less. This is the equivalent of Photoshop's *Indexed Color* mode change, where you're asked how you want to index the image. Figure 4-7 shows the *Quantization* dialog box.

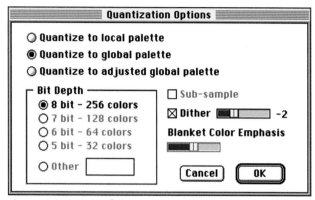

Figure 4-7. Importing full-color images brings up the *Quantization* dialog box.

The top three buttons in this dialog box let you choose how to index the image.

Quantize to local palette creates a local palette for the image.

Quantize to global palette uses the global palette (selected when you created the file or using the ***Project/Global Info*** menu option). If few or none of the colors in the image are in the global palette, GIFmation's quantizer will do its best to match colors. The results, however, could be unfortunate.

Quantize to adjusted global palette uses the global palette but adjusts it to better fit the image. After the image is added, GIFmation changes all of the other images using the global palette to adhere to this new global palette. This has several advantages when the frames of the image have widely varying color schemes.

Let's look at the effect of the adjusted global palette. Figure 4-8 shows two images with quite different color schemes and each image's adaptive palette. The problem is how to use both images in an animation while maintaining quality for both images. The simplest solution — and one that usually proves adequate — is to use the Netscape palette as the global palette. If the images' colors are far enough out of that palette's range, however, it may not be possible to maintain quality.

Why not just use each image's adaptive palette and let the browser figure out how to dither those colors to the Netscape palette? In most cases, that would provide decent results except for one little glitch. When you have images with local palettes, Netscape loads the local palette for the next image while the previous image is still displayed, effectively resulting in a palette swap and producing the gross results you see in Figure 4-9. This is not a problem with Internet Explorer.

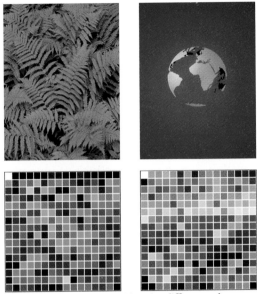

Figure 4-8. Two images with quite different color schemes as shown in the corresponding palettes. The problem is how to maintain quality for both images.

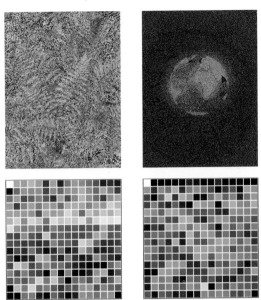

Figure 4-9. Netscape effectively swaps palettes when loading an image with a local palette, creating the unfortunate results shown here.

The adjusted global palette option offers a solution by creating a new global palette that mixes in colors from the image you're importing, as shown in Figure 4-10. While some of these colors won't be found in the Netscape palette, the advantage is that Netscape will just convert once from the adjusted global palette to the Netscape palette.

Bit Depth lets you choose how many colors the palette will have. If you use the Netscape palette, by definition the palette will have 8 bits.

You can choose to have GIFmation dither the image for better representation of continuous-tone images. If you click on the *Dither* checkbox, a slider bar lets you specify how much dithering to do. The default is –2,

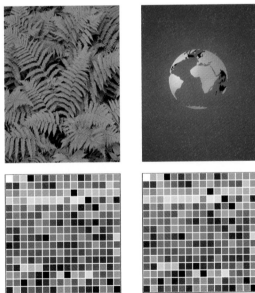

Figure 4-10. GIFmation's adjusted global palette changes the global palette to include colors from both images.

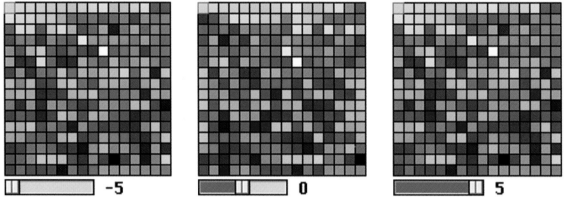

Figure 4-11. These three palettes show the effect of the Blanket Color Emphasis setting. It's hard to see much of a difference among them, but if you look closely you'll notice some more beige pixels in the left-hand palette (in which blanket emphasis is set to –5) than in the center or right-hand palettes. Given the subtlety of the effect, there doesn't seem to be much advantage to changing the default setting.

and works fine in most cases. Higher numbers do more dithering, lower numbers do less.

Blanket Color Emphasis is a techy term for a function that lets you reduce the number of colors used for large background areas and increase the number of colors used for detailed portions of the image. *Blanket Color Emphasis* is only enabled when the image is set to quantize to local palette. The effect is subtle, as shown in Figure 4-11.

The *Sub-Sample* box, which is grayed out in our screen shot in Figure 4-7 (it's enabled when quantization is set to local palette), lets the software sample the image without checking every pixel. There doesn't seem to be any noticeable loss of quality in using subsampling, and it is quite a bit faster.

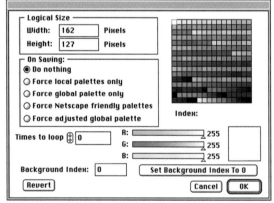

Figure 4-12. The *Global Settings* dialog box.

Changing global settings

To change the global settings for your animation, select **Project/Global Settings** or click on the *i* box in the top left of the window. Figure 4-12 shows the *Global Settings* dialog box.

There are a lot of elements in this dialog box, so we'll try to break it down into bite-size chunks.

Logical Size. The size of the full animation, not any single image, in pixels.

Global palette. The actual global palette is displayed in the upper right. This is the Mac system palette.

On Saving. This section consists of five possible options that will take effect when you save your project as a GIF file.

> **Do Nothing.** Naturally enough, this option leaves all the settings the way they are.

> **Force local palettes only.** If you select this option, every frame will use its local palette. In general this is not a good idea as (in Windows anyway), every local palette will be dithered to the Netscape palette. If you're working with images with dramatically different palettes, this means that some images will look rotten, while others will look fine.

> To make matters worse, a bug in Netscape causes a flash between frames as it loads each new local palette. GIFmation offers a fix to this problem, however, with the *Force Netscape friendly palettes* option detailed below.

> **Force global palette only.** All frames will use the global palette.

> **Force Netscape friendly palettes.** The reason you get the flashing effect when using local palettes in Netscape is that Netscape replaces the local palette for the next image while the current image is still displayed. "The results are a little more than hideous," notes Travis Anton of BoxTop Software, "in most cases making it impossible to reliably use normal local palettes."

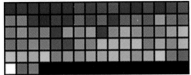

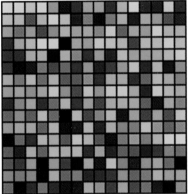

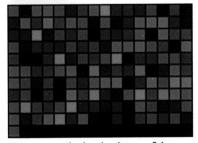

Figure 4-13. The local palettes of these images are dramatically different. Netscape will flash as it switches between the palettes.

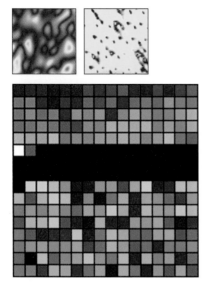

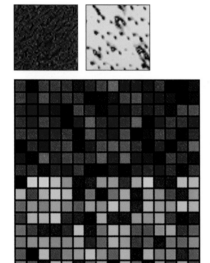

Figure 4-14. The Netscape friendly palettes combine palettes of two images into one, eliminating the flash effect.

This option gets around that problem by essentially creating mixed local palettes, with half the palette devoted to the current image and half devoted to the previous image.

What GIFmation does is condense the 256-color local palette for a given image down to 128 colors. Those are the colors that will actually be used on the image. The rest of the palette is used for the 128-color palette of the previous image. So when Netscape preloads the local palette for the next image, all those colors will still be loaded, and there will be no flash. A pretty clever little trick.

This is perhaps best understood by looking at the palettes this option generates.

We used the Texture Explorer from Kai's Power Tools (a Photoshop plug-in described in Chapter 8) to create three images with dramatically different color schemes. Figure 4-13 shows the images with their normal local palettes. In Figure 4-14, which shows the Netscape friendly palettes, you can clearly see how GIFmation combines the reduced palettes into one.

Travis adds: "Our trick lets you use up to 128-color local palettes with no nasty palette shifts and 128-color local palettes provide better overall image quality than a 256-color super palette divided among many images."

Force adjusted global palette. This creates the "super palette" that Travis refers to above. It's a two-pronged effect. First, all images using local palettes are assigned the global palette. Second, the global palette is altered so that colors from all frames are included. This will give better results than a straight global palette when frames have drastically different colors.

Times to loop. This setting controls the looping. 0 means the animation will play forever. In a browser that correctly implements the GIF spec, entering a number in this field dictates the number of times the animation plays. Putting 1 in the field means the animation plays once, 2 means it plays twice, and so on.

Figure 4-15. GIFmation's image editing tool set.

Netscape, however, fails to implement this feature, so animations loop forever, no matter what you enter in this field. Microsoft Internet Explorer 3.0 almost gets it right. You can set the number of times the animation plays, but if you ask for one loop, Internet Explorer will play it twice. if you ask for two loops, it plays three times, and so on.

Background color. The RGB sliders let you mix and set a background color for the animation. This is the GIF file's background color, not the HTML page's, which is what Netscape and Internet Explorer use.

Background index. This specifies a palette color as the background color for the animation. (Again, Netscape ignores this and simply uses the background of the HTML page.) The possible values are 0 to 255 for the 256 colors in a palette.

Changing local settings

There are two sets of controls for individual images. One set is in the toolbar in the animation strip. More controls are located under the *Image/Local Info* menu.

The tools

The four image editing tools, pictured in Figure 4-15, are located on the bottom right of the animation strip. The tools are (from left to right):

- Pointer
- Cropping tool
- Transparency dropper
- Defuzz tool

Figure 4-16. Clicking on a color with the dropper turns pixels of that color transparent.

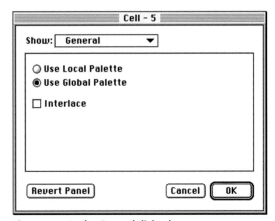

Figure 4-17. In the General dialog box, you can specify whether the image will use a local palette or global palette.

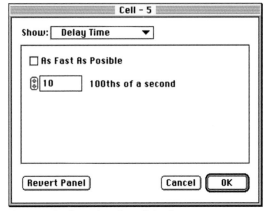

Figure 4-18. The Delay Time dialog box.

Pointer. With the pointer tool, you can click-and-drag images into position within the animation frame. To check the coordinates of the new position, use *Image/Alignment/To Coordinates.*

Cropping tool. With the cropping tool, you can cut away part of the image. This is handy for doing away with redundant image parts. To crop an image, select the cropping tool and click-and-drag to select the cropped area. Releasing the tool crops the image. Command-Z undoes the crop.

Transparency dropper. The transparency dropper makes it very easy to make one or more colors transparent. Just select the dropper and click on a color in the image. You'll see all pixels with that color turn gray. Figure 4-16 shows what happens when we click on a colored object. This example is taken from the Flavor Graveyard page of Ben & Jerry's Web site. You can view the page at *http://www. benjerry.com/graveyard/.*

To deselect the color, click in the area while pressing the *Option* key. To make an additional color transparent, click on the image while pressing the *Shift* key.

In Figure 4-16, notice that a pink fringe remains around the hats. If you look carefully at the left-hand image, you'll see that there are black pixels mixed in with the pink pixels at the edges of the hats.

Defuzz tool. You can use the defuzz tool to get rid of this fringe. You use it by running it along the pixels you want to make transparent and then releasing the mouse. It's easy to overdo it, though, and lose the shape of the object. So go in small increments and keep your fingers close to Command-Z, so you can undo work if you go too far. The defuzz tool is simply adding pixels to the transparent area, so you can also use it to make any unwanted area transparent.

Another solution to this problem is to use the dropper tool with the *Shift* key depressed. As mentioned above, this makes additional colors transparent.

The Local Image menu

To control settings for individual images, select a frame and click on the *i* icon at the bottom right of each frame, or choose *Image/Local Info.*

This dialog box is really four boxes in one. A pop-up menu lets you choose from:

- General
- Delay Time
- Disposal Method
- Local Palette

In the *General* dialog box, shown in Figure 4-17, you can specify whether the image will use the global palette or a local palette. There's also a checkbox to interlace the image (not advised in animation). The *Revert Panel* button reverts to the default settings: *global palette, no interlacing.*

The *Delay Time* dialog box, shown in Figure 4-18, lets you set the interframe delay or choose *As Fast As Possible.* The default is an interframe delay of 10/100ths of a second.

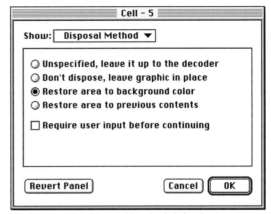

Figure 4-19. The Disposal Method dialog box.

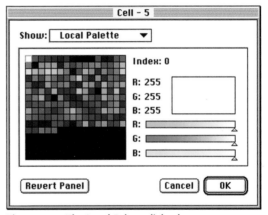

Figure 4-20. The Local Palette dialog box.

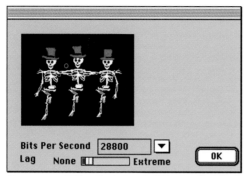

Figure 4-21. GIFmation's bandwidth simulator lets you see how quickly your animation will come down the line.

The *Disposal Method* dialog box, shown in Figure 4-19, is where you set the disposal method for the frame. The possible disposal methods are discussed in detail in Chapter 2.

The checkbox *Require user input before continuing* is irrelevant for the Web, since browsers do not support this feature. If it did work, it would pause the animation at this frame until the user clicked to continue.

The *Local Palette* dialog box, shown in Figure 4-20, displays the local palette for the selected frame and lets you edit it. To edit, select a color on the palette to see its RGB values. You can then mix a new color by moving the RGB sliders. The mixed color displays in the large swatch and in the selected cell of the palette.

The bandwidth simulator

One particularly nice feature of GIFmation is a preview that simulates performance at different bandwidths. To preview your animation, just select **Project/Preview.** Figure 4-21 shows the dialog box that appears.

Click on the pop-up menu to select different baud rates, from 9600 to T1. A slider bar also lets you simulate server load. If you know your site is heavily used, move the slider bar toward *Extreme.* If you have little traffic, you can leave the slider bar at *None.*

This previewing will tell you whether your animation's performance will be acceptable at lower bandwidths. For instance, you may know that many users hit your site at 14.4K. You'll want to make sure that the frames come down acceptably fast at that baud rate, but you may not care what it looks like at 9600.

Saving the file

Once everything's set the way you want it, just choose
File/Save or *File/Save As* and enter the filename in the
dialog box. Unlike GIFBuilder, GIFmation doesn't generate
your HTML code; you'll have to take the height and width
information from the top of the animation strip and enter
it by hand.

5

Palettes, Colors and Photoshop

Adobe Photoshop 3.0

Mac and Windows demo versions of Photoshop are included on the CD-ROM. You can do anything with these demo versions that you can do with the full versions except save and print your work. The software is located in the Software folder.

Adobe Systems Inc.
1585 Charleston Road
Mountain View, CA 94039
(800) 833-6687
http://www.adobe.com/

Even though it can't create GIF animations, Adobe Photoshop is the core tool for preparing images before importing them into your GIF editing program. Use Photoshop to create custom palettes, to dither colors, and to apply filters for animation effects. Photoshop is available on Mac, Windows and certain Unix platforms. A demo version (you can't save or print) is included on the CD for both Mac and Windows.

Creating GIFs in Photoshop

A GIF is a bitmap image with a pixel depth of 8 bits or less. GIFs use a color table, or palette, to specify which colors will be displayed. The more bits associated with a pixel, the greater the color possibilities for the image. The possible colors grow exponentially as bit depth is increased. Each bit has 2 possible values (on or off) and the number of possible colors is calculated by taking 2 to the power of the number of bits. That is, with a bit depth of 1 (2^1) there are two possible values — black or white. With 2 bits, there are 4 possible values (2^2). With 3 bits there are 8 possible values (2^3). All the way up to 8 bits (2^8), where there are 256 colors. The chart in Figure 5-1 shows the number of colors associated with the various pixel depths.

The basic issue in creating GIFs for the Web, whether static or animated, is getting images to look good in 256 colors on both Macs and Windows computers. In this section, we'll go through the steps of converting a 24-bit image to a GIF file suitable for use on the Web. Figure 5-2 shows the original image, a 24-bit PICT file.

To create a GIF in Photoshop, select **Mode/Indexed Color.** This brings up the dialog box shown in Figure 5-3. Now let's take a look at the options in the dialog box.

Resolution. This is where you choose the bit depth of the image. When the dialog box comes up, the resolution is already set, based on Photoshop's evaluation of the image. If your original image had more than 256 colors, the resolution will be set to 8 bits per pixel. At 8 bits per pixel your image will have 256 colors, the maximum number.

If your image contains 256 colors or fewer, a different bit depth will be selected. If the number of colors corresponds to a bit depth, that bit depth is selected. If there are an odd number of colors (or if there are exactly 256 colors), the *Other* option is selected and the exact number of colors is displayed in the accompanying field.

Palette. In this section, you choose the appropriate color palette for your image. The options are:

Bits	Colors
1	2
2	4
3	8
4	16
5	32
6	64
7	128
8	256

Figure 5-1. Bit depths and corresponding colors.

- **Exact.** Creates a palette consisting of only the colors in the image. (This option is unavailable unless *Other* is selected in the *Resolution* area.)
- **System.** Uses your platform's system palette.
- **Adaptive.** Creates a palette consisting of the actual colors used in the image.
- **Custom.** Opens a dialog box where you can load a custom palette.
- **Previous.** Uses the same palette as the last image.

Dither. In this section, you determine how Photoshop will dither the image. Dithering is the mixing of pixels to approximate colors not actually in the palette. The choices are *none, pattern* and *diffusion*. The best option is diffusion.

Figure 5-2. The original
24-bit image.

Figure 5-4. An 8-bit image with
adaptive palette and diffusion
dithering.

Ordinarily, the best setting is *Adaptive Palette, Diffusion Dithering.* Figure 5-4 shows the image created with those options.

It looks quite good, not quite as good as the 24-bit image, but not at all shabby. Actually, we can only say that it looks good in Photoshop and other GIF viewers. How it looks in Web browsers is quite a different story.

The Netscape palette

While image editing software only has to worry about one image at a time, Web pages routinely have multiple images on a single page. Of course they can't use more than one image's palette at the same time. So the browser has to pick a palette and force all the images into that one palette.

On a Macintosh in 8-bit mode, Netscape uses the Mac system palette. But Windows doesn't have a system

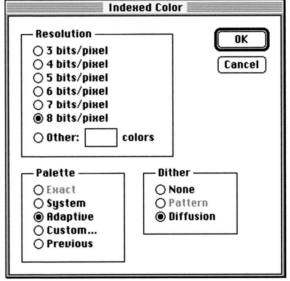

Figure 5-3. Photoshop
Indexed Color dialog box.

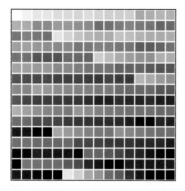

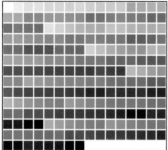

Figure 5-5. Netscape and Internet Explorer on the Mac use the Mac system palette (top). In Windows they use a 216-color version of the Mac system palette, known as the Netscape palette (bottom).

palette to speak of. In Windows, each application creates its own palette. Fortunately for Web designers, Netscape uses a truncated version of the Mac system palette for its Windows application palette, and Microsoft followed suit with Internet Explorer. The Windows palettes for both Netscape and Internet Explorer use the first 216 colors of the Mac system palette. The Mac and Windows palettes are shown in figure 5-5.

(Interestingly enough, Netscape does use the adaptive palette when displaying the GIF file itself; it's only when the image is placed in an HTML document that the Netscape palette takes over. But on the Mac, the Mac system palette is always in effect. Internet Explorer always uses the Netscape palette.)

What happens when an image with one palette is forced into the Netscape palette? The browser tries to accommodate the colors that aren't in the Netscape palette by dithering. So if you use an image that is dramatically different than the Netscape palette, you may suffer the slings and arrows of outrageous dithering.

To recap, when you put your image on the Web, it's being forced into the Netscape palette in Windows and the Mac palette on the Mac. Figure 5-6 shows what that beautiful still life looks like when displayed in a Windows Web browser.

The solution to this problem, is to reduce the amount of dithering that the browser performs by using the Netscape palette, or something close to it, from the beginning.

To load the Netscape palette:

1. Select *Custom* in the *Indexed Color* dialog box.
   This brings up the *Color Table* dialog box.

2. In the *Color Table* dialog box, select the *Load* button.

3. Find the Netscape Palette file in the **Samples/ Chapter5** folder.

4. Click *OK*.

Alternatively, you could save with the adaptive palette and load the Netscape palette in your GIF editor, but a high-end program like Photoshop will do a better job of dithering than your freeware GIF animation program.

When you bring your image with the Netscape palette into GIFBuilder or another GIF editor, the Netscape palette will already be selected.

Painting with the Netscape palette

If you're adding colors to an image or creating an image from scratch with Photoshop's painting and drawing tools, you can be sure you're using Netscape colors by loading the Netscape palette as swatches.

1. If you're dealing with an existing image, first load the Netscape palette either through the *Indexed Color* dialog box or the *Color Table* dialog box.

2. Display the *Swatches* palette **(Window/Palettes/Show Swatches).**

3. Click on the pop-up menu in the *Swatch* window and select *Load Swatches.* Then select the 6x6x6 Palette file from the **Support Files/Chapter5** folder.

4. The Netscape palette will be displayed in the swatches palette (shown in Figure 5-7). You can then use the eyedropper tool to select foreground color or press the *Option* key (Mac) or *Alt* key (Windows) to select the background color.

Figure 5-6. The colors of this image's adaptive palette have been dithered to the Netscape palette.

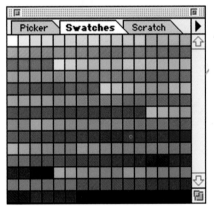

Figure 5-7. The Netscape palette loaded as Photoshop swatches.

Specifying hexadecimal colors

Another great mystery about Web pages is the hexadecimal color system; that's the system you use to specify the body background color or text colors in your HTML page. The tag looks like this.

```
<BODY BGCOLOR="#FFFFFF">
```

That code gives the page a white background.

How do you convert RGB values, in a program like Photoshop, to hexadecimal? Well, there's the easy way and there's the hard way.

The easy way is to forget about the math and use one of the many tools that calculate the conversion for you. Some of these are on the disk.

The hard way (which really isn't all that hard) is to understand how to do the conversion yourself.

The hexadecimal system is a base-16 system, as opposed to the base-10 system that we're all used to. Hex is often used in computer applications because it's more compact than base-10. It only takes six characters in hex, compared to nine characters in RGB, to describe a color.

In order to use RGB values from Photoshop as a BGCOLOR, they must first be converted to hexadecimal. The BGCOLOR attribute uses a six-character set. The first two characters represent the red value, the next two characters green, and the last set of two represent the blue value.

To convert a red, green or blue value to hexadecimal, you first divide the value by 16 and subtract the integer to get the first character of the pair. For the second character, you multiply the remainder by 16. If that seems obtuse, a quick example should make it all clear.

Figure 5-8 shows an RGB color displayed in Photoshop's Color Picker. It has a red value of 212, a green value of 159, and a blue value of 85. (Each channel has 256 possible values, from 0 to 255).

Color Pickers

If you know the RGB value for the color you'll use for your page's background, you can use the color pickers included on the CD-ROM to figure the hexadecimal value. You can also use these tools to figure the RGB value of hexadecimal colors — useful for setting the background color in your GIF editing software. Both tools are located in the *Support Files/Chapter5* folder of the CD-ROM.

The first tool is an HTML-based color picker that displays RGB and hexadecimal values when you pick a color in the Netscape palette. It is called *nspalette.html (!nspalette. html* in Windows).

The other tool is a self-running Director movie called *rgb2hex (rgb2hex.exe* in Windows) that converts color values from one system to the other. So, if you enter the RGB values of a color, the program will generate the hex value.

We'll start with the red value of 212. Divide 212 by 16 and you get 13.25. So 13 is the first value of the two-character set. It doesn't matter what numbers come after the decimal point; you don't round up or down. In hexadecimal, 13 is represented as D. The chart in Figure 5-9 shows the base-16 equivalents of base-10 numbers.

Next, take the remainder (.25) and multiply it by 16 to get the value of the second character .25 x 16 = 4, so the RGB value of 212 equals D4 in hexadecimal.

Now, repeat the steps for the other two values. You'll end up with D4 for red, 9F for green, and 55 for blue. So the body tag for this color is:

`<BODY BGCOLOR="#D49F5">`

Managing frames in Photoshop

As we said in Chapter 2, you should make a separate folder for each animation and put numbered frames in that folder. The only problem with that method is that it's a bit hard to visualize what's happening from frame to frame.

One technique that makes managing your animation a bit easier is to put each frame on a separate Photoshop layer. When you import a multi-layer Photoshop file into GIFBuilder 0.4, each layer is loaded as a subsequent frame. The background layer is the first frame, the next layer is the second frame, and so on.

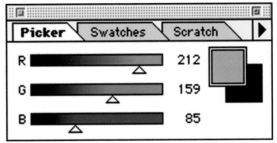

Figure 5-8. A color broken into red, green and blue components in Photoshop's Color Picker.

Base-10	Base-16
0	0
1	1
2	2
3	3
4	4
5	5
6	6
7	7
8	8
9	9
10	A
11	B
12	C
13	D
14	E
15	F

Figure 5-9. Base 16 equivalents for the numbers 0-15.

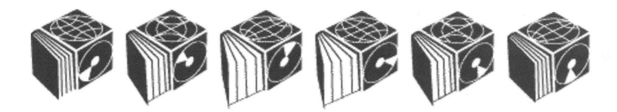

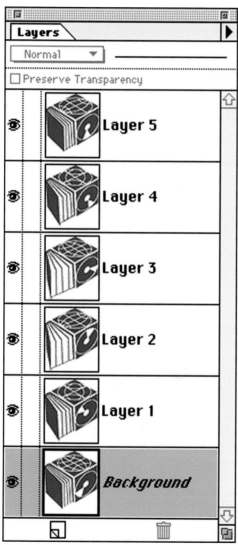

Figure 5-10. You can create all the frames for an animation in one Photoshop file by putting each frame on a separate Photoshop layer.

With this technique, you have only one file to worry about instead of dozens; you don't have to bother with the drudgery of converting lots of images from RGB to Indexed Color and saving GIF files in Photoshop; and you can easily test layering effects by simply turning layers on and off.

Figure 5-10 shows the *Layers* palette for creating a simple animation with this technique. This animation is taken from Reed Exhibition Companies' page for the American Bookseller's Association's Convention and Trade Exhibit *(http://aba.reedexpo.com/)*. This technique only works with GIFBuilder 0.4 and higher. As of this writing, no other GIF animation editor supports this feature.

6

Assorted Tips and Tricks

Your Web page can be a lot more fun if it's not always crystal clear exactly *what* is going on. It's only good design sense to try to hide the square boundaries of your GIF file (typically by using a transparent background or by matching the background color of the GIF to the *BGCOLOR* of the Web page), so your readers aren't constantly going, "Look, that graphic's moving! It must be an animated GIF."

But there are a number of other tricks you can use with GIF animation.

Fun with timing

One strategy is to make the movement irregular or infrequent. Someone might be looking at your page, not noticing anything out of the ordinary, when they see something move — just for a second — out of the corner of their eye. If you can surprise and delight your reader, you've accomplished something, especially given the competition for reader attention on the Web.

The blinking alien

One good example of that element of surprise is the little alien character designed by Audrey Witters,

To see the alien in action, start up your browser and open *alien.gif*, located in the *Animations/Samples/Chap3* folder of your CD. Or check out Audrey's page at *http://www.metatools.com/ webtips/anitip/size.html*. But don't blink or you'll miss it. Also check out Audrey's tips on GIF animation at *http://www.metatools.com/ webtips/anitip/what.html*.

"Web engineer" at MetaTools, publishers of Kai's Power Tools and other cool products. We'll hear more about Audrey in Chapter 8, *Rolling Textures.*

As you can see in the graphic at the top of this page, the only thing that happens is that the alien blinks occasionally with his different eyes. Nothing too brilliant there. But the trick is that Audrey has programmed long intervals between quick blinks, so that you might not even notice anything unusual at first.

Frames						
8 frames	Length: 12.30 s		Size: 79×111			Loop: forever
Name	Size	Position	Disp.	Delay	Transp.	
Frame 1	79×111	(0 ; 0)	N	300	-	
Frame 2	79×111	(0 ; 0)	N	10	-	
Frame 3	79×111	(0 ; 0)	N	500	-	
Frame 4	79×111	(0 ; 0)	N	10	-	
Frame 5	79×111	(0 ; 0)	N	200	-	
Frame 6	79×111	(0 ; 0)	N	10	-	
Frame 7	79×111	(0 ; 0)	N	100	-	
Frame 8	79×111	(0 ; 0)	N	100	-	

Figure 6-1. The alien animation uses very irregular interframe delays.

Figure 6-1 shows how Audrey programmed the irregular interframe delays in GIFBuilder.

For the first three seconds, nothing happens. Then the alien blinks his second eye. The blink only lasts a tenth of a second. He then keeps his eyes wide open for a full five

seconds. Then comes the two-eyed blink in Frame 4, a two-second wait, the middle-eye blink, and a one-second wait for the final blink, which he holds for a full second before the loop starts over.

The Stim home page

The blue diode animations on the Stim home page ("Where sugar is a state of mind") are anything but subtle. They blink, throb and dance in a most attention-getting manner.

What's interesting about this page is the use of a few small files and creative timing to create a fun and busy look.

Figure 6-2 shows a screen shot of the page.

Figure 6-2. Stim designer Georgia Rucker alternated the timing of the two diodes.

The page is built as an HTML table, with a column of buttons on the left, the main graphic and "Welcome to Stim" text in the middle, and another column of buttons on the right.

There are only two GIF animations on the page, called *bluediode.gif* and *bluerdiode.gif.* Each consists of only three frames — an on state, a glowing state, and an off state — as shown in Figure 6-3.

Figure 6-3

Frames

3 frames	Length : 0.35 s		Size : 20×20		Loop : forever	
Name	Size	Position	Disp.	Delay	Transp.	
Frame 1	20×20	(0 ; 0)	N	5	–	
Frame 2	20×20	(0 ; 0)	N	5	–	
Frame 3	20×20	(0 ; 0)	N	25	–	

Figure 6-4. GIFBuilder Frames window shows interframe delays for *bluediode.gif*.

Frames

3 frames	Length : 0.75 s		Size : 20×20		Loop : forever	
Name	Size	Position	Disp.	Delay	Transp.	
Frame 1	20×20	(0 ; 0)	N	60	–	
Frame 2	20×20	(0 ; 0)	N	5	–	
Frame 3	20×20	(0 ; 0)	N	10	–	

Figure 6-5. Interframe delay for *bluerdiode.gif*, the second animation.

Changes, changes

Shortly before we went to press, Stim completely changed their home page. Art director Georgia Rucker promises the diodes will return in various permutations, however. They've already returned as white diodes on an article about "computer-mediated oracles."

Stim

http://www.stim.com/

Get In on the New-Age Goodness!
http://www.stim.com/STIM-X/o696June/ Phenom/newage.html

Once again, the skill is all in the timing. Figures 6-4 and 6-5 show the timings for *bluediode.gif* and *bluerdiode.gif.*

The first animation runs only .35 seconds, while the second runs .75 seconds. In the first animation, the first and second frames (the lit and glowing states) last only 5/100ths of a second. The third frame lasts 25/100ths of a second before the animation loops again.

The second animation is almost exactly the opposite. Here the lit state lasts 60/100ths of a second, the glowing state lasts 5/100ths of a second, and the dark state lasts only 10/100ths of a second. Together the two files create that on-and-off illusion.

Animated imagemaps

GIF animations don't have to be just window-dressing. If you turn your animation into an imagemap, users can click on different areas of your animation to go to various pages on your site. You can customize your animation for use on different pages, thereby reminding people of where they are on your site, or encouraging them to click on a specific link.

![Animated toolbar showing Home, Services, Contact, Clients]

Figure 6-6. Animated toolbar for the H.A. USA site, caught mid-way through the animation.

The trick is to use an imagemap, standard fare on the Web. The new wrinkle is to use a *client-side imagemap.* This is a relatively new addition to HTML that is supported in current versions of both Netscape and Internet Explorer.

In an imagemap, users can click on different parts of an image to go to different URLs. In the old method, this was done on the server. The Web server ran a CGI (common gateway interface, if you must know) script that interpreted which coordinates the user clicked on, looked up what URL those coordinates were mapped to, and told the server what URL to send.

With client-side imagemaps, the coordinate and URL information is put directly into the HTML, thus leaving it up to the browser to decide which URL to display.

Figure 6-6 shows a toolbar created by R. Matthew Peyton for the H.A. USA site *(http://www.hausa.com)*. It's a simple animation of a wave rolling across the image, as shown in Figure 6-7.

The toolbar links to four different pages. On each page is a different version of the animation. On the home page,

Figure 6-7. The animation for H.A. USA's Services page. The wave rolls from left to right, splashes back and finally settles in the Services tile. Note that the word services is colored red in the first frame. Some browsers display only the first frame of a GIF animation, so coloring the text identifies the page for those users.

```
<MAP NAME="button1">
<AREA SHAPE=rect COORDS="1,1,113,56" HREF="http://www.hausa.com/home/">
<AREA SHAPE=rect COORDS="115,0,229,56" HREF="http://www.hausa.com/services/">
<AREA SHAPE=rect COORDS="231,0,344,56" HREF="http://www.hausa.com/contact/">
<AREA SHAPE=rect COORDS="346,0,459,56" HREF="http://www.hausa.com/clients/">
</MAP>
<IMG BORDER=0 SRC="anime1.gif" USEMAP="#button1" ALT="Surf's Up!">
```

Figure 6-8. HTML coding for the "home" version of the animated imagemap.

the wave lands on the "home" tile; on the support page, it lands on the "support" tile, and so on.

Matthew used client-side imagemaps to get the animation to link to the different pages. Figure 7-8 shows the HTML for the home version.

There are two parts to this HTML example. The first part is the imagemap, which uses the *MAP* tag. The second part is the *IMG* tag for the GIF file, which uses the *USEMAP* attribute.

Let's look at the map portion first.

<MAP NAME="button1"> starts a client-side imagemap and names it "button1."

The *AREA* tag starts the description of an area. *SHAPE* defines the geometric shape of the area (in this case, *"rect"* for rectangle). *COORDS* give the XY coordinates of the area. (X is the horizontal axis and Y is the vertical axis.) In this case, where a rectangle is being used, the two sets of numbers define the top left and bottom right corners of the rectangle.

So, in the first entry, 0,0,113,56 describes a rectangle that starts at the top left corner of the image (0,0); the bottom right corner is at 113,56.

The "services" tile starts at 115,0 (skipping two pixels for the dividing line) and ends at 229,56. There are also entries for the "contact" and "clients" tiles.

Then, *HREF* gives the URL to link to. It can be either a

Various programs on all platforms let you find the XY coordinates of a point in a graphic.

Some common ones are WebMap for the Mac, Mapedit for Windows and XV for Unix.

Assorted Tips and Tricks

75

relative or absolute URL. In the above map, the first area (the home tile) points to *http://www.hausa.com/home/.* The second area (the services tile) points to *http://www.hausa. com/services/,* and so on.

After you've specified all the areas, simply end the map with *</MAP>*.

You also have to add the *USEMAP* attribute to the *IMG* tag. *USEMAP* associates a map with the image. Here, we have *USEMAP="#button1."* The pound sign indicates that you're pointing to a map defined within the same HTML file, not a different file. If you were using a map embedded in a different file, you would need to specify both the location and the map name.

Besides rectangles, you can also use circles and polygons. Circles have three coordinate numbers: the X and Y points of the center, followed by the length of the radius in pixels. For polygons, use a series of coordinates for each point in the polygon.

It's fine to have two regions that overlap. If the user clicks in the overlap area, the region listed first in the map file takes precedence.

Finally, what happens to users whose browsers don't support client-side imagemaps? It's a simple matter to add support for server-side imagemaps, as well. You do this by adding a link to a map file on the server and adding the *ISMAP* attribute, as follows:

```
<A HREF="http://www.hausa.com/cgi-bin/wrmaps/wave.map">
<IMG SRC="anime1.gif" USEMAP="#button1" ISMAP></A>
```

7
Combining Animations and Static Images

Pepsi's Jetscream site (shown in Figure 7-1), designed by New York-based Razorfish Inc., confronts the viewer with an animation "wall" that grabs the attention without overwhelming the senses.

Figure 7-1. The Jetscream opening page.
http://www.pepsimax.com

"The mission of the site is to 'expose' the PepsiMax brand in the same way that the TV commercials do, to the same target audience — male youth outside the US," explains Craig Kanarick, a principal at Razorfish.

"We feel that the site speaks with a voice that will appeal to this audience, and that the Jetscream experience is one that makes sense for this audience. It reinforces the brand as an exciting, vibrant beverage," according to Craig.

This PepsiMax site is part of a Pepsi international advertising effort, says Craig.

Constructed out of nine GIFs, only two of which are

Toolbox

Platform: Macintosh
Adobe Photoshop
Adobe Illustrator
Debabelizer
GIFBuilder

Razorfish Inc.

http://www.razorfish.com/

Razorfish was started in the fall of 1994 as a dynamic digital design firm. They currently have about 23 employees, located mostly in lower Manhattan. The company designs and produces digital media across a wide variety of platforms: not just the World Wide Web, but also CD-ROM, kiosk, interactive TV, etc.

Clients include Time-Warner, America Online, IBM, Viacom Interactive Services, Prodigy, Pepsi International, Microsoft and Ralph Lauren.

animated, the whole image hints at the international aspect of the site without spelling it out. One animation displays the word *presents* in different languages while the other overlays various permutations of the word *Jetscream.*

For a high-energy site like Jetscream, animation was the way to go, Craig says. "Animation means action, and this site is about action. In fact, there are many pages with over four simultaneous animations, something not found on many other sites."

There are several advantages to the way Razorfish handled this animation.

First, breaking the animation into pieces allows different parts to run at different speeds, which makes the whole page seem more dynamic. Using several small GIFs instead of one large one also requires less bandwidth. Indeed, Craig says that bandwidth efficiency was the primary reason for breaking the animation up into parts. Finally, having parts of the image point to different URLs would be impossible with a single GIF.

Making the Jetscream animations

Three things come together to make this page work: the quality of the images, the timing of the animations, and the layout of the animations and static images in a table.

Illustrator was used to lay out the type, which was then imported into Photoshop. The images of Chazz (the male figure) were taken by a professional photographer using a commercial-grade digital camera and a Sony PC Cam video camera. After the images were "massaged" in Photoshop, they were broken up and re-assembled using GIFBuilder. The images were then judged to be too large, so they were shrunk using Debabelizer, and then the animations were reassembled using GIFBuilder.

First, let's look at the component images of the Jetscream animation, which was called *jetscream.gif.* Figure 7-2 shows all seven frames of the animation.

Designer Thomas Mueller created the type for the animation in Adobe Illustrator, then imported the type into Photoshop to apply special effects and design the layering effect.

Thomas used Photoshop 3.0's *Layers* feature to design the images. Using layers, he was able to arrange the various pieces of type quickly and easily.

Between the first and second frames, Thomas simply blurs the large serif gray type in increasing increments, which also has the effect of darkening the yellow type.

In the third frame, he brings in the word *Jetscream* in the official Pepsi type. Note that the type is slightly transparent.

In the next frame he brings in another version of the word, heavily blurred, behind the Pepsi type. In the next frame he layers yet another copy of the sans serif type directly over the previous version, creating a rich blurry outline effect.

The next frame adds the word in a small type size in yellow. And to create the *final* frame, Thomas laid in the word *Jetscream* underlined in red.

The image layout

Thomas put the animated and static images together using an HTML table. By breaking up the total image into a series of several small images, Thomas substantially reduced the length of time it would take users to start seeing the page. By putting the animations in separate files, Thomas could control the timing of the animations.

Figure 7-2. Different treatments of the word *Jetscream* are layered on the top of each other in one of the animations.

Since the table is so important here, we'll take a look at how it was constructed. Here's the code for the table:

```
<CENTER>
<TABLE BORDER=0 CELLPADDING=0 CELLSPACING=0>
```

This opening code creates a table with no borders between cells, no spacing between cells, and no padding within cells.

```
<TR ALIGN=TOP>
```

This line creates a row and aligns the content to the top of the row.

```
<TD VALIGN=TOP COLSPAN=2>
```

This line defines the first cell in the row. The cell spans two columns and the content is vertically aligned to the top of the cell.

```
<IMG SRC="images/pepsimaxone.gif" WIDTH=122
HEIGHT=64>
<A HREF="form.html">
<IMG SRC="images/register.gif" WIDTH=122 HEIGHT=64
BORDER=0>
</A>
<IMG SRC="images/hostfrance1.gif" WIDTH=122
HEIGHT=64>
<IMG SRC="images/pepsimaxthree.gif" WIDTH=122
HEIGHT=64>
</TD>
</TR>
```

The above code inserts four images into the first row of the table. Also notice the *BORDER = 0* attribute in the image tag. Normally, linked images have a color border indicating that they are clickable. The *BORDER* attribute of the *IMG* tag lets you set the width of this border. So, *BORDER = 0* turns off the border entirely, while *BORDER = 2* sets the border to two pixels wide. Figure 8-3 shows what the first row looks like.

Notice that they've cut the French image in half, with only the top of image in this row. The bottom half appears in the next row.

```
<TR VALIGN=TOP>
<TD VALIGN=TOP COLSPAN=2>
```

Figure 7-3. The first row of the animation wall.

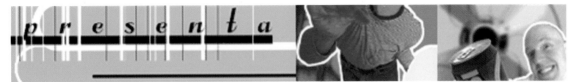

Figure 7-4. The second row of the animation wall.

Figure 7-5. The third row of the animation wall.

Figure 7-6. The final row of the animation wall.

```
<IMG SRC="images/presents.gif" WIDTH=245 HEIGHT=64>
<IMG SRC="images/hostfrance2.gif" WIDTH=122
HEIGHT=64 ALIGN=TOP>
<IMG SRC="images/hostargentina1.gif" WIDTH=122
HEIGHT=64 ALIGN=TOP>
</TD>
</TR>
```

Here in the second row, the first image is the animation of
the word *presents,* which is twice as wide as the other

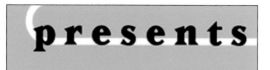

Figure 7-7. The other animated GIF in the wall flips between four different variations of the word "presents" as shown here.

graphics. Figure 7-4 shows what the second row looks like.

```
<TR VALIGN=TOP>
<TD ROWSPAN=2>
<IMG SRC="images/hostgreece.gif"
WIDTH=122 HEIGHT=128>
</TD>
<TD>
<IMG SRC="images/jetscream.gif"
WIDTH=245 HEIGHT=64>
<IMG SRC="images/hostargentina2.gif"
WIDTH=122 HEIGHT=64 ALIGN=TOP>
</TD>
</TR>
```

In the third row, the content spans two rows. This is because the first image, *hostgreece.gif,* is twice as deep as the other images. Figure 7-5 shows what this row looks like.

```
<TR VALIGN="TOP">
<TD>
<A HREF="noreg.html">
<IMG SRC="images/come.gif" WIDTH=122
HEIGHT=64 BORDER=0>
</A>
<IMG SRC="images/pepsimaxtwo.gif"
WIDTH=122 HEIGHT=64>
<A HREF="prot/max/airport/">
<IMG SRC="images/done.gif" WIDTH=122
HEIGHT=64 BORDER=0>
</A>
</TD>
</TR>
</TABLE>
<P>
</CENTER>
```

The final row contains the last three images, as shown in Figure 7-6.

Timing the animations

The timing of the animations is very simple. The *presents* animation *(presents.gif)* changes images every 50/100ths of a second and lasts 2 seconds, while the *Jetscream* animation *(jetscream.gif)* changes images every 73/100ths of a second, and lasts 5.11 seconds.

With the two animations staggered like this, they never actually sync up. They come close at the 10-second mark but don't sync up, because *presents* loops through five times in 10 seconds, but *Jetscream* doesn't finish its second loop until 10.22 seconds.

It's this staggered timing that keeps the page interesting, even after the animations have looped numerous times.

8

Rolling Textures

Toolbox

Platform: Macintosh
Adobe Photoshop 3.0
Kai's Power Tools 3.0
GIFBuilder

It's fairly simple to create scrolling text animations (just inch the type across the frame) or type effects (just incrementally apply Photoshop filters, as shown in Chapter 12). But here's a really cool type effect that's a little more complicated.

In this "rolling texture" effect, the type doesn't change, but what's inside does. Audrey Witters demonstrated this technique on her Web page on the MetaTools site, and her explanation provides the basis for this chapter.

To create the effect, we used the Texture Explorer module from Kai's Power Tools 3.0 — a powerful set of plug-ins for Photoshop and compatible programs. Although we did this project on a Macintosh, both KPT and Photoshop are available for Windows as well as Macintosh.

A look at KPT Texture Explorer

To make this animation, Audrey created a texture in KPT Texture Explorer and then used Photoshop to make the individual frames for the movement sequences. If you're not familiar with KPT, it's worth getting familiar with the innovative but somewhat strange interface.

Texture Explorer generates random textures algorithmically. In Figure 8-1, the currently selected

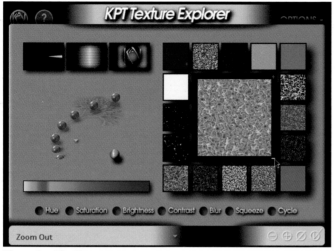

Figure 8-1. The Texture
Explorer interface.

Kai's Power Tools

Save-disabled demo versions of
both Kai's Power Tools 3.0 and
Photoshop 3.0 for Macintosh
and Windows are on the CD-
ROM. Check the *Software* folder
for the *KPT* and *Photoshop*
folders, respectively.

Kai's Power Tools
MetaTools
6303 Carpinteria Ave.
Carpinteria, CA 93013
(805) 566-6200
http://www.metatools.com/

texture appears in the large
square on the right. Variations of
the texture appear in the smaller
tiles surrounding the large
square. Texture Explorer
calculates the variations based
on the amount of "mutation" you
ask for by selecting one of the
balls on the tree to the left.
The lowest ball gives the least
amount of variation, the highest
ball the most. In this case, we've
selected maximum mutation,
and you can see that the
variations are quite different from the active texture.

To create the texture you want, you pick one of the
variations as the new active texture. This generates a new
set of variations. By gradually reducing the amount of
mutation, you create more and more subtle variations.
Eventually you get just the right look.

You can also control the direction, opacity and
"apply mode" (the method for combining pixels of two
layered images).

Creating the texture

The first step in creating a rolling texture mask is to create the
texture. Then we'll use Photoshop to set type, create a mask,
and move the texture around. The last step is to import the
various frames into a GIF editing program and build the
animation.

The "wacky" type animation is included on your CD in the *Animations/Samples/Chap8* folder.

Run Photoshop and create a new file *(File/New).* You need to make this file larger than your final image. We made this file 600 x 400 pixels for a final image of 240 x 120. Our New dialog box is shown in Figure 8-2.

Then choose the KPT Texture Explorer *(Filters/KPT3.0/Texture Explorer)* and you'll see the interface shown in Figure 8-1.

Kai's Power Tools includes a feature called "presets." Once you have a texture you like, you can save it as a preset. Over 100 presets come with Kai's Power Tools. We used

one of those factory-installed presets, *Seussian fribbldig- niggets,* so-named for the Dr. Seuss-like shapes and colors in the texture.

There are two modes for selecting presets — a graphical mode and a text list. The graphical list lets you preview the actual textures but is really difficult to navigate. The text list is somewhat unwieldy since it's not divided up into categories (a feature that did exist in earlier versions of the program), but is in general an easier way to navigate.

To use the text mode, press Command-P (Control-P in Windows) to bring up the *Preferences* dialog box. Once in the *Preferences* dialog box, uncheck the *Graphical Presets* option.

Now, to load the texture for this example, click on the arrow in the middle of the bottom bar to bring up a list of all the presets. Scroll down and select *Seussian fribbldigniggets.*

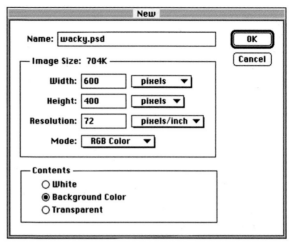

Figure 8-2. Creating a new Photoshop file.

For Mac users

As an extra value, we asked Audrey to create some special texture presets just for this book. This presets file, called *Audrey's Presets,* is located in the *Support Files/Chap8* folder. To load *Audrey's Presets,* run Texture Explorer and click on the minus icon in the bottom right of the screen. This will bring up the Presets Manager. Click on the *Import* button, find the file *Audrey's Presets,* and click OK.

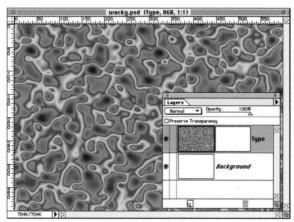
Figure 8-3. Adding a layer mask to the texture.

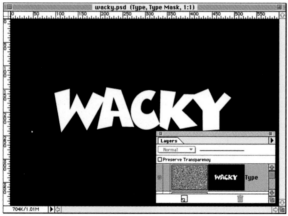
Figure 8-4. Text mask for the animation.

What's a mask?

A mask is an art technique that allows you to work on part of an image, while protecting the rest of the image. Think of it like a stencil that overlays the base image. If we make a type mask, then everything but the type is blocked out and the effect is type filled with the underlying texture.

Of course you don't have to use any preset texture. Feel free to muck about in Texture Explorer until you find something you like. When you've chosen your texture, click on the checkmark to apply the texture.

Add the text mask

In this section, we'll create a text mask. In Photoshop, choose *Windows/Palettes/ Layers* to display the layers palette. On the layer with the texture, select *Add Layer Mask* from the layer palette's pop-up menu. (Note: You can't add a layer mask to the background layer, so you need to make sure your texture is on a layer other than the background.)

An empty thumbnail box will appear to the right of the texture thumbnail, as shown in Figure 8-3. That's the layer mask icon.

To see what's going on while the layer mask is selected, option-click on the layer mask icon. This will display just the layer mask, so the image will turn white.

Now, using the type tool, set a font and point size and type in your text. We used Comics Car Toon, 100 pt. After you set the type, you may have to resize it with the *Image/Effects/Scale* function. The text should be white on a black background. Option-click on the layer mask again to return to regular view. Figure 8-4 shows the text mask.

Picking a texture

There are a few considerations to keep in mind as you choose the settings for your texture.

- Setting direction. The animation effect can be quite different depending on the texture's direction. Some textures are fairly uniform throughout, while others are quite varied. You'll have to play with how direction affects various textures, but a good rule of thumb is to orient the texture so that the fastest-changing areas of the texture are perpendicular to the direction of animation.

  Figure 8-5 shows a texture that varies fastest from top to bottom and more slowly from left to right. The texture's direction is set to 90 degrees, so this texture should move to the right or left.

  To set direction, click on the *Direction* tile in the top left and drag the direction indicator around. Exact values appear at the bottom of the window as you drag.

Figure 8-5. Setting a texture's direction in Texture Explorer.

- Color variation. Make sure there's enough variation in color between the texture and the background. The texture back in Figure 8-3 is heavy on the blue, so avoid using blue as the background color on the HTML page.

- Zooming. You can zoom in and out of the texture using plus and minus buttons on the main display. "If you zoom out too far, so that your texture has a lot of very small elements, the jumps between frames will be more noticeable," Audrey notes. "If you zoom in too close, the effect will be very subtle. Since each texture is different, you'll probably need to experiment to find the right level of zoom." In the "wacky" example, we zoomed out three levels from the default setting.

Figure 8-6. Type mask over texture background.

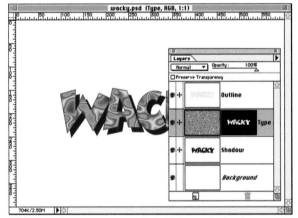

We've gussied up our type a little bit beyond what is described here. Using the *Layers* palette, we added a drop shadow (filled with a dark blue) and a type outline (using the *Stroke* command, 1 pixel, inside).

Next, add a new layer behind the masked texture layer. Fill this layer with the same color as the color of the page: in this case, white. Figure 8-6 shows the final image of a masked texture on a white background.

Create the frames

Now that the image is complete, it's time to move the texture around and create the component images. First of all, center the type in the window. That's your first frame; save it with a name like *01.psd*.

Next, we'll move the texture around in increments to create the component frames of the animation. To create the second frame, duplicate the image *(Image/Duplicate)* and click the *Merge Layers* box. The *Duplicate* dialog box is shown in Figure 8-7.

Select the texture layer in the *Layers* palette (make sure you select the actual texture icon, not the type icon) and select the entire image *(Select/All).* Then, using arrow keys, move the texture 5 to 10 pixels in the direction you'd like it to roll. We

moved the texture down 5 pixels and to the right 5 pixels for each frame.

Once you've moved the texture, save a new version of the file — *02.psd.* Repeat this process for each frame of your animation.

How many frames should this sort of animation run? Probably somewhere between 12 and 20. If there are too few frames, the animation will seem jumpy. If there are a lot of frames, the file size will be too big.

To recap the procedure:

- Duplicate the image.
- Move the texture.
- Save a new file.

The next step is to crop these large files down to just the size you want for your GIF file. If you've centered the text, you can do this easily with the *Canvas Size* command *(Image/Canvas Size).*

Use the *Info* palette to determine what size your final image will be. Select the marquee tool and select a rectangle as if you were going to crop the image. The *Info* pallete will

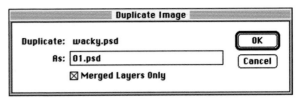

Figure 8-7. The *Duplicate* dialog box.

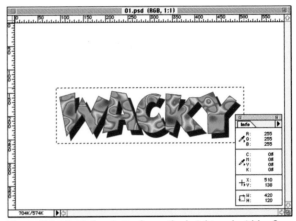

Figure 8-8. The *Info* palette shows the height and width of a marquee selection.

Here's another example of a rolling texture within type. This file is in the *Animations/Samples/Chap8* folder on the CD.

display the width and height of your selection, as shown in Figure 8-8.

Once you know the width and height, you can use the *Canvas Size* command to quickly resize the images. Simply enter the width and height of the new size in the *Canvas* dialog box and click *OK*. Boom, the image is cropped.

Once you've saved all the cropped images, you can save them as GIFs with the appropriate palettes and color settings. Or you can just import the Photoshop files directly into GIFBuilder, which will automatically convert them to GIFs.

Finally, import the frames into GIFBuilder and set the timing, transparency, etc. We gave all the frames a delay of 25, except the last one which has no delay, in order to account for the loading of the image.

Animation rocks

Audrey has more fun animation on her Web pages using other KPT tools. Check out the glowing button at *http://www.metatools.com/webtips/anitip/what.html.*

9 Creating an Animation Wall

When museums create online versions of their real-world exhibits, the results are often disappointing. They put up a few photos of some pieces from their permanent collections and page after page of information on

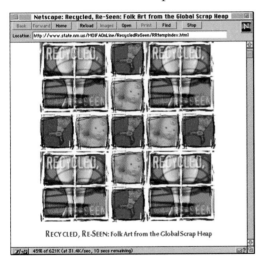

how to buy a museum T-shirt or donate money. The Museum of International Folk Art is clearly different. *RECYCLED, RE-SEEN: Folk Art from the Global Scrap Heap* is one of the best online exhibits from any museum.

The exhibit, designed by Zoom Interactive Design, boasts a GIF animation "wall" that works like a fast-moving montage of the recycled art in the exhibit.

Zoom hired independent designer Erik Josowitz to create the animation wall. Erik also built an interactive game called *Consider the Source,* using mBED, a new format for presenting interactivity, animation and sound on the Web.

Toolbox

Platform: Macintosh
Adobe Photoshop 3.0
Adobe After Effects
Debabelizer
GIFBuilder

Defining the concept

"The folks at Zoom had me focus on the opening screen animation and games while they designed the site," Erik relates. "The real exhibit, in Santa Fe, has a video wall showing images of objects that are actually in the exhibit. We

Figure 9-1. Erik created the background image for the tiles by layering a lighter version on top of a darker one. He used a third layer, containing scratch imagery, as a mask.

The following pages show all the frames from just one of the *Recycled* site's animations. As you go through them, notice how just one tile at a time changes, yet over time the entire image changes dramatically.

wanted to achieve the same effect online but with images more stylistically related to those in the exhibit and with an eye more toward a stylistic interpretation of *folk art* and *junk art.*"

The Zoom designers went out to a junk shop in Houston and shot about 50 images of various old bottle caps, license plates, and other general detritus. They sent JPEG files of these photos to Erik with a vague directive to make things work. "At that point the online exhibit really was a loose collection of text and images but had no real unifying style. The home page animations really served to set a style for the rest of the site and for the games," Erik says.

Erik mapped out a rough plan for the video wall which would try to maximize bandwidth-to-surface area by using only two animated GIFs. One would be small and would repeat a number of times. The other would be a larger four-square animation, which maximized bandwidth by positioning individual squares within the animation frame. "In other words, the larger GIF would look like four smaller animated GIFs but would not replace the entire area at any point in the animation," Erik says.

This offered two benefits: it would make the animation move more quickly than if the entire area changed every frame and it would allow Erik to synchronize the four frames — something that would not be possible if he had four separate animated GIFs loading over the wire.

With this plan in mind, Erik took the Zoom designers' photographs of junk and set about to develop the rough, scratched-out look that you see on the site. Erik created the look by using scratch imagery as a mask using Photoshop's *Layers* palette. Figure 9-1 shows the background image Erik worked from.

PLAY: CONSIDER THE SOURCE

BEAR ▶

MATCHES

TOILET PAPER

TOOTHPICKS

Place the bear over its source material and click the mouse button.

Creativity in recycling

"This exhibition pays tribute to the creativity and ingenuity of folk 'recyclers' from Africa to Asia to the Americas," according to the museum's Web site. "Though these artists live in widely dispersed places and diverse cultures, they all share one thing: they take throwaways and transform them into objects of renewed beauty, utility and meaning. They may not think of what they do as recycling, but each of them sees potential where others see only useless junk.

"If trash is the raw material of this folk art, mass production is its driving force. Planned obsolescence spurs sales of products but their remains quickly wind up in the scrap heap.

"Find out how and why people from around the world transform junk in different ways. Come in and take a global tour of creativity at work in the arts of recycling. You may never look at a bottle cap in quite the same way again!"

The online exhibit is at *http://www.state.nm.us/MOIFAOnLine/ RecycledReSeen/RRtempindex.html.*

The game *Consider the Source* **is at** *http://www.state.nm.us/MOIFAOnLine/.*

To get the mBED plug-in and for more information on mBED, check out the mBED Web site at *http://www.mbed.com/.*

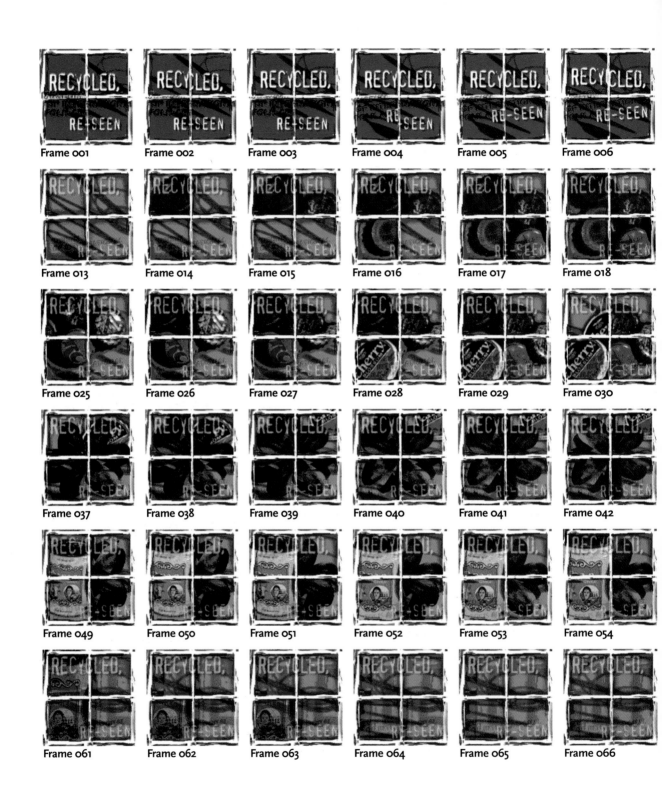

Frame 001 Frame 002 Frame 003 Frame 004 Frame 005 Frame 006

Frame 013 Frame 014 Frame 015 Frame 016 Frame 017 Frame 018

Frame 025 Frame 026 Frame 027 Frame 028 Frame 029 Frame 030

Frame 037 Frame 038 Frame 039 Frame 040 Frame 041 Frame 042

Frame 049 Frame 050 Frame 051 Frame 052 Frame 053 Frame 054

Frame 061 Frame 062 Frame 063 Frame 064 Frame 065 Frame 066

Frame 007 Frame 008 Frame 009 Frame 010 Frame 011 Frame 012

Frame 019 Frame 020 Frame 021 Frame 022 Frame 023 Frame 024

Frame 031 Frame 032 Frame 033 Frame 034 Frame 035 Frame 036

Frame 043 Frame 044 Frame 045 Frame 046 Frame 047 Frame 048

Frame 055 Frame 056 Frame 057 Frame 058 Frame 059 Frame 060

Frame 067 Frame 068 Frame 069 Frame 070 Frame 071 Frame 072

Creating an Animation Wall

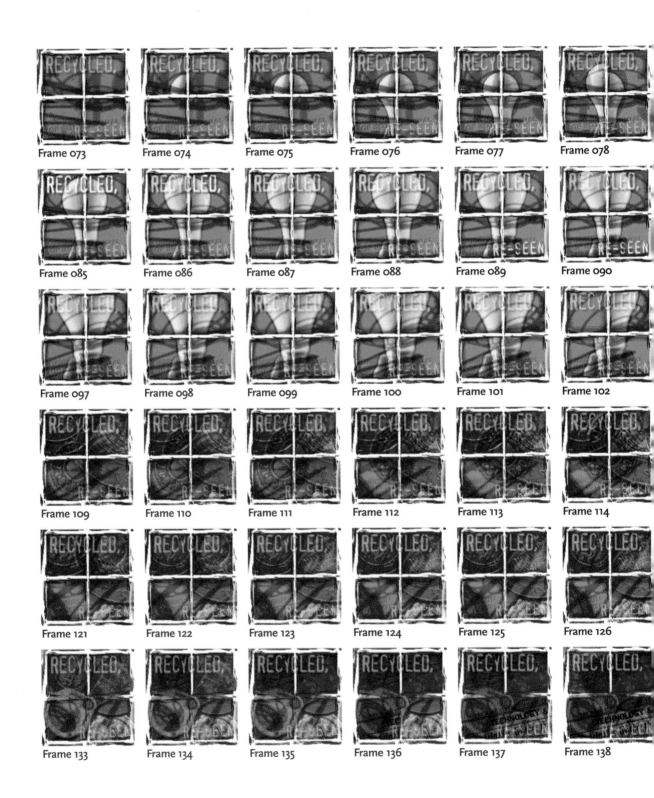

Frame 073 Frame 074 Frame 075 Frame 076 Frame 077 Frame 078

Frame 085 Frame 086 Frame 087 Frame 088 Frame 089 Frame 090

Frame 097 Frame 098 Frame 099 Frame 100 Frame 101 Frame 102

Frame 109 Frame 110 Frame 111 Frame 112 Frame 113 Frame 114

Frame 121 Frame 122 Frame 123 Frame 124 Frame 125 Frame 126

Frame 133 Frame 134 Frame 135 Frame 136 Frame 137 Frame 138

GIF Animation Studio

Frame 079 Frame 080 Frame 081 Frame 082 Frame 083 Frame 084

Frame 091 Frame 092 Frame 093 Frame 094 Frame 095 Frame 096

Frame 103 Frame 104 Frame 105 Frame 106 Frame 107 Frame 108

Frame 115 Frame 116 Frame 117 Frame 118 Frame 119 Frame 120

Frame 127 Frame 128 Frame 129 Frame 130 Frame 131 Frame 132

Frame 139 Frame 140 Frame 141 Frame 142 Frame 143 Frame 144

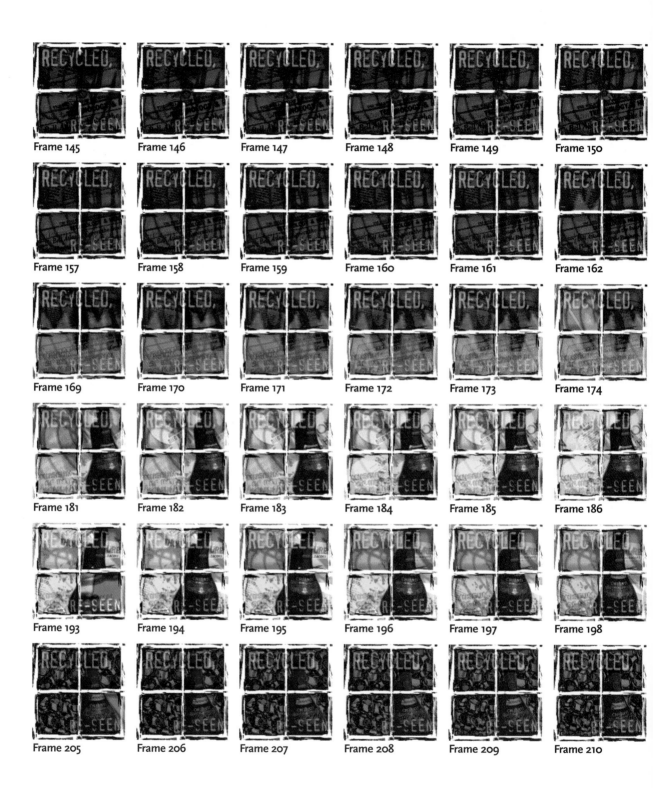

Frame 145   Frame 146   Frame 147   Frame 148   Frame 149   Frame 150

Frame 157   Frame 158   Frame 159   Frame 160   Frame 161   Frame 162

Frame 169   Frame 170   Frame 171   Frame 172   Frame 173   Frame 174

Frame 181   Frame 182   Frame 183   Frame 184   Frame 185   Frame 186

Frame 193   Frame 194   Frame 195   Frame 196   Frame 197   Frame 198

Frame 205   Frame 206   Frame 207   Frame 208   Frame 209   Frame 210

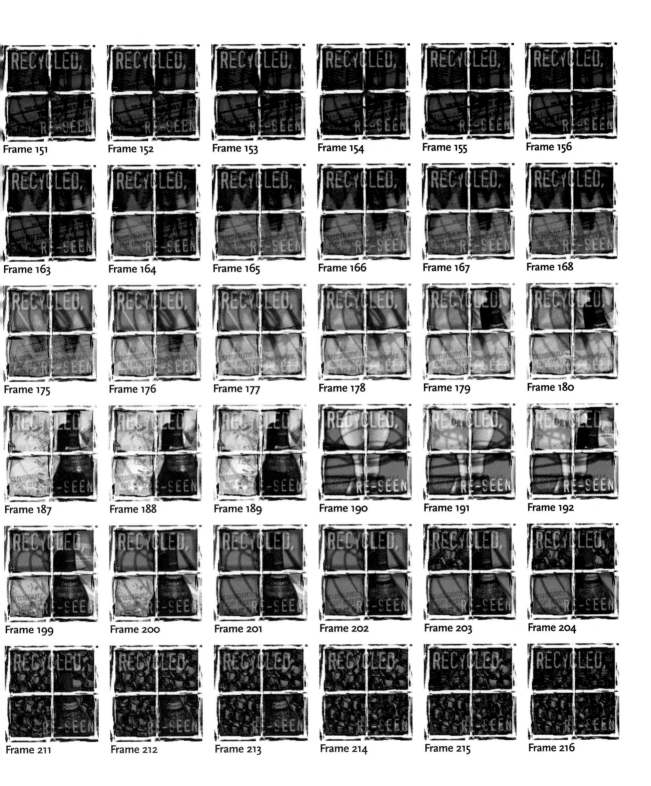

Frame 151 Frame 152 Frame 153 Frame 154 Frame 155 Frame 156

Frame 163 Frame 164 Frame 165 Frame 166 Frame 167 Frame 168

Frame 175 Frame 176 Frame 177 Frame 178 Frame 179 Frame 180

Frame 187 Frame 188 Frame 189 Frame 190 Frame 191 Frame 192

Frame 199 Frame 200 Frame 201 Frame 202 Frame 203 Frame 204

Frame 211 Frame 212 Frame 213 Frame 214 Frame 215 Frame 216

Creating an Animation Wall

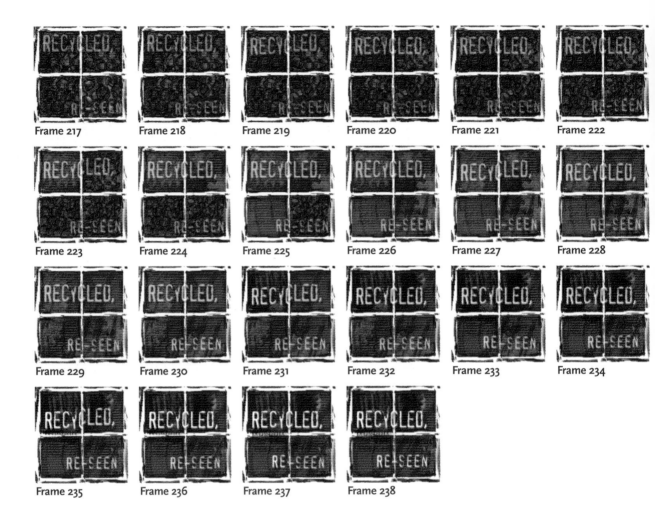

Frame 217 Frame 218 Frame 219 Frame 220 Frame 221 Frame 222

Frame 223 Frame 224 Frame 225 Frame 226 Frame 227 Frame 228

Frame 229 Frame 230 Frame 231 Frame 232 Frame 233 Frame 234

Frame 235 Frame 236 Frame 237 Frame 238

"Once I had the basic layered layout in Photoshop, I moved into Adobe After Effects and began animating," Erik says. After Effects is post-production video editing software from Adobe Systems. As shown in Figure 9-2, it allows you to set timelines for different image layers and specify how the layers are combined.

"Once I had an animation that worked roughly the way I wanted it to, I exported the individual frames as PICT files. These PICT files were then run through a couple of

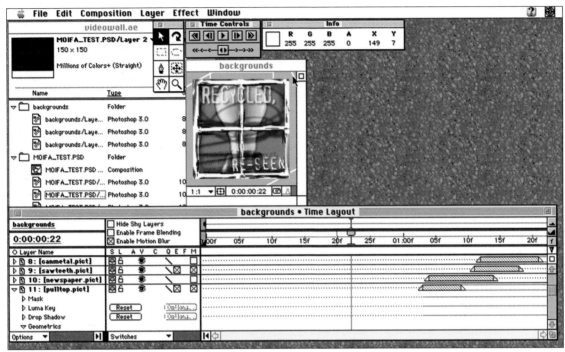

Figure 9-2. Designing the four-frame animation in After Effects.

Debabelizer scripts which converted them to the Netscape palette, dithered them to roughly 70%, and chopped them into quadrants, finally saving them as numbered GIF files," Erik explains.

Now that he finally had component GIF files, Erik pulled them into GIFBuilder and set the timing, offset and looping specs. "After repeating this process a few times, going back into After Effects and tweaking the animation, going back to DeBab and tweaking the dither, and so on, the final frames and animated GIFs were produced," Erik says.

The job still wasn't over, though. After the animations were finished, the page still had to be laid out. The page uses HTML tables, which we explain in some detail below.

"The whole page was then tested in Netscape Navigator and Internet Explorer," Erik explains. "We found then, to our

Figure 9-3. Each of the three component images of the animation wall are outlined above in red.

Frames					
18 frames	Length: 5.40 s	Size: 75x75			Loop: forever
Name	Size	Position	Disp.	Delay	Transp.
Frame 1	75x75	(0; 0)	N	30	-
Frame 2	75x75	(0; 0)	N	30	-
Frame 3	75x75	(0; 0)	N	30	-
Frame 4	75x75	(0; 0)	N	30	-
Frame 5	75x75	(0; 0)	N	30	-
Frame 6	75x75	(0; 0)	N	30	-
Frame 7	75x75	(0; 0)	N	30	-
Frame 8	75x75	(0; 0)	N	30	-
Frame 9	75x75	(0; 0)	N	30	-
Frame 10	75x75	(0; 0)	N	30	-
Frame 11	75x75	(0; 0)	N	30	-
Frame 12	75x75	(0; 0)	N	30	-
Frame 13	75x75	(0; 0)	N	30	-
Frame 14	75x75	(0; 0)	N	30	-
Frame 15	75x75	(0; 0)	N	30	-
Frame 16	75x75	(0; 0)	N	30	-
Frame 17	75x75	(0; 0)	N	30	-
Frame 18	75x75	(0; 0)	N	30	-

Figure 9-4. Frames window for the small animation.

Frames					
234 frames	Length: 23.80 s	Size: 150x150			Loop: forever
Name	Size	Position	Disp.	Delay	Transp.
Frame 1	150x150	(0; 0)	N	50	-
Frame 2	75x75	(0; 0)	N	10	-
Frame 3	75x75	(75; 0)	N	10	-
Frame 4	75x75	(0; 75)	N	10	-
Frame 5	75x75	(75; 75)	N	10	-
Frame 6	75x75	(0; 0)	N	10	-
Frame 7	75x75	(75; 0)	N	10	-
Frame 8	75x75	(0; 75)	N	10	-
Frame 9	75x75	(75; 75)	N	10	-
Frame 10	75x75	(0; 0)	N	10	-
Frame 11	75x75	(75; 0)	N	10	-
Frame 12	75x75	(0; 75)	N	10	-
Frame 13	75x75	(75; 75)	N	10	-
Frame 14	75x75	(0; 0)	N	10	-
Frame 15	75x75	(75; 0)	N	10	-
Frame 16	75x75	(0; 75)	N	10	-
Frame 17	75x75	(75; 75)	N	10	-
Frame 18	75x75	(0; 0)	N	10	-

Figure 9-5. Frames window for the large animation.

dismay, that IE2 did not correctly interpret the offsets and just stacked animation frames on top of one another. A couple of calls later we had been reassured that IE3 would correctly support GIF animation offsets. So we called it finished."

A closer look

As we just discussed, the animation wall consists of three GIF files — two animations and one static image. Figure 9-3 shows the component images of the animation.

The one-tile animation contains 18 frames, with a 30/100th of a second delay between frames, looping forever. Each frame is 75 x 75 pixels. The animation uses the Netscape palette. The animation runs 5.4 seconds. The file size is 47K. Figure 9-4 shows GIFBuilder's Frames window for this animation.

The four-tile animation is quite a bit more complex, using location coordinates and timing variations. The animation uses *Do Not Dispose* as the disposal method. (Disposal methods are explained in Chapter 2.) Figure 9-5 shows GIFBuilder's Frames window for the large animation.

The animation starts with a single image displayed over four tiles and held for half a second.

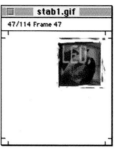

Figure 9-6. At frame 45, one image covers all four squares.

Figure 9-7. Each subsequent image is offset to one of the four tile positions.

The subsequent four frames replace each tile, one at a time, in series. First the top left tile (0,0), then the top right (75,0), then the bottom left (0,75), and finally the bottom right (75,75). By having each frame contain just the tile that changes, rather than the whole four-tile image, Erik was able to reduce the file size of each frame significantly.

And it's the file size of each frame — rather than the size of the whole GIF file — that's important. This is because GIF animations stream in; as soon as one image is complete, the browser displays it. So even though the file is very large — this one is over 600K, with over 300 frames — if the individual images are relatively small, the animation should work fairly well. In fact, it's especially important with a long animation like this (almost 12 seconds), since some users will only stay with it a few seconds — not long enough for it to be cached on the hard disk.

If you're thinking about creating animations on this scale, it's probably a good exercise to run them through the bandwidth simulator in GIFmation to see how they'll display at different connection speeds. (See Chapter 4 for more information on GIFmation.)

Let's take a look at how Erik changes the imagery in each of the tiles, creating a quick-cut effect. The fact that he subtly changes the image, without completely changing

GIF Animation Studio

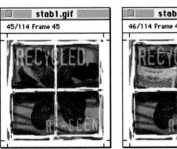

Figure 9-8. Each subsequent frame changes one tile at a time, while leaving the rest of the image intact.

the entire picture, captures the sense of recycling material.

Let's start with the animation at frame 45, as shown in Figure 9-6. Figure 9-7 shows the subsequent images.

Note that each of these images has a different position:

Frame 46   0,0
Frame 47   75,0
Frame 48   0,75
Frame 49   75,75

As each frame is displayed, it replaces only the part of the image that it overlays. Thus the user sees each tile changing one by one but, with only a 10/100ths of a second delay between each frame, the change happens quite quickly. Figure 9-8 shows what the user sees as each new frame is displayed.

Repeating images

To create the whole animation wall, Erik repeated the animations in a pattern by placing the images in a table. Here's the HTML he used:

```
<TABLE CELLSPACING=0 CELLPADDING=0 BORDER=0>
    <TR>
    <TD ROWSPAN=2 COLSPAN=2>
    <IMG SRC="stab1.gif" HEIGHT=150 WIDTH=150>
    </TD>
```

Figure 9-9 The first row of the animation wall.

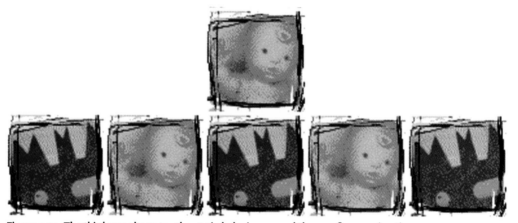

Figure 9-10. The third row alternates the static baby image and the one-frame animation.

Figure 9-11. The next two rows of the table repeat the first two rows.

GIF Animation Studio

The table starts with the four-tile animation *(stab1.gif)*, which spans two rows and two columns.

```
<TD>
<IMG SRC="smallframe.gif" HEIGHT=75 WIDTH=75>
</TD>
```

Then comes the one-tile animation.

```
<TD ROWSPAN=2 COLSPAN=2>
<IMG SRC="stab1.gif" HEIGHT=150 WIDTH=150>
</TD>
```

And *stab1.gif* is repeated.

```
</TR>
```

Figure 9-9 shows what we have so far.

```
<TR>
<TD>
<IMG SRC="baby1.gif" HEIGHT=75 WIDTH=75>
</TD>
</TR>
```

This row contains only the baby image, which fills in the blank space in the second row.

```
<TR>
<TD>
<IMG SRC="smallframe.gif" HEIGHT=75 WIDTH=75>
</TD>
<TD>
<IMG SRC="baby1.gif" HEIGHT=75 WIDTH=75>
</TD>
<TD>
<IMG SRC="smallframe.gif" HEIGHT=75 WIDTH=75>
</TD>
<TD>
<IMG SRC="baby1.gif" HEIGHT=75 WIDTH=75>
</TD>
<TD>
<IMG SRC="smallframe.gif" HEIGHT=75 WIDTH=75>
</TD>
</TR>
```

This row alternates the one-frame animation with the static baby picture. Figure 9-10 shows this row.

```
<TR>
<TD ROWSPAN=2 COLSPAN=2>
<IMG SRC="stab1.gif" HEIGHT=150 WIDTH=150>
</TD>
<TD>
<IMG SRC="baby1.gif" HEIGHT=75 WIDTH=75>
</TD>
<TD ROWSPAN=2 COLSPAN=2>
<IMG SRC="stab1.gif" HEIGHT=150 WIDTH=150>
</TD>
</TR>
<TR>
<TD>
<IMG SRC="smallframe.gif" HEIGHT=75 WIDTH=75>
</TD>
</TR>
</TABLE>
```

This section simply repeats the HTML for the first two tables, as shown in Figure 9-11.

Erik's work on this site represents a very interesting combination of textured imagery, offset positioning, and repetition in a table.

10

Voyager's Morphing A

One of the best uses of GIF animation we've seen is a morphing animation of the letter A for the Voyager Company's online font shop *(http://www.voyagerco.com/)*. Unlike a lot of other animated sites (including several mentioned in this book), the Voyager site doesn't make a big deal of GIF animation. Instead of emblazoning animation over the top of the page, the *fount* animation, which links to Voyager's Online Font Shop, is located at the center of a group of tiles about halfway down the page.

Toolbox

Platform: Macintosh
Adobe Photoshop
Elastic Reality
GIFBuilder

Shown in Figure 10-1, this group of tiles provides links to several standard areas of the site, while the top of the page contains daily changing links to highlighted parts of the site.

The Font Shop is where Voyager sells their original typefaces. The fount animation is especially effective because it shows off the actual typefaces being offered for sale. "It's not just cool, it's content," says Peter Merholz, who designed the animation while at Voyager. (He has since left to join San Francisco-based Studio Archetype, headed by designer Clement Mok.) "It tells you what you're going to see before you go there."

The animation communicates what's behind the link by displaying the letter A in each of the eight typefaces and *morphing* between them. Users of the site get an instant

What's a morph?

Morphing is an animation technique in which one image changes into another by gradually merging the two images. Computer-based morphing creates a series of intermediate images in which the first image is gradually changed to resemble a second image. Shape, texture, color and other attributes all change as one image is morphed into another.

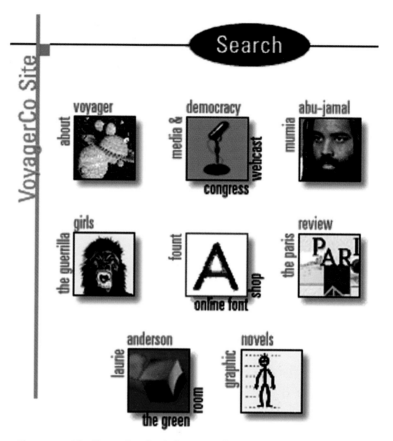

Figure 10-1. The font animation is just one of several tiles in the center of the Voyager page.

preview of the available typefaces, and the morphing effect gives the animation a fluid movement.

Let's take a look at the morphing effect from one typeface to another. Figure 10-2 shows the actual A characters from the eight fonts. The names of the fonts give a hint of the typography style represented here: Dirt Devil, Graham, Intention, Oogabooga, Ribjoint, Square 40, Superior and Ultra Bronzo.

Figure 10-3. The morphing A in action.

GIF Animation Studio

The animation moves from one font to the next. Figure 10-3 shows all the steps of the morph from the GIF animation.

How he did it

It was not a simple process to create this animation. Peter went through a number of steps including setting the original type, creating the morphs, turning a QuickTime movie into separate files, and finally creating the GIF animation.

Setting the type

Using Adobe Photoshop, he created a PICT file of the letter A in each of the eight typefaces. He set the type at 48 points, antialiased. If you're working in Windows, you can save your files in the BMP format. Figure 10-4 shows the options for setting the Dirt Devil A in Photoshop.

It's important to antialias the type to create that smooth letterform. In the first place, antialiasing creates type that's attractive, not jaggy. But as you morph between the letters, if you don't antialias the type you'll get especially unattractive images as the jaggies from one letter merge with the jaggies of the next. We should note, however, that antialiasing increases file size.

Creating the morphs

He imported those files into a morphing program from Avid Technologies called Elastic Reality and had it morph through the eight PICT files in six seconds. He used the program's default settings.

"I learned just enough about Elastic Reality to do what I wanted to do," Peter says. Elastic Reality is just one morphing program. There are several others for both Mac

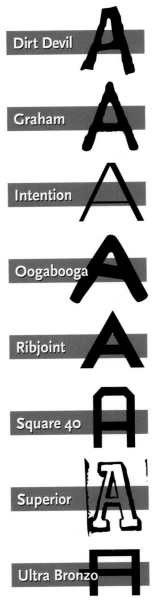

Figure 10-2. The original A's from the eight Voyager fonts.

Voyager Company

Voyager's home page is at *http://www.voyagerco.com*. But you won't see this animation on the home page. Just before press time, Voyager changed the icon for the Font Shop. But you can still see the animation at this URL: *http://www.voyagerco.com/fount/gifs/none.gif* And we've included the animation on the CD in the *Samples/Chapter10* folder.

Elastic Reality

Avid Technology, Inc.
Metropolitan Technology Park
One Park West
Tewksbury, MA 01876
(800) 949-AVID
(508) 640-6789

Avid recently stopped production of its low-end version of Elastic Reality for Macintosh and Windows. They continue to sell a high-end version for Silicon Graphics workstations. A new version for Mac and Windows will be released in the first quarter of 1997, which will have all the features previously available only on the SGI platform.

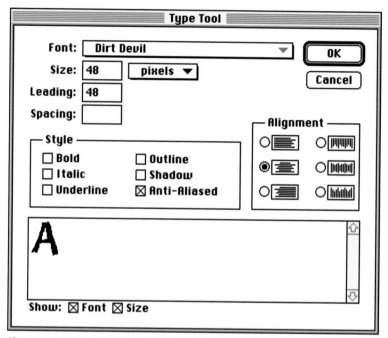

Figure 10-4. Setting the letter A in Photoshop.

and Windows, many under $100. The basic concept of morphing is to take two images and interpolate a number of intermediary steps between them, giving the impression of one image transforming into another.

Figure 10-5 shows setting the morph between the Dirt Devil A and the Graham A. The first font is set in the "A roll" and the second font is set in the "B roll". The FX roll specifies the number of frames that the morph will last. Figure 10-6, the *Edit* window, shows the two letter forms overlaid.

Once Peter finished the morph sequence in Elastic Reality, he exported it as a QuickTime movie, again using Elastic Reality's default settings.

He imported the QuickTime movie into DeBabelizer (a file conversion program from Equilibrium Technologies). DeBabelizer displayed each of the individual frames of the QuickTime movie, which Peter saved as separate GIF files.

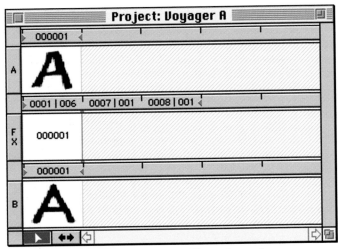

Figure 10-5. The two letter forms that will morph together.

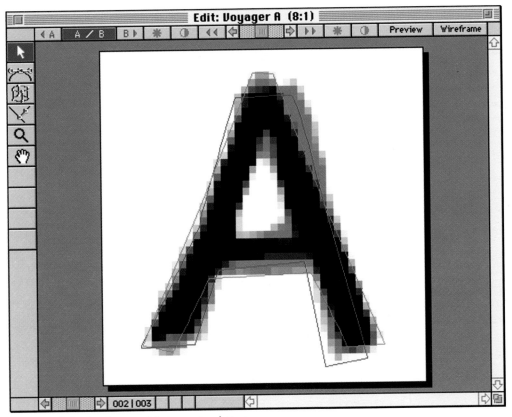

Figure 10-6. Setting the morph between two letters.

Frames					
46 frames	Length : 4.60 s		Size : 48x84		Loop : forever
Name	Size	Position	Disp.	Delay	Transp.
frame 1	48x84	(0 ; 0)	N	10	-
frame 2	48x84	(0 ; 0)	N	10	-
frame 3	48x84	(0 ; 0)	N	10	-
frame 4	48x84	(0 ; 0)	N	10	-
frame 5	48x84	(0 ; 0)	N	10	-
frame 6	48x84	(0 ; 0)	N	10	-
frame 7	48x84	(0 ; 0)	N	10	-
frame 8	48x84	(0 ; 0)	N	10	-
frame 9	48x84	(0 ; 0)	N	10	-
frame 10	48x84	(0 ; 0)	N	10	-
frame 11	48x84	(0 ; 0)	N	10	-
frame 12	48x84	(0 ; 0)	N	10	-
frame 13	48x84	(0 ; 0)	N	10	-
frame 14	48x84	(0 ; 0)	N	10	-
frame 15	48x84	(0 ; 0)	N	10	-
frame 16	48x84	(0 ; 0)	N	10	-
frame 17	48x84	(0 ; 0)	N	10	-
frame 18	48x84	(0 ; 0)	N	10	-
frame 19	48x84	(0 ; 0)	N	10	-
frame 20	48x84	(0 ; 0)	N	10	-
frame 21	48x84	(0 ; 0)	N	10	-
frame 22	48x84	(0 ; 0)	N	10	-
frame 23	48x84	(0 ; 0)	N	10	-
frame 24	48x84	(0 ; 0)	N	10	-
frame 25	48x84	(0 ; 0)	N	10	-
frame 26	48x84	(0 ; 0)	N	10	-
frame 27	48x84	(0 ; 0)	N	10	-
frame 28	48x84	(0 ; 0)	N	10	-
frame 29	48x84	(0 ; 0)	N	10	-
frame 30	48x84	(0 ; 0)	N	10	-
frame 31	48x84	(0 ; 0)	N	10	-
frame 32	48x84	(0 ; 0)	N	10	-
frame 33	48x84	(0 ; 0)	N	10	-
frame 34	48x84	(0 ; 0)	N	10	-
frame 35	48x84	(0 ; 0)	N	10	-
frame 36	48x84	(0 ; 0)	N	10	-
frame 37	48x84	(0 ; 0)	N	10	-
frame 38	48x84	(0 ; 0)	N	10	-
frame 39	48x84	(0 ; 0)	N	10	-
frame 40	48x84	(0 ; 0)	N	10	-
frame 41	48x84	(0 ; 0)	N	10	-
frame 42	48x84	(0 ; 0)	N	10	-
frame 43	48x84	(0 ; 0)	N	10	-
frame 44	48x84	(0 ; 0)	N	10	-
frame 45	48x84	(0 ; 0)	N	10	-
frame 46	48x84	(0 ; 0)	N	10	-

Figure 10-7. The GIFBuilder frames window for the fount animation.

He saved the GIFs as 8-bit images and limited the number of colors to 3. (See Chapter 5 for more about bit depth, color palettes and so on.)

None of this is necessary anymore, since Elastic Reality can export numbered PICT files or PICS files, both of which are suitable for importing into the latest version of GIFBuilder. In version 0.4, you can even import QuickTime movies.

To create the GIF animation, Peter opened GIFBuilder and imported all 46 individual GIFs created in DeBabelizer. He selected all the frames (Command-A) and gave each a delay of 10/100ths of a second *(Options/Interframe Delay,* value of 10). Finally he output the GIF animation *(File/Save As).*

Fluid transitions

Peter's animated A stands out because of the fluid effect created by morphing between the letters rather than just flipping through them.

"The morphing was very important for the feel of it. That's the cool aspect. I don't have a problem with cool as long as it's nonobtrusive. If it excites the user, if it draws them in, it does a better job than a static image," he says.

Another effect of the morphing is more conceptual. "It shows all the forms of the letters and how they are linked to each other but different. It shows off the archetypal form of the letter A, the fluidity of typefaces. That wasn't a stated goal of mine in the beginning, but it was probably rattling around somewhere in my subconscious."

11 Hare Krishna Cyclotron

Our final example is something called "Hare Krishna Cyclotron" by renowned illustrator Henrik Drescher. The Danish-born Drescher has written and illustrated more than 20 children's books and done editorial illustrations for *The New York Times* and other prestigious publications. At the time of this writing, Drescher was living in Bali, Indonesia, where his wife Lauren was working as an apprentice midwife while he continued to work on children's books and magazine illustrations.

Figure 11-1. The cyclotron animation at the end of its cycle.

Drescher created this animation for the Summer '96 issue of @tlas, a Web site concerned with design and visual arts.

"The animation is based on a cremation ceremony that I attended in Bali (where we spend a lot of time). I've always loved the corny dioramas that Hare Krishnas use to illustrate the birth/death cycle, and this was my inspiration and tribute to these," he explains.

The animation depicts a life cycle, from a baby exiting the womb to a skeleton falling apart. The various stages of

@tlas

http://atlas.organic.com/

life are depicted circling a pocket watch, which shows the relentless forward movement of time. Figure 11-1 shows the animation in its final stage (so to speak).

The animation consists of a very large black frame with the pocket watch in the center and separate images of the body positioned to form a circle. Drescher makes use of the *As Fast As Possible* setting (under **Options/Interframe Delay** in GIFBuilder) to create the illusion that two separate images are appearing simultaneously. Figure 11-2 shows the GIFBuilder Frames window for this animation. The frames with a dash under the Delay column are set to change as fast as possible.

While the animation frame itself is huge, 775 pixels wide by 550 high, the individual images are relatively small. The watch is the largest image, at 195x142. The entire animation has a black background (set in **Options/Background Color** in GIFBuilder) and all frames are set to

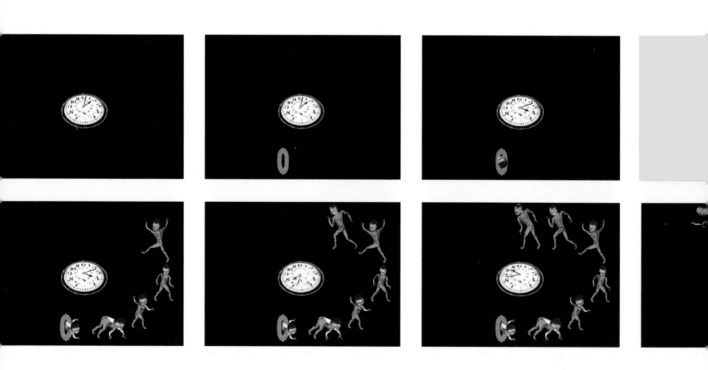

Henrik Drescher

Collections of Drescher's work have been exhibited at the Library of Congress, the Museum of Modern Art, The Getty Museum (Los Angeles), the New York Public Library and the Walker Art Center (Minneapolis).

His *Simons Book* (1983) was picked as one of the 10 best illustrated children's book by *The New York Times* and won the Parent's Choice Award. Three of his other children's books were in the *Times'* 10 best list in 1982, 1987 and 1993.

Drescher has won gold and silver awards for his illustrations from the Toronto Art Directors Club, the Society of Illustrators Annual Exhibition (New York) and the Art Directors Club of New York. He also won four awards of excellence from *Communications Arts* magazine.

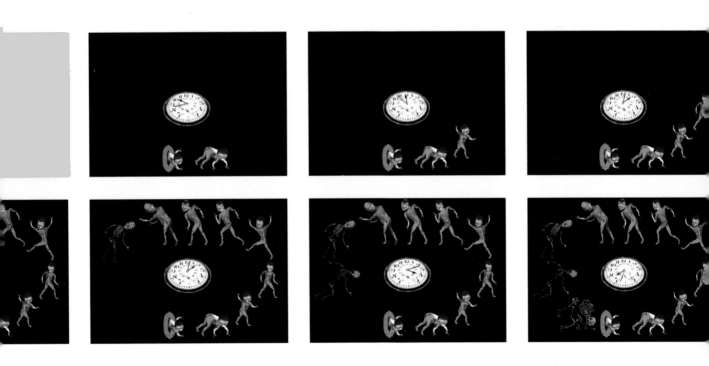

Hare Krishna Cyclotron

Frames					
26 frames	Length: 5.55 s		Size: 775x550		Loop: forever
Name	Size	Position	Disp.	Delay	Transp.
Frame 1	195x142	(286 ; 222)	N	-	-
Frame 2	59x113	(281 ; 427)	N	75	-
Frame 3	195x142	(286 ; 222)	N	-	-
Frame 4	59x113	(281 ; 427)	N	40	-
Frame 5	195x142	(286 ; 222)	N	-	-
Frame 6	89x113	(281 ; 427)	N	40	-
Frame 7	195x142	(286 ; 222)	N	-	-
Frame 8	142x99	(410 ; 433)	N	40	-
Frame 9	195x142	(286 ; 222)	N	-	-
Frame 10	100x142	(564 ; 347)	N	40	-
Frame 11	195x142	(286 ; 222)	N	-	-
Frame 12	87x149	(655 ; 235)	N	40	-
Frame 13	195x142	(286 ; 222)	N	-	-
Frame 14	120x177	(606 ; 60)	N	40	-
Frame 15	195x142	(286 ; 222)	N	-	-
Frame 16	133x184	(479 ; 6)	N	40	-
Frame 17	195x142	(286 ; 222)	N	-	-
Frame 18	107x177	(358 ; 5)	N	40	-
Frame 19	195x142	(286 ; 222)	N	-	-
Frame 20	168x170	(184 ; 12)	N	40	-
Frame 21	195x142	(286 ; 222)	N	-	-
Frame 22	137x163	(47 ; 83)	N	40	-
Frame 23	195x142	(286 ; 222)	N	-	-
Frame 24	185x163	(15 ; 234)	N	40	-
Frame 25	195x142	(286 ; 222)	N	-	-
Frame 26	157x135	(117 ; 378)	N	40	-

Figure 11-2. The settings for the cyclotron animation as shown in GIFBuilder.

Do Not Dispose. These settings eliminate the need to create a huge image as the first frame, which reduces file size.

The first image is the watch (set to 2:00) as seen on the previous pages. The second frame is the womb image, which appears at virtually the same time as the first frame.

In subsequent images we see the baby's head and then the baby's body emerge from the womb as the time on the watch changes. Then the wonderfully strange images (with the skeleton ever-present) as the baby grows into a man and fades into non-existence.

GIF Animation Studio

12

Animating with Photoshop Filters

A simple and effective way to create animations is to incrementally apply Photoshop filters to your image. This chapter is mostly pictures. We take the same image and try to simulate the animation effects by slowly applying the filter from frame to frame. The image we're using was taken by Tom Page, a San Diego-based photographer. It's a product shot of some space-age pacifiers.

Tom Page Photography's site is http://www.redrom. com/tom/

As Tom tells it: "I was hired by Quiet Time, Inc. to shoot a series of product shots illustrating their groovy re-invention of the baby pacifier. It seems that there are moms in the world who get seriously grossed out when anything touches the working end of their little lugnut's 'pluggy.' You see, when the pacifier is not in use, the xylophonic sheath is extended keeping the nipple free of disgusting debris. When your little squealer needs pure sucking satisfaction, retract the sheath to expose the most sanitary object of desire. (A high tech latex strep-sickle.) The product was designed by Charles and Andrew at DesignDesign in Cardiff, CA."

We used the standard Photoshop filters and some filters from Kai's Power Tools. There are many more third-party Photoshop filters, of course. So pull up your favorite filters and experiment.

Crystallize

The Crystallize filter creates crystal-like formations. The animation builds up to the highest distortion (15 pixels), then slowly returns to normal.

  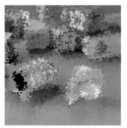 

Displace

The Displace filter uses a displacement map to create the distortion. Here we use the mezzo effect displacement map with 40-pixel distortion in both the horizontal and vertical axis.

Edges

Here we used the KPT Edge f/x filter from Kai's Power Tools 3.0. Opacity was set to 100% for all images and the effect intensity was gradually turned up to 100%.

Emboss

The Emboss filter was applied in increasing increments. The filter lets you choose angle, effect height (up to 10 pixels), and amount (from 0% to 500%).

Fade-In

We didn't use any filters for this effect. We just gradually increased the opacity of the image from 0% to 100%, using the Opacity slider on the Layers palette.

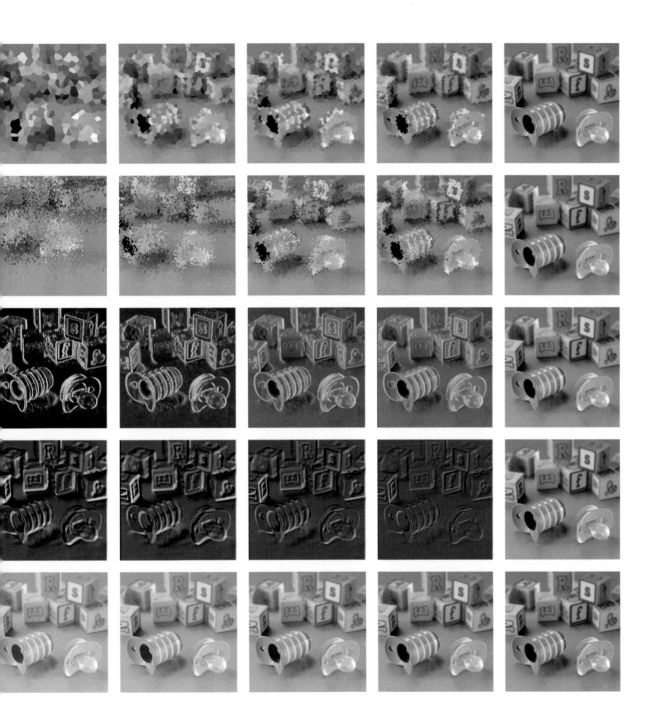

Animating with Photoshop Filters

Gaussian Blur

We used the Gaussian Blur f/x filter from KPT here, gradually building up to about 40% blur.

KPT Pixel

KPT's Pixel f/x filter appears to break an image into tiny dots. There are several different apply modes, as well as an option to apply in one or two directions.

    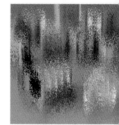

Median

Median creates a softening effect. Again, we gradually increased the effect and then decreased it, returning to the original image.

Mosaic

This filter "pixelates" the image, making it look like it's made of large squares.

Motion Blur

We applied Motion Blur at a 40° angle. We used 60 pixels for the most extreme setting.

   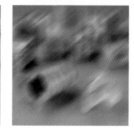 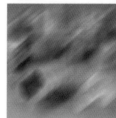

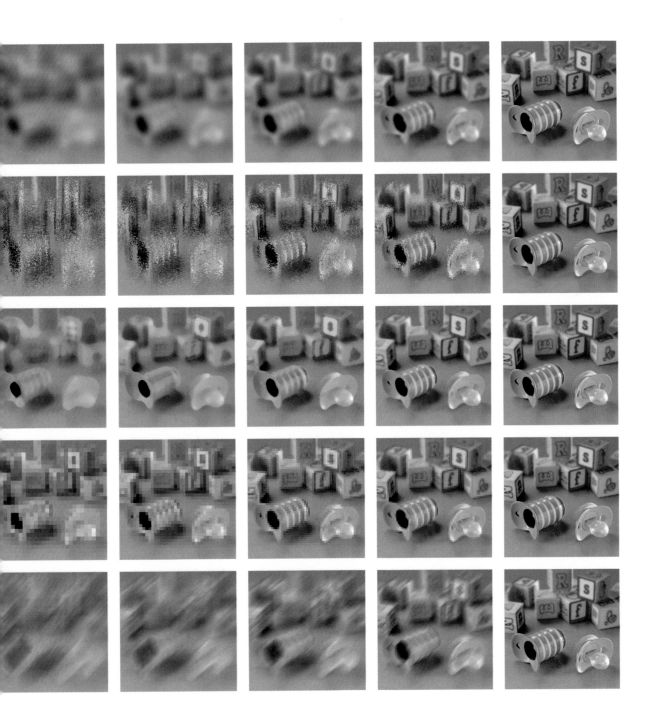

KPT Page Curl

This example unfurls an image using KPT Page Curl. In the first image, the effect is set at 100% and is gradually reduced until the entire image is displayed.

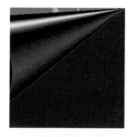 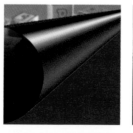  

KPT Planar

Here we get the effect of the image falling back to unveil a seemingly infinite number of images stretch out to a horizon. The example uses the filter's *Perspective Tiling* option.

Pointilize

As you apply this filter, the image is broken into Impressionist-like points. We used 5 pixels for the most extreme setting.

 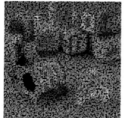 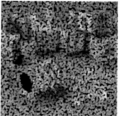 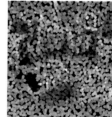

Radial Blur

This filter has options for creating a *spin* blur or a *zoom* blur. We used the spin setting, best quality. We used 30 pixels for the most extreme setting.

   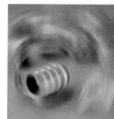

Ripple

In the Ripple filter, there are options for small, medium or large waves. We used medium waves and a value of 600 for the most extreme setting.

  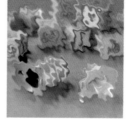 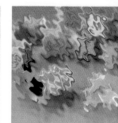

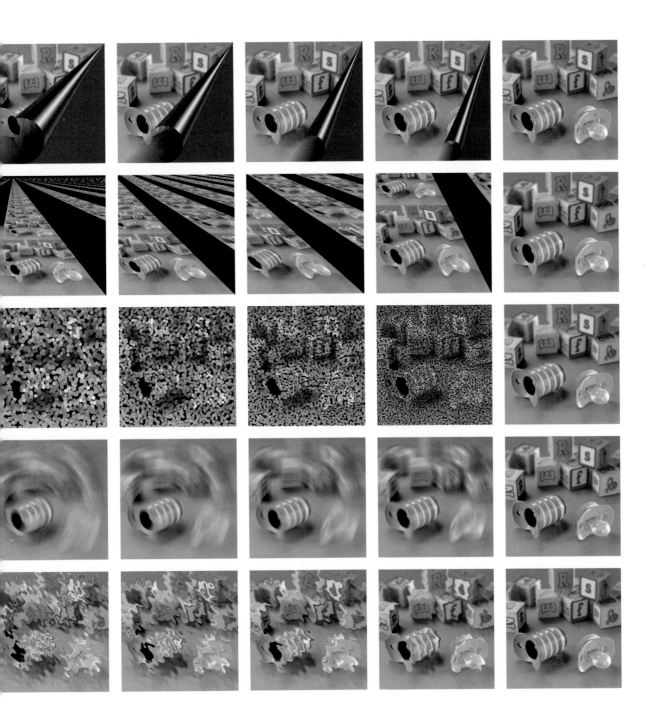

Shear

This is a path-based effect. In this example, we first pulled the image to the right, then pulled just the bottom of the image to the left.

KPT Smudge

Created with KPT Smudge f/x, this example incrementally smudges the image at a 0° angle.

Twirl

The Twirl filter was applied with a setting of 400 in the most extreme frame.

Wave

This is a complex filter, with settings for numbers of waves, amplitude, wavelength and scale. There's also a randomize option, which we used in this example.

 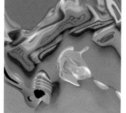 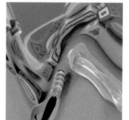 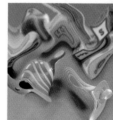

Zig Zag

With the Zig Zag filter you choose the number of ridges and amount of distortion. Here we used the *Pond Ripples* setting, 5 ridges and an amount of 10.

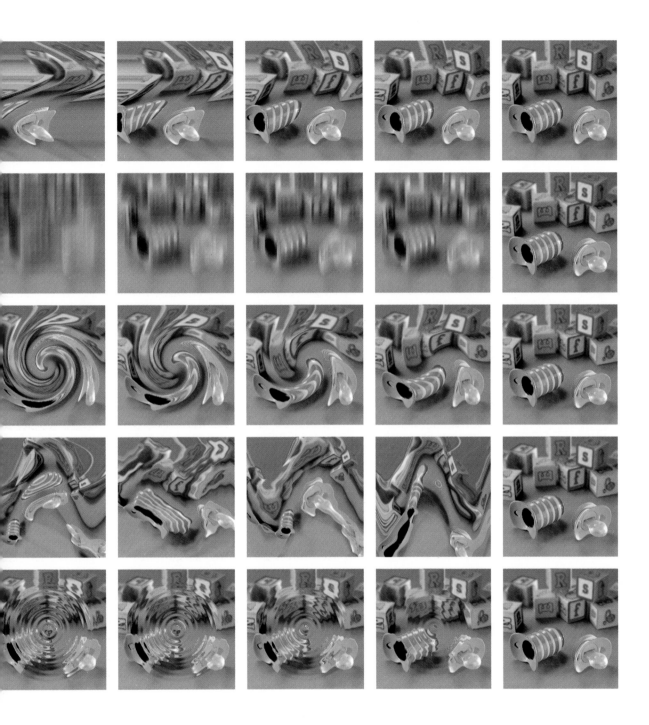

A Software Installation Instructions

The companion CD-ROM is readable by both Macs and Windows 95/NT PCs. Windows 3.1 users will *not* be able to read the CD!

Macintosh. Mac users will find the software in the *Software* folder. The color picker tools and KPT presets are located in the *Support Files* folder. To view the sample files, open the *Animations* folder and load the *index.html* file in a Web browser. This document provides links to all of the animation samples on the disc. The actual GIF and HTML files are located in the *Animations/Samples* folder.

Windows 95/NT. Windows users will find the software in the *Programs/Software* folder. The color picker tools are located in the *Programs/Support* folder. To view the sample files, open the *Files* folder and load the *index.html* file in a Web browser. This document provides links to all of the animation samples on the disc. The actual GIF and HTML files are located in the *Files/Samples* folder.

rgb2hex (Mac and Windows)
This is a self-running application for converting RGB values to hexadecimal values. Double-click on the program to launch it.

6x6x6 palette (Mac), 6x6x6.act (Windows)
To use the Netscape palette in Photoshop, load this file in the *Indexed Color* or *Color Table* dialog boxes.

Netscape Palette Color Picker

Use this tool to select colors from the Netscape palette, learn the hexadecimal values, and get the BODY tag code to insert in your HTML pages. Mac users, load the *nspalette.html* file (found in *Support Files/Chapter 5/Color Converters/nspalette*) in your Web browser. Windows users, load the *!nspalette.html* file (found in *Support/HexTool.*)

Mac Software

Software programs are located in individual folders in the *Software* folder. In general, copy the program folder to your hard disk before running the program.

GIFBuilder

Copy the entire *GIFBuilder* folder from the CD-ROM to your hard disk. Double-click on the GIFBuilder icon to launch the program. This is fully functional freeware.

WebPainter

Copy the *WebPainter* folder from the CD-ROM to your hard disk. Double-click on the *WebPainter* icon to launch the program. This is a 90-day demo version.

GifGifGif

Copy the *ggg* folder from the CD to your hard disk. Double-click on the application icon. This is a 30-day demo version.

Kai's Power Tools

Double-click on the *KPT 3.0 Demo* icon to open the demo software folder. Double-click on the *KPT3 Demo Install.1* icon to install the software. Select Photoshop's plug-ins folder and click *Install.*

Adobe Photoshop

Open the *Adobe Photoshop 3.0.5 Tryout Folder* and the *Install-Part 1* folder. Double-click on the *Install Adobe Photoshop* icon. When the installer comes up, select the disk and folder you want to install on to, and click *Install.*

Windows 95/NT Software

Ulead PhotoImpact

In addition to PhotoImpact GIF Animator, a number of other Ulead products are included on the disc. All programs are 30-day trial versions. The programs are:

- PhotoImpact with WebExtensions (full-featured image editor) — *PhotoImpact/setup.exe.*
- PhotoImpact GIF Animator — *Webutil/Ga12t.exe.*
- PhotoImpact GIF/JPEG SmartSaver (graphics compression utility) — *Webutil/Uss11at.exe.*
- PhotoImpact Screen Capture (screen capture utility) — *Webutil/Pisc30t.exe.*
- PhotoImpact Album (image browser) — *Webutil/Piabm30t.exe.*
- WebExtensions for Photoshop — *Webutil/We4ps14t.exe.*

To install PhotoImpact with Web Extensions, open the *PhotoImpact* folder and run *setup.exe.*

To install the other programs open the *Webutil* folder and run the appropriate installer program and follow the directions.

VideoCraft GIF Animator

In the *Vidcraft* folder, run the installer file, *vidgif32.exe,* and follow the directions. This is a 30-day trial version.

WebPainter

In the *Webpaint* folder, run the installer file, *wp10demo.exe.* Follow the directions. This is a 30-day trial version.

CelAssembler

CelAssembler is a new product from Gamani Productions. It was released too late for coverage in the text but a 30-day trial version is included on the CD. In the *Gamani* folder, run the installer program, *celasm11.exe,* and follow the installation directions.

Gif•Gif•Gif

Open the *Software/ggg* directory and double-click on the *setup.exe* icon to run the Setup program.

Photoshop

Open the *Photoshop/Disk1* folder and run the *setup.exe* program. Then follow installation instructions. This is a save-disabled version of Photoshop.

Kai's Power Tools

In the *KPT* folder run the *setup.exe* program and follow the directions. This is a save-disabled version.

B GIFBuilder 0.4 Developer's Notes

This appendix consists of the read-me files supplied by Yves Piguet with GIFBuilder. This information is included in the Documentation and Release Notes files in the GIFBuilder folder.

GifBuilder is a scriptable utility for creating animated GIF files. Its input is an existing animated GIF, a bunch of PICT, GIF, TIFF and/or Photoshop files, a QuickTime movie, a PICS file, an Adobe Premiere FilmStrip 1.0 file, or the layers of an RGB or grayscale Adobe Photoshop 3.0 file, and its output is a GIF89a file with multiple images.

Options include pixel depth, color palette, interlacing, transparency, interframe delay, disposal method, frame offset, looping and dithering.

GifBuilder should ultimately be placed onto many ftp archives, including Info-Mac (in gst/grf), Umich (in graphics/graphicsutil) and their mirrors.

Please read this document carefully if you want to get the best of GifBuilder. There are several shortcuts which can make your work much easier.

Basic Usage

1. Draw each frame — Use any drawing program able to save as PICT, GIF, TIFF or Photoshop 2.5/3.0. Save frames in a new folder to make their retrieval easier. If you name them in alphabetical order (e.g. 0001.tiff, 0002.tiff, etc.), you can easily sort them later.

2. Collect frames in GifBuilder — Launch GifBuilder, be sure that there are no frames from a previous animation in the Frames window (if that's the case, choose *File/New*), and drag the frames from the Finder into the Frames window. Supported files are PICT, GIF, TIFF (baseline) and Photoshop 2.5 or 3 (bitmap, grayscale, indexed or RGB). If you don't have the Drag Manager (standard since MacOS 7.5), you can add each frame by choosing Add Frame in the File menu. You can also copy a picture from another application, or drag it. Then, check that they're in the correct order and, if necessary, change their order by dragging frames. You can also remove the selected frame(s) by choosing *Edit/Clear* or hitting Backspace, sort them and reverse their order. Double-clicking a frame will open it in its own application; if you modify it, save it and choose *File/Reload Frames* to update your changes (the Save command always uses the disk copy).

3. Set the options — Set the standard graphic options (pixel depth, color palette and dithering); the GIF options (size, interlacing, transparency); and the animation options (interframe delay, disposal method, frames position and looping). Some of these properties (transparency, interframe delay, disposal method and position) are attached to individual frames; select the frame or group of frames before changing them. If no frame is selected, the settings will apply to the default values used for images you import. See below for more details.

You can save the default options by choosing *Options/Save Options.*

Tip: Most options displayed in the Frames window can be changed by clicking or double-clicking them.

4. Check the animation — Choose Animation/Run. To display a specific frame, stop the animation and select it in the Frames window. You can also use the Home, End,

GIF Animation Studio

Up and Down keys. To start from the first selected frame, choose Continue. In the Animation window, you can move a frame by dragging it (the frame will be drawn on an onion skin if you hold down the Option key), or select the transparent color by Shift-clicking it (you can do it even when the animation is running, but depending on the speed, you'd better stop it first!). To position precisely the selected frames, choose Frame Position in the Options menu, or use the arrow keys (hold down the Option key if the Frames window is active).

    5. Build the animation — Choose *File/Save As.*

    6. Add an image tag to your HTML page — Choose *Edit/Copy HTML Image Tag,* and paste the resulting IMG tag in your HTML page. IMG fields contain a relative URL with the current name of the animation as well as the width and height. Of course, you can edit the tag to change the path of the image or add optional fields like ALT and ALIGN.

Options

Interlaced: With interlacing, a first rough image is loaded first, and then the vertical resolution improves in three additional passes. It isn't very useful for animations.

    Colors and Depth: For cross-platform web animations, the 6x6x6 color table is recommended. The system (or grayscale) 1 bit/pixel table should be used for black and white images. Images created with other settings are likely to be dithered on color-table-based machines. Set the Remove Unused Colors option in the Colors submenu to let GifBuilder keep only the colors present in the animation; this may reduce the file size a bit.

    Dithering: Dithering is a way to simulate intermediate color shades with clouds of points. It should be used with continuous-tone images. With dithering, the color table should be chosen so that the image isn't dithered a second time on the target machine (see above), and transparency should be off.

Image Size: When Minimum Size is on, the size is calculated so that the animation's bottom right corner corresponds to the rightest lowest frame. Frames are always cropped to fit in the animation bounding box.

Background Color: The Background Color is the color used to paint the animation bounding box where no frame is displayed. With some Web browsers, the page background is used instead.

Loop: The Loop option specifies how many times the animation is repeated. Some browsers don't recognize this option, while others loop an unlimited number of times if the setting is more than 1.

Transparent Background: All pixels which have the color specified by Transparent Background are left untouched when the frame is rendered.

Frame Position: Each frame can be shifted by an arbitrary amount. The Frame Position specifies the horizontal and vertical distances between the top left animation corner and the top left frame corner. Positive values push the frame to the left and to the lower part. Negative values result in a cropped frame.

Interframe Delay: The Interframe Delay is the delay between the current frame and the following frame renderings. It's specified in hundredths of seconds (i.e. 100 means 1 second).

Disposal Method: The Disposal Method specifies what each frame becomes once the interframe delay is elapsed. Use Unspecified when transparency is off and each frame covers the whole animation, Do Not Dispose when you want to add some bits of image to the previous animation state, Revert to Background for moving objects on a transparent background, and Revert to Previous for moving objects on a background you've drawn with an earlier large frame. Note that Revert to Background isn't supported by some browsers.

Frame Optimization: The Frame Optimization option crops each frame (but the first one) to the part that has changed. This can result in tremendous file size savings. If some, but not all, of the frames have the Disposal Method set to Revert to Background, you are warned that this may give unexpected results.

Frame Expansion: The Frame Expansion option does the opposite of Frame Optimization, i.e. it saves only whole frames. You shouldn't have to use it, but it can help with some GIF decoders (like old versions of Internet Explorer) that don't interpret correctly the frame position.

Notes

New: After asking if you want to save your previous animation, New removes all the frames and reads the default settings from the Preference file.

Open: You can open an existing animation, or append to the end of the current animation by holding down the Shift key and choosing *File/Open* or typing Command-Shift-O. Frames displayed in italic are loaded in memory, while those displayed in roman correspond to separate files.

Save Selection: Only the selected frames are saved. Can be used to export single frames as GIF files.

Convert: You can convert a QuickTime movie, a PICS or a FilmStrip directly to an animated GIF without opening it, by choosing Convert in the File menu. This saves a lot of memory, but is less flexible: the current options are used, all the frames are saved, and no frame optimization is performed.

Clear: Clear (in the Edit menu) or the Backspace key deletes the selected frames. To preserve the timing, hold down the Shift key and choose Special Clear or type delete.

Undo: Undo allows to return to the state just before the last operation which changed the frames or frame order.

Color palette: System Palette and Gray Shades are fixed palette. Best Palette is optimized for all the frames simultaneously. 6x6x6 Palette is a subset of the System palette where each component takes the six values 0, 51, 102, 153, 204 and 255; it has 6x6x6 = 216 entries. It's the palette used by Netscape for Windows, so you might want to choose it to avoid additional dithering on both Macintosh and Windows machines.

Load Palette lets you use a Photoshop-compatible palette file. Three such palettes are included with GifBuilder: *Gray from 6x6x6 Palette* (six gray values of the 6x6x6 palette), *2x2x2 Palette* (eight basic colors where each component is 0 or 255), or *16 from 6x6x6 Palette,* superset of the previous one with eight additional colors: (153,153,153), (0,153,255), (255,51,0), (51,153,0), (255,153,255), (153,204,255), (255,255,153) and (204,204,204) (see below). All of them should give good results on both the Mac and Windows.

Note that the 4-bits-per-pixel System palette has some intermediate colors and shouldn't be used if you're concerned about cross-platform issues.

To reuse the color palette of an existing GIF, open the GIF file with Open (in the File menu) and save the palette with Save Palette (in the Colors submenu of the Options menu). The GIF file doesn't have to contain multiple frames.

The format of palette file is 256 entries of three bytes which represent the red, green and blue values of the corresponding index. 0 is black, and 255 is the maximum intensity. For palettes of less than 256 colors, fill the unused entries with the last used one. The file type is '8BCT', and the file creator should be 'gfBr' (GifBuilder's) to have a nice icon. Note that in AppleScript, RGB values are in the range 0-65535; to convert them from a byte value, multiply them by 257.

When you load a palette, you can't choose the depth anymore. Choose a System, grayscale or best palette before changing the depth.

Scripting

Warning: scripting support is experimental. Some functionality is missing. This should be fixed in future releases.

The core AppleEvents and a rudimentary object model are partially implemented, allowing you to create new and modify existing animations. Here is an example of what can be done:

```
tell application "GifBuilder"
    open file "animation.gif" — opens an existing animation
    make new frame at the beginning Â
        with data {contents:somePictObject}
-- prepends a new frame with default frame options
    make new frame at the end Â
        with data {contents:file "lastFrame.tiff",
        translation:{10, 10},
        transparency:first pixel,
        disposal method:restore to background,
        interframe delay:50}
-- appends another frame, with specified options
    make new frame before 5th frame with data
    {contents:file "newFrame.pict"}
-- inserts a frame
save in file "animation2.gif"
-- saves the animation in a new file
end tell
```

The color values are in the range 0 (black) - 65535 (maximum intensity). The PICTs can be created by any good graphic (and many other) applications.

And here is a "real" example that creates a bouncing ball on a transparent black background with clip2gif:

```
property w : 10
property h : 95
tell application "GifBuilder"
        new
        repeat with t from -13 to 12
        set y to t * t / 2
        tell application "clip2gif-ppc" to set p to save {w, h}
        in picture
            drawing {{rectangle:{0, 0, w, h}}, {disk:{0, y, w, y +
            w}, color:{65535, 0, 0}}}
        make new frame at end
            with data {contents:p, transparency:first pixel,
            disposal method:restore to background}
```

```
        end repeat
            set loop to 0
            save in new file
            run animation
    end tell
```

Results

Some option combinations can give unexpected results; this may be caused by strange features, viewer bugs, or GifBuilder bugs. If you don't succeed in creating files that load correctly in Netscape, choose Reset to Factory Settings in the Options menu and import your frames again.

One of the main goals of GifBuilder is to stick as closely as possible to the GIF 89a specifications, not to reproduce the way animations are performed on some particular browser.

Requirements

GifBuilder requires System 7 or above and 32-bit Color QuickDraw. The Drag Manager (which comes with PowerTalk and System 7.5) is recommended. AppleScript is obviously needed to Apple-script GifBuilder. On the PowerMacs, the file ObjectSupportLib is needed in the Extensions folder; it should be included with the System and AppleScript installer. QuickTime is needed for importing QuickTime movies. If Convert (in the File menu) is dimmed, QuickTime is not correctly installed.

The animation, as well as the individual frames if they're loaded, must fit in RAM; set the application memory partition appropriately (Get Info in the Finder). GifBuilder shouldn't crash in low memory conditions; but if it does, try to increase the memory partition to some high value (if you can) before sending me a bug report.

Frequently Asked Questions

Local animations are OK, but when I use an HTTP server, they don't loop and the end of the last frame is corrupted. What happens?

You probably corrupted the file when you uploaded it to the server. Be sure that you choose the binary mode (not MacBinary) for your file transfer.

Can I choose which frame is displayed by old browsers?

No. Some GIF decoders display only the first frame, while others render all the images but don't recognize the looping Netscape 2.0 extension.

Netscape doesn't display correctly transparent animations. Is there a trick?

Try to set the Disposal Method of all the frames to Revert to Background, and specify a background GIF to be tiled behind the HTML page with the <body> tag: <body background=tile.gif>.

There is a flash when the animation loops. What can I do?

Try to remove interlacing and to use a cross-platform color palette (e.g. the 6x6x6 Palette).

Is it possible to have an animated background?

Not with the current versions of Netscape..

Should I put the original images on my server?

No. Animated GIFs are completely self-contained. They don't contain any references to the original files.

How can I stop animations in Netscape 2.0 for the Mac?

You should hold down the Command key and hit the dot key exactly when Netscape reloads the image from its cache.

I want to keep the color palette of my frames, which are GIF files. What should I do?

Open one of your frames in GifBuilder with Open, add the other frames and set their options, and save the result.

Why can't I choose a System Palette with a depth of 3, 5, 6 or 7 bits/pixel, or a 6x6x6 Palette with a depth smaller than 8?

Because there are no such palettes.

Why is the transparency set to First Pixel even if I specify a color?

In GIF files, the transparency is always based on a color. When GifBuilder reads an animation, it looks at the first pixel to see if it's the transparent color, and if so reports that the transparency is based on it.

Why do I get the error "File not found" when I save the animation?

For disk-based frames (whose name is displayed in roman), GifBuilder uses the content of the files when it builds the animation or when you choose Reload Frames in the File menu. You should leave the files where they were when you imported them.

Why do I get an error message saying that a feature isn't supported when I import a TIFF or Photoshop image?

Because GifBuilder supports only the most common, publicly documented and patent-free formats. Supported TIFF files include bitmap, grayscale, indexed and RGB, uncompressed or compressed with Packbits. Supported Photoshop files include bitmap, grayscale, indexed, RGB and duotone (read as grayscale), version 2.5 or 3.0.

How can I choose the comment displayed by JPEGView and other utilities?

You can't. GifBuilder adds a fixed comment containing its and my names. This is deliberate.

I've found a GifBuilder bug! Revert to Previous doesn't work!

If your browser doesn't handle correctly a feature, this isn't necessarily a GifBuilder bug. This one, for instance, is most probably not.

Images are dithered even if I don't select it in GifBuilder! Why?

Images are usually dithered by the browser if its palette isn't the same as the GIF's. You'd better use the 6x6x6 palette provided with GifBuilder, which is used by several browsers on the Mac as well as on alien machines, and let GifBuilder do the dithering if you need to.

I don't use Windows 3.1 anymore. Are you working on a Windows NT version?

GifBuilder runs on the Mac. I don't intend to port it to any currently available operating system (I might have ideas about new ones, however).

So give me the source, I'll port it.

First, I don't make the source code available. Second, even if it was, the GIF part is about 10% of the whole program. The remaining is closely tied to the Mac user interface and graphical model.

Compatibility with other programs

Programs are mentioned here for information only. Some of them are quite good (imo), others aren't (imho); don't try to deduce which ones I like or love.

Netscape Navigator 2.01 for Mac

Netscape Navigator 2.01 for Mac doesn't support all the GIF89a features. Features not supported include Revert to Previous, all the transparency specifications except the one for the first frame (which is applied globally to all the frames), transparency without a background GIF in the <body> tag (use <body background=tile.gif>), and the number of loops.

Microsoft Internet Explorer 2 for Mac

Neither the frame position nor the looping is taken into account. Use Expand Frames.

NCSA Mosaic 2.0.1 for Mac

Only the last frame is displayed. Partial frames result in corrupted images (version 3.0A2 has the same problems). Use Expand Frames.

Apple Cyberdog 1.0

Neither the looping nor the timing info is taken into account. At the end, the last frame is displayed.

Adobe Photoshop 3.0

You can create individual frames in Photoshop and save them as Photoshop bitmap, grayscale or RGB files, and drag them from the Finder to the GifBuilder Frames window (duotone files can also be imported, but color information is lost). PICT, GIF and TIFF files are of course also possible.

GifBuilder can also load the layers of a grayscale or RGB Photoshop 3.0 file. Each layer is rendered onto a white opaque background. To create the animation, you can draw the first frame on the Background layer. Then for each new frame, choose Duplicate Layer, hide the other layers, and edit the new one.

Adobe Premiere 4.0

You can save animations as QuickTime movies, FilmStrips or bunches of numbered PICT files. The FilmStrip format is recommended, because it's more convenient than several PICT files and guaranties that no lossy compression method is used. You can also edit it in Photoshop.

Specular Infini-D 3.0 and LogoMotion 2.0

You can save animations either as QuickTime movies or PICS, and open them in GifBuilder to save them as animated GIF. The PICS format is recommended, because it guaranties that no lossy compression method is used.

Release Notes

For each release, main improvements are listed first, followed by minor modifications and bug fixes.

0.4 (7/8/96)

- PICS, Adobe Premiere FilmStrip 1.0 and Adobe Photoshop 3.0 RGB and grayscale layers import (as animation)
- Photoshop bitmap, grayscale (or duotone), indexed and RGB files input (as frames)
- Built-in 6x6x6 palette
- Optional suppression of unused colors
- Frame expansion
- Option + arrow keys to position precisely the frames
- Onion skin during frame positioning with the Option key
- Save Selection
- New stops the animation
- "create GIF" AppleScript command removed (use the object model instead)
- Minor cosmetic improvements
- Crashes when one drags too many frames fixed
- QuickTime movie conversion fixed (memory leak fixed, interruptible)
- Frames window automatic scrolling
- Explanation when ObjectSupportLib is not found
- Frame crop marks
- Transparency based on the first pixel wasn't always rendered correctly in the Animation window; fixed
- Error message for error -43 (file nor found)
- Memory leak when an error occurred during the animation creation fixed
- Import Frame didn't display the imported frame; fixed
- No error message for corrupted TIFF file or unsupported TIFF feature; fixed
- The set data AppleEvent didn't work with boolean settings; fixed
- Animation size is frozen when a frame is dragged around.

Index

W

Index

More Titles from O'REILLY™

Web Publishing

Shockwave Studio: Designing Multimedia for the Web

By Bob Schmitt
1st Edition March 1997
200 pages, Includes CD-ROM
ISBN 1-56592-231-X

This book, the second title in the new Web Studio series, shows how to create compelling and functional Shockwave movies for Web sites. The author focuses on actual Shockwave movies, showing how the movies were created. The book provides and explains the actual Lingo source code for the movies. It takes users from creating simple time-based Shockwave animations to writing complex logical operations that take full advantage of Director's power. Glossaries of Net-specific Lingo commands and a poster that provides a quick reference to the Director interface are included. CD-ROM includes demo version of Director and other software sample files.

The Web Studio series—published by O'Reilly & Associates' affiliate company, Songline Studios, publishers of the groundbreaking Web sites Web Review and Ferndale—demystifies the complexities of publishing multimedia on the Web. The series is aimed at creative Web professionals and enthusiasts—the people creating graphics, animation, sound, and multimedia on the Web.

HTML: The Definitive Guide

By Chuck Musciano & Bill Kennedy
2nd Edition Winter 1997
420 pages (est.), ISBN 1-56592-175-5

HTML: The Definitive Guide, second edition, is a complete guide to creating documents on the World Wide Web. This book describes basic syntax and semantics and goes on to show you how to create beautiful, informative, and dynamic Web documents you'll be proud to display.

The second edition covers the most up-to-date version of the HTML standard (the proposed HTML version 3.2), Netscape 3.0 and Internet Explorer 3.0, plus all the common extensions, especially Netscape extensions. The authors cover each and every element of the currently accepted version of the language in detail, explaining how each element works and how it interacts with all the other elements. They've also included a style guide that helps you decide how to best use HTML to accomplish a variety of tasks, from simple online documentation to complex marketing and sales presentations. Readers of the first edition can find the updates for the second edition on the Web at *www.ora.com*.

Designing for the Web: Getting Started in a New Medium

By Jennifer Niederst with Edie Freedman
1st Edition April 1996
180 pages, ISBN 1-56592-165-8

Designing for the Web gives you the basics you need to hit the ground running. Although geared toward designers, it covers information and techniques useful to anyone who wants to put graphics online. It explains how to work with HTML documents from a designer's point of view, outlines special problems with presenting information online, and walks through incorporating images into Web pages, with emphasis on resolution and improving efficiency.

JavaScript: The Definitive Guide

By David Flanagan
1st Edition Winter 1997
700 pages (est.), ISBN 1-56592-234-4

This definitive reference guide to JavaScript, the HTML extension that gives Web pages programming language capa-bilities, covers JavaScript as it is used in Netscape 3.0 and 2.0 and in Microsoft Internet Explorer 2.0. Learn how JavaScript really works (and when it doesn't). Use JavaScript to control Web browser behavior, add dynamically created text to Web pages, interact with users through HTML forms, and even control and interact with Java applets and Navigator plug-ins.

Building Your Own WebSite

By Susan B. Peck & Stephen Arrants
1st Edition July 1996
514 pages, ISBN 1-56592-232-8

A hands-on reference for Windows® 95 and Windows NT™ desktop users who want to host their own site on the Web or on a corporate intranet. This step-by-step guide will have you creating live Web pages in minutes. You'll also learn how to connect your web to information in other Windows applications, such as word processing documents and databases. Packed with examples and tutorials on every aspect of Web management. Includes highly acclaimed WebSite™ 1.1—all the software you need for Web publishing.

For information: **800-998-9938**, 707-829-0515; **info@ora.com; http://www.ora.com/**
To order: **800-889-8969** (credit card orders only); **order@ora.com**

Stay in touch with O'REILLY™

Visit Our Award-Winning World Wide Web Site

http://www.ora.com/

VOTED

"Top 100 Sites on the Web" —*PC Magazine*
"Top 5% Websites" —*Point Communications*
"3-Star site" —*The McKinley Group*

Our Web site contains a library of comprehensive product information (including book excerpts and tables of contents), downloadable software, background articles, interviews with technology leaders, links to relevant sites, book cover art, and more. File us in your Bookmarks or Hotlist!

Join Our Two Email Mailing Lists

LIST #1   NEW PRODUCT RELEASES: To receive automatic email with brief descriptions of all new O'Reilly products as they are released, send email to: listproc@online.ora.com and put the following information in the first line of your message (NOT in the Subject: field, which is ignored): **subscribe ora-news "Your Name" of "Your Organization"** (for example: **subscribe ora-news Kris Webber of Fine Enterprises)**

List #2   O'REILLY EVENTS: If you'd also like us to send information about trade show events, special promotions, and other O'Reilly events, send email to: **listproc@online.ora.com** and put the following information in the first line of your message (NOT in the Subject: field, which is ignored): **subscribe ora-events "Your Name" of "Your Organization"**

Visit Our Gopher Site

- Connect your Gopher to **gopher.ora.com**, or
- Point your Web browser to **gopher://gopher.ora.com/**, or
- telnet to **gopher.ora.com** (login: **gopher**)

Get Example Files from Our Books Via FTP

There are two ways to access an archive of example files from our books:

REGULAR FTP — ftp to: **ftp.ora.com** (login: **anonymous**—use your email address as the password) or point your Web browser to: **ftp://ftp.ora.com/**

FTPMAIL — Send an email message to: **ftpmail@online.ora.com** (write "help" in the message body)

Contact Us Via Email

order@ora.com — To place a book or software order online. Good for North American and international customers.

subscriptions@ora.com — To place an order for any of our newsletters or periodicals.

software@ora.com — For general questions and product information about our software.
- Check out O'Reilly Software Online at **http://software.ora.com/** for software and technical support information.
- Registered O'Reilly software users send your questions to **website-support@ora.com**

books@ora.com — For General questions about any of our books.

cs@ora.com — For solutions to problems regarding your order or our products.

booktech@ora.com — For book content technical questions or corrections.

proposals@ora.com — To submit book or software proposals to our editors and product managers.

international@ora.com — For information about our international distributors or translation queries.
- For a list of our distributors outside of North America check out: **http://www.ora.com/www/order/country.html**

O'REILLY™

101 Morris Street, Sebastopol, CA 95472 USA
TEL 707-829-0515 or 800-998-9938 (6 A.M. to 5 P.M. PST)
FAX 707-829-0104

Listing of Titles from O'REILLY™

INTERNET PROGRAMMING

CGI Programming on the World Wide Web
Designing for the Web
Exploring Java
HTML: The Definitive Guide
Web Client Programming with Perl
Learning Perl
Programming Perl, 2nd Edition (Fall '96)
JavaScript: The Definitive Guide,
    Beta Edition
Webmaster in a Nutshell
The World Wide Web Journal

USING THE INTERNET

Smileys
The Whole Internet User's Guide and Catalog
The Whole Internet for Windows 95
What You Need to Know:
    Using Email Effectively
Marketing on the Internet (Fall '96)
What You Need to Know: Bandits on the
    Information Superhighway

JAVA SERIES

Exploring Java
Java in a Nutshell
Java Language Reference (Fall '96 est.)
Java Virtual Machine

WINDOWS

Inside the Windows '95 Registry

SOFTWARE

WebSite™ 1.1
WebSite Professional™
WebBoard™
PolyForm™
Statisphere™

SONGLINE GUIDES

NetLearning
NetSuccess for Realtors
NetActivism
Gif Animation
Shockwave Studio (Winter '97 est.)

SYSTEM ADMINISTRATION

Building Internet Firewalls
Computer Crime:
    A Crimefighter's Handbook
Computer Security Basics
DNS and BIND
Essential System Administration,
    2nd Edition
Getting Connected:
    The Internet at 56K and Up
Linux Network Administrator's Guide
Managing Internet Information Services
Managing Usenet (Fall '96)
Managing NFS and NIS
Networking Personal Computers
    with TCP/IP
Practical UNIX & Internet Security
PGP: Pretty Good Privacy
sendmail
System Performance Tuning
TCP/IP Network Administration
termcap & terminfo
Using & Managing UUCP
Volume 8: X Window System
    Administrator's Guide

UNIX

Exploring Expect
Learning GNU Emacs, 2nd Edition (Fall '96)
Learning the bash Shell
Learning the Korn Shell
Learning the UNIX Operating System
Learning the vi Editor
Linux in a Nutshell (Fall '96 est.)
Making TeX Work
Linux Multimedia Guide (Fall '96)
Running Linux, 2nd Edition
Running Linux Companion CD-ROM,
    2nd Edition
SCO UNIX in a Nutshell
sed & awk
Unix in a Nutshell: System V Edition
UNIX Power Tools
UNIX Systems Programming
Using csh and tsch
What You Need to Know: When You Can't
    Find Your UNIX System Administrator

PROGRAMMING

Applying RCS and SCCS
C++: The Core Language
Checking C Programs with lint
DCE Security Programming
Distributing Applications Across
    DCE and Windows NT
Encyclopedia of Graphics File Formats,
    2nd Edition
Guide to Writing DCE Applications
lex & yacc
Managing Projects with make
ORACLE Performance Tuning
ORACLE PL/SQL Programming
Porting UNIX Software
POSIX Programmer's Guide
POSIX.4: Programming for the Real World
Power Programming with RPC
Practical C Programming
Practical C++ Programming
Programming Python (Fall '96)
Programming with curses
Programming with GNU Software
    (Fall '96 est.)
Pthreads Programming
Software Portability with imake
Understanding DCE
Understanding Japanese Information
    Processing
UNIX Systems Programming for SVR4

BERKELEY 4.4 SOFTWARE DISTRIBUTION

4.4BSD System Manager's Manual
4.4BSD User's Reference Manual
4.4BSD User's Supplementary Docs.
4.4BSD Programmer's Reference Man.
4.4BSD Programmer's Supp. Docs.

X PROGRAMMING
THE X WINDOW SYSTEM

Volume 0: X Protocol Reference Manual
Volume 1: Xlib Programming Manual
Volume 2: Xlib Reference Manual
Volume. 3M: X Window System User's Guide,
    Motif Edition
Volume. 4: X Toolkit Intrinsics
    Programming Manual
Volume 4M: X Toolkit Intrinsics
    Programming Manual, Motif Edition
Volume 5: X Toolkit Intrinsics
    Reference Manual
Volume 6A: Motif Programming Manual
Volume 6B: Motif Reference Manual
Volume 6C: Motif Tools
Volume 8 : X Window System
    Administrator's Guide
Programmer's Supplement for Release 6
X User Tools (with CD-ROM)
The X Window System in a Nutshell

HEALTH, CAREER, & BUSINESS

Building a Successful Software Business
The Computer User's Survival Guide
Dictionary of Computer Terms
The Future Does Not Compute
Love Your Job!
Publishing with CD-ROM

TRAVEL

Travelers' Tales: Brazil (Fall '96)
Travelers' Tales: Food (Fall '96)
Travelers' Tales: France
Travelers' Tales: Hong Kong
Travelers' Tales: India
Travelers' Tales: Mexico
Travelers' Tales: San Francisco
Travelers' Tales: Spain
Travelers' Tales: Thailand
Travelers' Tales: A Woman's World

TO ORDER: **800-889-8969** (CREDIT CARD ORDERS ONLY); **order@ora.com**; **http://www.ora.com/**
OUR PRODUCTS ARE AVAILABLE AT A BOOKSTORE OR SOFTWARE STORE NEAR YOU.

International Distributors

Customers outside North America can now order O'Reilly & Associates books through the following distributors. They offer our international customers faster order processing, more bookstores, increased representation at tradeshows worldwide, and the high-quality, responsive service our customers have come to expect.

EUROPE, MIDDLE EAST AND NORTHERN AFRICA
(except Germany, Switzerland, and Austria)
INQUIRIES
International Thomson Publishing Europe
Berkshire House
168-173 High Holborn
London WC1V 7AA, United Kingdom
Telephone: 44-171-497-1422
Fax: 44-171-497-1426
Email: **itpint@itps.co.uk**

ORDERS
International Thomson Publishing Services, Ltd.
Cheriton House, North Way
Andover, Hampshire SP10 5BE,
United Kingdom
Telephone: 44-264-342-832 (UK orders)
Telephone: 44-264-342-806 (outside UK)
Fax: 44-264-364418 (UK orders)
Fax: 44-264-342761 (outside UK)
UK & Eire orders: **itpuk@itps.co.uk**
International orders: **itpint@itps.co.uk**

GERMANY, SWITZERLAND, AND AUSTRIA
International Thomson Publishing GmbH
O'Reilly International Thomson Verlag
Königswinterer Straße 418
53227 Bonn, Germany
Telephone: 49-228-97024 0
Fax: 49-228-441342
Email: **anfragen@arade.ora.de**

AUSTRALIA
WoodsLane Pty. Ltd.
7/5 Vuko Place, Warriewood NSW 2102
P.O. Box 935, Mona Vale NSW 2103
Australia
Telephone: 61-2-9970-5111
Fax: 61-2-9970-5002
Email: **info@woodslane.com.au**

NEW ZEALAND
WoodsLane New Zealand Ltd.
21 Cooks Street (P.O. Box 575)
Wanganui, New Zealand
Telephone: 64-6-347-6543
Fax: 64-6-345-4840
Email: **info@woodslane.com.au**

ASIA *(except Japan & India)*
INQUIRIES
International Thomson Publishing Asia
60 Albert Street #15-01
Albert Complex
Singapore 189969
Telephone: 65-336-6411
Fax: 65-336-7411

ORDERS
Telephone: 65-336-6411
Fax: 65-334-1617

JAPAN
O'Reilly Japan, Inc.
Kiyoshige Building 2F
12-Banchi, Sanei-cho
Shinjuku-ku
Tokyo 160 Japan
Telephone: 81-3-3356-5227
Fax: 81-3-3356-5261
Email: **kenji@ora.com**

INDIA
Computer Bookshop (India) PVT. LTD.
190 Dr. D.N. Road, Fort
Bombay 400 001
India
Telephone: 91-22-207-0989
Fax: 91-22-262-3551
Email: **cbsbom@giasbm01.vsnl.net.in**

THE AMERICAS
O'Reilly & Associates, Inc.
101 Morris Street
Sebastopol, CA 95472 U.S.A.
Telephone: 707-829-0515
Telephone: 800-998-9938 (U.S. & Canada)
Fax: 707-829-0104
Email: **order@ora.com**

SOUTHERN AFRICA
International Thomson Publishing Southern Africa
Building 18, Constantia Park
240 Old Pretoria Road
P.O. Box 2459
Halfway House, 1685 South Africa
Telephone: 27-11-805-4819
Fax: 27-11-805-3648

O'REILLY™

Here's a page we encourage readers to tear out...

The Web Review Studio series...

demystifies the complexities of publishing on the Web. Unlike other Web books, Web Review Studio books don't just tell you how to create Web content; we show you how leading designers are implementing technology for compelling communication. Upcoming books will cover Shockwave for Director, Java, streaming audio, and other topics.

TELL ME ABOUT UPCOMING STUDIO BOOKS

Thank you for purchasing *Gif Animation Studio*

Where did you buy this book?
- ❑ Bookstore
- ❑ Tradeshow
- ❑ Direct from O'Reilly
- ❑ Online
- ❑ Class/Seminar
- ❑ Other _____

What operating system do you use?
- ❑ Macintosh
- ❑ Windows NT
- ❑ Windows 95
- ❑ Other _____

What is your job description?
- ❑ Designer/Art Director
- ❑ WebMaster/Developer
- ❑ Marketing Communications
- ❑ Other _____

What other Web development topics interest you?
- ❑ Java
- ❑ HTML
- ❑ Audio
- ❑ ActiveX
- ❑ Video
- ❑ Web Design
- ❑ Other _____

Name _____ Company/Organization _____

Address _____

City _____ State _____ Zip/Postal Code _____ Country _____

Telephone _____ Internet or other email address (specify network) _____

Songline Studios specializes in developing innovative, interactive content for online audiences. Visit the many online and print properties created by Songline Studios through their Website located at http://www.songline.com

POST CARD

Songline Inc., 101 Morris Street, Sebastopol, CA 95472-9902

BUSINESS REPLY MAIL
FIRST CLASS MAIL   PERMIT NO. 80   SEBASTOPOL, CA

Postage will be paid by addressee

O'Reilly & Associates, Inc.
101 Morris Street
Sebastopol, CA 95472-9902

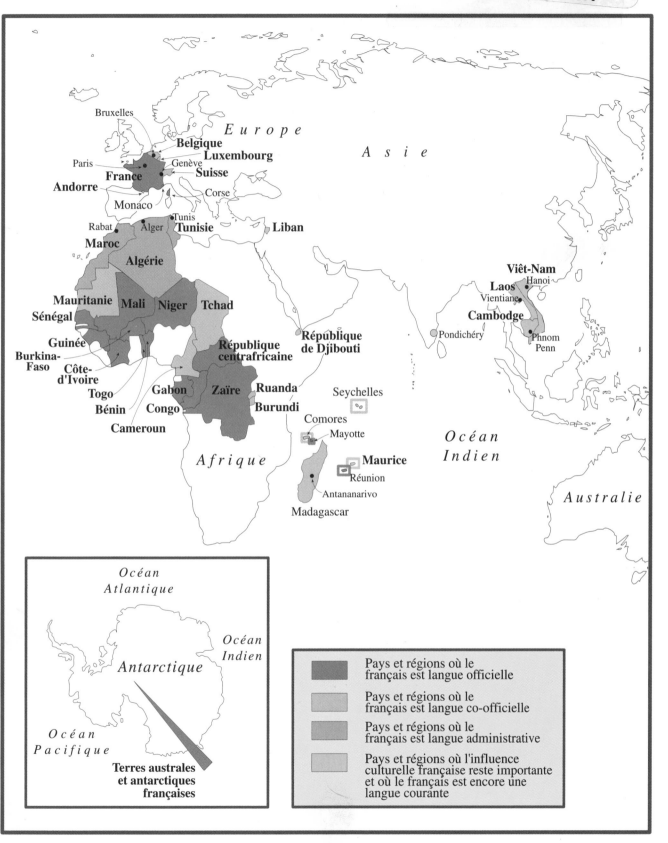

W9-DHV-917

Europe

Bruxelles
Belgique
Luxembourg
Paris   Genève
France   **Suisse**
Andorre
Monaco   Corse

Asie

Tunis
Rabat   Alger   **Tunisie**   **Liban**
Maroc
Algérie

Viêt-Nam
Hanoi
Laos
Vientiane
Cambodge
Phnom
Penn

Mauritanie   **Mali**   **Niger**   **Tchad**
Sénégal
Guinée
Burkina-
Faso
Côte-
d'Ivoire
Togo   **Gabon**   **Zaïre**   **Ruanda**
Bénin   **Congo**   **Burundi**
Cameroun

République
centrafricaine

République
de Djibouti

Pondichéry

Seychelles

Comores
Mayotte

Océan
Indien

Maurice
Réunion

Australie

Antananarivo
Madagascar

Afrique

Océan
Atlantique

Océan
Indien

Antarctique

Océan
Pacifique

Terres australes
et antarctiques
françaises

Pays et régions où le
français est langue officielle

Pays et régions où le
français est langue co-officielle

Pays et régions où le
français est langue administrative

Pays et régions où l'influence
culturelle française reste importante
et où le français est encore une
langue courante

Voilà!

An Introduction to French

THIRD EDITION

L. Kathy Heilenman
University of Iowa

Isabelle Kaplan
Bennington College

Claude Toussaint Tournier
Northwestern University

 HH Heinle & Heinle Publishers
Boston, Massachusetts 02116 U.S.A.

I T P A division of International Thomson Publishing, Inc.
The ITP logo is a trademark under license.

Albany - Bonn - Cincinnati - Detroit - Madrid - Melbourne - Mexico City - New York - Paris - San Francisco - Singapore - Tokyo - Toronto - Washington

The publication of VOILÀ! was directed by the members of the Heinle & Heinle College Foreign Language
Publishing Team:

Wendy Nelson, Editorial Director
Amy R. Terrell, Market Development Director
Gabrielle B. McDonald, Production Services Coordinator
Diana Bohmer, Associate Developmental Editor

Also participating in the publication of this program were:

Publisher:	Vincent Duggan
Managing Editor:	Beth Kramer
Managing Developmental Editor:	Amy Lawler
Project Manager:	Anita L. Raducanu/A+ Publishing Services
Photo/Video Specialist:	Jonathan Stark
Associate Market Development Director:	Melissa Tingley
Production Assistant:	Lisa Winkler
Manufacturing Coordinator:	Wendy Kilborn
Photo Coordinator:	Martha Leibs
Illustrator, Third Edition:	Len Shalansky
Interior Designer:	Sue Gerould/Perspectives
Cover Illustrator:	David Loftus
Cover Designer:	Sue Gerould/Perspectives

Manufactured in the United States of America

Student edition ISBN: 0-8384-6603-6
10 9 8 7 6 5 4 3 2 1

Instructor's annotated edition ISBN: 0-8384-6605-2
10 9 8 7 6 5 4 3 2 1

Table des matières

Instructor's Guide

The VOILÀ! Program

- ◆ Student Text
- ◆ Text Tape
- ◆ Instructor's Annotated Edition
- ◆ Instructor's Resource Manual:
  - – Teaching suggestions
  - – The Video Guide
  - – Text Tape Script and Laboratory Tape Script
- ◆ Cahier d'activités écrites et orales

- ◆ Laboratory Tapes
- ◆ VOILÀ! Video
- ◆ Overhead Transparency Masters
- ◆ *Parle-moi un peu!* Information Gap Activities for Beginning French Classes
- ◆ Computerized Test Bank
- ◆ CD-Rom: «Un Meurtre à Cinet»
- ◆ Système-D: Writing Assistant for French

VOILÀ!: An Introduction to French, Third Edition, is a complete program for first-year courses. *VOILÀ!* takes a communicative, functional approach to the teaching and learning of French and provides materials to help instructors plan effective sequences of instruction. The materials in *VOILÀ!* were designed with three goals in mind:
- to help students develop basic communicative skills;
- to give them the intellectual experience of understanding how French functions as a language;
- to introduce students to the Francophone world.

VOILÀ! helps instructors to achieve all of these objectives. Classroom-tested, innovative activities help develop student proficiency in using French. At the same time, clear explanations and exercises encourage students to learn about French. And

finally, authentic materials, photos, and maps, cultural notes, World Wide Web projects, and activities develop cultural awareness and provide a context for learning and understanding French as a world language. With *VOILÀ!*, students will gain an intellectual control of French structure, an awareness of French and Francophone cultures, and the motivation and ability to keep using French, even after the final exam!

VOILÀ!, the Third Edition

The philosophy and principles underlying the first and second editions of *VOILÀ!* remain unchanged in the third edition. Based on feedback and reactions from students and instructors using the first and second editions of *VOILÀ!*, the following changes have been incorporated into the third edition.

Reduction in number of lessons

As we have learned more about how second languages and cultures are acquired, it has become apparent that simply racing through materials linearly is counterproductive. Less is indeed more! *VOILÀ!*, in its third edition, has evolved to complement current classroom realities. Twenty, instead of twenty-four, lessons provide sufficient but not overwhelming materials to suit almost any instructional environment. This reduction in amount of material covered has been accomplished by eliminating structural points not essential to the development of basic communicative competence (e.g., the compound tenses, the **passé simple, dont,** the present participle). While reducing the number of structural points covered, we have not, however, compromised the richness or the flexibility of the materials. Instead we have incorporated crucial vocabulary into various lessons and we have continued to provide instructors with a wide range of materials from which to build effective instructional sequences.

Appendice de grammaire

An appendix, *L'Appendice de grammaire,* provides instructors with additional flexibility in syllabus planning. This section contains brief explanations of structural points not covered in the main text (**les temps composés, le passé simple, le participe présent, l'infinitif, les pronoms relatifs *dont* et *ce dont*, les pronoms démonstratifs, les pronoms possessifs, l'ordre des pronoms d'objet, les adjectifs qui changent de sens selon leur place**). Instructors can choose to teach these structures for passive or active recognition or to refer students to them as necessary. Activities to accompany each grammar point are provided in the *Cahier d'activités écrites et orales.*

Vocabulary

Vocabulary presentations have been brought up to date and revised to make them more user-friendly. Photographs have replaced many drawings. Vocabulary has been systematically recycled with words and expressions first seen in the *Vocabulaire supplémentaire* (receptive vocabulary) later reappearing on a regular basis in the *Vocabulaire de base* (productive vocabulary).

Grammar scope and sequence

Several changes have been made in the scope and sequence of structures presented in *VOILÀ!* While retaining the clear, concise grammar explanations of previous editions, several items have been moved earlier in the grammatical syllabus (**les adjectifs possessifs, les pronoms d'objet direct, les verbes *pouvoir* et *devoir*, le passé composé avec *avoir*, les pronoms relatifs *qui* et *que***). In addition, several items have been added to *Les notes de vocabulaire* (for example, **il faut, aussi et donc, parce que, c'est et il est**) in order to facilitate early use of French. Each grammar point is accompanied by several activities that provide practice in controlled as well as communicative contexts. Recycling is frequent and systematic as it was in the first and second editions. An additional review section on personal pronouns has been added in Lesson 18.

Culture integrated into each lesson

Every lesson in *VOILÀ!* has a cultural component worked in throughout. Vocabulary presentations deal with daily life, families, routines, schooling, work, and other cultural issues. Wherever possible, activities are based on cultural information (for example, an activity in Lesson 5 where students are asked to interpret statistics and photographs depicting the relationship between age/generation and height among the French). Two new sections— *Entrée en matière* and *Découvertes culturelles*— help students learn how to read, interpret, and analyze cultural information. In addition, brief cultural topics are treated in notes called *Info plus.* Finally, four revised and enhanced *Magazines francophones* provide additional material for cultural learning.

Entrée en matière

Each lesson begins with a two-page introduction concentrating on a major lesson theme. These center on authentic materials and provide a transition between work done previously (vocabulary and structure) and work to come (new theme). For example, the *Entrée en matière* for Lesson 4 is centered around a brochure for a **station de ski.** Activities focus on using the French words and structures students have learned in Lessons 1–3 (seasons, colors, descriptions of persons) to lead students to a simple discussion of seasons and holidays within a French context. At the same time, this authentic document introduces leisure activities, one of the themes of the lesson.

Découvertes culturelles

This section focuses on the reading and interpretation of authentic cultural documents and serves to tie together various lesson themes. Each section contains two thematically-related documents accompanied by prereading, reading, and postreading activities. The documents in this section provide students with the opportunity to investigate and hypothesize about Francophone culture, thus enabling them to understand the process of learning about culture. For example, Lesson 4 provides two documents about music (**Radio: du rock, du rap... mais en français** and **30 ans de musiques africaines pour les 10 ans d'Africa N° 1**) that introduce students to the issue of French vs. English in music as a culturally specific phenomenon and music as an international language.

Magazines francophones

These four full-color sections represent a unique tool for introducing students to the richness and variety of Francophone culture while providing them with additional practice in dealing with authentic language. The *Magazines* have been revised in the third edition to reflect Francophone cultures and to provide students with an interesting and intellectually rich context for learning. Each *Magazine* is based on one primary and one or more secondary themes related to the preceding lessons (for example, *Magazine 1,* **les fêtes** and **Sénégal;** *Magazine 2,* **Québec** and **la famille),** and each contains a literary section *(Les arts et les lettres).* A page of activities completes each *Magazine* section. The *Magazine* sections are correlated to the *Video Magazines* that accompany *VOILÀ!* and can be expanded and combined with the video materials.

Text Tape

A Text Tape is packaged with each copy of *VOILÀ!* For each lesson, this tape contains a sample dialogue based on the textbook activity *Conversation en français,* and pronunciation of the words contained in the *Vocabulaire de base* list at the end of the lesson.

The VOILÀ! www home page

Instructors should consult the *VOILÀ!* home page for meaningful, task-based activities that help students explore the riches of the World Wide Web in conjunction with each lesson of *VOILÀ!* These activities will serve to enrich the cultural content of *VOILÀ!* by widening its scope to the world itself, and they will provide instructors with the resources to enhance the learner-centered approach of *VOILÀ!* Activities can either be assigned as homework or used as a collaborative in-class exercise. Each activity is self-contained and includes learner objectives, a contextual introduction, and an Internet task (with all links provided). Each activity also includes a communicative task *(Expansion)* where students are encouraged to share their Internet discoveries with each other.

Parle-moi un peu!
Information Gap Activities for Beginning French Classes

These activities provide instructors with true information gap activities that correspond to each lesson in *VOILÀ!* These activities give students the opportunity for fun and lively interaction in the classroom as they use pertinent grammar structures and vocabulary to engage in authentic negotiation for meaning.

Revised overhead transparencies masters

The transparencies from the second edition have been updated and now include new maps of the Francophone world.

Software

Using characters from *VOILÀ!*, «*Un Meurtre à Cinet*» provides a multi-faceted, multimedia environment to encourage and motivate the study of French by providing task-based, whole language activities. There are three components to this software package:

• e-mail Activity: «Un Meurtre à Cinet»

Students engage in role-play in order to solve the murder of Virginie Collin. In a series of four rounds, students discover more about the activities of their own characters, and (by questioning their classmates via e-mail) about the activities of other suspects/students. Each round is also supplemented by "evidence" distributed via the World Wide Web (see *Cinet à l'Internet* below). «*Un Meurtre à Cinet*» provides the opportunity for students to improve reading and writing skills in a meaningful and exciting environment.

• «Un Meurtre à Cinet» CD-ROM

The CD-ROM, which interfaces with the Cinet Web Site (see *Cinet à l'Internet* below), includes a variety of activities. By completing structural and vocabulary exercises at the **École,** students earn the money necessary to complete the tasks assigned at the **Lycée.** These real-life tasks include purchasing a **télécarte** at the **tabac** or post office, shopping for dinner, planning a trip, etc. As a complement to the activities provided on the *VOILÀ!* home page (where information at the linked sites changes regularly), the tasks assigned at the **Lycée** focus on day-to-day life in France.

• «Cinet à l'Internet»

Based upon the map of Cinet, this World Wide Web site can be added to your own Internet or local server. As a "home base" for the other components of the package, *Cinet à l'Internet* provides a seamless interface between CD-ROM and Internet activities. Each site (**poste, mairie,** etc.) has three components: *Explorez le monde* (with links to Web sites around the world), *Visitez...* (each site provides links to locally based information — the **gare,** for example, has links to train schedules and the **Syndicat d'initiative),** and *Activités* (a seamless interface to the CD-ROM and its activities).

VOILÀ!, an Overview

Although much has changed in the third edition of *VOILÀ!,* much that was successful in earlier additions has remained the same or has been only slightly modified. The vocabulary has been updated, minor changes have been made to activities already proved successful, annotations have been reviewed in order to provide an even better instructor aide, and the ancillary package has been expanded and revised. Here is an overview of the philosophy and theory underlying *VOILÀ!*

Teaching/learning about language

VOILÀ! provides clear grammar explanations and effective grammar exercises. This allows students to develop a conceptual grasp of French as a language along with an appreciation of how languages convert function and meaning into linguistic form. The exercises and activities in the grammar sections are designed to promote linguistic accuracy. The focus here is on form, but *VOILÀ!* goes even further by consistently tying form to context. Grammar explanations are pedagogical rather than comprehensive. *FYI* sections in the **Instructor's Resource Manual** provide instructors with further information about the structure of French.

Teaching/learning how to use the language

VOILÀ! does not assume that teaching and learning about a language are identical to teaching and learning how to use that language. Although students need practice manipulating vocabulary and grammar, they also need extensive practice using French in meaningful situations. For that reason, each lesson in *VOILÀ!* contains varied and motivating activities that focus on language use rather than grammatical form. In addition, communicative activities in the *Vocabulaire* and *Structure* sections of each lesson as well as in the *Entrées en matière,* the *Découvertes culturelles,* and the *Magazines francophones* provide practice in using French as a communicative tool. Students engage in speaking, reading, writing, and listening activities in very much the same way they would in real life, obtaining information, expressing ideas and feelings, observing and describing cultural phenomena, and negotiating meaning with their classmates and instructors. These activities focus on fluency and help develop students' confidence in their ability to use French to express their own ideas and needs.

Teaching/learning about Francophone culture

The teaching and learning of culture is central to *VOILÀ!* Vocabulary appears within a Francophone context in the *Magazines francophones* and cultural information appears as brief and informative *Info plus* sections. The vocabulary presentations introduce students to people from throughout the Francophone world and from various walks of life. There are farmers and workers as well as lawyers and doctors; the young, the not-so-young, and the elderly are also represented. Exercises and activities throughout *VOILÀ!* encourage students to learn how Francophone peoples live and think, and to discover the similarities and the differences with their own ways of living and thinking. Maps of the Francophone world and photos throughout the book provide students with an expanded view of the world.

The grammatical syllabus of VOILÀ!

To many instructors, the first year of French has become a race against grammar with little time left for skill acquisition. In order to enhance the lexical content of *VOILÀ!* and to provide a variety of functional activities, the grammatical syllabus has been streamlined. The following items are not treated as explicit grammatical points, although they appear for comprehension in authentic documents and are listed in the *Appendice de grammaire:* compound tenses, the **passé simple,** the present participle, the infinitive, the pronouns **dont** and **ce dont,** possessive and demonstrative pronouns, the use of double object pronouns, and additional information on adjective placement. These items were chosen to be eliminated from the first-year grammatical syllabus of *VOILÀ!* in view of the relatively small return for time expended. That is, students develop little control over these constructions in comparison to the amount of time they devote to them, although in many cases (double object pronouns, for example), their recognition and comprehension are achieved with relative ease.

Recycling of vocabulary

VOILÀ! aims toward a cyclical syllabus where lexical themes and vocabulary items are presented in incremental steps rather than as monolithic wholes and where new material builds on the familiar. Here is an example of a cyclical presentation of vocabulary concerning the family.

Family members	Lessons 4, 5, 7
Family living arrangements	Lesson 11
Daily routines in a family context	Lesson 15
Love, marriage, children	Lesson 16
Families, children, and the outside world	Lesson 20

Family vocabulary is also indirectly recycled in activities and exercises in lessons where it is not the direct focus of attention. The same care with cycling and re-entry has been taken with topics such as clothing, housing, food and meals, jobs and professions, and describing people and places.

Recycling of grammar

As with vocabulary, *VOILÀ!* also recycles grammatical concepts and expands students' understanding through a spiral presentation of critical points.

For example, expressing past time:

Lexical items using past time	Lessons 6, 7
Passé composé with **avoir**	Lesson 10
Passé composé with **être**	Lesson 11
Imparfait (formation and basic use)	Lesson 12
Imparfait vs. **passé composé** (1)	Lesson 12
Recent past	Lesson 13
Past participle agreement	Lesson 14
Reflexive (pronominal) verbs in the past	Lesson 16
Savoir/connaître in the past	Lesson 16
Passé composé vs. **imparfait** (2)	Lesson 17

Past time in Lessons 10 and 11 is practiced in very controlled activities so as to prevent the need for the **imparfait.** Those verbs that students tend to overuse or to use inappropriately in the **passé composé (avoir, être, devoir, pouvoir,** and **vouloir)** do not appear in Lessons 10 and 11. When students first encounter the **imparfait** in Lesson 12, exercises and activities are strictly controlled. Student expression of past time is limited to guided narration and description in the past. In Lessons 13 and 14, activities encourage students to continue "getting a feel" for the past tenses in French. Then, Lesson 16 introduces reflexive (pronominal) verbs in the past, providing additional contexts for past narration and description. The explanation of the difference in meaning between the **passé composé** and **imparfait** forms of **connaître** and **savoir** also in Lesson 16 prepares the ground for the conceptual discussion of the distinctions between these two tenses for the verbs **avoir, être, devoir, pouvoir,** and **vouloir** in Lesson 17. Experience with this type of cyclical presentation has shown that students gain a much better grasp of how past time is expressed in French and that they improve their ability to use these structures more readily than when the syllabus makes no provision for re-entry of material. Similar cyclical presentations are used for interrogative constructions and the article system.

Levels of language

The question of what kind of French to use is a difficult one. Do we teach students "standard, written French" and have them "sound like a book" or do we teach them informal spoken French, **français familier**, and risk inappropriate language use? How, for example, should question formation be treated? Which of the following do we teach?

> **Où ton père va-t-il?**
> **Où est-ce que ton père va?**
> **Où va ton père?**
> **Où il va, ton père?**
> **Ton père, où il va, lui?**
> **Il va où, ton père?**
> **Ton père, il va où?**

And, do we tell students that although **voiture, argent,** and **se promener** are indeed standard French, they are very likely to hear **bagnole, fric,** and **se balader** used by native speakers instead? There are no easy answers. *VOILÀ!* does not, however, sidestep the issue. Instead, it sensitizes students to levels of language, both in English and in French, and gives them passive knowledge of colloquial language in *Le français familier. VOILÀ!* avoids overemphasizing structures that are more appropriate to the written than to the spoken language. For example, it treats inversion as a means of question formation in two ways: first, as it is used in fixed expressions (**Quelle heure est-il?**), and secondly, as a more formal alternative to intonation and **est-ce que** questions. Students are not asked to produce inversion questions in communicative activities since this would be largely inappropriate in normal, everyday language use. They are, however, encouraged to observe the use and non-use of inversion in the authentic texts that appear in activities and readings throughout the book. In addition, the *Vocabulaire supplémentaire* has a special section for common expressions *(Le français tel qu'on le parle)* as well as a section for familiar slang words *(Le français familier)* today's students need to know to be able to understand spoken and even written French. These words are presented for recognition only; students are not asked to produce them. Finally, a section called **On entend parfois...** presents words and expressions characteristic of the French spoken outside of France.

In the most general way, *VOILÀ!* addresses this issue of language use by providing natural-sounding examples of the vocabulary and structure items taught.

How VOILÀ! is Organized

Each lesson of *VOILÀ!* has the same organization.

En bref

Each lesson opens with a photograph and an overview of the theme, function, vocabulary, and structure to be taught. The photograph may be used as a warm-up, to present vocabulary, or as the basis for a culminating activity once the lesson is finished.

Entrée en matière

The *Entrée en matière* section presents an authentic document whose theme foreshadows a theme in the lesson, but with activities that require the French learned in previous lessons. Instructors can use these activities as an opener for the lesson or can return to them later for a more in-depth coverage once the lesson content has been taught.

Vocabulaire

The text's extensive attention to lexical development is central to its approach. Each lesson features an illustrated presentation of vocabulary in context. *Notes de vocabulaire* contain information about the words and expressions used in each lesson.

Frequently, items that have traditionally been considered "grammar," but which can also be treated as words in their own right, are presented as lexical items in this part of the lesson, and are then taken up in a *Structure* section in a later lesson. For example, the introduction of **et toi?** and **pas moi!** as rejoinders prepares the ground for stressed or disjunctive pronouns and the appearance of selected past tense forms as lexical items (**j'ai oublié, j'ai trouvé, j'ai rencontré**) as lexical items foreshadows the explanation of the passé composé.

The practice materials in the vocabulary section begin by developing students' receptive skills. These initial exercises, found in the *D'accord?* section, demand only limited oral or written production. Students find words that don't belong, classify objects by categories, or respond with expressions such as **oui, moi aussi,** or **pas moi.** These comprehension-based exercises are followed by activities, in the *Mise en pratique* section, that require one- or two-word answers along with open-ended creative activities for which students may or may not produce complete sentences, depending on what would be appropriate to that particular language activity.

Structure

The *Structure* section presents grammatical points in a clear, student-oriented manner. The explanations are written in English and are accessible to all students, even those with mediocre language abilities, without an instructor's help. At first, they may seem overly simplified to some instructors and students. This is deliberate. Better that students who are gifted at linguistic analysis be able to skip over explanations than that their less-gifted classmates be handicapped by presentations that are unclear or incomplete. Frequent *Rappels* remind students of material previously studied. For example, when the interrogative pronoun **qu'est-ce que** is introduced, students are reminded that **quel,** although it may also mean *what,* is not interchangeable with **qu'est-ce que.**

Each grammar explanation is followed by one or two *Vous avez compris?* exercises, meant to verify student understanding of the point(s) just studied. These are straightforward, but hopefully interesting, grammar exercises. Students are expected to use the structures just covered to speak or write in full sentences and to focus on form. Further discrete-point exercises are provided in the **Cahier d'activités écrites et orales** as well as the accompanying software. Additional, communicatively-oriented activities follow in a section called *Continuons!* Some of these activities are brief, but others, designed to develop fluency, can easily run much longer. This selection provides instructors with materials that can easily be adapted to different educational settings.

Découvertes culturelles

Reading in *VOILÀ!* is treated as a functional activity whose utility is seated in culture. The selected texts are authentic, introducing students to the ways people in Francophone cultures communicate with one another. These documents are either personal, administrative, or artistic and offer students a range of cultural discoveries. Because some of these texts may appear initially difficult, students are guided through progressive sets of activities that help them extract meaning and discover the ways in which meaning is controlled. Prereading activities, skimming and scanning sections, and follow-up activities where students apply their understanding of the world to their understanding of the text are provided.

Orthographe et prononciation

This section presents the basic systems of French spelling and pronunciation. The laboratory program includes additional French pronunciation information and exercises.

Listes de vocabulaire

In order to give students maximum flexibility but, at the same time, avoid overwhelming them, the vocabulary in each lesson of *VOILÀ!* is divided into two lists. The *Vocabulaire de base* contains active vocabulary that students are expected to be able to understand as well as to produce on tests. The *Vocabulaire supplémentaire* is primarily for recognition. These words and expressions appear in exercises and activities but students should not be required to produce them from memory on a test. A third list, *Vocabulaire facultatif,* appears in the **Cahier d'activités écrites et orales** as well as in the **Instructor's Resource Manual.** Although they may not interest all students equally, the words in this list are frequently requested by students in order to talk about specific things and personal subjects.

Leçon	Entrée en matière	Vocabulaire
1 Qui êtes-vous?	Le français dans le monde	greetings, leave-takings / **j'aime** and **je déteste** / dates / numbers from 0 to 39
2 Comment êtes-vous?	Qui sont-ils?	descriptive adjectives / comparison / likes and dislikes
3 Comment est votre chambre?	La chambre Valérie	rooms and offices / color / adjectives
4 Qu'est-ce que vous aimez?	Les saisons et les sports	Dubois family / things to do / descriptive adjectives / **c'est** and **il est**
5 Les âges de la vie	Les jeunes	numbers from 40 to 100 / people / prepositions / other families
6 L'espace et le temps	Un espace historique	time / places (town/country) / **avoir** expressions (**chaud, froid, sommeil**) / **quel**
7 Famille, familles...	Tel père, tel fils?	expressions with **faire** (**ménage, vaisselle, cuisine**) / weather / family
8 Vous êtes artiste ou sportif?	En visite à Montréal	sports, music, and art
9 Qu'est-ce qu'on mange?	Produits naturels et régionaux	food / meals
10 Qu'est-ce que vous portez?	Des vêtements pour tous	clothing / prices / colors (additional) / numbers from 100 to 1,000
11 Où est-ce que vous habitez?	Maisons en France	house / furniture / more about families / map of Cinet / directions / numbers above 1,000
12 Au travail!	Hommes et femmes au travail	professional life / jobs
13 Une invitation chez les Dumas	Invitations, annonces...	restaurants / stores / hospitality / not feeling well
14 Que faire un jour de pluie?	Pour communiquer	post office / telephone / newspapers / magazines
15 Chez les Hanin	Être père	parts of the body / daily routine
16 Une histoire d'amour	Je t'aime un peu, beaucoup, pas du tout	love and courtship / marriage and divorce
17 Une soirée devant la télévision	Devant la télévision	television / radio / movies
18 Le tour du monde en 365 jours	Voyageur 1	means of transportation / countries / travel vocabulary /
19 Le Tour de France	Tourisme en France	weather expressions (additional) / French regions and countryside / **Tour de France**
20 Le bonheur, qu'est-ce que c'est?	Le bonheur quand même!	feelings, happiness, sadness / world problems

Appendice de grammaire

Notes de vocabulaire	Structure	Découvertes culturelles
comment poser des questions	les phrases / genre / pluriel des noms (article défini)	Calendrier du mois / Monuments aux morts
comparison (**plus, moins, aussi... que**) / **aussi** et **donc**	**être** / forme négative / formation des adjectifs	Faire-part de naissance / La France vous est-elle sympathique ou antipathique?
on / **voilà** et **il y a** / pluriel des noms irréguliers / **orange**	article indéfini / articles après **ne... pas** / **avoir**	L'Université Libre de Bruxelles / Deux hôtels très parisiens
beaucoup (de) / parler français / **écouter et regarder** / la place des adjectifs / l'infinitif / **c'est** et **il est**	verbes en **-er** / adjectifs possessifs / questions à réponse affirmative ou négative	Radio: Du rock, du rap... mais en français / 30 Ans de Musiques Africaines pour les 10 Ans d'Africa N° 1
préposition **de** / **de** + article défini / **avoir** + **ans** / **habiter** / place des adverbes / **combien de**	verbes comme **sortir** / place des adjectifs / **bel** et **vieil** / pronoms toniques	Devenir adulte / Être majeur
préférer / **commencer** / **dans** et **en** / **quel** / **le lundi** / **jour** et **journée**, etc. / **téléphoner à**	**aller** / **à** et **de** + article défini / questions pour demander des renseignements	Les activités de la journée / Les loisirs des Français
le temps / **qui** interrogatif et relatif / dates (dix-neuf cent...) / **si** et **oui**	**faire** / **vouloir** / pronoms d'objet direct	La famille et l'argent / La famille wolof
faire une promenade, etc. / **jouer** et **faire** + sports, etc. / **jouer** et musique / **avoir envie de** / **ce** / parler au passé (lexical)	**pouvoir** et **devoir** / pronoms interrogatifs / expressions negatives	Quels sports préfèrent-ils? / Les loisirs des jeunes
avant et **après**, **devant** et **derrière** / **bon (meilleur)** et **mauvais** / **acheter** / **il faut** + infinitif / **avoir** + **faim, soif**	**boire** et **prendre** / article partitif / article partitif et article indéfini après une expression négative	Manger au restaurant / Un bon plat sénégalais
avoir besoin, l'air, le temps de / **nouveau** / **fois** et **temps** / **long**	verbes comme **finir** / **mettre** / passé composé avec **avoir**	Chic et propre pour pas cher / Les Français pantouflards
nombres ordinaux / **dernier** + jour, semaine, année / **une pièce** / **si** / place des adverbes au passé composé / demander votre chemin	verbes comme **vendre** / passé composé avec **être** / passé composé à la forme négative et interrogative	Dessine-moi une maison / Une tradition française: la résidence
les affaires / **c'est** et **il est** + métier	imparfait (formation) / imparfait (usage) / pronoms relatifs **qui** et **que**	La revanche d'un cancre / Le temps perdu
payer / **tout** / **avoir mal à**	**venir** et **venir de** / expressions de quantité / **voir**	Pour un beau dîner / Une tradition sénégalaise
cher / **envoyer** / téléphoner / écrire son courrier	**dire, lire, écrire** / pronoms d'objet indirect / accord du participe passé	Le Minitel / La numérotation à 10 chiffres
verbes réfléchis / **cheveux** / décrire des personnes / **les dents** et **ses dents** / **essayer** et **emmener**	verbes réfléchis / verbes réfléchis à l'impératif / **savoir** et **connaître**	Crèches et haltes-garderies / Les parents au travail
verbes réciproques / **que** conjonction / **quelqu'un** et **quelque chose de** + adj. / **quitter, partir, sortir** / **parce que** et **à cause de** / **pendant que** et **pendant**	verbes réciproques / verbes réfléchis et réciproques au passé / comparaison des adjectifs et adverbes	Les travaux ménagers / Vacances à Marrakech
avoir peur / **ne rien** et **personne de** / à la télé et à la radio / **même** / **victime** / verbes composés	**en** / verbes **être, avoir, vouloir, devoir** et **pouvoir** au passé / **croire, vivre** et **suivre**	La télévision / Les jeunes choisissent
conduire / pays / prépositions avec pays / **ce** et **quel** / en avion, etc. / **place** / **rapide** et **vite** / **découvrir**	le futur / **y** / récapitulation: pronoms personnels	Les voyages à l'étranger / Un voyage autour du monde
directions / **on, gens, personne, monde** / **meilleur** et **mieux**	le conditionnel / phrases avec **si** / **ce qui** et **ce que**	Les sites touristiques en France / Une grande ville: Strasbourg
s'intéresser à et **intéresser** / **avoir raison, tort** / **souffrir**	le subjonctif	Plus ça change... / Les jeunes et le bonheur
	temps composés / passé simple / participe present / infinitif / **dont, ce dont** / pronoms démonstratifs et possessifs / ordre des pronoms / place des adjectifs	

Organizing a Course Using VOILÀ!

VOILÀ! is easily adaptable to either a semester or a quarter system. Exactly how you choose to organize a course will depend on the kinds of students you have, the time available, the goals of the course, and your own personal style. Since there are 20 lessons, one possible solution is to divide the material 10–10 for a school on the semester system, or 8–6–6 (7–7–6) (see below) for a school on the quarter system. You may, however, want to experiment with various options. Keep in mind that the first few lessons are usually perceived as being more easily assimilated than are later ones. This is so for two reasons. First, later lessons, since they depend on students having learned material in earlier ones, bear the burden of being cumulative. In addition, many structural points found in later lessons inevitably increase the learning burden geometrically. Learning about direct object pronouns, for example, involves learning not only the forms and the placement rules but also how to structure coherent and cohesive discourse. Likewise, learning the **passé composé** and the **imparfait** involves more than learning forms; it also involves learning the functions of narration and description in the past. Instructors may, then, want to allow additional time later in the sequence in order to give students the time to assimilate these structures.

Here are some suggestions for organizing courses using *VOILÀ!*

True beginners

If the majority of your students are true beginners, you may want to divide the lessons in *VOILÀ!* as follows:

SEMESTERS
11–9

QUARTERS
7–7–6 (or to give yourself more time toward the end, 8–6–6)

This provides you with a sort of jump start to the instructional sequence and allows additional time later when it will be needed. You will probably need at least four classes per lesson and you may find it necessary to eliminate some sections or assign them

for home study. Assuming that one lesson per week is to be completed, here is one possible lesson organization.

Day 1: Introduce the lesson by using the ***Entrée en matière.***
Introduce vocabulary.
Begin vocabulary exercises.
Assign vocabulary exercises and one or two structural points for homework.

Day 2: Go over vocabulary exercises.
Do structure exercises selected for class interest.
Work in groups checking comprehension of structural points.
Assign one or two exercises for homework.

Day 3: Do exercises or activity prepared at home or quickly go over exercises assigned using board or overhead.
Assign the first ***Découvertes culturelles*** activity to be prepared at home (begin work in class).

Day 4: Use assigned material as basis for class activity.
Continue using second ***Découvertes culturelles*** section.
Review using exercises and activities not previously covered.
Briefly go over ***Orthographe et prononciation*** section.

False beginners

If your students are largely **faux débutants,** you will want to go very rapidly at the beginning and slow the pace later to concentrate on activities in later lessons. Here is one suggested division:

SEMESTERS
13–7

QUARTERS
8–6–6 (or even 9–6–5 if you want even more time at the end)

This will provide you with the time necessary to complete the more involved activities found later in the instructional sequence while, at the same time, rapidly reviewing materials the majority of students have already studied.

It is also possible to use *VOILÀ!* as a one-semester or two-quarter course for false beginners. In this case, you might cover 13 lessons by mid-term and 7 after, or, for a two-quarter course, complete 12 or 13 lessons the first quarter and 8 or 7 the second. In these "accelerated" courses, the first lessons can be done at a pace of one per day. Here, the instructor's role is less one of teaching and more one of verifying that students have actually gone over the material. The assumption is that this material is actually a review. As you reach later lessons, slow the pace, working on the assumption that this material is either new or very imperfectly mastered.

Adapting VOILÀ! to Course Goals

VOILÀ! is organized so that instructors can pick and choose to emphasize specific goals. The *Vocabulaire* and *Structure* sections form the core of the course and, since they are sequential, will probably need to be included in any scheme. Beyond that, however, the various elements of *VOILÀ!* can be tailored to suit your needs. For example, if time is short or your course meets only three days a week, you may want to use the various sections selectively, picking and choosing according to class interests and time available. Keep in mind that all the exercises and activities, even in the *Vocabulaire* and *Structure* sections, do not have to be done. Select what best suits your situation.

Written testing

We suggest brief quizzes after each lesson and an hour test after every three or four lessons. Ideas for test formats can be found in the **Instructor's Resource Manual.** The **Computerized Test Bank** contains testing materials for each topic within a lesson. Designed for maximum flexibility, it allows instructors to create tests appropriate for their teaching styles.

Oral testing

Oral testing based on the material in *VOILÀ!* is not difficult to organize. The **Instructor's Resource Manual** contains questions, situations/conversations, and scoring scales that have been extensively classroom tested.

Things to Keep in Mind When Using VOILÀ!

You have a choice

There are more exercises and activities in *VOILÀ!* than even a class meeting five times a week can cover! Look over the possibilities and choose according to your own teaching style, the kind of class you have, and the time frame available. Keep in mind that many of the exercises can be done very rapidly. Keep up the pace and if students are beginning to get restless, go on to something else.

Maximize class time

Try not to use class time to explain grammar. The explanations in *VOILÀ!* have been class-tested and students can learn them on their own. One approach is to assign certain grammar points plus exercises to be done at home. Then, during the last 15 minutes of class, have students work in groups correcting their assignments. Circulate among the groups answering questions, and then collect (corrected!) assignments at the end of the hour. This approach encourages students to prepare outside of class, to help each other, and to learn better through explaining to others. It saves the time that is normally wasted answering individual questions in a whole-class format. And finally, if you do decide to explain grammar in class, try doing it only during the last 10 or 15 minutes. You'll find that if you begin the class with a grammar explanation, you'll have real difficulty getting students to switch to more communicative activities. Grammar expands to fill the time available; keep it under control.

English or French?

Which language should you use and when? If you prefer to use French exclusively, go ahead. You may, however, prefer to use English to discuss grammatical and cultural concepts that students cannot cope with in French yet. If this suits your style, fine—-but be careful. English, like grammar, tends to take over the classroom. Try always starting class with some kind of communicative activity and reserving grammar and English for the last 10 to 15 minutes. Another idea is to begin each class by asking students if they need anything "cleared up" in English.

Supplements to VOILÀ!

VOILÀ! is supported by a complete teaching and learning package that includes the following:

◆ The **Instructor's Annotated Edition** provides on-page teaching tips, suggestions for effective lesson planning, and alternate class activities.

◆ The **Instructor's Resource Manual** includes the following:
  – Suggestions for teaching culture, listening, speaking, reading, and writing skills, lesson-by-lesson teaching tips, ideas for teaching the *Magazine francophone* sections, additional information about French, and an oral testing program.
  – The Video Guide
  – The Text Tape Script and Laboratory Tape Script

◆ The **Text Tape,** packaged with the student text, provides students with sample dialogues in normal, spoken French, that correspond to each lesson's *Conversation en français.* The script of a second version, in standard French, is included in the **Instructor's Resource Manual.** Also on the Text Tape are readings of the *Vocabulaire de base* in each lesson of the textbook.

◆ The **Cahier d'activités écrites et orales** is a combined workbook and laboratory manual. The workbook section contains exercises and activities that use the vocabulary and structures of each lesson, **thème et version** exercises, and a guided writing activity. A list of words that expands upon those in the textbook (*Vocabulaire facultatif*) concludes each lesson of the workbook. The laboratory manual section contains pronunciation exercises, focused listening activities, practice with the vocabulary and structures for each lesson, and contextualized listening-for-gist activities. These latter (*À l'écoute de...*) have been revised and simplified for the third edition. This book can be ordered with or without the Answer Key.

◆ The **Laboratory Tapes,** fully coordinated with the laboratory manual, are available for duplication by adopters or for individual student purchase. A complete Tape Script is provided in the **Instructor's Resource Manual.** Adopters may request sample tapes from the local Heinle & Heinle sales representative.

◆ The *VOILÀ!* **Video,** produced especially for *VOILÀ!*, features a variety of authentic footage coordinated in theme with the *Magazines francophones.* The accompanying Video Guide, included in the **Instructor's Resource Manual,** provides a script and classroom activities.

◆ **Overhead Transparencies Masters** of text illustrations and maps allow for closed-book presentation of vocabulary and art-based exercises.

◆ **Parle-moi un peu! Information Gap Activities for Beginning French Classes** provide instructors with lively activities that facilitate real communication between and among students.

◆ **The Computerized Test Bank** contains testing materials for each topic within a lesson. Designed for maximum flexibility, it allows instructors to create tests appropriate for their teaching styles.

◆ **CD ROM: «Un Meurtre à Cinet»**

◆ **Système-D: Writing Assistant for French,** a software program for writing in French, can be used with both the student text and workbook.

Voilà!

An Introduction to French

THIRD EDITION

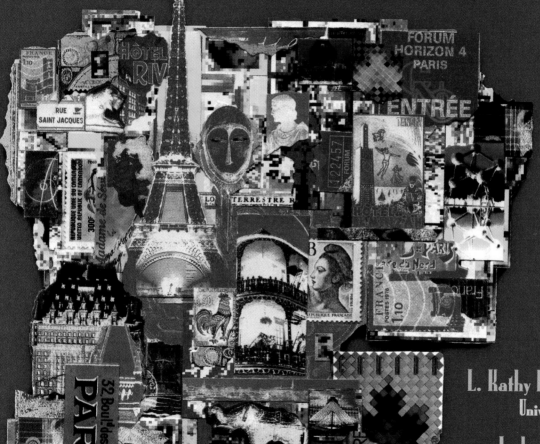

L. Kathy Heilenman
University of Iowa

Isabelle Kaplan
Bennington College

Claude Toussaint Tournier
Northwestern University

HH Heinle & Heinle Publishers
Boston, Massachusetts 02116 U.S.A.

ITP A division of International Thomson Publishing, Inc.
The ITP logo is a trademark under license.

Albany - Bonn - Cincinnati - Detroit - Madrid - Melbourne - Mexico City - New York - Paris - San Francisco - Singapore - Tokyo - Toronto - Washington

The publication of VOILÀ! was directed by the members of the Heinle & Heinle College Foreign Language Publishing Team:

Wendy Nelson, Editorial Director
Amy R. Terrell, Market Development Director
Gabrielle B. McDonald, Production Services Coordinator
Diana Bohmer, Associate Developmental Editor

Also participating in the publication of this program were:

Publisher:	Vincent Duggan
Managing Editor:	Beth Kramer
Managing Developmental Editor:	Amy Lawler
Project Manager:	Anita L. Raducanu/A+ Publishing Services
Photo/Video Specialist:	Jonathan Stark
Associate Market Development Director:	Melissa Tingley
Production Assistant:	Lisa Winkler
Manufacturing Coordinator:	Wendy Kilborn
Photo Coordinator:	Martha Leibs
Illustrator, Third Edition:	Len Shalansky
Interior Designer:	Sue Gerould/Perspectives
Cover Illustrator:	David Loftus
Cover Designer:	Sue Gerould/Perspectives

Student edition ISBN: 0-8384-6603-6
10 9 8 7 6 5 4 3 2 1

Instructor's annotated edition ISBN: 0-8384-6605-2
10 9 8 7 6 5 4 3 2 1

Table des matières

1 Qui êtes-vous?   1

CULTURE	VOCABULAIRE ET COMMUNICATION	STRUCTURE	ORTHOGRAPHE ET PRONONCIATION
Entrée en matière 2 Le français dans le monde **Découvertes culturelles:** **Le temps et l'histoire** 22 Calendrier du mois • Monuments aux morts **Info plus** Les chiffres 7 et 1 • Les mots et la culture • Les fêtes	**Vocabulaire** 4 Se saluer et se présenter • Compter de 0 à 39 • Parler des jours, des mois et des saisons **Notes de vocabulaire** 9 Mots et expressions utiles • Anglais/français • Les niveaux de langue: **tu** ou **vous?** • Les niveaux de langue: le français familier • Monsieur, Madame, Mademoiselle • Mots et contexte • Comment poser une question • Prononcer les chiffres • Le calendrier français **Vocabulaire de base** 27 **Vocabulaire supplémentaire** 28	**Structure** 17 Les phrases et les mots • L'article défini (genre, nombre, le pluriel des noms) • L'usage de l'article défini	L'alphabet français 26

2 Comment êtes-vous?   29

CULTURE	VOCABULAIRE ET COMMUNICATION	STRUCTURE	ORTHOGRAPHE ET PRONONCIATION
Entrée en matière 30 Qui sont-ils? **Découvertes culturelles: Identités sociales et nationales** 44 Faire-parts de naissance • La France vous est-elle sympathique ou antipathique? **Info plus** *Le Nouvel Obsrvateur* • Sir John Macdonald • L'argot	**Vocabulaire** 32 Décrire et comparer les personnes • Parler de ce qu'on aime **Notes de vocabulaire** 33 Mots et expressions utiles • **Ou / où** • **Aimer / aimer bien** • Singulier ou pluriel? • La prononciation • La comparaison • **Très / trop** • Les fêtes • **Aussi / donc** • **Parce que** **Vocabulaire de base** 48 **Vocabulaire supplémentaire** 48	**Structure** 37 Le verbe **être** • La forme négative • La formation des adjectifs	Les signes diacritiques 47

3 Comment est votre chambre?   49

CULTURE	VOCABULAIRE ET COMMUNICATION	STRUCTURE	ORTHOGRAPHE ET PRONONCIATION
Entrée en matière 50 La chambre Valérie **Découvertes culturelles: Où loger?** 64 L'Université Libre de Bruxelles • Deux hôtels très parisiens **Info plus** Porte ouverte ou porte fermée? • La chambre d'étudiant • Arthur Rimbaud • Le logement dans les universités • Le franglais	**Vocabulaire** 52 Décrire sa chambre et son bureau **Notes de vocabulaire** 56 Mots et expressions utiles • **On** • **Voilà / il y a** • Le pluriel des noms irréguliers • **Orange** **Vocabulaire de base** 70 **Vocabulaire supplémentaire** 71	**Structure** 58 L'article indéfini • Les articles après **ne... pas** • Le verbe **avoir**	Les autres signes diacritiques 69

Preface

VOILÀ!: An Introduction to French, Third Edition, is a complete program for teaching introductory French at the college level. It embodies a contemporary approach to language learning, one that is based on the most relevant current knowledge about language acquisition. At the same time, it draws upon a variety of proven methods, approaches, and materials.

VOILÀ! provides a balanced program that promotes proficiency in the four skill areas: listening, speaking, reading, and writing. Since learning French also involves learning about people who speak French, *VOILÀ!* presents a wealth of cultural materials in photographs, authentic documents, activities, cultural notes, and maps found throughout the book, as well as in special sections— *Magazines francophones*—devoted to the French-speaking world.

Every lesson of *VOILÀ!* is built around a theme that provides a meaningful focus for new material. Vocabulary is presented visually and in brief narratives that provide a natural and engaging context for its acquisition. Vocabulary notes teach the distinction between formal and informal vocabulary and give insight into the cultural aspects of language.

The grammar explanations in *VOILÀ!* are written in clear, concise English. They help you understand how languages work in general as well as how French works in particular. The variety of practice materials in *VOILÀ!* expands and reinforces your growing linguistic abilities. These materials include structured exercises that lead you toward grammatical accuracy, contextualized activities that provide meaningful practice, and open-ended activities that develop communicative skills.

VOILÀ! teaches reading and writing as active processes using authentic contemporary materials from Francophone newspapers, magazines, and other documents to train you in strategies that will make you an independent reader. It takes a unique approach to teaching writing skills, with activities that guide you step-by-step through the process of writing.

The language in *VOILÀ!* is fresh, familiar, and vital. It reflects the way French is actually spoken and written. With *VOILÀ!* you learn French that has the ring of authenticity and a spark of humor.

How VOILÀ! is Organized

Each lesson in *VOILÀ!* is organized as follows:

SECTION TITLE	OBJECTIVES	CONTENT
En bref	To introduce the thematic content of each lesson.	The accompanying photo introduces vocabulary or begins start-up activity.
Entrée en matière	To link theme of current lesson with language and culture learned in previous lessons. To introduce the current lesson theme.	An authentic document with accompanying activities.
Vocabulaire	To introduce vocabulary using photographs, drawings, and narrative storyline.	Photographs, drawings, narratives, questions, and activities help you internalize vocabulary while expressing your own feelings and ideas.
Notes de vocabulaire	To expand your understanding of vocabulary and to build links between vocabulary, structure and culture.	Information about vocabulary items.
Info plus	To expand your knowledge of Francophone culture and to build awareness of the cultural context of language.	Notes accompanying presentations and activities.
Structure	To explain grammar clearly in English. To practice the structures presented.	Explanations, exercises, and activities that enable you to practice grammar in interesting and communicative contexts.
Découvertes culturelles	To help you learn to extract information from authentic materials. To help you develop an awareness of cultural similarities and differences. To expand language use in a meaningful context.	Authentic documents accompanied by activities including writing activities.
Orthographe et prononciation	To explain important and interesting aspects of French pronunciation and spelling.	Information accompanied by activities for practice.
Listes de vocabulaire	To distinguish words to be learned for active use and those to be learned for passive recognition.	Words appear in two lists (**de base** and **supplémentaire**) at the end of each lesson.

To supplement the 20 lessons, the third edition of *VOILÀ!* contains four full-color sections, *Les Magazines francophones.* These *Magazines* offer the opportunity to use newly developed linguistic skills for reading, discussing, and learning. Each *Magazine* contains an editorial plus a variety of brief authentic documents and literary selections.

Supplements to VOILÀ!

VOILÀ! is supported by a complete learning package that includes the following:

◆ The **Cahier d'activités écrites et orales** is a combined workbook and laboratory manual. The workbook section contains exercises and activities that use the vocabulary and structures of each lesson, *thème et version* exercises, and a guided writing activity. A list of words that expands upon those in the textbook *(Vocabulaire facultatif)* concludes each lesson of the workbook. The laboratory manual section contains pronunciation practice, focused listening activities, practice with the vocabulary and structures for each lesson, and contextualized listening-for-gist activities.

◆ The **Lab Tapes,** fully coordinated with the laboratory manual, are available for duplication by adopters or for individual student purchase. A complete tapescript is included in the **Instructor's Resource Manual.**

◆ The **Video,** produced especially for *VOILÀ!,* features authentic footage coordinated with the *Magazines francophones.*

◆ The **Text Tape,** packaged with each copy of *VOILÀ!,* provides sample dialogues based on the textbook activity *Conversation en français* as well as the words contained in the *Vocabulaire de base* read aloud for student practice.

◆ **Software.** Using ancillary characters from *VOILÀ!,* «**Un Meurtre à Cinet**» provides a multi-faceted, multimedia environment to encourage and motivate study of French by providing task-based, whole language activities. There are three components to this software package:

   • «**Un Meurtre à Cinet**»: In this e-mail activity you will engage in role-play with classmates to solve the murder of Virginie Collin. In a series of four rounds you will discover more about the activities of your own character and (by questioning your classmates via e-mail) about the activities of the other suspects. Each round is supplemented by "evidence" distributed via the World Wide Web (see «**Cinet à l'Internet**» below).

   • **Cinet CD-ROM:** The CD-ROM, which interfaces with the Cinet Web Site (see «**Cinet à l'Internet**» below), includes a variety of activities. By completing structural and vocabulary exercises at the **École,** you earn the money necessary to complete the tasks assigned at the **Lycée.** These real-life tasks include purchasing a **télécarte** at the **tabac** or post office, shopping for dinner, planning a trip, etc. As a complement to the activities provided on the *VOILÀ!* Home Page (where information at the linked sites changes regularly), the tasks assigned at the **Lycée** focus on day-to-day life.

   • «**Cinet à l'Internet**»: Based upon the map of Cinet, this World Wide Web site can be added to your own internet or local server. As a "home base" for the other components of the package, «**Cinet à l'Internet**» provides a seamless interface between CD-ROM and Internet activities. Each site (**poste, mairie,** etc.) has three components: *Explorez le monde* (with links to Web sites around the world), *Visitez...* (each site provides links to locally based information — the **gare,** for example, has links to train schedules and the **Syndicat d'initiative),** and *Activités* (a seamless interface to the CD-ROM and its activities.

◆ *Système-D, Writing Assistant for French,* a software program for writing in French, can be used with writing activities in *VOILÀ!*

Acknowledgements

> À Michel, Dan et Harold

We would like to thank the following instructors, whose suggestions and criticisms were invaluable in developing *VOILÀ!*:

Carl Blyth, The University of Texas at Austin
Webb Donaldson, Tulane University
Kevin Elstob, Cleveland State University
Timothy Farley, Northeast Missouri State University
Christine Gaudry-Hudson, Millersville University
Hélène Germain-Simöes, University of Kansas
Brenda Glazer, Mount Royal College
Claude Grangier, University of Chicago
Thierry Gustave, Boston College
Elisabeth Guthrie, University of California, Irvine
Joyce Hanks, University of Scranton
Margaret Haggstrom, Loyola College
Katie Jewett, The University of Michigan
Nicole Kennedy, Northern Michigan University
Cheryl Krueger, University of Virginia, Charlottesville
David Lee, Southwestern Missouri State University
Anne Lutkus, University of Rochester
Patricia Kyle Mosele, Michigan State University
Sharon Neal, University of New Hampshire
Hélène Neu, The University of Michigan
Channa Newman, Point Park College, Pittsburgh
Laurie Ramsey, University of Southern Tennessee
Sonia Spencer, Rowan College of New Jersey
Kathryn Stewart, Oakland Community College
David Uber, Baylor University

In addition, we would like to thank the many teaching assistants, instructors, and students at Northwestern University, Louisiana State University, Bennington College, the University of Michigan, and the University of Iowa whose questions and comments during classroom testing added immeasurably to the effectiveness of the materials in *VOILÀ!* We would also like to especially thank Virginie Delfosse-Reese whose patience and expertise in dealing with permission issues was invaluable.

VOILÀ!, the third edition, is the result of the time, inspiration, and energies of many people besides the authors. We would like to thank the editorial and production staff at Heinle & Heinle for their contributions. Thanks all! Without you, it would have never happened!

L. Kathy Heilenman
Isabelle Kaplan
Claude Toussaint Tournier

Qui êtes-vous?

En bref

Dans cette leçon...

- Saluer
- Les dates: jours de la semaine, mois de l'année et saisons
- Les chiffres jusqu'à 39
- Les mots et les phrases
- Les noms et les prénoms
- Les articles définis (**le, la, les**)
- Le calendrier, les fêtes et les anniversaires
- Histoire: Monuments aux Morts
- L'alphabet français

In this lesson...

- Greeting and leave-taking
- Dates: days of the week, months, and seasons
- Counting up to 39
- Words and sentences
- First and last names
- Definite articles (**le, la, les**)
- The calendar, holidays, and birthdays
- History: War memorials
- French alphabet

www explore!
http://voila.heinle.com

Develop writing skills with Système-D software!

Practice listening and pronunciation skills with the Text Tape!

Discover the Francophone world!

Build your skills!

INTERNET

SYSTÈME-D

TEXT TAPE

VIDEO TAPE

CD-ROM

Students have an open-ended writing activity in the **Cahier** suitable for use with **Système-D**.

Entrée en matière: Le français dans le monde

Le document.
Voici le monde. Voici l'Afrique, l'Europe, la France, l'Espagne, la Russie, le Pôle Nord. Qu'est-ce que c'est? RFI, c'est le nom d'une radio. Une radio internationale. Mais c'est une radio française aussi.

Complétez le tableau.

R =	
F =	
I =	
Adresse de RFI?	
Code postal de RFI?	
Téléphone de RFI?	
Code téléphonique France?	
Code téléphonique Paris?	
Numéro du programme?	
Date du programme?	

Une radio francophone.
—*R*, c'est pour quel mot? Et *F?* Et *I?* RFI, c'est une radio en français? Où est Radio France Internationale? Et son adresse? Est-ce que Radio France a un numéro de téléphone?
—Oui, voilà le numéro de téléphone. 33, c'est pour la France; 01, c'est pour Paris; et 44-30-89-69, c'est pour RFI. Il y a aussi un code postal. Voilà le code postal pour Paris: 75016. Et voilà la date. Le 26, c'est le jour; mars, c'est le mois, et septembre aussi.
—Est-ce que RFI est une radio américaine? une radio canadienne? une radio européenne?
—C'est une radio internationale et elle est en France, en Afrique, en Amérique et dans le Pacifique.
—Pourquoi? Il y a des Français en Afrique?
—Oui, bien sûr! Il y a des Français et il y a des francophones en Afrique. Il y a des personnes qui parlent français.
—Est-ce qu'on parle français au Maroc? au Sénégal? Et où encore est-ce qu'on parle français?

Les photos.
Il y a trois personnes: un Européen, une Africaine, une petite Asiatique. D'où est l'Européen probablement? du Canada? d'Italie? de France? Et l'Africaine, d'où est-elle ? Et l'Asiatique? L'Européen, c'est un homme. L'Africaine, c'est une femme. Et l'Asiatique? C'est un enfant ou une enfant? Il ou elle?

Programmes & Fréquences

N°59 du 26 MARS au 23 SEPTEMBRE

RFI RADIO FRANCE INTERNATIONALE

CDF
nce Telecom

RFI la radio mondiale

BP 9516 ■ 75016 Paris FRANCE ■ 33 (01) 44 30 89 69 / 70 / 71

EXPANSION: Have students give names of countries in Europe where people speak French. As they give the name in English, give it in French, and give the name of the nationality as well. Expand to other countries: **Québec, Louisiane, Saint-Pierre et Miquelon** for the European-looking man; **la Guadeloupe, la Martinique, Madagascar** for the African woman; **le Vietnam, les Îles du Pacifique** for the Asian child.

Vocabulaire

A. Bonjour. Au revoir.

—Salut, Anne-Françoise, ça va?
—Oui, ça va, et toi?
—Pas mal... salut, à tout à l'heure.
—Oui, à tout à l'heure.

—Bonjour, Madame.
—Bonjour, Patrick. Comment allez-vous?
—Très bien, merci, et vous?
—Bien, merci.

—Merci, Madame. Au revoir.
—Au revoir, Patrick. À bientôt.

— Tu t'appelles comment?
— Frédéric, et toi?
— Géraldine. Tu es d'où?
— De Lyon, et toi?
— De Marseille.

—Et vous, Monsieur?
—Moi?
—Oui, vous! Comment vous
    appelez-vous?
—Je m'appelle Stéphane Abiragi.
—Stéphane comment?
—Abiragi.
—Avec un H?
—Non, non... A-B-I-R-A-G-I.
—D'accord! Ça y est!

The alphabet is found in the *Orthographe et prononciation* section on page 26 of this lesson.

• Et vous, ça va? Vous vous appelez comment? Vous êtes d'où?

B. Les chiffres

un professeur

deux chiens

trois affiches

quatre fleurs

cinq étudiants

six cahiers

sept livres

huit stylos

TRANSPARENCY:
1-3

LISTENING COMPREHENSION DRILL:
Ask students to write down how
many there are of each:
**deux professeurs / douze fleurs /
seize poissons / six chats /
cinq étudiants / quinze affiches /
treize stylos / trois chiens.**

neuf chats

dix poissons

Info plus

Les chiffres 7 et 1.
In French handwriting, sevens are barred
to distinguish them from ones:

7 1

0 zéro	11 onze	21 vingt et un
1 un	12 douze	22 vingt-deux
2 deux	13 treize	23 vingt-trois
3 trois	14 quatorze	29 vingt-neuf
4 quatre	15 quinze	30 trente
5 cinq	16 seize	31 trente et un
6 six	17 dix-sept	32 trente-deux
7 sept	18 dix-huit	33 trente-trois
8 huit	19 dix-neuf	39 trente-neuf
9 neuf	20 vingt	
10 dix		

C. Les jours de la semaine

lundi   mardi   mercredi   jeudi   vendredi   samedi   dimanche

D. Les mois de l'année

janvier   avril   juillet   octobre
février   mai   août   novembre
mars   juin   septembre   décembre

SEPTEMBER/SEPTEMBRE

SUNDAY	MONDAY	TUESDAY	WEDNESDAY	THURSDAY	FRIDAY	SATURDAY
				1	2	3 ☾
4	5	6	7	8	9	10
11●	12	13	14	15	16	17
18	19 ☽	20	21 LA FETE A FLOYD	22	23	24
25 ☷	26	27	28	29	30 FESTIVALS ACADIENS LAFAYETTE, LOUISIANA	

OCTOBER/OCTOBRE

						1
2 ☾	3	4	5	6	7	8
9	10●	11	12	13	14	15
16	17	18 ☽	19	20	21	22
23	24	25 ☷	26	27	28	29
30	31			FULL MOON ☷	FIRST QUARTER ☽	NEW MOON ●	LAST QUARTER ☾
DIMANCHE	LUNDI	MARDI	MERCREDI	JEUDI	VENDREDI	SAMEDI

TRANSPARENCY:
1-4

This calendar page is from *Floyd Sonnier's Beau Cajun Calendar.* Ask students why the page is in both French and English. If desired, explain about the Acadians and their flight from Canada to Louisiana.

- C'est quel jour aujourd'hui? Quelle est la date aujourd'hui? C'est quand, votre anniversaire?

E. Paris et les saisons de l'année

l'hiver

le printemps

l'été

l'automne

If desired, explain the allusions to Voltaire's **Candide** and Molière's **Alceste** (**Candide:** the optimistic and initially naïve hero of the philosophical novel *Candide ou l'Optimisme,* 1759; **Alceste:** the cynical hero of the comedy *Le Misanthrope,* 1666). These two characters will reappear throughout *VOILÀ!*

F. Alceste et Candide

CANDIDE	J'adore l'automne!
ALCESTE	Pas moi.
CANDIDE	Tu aimes le printemps? avril? mai?
ALCESTE	Pas du tout!
CANDIDE	Et l'hiver?
ALCESTE	Ah non! Et je déteste l'été aussi.
CANDIDE	Je ne comprends pas.

- Et vous, vous aimez l'automne? le printemps? l'hiver? l'été?
- Vous aimez janvier? juin? juillet? décembre?

Info plus

Les mots et la culture.

Words do not exist in a vacuum. They are an integral part of the life, customs, habits, and surroundings of the people who use them. For example, if you look in a French-English dictionary or phrase book to find out how to say the word *bread*, you will certainly find the word **pain.** If you stop there, however, you will have barely scratched the surface. Look at the two pictures. Can you explain why the French word **pain** is only a rough equivalent of the English word *bread*?

Encourage students to find similarities as well as differences. Ask for connotations or associations with American-style bread (slices, plastic, soft, etc.) and French-style bread (crusty, long, etc.).

Notes de vocabulaire

The **Notes de vocabulaire,** or *vocabulary notes,* contain information about the use of some of the words in the vocabulary for each lesson. You should always study them carefully.

1. Mots et expressions utiles.
Here are some useful words and phrases not included in the preceding vocabulary presentation.

à demain	*see you tomorrow*
bon week-end	*have a nice weekend*
ça dépend	*that depends*
j'aime*	*I like*
je comprends	*I understand*
je ne sais pas	*I don't know*
Mademoiselle (Mlle)	*miss, Miss*
moi aussi	*me too, so do I*
moi non plus	*me neither, neither do I*
pour	*for, in order to*

*Note that in **j'aime** and **tu aimes, aime** and **aimes** sound alike.

2: Ask students to find other examples from this lesson where literal translation works or doesn't work.

3: Point out (or ask students to hypothesize about) the differences between the various ways of asking someone's name in English.

See the **Instructor's Resource Manual** for more information.

3: If desired, point out that it is possible to use **vous** with someone addressed by their first name (a colleague for example). You may also wish to point out that the decision to use **tu** or **vous** is often a delicate one even for native speakers of French.

2. Anglais/français.
As you have probably already realized, French is not simply English written in code. Learning a language is more than learning simple vocabulary equivalents. For example, if you want to ask someone what his or her name is, you have to ask, **"Comment vous appelez-vous?,"** which in English has the literal meaning of *"How do you call yourself?"*! Although you will frequently be able to come up with acceptable (or at least understandable) French by plugging French words into an English sentence, you should be aware that this is not always the case.

3. Les niveaux de langue.
The language you use is never completely neutral. Your choice of words, expressions, and structures, as well as your tone of voice or gestures, all reflect social values and social relationships. You will, for example, certainly talk and write differently to an adult you do not know very well than you will to a friend your own age whom you have known for a long time. These registers or levels of language (**niveaux de langue**) exist in all languages.

In general, the French you are learning to use here is standard French. It is relatively neutral in that it represents the French least likely to give offense or to sound either too familiar or too formal. If, however, you have the opportunity to interact with French-speaking people, you will rapidly realize that there are many different registers or levels in use. Gradually, if you pay attention, you will learn how to vary your French according to the situation in which you find yourself.

Tu ou *vous?* A basic example of levels of language in French is found with the use of **tu** or **vous.** Your choice of either **tu** or **vous** when addressing someone indicates the status of your relationship with that person. In the dialogues above, can you guess why **tu** or **vous** was used?

Use **tu:**

• with people with whom you are on a first-name basis

• with children

• with animals

• with students your own age

Use **vous:**

• with people you address by their last name

• with people you are just meeting

• with people who are older than you

If in doubt, use **vous**—better too much respect than too little!

4. Les niveaux de langue: le français familier.

The use of informal French, like the use of informal English, depends on the relationship between the people speaking. Since informal French speech can be very different from its written equivalent, you will need to be aware of the characteristics of **le français familier**. Here are three of these characteristics:

a. Pronunciation characteristic of rapid or relaxed speech (**chais pas** for **je ne sais pas**, or **ouais** for **oui**).

b. Omission of words or sounds (**j'comprends pas** for **je ne comprends pas** or **t'aimes** for **tu aimes**).

c. Use of different words (**bouquin** for **livre** or **salut** meaning both *hello* and *good-bye*).

Some words and expressions characteristic of **le français familier** will be found listed at the end of each lesson.

4: Students are not expected to reproduce **le français familier** but should be able to understand it. Ask students to find similar phenomena in English (e.g., *gonna* for *going to*, *ya wanna* for *do you want to*, *bread* for *money*, etc.).

 See the **Instructor's Resource Manual** for more information.

5. Monsieur, Madame, Mademoiselle.

Monsieur is used to address a man. **Madame** is used to address a married woman and **Mademoiselle** to address a young or unmarried woman. As in English, older women are addressed with **Madame** whether they are married or not. When greeting or saying good-bye to someone, you should use **bonjour** or **au revoir** plus **Monsieur, Madame,** or **Mademoiselle.** Do not use the family name.

5: If desired, teach the abbreviations **M., Mme,** and **Mlle.** Note that abbreviations are used with names, never alone.

Bonjour, Monsieur.	*Hello.* (to a man)
Bonjour, Madame.	*Hello.* (to a woman)
Au revoir, Mademoiselle.	*Good-bye.* (to a young woman)

6. Mots et contexte.

When we speak, we frequently depend on context, intonation, gesture, and other such devices to make our meaning clear. Expressions in French (and in English) can have more than one meaning depending on the context in which they're used. Compare the following:

D'accord.	*OK. (I agree.)*
D'accord?	*OK? (Do you agree?)*

7. Comment poser une question.

There are several ways to ask questions in French. The easiest and the one found most frequently in informal conversation is the use of intonation. As in English, a statement can be turned into a question simply by raising your voice at the end.

Ça va?

Oui, ça va.

7: Question formation using **est-ce que** and inversion will be treated in *Leçon 4*.

8. Prononcer les chiffres.

The pronunciation of numbers depends on whether they are said in isolation, followed by a word beginning with a consonant, or followed by a word beginning with a vowel. Letters with a slash through them (∅) are not pronounced. The letters between slashes (/s/) indicate pronunciation.

NUMBER ALONE	NUMBER + CONSONANT	NUMBER + VOWEL
un	un chat	un hôtel (hotel) /n/
deux	deux chiens	deux années /z/
trois	trois stylos	trois affiches /z/
quatre	quatre professeurs	quatre hôtels
cinq /k/	cinq fleurs	cinq années /k/
six /s/	six poissons	six affiches /z/
sept /t/	sept cahiers /t/	sept étudiants /t/
huit /t/	huit livres	huit affiches /t/
neuf /f/	neuf chats /f/	neuf étudiants /f/
dix /s/	dix chiens	dix hôtels /z/

8: Many speakers do not make this distinction for **cinq** and **huit**, pronouncing the final consonant in all cases (**cinq** /k/ **fleurs**, **huit** /t/ **livres**). The **f** of **neuf** is pronounced /f/ except when the following word is felt to be closely bound, in which case it is pronounced /v/.

  neuf ans
    /v/
  neuf heures
    /v/]

9. Le calendrier français.

a. Dates are written differently in French and in English.

  6.3　　Le six mars, c'est l'anniversaire de Candide.
  12.9　Le douze septembre, c'est l'anniversaire d'Alceste.

b. Days of the week and months are not capitalized in French.

  C'est lundi?　　　　　　*Is it Monday?*
  Non, c'est mardi.　　　　*No, it's Tuesday.*
  Et la date?　　　　　　 *And the date?*
  C'est le 24 octobre.　　 *It's October 24.*

c. English has two ways to express dates, French only one. The *of* in English is never translated.

  le 21 octobre　　　　　　*October 21, the 21st of October*

d. Use **premier** for the first day of a month.

  C'est le premier mai.　　*It's May 1. It's the first of May.*

9a: You may want to point out the lack of **élision** in **le huit** and **le onze**.

9d: If desired, point out to students that **premier** is not used with the 21st and 31st of each month.

D'accord?

Each lesson will contain several activities using the words and expressions you have learned. In this part, you will be asked to understand new vocabulary words and to speak or write them in a limited way.

Additional exercises using the vocabulary in the *Vocabulaire* sections can be found in the **Cahier d'activités écrites et orales.**

As students progress, instructions for activities will be given in French and a model provided (except where complexity of instructions makes the use of French unfeasible). Beginning with *Leçon 9*, all instructions will be in French.

A. À VOUS Which photo goes with which caption?

a.

b.

c.

d.

1. — Au revoir, à bientôt.
   — Oui, à bientôt.

2. — Ça va?
   — Oui, oui, ça va.

3. — Comment vous appelez-vous?
   — Arlette Brasseur.

4. — Bonjour, Monsieur, comment allez-vous?
   — Très bien, merci, et vous?

B. En français

1. **Répondez.** What might you expect to hear after each of the following?

   a. Bonjour, Mademoiselle.
   b. Tu t'appelles comment?
   c. À tout à l'heure.
   d. Salut, Anne!

   e. Comment allez-vous?
   f. Comment ça va?
   g. Tu es d'où?
   h. Bon week-end.

2. *Tu ou vous?* Can you characterize the degree of familiarity between the speakers in each situation in part 1? Would each speaker be likely to use **tu** or **vous** to address the person he or she is talking to? Are there cases where you cannot tell?

C. Jours, mois, saisons

1. **Trouvez.** Find the following in the list of words below:

   a. les jours de la semaine
   b. les mois

   c. les saisons
   d. les chiffres

   novembre / six / stylo / dimanche / dix / janvier / printemps / vendredi / lundi / août / vingt / chien / mars / un / septembre / décembre / automne / seize / mercredi / mai / octobre / cahier / mardi / quatorze / livre / samedi / avril / douze / juillet / affiche / hiver / anniversaire / huit / jeudi / professeur / chat / juin / fleur / poisson / étudiant / vingt-neuf / été / février / trente

2. **J'aime/je déteste.** Put the months of the year along the scale below according to your own personal preferences. Compare your answers to others'.

j'adore	j'aime	je déteste

3. **Et les saisons?** Put the seasons along the scale below according to your own personal preferences. Compare your answers to others'.

j'adore	j'aime	je déteste

Act. D: If assigned as homework, be sure to specify whether you want students to complete using numbers (2, 3, etc.) or words (**deux, trois**, etc.).

D. L'année en chiffres

Complete the following:

1. un mois = ... jours
2. un mois = ... semaines
3. une année = ... mois
4. une semaine = ... jours
5. une saison = ... mois
6. un week-end = ... jours
7. un mois = ... week-ends

E. Combien de... ? Look at the picture. How many are there of each of the following?

1. professeurs
2. étudiants
3. chats
4. chiens
5. fleurs

F. Combien font? Do the arithmetic orally.

1. 4 − 1 = ?
2. 8 + 1 = ?
3. 25 + 11 = ?
4. 6 + 2 = ?
5. 6 + 6 = ?
6. 14 + 14 = ?
7. 2 + 2 = ?
8. 12 + 4 = ?
9. 20 − 2 = ?

Act. F: Teach **plus**, **moins**, and **font**, or ask for answers by item number.
CONTINUATION:
  35 + 4 = ?
  30 − 5 = ?
  25 + 2 = ?
  5 − 4 = ?
  19 − 8 = ?
  15 + 15 = ?
  39 − 16 = ?
  18 + 3 = ?
  20 − 6 = ?
  17 − 2 = ?

G. Les dates Read the dates.

Modèle 2.12
        le deux décembre

1. 20.3
2. 16.8
3. 30.10
4. 24.1
5. 12.4
6. 3.2

Act. G: CONTINUATION: 5.5, 10.6, 8.9, 19.11, 4.7, 25.12.

Mise en pratique

This section provides you with opportunities to do things and to express yourself with the vocabulary words you have learned.

A. Quelle est la saison? What season is it?

Modèle   le huit octobre
             C'est l'automne.

1. le vingt février
2. le dix mai
3. le vingt-cinq novembre

4. le quatorze juillet
5. le trente mars
6. le quinze juin

B. Les anniversaires

Act. B: Do not ask for complete sentences. Note that although students do not know the preposition **en**, you should not hesitate to use it as you speak.

1. **Quelle saison?** Find all the students in the class who have birthdays in each season.
   a. le printemps
   b. l'automne
   c. l'hiver
   d. l'été
2. **Quel mois?** Now group all the students in the class by the month of their birthday.
3. **Quel jour?** Are there students who were born on the same day in your class?

C. Mais qu'est-ce qu'ils disent? Write a dialogue for each photo.

Act. C: Students can be asked to role-play these situations.

Act. D: The student's **Text Tape** contains a dialogue that serves as a model for the *Conversation en français* for each lesson. The scripts of the dialogues are found in the **Instructor's Resource Manual**.

TEXT TAPE:
Conversation en français

D. Conversation en français You see someone in the school cafeteria sitting alone and reading the magazine *Paris-Match*. Approach, start a conversation, and, eventually, extricate yourself politely.

Structure

CD-ROM:
Build your skills!

▶▶ Les phrases et les mots

A sentence (**une phrase**) contains a subject (**un sujet**) and a verb (**un verbe**).

> *subject* = the person or thing the sentence is about
> (who or what performs the action)
> *verb* = what the person or thing is doing,
> how the person or thing is

Je comprends.
s   v

I understand.
s   v

Je ne comprends pas.
s   v

I don't understand.
s   v

Tu aimes le printemps?
 s   v

Do you like spring?
  s
 v

A sentence may also contain a complement (**un complément),** which completes the thought of the sentence.

J'aime l'été.
     c

I like summer.
     c

Je ne comprends pas le professeur.
          c

I don't understand the teacher.
         c

Il s'appelle Paul.
     c

His name is Paul. (He calls himself Paul.)
     c

Une phrase complète?

People usually use complete sentences when they write. When speaking, however, it is frequently acceptable to use a few words or a fixed expression instead of a complete sentence. In the dialogue below, there is only one complete sentence. Can you find it?

> — Bonjour, Monsieur. Comment allez-vous?
> — Bien, merci, et vous?
> — Pas mal.

This section may be skipped or assigned for home study according to class needs.

Ask students where, in writing, they might find incomplete sentences used (plays, scripts, etc., where speech is reproduced).

Qui êtes-vous?   **17**

Additional exercises using the grammar in the *Structure* sections are in the **Cahier d'activités écrites et orales.**

Vous avez compris?: These exercises are provided for brief form-based practice. Communicative activities are in the more extensive section, *Continuons!* that follows.

Vous avez compris? (Did you understand?)

A. Sujet, verbe, complément? Find the subject and verb in each sentence. If there is a complement, find it also.

1. Marc adore les chiens.

2. Je ne sais pas.

3. Je ne comprends pas le professeur.

4. Ça dépend.

B. Les phrases complètes Look again at the dialogue between Candide and Alceste, reproduced below. Pick out the complete sentences. When are incomplete sentences used? Can you explain?

—J'adore l'automne.

—Pas moi.

—Tu aimes le printemps? avril? mai?

—Pas du tout!

—Et l'hiver?

—Ah non! Et je déteste l'été aussi.

Continuons!

Le dialogue continue!: Suitable for pair or group work. If desired, have students act out the dialogue they reconstitute.

Le dialogue continue! Here are portions of an exchange that took place between Alceste and Candide. Decide whether Candide (**l'optimiste**) or Alceste (**le pessimiste**) said each line. Then put the lines in order so that they make sense.

—Je ne sais pas.

—JE NE SAIS PAS!

—C'est quel jour aujourd'hui?

—Pardon? Comment?

—D'accord! Ça va! Ce n'est pas important!

►► L'article défini

In English the definite article has only one form, *the.* In French, the definite article has four forms—**le, la, l', les.** The form you use depends on the gender, number, and initial sound of the noun it precedes.

Genre

All nouns in French belong to one of two groups: *masculine* or *feminine.* This group membership is called *gender* and is indicated by the form of the article used with the noun.

See the **Instructor's Resource Manual** for more information.

le + masculine singular nouns	**le** professeur, **le** chat
la + feminine singular nouns	**la** fleur, **la** saison, **la** semaine
l' + masculine or feminine singular nouns beginning with a vowel sound	**l'**étudiant, **l'**affiche, **l'**année

Exceptions: **le huit, le onze.** A discussion of **h aspiré** is in the *Orthographe et prononciation* section of *Leçon 9*.

Note that most words beginning with **h-** in French are considered to begin with a vowel since the **h-** is not pronounced.

    l'hiver   **l'**histoire   **l'**hôtel

The gender of each noun is indicated in the vocabulary list and in the end vocabulary. You should learn the gender of a noun along with its meaning. The simplest way to do this is to learn the article along with the noun—learn **la fleur** or **le professeur,** for example, not **fleur** *(f.)* or **professeur** *(m.).*

Nombre

Number refers to whether a word is singular or plural. The definite articles **le, la,** and **l'** are used in front of singular nouns. The definite article **les** is used in front of all plural nouns, both masculine and feminine.

les + all plural nouns	**les** chiens, **les** fleurs, **les** affiches

Note that when **les** is used in front of a noun beginning with a vowel sound, the **-s** of **les** links with the vowel and is pronounced like a **z.**

les chiens	*but*	le**s** affiches
		/**z**/

les chats	*but*	le**s** hôtels
		/**z**/

Le pluriel des noms

Remind students that the **-s** of **les** is silent before a consonant (**les chiens**).

Do a quick discrimination drill. Have students indicate whether what you are saying is singular or plural: **le chien / les fleurs / la fleur / les professeurs / le chat / les chiens / les chats / l'affiche / les années.**

As a general rule, the plural of a noun is formed by adding **-s** to the singular. If the singular form of a noun already ends in **-s** (for example, **le mois**), do not add an additional **-s** (for example, **les mois**). Note that the **-s** is not pronounced. This means that you have to listen to the article at the front of the word to find out if you are dealing with one or more than one, not the end as in English.

le chat	**les** chats
la fleur	**les** fleurs
l'affiche	**les** affiches
l'hiver	**les** hivers

Vous avez compris?

Masculin singulier, féminin singulier ou pluriel?: The aim is to sensitize students to the idea of gender and number marking. Do the exercise rapidly, asking students to justify. You can do this in French if you remain simple and restrict student responses to **oui/non**/article + noun (**La date? C'est pluriel? Non, c'est singulier. C'est féminin? Oui, c'est féminin; la c'est féminin et c'est singulier.**)
Ask students to quickly give you the plural forms for the following nouns (may be done orally or as a quick dictation): **le chat / la fleur / le professeur / le chien / la semaine / l'étudiante / l'affiche / le jour / le week-end / la saison / le stylo / l'hiver.**
VARIATION: Go from plural to singular or mix singulars and plurals.

Masculin singulier, féminin singulier ou pluriel? For each underlined noun, decide if it is masculine singular, feminine singular, or plural.

1. —Quelle est <u>la date</u> aujourd'hui?
   —C'est <u>le premier</u> novembre.

2. —Tu aimes <u>le printemps</u>?
   —Oui, j'adore <u>les fleurs</u>.

3. —C'est <u>le livre</u> de Michel?
   —Non, c'est <u>le cahier</u> de Monique!

4. —Je déteste <u>les chiens</u>!
   —Moi aussi, mais j'adore <u>les chats</u>!

Continuons!

Masculin? Féminin? Pluriel?: Read each word in the list first along with the appropriate article. Ask students to indicate whether each is **masculin, féminin,** or **pluriel.** Then ask students to read the list of words with the articles.

Masculin? Féminin? Pluriel? Read the list of nouns putting the appropriate definite article (**le, la, l', les**) in front of each.

fleur	printemps
anniversaires	date
stylos	jours
poisson	week-end
année	automne
cahier	mois
saisons	semaines
chien	affiche
étudiantes	chats
livre	professeur
hiver	

▶▶ L'usage de l'article défini

In French, as in English, the definite article is used to refer to a person or object that has already been specified.

C'est **le** professeur?	*Is that the teacher?*
Oui, c'est **le** professeur!	*Yes, that's the teacher.*

Ask students to tell you why the definite article is used here in English.

In French, however, unlike English, the definite article is also used to refer to something in general or in the abstract or to things you like or do not like. English uses no article in this case. Compare:

J'aime **le** printemps.	*I like spring.*
Tu détestes **les** chats?	*Do you hate cats?*
C'est **la** vie.	*That's life.*

Draw students' attention to the fact that one language is never the exact word-for-word translation of another. Ask them to find examples of this in the dialogues at the beginning of the lesson.

Vous avez compris?

L'article défini Use a form of the definite article to complete each sentence.

L'article défini: If desired, ask students to explain why the definite article was used. This can be done briefly in English in order to help students see the difference in usage between the two languages.

1. —Tu aimes ..... chats?
   —Non, je déteste ..... chats mais j'adore ..... chiens.

2. —Et ..... jours de la semaine?
   —Lundi, mardi...

3. —J'adore ..... été et je déteste ..... hiver. Et toi?
   —Moi? J'aime ..... automne et ..... printemps, mais pas ..... hiver!

4. —Quelle est ..... date aujourd'hui?
   —C'est ..... 22 septembre.

Continuons!

A. Réagissez Vous adorez, vous aimez ou vous détestez...

Act. A: If desired, teach cognates to extend the activity (**les vacances, le tennis, l'opéra, le golf, les examens,** etc.).

Modèle l'hiver
>   ***Je déteste l'hiver. / J'aime l'hiver.***

1. les lundis
2. les chiens
3. les professeurs
4. les chats
5. les mercredis
6. les dimanches
7. l'été
8. les vendredis

See the **Instructor's Resource Manual** for more information.

B. Interrogez Choose one of your classmates to interview. Find out how he or she feels about various days of the week, seasons, animals, and so on. Ask as many questions as possible.

Act. B: If desired, give students additional vocabulary so that they can nuance their answers (**bien sûr, absolument, pas du tout,** etc.).

Modèle — ***Tu aimes l'été?***
  — ***Oui. / Non. / Ça dépend.***

Découvertes culturelles: Le temps et l'histoire

➤ Calendrier du mois

Both texts deal with the concepts of time and identity. They are not sequential. You may elect to use either of them in any order.

Act. A: Since students have not yet studied indefinite articles, you may want to avoid the more natural **Le 3 septembre, c'est un mardi.**

A. C'est quel jour?

Modèle le 3 septembre
mardi

1. le 4 janvier
2. le 7 septembre
3. le 13 janvier
4. le 15 septembre
5. le 20 janvier
6. le 22 septembre
7. le 25 janvier
8. le 28 septembre

B. C'est quelle date?

Modèle les mardis
le 4 septembre, le 11 septembre, le 18 septembre

1. les jeudis
2. les samedis
3. les vendredis
4. les mercredis

Act. C: Students will have to guess the meaning of **dernier** from context.

C. La semaine. Comparez les semaines françaises et les semaines chez vous *(where you live)*.

	Chez moi	En France
Le premier jour de la semaine, c'est...		
Le dernier jour de la semaine, c'est...		*dimanche*
Les jours de classes sont...		

Act. D: Ask students for ideas as to why there are names on a French calendar.
  You may want to ask students if some names are not typically French (Ingrid, Raïssa, Davy, Hermann, Venceslas).

D. Féminins, masculins. Organisez les prénoms du mois de septembre.

1. Les prénoms masculins: Gilles, . . .
2. Les prénoms féminins: Inès, . . .
3. Les prénoms bizarres: . . .
4. Les prénoms nouveaux *(new for you)*: . . .
5. Votre prénom préféré: . . .

JANVIER

Les jours augmentent de 1 h 03

1	L	JOUR DE L'AN	01
2	M	Basile	
3	M	Geneviève	
4	J	Odilon	
5	V	Edouard	PL
6	S	Mélaine	
7	D	Epiphanie	
8	L	Bapt. du Seign.	
9	M	Alix	
10	M	Guillaume	
11	J	Paulin	
12	V	Tatiana	
13	S	Yvette	DQ
14	D	Nina	
15	L	Rémi	
16	M	Marcel	
17	M	Roseline	
18	J	Prisca	
19	V	Marius	
20	S	Sébastien	NL
21	D	Agnès	
22	L	Vincent	
23	M	Barnard	
24	M	François de Sa	
25	J	Conv. s. Paul	
26	V	Paule	
27	S	Angèle	P
28	D	Thomas d'Aq	
29	L	Gildas	
30	M	Martine	
31	M	Marcelle	

LA POSTE

SEPTEMBRE

Les jours diminuent de 1 h 42

1	D	Gilles	
2	L	Ingrid	36
3	M	Grégoire	
4	M	Rosalie	DQ
5	J	Raïssa	
6	V	Bertrand	
7	S	Reine	
8	D	Nativité de N.-D.	
9	L	Alain	37
10	M	Inès	
11	M	Adolphe	
12	J	Apollinaire	NL
13	V	Aimé	
14	S	Sainte Croix	
15	D	Roland	
16	L	Edith	38
17	M	Renaud	
18	M	Nadège . QT	
19	J	Émilie	
20	V	Davy	PQ
21	S	Matthieu	
22	D	Maurice/Aut.	
23	L	Constant	39
24	M	Thècle	
25	M	Hermann	
26	J	Côme/Damien	
27	V	Vincent de P.	PL
28	S	Venceslas	
29	D	Michel/Gabr./Raph.	
30	L	Jérôme	40

LA POSTE

E. Les fêtes et les dates.

Each day of the calendar has a saint's day listed for it. Give the date for the following saints for the months of September and January.

Modèle La Sainte-Ingrid?
  C'est le 2 septembre.

1. La Saint-Bertrand?
2. La Saint-Gilles?
3. La Saint-Renaud?
4. La Sainte-Geneviève?
5. La Sainte-Marcelle?

Act. E: Ask students to speculate why the names of saints are found on French calendars. You may want to point out that virtually all French calendars contain the names of saints and that these calendars are published by, for example, the postal service, and not the Catholic church. For the vast majority of French people, the fact that calendars contain the names of saints is a cultural rather than a religious phenomenon.

Act. E: La is used even for masculine saints since reference is to the word **fête**.

Info plus

Les fêtes

Both **fêtes** and birthdays are celebrated by many families in France. Flowers or candy often mark the event. Neither celebration is as important for the individual as in the U.S. The number and size of presents for birthdays are also more modest than in the U.S., even for children.

— Eugène...
une surprise pour toi !

F. Bonne fête! In France, each person has a birthday and a saint's day (date for the saint with the person's first name). Listen to the following greetings and identify the date in French.

Modèle VOTRE PROFESSEUR: Bonne fête, Rosalie!
VOUS: *C'est le 4 septembre!*

Act. F: Use this as a listening activity: **Bonne fête, Grégoire! / Bonne fête, Gilles! / Bonne fête, Roland! / Bonne fête, Alain! / Bonne fête, Aimé! / Bonne fête, Maurice!**
Then have students quote some **fêtes** while the others find the dates.
You can also play this as a game. Divide the class into two teams. The first team to answer correctly gets two points; answers with a mistake get only one point. Give a time limit. The team with the most points wins.

[Voilà!] **Act. F:** See **Video Magazine 1**, *Interviews. Interview 8* refers to **fêtes** and birthdays.

[Voilà!] **Act. G:** See **Video Magazine 1**, *Interviews. Interview 7* includes **prénoms** from the Maghreb.

G. Les prénoms. According to an article published in the magazine *L'Avenir* in 1994, here is a list of **prénoms déjà dépassés** *(first names already out of fashion)* and **prénoms originaux** *(new, original first names)*. How does this chart compare with your perception of "in" and "out" first names in your culture? Work in pairs and make a chart to present a comparison of first names in the two cultures.

Des prénoms dépassés		Des prénoms originaux	
FILLE	**GARÇON**	**FILLE**	**GARÇON**
Camille	Benjamin	Brigitte	André
Charlotte	Benoît	Claude	Bernard
Claire	Damien	Denise	Claude
Déborah	Guillaume	Françoise	Étienne
Fanny	Jérémy	Joëlle	Georges
Jessica	Jonathan	Laure	Jean-Yves
Lucie	Kévin	Marianne	Noël
Marie	Martin	Noëlle	René
Noémie	Rémy	Odile	Serge
Sarah	Thomas	Solange	Yvon

➤ Monuments aux morts

A. Comment? How are heros commemorated in your culture?

Avec des monuments? des fleurs? des universités? des affiches? des parcs?

Voilà des monuments historiques. Voilà des dates importantes. Voilà des dates importantes pour les Français. Voilà des noms. Voilà des noms français. Voilà des noms de soldats. Les soldats sont français. Ce sont des Monuments aux morts français.

Present this document briefly using cognates.

T.O.E = théâtres d'opérations extérieures

B. Pour comprendre. In order to better understand the two photographs, match the items in the column on the left with the items in the column on the right. You'll have to guess the meanings of some words.

1939–1945	les soldats
1914–1918	la ville où sont nées ces personnes
Indochine	les dates de la Deuxième Guerre mondiale
les Morts	la France
Salies-du-Salat	les dates de la Première Guerre mondiale
la Patrie	la guerre d'Indochine (1946–1954)

FRANCE

Salies-
du-Salat

Act. C: If desired, discuss the role of the two World Wars and the Indochina War. Overall, 1,357,800 French soldiers died or were missing in action in WWI. In WWII, 210,671 died. In the Indochinese War, there were 74,200 casualties on the French side (figures from *QUID*, 1994, pp. 669, 676; and *QUID*, 1991, p. 1133 for Indochina). Note that another war, **la guerre d'Algérie** (1954–1962), is not mentioned here.

All tourist villages in France, however small, have a **Monument aux morts.**

Act. D: This will need to be done briefly in English.

www explore!
http//voila.heinle.com

C. Les soldats.

1. Combien de soldats de Salies-du-Salat sont morts *(died)* pendant la Première Guerre mondiale? pendant la Seconde Guerre mondiale? pendant la guerre d'Indochine?

2. Il y a combien de soldats qui figurent sur le Monument aux morts qui s'appellent Ramirez? Caubet? Debax? Dubuc? Ducos? Larroque? Noguès? Caperan? Dupeyron? Quels noms ne sont pas d'origine française? D'où sont les noms? La population française est-elle homogène?

D. Discutons. Are there **Monuments aux morts** where you live? What do they commemorate? Where are they located? What kinds of inscriptions are there?

Orthographe et prononciation

An *Orthographe et prononciation* section will be found at the end of each lesson. These brief notes are intended to provide students with useful information about the French spelling system and its relation to the spoken language.

Pronunciation exercises can be found in the **Cahier d'activités écrites et orales** and the accompanying cassettes.

Have students listen while you pronounce the letters of the alphabet. Then have them repeat. Note that the pronunciation guide respects French orthography; it is not a phonetic transcription.

See the **Instructor's Resource Manual** for more information.

▶▶ L'alphabet français

Although French is written using the same alphabet as English, the sounds corresponding to many of the letters are different.

a	(ah)	n	(en)
b	(bé)	o	(o)
c	(cé)	p	(pé)
d	(dé)	q	(ku)
e	(euh)	r	(er)
f	(ef)	s	(es)
g	(gé)	t	(té)
h	(ach)	u	(u)
i	(i)	v	(vé)
j	(ji)	w	(doublevé)
k	(ka)	x	(iks)
l	(el)	y	(igrec)
m	(em)	z	(zed)

Activité

À l'aéroport You are the tour guide who will be meeting several tourists at Roissy-Charles de Gaulle. Find out how to spell each person's name.

Modèle   M. Smith?
           Oui, Monsieur Smith, S-M-I-T-H.

1. M. et Mme Zweig?
2. Mlle Wiltberger?
3. Mlle Matecki?
4. Mme Jakada?
5. Mme Hawthorne?
6. M. Buxton?
7. M. Quigley?

À l'aéroport: If desired, explain the rule for using periods in French abbreviations. (A period is not used when the last letter of the abbreviation is the same as the last letter of the word abbreviated.)

See the **Instructor's Resource Manual** for an activity using **sigles** (acronyms such as **ONU** or **PDG**).

Vocabulaire de base

The ***Vocabulaire de base*** *(basic vocabulary)* for each lesson contains the words and expressions that you are responsible for learning to use in speaking and in writing. (NOTE: *m. = masculine; f. = feminine*)

TEXT TAPE:
Vocabulaire de base

Refer students to the student **Text Tape** for a recording of the words in the *Vocabulaire de base.*

The *Vocabulaire de base*, or basic vocabulary, is intended to limit the number of words students feel they must memorize for a test.

les chiffres de 0 à 39 (voir page 6)
les jours de la semaine (voir page 7)
les mois de l'année (voir page 7)
les saisons de l'année (voir page 8)

NOMS

le cahier *notebook*
le chat *cat*
le chien *dog*
l'étudiant *(m.)*, l'étudiante *(f.)*
    student (male), student (female)
le livre *book*
le professeur *teacher*
le stylo *pen*

DIVERS

à bientôt *see you soon*
à demain *see you tomorrow*
au revoir *good-bye*
aussi *also*
avec *with*
bien *fine, good, well*
bonjour *hello*

Ça va? *How's it going?*
c'est le huit janvier *it's January 8 /
    it's the eighth of January*
c'est le premier octobre *it's
    October 1 / it's the first of October*
c'est lundi *it's Monday*
Comment allez-vous? *How are you?
    (formal)*
Comment ça va? *How's it going?*
d'accord *all right, OK*
de *of, from, about*
et *and*
Et toi? *What about you? (to a friend)*
Et vous? *What about you? (to an
    adult)*
j'adore *I love*
j'aime *I like, I love*
je déteste *I hate*
je m'appelle *my name is*

je ne comprends pas *I don't
    understand*
je ne sais pas *I don't know*
Madame (Mme) *ma'am (Mrs.)*
Mademoiselle (Mlle) *miss, Miss*
mais *but*
merci *thank you*
moi *me*
Monsieur (M.) *sir, Mr.*
non *no*
oui *yes*
pardon *excuse me*
pas mal *not bad*
pour *for, in order to*
premier *first*
salut *hi, bye*
très bien *fine, good, very good*
tu adores *you love*
tu aimes *you like, you love*

Vocabulaire supplémentaire

The *Vocabulaire supplémentaire* for each lesson contains words and expressions that you should be able to recognize when you hear them or when you read them. You may want to learn some of these words and expressions and start using them when you speak and write.

NOMS

l'affiche *(f.)* poster
l'année *(f.)* year
l'anniversaire *(m.)* birthday
la date *date*
la fleur *flower*
le jour *day*
le mois *month*
le poisson *fish*
la saison *season*
la semaine *week*
le week-end *weekend*

DIVERS

à tout à l'heure *see you later*
aujourd'hui *today*
Bon week-end! *Have a nice weekend!*
ça dépend *that depends*
Ça y est! *That's it/done/finished!*
C'est quand, ton anniversaire? *When's your birthday? (to a friend)*
C'est quel jour aujourd'hui? *What day is it today?*
Comment? *What did you say?*
Comment t'appelles-tu?, Tu t'appelles comment? *What's your name? (to a friend or a child)*
Comment vous appelez-vous? *What's your name? (to someone you don't know well)*
je comprends *I understand*
moi aussi *me too, so do I*
moi non plus *me neither, neither do I*
pas du tout *not at all*
pas moi *not me*
Quelle est la date aujourd'hui? *What's the date today?*
Tu es d'où? *Where are you from?*
Vous aimez...? *Do you like . . . ?*
Vous êtes...? *Are you . . . ?*

LE FRANÇAIS TEL QU'ON LE PARLE

This section contains words and expressions characteristic of spoken French. Spelling for some of these words and expressions is not standardized and you will not find them in dictionaries. This is similar to the situation in English for words like *gonna* or *whatcha* which are common in spoken English. These are presented here in order to help you understand French as you will hear it both in and out of the classroom.

chais pas = je ne sais pas
j'comprends pas = je ne comprends pas
t'aimes = tu aimes
ouais = oui

LE FRANÇAIS FAMILIER

This section contains words and expressions characteristic of the informal French spoken by friends, within families, or by young people. Although it is probably not advisable for learners of French as a second language to use these words and expressions until they are very sure of their nuances, you may need to be able to understand them.

le bouquin = le livre
le prof = le professeur

ON ENTEND PARFOIS...

Although English is spoken in both the United States and Great Britain, there are some differences, particularly in vocabulary. For example, in the United States you rent an *apartment* and you buy *gas* for your car. In Great Britain, however, you rent a *flat* and you buy *petrol.* There are similar kinds of differences in countries where French is spoken. The section **On entend parfois...** *(You sometimes hear . . .)* contains a selection of words along with the French-speaking country where they're used.

la fin de semaine (Canada) = le week-end
bonjour (Canada) = au revoir
la fête (Canada) = l'anniversaire

Comment êtes-vous?

En bref

Dans cette leçon...
- Description: parler de soi, de ses amis
- Goûts et préférences
- Niveaux de langue
- Le verbe **être**
- Pour dire **non**
- Les adjectifs
- Comparaisons
- Pratiques sociales en France: Faire-parts de naissance
- Les stéréotypes

In this lesson...
- Talking about what you and your friends are like and not like
- Likes and dislikes
- Levels of language in French
- The verb **être** *(to be)*
- Saying *no*
- Adjectives
- Comparisons
- Social traditions in France: Birth announcements
- Stereotypes

www explore!
http://voila.heinle.com

Develop writing skills with Système-D software!

Practice listening and pronunciation skills with the Text Tape!

Discover the Francophone world!

Build your skills!

 INTERNET
 SYSTÈME-D
 TEXT TAPE
 VIDEO TAPE
 CD-ROM

Students have an open-ended writing activity in the **Cahier** suitable for use with **Système-D**.

DOSSIER

Ils sont le nouveau pouvoir mondial

Les **50** hommes les plus influents de la planète

Ils sont intellectuels ou mafieux, chercheurs ou banquiers, créateurs ou espions. Aux États-Unis, en Europe mais aussi au Japon ou en Chine, «le Nouvel Observateur» a sélectionné 50 chefs de file de ces nouvelles Internationales de la finance, des médias, de la mode, de la recherche ou du crime.

Le Nouvel Observateur

Use this document to introduce adjectives and involve students in a brief discussion about what they know of the world. The use of cognates should aid comprehension. Students will only need to cite the names of important people they know or answer **oui** or **non**.

Suggestions for presenting the text: Speak slowly and use visuals, gestures, and repetition of key words to aid student comprehension. You may want to ask questions and then provide answers yourself.

Some of the top 50 are: Michel Camdessus, Alan Greenspan (Finance); Hans Zacher, John Maddox (Science); Samuel Huntington, Newt Gingrich, Ted Turner (Public Opinion Leaders); Rupert Murdoch, Bill Gates (Communication).

See the **Instructor's Resource Manual** for the complete list. You may want to put the list on a transparency.

L'illustration. Quels continents est-ce qu'il y a sur le globe terrestre? l'Afrique? l'Europe? l'Australie? l'Amérique du Nord? l'Amérique du Sud?

Est-ce qu'il y a des humains? Oui, il y a un humain... Est-ce qu'il est masculin ou féminin? Est-ce que c'est typique? Est-ce que c'est traditionnel?

Le texte. Quels sont les domaines d'influence considérés dans le texte? Soulignez *(underline)* les mots *(words)* et les catégories mentionnées dans le texte.

Domaine d'influence	Adjectifs descriptifs
_____ science	a. intellectuel
_____ crime	b. mafieux
_____ mode	c. chercheur
_____ finance	d. banquier
	e. créateur
	f. espion

Assemblez les adjectifs descriptifs avec les domaines d'influence.

Crime	_____
Finance	_____
Médias	_____
Mode	_____
Recherche	_____

Utilisez des chiffres (1, 2, 3, 4, 5; 1 = la catégorie la plus importante) pour indiquer quelles sont les catégories les plus importantes pour vous.

Et pour vous? Quel est l'homme le plus important de la planète pour vous? Est-ce qu'il est intellectuel? mafieux? chercheur *(scientist)?* banquier? créateur? espion? Qui sont les hommes influents de la planète aujourd'hui pour vous?

Et les femmes? (Les femmes sont du sexe féminin.) Donnez des noms de femmes très influentes. Dans quel domaine est-ce qu'elles sont influentes?

Le prix de l'influence planétaire!
Donnez un prix *(award)* à la personne la plus influente pour vous.

1er Prix

Info plus

Le Nouvel Observateur.
Le Nouvel Observateur is a weekly liberal magazine that is widely read in France.

Point out the roots of these words: **mafia / intelligence / chercher / banque / création / épier ou espionner** *(to spy).*

Have students rank the categories according to their own priorities using numbers. Put the list on the board or on a transparency and compare student responses. You may want to provide French words for other categories suggested by students in their native language.

Have students brainstorm to make a list of influential people. Then have them categorize them by countries or continents and category of influence.

Have students give names and categories: **finance, médias, mode, recherche, crime,** or other. You may need to provide new categories. Take a tally to see the category and the person most cited by students.

Vocabulaire

[In French, adjectives change their form according to the gender of the noun they go with or modify. Traditionally, the masculine, singular form is the base form (the form used for dictionary entries) and feminine and plural forms are derived from it. To make things easier, the vocabulary section here deals with masculine singular and plural forms only. Feminine singular and plural forms will be found in the **Structure** section.]

A. Ils sont...

Voilà Patrick. Il est grand et brun. Il est sérieux, travailleur et raisonnable. Il est aussi sympathique parce qu'il est équilibré et généreux.

Voilà Jean-Paul. Il est petit et blond. Maintenant, il est méchant, pénible et égoïste parce qu'il est fatigué.

Voilà Michel. Il est mince. Aujourd'hui, il est malade donc il est fatigué et déprimé.

Voilà Bertrand. Il n'est pas très âgé mais il n'est pas jeune. Il est intelligent mais il est paresseux. Il est aussi sociable et équilibré.

Voilà Robert. Il est beau mais il est trop timide et il est très naïf.

Voilà Émile. Il est laid, bizarre et bête. Mais il est très amusant!

Voilà Candide et Alceste. Candide est heureux mais Alceste est malheureux.

Voilà Pierre. Il est sportif et très occupé.

Voilà Napoléon.
Il est français.

Voilà Daniel Boone.
Il est américain.

Voilà John Macdonald.
Il est canadien.

Info plus

Sir John Macdonald.
Sir John Macdonald was the first prime minister of Canada. He led Canada through its period of consolidation in the nineteenth century.

TRANSPARENCY:
2-3

- Patrick est plus sympathique que Jean-Paul. Émile est moins beau que Robert et Pierre. Et Alceste? Il est aussi beau que Robert? Qui est plus mince, Michel ou Bertrand? Qui est plus grand, Napoléon ou Daniel Boone? Qui est moins sportif, Pierre ou Bertrand? Qui est aussi heureux que Candide aujourd'hui? Qui est aussi malheureux qu'Alceste? Comment est Napoléon? Comment est Daniel Boone? Comment est John Macdonald?

B. Qui aime...

TRANSPARENCY:
2-4

les cours?

les devoirs?

les examens?

les fêtes?

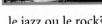

la musique classique?

le jazz ou le rock?

l'université?

les vacances?

- Et vous, vous aimez les cours? le rock? les fêtes? la musique classique?

Notes de vocabulaire

1. Mots et expressions utiles. Here are some useful words and expressions not included in the preceding vocabulary presentation.

c'est bizarre	*that's weird (odd, strange)*
c'est normal	*that's normal*
c'est tout	*that's all*
il/elle adore	*he/she loves*
il/elle aime	*he/she likes, he/she loves*
il/elle déteste	*he/she hates*
où	*where*
plus ou moins	*more or less*

1: You may want to present these words using examples, mime, and simple drawings. For example: **c'est bizarre/c'est normal: les examens le dimanche vs les examens le vendredi; c'est tout: un livre qu'on ferme; aimer/détester: en général, on aime (les étudiants aiment) le chocolat mais on n'aime pas (les étudiants n'aiment pas) les examens;** etc.

2: For **où**, point out the expression students saw in *Leçon 1* (Tu es d'où?).
Accent marks are discussed in the ***Orthographe et prononciation*** sections of *Leçons 2* and *3*.

3: Point out that **aimer bien** is used when there is ambiguity. Context is usually sufficient to distinguish between *like* and *love*.

4: If desired, point out that **le devoir** can also mean *duty*.

6: Comparison of adjectives and adverbs is treated in more detail in *Leçon 15*.

2. Ou / où.
Ou (no accent) means *or*; **où** (with an accent) means *where*.

— Où est Michèle?   "Where's Michèle?"
— Michel ou Michèle?   "Michel or Michèle?"

3. Aimer / aimer bien.
If you want to say that you love someone, use the verb **aimer.** If, however, you want to emphasize the fact that you like that person as opposed to loving them, use **aimer bien.**

J'**aime bien** Marc mais c'est   *I like Marc but I love Christophe.*
   Christophe que j'**aime.**

4. Singulier ou pluriel?
Some words that are used in the singular in English are used in the plural in French, and vice versa.

Le devoir/les devoirs. A **devoir** is an assignment. **Les devoirs** refers to homework in general.

Je déteste **les devoirs.**   *I hate homework.*
Le devoir est bizarre!   *The assignment is strange!*

Les vacances. The word **vacances** is always plural in French.

J'adore **les vacances.**   *I love vacation(s).*

5. La prononciation.
Spelling differences do not always indicate differences in pronunciation. In the example below, the words in boldface type are both pronounced alike.

Il **aime** le jazz.   Tu **aimes** le rock?

The same is true in **j'adore, tu adores,** and **il/elle adore** as well as for **je déteste, tu détestes,** and **il/elle déteste.**

6. La comparaison.
Use **plus/plus... que, moins/moins... que** and **aussi/aussi... que** to make comparisons.

Qui est **plus** mince, Michel   *Who's thinner, Michel*
   ou Bertrand?   *or Bertrand?*

Jean-Paul est **plus** égoïste   *Jean-Paul is more selfish*
   que Patrick et il est   *than Patrick, and he is*
   moins sympathique.   *less likable.*

Michel est **aussi** malheureux   *Michel is as unhappy*
   qu'Alceste aujourd'hui.   *as Alceste today.*

7. Très / trop.
Très and **trop** are adverbs that can be used to qualify an adjective.

Il est **très** intelligent.   *He's very intelligent.*
Il est **trop** généreux.   *He's too generous.*

8. Les fêtes.
The word **fête** may refer to a holiday or simply to a party.

9. Aussi / donc. **Aussi** is an adverb and means *also* or *as*. **Donc** is a conjunction (coordinates clauses) and means *so* or *therefore*. Use **donc** to introduce a conclusion or consequence, as in Descartes' famous **"Je pense donc je suis"** *(I think therefore I exist)*. Use **aussi** to express *also* or a comparison of equality. **Aussi,** in these uses, is never found at the beginning of a sentence or clause.

Alceste est malade **donc** il est malheureux et déprimé.
Alceste is sick, so he's unhappy and depressed.

Candide est **aussi** malade **qu'**Alceste mais il n'est pas **aussi** malheureux.
Candide is as sick as Alceste, but he's not as unhappy.

Moi, je suis malade **aussi!**
I'm sick too!

10. Parce que. The **-e** of **que** is dropped when **parce que** is used in front of a word beginning with a vowel.

Alceste est malheureux **parce qu'**il est malade.
Alceste is unhappy because he's sick.

9: The information in this note (aussi et donc) is obviously oversimplified. If desired, give more information about aussi and donc.

See the **Instructor's Resource Manual** for more information.

D'accord?

A. Positif ou négatif? Decide which of the following adjectives have positive or negative connotations. Are there some adjectives that are both negative and positive or that are otherwise difficult to classify?

amusant / sportif / timide / naïf / déprimé / méchant / beau / bête / bizarre / égoïste / grand / généreux / intelligent / sérieux / malade / heureux / malheureux / équilibré / occupé / paresseux / pénible / raisonnable / sociable / sympathique / travailleur / normal

Act. A: Some adjectives, such as **gros, mince, petit, âgé,** and **laid,** are not included in order to avoid hurting or embarrassing students. You could, however, add the adjectives **français** and **américain** if you want to know your students' feelings about the French people and to start a discussion on stereotypes.

ADJECTIFS POSITIFS	ADJECTIFS NÉGATIFS	ADJECTIFS DIFFICILES À CLASSER

B. Comment est... ? Describe each person. Base your description on what you know. Then add other possible characteristics.

1. Robert
2. Émile
3. Patrick
4. Jean-Paul
5. Michel
6. Bertrand
7. Napoléon
8. Daniel Boone
9. John Macdonald
10. Le président américain

Act. B: Ask students to describe each person without looking back at the pictures. Encourage elaboration. Later, they may want to verify their descriptions with the drawings. ALTERNATIVE FORMAT: Use a transparency to encourage students to base their descriptions on the drawings alone.

C. Qui est... ?

1. Qui est plus intelligent, Émile ou Patrick?
2. Qui est plus âgé, Jean-Paul ou Patrick?
3. Qui est moins sportif, Daniel Boone ou Bertrand?
4. Qui est moins beau, Napoléon ou Pierre?
5. Qui est plus heureux, Candide ou Michel?
6. Qui est plus malheureux, Robert ou Alceste?
7. Qui est plus sérieux, Bertrand ou John Macdonald?
8. Qui est aussi mince que Pierre?

D. Ils aiment?

For each person in the *Vocabulaire* section on page 32, decide whether or not he likes each of the following. Then, group the people according to how you feel about them.

Il aime...	les chiens	les vacances	les devoirs	les fêtes	les fleurs
Patrick					
Jean-Paul					
Bertrand					
Robert					
Émile					
Alceste					

Ils sont *(they are)* sympathiques:
Ils ne sont pas *(they aren't)* très sympathiques:

Mise en pratique

A. Expliquez!

Modèle   Il est méchant.
   Donc il est pénible, égoiste,...

1. Il est sérieux.
2. Il est amusant.
3. Il est sociable.
4. Il est bizarre.
5. Il est heureux.
6. Il est malheureux.
7. Il est équilibré.
8. Il est pénible.

B. Qui est-ce?

Work in pairs. One student selects a character from the *Vocabulaire* section on pages 32–33 and describes him without giving his name. The other partner identifies who was selected.

Modèle   ***—Il est français, il est petit, il n'est pas timide!***
   —Napoléon!

C. Comparez

Compare the following people:

1. Michel et Bertrand
2. Patrick et Jean-Paul
3. Pierre et Alceste
4. Robert et Candide
5. Napoléon et Daniel Boone
6. Émile et vous

Act. D: CONTINUATION: **les chats / les poissons / les professeurs / les cours de français / les livres / les examens / la musique classique / le rock / le jazz / l'hiver / l'été / l'université.** Ask students to justify their opinions (**Jean-Paul est sympathique parce qu'il aime les chiens,** etc.). If desired, put students in pairs to interview one another about their likes and dislikes and to report back to the class.

Act. A: Can be used as a writing activity or assigned for homework. To encourage a wide use of adjectives, put a list of those that students already know on the board or a transparency for them to choose from.
   CONTINUATION: **Il est grand et sportif. / Il est petit et beau. / Il est généreux et amusant. / Il est amusant et heureux.**

Act. C: You may want to prepare this activity by first having students describe each character from memory. They can then compare their descriptions with those given in the *Vocabulaire* section. Comparisons are possible by using **plus... que / aussi.. que / moins... que** or by using two sentences connected by **mais.**

Act. C, 6: Since students do not know **je suis,** have them start the comparison with Émile's name. If desired, teach **je suis** as a lexical item.

Structure

 CD-ROM:
Build your skills!

▶▶ Le verbe *être*

Here are the forms of the verb **être** *(to be).*

je suis	*I am*
tu es	*you (familiar) are*
il est	*he (it) is*
elle est	*she (it) is*
nous sommes	*we are*
vous êtes	*you (formal or plural) are*
ils sont	*they are*
elles sont	*they are*

Note that the **-s** of **vous** is pronounced as a **z** in front of the vowel **ê-** in **êtes.**

vous êtes
   /z/

Use **ils** to refer to any group that includes a male. **Elles** is used only to refer to groups that are composed exclusively of females. Note that the **-s** of **ils** and **elles** is not pronounced in front of a consonant.

There are also three *imperative* or *command* forms of the verb **être.**

Sois raisonnable!	*Be reasonable! (said to a person you would address using **tu**)*
Soyez raisonnable(s)!	*Be reasonable! (said to a person you would address using **vous** or to more than one person)*
Soyons raisonnables!	*Let's be reasonable!*

SUBSTITUTION DRILL: **Tout le monde est occupé! Le professeur est occupé. (je / Alceste / nous / Robert et Aline / vous / tu)**

Treat the imperative forms rapidly and as straightforwardly as possible. *VOILÀ* introduces these forms as part of the verb conjugations as verbs are presented.

Vous avez compris?

A. *C'est qui?* Choose one of the pronouns in parentheses to complete each sentence appropriately.

1. (Vous / Ils / Nous) sommes américains.
2. (Tu / Vous / Elles) êtes sympathique.
3. (Je / Il / Nous) suis malade.
4. (Elle / Ils / Tu) es timide.
5. (Nous / Elles / Vous) sommes raisonnables.
6. (Je / Tu / Elle) est bête!
7. (Il / Ils / Je) est occupé.
8. (Il / Ils / Vous) sont malades.

B. Être! Complete each sentence with the correct form of the verb être.

1. Tu ..... très égoïste!
2. Il ..... grand et gros.
3. Vous ..... américains?
4. Elles ..... étudiantes?
5. Nous ..... trop occupés.
6. Je ..... plus mince que Bertrand!
7. Elle ..... trop timide.

Continuons!

Je suis comme je suis! Sometimes people are just like they are! Combine elements from the two columns with a form of **être** to make complete sentences.

je	bête
tu	bizarre
Alceste	malade
Candide	mince
le professeur	pénible
	raisonnable
	sociable
	sympathique
	timide

*Je suis comme je suis!: Adjectives are limited to singular forms with no spelling or pronunciation change in masculine/feminine forms. Encourage students to make as many sentences as possible and to link sentences where possible using **et**, **mais**, and **donc**.*

▶▶ La forme négative

To make a verb negative in French, put **ne** in front of the verb and **pas** after it.

> **ne** + verb + **pas**

*To check assimilation of forms, have students write out affirmative and negative conjugations of **être** and **aimer**.*

Here are the negative forms of **détester**.

je **ne** déteste **pas**   *I don't hate*
tu **ne** détestes **pas**   *you don't hate*
il ⎱
elle ⎰ **ne** déteste **pas**   *he* ⎱
                                     she ⎰ *doesn't hate*

*DRILL: Have students make these sentences negative: **Paulette aime le rock. Nous sommes timides. Vous êtes intelligent. Alceste et Candide sont contents. Tu aimes les vacances. Je suis travailleur.***

Note that the **-e** of **ne** is dropped in front of a verb form beginning with a vowel.

—Tu **n'**es pas heureux?
—Non. Ça ne va pas du tout. Patrick **n'**aime pas les chats et moi je **n'**aime pas les chiens!

Vous avez compris?

Oui ou non?
Read the exchanges. Is the reply **oui** or **non?** You won't know all the words, but you should be able to guess the general intent.

Oui ou non?: This activity is meant to sensitize students to how negation is expressed in French. If desired, ask students how they decided whether the answer was **oui** or **non.** You can also ask for guesses as to the meaning of each exchange.

1. —C'est clair? Tu comprends?
   — . . . . . , je comprends maintenant.

2. —Vous permettez que je fume?
   —Je suis désolé mais, ... , ce n'est pas permis.

3. —Jeanne est là?
   — . . . . . , elle n'est pas là.

4. —Ça va? Vous êtes d'accord?
   — . . . . . , ça va, je suis d'accord.

5. —Tu sais où est le supermarché?
   — . . . . . , je ne sais pas.

Continuons!

A. L'esprit négatif
Candide sees life through rose-colored glasses. Alceste does not. Say what Alceste would say.

Act. A: It is possible to make these sentences negative by lexical means. Ask students to do this as a follow-up.

Modèle   CANDIDE   Je suis heureux!
           ALCESTE   ***Et moi, je ne suis pas heureux.***

1. CANDIDE   J'aime les chats!
2. CANDIDE   Les chiens sont sympathiques!
3. CANDIDE   L'automne est beau!
4. CANDIDE   Le professeur est très intelligent!
5. CANDIDE   Les étudiants sont sérieux!
6. CANDIDE   J'aime le printemps!
7. CANDIDE   Je suis généreux!
8. CANDIDE   Ça va!

B. J'aime...
Et vous, est-ce que vous aimez... ?

Modèle   les chats?
           Oui, j'aime les chats. / Non, je n'aime pas les chats.

les chiens?
les poissons?
les vacances?
les examens?
les fêtes?
les devoirs?
la musique classique?
le rock?
les professeurs?
les cours?

*Amphithéâtre Richelieu
La Sorbonne, Paris*

➤➤ La formation des adjectifs

In French, adjectives agree in number and gender with the person or object to which they refer. Thus adjectives may change form depending on whether the person or object they refer to is singular or plural, masculine or feminine.

Paul est **grand** et **beau**.   Paul et Marc sont **grands** et **beaux**.
Nicole est **grande** et **belle**.   Nicole et Marie sont **grandes** et **belles**.

Adjectifs comme **mince**

Adjectives whose masculine singular form ends with a mute -**e** (an -**e** that is not pronounced) are spelled identically in the masculine and feminine forms. They add -**s** to form the plural. These changes affect spelling only; all four forms are pronounced identically.

	MASCULINE	FEMININE
SINGULAR	Il est mince.	Elle est mince.
PLURAL	Ils sont minces.	Elles sont minces.

Other adjectives like **mince** are **bête, bizarre, égoïste, malade, raisonnable, sociable, sympathique,** and **timide.**

Adjectifs comme **fatigué**

Adjectives that end in -**é** form their feminine by adding a silent -**e.** Their plurals end in a silent -**s.** Changes involve spelling only; all four forms are pronounced identically.

	MASCULINE	FEMININE
SINGULAR	Il est fatigué.	Elle est fatiguée.
PLURAL	Ils sont fatigués.	Elles sont fatiguées.

Other adjectives like **fatigué** are **âgé, déprimé, équilibré,** and **occupé.**

Adjectifs comme **grand** et **français**

The majority of adjectives that end in a silent consonant (rather than a mute -**e** or an -**é**) form their feminine by adding -**e.** The addition of this -**e** causes the preceding consonant to be pronounced.

	MASCULINE	FEMININE
SINGULAR	Il est grand. (-**d** not pronounced)	Elle est grande. (-**d**- pronounced)
	Il est français. (-**s** not pronounced)	Elle est française. (-**s**- pronounced)

Point out that certain adjectives also have a change in the pronunciation of the vowel preceding the consonant: **brun / brune, américain / américaine, canadien / canadienne.**

If desired, point out that the oral masculine form can be derived from the feminine by dropping the final consonant sound.

Plurals are formed by adding **-s** to the singular form (unless that form already ends in **-s,** in which case nothing is added). The plural **-s** is never pronounced.

	MASCULINE	FEMININE
PLURAL	Ils sont grand**s**.	Elles sont grande**s**.
	Ils sont français.	Elles sont françai**ses**.

Other similar adjectives include **américain, amusant, blond, brun, content, intelligent, laid, méchant,** and **petit.**

D'autres adjectifs

Some adjectives have feminine and/or plural forms that do not fall into the three categories just discussed. The forms of adjectives that do not follow one of these three patterns are always given in the vocabulary list. You should learn them as you encounter them.

Encourage students to start and keep their own lists. The form **bel** will be introduced in *Leçon 5.*

Here are the forms of irregular adjectives in this lesson.

MASC. SING.	FEM. SING.	MASC. PL.	FEM. PL.
-eux	**-euse**	**-eux**	**-euses**
généreux	généreuse	généreux	généreuses
paresseux	paresseuse	paresseux	paresseuses
sérieux	sérieuse	sérieux	sérieuses
-s	**-sse**	**-s**	**-sses**
gros	grosse	gros	grosses
-f	**-ve**	**-fs**	**-ves**
naïf	naïve	naïfs	naïves
sportif	sportive	sportifs	sportives
-ien	**-ienne**	**-iens**	**-iennes**
canadien	canadienne	canadiens	canadiennes
-eur	**-euse**	**-eurs**	**-euses**
travailleur	travailleuse	travailleurs	travailleuses
-al	**-ale**	**-aux**	**-ales**
normal	normale	normaux	normales
beau	belle	beaux	belles

Model pronunciation of **canadien, canadienne.**

Vous avez compris?

Act. A: Do rapidly. Point out how gender and number link across words in French, for example, Oui, il est beau, le chat, or, Oui, le chat il est beau, or, L'affiche, elle est belle.

A. Vous parlez de quoi? Use the pronouns and adjective endings to decide what each person is talking about.

1. Il est beau! (le chat ou l'affiche?)
2. Elles sont laides! (les livres ou les fleurs?)
3. Il est grand! (le poisson ou l'université?)
4. Elle est belle! (l'affiche ou le livre?)
5. Elles sont grandes! (les fleurs ou les chats?)
6. Il est âgé! (Monsieur Dumont ou Madame Vital?)

Act. B: CONTINUATION: Robert est travailleur. Et Richard? Sabine est petite. Et Suzanne? Marc est déprimé. Et Marianne? Catherine est naïve. Et Charles? Bruno est beau. Et Bernadette? Évelyne est brune. Et Éric?

B. Des jumeaux et des jumelles Here are some sets of twins. You already know what one twin is like. What is the other twin probably like?

Modèle   Sophie est intelligente. Et Marc?
             Il est intelligent.

1. Jacques est timide. Et Jacqueline?
2. Béatrice est sociable. Et Bernard?
3. Monique est sportive. Et Marie?
4. Paul est laid. Et Pierre?
5. André est généreux. Et Anne?
6. Claudine est grosse. Et Charles?

C. Comment sont... ? Refer to activity B to tell what each pair of twins is like.

Modèle   Sophie et Marc?
             Ils sont intelligents.

1. Jacques et Jacqueline?
2. Béatrice et Bernard?
3. Monique et Marie?
4. Paul et Pierre?
5. André et Anne?
6. Claudine et Charles?

Continuons!

A. Et les sœurs? Look at the pictures on page 32. Each of these people has a sister. What are the names of these sisters? What is each one like? Use your imagination!

Modèle   ***Jean-Paul? Il est petit et blond. Il est méchant et égoïste.***
             Et sa (his) sœur? C'est Marie-Jeanne. Elle n'est pas petite.
             Elle est grande et blonde. Elle est sympathique et sociable.

B. Comment est... ? With a partner or in groups, find out as much as possible about each other using the vocabulary you already know. Find out where your classmates are from, what they like, what they do not like, and what they are like. Be ready to tell the class one or two interesting things about the people to whom you have been talking.

Act. B: Ask students to write a short paragraph about the person or persons to whom they have been talking. Encourage them to link sentences and to compare and contrast.

C. Comparez-les In small groups, compare the people in photos A and B. Then, compare the two people in photo C. Put your ideas together to write a short paragraph about each pair. Don't forget words like **et, mais, très, trop,** etc.

A

Dominique

B

Sandrine

C

M. Challibi   *M. M'Somwé*

Act. C: CONTINUATION: Ask students to describe and contrast TV characters from soap operas and other popular shows.

D. Conversation en français You are talking to a friend who has a knack for writing personal ads. Tell this friend about yourself. Keep in mind that absolute truth may not be to your advantage in this situation.

TEXT TAPE:
Conversation en français

Découvertes culturelles: Identités sociales et nationales

▶ Faire-parts de naissance

Act. A: Do this activity with students before they open their books.

A. Préparation. Have you ever sent or received a printed announcement? What was it for? What kind of information did it contain? On what other occasions are printed announcements appropriate?

Le Capitaine Bruno Beth et Madame née Hélène Claret ont la joie de vous annoncer la naissance et le Baptême de

Matthieu

23 Mai - 2 Juin 1996

8, Allée des Rosiers
04400 Barcelonnette
04.92.81.31.31.

Monsieur Christian Debay et Madame née Françoise Beth, laissent à Benoist, Marie et Arnauld la joie de vous annoncer la naissance et le baptême de leur petite sœur

Alix

les 8 et 13 Février 1996

14, rue des Condamines
78000 Versailles

Le Lieutenant et Madame Frédéric Beth laissent à Bénédicte la joie d'annoncer la naissance et le baptême de

Guillaume

14 - 29 Avril 1996

7, avenue Maréchal Fayolle
56380 Coëtquidan

B. Les données principales. Select the kind of information found on these cards.

☐ baptême   ☐ prénoms *(first names)*   ☐ religion

☐ saison   ☐ profession   ☐ événement

☐ famille   ☐ adresse   ☐ nationalité

☐ chiffres   ☐ noms *(last names)*   ☐ date

C. Quel événement? Match each event with its date.

la naissance de Matthieu   14/4
le baptême d'Alix   23/5
la naissance de Guillaume   13/2

D. Quelques détails. Complete the chart to map out the information contained in these three cards. What do these cards have in common?

	Qui?	**Quoi?** *(What?)*	**Quand?** *(When?)*	**Où?**
Carte 1				
Carte 2				
Carte 3				

Act. D. Ask students, in English, for each card: Was it a boy or a girl? Which of these babies is the youngest? the oldest? Which of these people are brothers? sisters? brothers-in-law? first cousins? How do you know?

E. Apprenons.

1. **Mots et expressions.** Can you guess the meaning of these words? **baptême? naissance? Madame, née Françoise Beth?**
2. **Quelle famille?** Use format, presentation, and context to identify the social position of these families.
3. **Quelle adresse?** How are addresses written in France?
4. **Décidons.** What would you do if you received this announcement? Telephone? Write a note? What else? If you were living in France, what would you do?

Act. E, 1: If desired, give students the following information about the relationship between English and French. Since 1066, when William the Conqueror invaded England, a number of French words have infiltrated and survived in English, often with the same meaning and the same or similar spelling. These words are called *cognates.*

F. Une bonne nouvelle. If you had been born in France, what do you think your parents might have put on your birth announcement? Make a card in French announcing your birth!

Act. E, 3: Have students decide what they would do other than assume that their own customs would automatically be right. Ask a native informant? Ask about type of gifts?

La France vous est-elle sympathique ou antipathique?

This text and accompanying activities deal with stereotypes. You may want to set aside some time in English to discuss the issues surrounding stereotypes (how they arise, where they come from, degree of truth, etc.).

Act. B: Do quickly. This activity serves to give students vocabulary they will need later on.

A. Stéréotypes! Quels stéréotypes existent dans votre culture?

Les Italiens sont...
Les Anglais sont...

B. Qui sont-ils? Comment s'appellent-ils?

Modèle   Ils sont d'Italie.
        Les Italiens.

1. Ils sont de Russie.
2. Ils sont du Québec.
3. Ils sont de Belgique.
4. Ils sont du Japon.
5. Ils sont d'Espagne.
6. Ils sont d'Angleterre.

La France vous est-elle sympathique ou antipathique?

LES JAPONAIS
● LA FRANCE VOUS EST-ELLE SYMPATHIQUE OU ANTIPATHIQUE?

Sympathique 22
Antipathique 5
Ni antipathique, ni
    sympathique . . .71
Sans opinion 2

LES ANGLAIS
● LA FRANCE VOUS EST-ELLE SYMPATHIQUE OU ANTIPATHIQUE?

Sympathique 29
Antipathique 17
Ni antipathique, ni
    sympathique . . .51
Sans opinion 3

LES BELGES
● LA FRANCE VOUS EST-ELLE SYMPATHIQUE OU ANTIPATHIQUE?

Sympathique 77
Antipathique 4
Ni antipathique, ni
    sympathique . . .16
Sans opinion 3

LES ITALIENS
● LA FRANCE VOUS EST-ELLE SYMPATHIQUE OU ANTIPATHIQUE?

Sympathique . . .58
Antipathique 15
Ni antipathique, ni
    sympathique . . .25
Sans opinion 2

LES RUSSES
● LA FRANCE VOUS EST-ELLE SYMPATHIQUE OU ANTIPATHIQUE?

Sympathique 78
Antipathique 1
Ni antipathique, ni
    sympathique . . .14
Sans opinion 7

LES ESPAGNOLS
● LA FRANCE VOUS EST-ELLE SYMPATHIQUE OU ANTIPATHIQUE?

Sympathique 36
Antipathique 18
Ni antipathique, ni
    sympathique . . .39
Sans opinion 7

LES QUÉBÉCOIS
● LA FRANCE VOUS EST-ELLE SYMPATHIQUE OU ANTIPATHIQUE?

Sympathique 32
Antipathique 3
Ni antipathique, ni
    sympathique . . .49
Sans opinion 16

Le Figaro

C. Comment sont les Français pour eux?

Pour qui les Français sont-ils très sympathiques?
Pour qui sont-ils moins sympathiques?
Pour qui sont-ils indifférents?

D. Comparaisons. Organisez ces nationalités d'après leur sympathie pour les Français.

Modèle   Les Russes
Pour les Russes, les Français sont très sympathiques.

E. Une enquête. Préparez des questions pour un tableau des stéréotypes dans votre culture.

Act. C: Have students rank **sympathiques** according to these categories: **très, assez** *(rather)*, **peu** *(a little)*, **pas du tout** *(not at all)*. This is limited production and prepares students for the next exercise.

Act. D: Students need not limit themselves to **sympathiques, antipathiques.** Suggest that they use other adjectives. Encourage students to give complete sentences.

Act. E: Students should formulate yes-no questions using various adjectives. Then have them imagine what each nationality would say. Could be group work.

www explore!
http//voila.heinle.com

*O*rthographe et prononciation

➤➤ Les signes diacritiques

French uses five diacritical signs: **l'accent aigu** (´), **l'accent grave** (`), **l'accent circonflexe** (ˆ), **la cédille** (̦) and **le tréma** (¨). Omitting, misplacing, or misusing a diacritical is the same as misspelling a word in French.

Here we will discuss **l'accent aigu** (´); the others appear in *Leçon 3.*

The **accent aigu** is found only over the letter **e.** It marks the sound represented by the **é** in the word **étudiant.**

Activités

A. Prononcez Here are some words whose spelling includes an **accent aigu.** Repeat them after your instructor.

1. la clé *(key)*
2. déprimé
3. occupé
4. agréable *(nice, pleasant)*
5. fatigué

B. Écrivez Here is a list of words that you have already learned. Rewrite them adding the **accents aigus** that are missing.

1. americain
2. genereux
3. penible
4. universite

Vocabulaire de base

 **TEXT TAPE:**
Vocabulaire de base

NOMS

le cours *course, class*
le devoir (les devoirs) *assignment*
    (homework)
l'examen *(m.)* *test, exam*
la fête *holiday, party*
le jazz *jazz*
la musique *music*
le rock *rock (music)*
l'université *(f.)* *university, college*
les vacances *(f.pl.)* *vacation*

ADJECTIFS

américain(e) *American*
beau, belle, beaux, belles *beautiful,*
    good-looking, handsome
bête *dumb, stupid*
bizarre *weird, strange, odd*
blond(e) *blond*
brun(e) *dark-haired*
canadien, canadienne *Canadian*

fatigué(e) *tired*
français(e) *French*
généreux, généreuse *generous*
grand(e) *tall*
gros, grosse *big, fat*
heureux, heureuse *happy*
intelligent(e) *smart, intelligent*
laid(e) *ugly*
malade *sick*
malheureux, malheureuse *unhappy*
mince *slim, thin*
naïf, naïve *naive*
occupé(e) *busy*
paresseux, paresseuse *lazy*
pénible *obnoxious*
petit(e) *short (stature), small*
raisonnable *reasonable, sensible*
sociable *sociable, gregarious*
sportif, sportive *athletic*
sympathique *nice, congenial, likable*
timide *shy*
travailleur, travailleuse *hardworking*

VERBE

être *to be*

DIVERS

aussi... que *as... as*
il/elle adore *he/she loves*
il/elle aime *he/she likes, he/she loves*
il/elle déteste *he/she hates*
donc *thus, so*
maintenant *now*
moins (moins... que) *less (less... than)*
ou *or*
où *where*
parce que *because*
plus (plus... que) *more (more... than)*
très *very*

Vocabulaire supplémentaire

NOMS

la musique classique *classical music*

ADJECTIFS

âgé(e) *old*
amusant(e) *fun*
déprimé(e) *depressed*
égoïste *selfish*
équilibré(e) *well-adjusted*
jeune *young*
méchant(e) *mean*
normal(e) *normal*
sérieux, sérieuse *serious, hardworking*

DIVERS

c'est tout *that's all*
Comment est Jean? *What is Jean like?*
plus ou moins *more or less*

qui *who*
trop *too (too much)*
voilà *there are/is (here are/is), there!*

LE FRANÇAIS FAMILIER

branché(e) = *"with it"*
crevé(e) = très fatigué(e)
la fac = l'université
marrant(e) = amusant(e)
sympa *(invariable)* = sympathique

ON ENTEND PARFOIS...

une ambiance (Zaïre) = une fête
assez, ben (Canada) = très
bolé(e) (Canada) = intelligent
cagou (Antilles) = malade
fatigué(e) (Maghreb) = malade
minçolet(te) (Suisse) = très mince
les tâches *(f.pl.)* (Suisse) = les devoirs

Ask students: What slang expressions do you use? When do you use them? With whom?

Info plus

L'argot.

Slang (**l'argot**) in French, as in English, serves to define speakers in relationship to their age group, social class, and other affiliations. It is unstable and changes from generation to generation and from group to group. Words that are common slang expressions in current French will be included in **Le français familier** lists. Such words include, for example, **bouquin, branché, crevé**, and **marrant**. Again, as was the case with informal French, you will want to be able to recognize these words, but you should be careful about using them with French speakers since such use may seem insensitive or inappropriate.

Comment est votre chambre?

En bref

Dans cette leçon...

- Décrire sa chambre
- Parler de ses affaires
- Les couleurs
- Les articles indéfinis (**un, une, des**)
- Le verbe **avoir**
- Hôtels en France
- Logement dans une université belge

In this lesson...

- Describing your room
- Talking about your possessions
- Colors
- Indefinite articles (**un, une, des**)
- The verb **avoir** (to have)
- Hotels in France
- Lodging at a Belgian university

www explore!
http://voila.heinle.com

Develop writing skills with Système-D software!

Practice listening and pronunciation skills with the Text Tape!

Discover the Francophone world!

Build your skills!

INTERNET

SYSTÈME-D

TEXT TAPE

VIDEO TAPE

CD-ROM

Students have an open-ended writing activity in the **Cahier** suitable for use with **Système-D**.

OFFRE SPECIALE OFFRE

Gagnez jusqu'à 960 F
sur la chambre complète !

D. la commode

A. le lit

C. l'armoire

B. la table de nuit

Style Louis Philippe

La chambre 1 personne
1699F le lit
+ **985**F la table de nuit
+ **3670**F l'armoire
~~6354F~~ **5854**F
ou **1462**F + 3 x 1464F sans frais

Maison et loisir

Le style Louis-Philippe is traditional middle-class furniture in France.

This document is used to introduce a few words **(une chambre, un lit, une commode, une armoire, une lampe, une table de nuit)** in context. Although several of the words used will be part of the vocabulary for this lesson, avoid treating the *Entrée en matière* as a vocabulary presentation. Its purpose is to set the theme and allow students an opportunity to see the lesson theme in context. Student responses should be limited to the very simple French they have already learned—don't spend too much time on this. Make sure students understand that this is a catalog page and not a real room.

L'illustration. Regardez et décidez.

—Voilà une chambre. Il y a un lit, une armoire, une commode et une table de nuit.
Il y a aussi une lampe.
—Une lampe? Non, il y a deux lampes.
—Vous aimez la chambre?

Pour qui est la chambre? un étudiant? une personne riche? une personne sportive?
un couple? un adulte? une personne jeune? une personne travailleuse? des
parents? une personne occupée?

L'illustration: Introduce la chambre
Valérie in simple French. Use a
transparency if possible to help students
focus on the drawing.

Encourage students to answer using **oui**
and **non**. (La chambre est pour un
étudiant? Oui? Non?) If desired,
introduce **peut-être** or use **oui et non** to
allow students to nuance their answers.

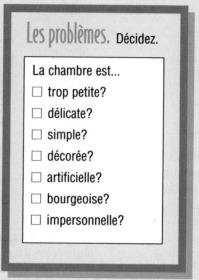

Les qualités de la chambre. Décidez.

Elle est...

☐ sympathique? ☐ prétentieuse?

☐ pratique? ☐ laide?

☐ simple? ☐ petite?

☐ classique? ☐ moderne?

☐ artificielle? ☐ confortable?

Les problèmes. Décidez.

La chambre est...

☐ trop petite?

☐ délicate?

☐ simple?

☐ décorée?

☐ artificielle?

☐ bourgeoise?

☐ impersonnelle?

Vous aimez les chambres modernes ou les chambres classiques?

Les qualités...: ALTERNATIVE FORMAT:
Make two lists: **elle est...** and **elle n'est
pas...**

Discussion.

Le style. Qui est Louis-Philippe? un décorateur? une personne célèbre?
un roi de France?

Choisissez. La chambre est une imitation ou elle est authentique?

Quel style préférez-vous? Le style moderne? classique? romantique? colonial?
art nouveau?

Comparez. Quel est l'équivalent du style Louis-Philippe dans votre culture?

Discussion: Students may have to use
some English to briefly discuss these
issues. You may want to point out the
omission of **de (chambre Valérie)**
where the name functions as an
adjective. Ask students what it is that
tells them this is a catalog page and not
a real room. Ask also for differences and
similarities between this room and what
they would expect to see in a catalog
from their own culture.

Vocabulaire

A. Voilà la chambre de Monsieur et Madame Mercier.

TRANSPARENCY:
3-1

You may want to point out that **grand** and **petit** mean *tall* and *short* when referring to people but *big* and *little* when referring to things.

Ask students: When do you close doors? In your home, what doors are more likely to be found open than closed?

Info plus

Porte ouverte ou porte fermée?
In many cultures the open door is a sign of friendliness. In France, there is a feeling that private areas of a home should remain private. For most French people, a closed door is a quite natural way of delineating private space. In a French home, it means that entering the room must be negotiated. A knock on the door and an invitation to come in and sit down are necessary and expected.

You may want to explain that a closed bathroom door in France does not necessarily mean that the facilities are in use!

TRANSPARENCY:
3-2

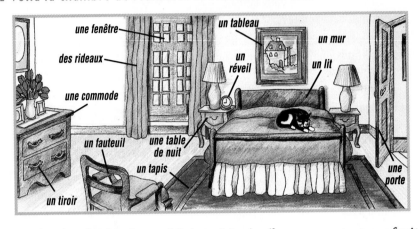

Dans la chambre de Monsieur et Madame Mercier, il y a une porte et une fenêtre avec des rideaux. Il y a aussi des meubles: un lit, deux tables de nuit, un fauteuil et une commode avec des tiroirs. Sur le mur, il y a un tableau et sur la table de nuit, il y a un réveil. Par terre, il y a un tapis. Et les couleurs? Les murs sont blancs, les rideaux et le fauteuil sont verts, le chat est noir et blanc, le tapis est bleu et vert, et les fleurs sont rouges.

- La chambre est grande ou petite? Elle est claire ou sombre? Elle est belle ou laide? Vous aimez les couleurs de la chambre?
- Quels *(what)* meubles sont grands? petits? pratiques? beaux?
- Vous aimez les tapis rouges? les murs verts? les rideaux noirs? les chats blancs? les fauteuils bleus?

B. Voilà la chambre de Jessica et de Susan.

Jessica est la camarade de chambre de Susan. Dans la chambre de Jessica et de Susan, il y a un placard, deux chaises, deux bureaux et deux étagères. Sur les bureaux, il y a un téléphone, une télévision, un dictionnaire et une cassette. Sur les murs, il y a des affiches et par terre, sous la chaise, il y a deux livres. Dans la chambre, il y a aussi une chaîne hi-fi, un réfrigérateur et une corbeille à papier, mais il n'y a pas de fauteuil. Et les couleurs? Le téléphone est orange, les bureaux sont bruns, les rideaux sont jaunes, les chaises sont orange et la corbeille à papier est blanche.

- La chambre de Jessica et de Susan est agréable? Elle est en ordre ou en désordre? Elle est grande ou petite pour deux personnes? Vous aimez les couleurs de la chambre?

- Quels *(what)* objets sont grands? petits? pratiques?
- Quels objets et meubles de la chambre sont blancs? orange? jaunes? bruns? rouges? verts? bleus?
- Jessica et Susan sont françaises ou américaines?

C. Voilà la chambre de Jean-Pierre.

Dans la chambre de Jean-Pierre, il y a un lavabo et un miroir. Il y a aussi une guitare, une radio et un disque. Il y a une lampe sur le bureau et une photo sur l'étagère. Il y a une armoire? Peut-être, c'est possible. Mais il n'y a pas de réfrigérateur et il n'y a pas de télévision!

- La chambre de Jean-Pierre est en ordre ou en désordre? Elle est grande ou petite? Elle est agréable? confortable? belle? pratique?
- De quelle couleur sont les rideaux? et la guitare? et le lavabo? et la lampe? et la chaise?
- Quels *(what)* objets importants pour vous ne sont pas dans la chambre?
- Vous aimez la chambre? les couleurs de la chambre?
- Jean-Pierre est français ou américain? étudiant ou professeur? travailleur ou paresseux?
- Qu'est-ce qu'il aime? Qu'est-ce qu'il n'aime pas?
- Comparez les trois chambres:
  J'aime la chambre de… parce qu'il y a… , mais je n'aime pas la chambre de….
  La chambre de… est plus/aussi/moins… que la chambre de…

Info plus

La chambre d'étudiant.

Traditionally, French universities have been urban institutions. They have always been centers of higher learning rather than centers of student life. These older universities are not organized in campuses where students move in for a period of time to live, study, and have fun before entering the professional adult world.

D. Voilà le bureau de Mme Bernstein.

un ordinateur

un crayon

une machine
à écrire

une clé

une calculatrice

un sac

- Qu'est-ce qu'il y a dans le bureau de Madame Bernstein? Le bureau est clair ou sombre? normal ou bizarre? Il est agréable? pratique? confortable?
- De quelle couleur sont les fleurs? et l'ordinateur? et le sac? et le téléphone? et le fauteuil?
- Quels objets et meubles sont jaunes? bruns? rouges? blancs?

E. Objets pour aujourd'hui

TRANSPARENCY:
3-5

Usage for many of the words referring to technology is not yet standardized in French.

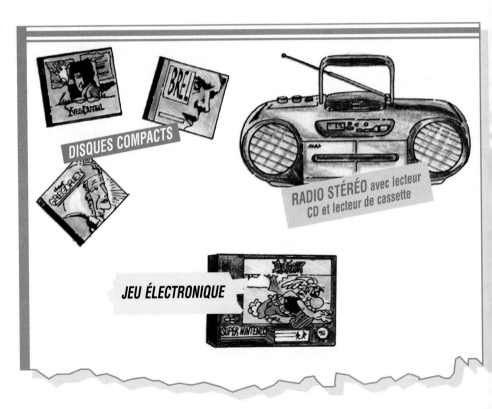

DISQUES COMPACTS

RADIO STÉRÉO avec lecteur
CD et lecteur de cassette

JEU ÉLECTRONIQUE

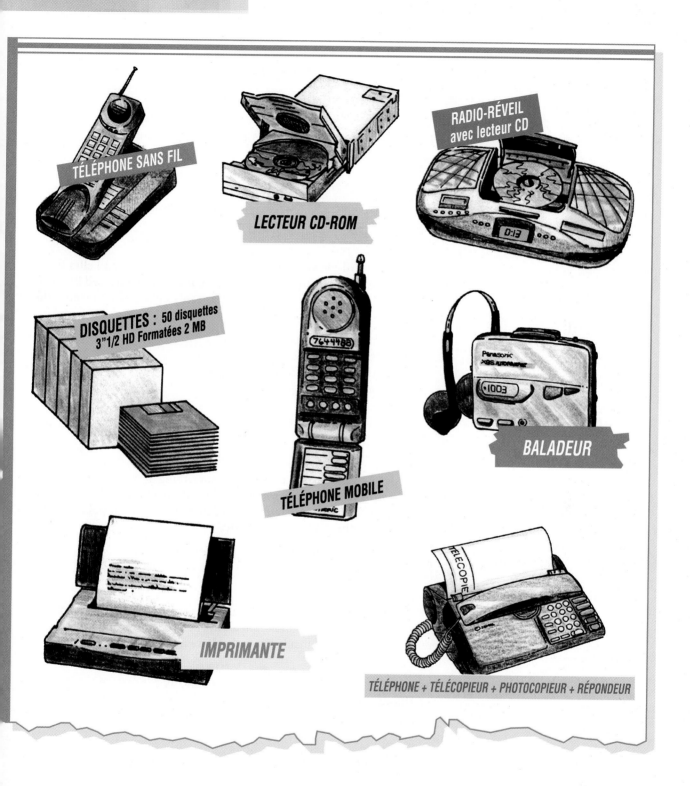

TÉLÉPHONE SANS FIL

LECTEUR CD-ROM

RADIO-RÉVEIL
avec lecteur CD

DISQUETTES : 50 disquettes
3"1/2 HD Formatées 2 MB

TÉLÉPHONE MOBILE

BALADEUR

IMPRIMANTE

TÉLÉPHONE + TÉLÉCOPIEUR + PHOTOCOPIEUR + RÉPONDEUR

- Quels objets sont pour les étudiants? pour les professeurs?
- Quels objets sont dans votre *(your)* chambre? ne sont pas dans votre chambre?

Notes de vocabulaire

1. Mots et expressions utiles.
Here are some useful words and expressions not included in the preceding vocabulary presentation.

impossible	*impossible*
on	*one, they, people, we*
une personne	*person*
qu'est-ce que c'est?	*what's this?/what's that?*
une salle de classe	*classroom*

2. On.
On is a third-person singular subject pronoun (like **il** and **elle**) that corresponds very roughly to the English *one*. **On** is commonly used in spoken French instead of **nous** or in cases where it is easily understood to whom the **on** refers.

On parle français et anglais à Montréal.
> *One speaks French and English in Montreal.*
> *They speak French and English in Montreal.*
> *French and English are spoken in Montreal.*

On a un examen aujourd'hui?
> *Do we have a test today?*

3. Voilà / il y a.
Voilà is used to point out something or someone. It can mean either *there is/there are* or *here is/here are*. **Il y a** is used to state that someone or something exists, to enumerate, and to describe. It does not point out. **Il y a** can mean either *there is* or *there are*.

Voilà la chambre d'Anne.	*There's Anne's room.*
Il y a deux chaises, un lit...	*There are two chairs, a bed . . .*

4. Le pluriel des noms irréguliers.
A small number of nouns do not form their plural by adding **-s**. These plurals will always be given in vocabulary lists. Here are the nouns you already know that have irregular plural forms.

SINGULAR	PLURAL
un bureau	des bureaux
un rideau	des rideaux
un tableau	des tableaux

5. Orange.
The adjective **orange** is invariable. It has only one form, even in the plural.

Les cahiers de Jean-Pierre sont **orange**.
> *Jean-Pierre's notebooks are orange.*

1: Tell students that the word **personne** is feminine even when it refers to a man.
    Students do not know **c'est** until *Leçon 4.* Do not expect complete sentence answers to questions with **qu'est-ce que c'est.**

2: On is presented here to facilitate students' comprehension of "normal" French as used by instructors. Students will not be likely to use it.

See the **Instructor's Resource Manual** for more information.

3: If desired, point out the use of **voilà** to mean *here* when handing something to someone.

See the **Instructor's Resource Manual** for more information.

5: Color names used as adjectives are theoretically invariable. Current usage, however, seems to be tending toward treating such words as real adjectives and having them agree with the noun they modify.

D'accord?

A. Les couleurs et vous
Make a list of colors in order of your own personal preferences. Compare with your classmates. What is the class' favorite color?

B. Les couleurs et les chambres

1. Dans votre (*your*) chambre, de quelle couleur sont les murs? les rideaux? le tapis? le téléphone? le bureau? les chaises? les lampes?
2. Et dans la chambre idéale, de quelle couleur sont les murs / les rideaux / le tapis?

C. Les meubles, les objets et vous
Classify the furniture and objects that you have learned in this lesson using the following categories:

• Ils sont pratiques:
• Ils sont confortables:
• Ils sont très importants pour moi:
• Ils ne sont pas très importants pour moi:

D. Lieux et objets
Qu'est-ce qu'il y a dans... ?

1. une chambre d'hôtel?
2. une salle de classe?
3. le bureau d'un professeur?
4. un sac d'étudiant?

E. Une chambre d'étudiant
Make two lists:

1. The things in a typical dorm room before a student moves in (**avant** = *before*).
2. The things that are added after a student moves in (**après** = *after*).

Act. E: Since students have not yet studied the use of **il n'y a pas de**, exercises involving what's not in various things are reserved for the *Structure* section where this concept is introduced.

Mise en pratique

A. Les couleurs et les voyelles: vision du poète

> «A noir E blanc I rouge U vert O bleu : voyelles
> Je dirai quelque jour vos naissances latentes ... »
> —Arthur Rimbaud

Et pour vous? Quelles couleurs pour les voyelles? Comparez avec les étudiants de la classe.

B. Les couleurs et l'imagination

1. What emotions or feelings do you associate with each color?
   bleu / rouge / vert / noir / blanc / jaune
   Modèle: *bleu = déprimé*

2. De quelle(s) couleur(s) sont: les lundis? les samedis? le printemps? l'été? l'automne? l'hiver? les vacances? les examens?

Info plus

Arthur Rimbaud.
Rimbaud was a famous 19th century poet who, by the age of 19, had produced his entire work.

Act. A: Have students ask different classmates: **Quelle couleur pour A? Quelle couleur pour E?** etc., until they find a student who has vision and imagination similar to their own.

Act. B: Have students compare their answers.

C. Décrivez

Qu'est-ce qu'il y a dans la chambre? La chambre est comment? C'est la chambre d'un étudiant? d'une étudiante? d'un professeur? Comment est-il/elle?

D. La chambre idéale What would the ideal bedroom (dorm room) be like? Make a drawing and label as many items as you can.

Structure

▶▶ L'article indéfini

In English, the indefinite articles *a (an)* and *some (any)* are used to refer to persons or objects whose identity is not specified. In French, the indefinite articles **un, une,** and **des** are used in the same way. Note the pronunciation of **des** before a vowel.

un + masculine singular noun	un livre; un hôtel
une + feminine singular noun	une chaise; une affiche
des + plural nouns	des livres; des chaises
	des hôtels; des affiches
	/z/ /z/

Dans **une** chambre, il y a **un** lit, **une** lampe et **des** livres.   *In a room, there's a bed, a lamp, and some books.*

In French, unlike English, the article must be used.

Il y a **des** chiens et **des** chats.   *There are (some) dogs and (some) cats.*

Rappel! Remember that when you are talking about things that you like or do not like (using verbs like **aimer, adorer,** and **détester**) or about things in general, you must use the definite article (**le, la, l', les**) in French, even though there is no article in English.

J'aime **les** chats mais je déteste **les** chiens.   *I like cats, but I don't like dogs.*

Act. C: FOLLOW-UP: Have students suggest colors for objects in the room. Have students imagine who might live in this room.

CD-ROM:
Build your skills!

See the **Instructor's Resource Manual** for more information.

If desired, explain that indefinite articles refer to something whose identity is assumed not to be known to both the speaker and listener; for example, **Vous avez un chat?** (speaker does not know if such a cat exists) versus **Où est le chat?** (both people know the cat in question).

Point out that **un** and **une** can indicate the number *one* as well as the article *a (an).*

If students ask, point out that the English *some,* as in the sentence *I like some animals* (but not others), is best translated by the adjectives **certains** or **quelques.**

Vous avez compris?

A. Chassez l'intrus In each list, one word does not belong because of its number (singular or plural) or its gender (masculine or feminine). Read each list aloud, adding the appropriate article (**un, une,** or **des**) in order to find the intruder.

Modèle chaise / photo / étudiante / livres
une chaise / une photo / une étudiante / ~~des livres~~

1. rideau / crayon / porte / livre
2. sac / table / étudiante / porte
3. lit / radios / chat / cahier
4. bureaux / étagères / tiroir / affiches

B. Cherchez le singulier! Give the singular for each plural.

Modèle des tables **une table**

1. des bureaux
2. des professeurs
3. des portes
4. des crayons
5. des tapis

Act. B: This activity helps students to focus on article choice and form. CONTINUATION: **des cahiers / des étudiants / des chaises / des stylos**

Continuons!

A. Inventaire Dans une salle de classe il y a un/une ou des...

Modèles professeur? ***Il y a un professeur.***
table? ***Il y a une table / Il y a des tables.***

1. chaise?
2. étudiante?
3. crayon?
4. fenêtre?
5. bureau?
6. porte?
7. livre?
8. stylo?
9. étudiant?
10. mur?

B. La chambre de Candide Use indefinite articles (**un, une, des**) and definite articles (**le, la, l', les**) to find out what Candide's room is like.

Act. B: FOLLOW-UP: Ask students: **Vous aimez la chambre de Candide?**

Il y a ..... fleurs dans ma *(my)* chambre. Pourquoi *(why)*? J'aime ..... fleurs, voilà pourquoi! Il y a aussi ..... radio pour ..... musique. Et il y a ..... affiches de Louis Armstrong sur ..... mur (j'adore ..... jazz). Sur ..... bureau, il y a ..... stylos, ... crayons, et ..... dictionnaire. Il y a aussi ..... livres. ..... livres sont par terre! Et ..... chambre? Comment est-elle? Elle est en désordre!

▶▶ Les articles après *ne... pas*

Un, une, and **des** become **de (d')** after a negative expression like **ne... pas.**

Il y a **un** chat?
Il y a **des** crayons?

Non, il n'y a pas **de** chat.
Non, il n'y a pas **de** crayons.

See the **Instructor's Resource Manual** for more information.

The definite articles (**le, la, l', les**) always stay the same.

J'aime **les** chats.

Je n'aime pas **les** chats.

Vous avez compris?

A. Vrai ou faux? C'est (probablement) vrai ou faux?

1. Dans la salle de classe, il y a des bureaux mais il n'y a pas de lits.
2. À l'université, il y a des étudiants mais il n'y a pas de professeurs.
3. Sur le bureau de M. Charaudeau, il y a des crayons mais il n'y a pas de chien.
4. Sur le bureau de Mme Besco, il y a un ordinateur mais il n'y a pas de télévision.
5. À l'université, il n'y a pas de professeurs sympathiques.

B. Alceste n'est pas content
Alceste is surveying the state of his room and he is not happy. Follow the model.

Modèle Il y a une machine à écrire, mais...
il n'y a pas d'ordinateur!

1. Il y a un fauteuil, mais...
2. Il y a une radio, mais...
3. Il y a des cassettes, mais...
4. Il y a une table, mais...
5. Il y a des livres, mais...
6. Il y a une chaîne hi-fi, mais...

Continuons!

A. Ce n'est pas normal! Name at least three things not normally found in each place.

Modèle Dans un bureau?
Il n'y a pas de chien, pas de lit, pas de chaîne hi-fi.

1. Dans une salle de classe?
2. Dans un réfrigérateur?
3. Dans un sac?

B. Une chambre bizarre What is not in this bedroom?

TRANSPARENCY: 3-7

Act. A: Ask students to reformulate these assertions to make them true and/or ask students to create additional items. After going through these items for "truth" value, ask students to find examples of affirmative and negative constructions and to note article usage with each.

Act. B: Il n'y a pas de fenêtre, de porte (pour la salle de bains), de placard, d'étagère, de téléphone et de réfrigérateur. Il y a un bureau, mais il n'y a pas de bureau pour le camarade de chambre, etc.

C. Vous êtes content(e) ou non? Give three reasons why you like or don't like your room.

Modèle *Il y a un fauteuil, mais il n'y a pas d'ordinateur.*

D. Chambres d'étudiants Tell what is and what is not in each room. Then give your overall impression of the rooms and of their occupants.

Il y a un/une/des...
Il n'y a pas de....
La chambre est....
L'étudiante est...

E. Salles de classe Tell what is and what is not in each room.

Il y a un/une/des...
Il n'y a pas de...

Act. E: Ask students which room is **une salle de classe française.** You may want to discuss similarities and differences.

F. Conversation en français Explain why you like or dislike your room. Give as many details as possible. You may want to begin with, **"J'aime (je n'aime pas) ma** *(my)* **chambre parce que..."**

▶▶ Le verbe *avoir* (to have)

LA FORME AFFIRMATIVE		LA FORME NÉGATIVE	
j'**ai**	nous **avons**	je n'**ai pas**	nous n'**avons pas**
tu **as**	vous **avez**	tu **n'**as pas	vous n'**avez pas**
il elle } **a**	ils elles } **ont**	il elle } **n'a pas**	ils elles } **n'ont pas**

Note the pronunciation of the plural forms.

nous avons	ils ont
/z/	/z/
vous avez	elles ont
/z/	/z/

Rappel! Remember that the articles **un, une,** and **des** become **de (d')** after a negative.

Je n'ai pas **de** radio mais   *I don't have a radio but*
  j'ai **une** chaîne hi-fi.   *I have a stereo.*

There are also three imperative or command forms for the verb **avoir.** These forms are not in common usage except in certain expressions (for example, **avoir peur** *[to be afraid],* **avoir de la patience** *[to be patient],* **avoir du courage** *[to be brave])* that you will learn later.

    Aie plus de patience!   *Have more patience! (said to a person you would address using **tu**)*

    N'**ayez** pas peur!   *Don't be afraid! (said to a person you would address using **vous** or to more than one person)*

    Ayons du courage!   *Let's be brave!*

Vous avez compris?

A. Être ou avoir? Décidez s'il s'agit de *(if it's about)* la description ou de la possession dans les phrases suivantes.

Modèle   J'ai trois chats.
        possession

1. Nous sommes déprimés mais nous aimons l'université.
2. Jean-Pierre n'a pas de téléphone dans sa chambre.

3. Les étudiants sont dans la chambre.
4. —Vous êtes d'où?
   —Moi, je suis de Dakar.
5. J'ai une belle chambre à l'université.

B. Les possessions
Use the verb **avoir** and combine items from the two columns to tell what everybody owns or does not own.

le professeur de français	une chaîne hi-fi
les étudiants	un radio-réveil
je	un/une camarade de chambre
elles	des affiches
ils	un dictionnaire de français
Alceste	un baladeur
tu	une télévision
vous	un chien
nous	des disques de rock
	des cassettes de Sinatra

Continuons!

A. Qu'est-ce qu'ils ont?
What might each person logically possess and not possess?

Modèle   Paul aime la musique classique.
   Il a des disques de Mozart. Il n'a pas de disques de rock.

1. Martine et Michel aiment les livres classiques.
2. Nicole aime les cours.
3. Julien aime le jazz.
4. Sophie est très sociable.
5. Marie-Laure aime les animaux *(animals)*.

B. Qui a...?
List the names of four or five students in the class. For each one, decide what he or she has and does not have. (Guess if you don't know.) When you have finished, find out how accurate your list is.

C. Nous avons tous...
In groups of three or four, find out what objects all of you possess (for example, each person in the group has some tapes). Report to the class.

D. Et le professeur?
Find out what your instructor's room is like. Ask as many questions as possible.

Modèle   VOUS   ***Vous avez une table?***
   LE PROFESSEUR   ***Oui, j'ai une table.***

Act. B or C: La chaîne. One student starts the game by saying «**Dans une salle de classe, il y a une table**» (or another object). A second student repeats this and adds another object. Keep going as long as possible.

Découvertes culturelles: Où loger?

➤ L'Université Libre de Bruxelles

Act A: This is a pre-reading activity whose purpose is to have students think about lodging possibilities for students, the subject of the text they will read.

A. À l'université. Quelles sont les options pour se loger (pour avoir une chambre) dans votre université? Lesquelles sont préférables?

☐ dans une cité universitaire? *(dormitory)* ☐ dans un hôtel?
☐ dans une famille? ☐ dans un appartement?
☐ dans un studio? ☐ chez les parents?

Act. B: Universities constructed recently tend to be on the outskirts of towns and to have a "campus."

Act. B, 2: At time of publication, one dollar was approximately 30 Belgian francs (FB).

B. À l'Université Libre de Bruxelles.

1. Quel type de logement offre l'université? Quel type de chambre offre l'université?
2. Quelques détails. Indiquez:

Le campus le plus grand:	
Le campus le plus petit:	
Combien de maisons au Campus Solbosch:	
Les maisons où les chambres sont individuelles:	
Le campus où les chambres sont les plus chères *(expensive)*:	
La date limite pour demander une chambre:	

Act. C, 1: Have students look at the photo and guess what else is probably there (un lit). Ask them to compare dormitory rooms they have known. What is usually provided? What not? Are there differences from region to region or from country to country?

Act. C, 3: Encourage students to look back at the *Entrée en matière*, *Vocabulaire*, and *Structure* sections for ideas. If desired, have students first sketch their room and then describe it. Make sure students finish by evaluating the room (C'est une chambre très confortable, etc.).

Act. C, 4: SUGGESTIONS: agréables, confortables, inconfortables, chères, belles, laides, sales, primitives, simples

Act. C, 5: Can be done as a role play.

C. Installation dans une cité universitaire. Vous allez *(go)* à L'Université Libre de Bruxelles.

1. **Préparation.** Préparez une liste des objets et meubles dans la chambre à votre arrivée.
2. **Installation.** Vous avez des objets de chez vos parents avec vous. Préparez une liste des objets que vous avez.
3. **La chambre.** Décrivez la chambre après votre installation.
4. **Comparez.** Comparez les résidences belges et les résidences dans votre université. Comparez les prix *(prices)* dans les universités belges et dans votre université. Quelles sont les différences?

   Modèle *En Belgique, les résidences sont... ; elles ne sont pas...*
   Le logement est plus... / moins....

5. **Questions.** Demandez à votre professeur quels sont les objets nécessaires pour votre année à l'ULB.

   Modèle *Est-ce qu'il y a des ordinateurs?*

Université Libre de Bruxelles

PAYS-BAS
ALLEMAGNE
Bruxelles ★
BELGIQUE
FRANCE
LUX.
Luxembourg
Paris ★

LE LOGEMENT

L'Université met à la disposition des étudiants environ 700 chambres groupées dans plusieurs maisons de logement et réparties à raison de 450 lits au campus de Solbosch, 150 lits au campus de la Plaine et 100 lits au campus Erasme (Anderlecht).

Les prix mensuels s'entendent par personne, toutes charges comprises, et varient selon qu'il s'agit d'une chambre individuelle ou d'une chambre double et selon le degré de confort. La location est contractée pour dix mois.

CAMPUS DU SOLBOSCH

Au campus du Solbosch, dans les maisons Elisée Reclus et Willy Peers, les chambres, doubles ou individuelles, sont spacieuses et équipées d'un lavabo. Des installations communes de douches et de toilettes sont disponibles à chaque étage et il existe une salle de télévision. Le loyer s'élève à 2.950 F pour une chambre double et 5.080 F pour une chambre simple. À la maison Nelson Mandela, avenue des Courses, toutes les chambres sont individuelles, confortables mais plus petites. Chacune d'elles dispose d'un cabinet de toilette comprenant douche et w.c. Le loyer est de 6.020 F.

CAMPUS DE LA PLAINE ET CAMPUS ERASME

Les chambres y sont individuelles. Les douches sont communes à deux chambres; des w.c. sont installés aux étages. Les studios de deux personnes sont équipés d'une douche, de w.c. et d'un coin cuisine. Le loyer s'élève à 5.870 F. Dans toutes les maisons de logement, des cuisines d'étage sont mises à la disposition des étudiants.

Le service médical de l'Université assure la surveillance médicale des étudiants qui logent sur place.

L'étudiant qui souhaite obtenir une chambre à l'Université demandera un formulaire d'admission à l'Administration des Maisons de Logement. Ce document, dûment complété, devra être renvoyé, avant le 15 juin de l'année d'inscription, à la même adresse. Une réponse sera donnée à l'étudiant dans le courant du mois de juillet.

Si vous préférez loger en ville, seul ou avec des amis, l'Office du Logement peut vous aider à trouver un domicile. Ce service centralise des centaines d'offres de logements de toutes catégories et donc à des prix variés.

En août et en septembre, le fichier des logements disponibles est le plus garni. Il vaut donc mieux s'y prendre à temps pour avoir le choix et bénéficier des meilleures conditions.

Si l'étudiant le souhaite, il peut également recevoir l'aide de ce service pour établir un contrat de location, un état des lieux et pour résoudre les divers problèmes posés par une location, tels que garantie, préavis...

Info plus

Le logement dans les universités.

L'ULB, ou **l'Université Libre de Bruxelles,** was created in 1834. Its early buildings were centrally located. More recently, with the growth of its student population, it has expanded into several campuses with many colleges, professional schools, and institutes, as well as a teaching hospital, an experimental park, and two industrial centers.

Similarly, French universities are old, urban institutions and do not have campuses such as those found at most North American universities. Many newer universities were built in the suburbs of towns outside Paris during the 1950s. Housing for these newer universities is subsidized, but very limited. This type of housing is usually reserved for students with scholarships or other form of financial aid.

▶▶ Deux hôtels très parisiens

Act. A: Ask students to look back at vocabulary lists for the first three lessons to find words for this activity.

A. L'hôtel idéal. Quelles sont les caractéristiques de l'hôtel idéal pour vous pendant (*during*) une visite touristique?

Modèle   *Il est...*
            La chambre est...
            La chambre a...

Act. B, 1: Have students use the list of preferences generated in activity A to compare the amenities they would like with those offered by these two hotels.

B. Un hôtel pour vous?

1. Est-ce que ces hôtels ont les caractéristiques que vous aimez dans un hôtel? Quel hôtel aimez-vous?

2. **Quelques détails.** Complétez la grille.

Nom de l'hôtel	Prix des chambres	Prix du petit déjeuner	Sports? (*oui / non*)	Téléphone? (*oui / non*)	Chiens? (*oui / non*)	Bar privé? (*oui / non*)
Hôtel des Tuileries						
Hôtel Voltaire						

Act. B, 3: Encourage students to use context when they guess.

3. **Mots nouveaux.** Devinez (*Guess*) le sens des mots suivants:
   a. (**Hôtel des Tuileries**) Ouvert / petit déjeuner / entre / demeure / restauré
   b. (**Hôtel Voltaire**) chaînes / proche

4. **Quel hôtel pour vous?** Choisissez un hôtel.
   a. Vous aimez les souvenirs historiques d'Europe.
   b. Vous aimez les activités sportives.
   c. Vous êtes un grand amateur d'art.
   d. Pour vous, regarder la télévision est une passion.
   e. Vous aimez le grand style et le luxe aristocratique.

Act. B, 5: Have students look at the plan of Paris on page 68. Although these questions appear complex, they can be answered quite simply. This activity will help prepare students for the activity that follows. You may want to allow a few moments of English in order to have students extract the values that the descriptions of these two hotels reflect (importance of history and historical references, importance of recent modernization, characteristics of each **arrondissement** of Paris, etc.).

5. **La culture française.** Regardez les adresses des hôtels. Le code postal vous indique dans quel arrondissement (*district of Paris*) sont situés les hôtels. Combien d'arrondissements y a-t-il à Paris (voir le plan, page 68)? Quels arrondissements sont historiques? Quels arrondissements sont plus modernes? Dans quels arrondissements sont les monuments principaux? Identifiez les gares (*train stations*) sur le plan de Paris. Où sont situés les deux hôtels? Quel hôtel préférez-vous? Pourquoi (*why*)?

Act. C: Ask students to use French to write a description of a local hotel in the style of the two texts reproduced here. What modifications will have to be made? What will stay much the same? How does this reflect cultural values?

C. Les clients. Quels types de clients choisissent (*chooses*) l'Hôtel Voltaire? l'Hôtel des Tuileries? Écrivez (*write*) des paragraphes.

Modèle   *Dans l'Hôtel Voltaire, on trouve des clients... qui (who) aiment... Les clients de l'Hôtel Voltaire sont... Ils ont aussi... Mais dans l'Hôtel des Tuileries, il y a... et les clients sont... Ils aiment... et ils ont...*

Hôtel des Tuileries

10 rue Saint-Hyacinthe - 75001 Paris
Tel.: 01.42.61.04.17
Fax: 01.49.2791.56 - Télex: 240 744

Mme Monique Poulle Vidal
Ouvert toute l'année
26 chambres de 490 F à 900 F (S.T.C.)
3 appartements de 1400 F à 1800 F (S.T.C.)
Petit déjeuner : 45 F

Entre les jardins des Tuileries, les Musées du Louvre et d'Orsay et de la place Vendôme, une authentique demeure XVIIIe siècle propriété de la Première Dame de la Reine Marie-Antoinette qui a logé sur place avec Louis XVI. Restauré en 87 autour d'un patio contemporain, salon des Jacobins, bar, chambres raffinées et silencieuses, le rêve y est permis.

Une situation exceptionnelle à Paris et le calme

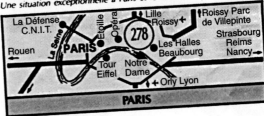

 oui
 oui non
 non oui non
 non non non

Hôtel Voltaire

110 boulevard de Courcelles
Tel.: 01.46.58.13.34
Fax: 01.46.58.78.06 - Télex: 637 963

Ouvert toute l'année
28 chambres de 450 F à 550 F (S.T.C.)
Petit déjeuner : 45 F

Hôtel de charme grand confort, calme absolu, tél. direct, TV cablée 19 chaînes. A 5 mn de l'Arc de Triomphe et des Champs-Elysées. A 10 mn du centre de Paris proche de la Porte de Versailles, Roland Garros, stade Coubertin, Parc des Princes. Possibilité garage, bar privé. Canal plus.

Un cadre raffiné et confortable

 non possibilité à proximité
 oui non à proximité
 non oui à proximité
 possibilité non non

Comment est votre chambre? 67

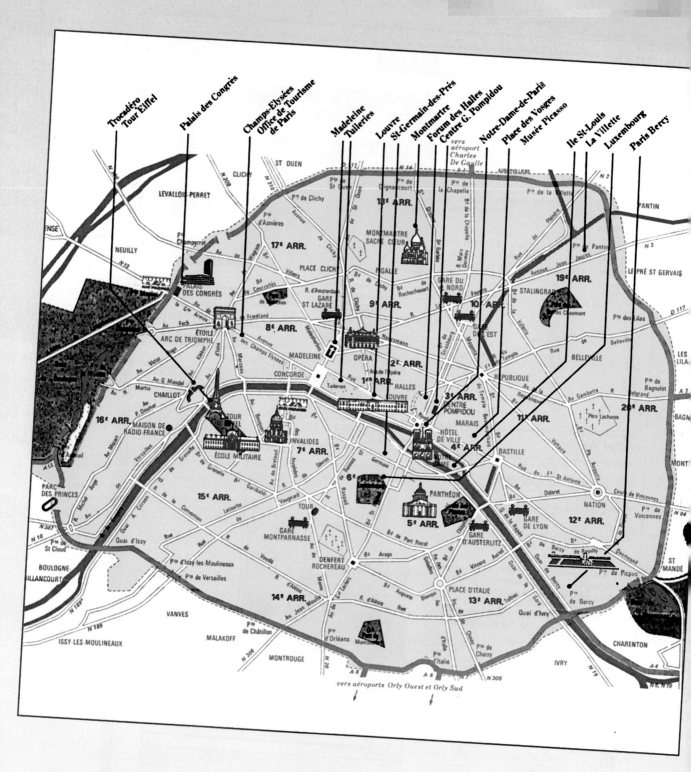

*O*rthographe et prononciation

▶▶ Les autres signes diacritiques

Rappel! **L'accent aigu** (´) represents the sound of the **é** in **étudiant.**

L'accent grave (`) represents the sound you hear for the second **e** in the word **étagère** and can also be found over letters other than **e.** In these cases, it serves to distinguish the written forms of several homonyms.

    à *(to, at)* **a** *(has)*   **là** *(there)* **la** *(the)*   **où** *(where)* **ou** *(or)*

L'accent circonflexe (^) indicates a letter was dropped from a (historically) earlier form of the word. Often the letter (usually an **-s-**) that disappeared still remains in the related English word. This accent does not change the sound of the vowel over which it appears. Do you now recognize these words?

    forêt   **hôpital**   **arrêt**   **bête**   **château**   **maître**

*Traditionally, a circumflex indicates that the vowel is long (**pâte** vs. **patte**). Many speakers, however, no longer maintain this distinction.*

Le tréma (¨) indicates that both vowels are pronounced.

    égoïste (é-go-ïste)   **naïf** (na-ïf)   **Noël** (No-ël)

The **cédille** (¸) or *cedilla,* is found only under the letter **c.** It marks a soft **c** or **s** sound.

    balcon   *no cedilla = hard **c** or **k** sound*
    garçon   *cedilla = soft **c** or **s** sound*

Activités

A. Prononcez Here are some words that you have already learned or will learn in *Leçons 4* and *5.* Repeat them after your instructor.

1. un garçon   *boy*
2. le théâtre   *theater*
3. un problème   *problem*
4. égoïste   *selfish*
5. à côté de   *next to*

B. Écrivez Rewrite the following words, adding any diacritical signs that are missing.

1. une fenetre
2. une etagere
3. ca depend
4. peut-etre
5. tres
6. naive
7. francais
8. etre

Vocabulaire de base

Quel article? Beginning with this lesson, you will find words listed with either the definite article (**le, la, l', les**) or with the indefinite article (**un, une, des**). Generally speaking, it is more natural, in a list, to use the indefinite article with things you can count (**une chaise, deux chaises,** etc.) and the definite article with things you do not usually count (**le jazz, la musique,** etc.). Note that you can use either article with any noun; it depends on what you want to say. Look at the sentences below. Can you tell why each article was used?

Candide aime **les** animaux. Il a **un** chat et **un** chien.
Alceste déteste **le** chat de Candide. Il n'aime pas **les** animaux.

NOMS

une affiche *poster*
un bureau, des bureaux *desk(s), office(s)*
un/une camarade de chambre
   roommate
une chaîne hi-fi *stereo*
une chaise *chair*
une chambre *bedroom*
une clé *key*
un crayon *pencil*
un disque *record, disc*
une étagère *bookcase, shelf*
une fenêtre *window*
une fleur *flower*
un lavabo *sink*
un lit *bed*
un ordinateur *computer*
une photo *photograph*
un placard *closet*
une porte *door*
une radio *radio*
un réveil *alarm clock*
un sac *sack, purse*
une salle de classe *classroom*
une table *table*
un tapis *area rug*
un téléphone *telephone*
une télévision *television*

ADJECTIFS

agréable *agreeable, nice, pleasant*
grand(e) *big, tall*
petit(e) *little, small, short*

ADJECTIFS DE COULEUR

blanc, blanche *white*
bleu(e) *blue*
brun(e) *brown, dark-haired*
jaune *yellow*
noir(e) *black*
orange *(invariable) orange*
rouge *red*
vert(e) *green*

VERBE

avoir *to have*

DIVERS

dans *in, within*
il y a; il n'y a pas de *there is, there are;*
there is no, there are not any
on *one, they, people*
peut-être *maybe, perhaps*
Qu'est-ce que c'est? *What is this/that?*
sous *under*
sur *on, on top of*
voilà *there is, there are, here is, here are*

Vocabulaire supplémentaire

NOMS

une armoire *wardrobe*
une calculatrice *calculator*
une commode *bureau, chest of drawers*
une corbeille à papier *wastepaper basket*
une couleur *color*
un dictionnaire *dictionary*
un fauteuil *armchair*
une guitare *guitar*
une lampe *lamp*
une machine à écrire *typewriter*
un meuble *piece of furniture*
un miroir *mirror*
un mur *wall*
un objet *object*
une personne *person*
un réfrigérateur *refrigerator*
un rideau, des rideaux *curtain(s)*
une table de nuit *nightstand, night table*
un tableau, des tableaux *painting(s)*
un tiroir *drawer*

ADJECTIFS

clair(e) *bright, full of light*
confortable *comfortable*
important(e) *important*
impossible *impossible*
possible *possible*
pratique *practical*
sombre *dark*

DIVERS

De quelle couleur est/sont... ? *What color is/are... ?*
en désordre *messy*
en ordre *straight, neat*
par terre *on the floor*
Qu'est-ce qu'il y a dans... ? *What is there in... ?*

OBJETS POUR AUJOURD'HUI

The list of **objets pour aujourd'hui** is provided to allow students to talk about their daily life.

Pour l'ordinateur:
   un cédérom *CD-ROM*
   une disquette *diskette, floppy disk*
   une imprimante *printer*
   un jeu électronique *electronic game, video game*
   un lecteur CD-ROM *CD-ROM player/drive*

Pour le téléphone:
   un répondeur *answering machine*
   un télécopieur *fax machine*
   un téléphone mobile *cellular phone*
   un téléphone sans fil *portable phone*

Pour la musique:
   un baladeur *walkman*
   une cassette *cassette*
   un disque compact (un CD) *CD, compact disc*
   un lecteur CD *CD player*
   un lecteur de cassette *cassette player*
   un radio-réveil *clock radio*

Info plus

Le franglais.

Here are some English words and expressions that have come from French and some French words that have come from English. Can you add to the lists?

French → English:
    restaurant, gauche, lingerie,...
English → French:
    un poster, le football, le rock,...

When two languages come into contact, there is a mutual borrowing of words, though meanings and pronunciation may be altered. This is the case with English and French. Although many people in France, including those in government, may try to avoid using franglais, the mutual borrowing of words between French and English has been going on for centuries.

Tell students that **le football** means *soccer*. **Le football américain** refers to football as played in the United States.

LE FRANÇAIS TEL QU'ON LE PARLE

T'as = tu as
T'as pas = tu n'as pas

LE FRANÇAIS FAMILIER

un dico = un dictionnaire
un fax - un télécopieur
un frigo = un réfrigérateur
une piaule = une chambre
un poster = une affiche
une télé = une télévision
un walkman = un baladeur

ON ENTEND PARFOIS

un auditoire (Belgique) = une salle de classe
une boîte à portraits (Louisiane) = une télévision
une sacoche (Canada, Belgique) = un sac

Qu'est-ce que vous aimez?

En bref

Dans cette leçon...

- Activités de tous les jours
- Les loisirs
- Décrire des personnes
- Une famille française:
  les Dubois
- Poser des questions
- Les verbes en **-er**
- Les adjectifs possessifs
- La musique francophone:
  France, Afrique

In this lesson...

- Talking about things you do
- Leisure activities
- Describing people
- Meeting the Dubois family
- Asking questions
- First conjugation (**-er**) verbs
- Possessive adjectives
- Francophone music: France, Africa

www explore!
http://voila.heinle.com

Develop writing
skills with
Système-D software!

Practice listening and
pronunciation skills
with the Text Tape!

Discover the
Francophone world!

Build your skills!

INTERNET

SYSTÈME-D

TEXT TAPE

VIDEO TAPE

CD-ROM

Students have an open-
ended writing activity in
the **Cahier** suitable for
use with **Système-D**.

73

Entrée en matière: Les saisons et les sports

Use the map of France, inside the back cover, to introduce French geography. Help students locate the various mountain ranges. The logo **Côte d'Azur** indicates that Valberg is in the southern Alps.

Using the photo numbers, ask students to identify the season for each photo. Use these numbers for other activities also in order to avoid problems. Encourage the use of **peut-être** (**c'est peut-être le printemps, l'été**, etc.).

Again using the photo numbers, recycle adjectives by asking students to give French names to the people and then to talk about them (**Jean-Luc est heureux, il est sympathique, beau, amusant**, etc.).

Valberg. D'après les indications de la brochure, où est Valberg? Dans les Pyrénées, les Alpes ou le Massif Central?

Les photos. C'est quelle saison? Quelle couleur est prédominante sur la photo 1? la photo 2? la photo 3? la photo 4? la photo 5?

Comment sont les personnes sur ces photos? Décrivez les personnes et décrivez la scène. Ils sont étudiants ou professeurs? Ils sont à l'université? Est-ce qu'ils sont au bureau ou en vacances? Valberg, c'est pour les vacances ou pour les études?

Informations générales. Où obtenir des informations générales? précises? Appelez pour faire une réservation. Appelez pour obtenir une information précise.

Des sports de glisse...
... aux sports d'été

RESERVATIONS :
OFFICE DU TOURISME
TEL : 04 93 23 24 25
MINITEL 36.15 VALBERG

36.15 VALBERG

VALBERG

Les activités.

Sur quelle photo on pratique...
    les promenades en forêt?
    les cours de ski avec un moniteur?
    le V.T.T. (vélo tous terrains) en montagne?
    les randonnées en haute montagne?

Quelle activité est pour l'hiver? pour l'été? Quelle activité préférez-vous? Pourquoi?

Quelles activités sont individualistes? familiales? difficiles? pénibles? dangereuses? agréables?

Et vous? Pour vos loisirs, est-ce que vous aimez les activités sportives ou les activités culturelles? Quel sport pratiquez-vous? Quelles activités culturelles aimez-vous? Il y a des activités culturelles à Valberg?

Have students decide, based on the seasons presented, why these people are here on vacation. Give students a list to choose from: **le week-end de Pentecôte, les vacances de Mardi Gras, les vacances d'été, les vacances de Pâques, les vacances pour les enfants, les vacances pour les jeunes.**

Have students use **parce que c'est...**

CONTINUATION AND EXPANSION: You may want to end with a quick **jeu de rôle** in pairs. Each student, either as the informant or the tourist, asks questions about Valberg's hotels and sports. Ex: **Les hôtels sont chers? Il y a une télévision dans les chambres?**

Vocabulaire

Ask students: Where were your grandparents born? Your great-grandparents? How can you guess about someone's origins?

Info plus

D'où venez-vous?

Although the name **Dubois** is typically French, the French population consists of people from diverse ethnic backgrounds, as can be seen on any page of a French phone book. See also *Monuments aux morts,* page 25.

C'est is contrasted with **il/elle est** in *Note de vocabulaire 8* of this lesson.

TRANSPARENCY:
4-1

Ask students: Do women keep the same name all their lives?

Info plus

Les femmes et les noms de famille.

French women may legally use either their maiden or married name, or both. For example, when Thérèse Ledoux got married, she could have chosen: Thérèse Dubois, Thérèse Ledoux, or Thérèse Dubois-Ledoux. Although traditionally women used to take their husbands' names, they kept their maiden names on official documents, followed by *wife of* and the husband's name. Now, however, many young French women, in particular professional women, tend to keep their maiden names when they marry.

TRANSPARENCY:
4-2

A. Voilà Vincent Dubois, agent immobilier.

Il a beaucoup d'amis. Pourquoi? C'est une personne sociable et sympathique. Il aime mieux sortir que travailler et il n'aime pas rester à la maison, surtout le samedi et le dimanche. Il aime parler, boire, fumer et danser. Il adore manger et il aime trop la cuisine française. Il aime aussi les films amusants parce qu'il adore rire. C'est un

homme très généreux et il aime donner des cadeaux. C'est le père de deux enfants: Céline et Jean-Marc.

- Qu'est-ce que Vincent aime? Qu'est-ce qu'il n'aime pas? Il a des enfants? Il est sympathique? Pourquoi?

B. Voilà Thérèse Dubois, psychologue.

C'est une femme très intelligente et équilibrée. Elle adore écrire des lettres et lire des livres sérieux. Elle aime aussi le théâtre classique et le cinéma. Elle adore marcher et elle aime beaucoup voyager. Elle parle anglais et elle étudie l'espagnol. C'est une personne très occupée et heureuse, mais elle déteste le ménage et les cigarettes de Vincent! Thérèse Dubois est la mère de Céline et de Jean-Marc.

- Comment est Thérèse Dubois? Elle est comme Vincent ou pas?

C. Voilà Céline Dubois.

Elle adore les animaux et donc elle a un chien, Youki, et un oiseau, Nestor. C'est une fille sportive et très sociable. Elle aime regarder les matchs de football à la télévision. Elle aime aussi chanter et elle adore écouter des chansons à la radio. Elle n'aime pas étudier, et elle déteste le français, mais elle aime les mathématiques et les sciences. Céline est la sœur de Jean-Marc.

- Céline a des frères et sœurs? Elle est comme Vincent ou comme Thérèse? Pourquoi?

TRANSPARENCY: 4-3

D. Voilà Jean-Marc Dubois.

See the **Instructor's Resource Manual** for more information.

C'est le frère de Céline. C'est un garçon sérieux et un peu timide, comme Thérèse. Il n'aime pas trop le sport. Il aime mieux lire et écouter des concerts à la radio. Il n'aime pas beaucoup les animaux, mais il a un chat, Minou. Il adore Minou, et Minou adore dormir sur le lit de Jean-Marc. Jean-Marc aime étudier, surtout le français, mais il n'aime pas trop les maths! Et il déteste ranger. Il est un peu comme Thérèse, n'est-ce pas?

- Jean-Marc est un peu comme Thérèse. Pourquoi?
- Et vous, vous êtes comme Vincent, Thérèse, Céline ou Jean-Marc? Pourquoi?
- Vous aimez danser? Vous aimez fumer? Vous aimez le cinéma? Et le sport?
- Vous aimez mieux sortir ou rester à la maison? Vous aimez mieux la cuisine française ou la cuisine américaine? Les films amusants ou les films sérieux? Le football ou le tennis? Les chats ou les chiens? Les mathématiques ou l'anglais? Les sciences ou le français?

Info plus

Les prénoms.
French people often have compound first names, such as **Anne-Françoise** or **Marie-Pierre**, or **Jean-Pascal** or **Jean-Marie**.

French children are also often given one or two additional names (**Olivier Xavier René Henri Dugué**, for example).

The **vous** form of first-conjugation verbs is presented in the *Structure* section of this lesson. Students need not produce it here.

Notes de vocabulaire

1. Mots et expressions utiles.
Here are some useful words and expressions not included in the preceding vocabulary presentation.

un/une camarade de classe	*classmate*
faux (fausse)	*false, untrue*
un nom (un nom de famille)	*name (last name)*
par exemple	*for example*
un prénom	*first name*
qu'est-ce que tu aimes?	*what do you like?*
votre nom, s'il vous plaît?	*your name, please?*
vrai(e)	*true, right*
c'est vrai / ce n'est pas vrai	*that's true / that's not true; you're kidding*

2. Beaucoup / beaucoup de.
Beaucoup means *a lot* or *much*. It is placed after the verb.

Il aime **beaucoup** le cinéma.	*He likes the movies a lot.*
Il n'aime pas **beaucoup** le théâtre.	*He doesn't like the theater much (a lot).*

Beaucoup de means *a lot of.* It is followed by a noun with no article. If the noun begins with a vowel sound, the **-e** of **de** is replaced with an apostrophe.

Elle a **beaucoup de** livres.	*She has a lot of books.*
Il n'a pas **beaucoup d'**amis.	*He doesn't have a lot of (many) friends.*
Il n'a pas **beaucoup de** devoirs.	*He doesn't have a lot of (much) homework.*

3. Parler français.
When you want to talk about *speaking a language,* the name of the language directly follows the verb **parler.** There is no article. When you want to talk about doing something else with a language, such as studying it, the definite article is used. Compare the following:

Il parle français et il étudie **l'**anglais.	*He speaks French and he's studying English.*

4. Écouter / regarder.
Écouter means *to listen to;* **regarder** means *to look at.* The *to* and the *at* are already included in the verb in French. You do not have to add them.

—Tu **regardes** la télévision?	*"Are you looking at (watching) television?"*
—Non, j'**écoute** la radio.	*"No, I'm listening to the radio."*

5. La place des adjectifs.
In general, adjectives in French follow the noun they modify.

C'est un homme **intelligent.**	*He's an intelligent man.*
C'est une étudiante **sérieuse.**	*She's a serious student.*

2: If desired, point out the difference in English between *a lot of* + count noun (*a lot of people*) and *much* + mass noun (*much money*).

5: Adjectives preceding the noun are treated in the **Structure** section of *Leçon 5*.

6. L'usage de l'infinitif.
Certain verbs (for example, **aimer**, **adorer**, and **détester**) can be followed by an infinitive. This is similar to English usage. Note that the **ne... pas** goes around the conjugated verb.

J'aime **parler**.	*I like to talk.*
Je **n'**aime **pas travailler**.	*I don't like to work.*

When you want to use the infinitive by itself (as in making a list, for example), **ne pas** is placed in front of the infinitive, as in these lists of things to do.

AUJOURD'HUI	TODAY
étudier	*study*
lire *L'Étranger*	*read* The Stranger
ne pas regarder la télé	*not watch TV*
ne pas fumer!	*not smoke!*

7. Verbes à ne pas conjuguer.
Many verbs can be used in conjunction with other verbs, such as **aimer** and **détester**. It will then be very useful for you to know the infinitive form of certain verbs even though you do not yet know how to conjugate them. For the moment, use the verbs listed here only in the infinitive form.

boire	*to drink*	dormir	*to sleep*
écrire	*to write*	lire	*to read*
rire	*to laugh*	sortir	*to go out*

8. C'est ou il/elle est?
Both **c'est** and **il/elle est** can mean *he / she / it is*. The table below gives some rules of thumb to help you use these structures appropriately.

	c'est	il est/elle est
être + noun	C'est une femme. C'est un chien. C'est un livre.	X
être + name	C'est Paul. C'est Paris.	X
être + profession, nationality, religion	+ *article* C'est un professeur.	*no article* Il est professeur.
être + **moi, toi**, etc.	C'est moi.	X
être + adjective	Ça, c'est beau. (*in general, nonspecific reference; adjective is always masculine singular*)	Elle est belle, ta chambre. (*for specific reference; adjective agrees with noun it refers to*)

9. Le lundi.
Use the definite article **le** in front of a day of the week to express the idea of *every Monday*, etc.

Je suis à l'université **le lundi, le mercredi** et **le vendredi**.
I'm at the university Mondays, Wednesdays, and Fridays.

8: The table given here provides a simple formula appropriate for beginning student use.

Students tend to assume that **c'est** is the equivalent of *it is,* while **il/elle est** means *he/she is.* Point out that the animate/inanimate distinction made by these pronouns in English does not hold for French. You may want to point out the pattern **il/elle est** + prepositional phrase (**Il est sur la table.**)

If desired, point out that the indefinite article does not change to **de** after the verb **être** since, here, the negation is absolute rather than partial (i.e., there *is* or there *isn't* in a total sense rather than *there is some* or *there isn't any*). **C'est un chat? Mais non, ce n'est pas un chat, c'est un chien!**

See the **Instructor's Resource Manual** for more information.

D'accord?

A. Catégories Organisez ces activités en catégories.

sortir / travailler / rester à la maison / parler / boire / fumer / danser / manger / rire / donner des cadeaux / écrire des lettres / lire / marcher / voyager / parler anglais / étudier / regarder la télévision / écouter la radio / ranger / dormir

1. activités d'intérieur ou d'extérieur

2. activités physiques ou intellectuelles

3. mes activités préférées

B. Associations What or whom do you associate with these activities?

écouter la radio	lire	écrire des lettres
danser	la musique classique	le football
le rock	regarder la télévision	parler anglais
voyager	donner des cadeaux	sortir
manger	boire	la cuisine
parler	les cadeaux	les mathématiques
le jazz		

C. Les stéréotypes C'est vrai ou c'est faux?

EXPRESSIONS UTILES: C'est vrai. / C'est faux. / Ça dépend.

1. Les filles aiment les enfants.
2. Les garçons aiment les sports.
3. Les Français aiment la cuisine.
4. Les étudiants américains aiment l'université.
5. Les chats n'aiment pas les chiens.
6. Les oiseaux détestent les chats.
7. Les chats détestent les oiseaux.
8. Les étudiants détestent travailler.
9. Les étudiants aiment les fêtes.

D. Préférences Qu'est-ce que vous aimez mieux?

Modèle Vous aimez mieux manger ou boire?
Manger. / Boire. / Ça dépend.

Vous aimez mieux...

1. boire ou manger?
2. regarder la télé ou écouter la radio?
3. lire une lettre ou écrire une lettre?
4. sortir ou dormir?
5. voyager ou rester à la maison?
6. ranger ou étudier?
7. parler français ou parler anglais?
8. chanter ou danser?
9. étudier les mathématiques, les sciences ou l'anglais?

Act. A: Note the use of cognates in instructions (**activités, préférées**). Students are not expected to actively produce these words but should be able to recognize them.
   Divide the class into two groups. One group works on the categories in 1; the other on those in 2. Each group then reports on its list and the other group corrects, agrees, or disagrees.
   For number 3, have students work alone and then in pairs. Model a sample exchange: **J'aime… Et toi?** Students may then report to the class: **J'aime… , mais Éric aime…** Repeat using the negative: **Je n'aime pas… Et toi? Je n'aime pas… , et/mais Jeanne n'aime pas…**

Act. B: Useful for recycling previous vocabulary. If time permits, add: **travailler / rire / fumer / marcher / étudier / ranger.** Encourage students to use words from previous lessons.
   FOLLOW-UP: Ask students: **Qui est associé à ces activités?** Do this in a conversational manner. For example, if you haven't heard of people mentioned by students, ask questions (**Épelez son nom, s'il vous plaît. Il/elle est américain(e)? français(e)?** etc. **D'où est-il/elle?**).

Act. C: Use as a listening activity with students reacting to these stereotypes. Ask students to contribute additional stereotypes for classmates to react to.
   CONTINUATION: **Les professeurs aiment travailler. Les enfants aiment dormir. Les femmes aiment le ménage. Les Français aiment boire. Les Américains aiment la télévision. Les femmes aiment parler.** You may also ask students what **les filles, les garçons, les professeurs, les chiens** and **les chats** like and dislike.

Act. D: Develop by occasionally asking: **Ça dépend de quoi? de la saison? du mois de l'année? du jour de la semaine? de la personne?**

E. C'est comment? Use **c'est** to construct sentences by matching words from each column.

Modèle   *Une guitare, c'est un beau cadeau.*

un professeur	pour chanter
un lit	amusant
une guitare	sérieux
une chanson	pour dormir
danser	un homme sérieux
un examen	pénible
la musique	un beau cadeau
travailler	pour écouter

Act. E: Ask students to add to both lists. Ask students to create **des phrases bizarres** (e.g., **Un examen, c'est amusant.**).

F. Beaucoup de... What do you have a lot of?

Modèle   Vous avez beaucoup de chiens?
Oui, j'ai beaucoup de chiens. / Non, je n'ai pas beaucoup de chiens.

Vous avez beaucoup de...

1. chats?
2. stylos?
3. amis?
4. professeurs?
5. cours?
6. tapis?
7. clés?
8. devoirs?

Act. F: Ask follow-up questions: **Combien de chiens est-ce que tu as?** Have students repeat the object in their responses, e.g., **J'ai deux chiens.** They have not yet learned **en** for responses such as **J'en ai deux.**

Mise en pratique

A. Les Dubois sont très occupés Dans la famille Dubois, qui est occupé et pourquoi?

Modèle   *Thérèse Dubois est occupée parce qu'elle aime marcher, lire, écrire...*

1. Et Vincent?
2. Et Céline?
3. Et Jean-Marc?

B. Les Dubois sont intelligents? Qui est intelligent? Pourquoi?

Modèle   *Jean-Marc Dubois est intelligent parce qu'il aime lire des livres.*

1. Et Vincent?
2. Et Thérèse?
3. Et Céline?

C. Les autres Qu'est-ce qu'ils aiment? Qu'est-ce qu'ils n'aiment pas?

1. un étudiant paresseux
2. un étudiant travailleur
3. un étudiant bizarre
4. un étudiant sérieux
5. un étudiant amusant
6. un étudiant égoïste

Act. C: Can be done in groups. Assign two items per group. Encourage students to include activities (**dormir**, etc.), things (**les livres**, etc.), and people (**un professeur**, etc). Suggest that students vary the verbs used (**adore / déteste / n'aime pas**, etc.).
CONTINUATION: **un père / une mère / un enfant / un oiseau / un chat / un chien / un professeur.**

D. Dis-moi ce que tu aimes, je te dirai qui tu es... Find out what three of your classmates like. Then draw conclusions about their personalities.

Modèle VOUS —*Tu aimes étudier?*
VOTRE PARTENAIRE —*Oui, et j'aime rester à la maison, et*
j'aime regarder la télévision. (**ou**)
Non, je déteste étudier, mais j'aime sortir!
VOUS —*Tu n'es pas raisonnable!*

E. D'après vous Qu'est-ce que vous aimez? Qu'est-ce que vous n'aimez pas?

Modèle *J'aime chanter mais je n'aime pas danser.*
Je n'aime pas boire et je n'aime pas les cigarettes.

Structure

➤➤ Les verbes en *-er*

A large number of French verbs have infinitives that end in **-er.** These verbs are called *first conjugation* or *-er verbs.* Some examples are verbs like **aimer, détester,** and **travailler.** The infinitive ending, **-er,** is pronounced like the é- in **étudiant.** The **-r** is never pronounced.

To write the forms of an **-er** or first conjugation verb, simply take off the infinitive ending (**-er**) and add the following endings:

je travaill**e**	nous travaill**ons**
tu travaill**es**	vous travaill**ez**
il ⎫ elle ⎭ travaill**e**	ils ⎫ elles ⎭ travaill**ent**

In spoken French, the forms ending in **-e, -es,** and **-ent** sound alike. Thus, although you can distinguish among five forms in written French, you hear only three in spoken French.

All **-er** verbs that begin with a vowel sound (for example, **aimer** or **écouter**) drop the **-e** of **je** and allow the **-s** of **nous, vous, ils,** and **elles** to link across to the vowel with a /z/ sound.

j'aime   nous_**a**imons
            /z/

tu aimes   vous_**a**imez
            /z/

il ⎫ elle ⎭ aime   ils**s** ⎫ elle**s** ⎭ **a**iment
                    /z/

The **nous** form of verbs ending in **-ger** adds an **-e-** in front of the **-ons** ending. This spelling change retains the soft **g** sound throughout the verb conjugation.

je mange	nous man**geons**
tu ranges	nous ran**geons**
il voyage	nous voya**geons**

DRILL: On n'aime pas travailler. Vincent ne travaille pas beaucoup. (nous / Céline et Jean-Marc / je / Alceste / tu)

To make **-er** verbs negative, put **ne** in front of the verb form and **pas** after it, just as you did for **être** and **avoir**. Remember to drop the **-e** of **ne** in front of verb forms beginning with a vowel.

Je **n'**écoute **pas**.	*I'm not listening.*
Ils **ne** travaillent **pas**.	*They don't work.*

Note that the present-tense form of these verbs can be translated several different ways in English.

Elle **parle** français.	*She speaks French.*
	She does speak French!
	She is speaking French.

There are also three imperative or command forms of **-er** verbs.

Écoute!	*Listen!* (said to a person you would address using **tu**)
Écoutez!	*Listen!* (said to a person you would address using **vous** or to more than one person)
Écoutons!	*Let's listen!*

Point out to students that you have regularly been using these forms as part of your classroom talk (**Écoutez, s'il vous plaît,**). Try to avoid making the explanation of the imperative complicated. If you treat it as a verb form with its own meaning and context, students will have little difficulty.]

Note the spelling difference.

Tu écoute**s**?	*Are you listening?* (verb form ends in **-s**)
Écoute!	*Listen!* (no **-s**)

Vous avez compris?

A. Chassez l'intrus Which verb form is pronounced differently?

1. écoute!	écoutes	écouter
2. regardez	regardent	regarder
3. parlons	parles	parlent
4. étudie	étudient	étudions
5. aimer	aimes	aimez

Act. A: Ask students first to mark the verb forms that aren't pronounced like the others. Then read the three forms aloud for students to check. Finally, have students read the three forms aloud.

B. C'est vrai ou c'est faux? Use the words below to make complete sentences. Then for each sentence, decide if it is generally true (**c'est vrai**) or false (**c'est faux**).

Modèle Je / ne pas / étudier / assez!
Je n'étudie pas assez! C'est vrai!

1. Les Français / fumer / trop.
2. Je / ne pas / aimer / travailler.
3. Le professeur / regarder / beaucoup / la télévision.
4. Candide / aimer mieux / regarder la télévision que travailler.
5. Je / danser / et / je / chanter / bien.
6. Les étudiants / manger / beaucoup.

C. Choisissons!
From among all the verbs that you have learned, including **être** and **avoir,** choose a verb that fits each sentence. There may be more than one verb possible. Use the correct form.

1. Dans la salle de classe, le professeur ..... et les étudiants .....
2. Nous ..... la télévision.
3. Céline ..... le match de football à la radio.
4. —Je ..... étudier. Et vous?
   —Ah non, je ..... étudier.
5. Est-ce que tu ..... danser?
6. ..... ! Je parle!
7. Lydie et Arnaud ..... la musique classique. Ils ..... le rock!
8. Vous deux! ..... ! C'est une personne très bizarre!
9. Anne ..... des amies canadiennes. Elles ..... sympathiques.
10. Nous ..... la cuisine, nous ..... beaucoup.

Act. D: Have students compare their stories when they are done. Can be given as homework assignment or done in class in pairs or small groups. Remind students to pay attention to form and encourage them to use negatives and to link using **mais, parce que,** etc.

D. Un peu d'ordre!
Use elements from the four columns to write some sentences about Julie's life. You may use any element you wish as many times as you wish. Reorganize and link your sentences to write a brief paragraph.

Julie

Une camarade de chambre	travailler dans la chambre	beaucoup	le week-end
Je	aimer	un peu	le lundi
Les amis	écouter	trop	en été
Olivier	regarder		en décembre
	voyager		dans un restaurant
	détester		la télévision
	manger		des disques
	fumer		lire et écrire des lettres
	être malade		espagnol
	s'appeler		dans la chambre
	marcher		
	parler		

Continuons!

A. Comme tout le monde!

Act A, 1: Have students work in pairs. Use the board or an overhead transparency to compile a list for the entire class. Encourage students to add details and to react to activities as you list them.

1. **Activités communes.** Use **-er** verbs in the infinitive form to make a list of six activities that all students in the class probably do or don't do. Add details as appropriate.

   Modèle *écouter la radio / ne pas fumer / regarder la télévision le week-end*

2. **Faire des phrases.** Now make as many sentences as you can to describe the activities of your class. Add details as appropriate.

   Modèle *Nous travaillons trop. Nous détestons étudier le week-end.*

3. **Les étudiants.** Identify six activities that seem characteristic of the life of a student on your campus. Then, prepare a report to introduce students from other countries to your campus.

   Modèle *Les étudiants aiment les sports. Ils travaillent beaucoup, mais pas le samedi.*

Act A, 3: Students can do this in groups, then exchange their work and correct it for each other. Alternatively, their work can be collected to be graded.

4. **Activités personnelles.** Divide the activities mentioned in your report into lists of those that do and do not apply to you. Rewrite your list to make a paragraph.

   Modèle *J'adore chanter. Je fume trop. Je n'écoute pas les matchs à la radio parce que je déteste les sports mais je...*

B. Les camarades de chambre

1. The ideal roommate is hard to describe, but try! Using the French you know, make a list of the qualities you would look for in a roommate. Include personal qualities, likes, dislikes, and so on.
2. You can't always get what you want. From your point of view, make a list of the attributes of the worst possible roommate—the person you would never want to have to share a room with!

Act. B & C: If your students have no roommate, change the situation to someone they are sharing an apartment with or a travel companion. Encourage students to stay within the French they know.

C. Conversation en français

You cannot stand it one more second, your roommate is driving you crazy. Tell the person in charge of housing why you can no longer room with your roommate.

 **TEXT TAPE:** *Conversation en français*

▶▶ Les adjectifs possessifs

Possessive adjectives are one way of specifying ownership. In English, a possessive adjective is a word such as *his* or *my*. The forms of the possessive adjectives in French are given below. In French, possessive adjectives have the same gender and number as the noun they modify.

Possessive pronouns are treated in the *Appendice de grammaire*.

MASCULIN SINGULIER	FÉMININ SINGULIER	PLURIEL	
mon	ma	mes	*my*
ton	ta	tes	*your (familiar)*
son	sa	ses	*his / her*
notre	notre	nos	*our*
votre	votre	vos	*your (formal or plural)*
leur	leur	leurs	*their*

Voilà Céline Dubois! **Son** père est agent immobilier et **sa** mère est psychologue.
There's Céline Dubois! Her father is a real estate agent and her mother is a psychologist.

Leurs enfants sont raisonnables mais **leur** chien est pénible.
Their children are sensible but their dog is obnoxious.

DRILL: C'est mon livre. (stylo / sœur / chien / table / affiche)

DRILL: Il habite avec sa mère. (sœur / ami Paul / amis Paul et Marc / frère)

Use the masculine singular forms in front of feminine nouns beginning with a vowel sound.

Ton amie est sympathique!   *Your friend is nice!*
Marie, c'est **son** enfant?   *Is Marie his/her child?*
C'est **mon** affiche.   *That's my poster.*

There is no way to distinguish between *her book* and *his book* or *her mother* and *his mother* simply by using a possessive adjective.

C'est **son** livre?   That's her/his book?
C'est **sa** mère?   That's his/her mother?

In French, the context usually prevents any misunderstanding since the people involved generally know who **son, sa,** or **ses** refers to.

Another way to express possession in French is to use the preposition **à** plus a noun or a pronoun, such as **qui** or **moi** or **toi.** Note the following expressions:

C'est **à qui?**   *Whose is it?*
C'est **à toi?**   *Is it yours?*
Non, c'est **à moi!**   *No, it's mine!*

Vous avez compris?

A. C'est mon stylo! Say that each object is yours. Follow the model.

Modèle   Le stylo, c'est à toi?
           Oui, c'est mon stylo!

Act. A: The goal of this activity is to accustom students to using the appropriate possessive adjective (masculine or feminine). Plurals have been omitted in order to avoid verb changes. Similarly, the full range of possessive constructions have not been used since students will not study all the **pronoms toniques** until **Leçon 5.**
CONTINUATION: le réveil / le disque / la guitare / l'animal / le lit / la photo / l'ordinateur

1. La fleur, c'est à toi?
2. Le bureau, c'est à toi?
3. La télévision, c'est à toi?
4. L'étagère, c'est à toi?
5. La radio, c'est à toi?
6. La clé, c'est à toi?

B. C'est à qui?

Modèle   Voilà un stylo. C'est à Marie?
           Oui, c'est son stylo.

           Voilà une guitare? C'est à Marc?
           Oui, c'est sa guitare.

1. Voilà un téléphone. C'est à Jean-Luc?
2. Voilà une affiche. C'est à Fatima?
3. Voilà un crayon. C'est à Marie?
4. Voilà une radio. C'est à Olivier?
5. Voilà un ordinateur. C'est à Rachid?
6. Voilà une fleur. C'est à Chantal?

Continuons!

Une famille idéale! Use **son, sa, ses,** or **leurs** to complete this portrait of an "ideal" family.

Une famille idéale!: Possessive adjectives will be recycled with the more extensive family vocabulary in **Leçon 7.**

1. Chantal adore ..... frère Bernard.
2. Bernard adore ..... sœur Chantal.
3. Chantal adore ..... père et ..... mère.
4. Chantal a un oiseau. Elle adore ..... oiseau aussi!
5. Bernard a un chat. Il adore ..... chat! Et ..... chat adore l'oiseau de Chantal!

⟫ Questions à réponse affirmative ou négative
(yes-or-no questions)

Information questions are treated in *Leçon 6;* interrogative pronouns in *Leçon 8.*

See the **Instructor's Resource Manual** for more information.

SUGGESTION: Teach intonation and **est-ce que** questions for active use. Teach questions with inversion for recognition and limited use only.

There are three ways to ask questions that can be answered by *yes* or *no:* intonation, the use of **est-ce que,** and inversion.

Intonation

To ask a question using intonation, raise your voice at the end. In writing, you add a question mark. If you expect to get a *yes* answer, **n'est-ce pas** can be added at the end. Questions with intonation are typical of informal, spoken French.

Tu parles français?	*(Do) you speak French?*
Il regarde la télévision, **n'est-ce pas?**	*He's watching television, isn't he?*

Point out that French does not have the variety of tag questions *(isn't it? don't you? wouldn't they?)* that English does.

Est-ce que

You can use **est-ce que** to ask a yes-or-no question by placing it at the beginning of the question. The final **-e** of **est-ce que** is dropped in front of a vowel.

- **Est-ce que** + *question*

Est-ce que tu parles français?	*Do you speak French?*
Est-ce qu'il aime danser?	*Does he like to dance?*

Inversion

You can also invert the verb and subject pronoun to ask a yes-or-no question. Inversion questions are typically found in writing and in formal contexts.

Parlez-vous français?	*Do you speak French?*
Est-elle sympathique?	*Is she nice?*

In addition, inversion is frequently seen in fixed questions dealing with topics such as greetings, name, age, and time. Here are some of the questions using inversion you have already seen.

Comment **allez-vous?**	D'où **est-il?**
Comment vous **appelez-vous?**	Comment **t'appelles-tu?**

The use of inversion to ask a question is relatively rare in spoken French. In general, questions with inversion are information questions rather than yes-or-no questions **(Que font-ils? Combien d'étudiants y a-t-il?).** Note, however, that in colloquial spoken French, this type of question is frequently formed by placing the question word at the end of the sentence **(Ils font quoi? Il y a combien d'étudiants?).** Students should be encouraged to use intonation and **est-ce que** to form questions at this stage. As their exposure to French increases, the use of inversion can be encouraged.

Note that:

1. Inversion is not generally used with **je.**

Est-ce que j'ai les clés?... oui!	*Do I have the keys? . . . yes!*

2. If the written form of a third-person singular verb does not end in the letter **-d** or **-t,** a **-t-** is placed between the verb and the subject.

A-t-elle la clé?	*Does she have the key?*

3. If the sentence has a noun subject, the word order is: (1) noun subject + (2) verb + (3) pronoun.

Patrick et Paul ont-ils un chien?	*Do Patrick and Paul have a dog?*

Vous avez compris?

A. Trouvez les formes interrogatives Here is an excerpt from an interview with the French movie star Christophe Lambert. What kinds of interrogative forms can you find? Make a list. (The interviewer is asking about Lambert's U.S. movie, *The Sicilian*.)

Info plus

Christophe Lambert.

Christophe Lambert has starred in several American films, including *Greystoke* (where he was the thirty-seventh Tarzan, and the only French one), *The Sicilian*, and *The Highlander* series.

Act. A: An interview excerpt is used here to show students interrogative forms used in context. Encourage students to note how questions are asked in other texts they encounter. Note that of the 74 questions in the total interview, 5.5% use **est-ce que**, 16% inversion, and 78% intonation.

This is not intended to be used as a reading. Do not expect students to do any more than get the gist and count verb forms.

Ask students to identify the various ways in which questions are asked.

Ask students to hypothesize about the use of **qu'est-ce qui** in line 7.

If desired, ask students to give you the gist of this excerpt.

M.M. C'est un film d'action avec de bons sentiments?

C.L. Mettons un film épique avec une belle histoire. C'est aussi un film de rêve dans le sens où l'on aimerait parfois que les adultes restent aussi simples et déterminés que les enfants.

M.M. Vous êtes adulte, vous?

C.L. Je ne sais pas, je ne m'analyse jamais.

M.M. En dehors du travail, qu'est-ce qui vous plaît, dans la vie?

C.L. Les gens.

M.M. Pas les livres?

C.L. Quand ça me prend.

M.M. La peinture?

C.L. Ah oui, ça dégage plus qu'un livre.

M.M. La musique?

C.L. J'aimerais en faire mais...

[...]

M.M. Quel acteur ancien admirez-vous particulièrement?

C.L. Spencer Tracy. J'aime les acteurs qui ne calquent pas la vie mais qui la subliment.

M.M. Vous croyez à l'amour plus qu'à l'intelligence?

C.L. L'amour est une forme d'intelligence, la plus belle...

M.M. Vous êtes courageux?

C.L. Je crois que je peux être lâche. Je serais peut-être courageux par rapport à de vraies injustices.

M.M. Vous avez des engagements politiques?

C.L. Comme je fais les choses à fond ou pas du tout, je n'ai pas le temps.

[...]

M.M. Alors, qu'est-ce que vous faites, vous, contre l'injustice?

C.L. Attention, c'est un choix.... Je déteste ceux qui font des choses en dilettante ou se contentent d'envoyer de l'argent....

M.M. Quelle est votre position par exemple par rapport à SOS Racisme?

C.L. Je suis forcément pour puisque je suis totalement contre la différenciation entre les êtres humains.

Christophe Lambert: «L'Important, c'est la passion»
Interview de Michèle Manceaux, *Marie-Claire*, novembre 1987, p. 350

B. Posez des questions Change the statements into questions using **est-ce que.** Then use the questions you have made to gather information from your classmates.

Modèle   Tu chantes bien.
> ***Est-ce que tu chantes bien? ... Martha, est-ce que tu chantes bien?***

1. Vous étudiez beaucoup.
2. Tu aimes le cinéma.
3. Jean-Marc a un chat.
4. Vous êtes américain.
5. Vincent et Thérèse aiment sortir.
6. Le professeur est pénible.
7. Les jeunes voyagent beaucoup.
8. C'est une salle de classe agréable.

Act. B: One possible organization would be first to have students formulate all the questions provided (i.e., do the activity as a straightforward, form-based exercise). Then ask students to formulate additional questions they want to ask. Finally, have each student select two or three questions and use them to gather information from their classmates and report back to the class.

Continuons!

A. Portrait d'un(e) camarade de classe

1. **Qu'est-ce qu'il /elle aime? Quelles activités?** Make a list of things you think he/she likes and doesn't like to do.

   Modèle   ***Il/elle aime sortir.***
   > ***Il/elle n'aime pas (déteste) le cinéma.***

2. **Dis-moi...** Ask questions about the activities that you have identified. Use rising intonation, **est-ce que,** or **n'est-ce pas?** Take notes.

   Modèle   ***Lisa, tu aimes danser?***
   > ***Lisa, est-ce que tu aimes sortir?***
   > ***Lisa, tu aimes sortir le samedi, n'est-ce pas?***

3. **Présentation.** Use your notes to give the class a short description of your classmate. Your classmate can agree or disagree using **C'est vrai!** or **Ce n'est pas vrai!**

Act. A: Have students form pairs. They can either create portraits of each other or pretend to be someone else. If desired, assign the final write-up as a homework activity.
   CONTINUATION: Do a similar activity focusing on the teacher (likes, dislikes, etc.).

B. Devinez: un personnage célèbre

1. **Comment est-il/elle?** In groups of two or three, select a well-known person and describe him or her in at least six sentences.
2. **Qui est-ce?** Try to guess the identity of the people chosen by the other groups.
   QUESTIONS UTILES: ***Est-ce que c'est un homme ou une femme? Il/elle est américain/français? D'où est-il/elle?***

C. Jeanne Calment, 121 ans
Jeanne Calment, a French woman from Arles, celebrated her 121st birthday on February 21, 1996. At the time, she was thought to be the oldest person in the world. Imagine that you are interviewing her for a local paper on the occasion of her 121st birthday.

1. In groups, prepare a list of questions that you would like to ask her about her life and her likes and dislikes.
2. Now, imagine the answers that she might give you.
3. Write a paragraph about Jeanne Calment.

Jeanne Calment

Info plus

Jeanne Calment.
In 1996, Jeanne Calment was living in a home for the elderly in Arles, France. She met Vincent Van Gogh and saw the Eiffel Tower while it was still under construction. She was married and had a daughter and grandson, who both died before her. She used to drink moderately and to smoke a cigarette once in a while. Her secret, according to her? She was always happy and never got mad. She made her first record at age 120 and planned to buy a mini-bus for her home with the benefits.

Découvertes culturelles: La musique pour tous

➤ Radio: Du rock, du rap... mais en français!

À L'AFFICHE

Radio
Du rock, du rap... mais en français!

Depuis le 1ᵉʳ janvier, une loi oblige les radios françaises à diffuser un minimum de 4 chansons sur 10 en langue française.

M. Rosenstiehl/Sygma

Alain Souchon pense qu'il est dommage d'avoir besoin de la loi pour défendre la chanson française.

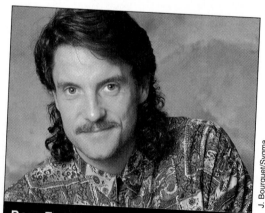

J. Bourguet/Sygma

Pour Francis Cabrel, la nouvelle loi permettra aux chanteurs français de *"continuer à vivre et à créer"*.

Quan
beau
Déso
de c
depu
les s
nouve
chans
que
doiven
Cette
chante
concu
Anglai
frança
qu'eux
Aider le
De plus
rap, les
mode.
à leurs
artistes
impose
chans
soient
chanteur
qui ont
disques.

Les Clés de l'Actualité Junior

A. La musique. Quelle musique écoutez-vous à la radio? Et vos parents? Qui sont vos chanteurs préférés? Pourquoi?

Act. A: OPTION: Do as a survey to identify the musical preferences of students.

B. Choisissez.

1. Dans cet article, on parle: ☐ de musique ☐ de politique ☐ d'études de médias.
2. Le rock et le rap sont normalement: ☐ en français ☐ en anglais.

C. Le sous-titre. Quel rock et quel rap est-ce qu'il y a à la radio française avant le 1er janvier? Et après *(after)*? Quel est le pourcentage des chansons en français avant le 1er janvier? Et après?

D. Mots nouveaux. Trouvez *(Find)* l'anglais pour:

1. depuis = *before / because / since / on*
2. une loi = *a director / a law / a programmer / a singer*
3. oblige = *prevents / encourages / selects / forces*
4. diffuser = *to sing / to broadcast / to play / to count*
5. chanson = *song / singer / program / show*

Act. E, 1: Have students support their opinions using the text: **Il y a trop de chanteurs américains, il n'y a pas assez de français à la radio, il y a trop d'anglais à la radio,** etc.

E. Débat.

1. **La protection.** Qu'est-ce que cette loi protège? Pourquoi?
2. **La loi et la liberté.** Construisez des phrases avec les groupes de mots de chaque colonne pour présenter des arguments en faveur ou contre le règlement sur la musique française.

Act. E, 2: Can be group work. Ask students to take a side and to develop two or three arguments for one side. Then alternate group reports so as to have each side represented.

Pour les Français	désirent protéger leur marché *(market)*
D'après le gouvernement français	en anglais ou en français, la musique, c'est la musique.
Pour les chanteurs français	il est nécessaire de protéger la musique française
Pour les radios françaises	les radios françaises jouent trop de musique américaine
Pour les auditeurs *(listeners)* français	le quota de chansons en français risque d'être dangereux
Les chanteurs français	la musique française est la meilleure

3. **Ils aiment...** Les chanteurs français aiment... / Les auditeurs français aiment... / Les radios françaises aiment... / Les chanteurs américains (anglais, australiens etc.) pensent que... / Les radios américaines pensent que...

4. Est-ce qu'il y a des lois semblables *(similar)* dans votre culture? À quel sujet? Pour protéger quoi? Quelles nationalités sont dangereuses pour les produits de votre culture?

Act. E, 4: You will need to provide the names of objects that are contentious in international trade. (**le pétrole, les automobiles, le logiciel, la musique,** etc.)

30 Ans de Musiques Africaines pour les 10 Ans d'Africa N° 1

Act. A: Encourage students to use cognates and to guess meanings. There may be more than one opinion as to the best way to commemorate an event.

A. Commémoration. Comment commémorer un événement important? Associez les éléments de la colonne de gauche avec les éléments correspondants de la colonne de droite.

LES ÉVÉNEMENTS	LES POSSIBILITÉS
l'anniversaire du débarquement américain en Normandie	un défilé militaire
	un beau discours *(speech)* par le président
l'anniversaire de la prise de la Bastille	un bal pour danser
l'anniversaire de l'indépendance de l'Algérie	un prix *(prize)*
un film magnifique	le nom d'une avenue
l'élection d'un président	une plaque sur la résidence
	une cérémonie avec musique et fleurs

30 ANS DE MUSIQUES AFRICAINES POUR LES 10 ANS D'AFRICA N° 1

Le 7 février prochain, Africa n°1 fête ses dix ans. La direction marque cet événement en célébrant, à sa manière, la musique africaine. Fin janvier, sort donc un disque rétrospectif des plus grands titres de la chanson et de la musique africaines des trente dernières années. Autant dire, depuis l'indépendance. Production Africa n°1; distribution Sonodisc. Ce sera un CD (disque compact) pour l'Europe et deux cassettes pour l'Afrique. La sélection des titres a été assurée par les programmateurs de la station. On peut citer Francis Bebey *(Kinshasa),* Elvis Kemayo *(Africa music non stop),* Pépé Kalé *(Pon Moun Paka Bongé),* San Fan Thomas *(African tipi),* Manu Dibango *(Soul Makossa),* Myriam Makeba *(Pata-Pata),* Franco aussi, bien sûr...
La pochette sera illustrée par un artiste gabonais primé lors du Salon d'octobre 1989.

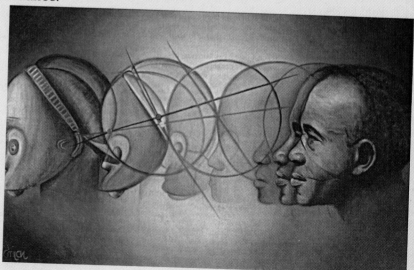

B. 30 Ans de Musiques Africaines.

1. Africa N° 1, qu'est-ce que c'est? Quels mots *(words)* dans les textes expliquent Africa N° 1?

Act. B, 1: Possible answers: station, KHX, fréquences, radio, etc.

2. **Âge.** Africa N° 1 existe depuis quand *(since when)*? Depuis quand est-ce que les pays africains sont indépendants?

3. **La fête.** Qu'est-ce qu'on fête le 7 février?

4. **L'objet.** Quel objet célèbre Africa N° l? Quel est le mois de sa production?

5. **La sélection.** Trouvez les mots en relation avec la musique.

6. **Les noms africains.** Trouvez une chanson avec le nom...

d'une grande cité africaine	
d'un chanteur avec un prénom américain	
d'un chanteur avec un nom français	
d'une chanteuse	

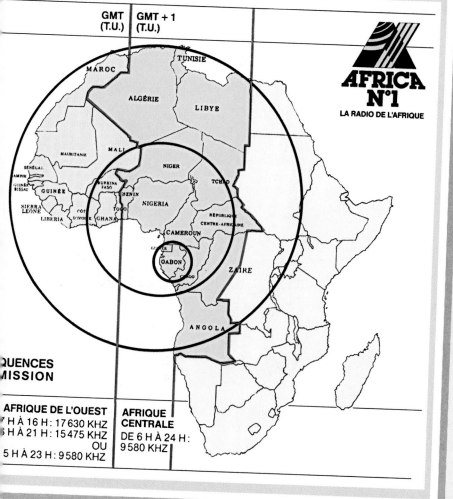

Jeune Afrique Économique

C. Mots nouveaux. Trouvez l'anglais.

1. prochain = *soon / next / quick*
2. la direction = *the director / the management / the way to go / the directions*
3. la pochette = *the art / the cover / the ad / the poster*

D. L'illustration.

Act. D: Answers: **Michel-Ange / un masque africain traditionnel / abstrait et symbolique**

Quel artiste imite l'artiste gabonais?

Quel objet est à l'origine de l'illustration?

Quel est le style de l'illustration? abstrait? réaliste? symbolique? impressionniste? représentatif?

Est-ce que vous aimez l'illustration? Pourquoi?

E. Interview. Préparez des questions pour interviewer un chanteur africain.

Act. E: You may want to bring some African music to class and play it for your students.

www explore!
http//voila.heinle.com

Orthographe et prononciation

▶▶ Les consonnes finales

Generally, final consonants are silent in French. A consonant plus **-e** is pronounced.

> gran**d**   *-d not pronounced*   grand**e**   *-d pronounced*

Four consonants, **-c, -r, -f,** and **-l** (think of the word *CaReFuL),* are frequently pronounced at the end of a word. In the words listed below, the letters in boldface are pronounced.

> par**c**   sporti**f**   su**r**   traditionne**l**

Frequently, the final consonant of French words adopted from other languages is pronounced. Here, the letters in boldface are pronounced.

> tenni**s**   ga**z**   campu**s**   shor**t**

Finally, note that the **-r** of the infinitive ending **-er** is not pronounced.

> étudie**r**   regard**er**

Activité

Chassez l'intrus Read each list aloud to find the words whose final consonant *is* pronounced.

1. enfant / fleur / tapis / blond
2. intelligent / français / animal / laid
3. cahier / devoir / étudier / travailler
4. sportif / parler / anglais / chat

If desired, point out that a consonant followed by any vowel is pronounced (e.g., **Anne, lundi, piano, vendu**).

See the **Instructor's Resource Manual** for more information.

Vocabulaire de base

TEXT TAPE: *Vocabulaire de base*

The word **ami** connotes a *good* or *best friend*. The word **copain** is closer to the American use of the word *friend* as in *going out with friends tonight*. **Copain** is generally used to refer to others in one's age group.

NOMS

un ami, une amie *friend*
un animal, des animaux *animal(s)*
un cadeau, des cadeaux *present(s), gift(s)*
un(e) camarade de classe *classmate*
le cinéma *movie theater, the movies*
un(e) enfant *child*
une femme *woman*

une fille *girl*
un frère *brother*
un garçon *boy*
un homme *man*
une mère *mother*
un nom *name*
un père *father*
une personne *person*
une sœur *sister*
le sport *sports*

ADJECTIFS

amusant(e) *fun*
anglais(e) *English*
espagnol(e) *Spanish*
sérieux, sérieuse *serious, hardworking*
vrai(e) *true, right*

VERBES

adorer *to love*
aimer *to like, to love*
aimer mieux (que) *to like better (than), to prefer*
chanter *to sing*
danser *to dance*
détester *to hate*
donner *to give*
écouter *to listen to*
étudier *to study*
fumer *to smoke*
manger *to eat*
marcher *to walk*

parler *to talk, to speak*
ranger *to straighten up, to clean up*
regarder *to look at, to watch*
travailler *to work*
voyager *to travel*

DIVERS

beaucoup *a lot, much*
beaucoup de *a lot of, many, much*
c'est / ce n'est pas *it is, he is, she is / it isn't, he isn't, she isn't*
c'est vrai / ce n'est pas vrai(!) *that's true / that's not true (you're kidding!)*

comme *like, as*
n'est-ce pas? *isn't it? / isn't he? / isn't she?, etc.*
parler anglais *to speak English*
parler espagnol *to speak Spanish*
parler français *to speak French*
rester à la maison *to stay home*
trop *too (too much)*
un peu *a little*
Votre nom, s'il vous plaît? *Your name, please?*

Vocabulaire supplémentaire

NOMS

un(e) agent immobilier *real estate agent*
une chanson *song*
une cigarette *cigarette*
un concert *concert*
la cuisine *cooking, cuisine*
un film *film, movie*
le football *soccer*
une lettre *letter*
un match *game*
les mathématiques *mathematics*
le ménage *housework*
un nom de famille *last name*
un oiseau, des oiseaux *bird(s)*
un prénom *first name*
un/une psychologue *psychologist*
les sciences *science*
le tennis *tennis*
le théâtre *theater*

ADJECTIF

faux, fausse *false*

VERBES À NE PAS CONJUGUER

(verbs that are not to be conjugated at this point)
boire *to drink*
dormir *to sleep*
écrire *to write*
lire *to read*
rire *to laugh*
sortir *to go out*

DIVERS

C'est à qui? C'est à moi, etc. *Whose is it? It's mine, etc.*
par exemple *for example*
Pourquoi? *Why?*
Qu'est-ce qu'il/elle aime? *What does he/she like?*
Qu'est-ce que tu aimes? *What do you like?*
surtout *especially*

LE FRANÇAIS TEL QU'ON LE PARLE

Chouette! *Great!*

LE FRANÇAIS FAMILIER

bosser = travailler
bûcher = étudier
C'est pas vrai! *Really! No kidding!*
le ciné = le cinéma
un copain, une copine = un ami, une amie
le foot = le football
un gars = un homme
un/une gosse = un/une enfant
maman = mère *(mom, mommy)*
les maths = les mathématiques
papa = père *(dad, daddy, pop)*
rigoler = rire
un(e) snob = snob
snob *(invariable)* = snobbish
un type = un homme

ON ENTEND PARFOIS

boumer (Zaïre) = danser

Although there are numerous slang terms for women, they are usually felt to be more vulgar than similar terms for men (such as **gars** or **type).** One term in current use that is not particularly vulgar is **nana.**

Magazine francophone

REVUE PÉRIODIQUE
PUBLIÉE À L'AIDE DE DOCUMENTATIONS INTERNATIONALES

Rédacteur en chef:
Isabelle Kaplan

Rédacteurs adjoints:
L. Kathy Heilenman
Claude Toussaint Tournier

NUMÉRO 1

REVUE EN FRANÇAIS POUR LES ÉTUDIANTS DE « VOILÀ! »

ÉDITORIAL

Étudier le français, pourquoi?

Étudier le français à l'université! Un an, deux ans? Pourquoi?

 Pour avoir un diplôme universitaire, c'est souvent obligatoire... Mais aussi...

 Pour parler et écouter des sons, des mots différents.

 Pour voyager et avoir beaucoup d'amis dans beaucoup de pays.

Peut-être pour travailler en France, en Amérique, dans un pays francophone, un jour...

 Pour découvrir une langue,

 une culture,

 un peuple,

 littératures et œuvres d'art...

 Pour avoir des idées différentes.

 Pour sortir de l'ethnocentrisme où nous sommes emprisonnés.

 Pour étudier des modes et des styles différents. Pour étudier des modes et des styles différents.

 Pour découvrir des horizons plus larges.

 Pour changer les stéréotypes et les idées conformistes de la tradition familiale.

Et vous? Pourquoi étudiez-vous le français? Le français est-il obligatoire? indispensable? nécessaire pour une éducation moderne? Pourquoi? Un an, deux ans, c'est assez?

L'été, à Paris, c'est le meilleur moment pour découvrir, loin de la foule, les rues et les monuments, pour voir les expositions et aller au concert tranquillement. Beaucoup de manifestations s'offrent à vous.

Paris

Paris-quartier d'été, du 14 juillet au 15 août

MUSIQUE

Festival "All Stars", du 4 au 27 juillet

Des groupes venus de tous horizons — Caraïbes, Amérique du Sud, États-Unis — se retrouvent au New Morning, rue des Petites-Écuries, pour l'amour du jazz. Invités : Caribbean Jazz Project, NG La Banda, Margareth Menezes, John Hammond, Ali Farka Touré, Arturo Sandoval...

Rens. : 01 45 23 56 39.

Bals-concerts, dans le parc de La Villette, les 23 et 30 juillet, 6 et 13 août

Concerts dans le kiosque à musique, de 17 à 21 h. Au programme, Sawt El Atlas, Olodum, Gramoun Lélé, Kanda Bongo Man, Zumbadera, Super Merengue, Ray Lema.

Rens. : 01 40 03 75 03.

Paris-quartier d'été.

DANSE

- Merce Cunningham Dance Company, cour d'Orléans au Palais Royal, à 22 h, du 3 au 6 août.
- Karine Saporta: "L'or ou le cirque Flamenco", au Cirque d'hiver, à 21 h, du 30 juillet au 2 août.

CINÉMA

Les Opéras de minuit, en plein air, sur le Parvis de la Défense, de 22 h à l'aube, du 20 au 22 juillet: Nuit Mozart, Nuit Carmen, Nuit Verdi.

Paris Quartier d'été: tél. 01 40 28 40 33.

Les fêtes...

en France

1er mai

La fête du Travail

Le 1er mai est un jour férié. Pourtant ce jour-là, on fête le travail...

Un jour de novembre 1884, les syndicats américains se réunissent dans la ville de Chicago, aux États-Unis. Ils décident que, à partir du 1er mai, ils ne travailleront plus que 8 heures par jour.

Interdit de travailler

Le 1er mai 1890, des manifestations sont organisées dans 138 villes d'Europe: des journées de 8 heures. La durée du travail est limitée par la loi. En France, depuis 1941, le 1er mai reste le symbole de ces luttes. Et ce jour-là, il n'est pas permis de travailler!

Sophie Cindel

Chaque 1er mai, tout le monde a le droit de vendre du muguet dans les rues. Comme cette Parisienne en 1925.

Pâques

Une fête pour deux religions

À Pâques, de nombreux enfants s'amusent à rechercher des œufs en chocolat dans leur jardin. Mais dans la religion juive et la religion chrétienne, cette fête très importante célèbre la liberté et le retour de la vie.

Pâques est une fête très importante dans la religion chrétienne et la religion juive. Mais ce mot n'a pas tout à fait le même sens, ni la même orthographe, pour les juifs et pour les chrétiens.

Selon la légende, les cloches de l'église Saint-Pierre de Rome quittent Rome à Pâques pour faire le tour du monde et lâcher des chocolats dans ton jardin.

La libération

Pour les juifs, le mot Pâque vient de l'hébreu "pessah" qui veut dire "passage". Il rappelle la libération par Dieu de leur peuple, quand les juifs étaient esclaves des pharaons égyptiens.

Le renouveau

Selon la tradition chrétienne, Pâques rappelle le retour à la vie de Jésus, trois jours après sa mort.
La période de Pâques est aussi celle du printemps et du réveil de la nature. Ainsi, cette fête est le symbole du renouveau de la vie.

---

et au Québec

La fête de l'Action de grâce

Comme les couleurs de l'automne qui l'auréolent de toute leur splendeur, la fête de l'Action de grâce est un véritable hymne d'extase et de gratitude.

Ses origines remontent au début du XVIIe siècle. À la fin de l'année 1620, le Mayflower, navire chargé d'immigrants britanniques, accoste dans un endroit sauvage de la Nouvelle-Angleterre, là où se trouve maintenant la ville de Plymouth, au Massachusetts. Cette manifestation de reconnaissance a été le point de départ d'une fête traditionnelle qui a lieu maintenant chaque année aux États-Unis, le quatrième jeudi de novembre; on l'appelle le "Thanksgiving Day". Au Canada, elle est célébrée le deuxième lundi du mois d'octobre.

La fête du travail

POUR LA FÊTE DU TRAVAIL, LE CANADA ET LES ÉTATS-UNIS DÉLAISSENT LA DATE DU 1ER MAI POUR LE PREMIER LUNDI DE SEPTEMBRE

VOYAGE AU SÉNÉGAL

CLIMAT

Climat tropical à nuance aride diminuant du nord au sud, chaud toute l'année (à Dakar 17° à 30° et en Casamance 16° à 37°). La meilleure saison pour voyager au Sénégal est la saison sèche qui s'étend de novembre à mai-juin. De juillet à octobre: quelques grosses averses brèves durant la journée. On se baigne toute l'année sur les plages du Sénégal avec des températures variant de 21° (février-avril) à 27° (octobre-novembre).

INFO

*VACCINATIONS:
Traitement antipaludéen et fièvre jaune recommandés.
DÉCALAGE HORAIRE:
En hiver, 1 heure de moins.
En été, 2 heures de moins.
MONNAIE:
Le franc CFA.*

PORTE OUVERTE SUR LE SÉNÉGAL

EXCURSIONS

Les prix sont donnés en francs français, à titre indicatif, mais réglables en francs CFA.

AU DÉPART DU DOMAINE DE NIANING

• **Dakar et l'île de Gorée:** la journée avec le déjeuner, environ 330 F.
Gorée, une île chargée d'histoire, témoignage de la traite des noirs et de l'esclavage.
• **Lac Rose de Retba:** la journée avec le déjeuner, environ 260 F. Visite d'une région de cultures maraîchères et de pêche traditionnelle.
• **Îles du Saloum:** la journée en car Safari avec ou sans déjeuner, entre 200 F et 360 F.

Le Saloum est un paradis pour les oiseaux de toutes sortes.

• **Balade broussarde en 4 x 4:** la demi-journée, environ 150 F. Une balade qui vous emmènera à travers des villages perdus au cœur de la brousse.

AU DÉPART DE KABROUSSE

• **Basse-Casamance Ziguinchor:** la demi-journée, environ 125 F.

Visite de la Basse-Casamance: Oussouye, Séléki, cases à impluvium. Brin et Ziguinchor.
• **Messe Diola Diembéring:** dimanche matin, environ 70 F. Excursion à Boucotte et Diembéring et service religieux, avec les villageois, à Diembéring.
• **Kachouane en 4 x 4 - pirogue:** la journée, environ 220 F.

---

page d'écriture

Deux et deux quatre
quatre et quatre huit
huit et huit font seize...
Répétez! dit le maître
5 Deux et deux quatre
quatre et quatre huit
huit et huit font seize.
Mais voilà l'oiseau-lyre
qui passe dans le ciel
10 l'enfant le voit
l'enfant l'entend
l'enfant l'appelle:
Sauve-moi
joue avec moi
15 oiseau!

Alors l'oiseau descend
et joue avec l'enfant
Deux et deux quatre...
Répétez! dit le maître
20 et l'enfant joue
l'oiseau joue avec lui...
Quatre et quatre huit
huit et huit font seize
et seize et seize qu'est-ce qu'ils font?
25 Ils ne font rien seize et seize
et surtout pas trente-deux
de toute façon
et ils s'en vont.

Jacques Prévert
Paroles
© *Éditions Gallimard*

Souleymane Keita, le peintre de Gorée

Souleymane Keita, peintre sénégalais, vit à Gorée, une petite île en face de Dakar.

Valérie Brierley

EXPOSITIONS

Souleymane Keita a exposé ses œuvres à:

• **Dakar** (Sénégal) 1969, 1972, 1973, 1981, 1986, 1992
• **Nouakchott** (Mauritanie) 1971
• **Ouagadougou** (Burkina Faso) 1972
• **Toronto** (Canada) 1975, 1979
• **New York** (USA) 1976, 1978, 1979, 1982, 1983, 1990
• **Gorée** 1987, 1988
• **Paris** 1991, 1992

D'UNE PAGE À L'AUTRE...
(Leafing through the Magazine...)

1. Leaf through the **Magazine** to identify its topics. Select the three words that best describe the articles: **les voyages / les vacances / l'art / la musique / l'Afrique / la correspondance / la religion / une célébration / les cités / l'histoire / la nationalité / le tourisme / travailler / les dates / le Québec.**

2. Find which articles mention: the calendar / food / politics / the Bible / history / art / travel / money / Italy / the U.S. / Canada / work / dancing /

seasons / climate / religion / mathematics / school / Paris / musical groups.

3. Find which articles share common elements and group them, identifying the element you chose.

   Modèle   *le tourisme: Paris, Sénégal*

4. Say in what order you would read the articles and give your reasons

   Modèle   *Article un: ... ; Il est facile, ...*

Les arts et les lettres

SOULEYMANE KEITA. Which word in this excerpt indicates Souleymane Keita's art? On how many continents is the man well known?

On a map, look at the location of the countries mentioned in this article. Do these countries have anything in common?

Modèle   *Paris est la capitale de...*

PAGE D'ÉCRITURE. First tell how many people are involved in this poem. How different are they?

Now read the poem and underline the words that you know. What sort of class does this poem refer to?

Next, underline in red the narrative portion of this poem. What words mark the beginning of the narrative?

Try to hear the voices of the people speaking. Underline in blue the direct speech. Are there interruptions?

What sort of student is the hero of this poem? Why?

Identify the elements of dramatic tension in the poem. Organize in pairs the words that are in opposition and that contribute to this tension. Does the author have an opinion on the scene? Which side is he on?

What object, person, or place has symbolic significance? What is it a symbol of?

Find words in the poem that illustrate the following ideas: **la liberté / l'oppression / la contrainte / la mémoire / l'imagination.**

Bravo! You have just read your first French poem!

À LA LOUPE
(A closer look)

L'ÉDITORIAL. What is the topic of the editorial? Which of the arguments presented is the one that brought you to this class? Which three arguments are the most persuasive? the least persuasive?

In the **Magazine,** find an article that is an example of each point of the editorial.

LES FÊTES. Decide which holidays are:

religious / political / family holidays / historical / socially-minded / familiar to you / different in your native culture.

Look at a calendar in your native culture and for each holiday give the day of the week and the date. Now do the same for the French and Québécois holidays.

Modèle   *La fête du travail, c'est le...*

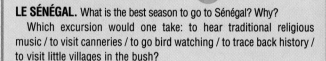

REGARDS SUR LE MONDE

LE SÉNÉGAL. What is the best season to go to Sénégal? Why?

Which excursion would one take: to hear traditional religious music / to visit canneries / to go bird watching / to trace back history / to visit little villages in the bush?

À VOTRE AVIS... *(According to you . . .)*

RECHERCHES.

1. Select one article and use the information presented to prepare six questions that relate to your article. The questions should lead to obtaining better knowledge of the main topic.

2. Select an article that raises problems or issues. Identify one issue and write three sentences about it.

3. Select one article and use it as the basis for an activity that you are going to do today (prepare a trip to Africa, go to a concert, celebrate a holiday, etc.). What questions will you ask to be able to conduct your activity?

ACTION.

1. Prepare a poster advertising a trip to Sénégal. Use what you have learned in both your textbook and the **Video Magazine.**

2. Interview Souleymane Keita. (This can be a role play.)

3. You are spending a year in France. Use the **Petites annonces** to find housing. Prepare four questions that you will ask when you call for more information. Will you take the room?

CORRESPONDANCE.

1. Write to Valérie or to Nadine to become her pen pal. Read all the letters that these girls receive. Who will each of them choose?

2. Write a response to the editorial. Use the argument of the editorial to articulate your own ideas.

3. You have been traveling in Sénégal and are now sending a postcard to your French teacher. What will you say?

POUR FINIR.

Say or write three things that you learned in this **Magazine.**

What words do you now associate with: **fête / Gorée / Paris / le français / juillet / travailler?**

Bravo! You have just finished reading your first **Magazine** in French!

Les âges de la vie

En bref

Dans cette leçon...

- Compter jusqu'à 100
- Décrire des enfants, des jeunes et des adultes
- Se situer dans l'espace (quelques prépositions)
- Des familles françaises
- Les verbes comme **sortir**
- Placer des adjectifs et des adverbes
- Employer les formes toniques des pronoms
- L'âge et les rites de passage

In this lesson...

- Counting to 100
- Describing children, young people, and adults
- Saying where you are (a few prepositions)
- French families
- Verbs like **sortir**
- Adjective and adverb placement
- Using stressed pronouns
- Age and rites of passage

www explore!
http://voila.heinle.com

Develop writing skills with Système-D software!

Practice listening and pronunciation skills with the Text Tape!

Discover the Francophone world!

Build your skills!

INTERNET

SYSTÈME-D

TEXT TAPE

VIDEO TAPE

CD-ROM

Students have an open-ended writing activity in the **Cahier** suitable for use with **Système-D**.

Entrée en matière: Les jeunes

Des jeunes. Qui sont ces jeunes? Où sont-ils? À l'université? Dans les rues de Paris? Ils sont vieux ou jeunes? Sont-ils très jeunes? 14 ans? 16 ans? 18 ans? 20 ans? 30 ans?

Et vous, est-ce que vous êtes plus ou moins vieux que ces jeunes?

Comment sont-ils?	
Combien sont blonds?	
Combien sont bruns?	

Combien *(How many)* sont-ils?	
Il y a combien de garçons?	
Combien de filles?	

Dans la rue. Est-ce qu'ils sont en vacances? Est-ce qu'ils sont sérieux? Pourquoi sont-ils dans la rue?

Et vous? Vous êtes quelquefois dans la rue? Pourquoi?

Pour chanter?		Pour marcher?	
Pour danser?		Pour regarder les gens?	
Pour parler?		Pour travailler?	
Pour étudier?		Pour protester?	

Une époque. De quelle couleur est leur banderolle *(banner)*? Pourquoi?

Contre *(Against)* qui est-ce qu'ils protestent? Qui est Monsieur Balladur? Le président de la France? Un ministre? Le premier ministre? Le ministre de l'éducation?

Conversation. Posez *(Ask)* trois questions à la jeune fille blonde.

-
-
-

Le portrait de votre génération. Quels sujets sont importants pour les jeunes de votre culture?

Nous sommes…   *Nous détestons…*

Nous aimons…   *Nous protestons contre…*

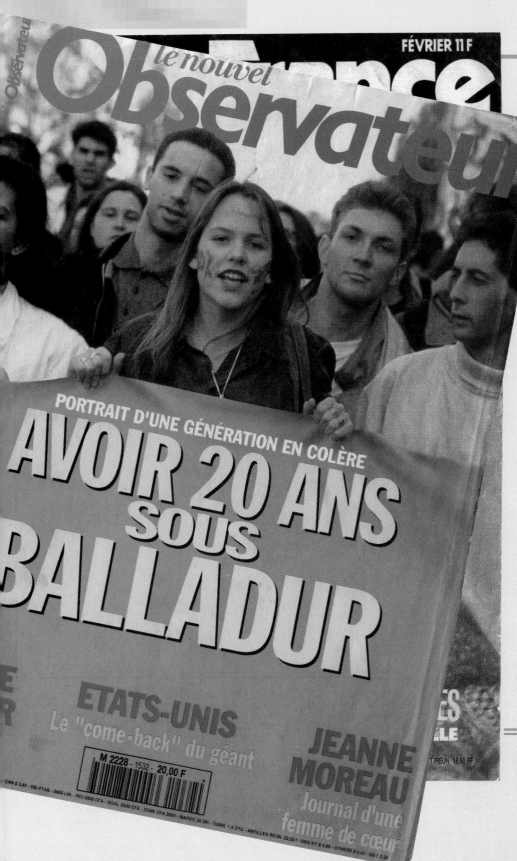

FÉVRIER 11 F

le nouvel
Observateur

PORTRAIT D'UNE GÉNÉRATION EN COLÈRE

AVOIR 20 ANS
SOUS
BALLADUR

ETATS-UNIS
Le "come-back" du géant

M 2228 - 1532 - 20,00 F

JEANNE
MOREAU
Journal d'une
femme de cœur

CAN $ 3,95 - 400 PTAS - 5500 LIR. - RCI 2000 CFA - SGAL 2000 CFA - ZONE CFA 2000 - MAROC 20 DH - TUNIS 1,5 DTU - ANTILLES REUN. 22,50 f - USA NY $ 3,95 - OTHERS $ 4,40 - GB £ 2,20

Info plus

Édouard Balladur.
Balladur was Jacques Chirac's Prime Minister after the 1995 election. He proposed financial reforms that affected the lives of students. They organized street demonstrations and caused his resignation.

TRANSPARENCY: 5-1

Vocabulaire

A. Les chiffres de 40 à 100

40	quarante	70	soixante-dix	82	quatre-vingt-deux
41	quarante et un	71	soixante et onze	90	quatre-vingt-dix
42	quarante-deux	72	soixante-douze	91	quatre-vingt-onze
50	cinquante	80	quatre-vingts	92	quatre-vingt-douze
60	soixante	81	quatre-vingt-un	100	cent

Info plus

Les départements.

European France is divided into 95 administrative departments which, in turn, are grouped into 22 **régions**. The system of **départements** has existed since the late 1700s, and the names of many **départements** are derived from geographical features. In fact, 60 **départements** are named after rivers and 13 after mountains (*QUID*, 1994, p. 721). **Départements** are listed alphabetically and license plates and postal codes incorporate **département** numbers. Someone who lived in **Finistère**, for example, would have a license plate ending in 29 and their postal code would begin with 29.

Départements

01	Ain				
02	Aisne				
03	Allier				
04	Alpes de Haute-Provence				
05	Hautes-Alpes				
06	Alpes-Maritimes				
07	Ardèche				
08	Ardennes				
09	Ariège				
10	Aube				
11	Aude				
12	Aveyron				
13	Bouches-du-Rhône				
14	Calvados				
15	Cantal				
16	Charente				
17	Charente-Maritime				
18	Cher				
19	Corrèze				
20	Corse				
21	Côte-d'Or				
22	Côtes-du-Nord				
23	Creuse				
24	Dordogne				
25	Doubs				
26	Drôme				
27	Eure				
28	Eure-et-Loir				
29	Finistère				
30	Gard				
31	Haute-Garonne				

32	Gers	48	Lozère	64	Pyrénées-Atlantiques	80	Somme
33	Gironde	49	Maine-et-Loire	65	Hautes-Pyrénées	81	Tarn
34	Hérault	50	Manche	66	Pyrénées-Orientales	82	Tarn-et-Garonne
35	Ille-et-Vilaine	51	Marne	67	Bas-Rhin	83	Var
36	Indre	52	Haute-Marne	68	Haut-Rhin	84	Vaucluse
37	Indre-et-Loire	53	Mayenne	69	Rhône	85	Vendée
38	Isère	54	Meurthe-et-Moselle	70	Haute-Saône	86	Vienne
39	Jura	55	Meuse	71	Saône-et-Loire	87	Haute-Vienne
40	Landes	56	Morbihan	72	Sarthe	88	Vosges
41	Loir-et-Cher	57	Moselle	73	Savoie	89	Yonne
42	Loire	58	Nièvre	74	Haute-Savoie	90	Territoire de Belfort
43	Haute-Loire	59	Nord	75	Ville de Paris	91	Essonne
44	Loire-Atlantique	60	Oise	76	Seine-Maritime	92	Hauts-de-Seine
45	Loiret	61	Orne	77	Seine-et-Marne	93	Seine-Saint-Denis
46	Lot	62	Pas-de-Calais	78	Yvelines	94	Val-de-Marne
47	Lot-et-Garonne	63	Puy-de-Dôme	79	Deux-Sèvres	95	Val-d'Oise

- Paris est dans le département de la Seine, 75. Marseille est dans le département des Bouches-du-Rhône, 13. Et Lyon? Strasbourg?

B. Les enfants

TRANSPARENCY:
5-2

Voilà Guillaume Firket. Il a 18 mois et il est très mignon. Il mange tout le temps et il aime dormir. C'est un bébé facile. Il est toujours content, mais il pleure quand il est fatigué.

- Comment est Guillaume? Il a quel âge? Qu'est-ce qu'il aime? Est-ce qu'il pleure souvent?

Voilà Sylvie Mabille. Elle a onze ans. Elle est jolie, mais c'est une enfant gâtée et difficile. Elle n'est pas souvent sage et c'est une petite fille mal élevée. Elle adore jouer mais elle n'a pas beaucoup d'amis parce qu'elle est égoïste: elle n'aime pas partager. Elle déteste l'école, mais elle aime l'histoire et la géographie. Aujourd'hui, elle est fâchée parce que c'est lundi.

- Comment est Sylvie? Elle a quel âge? Pourquoi est-ce qu'elle est gâtée? Qui aime les enfants gâtés? Pourquoi est-ce qu'ils n'ont pas beaucoup d'amis? Qu'est-ce qu'elle n'aime pas? Quand est-elle contente? Pourquoi?

Information questions (e.g., **Pourquoi est-ce qu'elle est gâtée?**) will be presented in the *Structure* section of *Leçon 6.* Students should be able to recognize them but should not be expected to produce them at this point.

François! Tu joues?

Voilà François Pinel. C'est un petit garçon typique de six ans. Très actif, il adore jouer et il a beaucoup d'amis parce qu'il est gentil. Il est sage et bien élevé. C'est un enfant heureux et bien équilibré. Comme Guillaume, il est toujours content.

- Quel âge a François? Est-ce qu'il est heureux ou malheureux? Pourquoi? Pourquoi est-il typique? Il est plus jeune ou plus âgé que Guillaume?

C. Les jeunes

Voilà Cédric Rasquin. Il a seize ans et il habite chez sa mère, à Toulouse. Il est parfois de bonne humeur et parfois de mauvaise humeur, et il n'est pas facile. C'est normal pour un adolescent, non? Il a des problèmes et il est malheureux. Il n'aime pas le lycée mais il aime lire et il adore la littérature. Il aime aussi les bandes dessinées! Il aime être seul, mais il joue de la guitare avec ses copains. Il est timide avec les filles et il n'a pas de petite amie.

- Quel âge a Cédric? Il habite où? Est-ce qu'il est content de sa vie? Expliquez (explain) ses problèmes. Qu'est-ce qu'il aime? Qu'est-ce qu'il n'aime pas?

Alors, on joue?

Maintenant???

Voilà Suzanne Mabille. Elle a dix-huit ans et elle étudie le droit à Bruxelles. Elle est souvent de bonne humeur. Elle est intellectuelle et elle adore parler, mais c'est aussi une jeune fille sportive et elle aime beaucoup le tennis. Elle ne mange pas trop parce qu'elle est au régime. Mais son copain, Abder, adore manger et fumer! Il est marocain et il étudie la médecine à Bruxelles aussi.

- Quel âge a Suzanne? Elle étudie où? Est-ce qu'elle est française? Et Abder? Qu'est-ce que Suzanne aime? Qu'est-ce qu'elle n'aime pas? Pourquoi? Et Abder, qu'est-ce qu'il n'aime pas? Pourquoi est-il à Bruxelles?

D. Les adultes

Voilà Béatrice Dubois. Elle a trente-sept ans et elle habite Toulouse. Elle aime être élégante. Elle n'est pas pauvre mais elle n'est pas très riche. C'est une femme énergique et débrouillarde, mais têtue. Elle a trois enfants. Avec ses enfants, elle est sévère mais compréhensive. Elle adore les langues étrangères et elle est professeur d'anglais dans un lycée. Elle a parfois des problèmes avec les adolescents de sa classe. Ils ne sont pas méchants, mais ils ne sont pas toujours polis et ils adorent rire.

• Où habite Béatrice Dubois? Elle est jeune ou vieille? Combien d'enfants est-ce qu'elle a? Quel âge ont-ils? Est-ce qu'elle est très occupée? Pourquoi? Pourquoi est-ce qu'elle n'est pas très riche? Comment sont les adolescents de sa classe?

Toulouse

TRANSPARENCY:
5-4

Voilà Jean Rasquin, dentiste, quarante-cinq ans. C'est le père de Cédric et il habite à Paris. Il est très bavard et il déteste être seul, mais il est souvent ennuyeux. Il adore les voitures, les vacances et les week-ends.

• Qui est Jean Rasquin? Il a quel âge? Est-ce qu'il est comme Cédric? Pourquoi? Il est sympathique?

Voilà Jacques Dubois. Il habite Nice, il a soixante-huit ans et il est retraité. C'est une personne âgée, mais il marche beaucoup et donc il est en forme. Il est calme, réservé et un peu pessimiste. Il est triste parce qu'il est seul et vieux.

Voilà Paulette Gilmard. Elle habite à Nice et elle est retraitée aussi, mais elle n'est pas comme Jacques: c'est une femme enthousiaste, sociable et optimiste. Elle aime la vie et elle n'est pas souvent déprimée. Elle a soixante-six ans, mais elle n'est pas vieille, n'est-ce pas?

TRANSPARENCY:
5-5

Gilmard is pronounced [ʒilmaʀ]. The first syllable is pronounced like the first syllable of girafe or gigantesque.

Nice

- Quel âge a Jacques Dubois? Il est jeune ou il est vieux? Il habite où? Est-ce qu'il a beaucoup d'amis? Pourquoi?

- Quel âge a Paulette Gilmard? Pour vous, est-ce qu'elle est jeune ou vieille? Et pour elle? Où est-elle? Qu'est-ce qu'elle aime? Pourquoi est-elle optimiste? Est-ce que c'est normal d'être optimiste quand on est vieux? Elle est comme Jacques?

- Et vous, quel âge avez-vous? Est-ce que vous êtes en forme aujourd'hui? Est-ce que vous êtes de bonne humeur ou de mauvaise humeur aujourd'hui? Est-ce que vous êtes débrouillard(e)? Est-ce que vous êtes optimiste ou pessimiste?

- Et dans le cours de français, qui joue de la guitare? Qui aime les bandes dessinées? Qui aime les voitures?

E. Les prépositions

Paulette est loin de Jacques.

Paulette est derrière Jacques.

Paulette est près de Jacques.

Paulette est devant Jacques.

Paulette est sur le banc.

Vous permettez?

Je vous en prie!

Jacques est sur le banc à côté de Paulette.

Je n'aime pas être seule.

Moi non plus!

Les deux chiens sont sous le banc.

- Est-ce que Jacques et Paulette sont amis maintenant?
- De quelle couleur est le chien de Paulette? Et le chien de Jacques? Est-ce que les deux chiens sont amis?
- Et dans la salle de classe, qui est près de la fenêtre? Qui est près de la porte? Qui est loin du professeur? Qui est devant le professeur?

LISTENING COMPREHENSION CHECK:
Ask questions about the location of people in class (**Qui est devant Mary? derrière Jack?** etc.).

Ask students to locate themselves in reference to other people in class (**Je suis devant Mary et à côté de Jack,** etc.).

Info plus

Près de, à côté de, loin de...

These prepositions all relate to space and distance. These concepts are not neutral and our perception of distance and space is culturally conditioned. When you watch a French movie or if you observe French people interacting, note how the French tend to stand closer to one another than would be comfortable for most people raised in the United States. In fact, someone from the United States talking to a French person will often move back to regain a comfortable distance, while the French person steps closer for exactly the same reason!

Notes de vocabulaire

1. Chez. The preposition **chez** means *at the house or home of.*

Il est **chez** Marie.	*He's at Marie's (house).*
Je suis **chez** moi.	*I'm at home.*

2. De. The preposition **de** can be used to express possession, to say where someone is from, or to qualify a noun. **De** is also used as a part of longer prepositions and to express the idea of playing a musical instrument.

a. **De** + noun expresses possession. This is the equivalent of **'s** in English.

C'est le cahier **de** Michel.   *It's Michel's notebook (the notebook of Michel).*

b. **De** + indication of place expresses origin.

D'où êtes-vous?	*Where are you from?*
Je suis **de** Dallas.	*I'm from Dallas.*

c. **De** + noun acts as an adjective and qualifies a noun.

C'est le professeur **d'**anglais.   *It's the English teacher (the teacher of English).*

Où est mon livre **de** maths?   *Where is my math book?*

d. Prepositions ending in **de.** Certain prepositions end in **de.**

Il est **à côté de** la fille.   *He's next to the girl.*
Vous habitez **près de** Fort Worth?   *Do you live near Fort Worth?*
J'habite **loin de** l'université.   *I live far away from school.*

e. **Jouer de** + instrument de musique.

Tu joues **de la guitare?**   *Do you play the guitar?*

3. De + article défini. The combination **de** + **le** contracts to become **du.** The combination **de** + **les** contracts to become **des.**

3: **De** will be taught as a grammar point in the *Structure* section of *Leçon 6.*
Point out that **de** does not change in combination with **la** and **l'**.

> de + le = du
> de + les = des

C'est le chat **du** garçon.   *It's the boy's cat.*
Je joue **du** piano.   *I play the piano.*
Il est à côté **du** professeur.   *He's next to the teacher.*
Les chats n'aiment pas être près **des** chiens.   *Cats don't like to be near dogs.*

4. L'âge. Use the verb **avoir** to say how old someone is. Be sure to include the word **ans.**

Elle **a** soixante **ans.**   *She's sixty (years old).*

To ask how old someone is, use these questions:

Quel âge avez-vous?
Quel âge as-tu?

4: If desired, point out other possible ways of asking someone's age (**Tu as quel âge? Quel âge est-ce que tu as?**).

5. Habiter (à) + ville. Use **habiter** with or without the preposition **à** to say that someone lives in a city.

Éric **habite** à Lomé.   *Éric lives in Lomé.*
Vous **habitez** Genève?   *Do you live in Geneva?*

6. La place des adverbes. Adverbs are placed after the verb.

Ils parlent trop!   *They talk too much!*
Il ne pleure pas souvent.   *He doesn't cry often.*

7. Combien de. To ask how many or how much a person has of something, use one of the following:

Elle a combien de chats?
Combien de chats est-ce qu'elle a?   *How many cats does she have?*
Combien de chats a-t-elle?

7: Although **est-ce que** and intonation questions with **combien de** are rejected by many prescriptive grammars, they are common in spontaneous spoken French.

D'accord?

A. Les chiffres Read each line aloud, filling in the missing numbers.

1. 40, __ , 42, 43, __ , 45, __ , 47
2. 58, __ , __ , 61, 62, 63, __ , 65
3. 9, __ , 11, __ , __ , 14, __ , 16

4. 69, __ , 71, __ , 73, __ , __ , 76
5. 78, 79, 80, __ , 82, __ , __ , 85
6. 89, __ , __ , 92, 93, __ , 95

B. Chassez l'intrus Find the word that does not belong.

1. un bébé / un enfant / un banc / un adolescent / un adulte
2. une chambre / une école / un lycée / une université
3. bavard / amusant / sociable / timide
4. triste / optimiste / fâché / déprimé
5. actif / énergique / réservé / enthousiaste
6. mignon / gâté / sage / bien élevé
7. méchant / gentil / égoïste / pénible
8. une bande dessinée / le droit / la médecine / les langues étrangères

C. C'est comment? Choose at least two of the following qualifications for each statement: **c'est normal / c'est bizarre / c'est facile / c'est difficile / c'est amusant / c'est triste.**

Modèle étudier le français   *C'est facile et c'est amusant.*
            ne pas avoir d'ordinateur   *C'est normal mais c'est difficile.*

1. être seul à 80 ans
2. être vieux à 20 ans
3. parler espagnol
4. avoir 50 chats
5. ne pas avoir la télévision dans sa chambre
6. ne pas aimer les fleurs
7. avoir un(e) camarade de chambre quand on est un étudiant américain
8. habiter chez ses parents à 45 ans
9. être malade tout le temps
10. avoir 15 ans

D. À quel âge? Where you live, how old are people when they do the following things?

Modèle habiter seul
            À 18 ans.

1. boire du vin *(wine)*
2. sortir avec une fille/un garçon
3. voyager seul
4. avoir un permis de conduire *(driver's license)*
5. travailler dans un restaurant
6. voter
7. se marier *(get married)*
8. étudier le droit ou la médecine

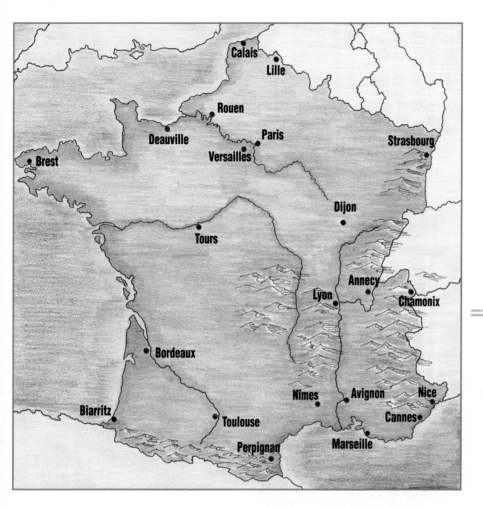

Ask students if they think of their country/state/province/town as having a geometric shape. If so, which one?
Show students the **Hexagone** on the map of France.

Info plus

L'Hexagone.
The line that joins the French cities of Brest, Calais, Strasbourg, Nice, Perpignan, and Biarritz forms a hexagon, and, in fact, France is often referred to as **l'Hexagone.** The concept of France as an ordered, geometric space with definite boundaries satisfies the French taste for a geometric ordering of space and gives a sense of natural destiny as well as a feeling of safety and protection.

E. Les villes de France C'est vrai ou c'est faux? Corrigez les phrases fausses.

Modèle   Cannes est près de Paris.
   C'est faux. Cannes est loin de Paris.

1. Nice est à côté de Cannes.
2. Nîmes est loin de Paris.
3. Rouen est loin de Paris.
4. Bordeaux est à côté de Strasbourg.
5. Avignon est à côté de Nîmes.

Act. E: CONTINUATION 1: Annecy est près de Chamonix. Lille est à côté de Toulouse. Brest est loin de Marseille. Deauville est loin de Rouen. Paris est près de Toulouse. Strasbourg est loin de Perpignan. Biarritz est près de Toulouse. CONTINUATION 2: Have students look at the world maps while you ask about countries (**La Belgique est loin de la France? Le Zaïre est près de la Suisse?** etc.).

F. Possessions Complete each dialogue with **de (d')** or **de** plus the definite article (**du, de la, de l', des**).

1. —C'est le cahier ..... Fatima?
   —Non, c'est le cahier ..... fille qui est derrière Fatima.
2. —C'est le stylo ..... Marc?
   —Non, c'est le stylo ..... professeur.
3. —C'est le livre ..... Anne?
   —Non, c'est le livre ..... étudiante qui est à côté ..... Anne.
4. —C'est la voiture ..... M. Mercier?
   —Non, c'est la voiture ..... amis ..... M. Mercier.

Mise en pratique

A. L'âge Pour vous, quel âge a quelqu'un *(someone)* qui est...

1. très jeune
2. jeune

3. adulte
4. vieux

B. L'âge et les tailles en France

Act. A: Have students work separately and then compare their answers in groups. Finish by doing a quick survey of class opinions. Ask students to give examples of people for each expression and to tell why **(Ma mère est jeune: Elle a 45 ans et elle aime le sport.)** *If desired, have students write a paragraph on the topic:* **Être jeune, c'est...** / **Être vieux, c'est...**

Plus on est jeune, plus on est grand

Taille moyenne par sexe en fonction de l'âge (en cm) :

173,4 173,0 172,0 169,8 168,8 172,0
162,0 161,0 160,0 157,8 156,3 160,0

18-24 ans 25-34 35-44 45-54 55 et + Moyenne

Renault

Robert Tournier (51 ans), Stéphane Tournier (27 ans) et Michel Tournier (49 ans)

1. Regardez les statistiques. Quelle est la différence (en centimètres) entre *(between)* un homme de 20 ans et un homme de 50 ans? Entre une femme de 18 ans et une femme de 60 ans? Pourquoi, à votre avis *(in your opinion)?* Est-ce qu'il y a les mêmes *(same)* différences entre les jeunes et les moins jeunes dans votre culture?
2. Regardez la photo. Quel âge a Robert Tournier? Et Stéphane? Et Michel? À votre avis, qui est Robert pour Stéphane? Et qui est Robert pour Michel? Est-ce que les statistiques sont vraies pour la famille Tournier?

C. Les gens et les âges
Ils ont quel âge? Ils sont comment? Qu'est-ce qu'ils aiment?

Paloma Toussaint et son grand frère François (Bruxelles, Belgique)

Madame Pinel, Madame Tournier et Monsieur Silici (Lavaur, France)

Monsieur et Madame Dumoulin (Paris, France)

Stéphanie Perrin et Khadiatou Diouf (Jardin du Luxembourg, Paris)

D. Les Américains et les Français
Voilà les idées des Américains sur les Français.

1. Devinez! *(Guess!)*
   - Une qualité, c'est positif ou négatif? Et un défaut?
   - Être entêté, c'est être...
   - Quand on est froid et distant, c'est peut-être parce qu'on est...
   - Être malhonnête, c'est ne pas être...
   - Être vieux jeu, c'est avoir des idées modernes ou traditionnelles?
2. Pour les Américains, quelles sont les trois plus grandes qualités des Français? Et les trois plus grands défauts? Est-ce qu'il y a des contradictions?
3. Et les Américains (ou les Canadiens), comment sont-ils? En groupes, faites une liste *(make a list)* par ordre d'importance des 10 qualités et des 10 défauts des Américains ou des Canadiens. Comparez avec la liste pour les Français: Est-ce qu'il y a des différences?

• QUELLES SONT LES PRINCIPALES QUALITÉS DES FRANÇAIS?		• QUELS SONT LES PRINCIPAUX DÉFAUTS DES FRANÇAIS?	
Sympathiques	38%	Bavards	21%
Intelligents	33%	Contents d'eux	20%
Travailleurs	28%	Froids, distants	16%
Accueillants	22%	Entêtés	14%
Débrouillards	19%	Hypocrites	13%
Énergiques	19%	Vieux jeu	11%
Propres	16%	Agressifs	10%
Honnêtes	16%	Menteurs	8%
Sérieux	14%	Paresseux	5%
Courageux	12%	Malhonnêtes	4%
Sans opinion	32%	Sans opinion	45%
(Réponses à l'aide d'une liste.)		(Réponses à l'aide d'une liste.)	

Figaro Magazine

TEXT TAPE:
Conversation en français

Act. E: Students may bring a picture
from a magazine if they prefer.

CD-ROM:
Build your skills!

Model pronunciation. Make sure
students notice that the stem consonant
in the plural is the same as the infinitive
consonant (dormir / dorment).

DRILL: On part demain. Nous partons
demain. (vous / tu / la famille Dubois /
Alceste et Candide / je)

DRILL: La forme négative. Make each
sentence negative. Je dors bien. Nous
sortons vendredi soir. Vous partez?
Richard dort en classe.

LISTENING DISCRIMINATION DRILL:
Singulier ou pluriel? 1. Il part
demain. 2. Elles sortent trop. 3. Elles
ne dorment pas. 4. Ils partent quand?
5. Elle part avec moi.

Point out that the imperative forms of
these verbs are identical in
pronunciation and spelling with the
indicative present forms.

E. Conversation en français Bring a picture of your mother, your father, your brother, your sister or one of your friends, and be ready to talk about him or her. Exchange photos with a partner and ask questions to find out about his or her family or friends.

Structure

▶▶ Les verbes comme *sortir*

Sortir *(to go out)* and two other common verbs, **dormir** *(to sleep)* and **partir** *(to leave)*, have identical endings in the present tense.

sortir	
je sors	nous sort**ons**
tu sors	vous sort**ez**
il elle } sort	ils elles } sort**ent**

partir		dormir	
je pars	nous part**ons**	je dors	nous dorm**ons**
tu pars	vous part**ez**	tu dors	vous dorm**ez**
il elle } part	ils elles } part**ent**	il elle } dort	ils elles } dorm**ent**

The singular forms sound identical. In the plural, the **-m-** or the **-t-** of the stem is pronounced.

il dor**t** (*-t not pronounced*)   elle sor**t** (*-t- not pronounced*)
ils dor**ment** (*-m- pronounced*)   elles sor**tent** (*-t- pronounced*)

Sortir indicates movement out of a place or going out as in going out, alone, with others, or on a date. **Partir** means simply *to leave.*

Il **sort** du bureau du professeur.   *He's coming out of the professor's office.*
Elle n'aime pas **sortir** seule.   *She doesn't like to go out alone.*
Nous **partons** demain pour   *We're leaving tomorrow for New York.*
     New York.

Here are the imperative or command forms of verbs like **sortir**.

Dors bien!   *Sleep well! (said to a person you would*
          address using **tu***)*

Partez maintenant!   *Leave now! (said to a person you would*
          address using **vous** *or to more than*
          one person)

Sortons ce soir avec Mamadou!   *Let's go out this evening with Mamadou!*

116 *Leçon 5*

Vous avez compris?

A. Des expressions Here are some expressions using **dormir, sortir,** and **partir.** Match each with its meaning.

1. Qui dort dîne.
2. partir de zéro
3. Ça sort du cœur.
4. dormir profondément
5. dormir bien/mal
6. Partir, c'est mourir un peu.
7. À vos marques! Prêts? Partez!
8. C'est parti!
9. sortir du lit
10. J'ai trop à faire, je n'en sors pas!

a. to sleep soundly
b. Sleeping is as good as eating.
c. to start from scratch
d. to sleep well/badly
e. Leaving is very difficult.
f. On your mark! Get set! Go!
g. to get out of bed
h. We're off!
i. I've got too much to do. I'll never get done!
j. That's straight from the heart.

Act. A: This activity is meant to help students internalize the meaning of these verbs. Students are not responsible for these expressions and they do not appear in the vocabulary lists. You may want to use this occasion to comment on the problems of idioms and translation between languages.

B. Complétez Complete each sentence with a form of **sortir, partir,** or **dormir.** In some cases, there may be more than one possibility.

1. Je ne ..... pas dans la classe de français.
2. Le professeur de français ..... pour Paris en juin.
3. Est-ce que vous ..... bien ici?
4. Nous ..... avec Pierre et Marie le week-end.
5. Tu ne ..... pas avec Anne demain?
6. Vous ..... pour Montréal?
7. Elle ..... avec Michel mais elle aime Pierre.
8. À demain! ..... bien!

Continuons!

A. Petit sondage Qui dans la classe...

1. dort souvent devant la télévision?
2. sort souvent le lundi soir?
3. sort toujours le week-end?
4. part souvent chez ses parents le week-end?
5. dort parfois en classe?
6. part toujours en vacances avec ses parents en été?
7. part parfois en vacances avec ses amis en été?
8. dort parfois quand il/elle regarde un match de baseball à la télé?

B. Et vous? Comment êtes-vous?

1. Quand est-ce que vous dormez beaucoup?
2. Quand est-ce que vous ne dormez pas beaucoup?
3. Quand est-ce que vous sortez beaucoup?
4. Avec qui est-ce que vous sortez?
5. En quel mois est-ce que vous partez en vacances?
6. Est-ce que vous aimez mieux étudier seul(e) ou avec un copain ou une copine?

➤ La place des adjectifs

Adjectifs qui suivent le nom

Most adjectives that are used to describe nouns follow the noun they modify.

Adjectives that change meaning according to placement are treated in the *Appendice de grammaire.*

Martine aime **la musique anglaise.**   *Martine likes English music.*
C'est **une chambre agréable.**   *It's a pleasant room.*

Adjectifs qui précèdent le nom

A small group of adjectives usually precede the noun they modify. You already know some of these. Others, as they occur, will be marked in the vocabulary list.

beau	*good-looking, beautiful*
grand	*big, tall*
gros	*big, thick, fat*
jeune	*young*
joli	*pretty*
petit	*small*
pauvre	*poor (to be pitied)*
vieux	*old*

C'est une **petite** chambre.   *It's a small room.*
La **pauvre** Monique!   *Poor Monique!*

If desired, point out the difference between **un grand homme** *(a great man)* and **un homme grand** *(a tall man);* **un pauvre étudiant** *(a "pathetic" student)* and **un étudiant pauvre** *(a "not well-off" student).* Note that a **grande maison** is a *big house.*

You may want to point out that strictly speaking, **de** (and not **des**) should be used before plural, preceding adjectives (**de beaux hommes**). However, both **de** and **des** are found. For example, **Il y a des gens qui ont des mauvais rêves** (C. Rochefort, *Le Repos du guerrier,* p. 110); **Des récents travaux en linguistique…** (L. Picabia in *Langue française,* Sept. 1971, p. 91).

See the **Instructor's Resource Manual** for more information.

Bel et vieil

The adjectives **beau** and **vieux** have alternative forms, **bel** and **vieil,** that are used before a masculine singular noun beginning with a vowel sound. They are pronounced the same as the feminine forms **belle** and **vieille.**

Minou est un **vieux** chat.   *Minou is an elderly (old) cat.*
Minou est un **vieil** animal.   *Minou is an old animal.*

Oscar est un **beau** chien.   *Oscar is a good-looking dog.*
Oscar est un **bel** animal.   *Oscar is a good-looking animal.*

Vous avez compris?

Act. A: Do this activity in three steps. (1) Read the items, asking students to express their preferences? **(Tu aimes la musique anglaise? Oui. / Non. / Ça dépend.** etc.) (2) Model the sentence pattern by telling students your preferences. **(Moi, j'aime la musique anglaise,** etc.) (3) Ask students to express their preferences.

A. Les goûts   Tell what you like and dislike. Pay attention to the agreement and placement of adjectives.

Modèle   les films (bizarre / amusant / classique / beau)
     J'aime les beaux films amusants. Je n'aime pas les films bizarres.

1. la musique (anglais / espagnol / américain / français / classique)
2. les professeurs (sympathique / raisonnable / bête / paresseux / travailleur / intelligent)
3. les chambres (vieux / joli / laid / petit / grand / clair)
4. les chiens (grand / petit / méchant / gentil)

5. les hommes (compréhensif / blond / brun / sportif / intellectuel / naïf / riche)
6. les femmes (compréhensif / blond / brun / sportif / intellectuel / naïf / riche)
7. les copains (égoïste / généreux / paresseux / sérieux / sociable / têtu / timide)
8. les voitures (grand / petit / américain / français / vieux / beau)
9. les livres (petit / gros / amusant / sérieux / classique)

B. Émile, le monstre Use adjectives to rewrite the paragraph about Émile so as to make it more descriptive. Choose from this list:

jeune / français / américain / canadien / petit / sombre / vieux / grand / sympathique / énergique / joli / clair / blond / gros / pauvre / fâché / beau / laid / travailleur

Modèle   Paul, l'ami d'Émile, est un étudiant. C'est un homme.
Paul, l'ami d'Émile, est un jeune étudiant français.
C'est un homme sympathique et travailleur.

Émile est un monstre. Il a une chambre. Il aime sa chambre parce qu'il y a une fenêtre et des rideaux. Il a une amie, Ernestine. C'est une femme. C'est une étudiante. Elle étudie l'histoire et la littérature.

Continuons!

A. La réalité Comment sont...

1. les enfants bien élevés?
2. les enfants mal élevés?
3. les adolescents de 15 ans?
4. les étudiants de l'université?
5. les professeurs de l'université?

B. Et le rêve Comment est...

1. la femme idéale?
2. l'homme idéal?
3. l'enfant idéal?

C. Et elle? Qui est-elle? Comment s'appelle-t-elle? Quel âge a-t-elle? Où est-ce qu'elle habite? Comment est-elle? Qu'est-ce qu'elle aime? Qu'est-ce qu'elle n'aime pas?

D. Le copain de Suzanne Describe Suzanne's boyfriend from the viewpoint of Suzanne, her parents, her sister (Abder's picture is at the beginning of this lesson).

Act. D: Begin by brainstorming to flesh out Abder's personality and lifestyle. Then, have students make a list of adjectives that each person (Suzanne, her parents, her sister) might use to describe Abder. Finally, students write a paragraph to describe Abder from the various viewpoints. Can be done as a group activity with different groups assigned different viewpoints from which to write.

▶▶ Les formes toniques des pronoms

Pronouns in French have separate *tonic* or stressed forms.

moi	*me, I*
toi	*you (familiar / singular)*
lui	*him, he*
elle	*her, she*
nous	*us, we*
vous	*you (formal / plural)*
eux	*them, they (all-masculine or mixed group)*
elles	*them, they (all-feminine group)*

See the **Instructor's Resource Manual** for more information.

If desired, point out that subject pronouns must always have a verb following them. They cannot stand alone.

Stressed pronouns are used in the following situations:

1. When there is no verb:

    —**Moi?**   "Me?"
    —Oui, **toi!**   "Yes, you!"
    —**Moi** aussi?   "Me too?"
    —Oui, mais pas **moi!**   "Yes, but not me!"

2. When they are the object of a preposition:

    —Il part **avec nous?**   "Is he leaving with us?"
    —Non, **avec eux.**   "No, with them."
    —Elle est **chez lui?**   "Is she at his house?"
    —Non, il est **chez elle!** "No, he's at her house!"

Point out that **ce sont** is used with **eux** and **elles** but not with **nous** and **vous**:
    —C'est vous?
    —Oui, c'est nous.
    —Ce sont eux?
    —Oui, ce sont eux.
C'est eux is also frequently used.

3. After **c'est:**

    —**C'est toi?**   "Is that you?"
    —Oui, **c'est moi.**   "Yes, it's me."

4. For emphasis:

    —**Moi,** je déteste danser.   "I hate dancing."
    —Mais tu danses bien, **toi!**   "But you dance well!"

5. After **c'est à** to indicate possession:

    —**C'est à eux?**   "Is it theirs?"
    —Non, **c'est à nous.**   "No, it's ours."
    —**C'est à qui?**   "Whose is this?"
    —**C'est à moi.**   "It's mine."

C'est à qui? can also mean *Whose turn is it?* or *Who's next?* **C'est à moi** can also mean *It's my turn* or *I'm next.*

Vous avez compris?

A. La vie de Jean Rasquin
Choose the noun that matches the stressed pronoun to find out more about the life of Jean Rasquin!

Modèle Il voyage avec lui. (son père / son père et sa mère)
son père

1. Il parle avec eux. (Cédric Rasquin / ses copains)
2. Il sort avec elle. (sa copine / Marie-France et Sonia / ses enfants)
3. Il mange chez lui. (sa mère et son père / son copain Marc)
4. Il part en vacances avec eux. (Cédric / Paul et Monique)

Act. A: This activity can be completed by focusing on grammatical information (**eux = ses copains**) or by using what students know about Jean Rasquin (**Il sort avec ses copains, oui, c'est vrai.**).

B. La vie de Jean Rasquin (suite)
Now, use stressed pronouns to say more about Jean Rasquin's life.

Modèle Il joue au tennis avec Rudolph.
Il joue au tennis avec lui.

1. Il habite avec *des amis.*
2. Il sort le week-end avec *Jérémy et Jimmy.*
3. Il écoute de la musique romantique avec *Mélanie.*
4. Il sort au restaurant avec *Mathilde et Maude.*
5. Il part aux États-Unis avec *Samantha.*

Continuons!

A. Qui... ?
Guess the preferences of your classmates. The person about whom you're talking confirms or denies your guess. Use stressed pronouns where possible.

Modèle Qui aime étudier?
—*Lui! Lui, il aime étudier!* (pointing to another student)
—*Moi? Non! Pas moi! / Moi? C'est vrai. Moi, j'aime étudier.*

1. Qui aime chanter?
2. Qui aime danser?
3. Qui étudie tout le temps?
4. Qui travaille beaucoup?
5. Qui regarde souvent la télévision?
6. Qui écoute toujours le professeur?
7. Qui parle une langue étrangère?
8. Qui aime les mathématiques?

Act. A: Encourage students to expand their questions and answers.
CONTINUATION: **Qui aime les films amusants? parler français? dormir? lire des livres sérieux? écrire des lettres? boire avec des copains? fumer?**

B. Les Dubois
Rewrite the paragraph below, replacing some (but not all) of the nouns in italics with pronouns. Use either subject pronouns (**je / tu / il / elle / on / nous / vous / ils / elles**), the pronoun **ce**, or stressed pronouns (**moi / toi / lui / elle / nous / vous / eux / elles**).

Voilà Vincent Dubois. *Vincent* est un homme sociable et *Vincent* adore sortir. *Vincent* a une femme. *Sa femme* s'appelle Thérèse. *Thérèse* n'aime pas sortir avec *Vincent.* Pourquoi est-ce que *Thérèse* n'aime pas sortir avec *Vincent?* Parce que *Vincent* adore boire, manger, parler et fumer. Et *Thérèse* aime lire et regarder des films classiques à la télé... et *Thérèse* déteste les cigarettes! Demain, *Vincent et Thérèse* partent pour New York. *Vincent* est content parce que *Vincent* adore New York. Et *Thérèse? Thérèse* est contente aussi. Pourquoi? Parce que *Thérèse* aime parler anglais et *Thérèse* adore voyager.

Act. B: Have students explain why they chose to retain certain nouns and not others.

Découvertes culturelles: L'âge et les rites de passage

▶▶ Devenir adulte

Have students use the pictures to determine the meaning of words.

A. Les difficultés des jeunes. Identifiez les cinq problèmes les plus importants des jeunes de 20 ans dans votre culture.

Modèle *Ils ont... ; ils sont... ; ils ne sont pas... ; ils n'aiment pas... ; ils aiment...*

B. Lire et apprendre.

Act. B, 1: Answers: les statistiques sur le logement: colonne 4, aussi colonnes 2 et 3; les statistiques sur le travail professionnel: la colonne 7, aussi la colonne 6; les statistiques sur les études: la colonne 1.

1. Regardez les illustrations et dites dans quelles colonnes sont:

   les statistiques sur le logement—la colonne 1 ou la colonne 4?
   les statistiques sur le travail professionnel—la colonne 7 ou la colonne 2?
   les statistiques sur les études—la colonne 1 ou la colonne 6?

2. Associez les mots suivants à leur équivalent anglais d'après les illustrations.

vit	*job*
seul	*lives*
emploi	*alone*

3. Regardez l'introduction. Quel mot français signifie:
   survey
   unemployment
   home

Act. C: Have students find and circle key words. They can then use these words for their answers.

C. Les jeunes Français. D'après ce tableau, quelles sont les grandes différences entre les années 83 et 93? Quels sont les problèmes des jeunes?

Modèle *Plus de jeunes sont... / ont... / n'ont pas...*
Moins de jeunes sont... / ont... / n'ont pas...

D. Les raisons. Trouvons les raisons de l'évolution économique. Complétez les phrases avec un des mots suivants:

âgés / parents / longtemps / active / stables / appartement / problèmes / pauvres / jobs / université

Il y a des ..... économiques maintenant et donc, il y a moins de ..... De plus, les emplois ne sont pas ..... Les jeunes vivent chez leurs ..... parce qu'ils sont trop ..... pour avoir un ..... Plus de jeunes continuent leurs études et ils entrent dans la vie ..... quand ils sont plus ..... Les études durent plus ..... et les jeunes sont à l'..... plus longtemps.

LE DIFFICILE PASSAGE À LA VIE D'ADULTE

Actuellement, il est plus difficile de trouver sa place dans la société qu'il y a vingt ans. Une enquête récente compare la situation des jeunes de 18 à 29 ans en 1975 et aujourd'hui. Prolongation des études et chômage retardent le départ du foyer familial et l'entrée dans la vie active.

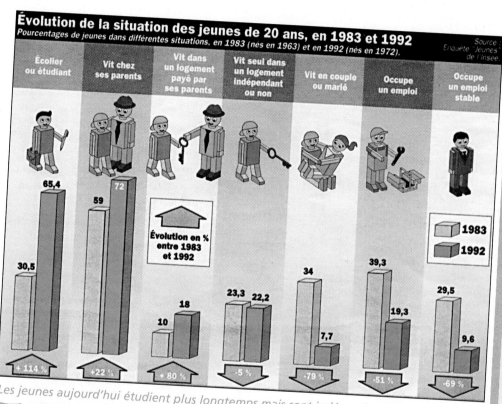

Évolution de la situation des jeunes de 20 ans, en 1983 et 1992
Pourcentages de jeunes dans différentes situations, en 1983 (nés en 1963) et en 1992 (nés en 1972).

Source : Enquête "Jeunes" de l'Insee.

Écolier ou étudiant	Vit chez ses parents	Vit dans un logement payé par ses parents	Vit seul dans un logement indépendant ou non	Vit en couple ou marié	Occupe un emploi	Occupe un emploi stable
30,5 / 65,4	59 / 72	10 / 18	23,3 / 22,2	34 / 7,7	39,3 / 19,3	29,5 / 9,6
+ 114 %	+22 %	+ 80 %	-5 %	-79 %	-51 %	-69 %

Évolution en % entre 1983 et 1992

1983 / 1992

Les jeunes aujourd'hui étudient plus longtemps mais sont indépendants plus tard.

Les Clés de l'Actualité

E. Les jeunes chez vous. Comparez la situation des jeunes chez vous avec la situation des jeunes Français.

Modèle *À 20 ans, nous sommes étudiants. Les Français aussi.*

Act. E: Have students use the text in the boxes above each category to come up with a sentence. Have students combine their sentences to write a brief paragraph.

➤ Être majeur

A. À la majorité. Quel est l'âge de la majorité chez vous? Quels sont les changements à la majorité? Dans laquelle des deux catégories—les droits ou les obligations—sont les changements que vous avez trouvés?

Modèle   *On a une voiture... On est...*

B. Les actions. Où trouver des informations sur les sujets suivants? Donnez le numéro de la section.

Modèle   voter?   *I*

- ☐ payer des impôts *(taxes)*?
- ☐ être militaire?
- ☐ partir de l'université?
- ☐ avoir un salaire?
- ☐ être jugé criminel?
- ☐ avoir un passeport?
- ☐ avoir un compte à la banque?

C. Lire et apprendre. Quels sont les mots?

1. Quand on a le droit de vote, on est... ? (paragraphe 1)
2. Quel mot est synonyme d'**habiter**? de **résidence**? (paragraphe 1)
3. Quels mots se réfèrent au mariage? à la banque? à l'armée? au travail? au logement? (paragraphe 2)
4. Quels mots se réfèrent à la justice? (paragraphe 3)

D. Vrai ou faux d'après le texte? À 18 ans en France...

	vrai	faux	
1.	☐	☐	c'est l'inscription pour le service militaire.
2.	☐	☐	les parents ont encore *(still)* le droit d'interdire le mariage.
3.	☐	☐	on a le droit de choisir où on habite.
4.	☐	☐	on a le droit de choisir son école.
5.	☐	☐	on a le droit d'arrêter l'école.
6.	☐	☐	on a le droit d'avoir un passeport.
7.	☐	☐	on a l'obligation de s'inscrire pour voter.
8.	☐	☐	les parents sont encore responsables des crimes des enfants.
9.	☐	☐	vos parents sont encore obligés de signer vos contrats.
10.	☐	☐	les parents sont toujours responsables de vos taxes et impôts.

E. Différences. Identifiez trois différences majeures entre votre culture et la culture française d'après le texte sur la majorité.

Modèle   *En France à 18 ans,... ; chez nous, à X ans,...*

F. Étude. Est-ce que c'est bien d'avoir 18 ans en France? Quels sont les avantages? les inconvénients? Quelle législation préférez-vous?

la majorité

Lorsque vous atteignez 18 ans, vous êtes majeur. Vous avez certains droits et vous êtes soumis à certaines obligations.

1. Sur le plan civique
Vous devenez électeur, sauf incapacité ou privation de vos droits. Vous devez vous faire inscrire sur les listes électorales de la mairie de la commune où vous résidez.

Vous devez également vous faire recenser à la mairie de votre domicile, en vue d'effectuer votre service national.

2. Sur le plan civil
L'autorité parentale cesse de s'exercer sur vous et vous pouvez:
— vous marier sans le consentement de vos parents;
— obtenir une carte nationale d'identité ou un passeport;
— vous inscrire dans un établissement scolaire, annuler cette inscription, choisir votre orientation;
— demander que vos notes et appréciations scolaires ne soient plus communiquées à vos parents;

— devancer l'appel pour le service national;
— signer un contrat de travail;
— percevoir votre salaire;
— ouvrir un compte bancaire ou postal et tirer des chèques;
— demander ou décliner la qualité de Français (en cas de double nationalité) ou demander votre naturalisation;
— faire partie d'une société;
— exercer un commerce;
— faire un emprunt;
— louer un appartement, une maison, etc.

3. Sur le plan pénal
Le juge ne peut plus prendre de mesures d'assistance éducative (placement dans un centre de rééducation, par exemple).

Vous êtes entièrement responsable des infractions que vous pourriez commettre.

4. Sur le plan fiscal
Lorsque vous atteignez 18 ans, vous pouvez choisir entre:
— être associé au foyer fiscal de vos parents;
— être imposé séparément (vous devez alors établir votre propre déclaration de revenus).

www explore!
http//voila.heinle.com

Orthographe et prononciation

➤➤ La liaison

La liaison (*linking*) is characteristic of spoken French. A liaison occurs when the final consonant of one word is pronounced along with the beginning vowel sound of the following word. This liaison consonant (the one pronounced) is not heard when it is followed by another consonant.

Comment‿allez-vous?
    liaison t

Comment ça va?
    silent t

Liaison consonants **-s** and **-x** are pronounced /z/.

les jeunes
    silent s

les‿écoles
    /z/

deux‿enfants
    /z/

The letter **h-** is silent, making liaison possible with the vowel that follows.

les‿hommes
/z/

deux‿hommes
/z/

Activités

A. Prononcez Repeat the following words after your instructor.

1. les affiches
2. deux adultes
3. C'est une femme.
4. Elles ont des enfants.
5. Elles sont étudiantes.
6. Nous avons des ordinateurs.

B. Trouvez les liaisons Say each pair of words aloud, then mark the liaisons.

1. trois ans; trois lits
2. les jeunes; les amis
3. des étagères; des clés
4. C'est un problème. C'est Paul.
5. Nous détestons sortir. Nous adorons jouer.
6. Ils ont des amis. Ils sont sympas.

Review liaison with numbers.

See the **Instructor's Resource Manual** for more information.

Vocabulaire de base

TEXT TAPE:
Vocabulaire de base

Les chiffres de 40 à 100 (voir page 104)
Les formes toniques des pronoms (voir page 120)

NOMS

un adulte *adult*
un an *year*
une école *school*
une guitare *guitar*
les jeunes *young people*
une jeune fille *girl (between about 15 and 25; not married)*
un lycée *high school*
une personne âgée *older person, senior citizen*
un petit ami, une petite amie *boyfriend, girlfriend*
un problème *problem*
la vie *life*
une voiture *car*

VERBES

dormir *to sleep*
habiter *to live (inhabit)*
jouer *to play*
partir *to leave*
sortir *to go out*

ADJECTIFS

âgé(e) *old, elderly*
bavard(e) *talkative*
compréhensif, compréhensive *understanding*
content(e) *glad*
débrouillard(e) *resourceful*
déprimé(e) *depressed*
difficile *difficult, hard to get along with*
égoïste *selfish*
équilibré(e) *well-adjusted*
facile *easy*
gentil, gentille *kind, nice*
jeune *(precedes noun) young*
joli(e) *(precedes noun) pretty*
méchant(e) *mean*
mignon, mignonne *cute*
normal(e) *normal*
pauvre *(precedes noun) poor, to be pitied*
riche *rich*
seul(e) *alone*
triste *sad*
vieux (vieil), vieille, vieux, vieilles *(precedes noun) old*

ADVERBES

parfois *sometimes*
souvent *often*
toujours *always*
tout le temps *all the time*

PRÉPOSITIONS

à *in, to, at*
à côté de *next to, beside*
chez *at the house of*
derrière *behind, in back of*
devant *in front of*
loin de *far from*
près de *near (to)*

DIVERS

avoir... ans *to be . . . years old*
C'est à qui? *Whose is it? Whose turn is it?*
combien de *how many, how much*
moi (toi...) aussi *me (you . . .) too, so do I (you . . .)*
moi (toi...) non plus *me (you . . .) neither, neither do I (you . . .)*
pas moi (toi...) *not me (you . . .)*
quand *when*

Vocabulaire supplémentaire

NOMS

un adolescent, une adolescente *adolescent, teenager*
un banc *bench*
une bande dessinée *comic strip, comic book*
un bébé *baby*
un/une dentiste *dentist*
un retraité, une retraitée *retired person*

Les études *studies*
le droit *law*
la géographie *geography*
l'histoire *history*
les langues étrangères *foreign languages*
la littérature *literature*
la médecine *medicine*

VERBES

partager *to share*
pleurer *to cry*

ADJECTIFS

actif, active *active*
bien élevé(e) *well-mannered*
calme *calm*
élégant(e) *elegant*

énergique *energetic*

ennuyeux, ennuyeuse *boring, annoying*

enthousiaste *enthusiastic*

fâché(e) *angry, mad, disgruntled*

gâté(e) *spoiled*

impoli(e) *impolite*

intellectuel, intellectuelle *intellectual*

mal élevé(e) *ill-mannered, rude*

marocain(e) *Moroccan*

optimiste *optimistic*

pessimiste *pessimistic*

poli(e) *polite*

réservé(e) *reserved, quiet*

sage *well-behaved*

sévère *strict*

têtu(e) *stubborn*

typique *typical*

DIVERS

être au régime *to be on a diet*

être de bonne humeur *to be in a good mood*

être de mauvaise humeur *to be in a bad mood*

être en forme *to be in shape, to feel great*

jouer de la guitare *to play the guitar*

Quel âge as-tu (avez-vous)? *How old are you?*

LE FRANÇAIS TEL QU'ON LE PARLE

alors (on joue?) *well, so (are we playing or not?)*

C'est pas marrant! *It's not funny! That's no fun!*

Hé! *Hey!*

je vous en prie *please do, of course (formal)*

Soyez sages! *Behave! Be good!*

Vous permettez? *May I? (formal)*

LE FRANÇAIS FAMILIER

une bagnole = une voiture

un bahut = un lycée

barbant(e) = ennuyeux, ennuyeuse

une BD = une bande dessinée

un copain, une copine = un petit ami, une petite amie *(meaning depends on context)*

fauché(e) = très pauvre

un gamin, une gamine = un(e) enfant

la géo = la géographie

un intello = un intellectuel

roupiller = dormir

ON ENTEND PARFOIS...

une blonde (Canada) = une petite amie

chéri-coco, chérie-coco (Sénégal) = petit(e) ami(e)

un chum, un tchomme (Canada) = un petit ami

être jaguar (Bénin, Togo) = être élégant

être jazz (Zaïre) = être élégant

huitante (Suisse) = quatre-vingts

jasant(e) (Canada) = bavard(e)

un (petit) mousse (Canada) = un petit garçon

niaiseux, niaiseuse (Canada) = pas très débrouillard, un peu bête

nonante (Suisse, Belgique) = quatre-vingt-dix

septante (Suisse, Belgique) = soixante-dix

L'espace et le temps

En bref

Dans cette leçon...

- L'heure (dire, donner l'heure)
- Ville et campagne; mer et montagne
- Avoir froid, chaud et sommeil
- Destinations et activités: le verbe **aller** et les prépositions **à** et **de**
- Obtenir des renseignements, poser des questions
- Le temps des Français actifs
- Un site historique: Versailles

In this lesson...

- Telling time
- City and country; sea and mountains
- Cold? hot? sleepy?
- Places to go and things to do: the verb **aller** *(to go)* and the prepositions **à** and **de**
- Getting information
- How the French spend time
- An historical site: Versailles

www explore!
http://voila.heinle.com

Develop writing skills with Système-D software!

Practice listening and pronunciation skills with the Text Tape!

Discover the Francophone world!

Build your skills!

INTERNET

SYSTÈME-D

TEXT TAPE

VIDEO TAPE

CD-ROM

Students have an open-ended writing activity in the **Cahier** suitable for use with **Système-D**.

Entrée en matière: Un espace historique

Une brochure. Versailles au Temps des Rois, c'est un concert? un spectacle? une visite? une promenade?

Les jours et les mois. Complétez avec les informations de la brochure.

Jours	
Saison(s)	
Mois	

Le prix. C'est combien pour visiter le parc? Pour tous *(for everybody)?* Qui est avantagé? Pourquoi?

Les spectacles. Combien de fêtes est-ce que la brochure annonce? Lesquelles *(which ones)*? Quand?

Les Grandes Nuits Vénitiennes au Temps des Rois

Où sont-elles? Est-ce que les personnes qui participent à la fête sont de France ou d'Italie? (D'où, en France ou en Italie?) Combien de spectacles est-ce qu'il y a pour Les Grandes Nuits Vénitiennes? Pourquoi est-ce qu'on appelle cette fête Les Grandes Nuits Vénitiennes?

Spectacle Théâtral

Qu'est-ce que c'est—un film? une pièce de théâtre *(play)*? un concert? un spectacle sons et lumières *(sound and light show)*? Quel est le sujet du spectacle? Qu'est-ce qu'il y a dans ce spectacle? Quelle est la date de cette fête? Où est-ce? Quelle musique est-ce qu'on joue pendant cette fête?

Promenades en gondoles

Quel type de promenades est-ce qu'il y a pendant les fêtes de Versailles? Quels jours? Combien de jours? En quelle saison? C'est comment, les promenades en gondoles?

VERSAILLES

OFFICE DE TOURISME DE VERSAILLES

Versailles.
Situated near Paris, Versailles is a famous palace built in the 17th century.

VERSAILLES AU TEMPS DES ROIS

SONS ET LUMIÈRE
ÉTÉ – AUTOMNE

FEU D'ARTIFICE ROYAL ET
GRANDE FÊTE DE NUIT AU BASSIN DE NEPTUNE
Tous les dimanches de juin à août après 22 heures

Droit de visite: Adultes: 17 F
Enfants de moins de 12 ans: 8 F
Familles nombreuses: 11 F

Pour revivre la majestueuse grandeur du Roi soleil

Autour des grands bassins de Neptune et d'Apollon
Dans le cadre historique de Versailles
LES GRANDES NUITS VÉNITIENNES
Vendredi 8, Samedi 9
et Samedi 16 Septembre à 21 heures 30

SPECTACLE THÉÂTRAL
illustré de textes historiques
et accompagné de Musique d'époque
7 et 21 Juillet à 22 heures

Sur le Grand Canal de Versailles
PROMENADES EN GONDOLES
Avec les gondoliers de Venise
**Du Samedi 5 Septembre au Dimanche 20 Septembre
de 11 heures à 17 heures**

INFORMATIONS ET RÉALISATION:
L'ASSOCIATION DE PROTECTION DES MONUMENTS HISTORIQUES
19, boulevard des Réservoirs Versailles

Hours may be expressed in numbers rather than written out: **Il termine à 3 heures.**

See the **Instructor's Resource Manual** for more information.

TRANSPARENCIES: 6-1, 6-2

L'heure

A. Les heures et les villes

à New York?
Il est huit heures du matin.

à Chicago?
Il est sept heures du matin.

à Denver?
Il est six heures du matin.

J'ai trouvé!

à San Francisco?
Il est cinq heures du matin.

à Paris?
Il est deux heures de l'après-midi.

à Moscou?
Il est quatre heures de l'après-midi.

"J'ai trouvé" is introduced here as a lexical item. Other regular, frequent verbs in the past will be introduced as lexical items in *Leçon 8* (j'ai gagné, j'ai rencontré) before the past is introduced as a *Structure* item in *Leçons 10, 11,* and *12.*

Info plus

L'heure d'été.
Daylight savings time **(l'heure d'été)** in France begins on the last Sunday in March and ends on the last Sunday in October. Current plans call for the possible phasing out of **l'heure d'été** in 1998.

à Tokyo?
Il est dix heures du soir.

à Sydney?
Il est onze heures du soir.

- Il est huit heures du matin et on mange à New York. Mais à Denver, il est six heures du matin et on dort. Est-ce qu'on dort à Paris à deux heures de l'après-midi? Est-ce que les enfants travaillent à Moscou à quatre heures de l'après-midi? Quelle heure est-il à Tokyo? C'est le jour ou la nuit? Et à Sydney?
- Cherchez: On mange à New York et aussi dans quelle ville? On dort à Denver et aussi dans quelle ville? On travaille à Paris et aussi dans quelle ville?
- Pour chaque (each) ville, quelle est la saison de l'année? C'est pendant la semaine ou pendant le week-end?

B. Quelle heure est-il?

Il est une heure.

Il est une heure cinq.

Il est une heure et quart.

Il est une heure vingt.

Il est une heure et demie.

Il est deux heures moins le quart.

Il est deux heures moins trois.

Il est deux heures.

Info plus

Les vingt-quatre heures.

In much of the world, including many French-speaking countries, official time schedules are based on a 24-hour rather than a 12-hour clock.

24-HOUR CLOCK	12-HOUR CLOCK
12 h 00	12 h (midi)
15 h 30	3 h 30 (de l'après-midi)
17 h 45	5 h 45 (de l'après-midi)
19 h 00	7 h (de l'après-midi)

When using the 24-hour clock, the expressions **et quart, et demie,** and **moins le quart** are not used.

20 h 15	vingt heures quinze
21 h 30	vingt et une heures trente
22 h 45	vingt-deux heures quarante-cinq
23 h 00	vingt-trois heures

Ask students where they hear expressions like "eighteen hundred hours."

Because of the influence of digital clocks, you will hear **une heure quarante-cinq** as well as **deux heures moins le quart.**

C. Midi ou minuit?

Il est minuit à Paris.

Il est midi à Caen.

- C'est quel jour aujourd'hui? Et quelle est la date? Quelle heure est-il maintenant? Et quelle heure est-il à Los Angeles? Et à Montréal (c'est comme à New York)? Et à Bruxelles (c'est comme à Paris)? Et à Tokyo? À Sydney maintenant, c'est aujourd'hui ou demain? Téléphoner à Paris maintenant, c'est un problème? Pourquoi ? Et téléphoner à Sydney?

Info plus

L'heure, c'est l'heure!

Just as space is perceived and used in different ways in different cultures, so is time. In North American culture, promptness is usually seen as a virtue. In France, however, this is not necessarily the case. The French instead obey their own set of culturally determined rules. Hosts, for example, do not expect their guests to arrive any earlier than 15 to 30 minutes after the given time, and guests would never think of arriving any earlier. However, arriving more than 30 minutes late is considered "being late" and requires an excuse. Appointments, on the other hand, require promptness. If you are to meet someone in his or her office at 3:00, you should be there at 3:00.

- Et vous? À quelle heure est-ce que vous commencez le cours de français? À quelle heure est-ce que vous terminez le cours de français? À quelle heure est-ce que vous mangez le matin? et le soir?

Où?

A. En ville

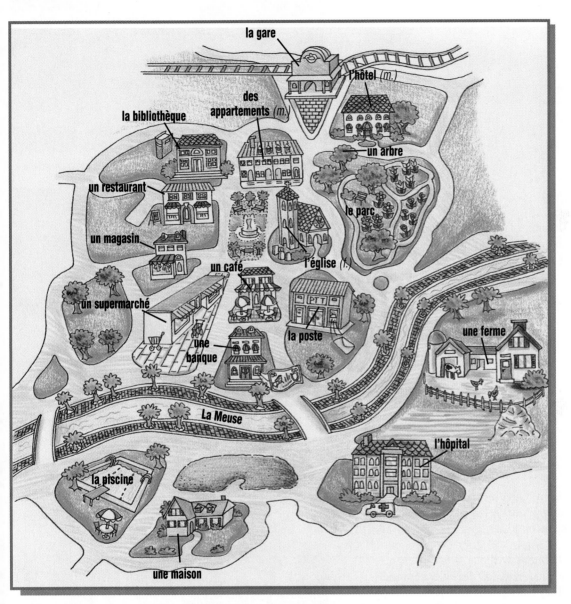

Voilà Cinet, une petite ville française. À Cinet, il y a des maisons, des appartements, une gare, une église, un parc, un supermarché, un hôpital, une piscine, des magasins, des banques, un hôtel, des restaurants, des cafés, une poste et une bibliothèque.

- Est-ce que l'église est près du café? Est-ce que la poste est à côté de la bibliothèque? Est-ce que le parc est loin de l'hôpital?

B. À la campagne

- Dans le village, est-ce qu'il y a une église? un supermarché? des appartements? des fermes? De quelles couleurs sont les vaches?

TRANSPARENCY:
6-5

Sur la photo, il y a un champ avec des vaches. Il y a aussi un village.

C. À la montagne

- Est-ce que vous aimez la neige à la montagne? et en ville? Est-ce qu'on skie sur la photo? Pourquoi ou pourquoi pas?

À la montagne, il y a... des montagnes! Sur la photo, il y a aussi un lac mais il n'y a pas beaucoup de neige parce que c'est l'été.

D. À la mer

- C'est quelle saison? Quel mois, peut-être? Est-ce qu'on nage sur la photo? À la plage, qu'est-ce qu'on regarde? Est-ce qu'on joue?

- Et vous, vous habitez en ville ou à la campagne? Qu'est-ce qu'il y a chez vous (des églises? la mer?...)? Qu'est-ce qu'il n'y a pas chez vous?

- Vous préférez la mer ou la montagne? Quel est votre endroit préféré pour un pique-nique? pour les vacances? pour habiter et travailler? pour être retraité?

À la mer, il y a... la mer! Sur la photo, il y a aussi une plage et des bateaux. Aujourd'hui, le ciel est bleu et le soleil brille. C'est une belle journée.

Expressions avec *avoir*

Alceste a froid.   Candide a chaud.   Alceste et Candide ont sommeil.

- Et vous? Est-ce que vous avez froid à la piscine en été? et au printemps? Est-ce que vous avez chaud quand vous jouez dans la neige en hiver? Est-ce que vous avez sommeil à huit heures du matin? et à onze heures du soir?

Notes de vocabulaire

1. Mots et expressions utiles. Here are some useful words and expressions.

une cité universitaire	*dormitory*
un laboratoire	*laboratory*
s'il te plaît	*please (familiar)*
trouver	*to find*
vous avez l'heure?	*do you have the time?*

2. Préférer. The verb **préférer** is a spelling-change verb. The **accent aigu** over the second **-e-** becomes an **accent grave** in all singular forms and the third person plural.

je préfère	nous préférons
tu préfères	vous préférez
il } elle } préfère	ils } elles } préfèrent

Other verbs that have the same spelling changes as **préférer** will be marked in the vocabulary lists.

3. Commencer. In order to retain the soft /s/ sound in the verb **commencer,** a cedilla is added to the **-c-** before the ending **-ons.**

je commence	nous commençons

4: If desired, point out that prepositions are notoriously treacherous items for second language learners. Give a few examples: **sur la photo** *(in the picture);* **à la télévision** *(on television);* **sous la pluie** *(in the rain),* etc.

See the **Instructor's Resource Manual** for more information.

4. Dans / en.

The English preposition *in* can be translated in French by either **dans** or **en,** depending on the context. In general, **dans** is used when it means or implies *within or inside of* (**dans la chambre),** while **en** is used in fixed expressions where there is no article (**en ville).**

The English prepositions *to* and *at* can usually be translated by the French preposition **à** (**à la plage).** In certain fixed expressions, however, **en** (with no article) is used (**en classe).** These expressions must simply be memorized.

Here are the most common fixed expressions using **en.**

en ville	*in town, downtown*
en vacances	*on vacation*
en classe	*in class*
en juillet, **en** avril, etc.	*in July, in April, etc.*
en automne	*in autumn*
en hiver	*in winter*
en été	*in summer*

BUT:

au printemps	*in spring*

5: **Quel** is treated here as a lexical item—an adjective—rather than a grammar point.

5. Quel.

Quel means *what* or *which.* It is an adjective. **Quel** may be separated from its noun by a form of the verb **être.** Like other adjectives, its form depends on the number and gender of the noun it modifies.

C'est **quel jour?** *(masculine singular)*
Quelle est **la date** aujourd'hui? *(feminine singular)*
Vous avez q**uels disques?** *(masculine plural)*
Quelles couleurs est-ce qu'il préfère? *(feminine plural)*

Note the use of **quel** to express an exclamation.

Quel hiver!	*What a winter!*
Quelles vacances!	*What a vacation!*

6:

See the **Instructor's Resource Manual** for more information.

6. Pour préciser le temps.

Note the following:

- **Jour/journée, an/année.** The words **jour** and **an** refer to periods of time that are countable.

Il y a **sept jours** dans une semaine.	*There are seven days in a week.*
Il a **14 ans.**	*He's 14 (years old).*

Journée and **année** refer to periods of time thought of as a whole.

Voilà **la journée** de Mme Dupont.	*That's Mrs. Dupont's day.*
Quelle **année!**	*What a year!*

- **Matin/après-midi/soir.** To specify *morning, afternoon,* or *evening,* use the following expressions:

Il est quatre heures **du matin.**	*It's four in the morning.*
Il est une heure **de l'après-midi.**	*It's one in the afternoon.*
Il est dix heures **du soir.**	*It's ten in the evening (at night).*

Le lundi / lundi. **Je travaille à la bibliothèque *le* lundi** means that *I work in the library **every** Monday.*

Je travaille à la bibliothèque *lundi* means that *I am working in the library **on Monday*** *(this coming Monday only).*

7. Téléphoner à + personne. The verb **téléphoner** is followed by the preposition **à** to mean *to telephone (to call) someone.*

Il **téléphone à** Paul. *He's calling Paul.*

D'accord?

A. Classons Groupez en catégories différentes et comparez vos catégories et les catégories de vos camarades.

Act. A: Can be group work.

ciel / supermarché / lac / vacances / lycée / lundi / mois / laboratoire / octobre / magasin / poste / juillet / dormir / nager / mer / matin / plage / ville / février / froid / café / chaud / affiche / camarade de chambre / skier / habiter / mars / mercredi / soir / minuit / parc / pique-nique / fête / hiver / mai / décembre / dimanche / heure / hôtel / jour / campagne / cours / gare / ferme

B. Chassez l'intrus Trouvez le mot qui ne va pas avec les autres mots.

1. université / maison / cours / bibliothèque / cité universitaire
2. vache / ville / village / campagne / champ
3. plage / mer / août / nager / froid
4. école / examen / cahier / juillet / laboratoire
5. café / restaurant / hôtel / supermarché / ciel
6. neige / noir / hiver / skier / montagne
7. poste / mer / hôtel / magasin / banque / gare

C. À votre avis C'est normal, c'est bizarre, ça dépend?

1. être à l'église le dimanche
2. avoir un cours de français le dimanche
3. être au théâtre le lundi matin
4. être en classe le mercredi
5. trouver des enfants à la piscine à deux heures du matin
6. être à la banque le vendredi
7. être à la poste le dimanche
8. sortir le samedi soir
9. avoir froid l'été

Act. C: CONTINUATION (can be done as listening comprehension): **avoir sommeil en classe / être à l'université en été / être en vacances en automne / avoir un lit dans une chambre / être fatigué le matin / être sportif et intellectuel / avoir des problèmes à l'université / commencer à étudier à minuit / trouver des étudiants à la bibliothèque**
Ask students to make up additional **c'est normal/c'est bizarre** situations.

D. À quelle heure? Donnez l'heure de ces activités.

1. Je mange . . . . .
2. La nuit, je dors de . . . . . à . . . . .
3. Le soir, j'étudie de . . . . . à . . . . .
4. Je suis de mauvaise humeur . . . . .
5. Je suis de bonne humeur . . . . .
6. Je pars le matin à . . . . .

E. Les sensations Quelles sont vos réactions dans les situations suivantes? Vous avez froid? chaud? sommeil?

Modèle Vous êtes au Pôle Nord.
J'ai froid.

1. Il est deux heures du matin et vous étudiez.
2. Aujourd'hui, la température est de −30 degrés.
3. Vous êtes à Miami en juillet.
4. Vous êtes à une fête très ennuyeuse et il est trois heures du matin.
5. Vous nagez dans un lac en Alaska.

F. Jour, mois, saison... Classez les jours, les semaines, et les saisons selon *(according to)* les critères suivants: travail / froid / chaud / vacances / agréable / pénible.

Act. F: Ask students to propose additional criteria and to justify their classifications (e.g., **Juillet et août sont des mois agréables parce que c'est l'été et on est en vacances**)

Possible questions to ask about days, months, and seasons: **Quel(s) jour(s) de la semaine est-ce que vous préférez? détestez? Quel(s) mois est-ce que vous préférez? détestez? Quels sont les jours de classe? les jours du week-end? Pendant quelle(s) saison(s) est-ce que vous avez froid? chaud? Quels sont les mois de vacances? de l'hiver? de l'été? de l'automne? du printemps?**

En quel mois ou quelle saison est **Noël? Pâques? la Toussaint? la fête nationale française? la fête nationale américaine? la fête des mères? la fête du travail en France? la fête du travail chez vous? le jour de l'an? votre anniversaire? Le Ramadan, c'est en quelle saison? (en hiver) C'est quand le Yom Kippour? (en automne)** See *Magazine 1* for more information on holidays and important dates in the Francophone world. A list of holidays is in the *Vocabulaire facultatif* for this lesson.

Mise en pratique

A. Et vous?

1. À quelle heure est-ce que vous commencez à étudier le soir?
2. Dans votre université, où est-ce qu'on trouve des professeurs? Où est-ce qu'on ne trouve pas de professeurs?
3. À quel âge est-ce qu'on commence l'école? le lycée? l'université? des études de médecine?
4. À quel âge est-ce qu'on commence à travailler?
5. Où est-ce qu'on trouve un livre? des clés? une chambre? une affiche? un cadeau?

À quelle heure commencent les visites de la basilique le matin?

B. Horaires d'ouverture Regardez la photo.

Quel jour est-ce que Claude Fabri ne travaille pas?
Quels jours est-ce que Claude Fabri ne travaille pas
l'après-midi? Que fait-il/elle le dimanche, à votre avis
(in your opinion)? et le samedi après midi? Et où est
cette personne le mardi après-midi, peut-être? À quelle
heure est-ce qu'il/elle mange? De quelle heure à quelle
heure est-ce qu'il/elle travaille? Quelle est sa
profession, à votre avis (dentiste / docteur /
psychologue / professeur / électricien / plombier)?
Quelles sont les heures de travail en France d'après
(according to) la photo? Maintenant, comparez avec les
heures de travail chez vous. Est-ce qu'on travaille plus
ou moins chez vous?

Et chez vous, de quelle heure à quelle heure est-ce
qu'on mange à midi? Et le soir, à quelle heure est-ce
qu'on mange?

Info plus

Horaires d'ouverture.

In France, many offices, stores, and schools are
closed between noon and 2 o'clock during the
week to give people time to go home for
lunch. In some parts of France, stores reopen
at 3 or 4 o'clock. The usual closing time is
between 6 and 7 or even 8. Although these
customs are changing in the larger French
cities, a long lunch hour and a late dinner hour
are still quite important to most French people.

C. Leur week-end, votre week-end! Voilà les moments préférés des Français le
week-end.

> 39% des Français préfèrent le dimanche après-midi; 32% préfèrent le
> samedi soir; 27% préfèrent le dimanche à midi; 24% préfèrent le
> dimanche matin; 21% préfèrent le samedi après-midi; 14% préfèrent le
> vendredi soir; 11% préfèrent le dimanche soir; 8% préfèrent le samedi
> matin; 4% préfèrent le samedi à midi.

Gérard Mermet, *Francoscopie 1995*

Quels sont les trois moments préférés des Français? Pourquoi, à votre avis? (ils
aiment dormir, jouer, etc.) Et quels sont les trois moments qu'ils n'aiment pas
beaucoup? Pourquoi? (ils n'aiment pas travailler, etc.)

Et chez vous? Quels sont les moments préférés du week-end dans votre culture?
Est-ce que ce sont les mêmes *(same)* moments que les Français? Pourquoi ou
pourquoi pas?

Modèle   *Chez nous, on préfère… parce qu'on aime…*

D. L'emploi du temps de Laure Laure a quatorze ans et elle est en quatrième *(eighth grade)*. Voilà son emploi du temps.

Classe de 4e:

jours / horaires	lundi	mardi	mercredi	jeudi	vendredi
8h à 9h	musique	espagnol	espagnol		anglais
9h à 10h	espagnol	sport	français	français	sciences physiques
10h à 11h	maths	sport	français	espagnol	maths
11h à 12h	français 12h 30	anglais	anglais	sciences physiques	sciences naturelles 12h 30
repas				13h 15	
13h45 à 14h45	permanence	assistante d'espagnol	Pas de cours	hist.-géo.	espagnol
14h45 à 15h45	technologie	hist.-géo.		maths	hist.-géo.
15h45 à 16h45	technologie	maths		sport	dessin

Laure Cunill, Orléans, France

1. **L'horaire.** Combien d'heures de cours a Laure par jour? C'est beaucoup? À quelle heure commencent les cours le matin? Jusqu'à *(until)* quelle heure? À quelle heure commencent les cours l'après-midi? À quelle heure est-ce Laure termine sa journée? Et le mercredi?

2. **Les cours.**
   - Est-ce que Laure a les mêmes *(same)* cours tous les jours *(every day)*?
   - Combien d'heures de français est-ce qu'elle a? de mathématiques? de sciences?
   - Combien de langues étrangères est-ce que Laure étudie? Combien d'heures par semaine a-t-elle pour chaque *(each)* langue? À quelle heure?
   - Est-ce qu'elle a des cours d'art? Combien d'heures par semaine?
   - Est-ce que le sport est très important dans son école?
   - À votre avis *(in your opinion)*, qu'est-ce qu'elle étudie en technologie? en histoire-géo?
   - Qu'est-ce que c'est, une permanence? une assistante d'espagnol?

3. **Les préférences.** Vous êtes Laure: quel(s) jour(s) préférez-vous? Quel(s) jour(s) n'aimez-vous pas? Pourquoi?

4. **Et chez vous?** Comparez avec les écoles dans votre culture: quelles sont les grandes différences entre les deux systèmes?

E. Endroits de vacances, endroits de rêve... Look at the pictures. What can you say about each place?

Guadeloupe

Bruxelles, Belgique

Québec, Canada

1. Quelle est la saison? Qu'est-ce qu'il y a sur les photos? Qu'est-ce qu'il n'y a pas?
2. Pour des vacances, vous préférez Bruxelles, la Guadeloupe ou le Québec? Pourquoi?

CD-ROM:
Build your skills!

Structure

➤➤ Le verbe *aller*

The verb **aller** (*to go*) is irregular.

je **vais**	nous **allons**
tu **vas**	vous **allez**
il } elle } **va**	ils } elles } **vont**

Aller can be followed by an infinitive to indicate future time or to express intention.

Nous **allons étudier**.　　　　　　*We're going to study.*

In the negative, **ne... pas** is placed around the conjugated form of **aller**.

Elle **ne va pas** aller à la plage.　　*She's not going to go to the beach.*

Rappel!　　**Aller** is also used to say how you are or to ask how someone else is.

—Comment **allez**-vous?　　　*"How are you?"*
—Je **vais** bien, merci.　　　*"I'm fine, thanks."*
—Ça **va?**　　　　　　　　*"How's it going?"*
—Oui, ça **va.**　　　　　　*"OK."*

The imperative or command forms of **aller** are **va, allons,** and **allez.**

Va dans ta chambre!　　　　　　*Go to your room!*
Allons manger!　　　　　　　　*Let's go eat!*
Allez étudier à la bibliothèque!　*Go study in the library!*

Here are some useful expressions with **aller.**

—On y **va?**　　　　　　　*"Shall we go?"*
—Oui, on y **va.**　　　　　*"Yes, let's go."*
—**Allons**-y!　　　　　　　*"Let's go!"*
—**J'y vais.**　　　　　　　*"I'm going, I'm leaving"*
—**Vas**-y (**Allez**-y).　　　*"Go on, go ahead."*
—**Allez!** Au revoir!　　　*"OK! Good-bye!"*

DRILL: Candide *va* à la bibliothèque (tu / nous / Alceste et Candide / je / vous).

DRILL: Give the negative. **Candide va à la mer. Alceste va à la plage. Nous allons à la banque. Tu vas en ville. Les étudiants vont à la cité universitaire. Vous allez à la campagne.**

Model these expressions for students. Explain that in French, you have to go "someplace" and that the **y** represents *there*. Point out the idiomatic use of **Allez!** as a conversation marker. If desired, ask students if they know another expression with an **y** in it (**il y a**).

144　　*Leçon 6*

Vous avez compris?

A. On y va! Use the suggestions to say where each person is going. Then evaluate each destination, from your own point of view, by using one of the following:

> c'est / ce n'est pas amusant
> c'est / ce n'est pas agréable
> c'est pénible
> c'est / ce n'est pas raisonnable
> c'est / ce n'est pas normal
> c'est / ce n'est pas ennuyeux

Modèle   Candide / chez les parents d'Alceste
Candide va chez les parents d'Alceste. C'est pénible!

1. Anne / à la plage
2. Tu / à l'hôtel pour le week-end
3. Nous / chez nous après l'école
4. Vous / à l'hôpital
5. Marie-Paule et Geneviève / manger en ville
6. Léon / en classe
7. Je / à Paris demain
8. On / à la bibliothèque pour étudier

B. Et demain? Some people never change. Say so following the model.

Modèle   Aujourd'hui, j'étudie et demain,...
... je vais étudier aussi.

1. Aujourd'hui, nous allons à la piscine et demain,...
2. Aujourd'hui, il téléphone à Myriam et demain,...
3. Aujourd'hui, vous avez froid et demain,...
4. Aujourd'hui, elles sont malheureuses et demain,...
5. Aujourd'hui, tu fumes et demain,...
6. Aujourd'hui, je travaille et demain,...
7. Aujourd'hui, nous sommes de mauvaise humeur et demain,...
8. Aujourd'hui, la vie est triste et demain,...

Continuons!

Projets! Make a list of five things that you are doing or not doing this year. Then make lists of five things that you are going to be doing or not going to be doing a year from now.

Projets!: Have the class compare their results and/or ask you about your plans.

Modèle   **_Maintenant: J'étudie le français, je ne joue pas au tennis,..._**

Dans un an: Je vais étudier le droit, je ne vais pas étudier l'espagnol...

➤➤ Les prépositions *à* et *de* et l'article défini

The prepositions **à** and **de** combine with two forms of the definite article, **le** and **les,** to form contractions. They do not contract with **la** or **l'** or when no definite article is present.

Students have already seen the contractions **du** and **des** in *Leçon 5.*

Remind students about **de** + proper noun (no article): **C'est le livre** *de* M. Bertrand. **C'est le livre** *du* professeur.

See the **Instructor's Resource Manual** for more information.

$$\boxed{\textbf{à + le = au}}$$

Il va **au** restaurant.   *He's going to the restaurant.*

$$\boxed{\textbf{de + le = du}}$$

C'est le livre **du** professeur.   *It's the teacher's book.*

$$\boxed{\textbf{à + les = aux}}$$

Elle parle **aux** plantes!   *She talks to plants!*

$$\boxed{\textbf{de + les = des}}$$

Où est la photo **des** professeurs   *Where's the picture of the English*
d'anglais?   *teachers?*

Note the pronunciation of **aux** and **des** when followed by a vowel sound.

Il va parler **aux‿e**nfants.   *He's going to talk to the children.*
    /z/

Voilà l'école **des‿e**nfants de Marie.   *There's Marie's children's school.*
    /z/

Rappel! Do not confuse the plural indefinite article **des** with the contraction of the preposition **de + les = des.** Although they are identical in spelling, they function very differently.

- **des** = plural, indefinite article

    Il y a **des** affiches sur le mur.   *There are some posters on the wall.*

- **des** = de + les

    Le professeur est à côté **des**   *The teacher is next to the students.*
    étudiants.

Vous avez compris?

A. Endroits Où sont-ils?

Modèle *Ils sont au parc.*

Act. A: Ask additional questions about the pictures to recycle vocabulary and structure.

1.

2.

3.

4.

5.

6.

B. Mais qu'est-ce que c'est? Complete using **de** alone or **de** plus the definite article. Pay attention to gender and number.

Modèle C'est l'appartement *des* filles.

1. C'est la bibliothèque ..... université.
2. C'est le bureau ..... professeur.
3. C'est le lit ..... enfants.
4. Ce sont les murs ..... chambre.
5. C'est le lac ..... Chicago.
6. C'est le disque ..... Olivier.
7. C'est l'anniversaire ..... M. Dupont.
8. C'est la porte ..... maison.
9. Ce sont les chaises ..... église.
10. C'est le premier jour ..... vacances.

Continuons!

A. Où va Vincent Dubois? The line on the map represents Vincent Dubois' activities. Describe his movements for the day.

Act. A: Ask students to say at what time and at what moment of the day: **matin, après-midi, soir,** etc. Ask students to speculate about why Vincent Dubois goes to each place.

Modèle 1–2
*Il va de chez lui
à la banque.*

1. 2–3
2. 3–4
3. 4–5
4. 5–6
5. 6–7
6. 7–8

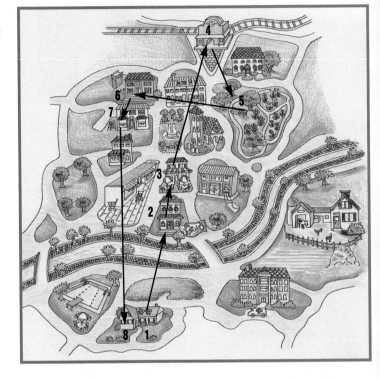

Act. B: A day in the life of Claudine (with whom Pierre has lunch on Monday) is included in the *Cahier d'activités écrites et orales.*

B. Où est-ce qu'il va? Look at Pierre's schedule and answer the questions.

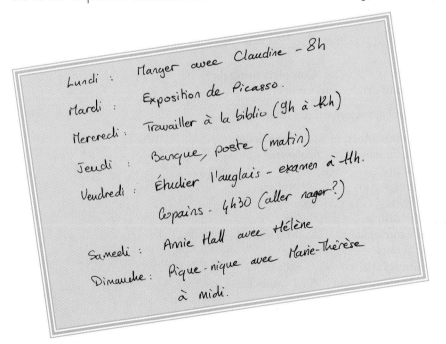

Lundi : Manger avec Claudine - 8h

Mardi : Exposition de Picasso.

Mercredi : Travailler à la biblio (9h à 11h)

Jeudi : Banque, poste (matin)

Vendredi : Étudier l'anglais - examen à 11h.

Copains - 4h30 (aller nager?)

Samedi : Amie Hall avec Hélène

Dimanche : Pique-nique avec Marie-Thérèse à midi.

1. Quel(s) jour(s) est-ce que Pierre va en ville?
2. Quel(s) jour(s) est-ce que Pierre va à l'université?
3. Quel(s) jour(s) est-ce que Pierre va sortir avec une jeune fille?
4. Où est Pierre vendredi après-midi? lundi soir? jeudi matin? dimanche matin? dimanche après-midi?
5. Comment est Pierre? (Draw as many conclusions as you can from what you know!)

C. Votre horaire
Say where you are and what you are usually doing at each of the following times.

Act. C: FOLLOW-UP: Have students say where they go on a regular basis; then ask where they're going today or after class.

Modèle   cinq heures, dimanche matin
À cinq heures, dimanche matin, je suis au lit. Je dors.

1. six heures, lundi matin
2. minuit, mercredi soir
3. onze heures, dimanche matin
4. huit heures et demie, samedi soir
5. trois heures, mardi après-midi
6. une heure, samedi matin

▶▶ Questions pour demander des renseignements

Information questions ask for information. In order to indicate what kind of information you are asking about, you need to use a question word (*how, what, when, where,* etc.). Here are some information questions. Can you find the question words?

Remind students of levels of language. Ask for English question variants *(Where are you going? Where ya' goin'? You goin' where?).*

Tu es d'où?	*Where are you from?*
Où est-ce que tu vas?	*Where are you going?*
Comment est Sébastien?	*What is Sébastien like?*
Pourquoi est-ce que tu es fatigué?	*Why are you tired?*
Quand part-il?	*When is he leaving?*
Vous avez combien de chats?	*How many cats do you have?*

Information questions such as these tend to be more frequent in inverted form than with **est-ce que**. Note, however, that qu- questions are more frequent with **est-ce que** (Qu'est-ce qu'il fait?). Since **est-ce que** preserves the subject-verb relationship, students usually find it easier to manipulate. You may want to encourage initial use of **est-ce que** while providing listening and reading experience with inverted forms.

You can use intonation, **est-ce que,** or inversion to form information questions, much as you did to form yes-or-no questions. The only difference is the addition of a question word.

Intonation

The question word can appear before or after the verb.

If desired, point out to students that **pourquoi** does not act in the same way as other interrogative adverbs in that it tends to appear only initially in intonation questions. *(Pourquoi tu manges?* is fine, but the acceptability of **Tu manges** *pourquoi?* is questionable.)

Comment tu t'appelles?   Tu t'appelles **comment?**

See the **Instructor's Resource Manual** for more information.

Est-ce que

The question word is placed in front of **est-ce que.**

question word + **est-ce que** + rest of sentence

Quand est-ce que tu pars?   *When do you leave (are you leaving)?*
Comment est-ce qu'on va à la   *How do you get to (go to) the library?*
   bibliothèque?

Inversion

The question word is placed at the beginning of the sentence.

Qui as subject is treated in a *Note de vocabulaire* in *Leçon 7*. Questions with both **qui** and **que** are treated in *Leçon 8.*

D'où est-elle?   *Where is she from?*
Quand pars-tu?   *When are you leaving (do you leave)?*
Comment va-t-on à la bibliothèque?   *How do you get to (go to) the library?*

Vous avez compris?

Act. A: Have students explain how they identified the interrogative portions of each exchange. If desired, discuss degrees of formality.

A. Pour poser une question... Find the question part of each exchange. How did you recognize it?

1. —Bonjour, Monsieur.
   —Bonjour, Aline. Comment allez-vous?
   —Bien merci, et vous?
2. —Pardon, Madame. Où est la poste, s'il vous plaît?
   —À côté de la banque, là.
   —Merci, Madame.
3. —Abder, c'est où la poste?
   —La poste? À côté de la banque, non?
   —OK, merci.
4. —Quand est-ce que tu pars?
   —Demain, toi aussi?
   —Non, non, aujourd'hui.

B. Posez des questions What would you say in French to find out the following?

Modèle   where the person you're talking to is going now
        Où est-ce que tu vas (vous allez) maintenant?

1. why the person you're talking to likes to watch television
2. when Martine and Jean-Pierre are leaving for New York
3. how many students there are in class
4. where Mme Mercier lives
5. when Alceste is leaving on vacation
6. how to get to the library

Continuons!

A. *Et des questions!* Ask as many questions as you can about the photograph.

B. *C'est vous le professeur!* Read the paragraph. What questions can you ask about it? See if your instructor or your classmates can answer your questions without looking at the text.

Alain et Annette habitent à la campagne, dans une petite maison très agréable. Alain a trente ans; il est grand, mince et blond. Annette est plus jeune. Petite et blonde, elle a vingt-six ans. Ils ont deux enfants (Adrien et Jean-Philippe), deux chiens (Olaf et Sacha) et un chat (Ouistiti). Alain est professeur dans un lycée en ville. Le matin, il part à six heures et demie parce que le lycée est loin de la maison. Les enfants ne sont pas toujours faciles et Alain est souvent fatigué le soir. Annette parle anglais et elle travaille avec des Américains. Le week-end, ils aiment rester chez eux. Ils mangent souvent avec des amis le samedi soir et ils adorent dormir tard *(late)* le dimanche matin. Mais c'est difficile parce que les enfants aiment jouer et ils ne sont pas calmes! Alain et Annette ne sont pas très riches, mais ils sont heureux parce qu'ils aiment la campagne, les enfants et les animaux!

C. *Emploi du temps* Take a moment to think about your weekly schedule. Then use these questions to find out about the weekly schedules of people in your class.

1. Combien d'heures de cours avez-vous?
2. Combien d'heures de laboratoire avez-vous?
3. Combien d'heures de sciences avez-vous? d'anglais? de français?
4. À quelle heure est-ce que vous allez au restaurant universitaire? à la bibliothèque? au cours le matin?
5. Où est-ce que vous êtes à 7 h du matin? à 3 h de l'après-midi? à 5 h du soir? à 10 h du soir? à minuit?
6. Quel jour est-ce que vous préférez? Quel jour est-ce que vous détestez? Pourquoi?
7. Quelle heure est-ce que vous préférez? Quelle heure est-ce que vous détestez? Pourquoi?

Act. C: Ask students to set up an ideal schedule. Have students ask you questions to determine your schedule.

D. *Conversation en français* You need to make an appointment to talk to your French teacher about some homework that you don't understand. Imagine a conversation where the two of you set up a time to meet.

TEXT TAPE:
Conversation en français

L'espace et le temps   **151**

Découvertes culturelles: Le temps des Français actifs

▶ Les activités de la journée

Act. A: Have students first look at the pictures and describe the people and what they are doing.

Suggest professions that are cognates: **docteur, dentiste, professeur, acteur,** etc. Have students draw up a fairly detailed **emploi du temps** as they conceive of it but focus on duration rather than on events. **De minuit à 6 heures: dormir,** etc. This will help avoid the need for verbs like **se réveiller,** etc.

Act. B: Use to recycle previous vocabulary. **Temps physiologique: on dort, on mange,** etc. Expand with questions such as: **À quelle heure? Quand? Pendant combien de temps? Qui, les hommes ou les femmes? Où, chez lui/elle ou au bureau? Quel jour? Quel mois?**

Act. C: Students will have to infer. Remind students of the expressions **moins de...** and **plus de...**

Act. D: Help students vary their questions: **Combien d'heures par jour? Quel jour de la semaine? Est-ce que vous travaillez le... ?** If time permits, have students do a survey in the class and compare their results to those given for the French.

A. Les horaires professionnels. Choisissez une profession dans votre culture et donnez l'emploi du temps de cette personne.

B. Qu'est-ce qu'ils font? Pour chaque catégorie, dites les activités des citadins actifs.

temps physiologique: on/ils...	
temps domestique: on/ils...	
temps libre: on/ils...	
temps professionnel: on/ils...	

C. Comparaisons. Comparez les emplois du temps des hommes et des femmes et expliquez les différences.

Modèle *Les femmes ont moins de temps libre que les hommes. C'est parce qu'elles...*

D. Questions d'enquête. Pour chaque catégorie de l'enquête *(survey)*, trouvez les questions de l'enquêteur.

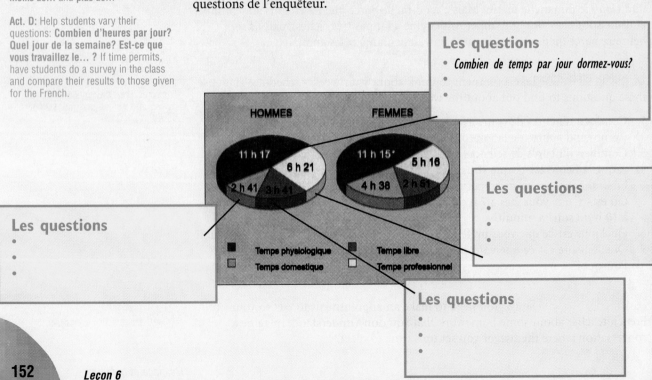

Les questions
- *Combien de temps par jour dormez-vous?*
-
-

Les questions
-
-
-

Les questions
-
-
-

Les questions
-
-
-

HOMMES FEMMES

11 h 17 6 h 21 11 h 15* 5 h 16

2 h 41 3 h 41 4 h 38 2 h 51

■ Temps physiologique ■ Temps libre
□ Temps domestique □ Temps professionnel

La journée des citadins actifs

Hommes et femmes de 18 à 64 ans:

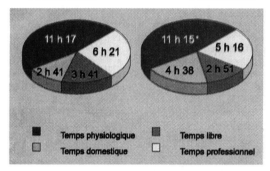

HOMMES   **FEMMES**

HOMMES: 11 h 17, 6 h 21, 2 h 41, 3 h 41

FEMMES: 11 h 15', 5 h 16, 4 h 38, 2 h 51

■ Temps physiologique   ■ Temps libre
□ Temps domestique   □ Temps professionnel

**Temps exprimés en heures et minutes.
Ces chiffres sont des moyennes incluant les
samedis et les dimanches.**

E. L'horaire des actifs. Choisissez un(e) Français(e) actif (active) et décidez: C'est un homme ou une femme? Quel âge a-t-il/elle? Il/elle est marié(e) ou non? Quelle est sa profession? Quel est son emploi du temps? (Choisissez un jour de la semaine précis et donnez les activités de sa journée en détails.)

Act. E: Refer students to other cultural information from documents and *Info plus* in previous chapters (leisure activities, eating habits etc.).

F. Votre horaire actif. Faites la liste de vos activités personnelles et évaluez leur durée. Préparez un cercle et comparez votre cercle à celui des Français. Quelles sont les différences?

⏩ Les loisirs des Français

A. Vos vacances préférées. Décrivez une journée de vacances idéale pour vous du matin au soir. Où êtes-vous? Où allez-vous?

B. Observation.

Act. B, 1: Ask students to determine their age, profession, personality, how they feel etc. Use also to review prepositions: **derrière, devant,** etc.)

1. **Les personnes.** Décrivez les personnes sur cette photo.
2. **L'environnement.** Où sont-ils? C'est quelle saison? Quel mois? Quel jour? Quel temps fait-il? Est-ce qu'ils ont froid ou chaud? Pourquoi? Qu'est-ce qu'il y a derrière eux? Qu'est-ce qu'ils font *(What are they doing)*?
3. **Les endroits de vacances.** Où est-ce que les Français aiment aller en vacances? Classez les endroits de vacances par ordre de préférence.

C. Étude: les vacances des Français.

Act. C, 1: Have students make simple sentences using Ils, e.g., **Ils aiment mieux la mer que la ville; Ils partent plus souvent en vacances maintenant.**

1. Utilisez les chiffres et les graphiques pour présenter les habitudes de vacances des Français.

Modèle *Les Français aiment les vacances à la mer.*

44 ÉCONOMIE >en couverture

>se distraire

L'art de vivre ses loisirs

> Des vacances plus souvent...
Taux de départ (en %)
56,2 59,1 62
1980 1990 1994

... mais moins longtemps
Congés d'été par personne (en jours)
24,8 23,3 22
1980 1990 1994

10 millio
de Français pratiquent la randonnée. 1 vacancier su en a effectué au moins un au cours de l'été 1994.

2. D'après les textes, ces phrases sont-elles vraies ou fausses? Corrigez les phrases qui sont fausses.

	vrai	faux	
a.	☐	☐	Les Français partent en vacances de moins en moins souvent.
b.	☐	☐	Ils partent deux jours de plus par an en 1994 qu'en 1980.
c.	☐	☐	Les habitudes dans les départs en vacances changent soudain en 1994.
d.	☐	☐	En 1980, une grande partie des Français ne part pas en vacances.
e.	☐	☐	Les Français préfèrent les petites vacances fréquentes et courtes.
f.	☐	☐	Pendant l'été, les Français restent chez eux au moins deux jours de plus par an.
g.	☐	☐	La randonnée est de plus en plus populaire en France.
h.	☐	☐	La mer, la plage et le soleil sont les formes de vacances préférées des Français.
i.	☐	☐	En 1994, les Français ont pratiqué au moins quatre randonnées.
j.	☐	☐	Les Français ne sont pas sportifs.
k.	☐	☐	Pour les Français, les activités dans la nature sont très importantes.

3. Quel est le plus grand changement dans les activités des Français?

>Ils se mettent au vert

81 % des vacanciers français sont partis en France au cours de l'été 1994. Où sont-ils allés ?

Montagne 14 %

Mer 46 %

Campagne 23 %

Villes, autres 9 %

Circuit 8 %

Le sport prend une place croissante dans la vie des Français : de 14 à 65 ans, plus de 2 sur 3 en font. Les mentalités ont changé : priorité à la détente, aux activités de plein air, à la nature, aux sports individuels, mais pratiqués en groupe.

L'Express International

D. Mots nouveaux.

Complétez les phrases avec les mots suivants:

au cours de / une place croissante / détente / congé.

> Lundi, mardi, mercredi, jeudi et vendredi sont des
> jours de travail, mais dimanche est un jour de . . . . .
> Aux USA, le samedi est aussi un jour de . . . . . , et on
> appelle ces deux jours le week-end. . . . . . ces deux
> jours, on joue au tennis, au football, etc.; on regarde
> la télé; on parle avec ses amis. En France, les jours de
> congé donnent . . . . . à la famille, parce que les
> activités sont souvent des activités familiales comme
> les randonnées, les pique-niques, etc.

E. Les valeurs.

Act. E, 1: Possible responses: l'importance du groupe, des sports, de la nature, et l'importance des loisirs.

1. Quelles valeurs ces pourcentages représentent-ils dans la culture française? (l'importance du groupe, le sport, la nature, les loisirs, la famille, la richesse, le luxe, la liberté) Est-ce que ce sont des valeurs nouvelles ou une nouvelle forme de valeurs traditionnelles?
2. Quelles connotations ont les mots **mer, campagne** et **montagne** pour les Français? Quels adjectifs sont associés à ces mots pour eux?
3. Et chez vous? Quels sont les pourcentages équivalents dans votre culture?

   Modèle *Chez moi, ...% des gens passent leurs vacances à...*

F. Échanges.

1. D'après les informations du texte, que font les Français pendant leurs vacances d'été?

...à la montagne?	
...à la campagne?	
...à la mer?	
...dans les villes?	
...pendant un circuit?	

Act. F, 2: Students need to keep culture in mind when they write. Provide suggestions.

Act. F, 4: Have students compare their sentences.

2. Imaginez que la photo est une bande dessinée *(comic strip)*. Dans une bulle *(bubble)*, imaginez une phrase pour chaque *(each)* personne de la photo.
3. **Dialogue.** Maintenant, imaginez un dialogue entre deux de ces personnes.
4. **L'album de photos de...** Une de ces personnes fait un album de photos de leurs vacances. Faites trois ou quatre phrases pour une photo (expliquez la photo).

www explore!
http//voila.heinle.com

*O*rthographe et prononciation

▶▶ L'élision

L'élision appears in spoken and written French. When the **-e** or **-a** in words such as **le, la, ne, je,** or **que** is followed by a vowel sound, the **-e** or **-a** is dropped. In writing, an apostrophe shows that **élision** has occurred.

NO ELISION	ELISION
un hôtel	**l'h**ôtel
une université	**l'u**niversité
Il ne cherche pas ses clés.	Il **n'é**coute pas la radio.
Est-ce que Jean est heureux?	Est-ce **qu'il** est heureux?

Activités

A. Prononcez Repeat the following after your instructor.

1. Ils ne sont pas à l'hôpital.
2. J'aime l'amie d'Élise.
3. Nous n'avons pas d'amis.
4. Voilà l'affiche d'Anne.
5. Est-ce qu'elle va à l'école?

B. Chassez l'intrus Put **le** or **la** before each noun. Which word does not fit?

Modèle   fille / femme / homme
    la fille / la femme / ~~l'homme~~

1. après-midi / matin / soir
2. magasin / parc / hôtel
3. église / campagne / bibliothèque
4. restaurant / hôpital / banque
5. plage / orange / lac

Vocabulaire de base

TEXT TAPE:
Vocabulaire de base

NOMS

une année *year*
un appartement *apartment*
un après-midi *afternoon*
une bibliothèque *library*
un café *café*
la campagne *country, countryside*
une cité universitaire *dormitory*
une heure *hour*
un hôtel *hotel*
un jour *day*
une journée *day (period of time)*
un lac *lake*
un magasin *store*
une maison *house*
le matin *morning*
la mer *sea, ocean*
un mois *month*
la montagne *mountain(s)*
la neige *snow*
la nuit *night, darkness*
un parc *park*
une piscine *swimming pool*
une plage *beach*
la poste *post office*
un restaurant *restaurant*
une semaine *week*
le soir *evening*
le soleil *sun*
un supermarché *supermarket*
un village *(rural) village*
une ville *city, town*

VERBES

aller *to go*
chercher *to look for, to search (for)*
commencer (à + infinitif) *to begin (to), to start (to)*
préférer *to prefer*
téléphoner (à quelqu'un) *to telephone, to call (someone)*
terminer *to finish, to end*
trouver *to find*

ADJECTIF

quel, quelle, quels, quelles *which, what*

DIVERS

à... heure(s) *at . . . o'clock*
À quelle heure? *At what time?*
aujourd'hui *today*
avoir chaud *to be hot*
avoir froid *to be cold*
avoir sommeil *to be sleepy*
C'est quel jour aujourd'hui? *What day is it today?*
comment *what, how*
demain *tomorrow*
en *in*
pendant *during*
pourquoi *why*
Quelle est la date aujourd'hui? *What's the date today?*
Quelle heure est-il? (Vous avez l'heure?) *What time is it? (Do you have the time?)*
s'il te plaît *please (familiar)*
s'il vous plaît *please (formal, plural)*

Vocabulaire supplémentaire

NOMS

un arbre *tree*
une banque *bank*
un bateau, des bateaux *boat(s)*
un champ *field*
le ciel *sky*
une église *church*
un endroit *place, spot*
une ferme *farm*
une gare *train station*
un hôpital *hospital*
un laboratoire *laboratory*
un pique-nique *picnic*
un restaurant universitaire *college cafeteria, dining hall*
une vache *cow*

VERBES

briller *to shine*
nager *to swim*
skier *to ski*

ADJECTIF

préféré(e) *preferred, favorite*

LE FRANÇAIS TEL QU'ON LE PARLE

J'ai trouvé! *I've got it! I've found it!*
Expressions avec aller
   Allons-y! *Let's go!*
   J'y vais! *I'm leaving! I'm going!*
   On y va? *Shall we go?*
   Vas-y! (Allez-y!) *Go on! Go ahead!*

LE FRANÇAIS FAMILIER

un appart = un appartement
une BU = une bibliothèque universitaire
une cité-u = une cité universitaire
un labo = un laboratoire
un restau, un resto = un restaurant
un restau-u = un restaurant universitaire

ON ENTEND PARFOIS...

le serein (Guadeloupe) = le soir

Famille, familles...

En bref

Dans cette leçon...

- La famille et les relations familiales
- Le temps qu'il fait
- Parler de vous et de vos activités
- Le verbe **faire**
- Exprimer la volonté et le désir **(vouloir)**
- Les pronoms d'objet direct
- La famille: tradition et modernité

In this lesson...

- Family relationships
- Weather
- Talking about you and what you do
- The verb **faire**
- Expressing will and desire **(vouloir)**
- Direct object pronouns
- The family: traditional and modern views

www explore! http://voila.heinle.com	Develop writing skills with Système-D software!	Practice listening and pronunciation skills with the Text Tape!	Discover the Francophone world!	Build your skills!

INTERNET

SYSTÈME-D

TEXT TAPE

VIDEO TAPE

CD-ROM

Students have an open-ended writing activity in the **Cahier** suitable for use with **Système-D**.

159

Entrée en matière: Tel père, tel fils?

Des Français. Combien sont-ils pour illustrer cet article? Combien sont jeunes? Il y a combien d'enfants? d'adultes?

Les enfants. Quel âge ont-ils? Comment sont-ils? Ils sont tristes? contents? surpris? Pourquoi?

Les adultes. Quel âge ont-ils? Où sont-ils? Ils sont heureux? Pourquoi?

L'article. Quel est le sujet de l'article? Choisissez:

☐ les couples mixtes	☐ la génétique
☐ le racisme	☐ la famille
☐ l'hérédité	☐ les étrangers

Dans quel type de magazine est probablement cet article? Pourquoi est-il écrit?

Trouvez dans le texte comment on dit en français: *to look like / twins / sky-blue / temperament / family resemblance / genetic laws*

A qui va-t-il

Les mystères de l'hérédité

Votre bébé est unique ! Vous vous en doutiez... et les lois de la génétique le confirment ! Et pourtant ce regard azur et ce caractère de tête brûlée ne vous sont pas étrangers. Qu'est-ce qui leur (et nous) donne donc cet air de famille ?

Sophie Pasquet.
Témoignages Anne Wieme-Dufour.

Le titre.
À qui est-ce qu'on pose la question du titre? Est-ce qu'il y a une réponse?

L'hérédité.

Les enfants blonds. À qui ressemble le premier garçon sur la photo de droite?

Les bébés. Dans le texte, à qui ressemble le premier bébé? et le deuxième *(second one)*?

Et vous? À qui ressemblez-vous physiquement? et de tempérament?

Seuls les vrais jumeaux ont le même bagage génétique. Leur caractère peut être cependant très différent!

ressembler?

La roulette génétique réserve bien des surprises aux couples mixtes; eh oui, un bébé noir et un blanc c'est possible !

Photos Gurfinkel / Rapho, Schäfer / Studio X Ekem. Joubert / Phanie, Rex / Sipa Press.

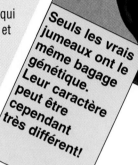

formes différentes. Ces vari[...]
me gène s'appellent les allèles. [...]
livrent bataille pour imposer l[...]
possèdent un caractère réces[...]
nant : certains s'effacent, d[...]
contraire, s'affirment.

Les cheveux blonds, ça peut sauter une gén[...]

En ce qui concerne la co[...]
par exemple, le bleu, réces[...]
le noir (ou le marron), [...]
qu'un caractère récessif [...]
que deux formes récess[...]
même gène se rencontren[...]
pas parce qu'il ne s'expr[...]
n'aura pas été transmis. B[...]
fant a le regard ténébreux [...]
n'est pas parce que sa mam[...]
donné de son regard d'azur, [...]
lui-ci s'est effacé devant la co[...]
dominante, de son père. Ma[...]
rité de la couleur bleue, qu[...]
ses gènes sans qu'elle n'app[...]
même aura une chance d'a[...]
fants aux yeux clairs s'il ren[...]
qu'un possédant égalem[...]
bleue dans son stock génét[...]
alors céderont-ils tous les [...]
fant la forme bleue du gène[...]
des yeux. Les cheveux blo[...]
l'oreille collé, les pieds palm[...]
ment un caractère récessif[...]

Info plus

Les mariages en France.
In France, in 1992, 11% of marriages were between a French person and a foreigner. About 30% of these marriages involve a European partner and 50% involve Africans, especially Africans from the Maghreb (Algeria, Tunisia, and Morocco).

Gérard Mermet, *Francoscopie 1995*

Integrate activities in the **D'accord?** section into your vocabulary presentation.

To recycle vocabulary and structure, ask students what they remember about these people. ALTERNATIVE: Divide students into as many groups as there are family members and give them a moment to find relevant information. Each group then reports to the class and the class combines information.

A. La famille Dubois en 1998

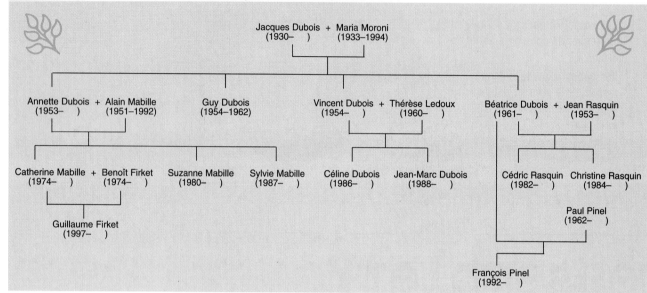

Jacques Dubois (1930–) + Maria Moroni (1933–1994)

Annette Dubois (1953–) + Alain Mabille (1951–1992)

Guy Dubois (1954–1962)

Vincent Dubois (1954–) + Thérèse Ledoux (1960–)

Béatrice Dubois (1961–) + Jean Rasquin (1953–)

Catherine Mabille (1974–) + Benoît Firket (1974–)

Suzanne Mabille (1980–)

Sylvie Mabille (1987–)

Céline Dubois (1986–)

Jean-Marc Dubois (1988–)

Cédric Rasquin (1982–)

Christine Rasquin (1984–)

Guillaume Firket (1997–)

Paul Pinel (1962–)

François Pinel (1992–)

TRANSPARENCY: 7-1

Info plus

Ask students to brainstorm very briefly on what the word *family* brings to mind to them (la famille = **parents, amour, problèmes,** etc.). Then compare with the information in the cultural note on **La famille.**

La famille.

France's origins as a Roman Catholic and rural society are reflected in the family structure. The traditional French family, based on father as provider and mother as caretaker, was formalized by the Napoleonic **Code civil** in the nineteenth century. The emergence of the women's movement, the dechristianization of France in the 20th century, and the arrival of immigrants from different ethnic and religious backgrounds have created new models of family. Nevertheless, the place of the family at the center of French life and its image as a source of individual happiness have remained strong.

Jacques Dubois   François Pinel   Vincent + Thérèse Dubois   Jean-Marc Dubois   Céline Dubois   Cédric Rasquin   Béatrice Dubois   Sylvie Mabille   Suzanne Mabille

Vincent Dubois. Il est né en 1954. C'est le fils de Jacques et de Maria Dubois. Il est marié. Lui et sa femme, qui s'appelle Thérèse Ledoux, ont deux enfants. Ils ont aussi six neveux et nièces: Catherine, Suzanne, Sylvie, Christine, Cédric et François. Vincent est leur oncle et Thérèse est leur tante.

- Qui sont les enfants de Vincent et de Thérèse? Qui sont les sœurs de Vincent? Qui est le frère de Vincent? Quand est-ce que son frère est né? Quel âge a Vincent?

Guy and Vincent Dubois are twins. If desired, teach **jumeau, jumeaux, jumelle, jumelles.**

Annette Dubois. Elle est née en 1953. C'est la fille de Jacques et de Maria Dubois et c'est l'aînée de leurs enfants. Elle est veuve: son mari, Alain Mabille, est mort en 1992. C'est la grand-mère de Guillaume Firket.

- Quel âge a Annette? Est-ce qu'elle a des enfants? Combien? Est-ce qu'elle a une petite-fille? Est-ce que c'est la tante de Vincent? Combien de neveux et de nièces est-ce qu'elle a?

Tell students that there is no **-e** after **grand-** in **grand-mère** but that there is an **-s** after **grand-** in **grands-parents.**

If desired, ask students their opinion of how centralized their government structure is. How much authority is local? National?

Info plus

L'état civil *(Legal status)*

Due to the highly centralized nature of French government, many areas of family life are the concern of the state. Subsidies to encourage couples to have children and to support the education of those children are a part of French life. These subsidies are seen by the French as a right due them from the government. One consequence of this degree of governmental involvement in French life is a great deal of bureaucratic paperwork. The **livret de famille, carte d'identité,** and **registre d'état civil** are documents that record an individual's birth, marriage(s), children, divorce(s), and death.

Jacques Dubois. Il est né en 1930. Il est veuf: sa femme, Maria, est morte en 1994. Il est grand-père: Catherine, Suzanne, Sylvie, Céline, Jean-Marc, Cédric, Christine et François sont ses petits-enfants. Il a une femme de ménage pour ranger la maison parce qu'il déteste faire le ménage.

- Est-ce que sa femme est en vie? Combien de petits-enfants est-ce qu'il a?
- Qui range la maison chez lui?

Guillaume Firket. Il est né en 1997 et c'est le plus jeune de la famille Dubois. C'est le petit-fils d'Annette Dubois. Ses parents sont Catherine et Benoît Firket. Il n'a pas de frère et il n'a pas de sœur. Il n'a pas de cousins mais sa mère, Catherine, a deux cousines, Céline et Christine, et trois cousins, Jean-Marc, Cédric et François.

- Est-ce que ses grands-parents sont en vie?

Guillaume is an only child **(fils unique).** One can say also **un enfant unique.** For a girl, one says **une fille unique** or **une enfant unique.**

Famille, familles... **163**

Jean Rasquin. Il est né en 1953. Il est célibataire maintenant parce qu'il est divorcé. C'est le père de Cédric et de Christine. On n'aime pas beaucoup Jean dans la famille Dubois parce que c'est un homme qui n'est pas très sérieux et Béatrice Dubois a beaucoup de problèmes avec lui.

- Quel âge a Jean Rasquin? Est-ce que c'est le père de François? Qui est le père de François?
- Et vous, vous avez une grande ou une petite famille? Combien de cousins est-ce que vous avez? Combien de cousines? Combien d'oncles? Combien de tantes? Est-ce que vous avez des neveux et des nièces? Quel âge ont-ils?

Ask students **Quel âge a François?** Since he has the same mother but a different father, François is the **demi-frère** of Cédric and Christine. Additional family vocabulary for this type of situation is in the *Vocabulaire facultatif* in the *Cahier d'activités écrites et orales* and in the **Instructor's Resource Manual**.

TRANSPARENCY: 7-2

Jacques Dubois, who lives in Nice, has met Paulette Gilmard on the **Promenade des Anglais**, in *Leçon 5,* p. 109. Have students speculate on what has happened between *Leçon 5* and now.

To review vocabulary and structure, ask students additional questions about the series of illustrations: **Où est le chien? Quelle heure est-il? Que fait Vincent?** etc.).

B. Grand-père arrive.

Dans la salle de séjour des Dubois:

Dans la cuisine:

- Et vous, vous aimez faire le ménage? Est-ce que vous aimez faire votre lit le matin? Est-ce que vous rangez souvent votre chambre? Vous préférez faire la cuisine ou faire la vaisselle? faire les courses ou faire la cuisine? ranger la maison ou faire la lessive? passer l'aspirateur ou faire les lits? faire la lessive ou repasser? Vous repassez souvent?

C. Le temps

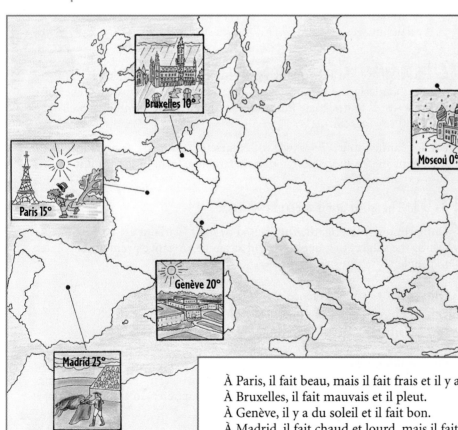

À Paris, il fait beau, mais il fait frais et il y a du vent.
À Bruxelles, il fait mauvais et il pleut.
À Genève, il y a du soleil et il fait bon.
À Madrid, il fait chaud et lourd, mais il fait gris: il y a des nuages.
Et à Moscou, il ne fait pas froid aujourd'hui? Mais si, il fait froid... Il neige!

- Quelle est la saison? Pourquoi?
- Et aujourd'hui, quel temps fait-il? Et chez vos parents?
- Et quelle est la météo pour demain? Il va faire beau? Il va neiger? Il va pleuvoir? Il va y avoir du vent? Il va faire chaud?

Famille, familles... **165**

There is no *Mots et expressions utiles* section for *Leçon 7*.

Notes de vocabulaire

1. Le temps.

In French, when referring to the weather, the verb **faire** is generally used.

Il **fait** beau!	*It's nice!*
Il ne **fait** pas froid.	*It's not cold.*

Faire is not used with the verbs **pleuvoir** and **neiger.**

Il **pleut.**	*It's raining.*
Il va **neiger?**	*Is it going to snow?*
Il va **pleuvoir?**	*Is it going to rain?*

Il y a is usually used with nouns.

il y a du soleil	*it's sunny*
il y a du vent	*it's windy*
il y a des nuages	*it's cloudy*

2. Les personnes.

In French, the word **femme** can mean either *wife* or *woman*. Similarly, the word **fille** may mean either *daughter* or *girl*. There are separate words to designate *husband* (**mari**) and *man* (**homme**) as well as *son* (**fils**) and *boy* (**garçon**).

Do not confuse **mari** *(husband)* with **marié(e)** *(married)*. **Femme** means *wife*. **Mari** means *husband*. There is no feminine form of the word **mari.**

3: Qui is presented here for recognition only. The interrogative pronouns will be presented as a structural point in *Leçon 8*. The relative pronouns **qui** and **que** will be presented as a structural point in *Leçon 12*. Activities in this lesson will not require the active use of **qui**.

3. Qui.

The word **qui** is used in two ways.

Qui: **pronom interrogatif. Qui** is used by itself (without **est-ce que**) to ask *who* as the subject of a question. **Qui** as an interrogative pronoun only refers to people.

Qui + verb + rest of sentence

Qui est fatigué aujourd'hui?	*Who's tired today?*
Qui va faire la vaisselle?	*Who's going to do the dishes?*

Qui: **pronom relatif. Qui** is also used to join two sentences or ideas together. When used in this manner, **qui** is called a relative pronoun because it relates two sentences or ideas. **Qui** as a relative pronoun refers to either people or things.

C'est lui **le professeur qui** parle anglais?
Is he the teacher who speaks English?

Les livres qui sont sur la table sont à moi.
The books that are on the table are mine.

4. Les dates. Here is one way to express years:

1950 (dix-neuf cent cinquante)
1715 (dix-sept cent quinze)
1988 (dix-neuf cent quatre-vingt-huit)

4: If desired, teach the alternative expression (**mil neuf cent cinquante,** etc.).

5. Si / oui. Use **si** instead of **oui** to answer *yes* to a negative question or to contradict a negative statement.

—Tu n'aimes pas chanter? *"You don't like to sing?"*
—**Si,** j'adore chanter. *"Yes (on the contrary), I love to sing."*

—Il n'est pas raisonnable, lui. *"He's not reasonable."*
—**Si,** il est raisonnable! *"Yes, he is!"*

D'accord?

A. Des groupes Refer to the family tree on page 162 and make groups as follows:

1. les femmes
2. les hommes
3. les vieux
4. les jeunes

B. Les relations de famille Vrai ou faux?

1. Jacques Dubois est l'oncle de Céline Dubois.
2. Guillaume Firket est le fils de Benoît Firket.
3. Céline Dubois est la sœur de Jean-Marc Dubois.
4. Jacques Dubois est le grand-père de Vincent Dubois.
5. Annette Dubois est la grand-mère de Guillaume Firket.
6. Céline Dubois est la tante de Sylvie Mabille.

Act. B: If desired, have students correct the false statements.
SUGGESTION: Have students open their books to the family tree, page 158, while you read the items.
CONTINUATION: **Thérèse Ledoux est la femme de Jean Rasquin. Suzanne Mabille est la petite-fille de Jacques Dubois. Cédric Rasquin et Sylvie Mabille sont les petits-enfants de Maria Moroni. Paul Pinel est le mari de Catherine Mabille. Béatrice Dubois et Jean Rasquin sont les parents de François Pinel.**

C. L'état civil Dans les familles Dubois, Mabille, Rasquin et Pinel...

1. Qui est marié?
2. Qui est célibataire?
3. Qui est divorcé?
4. Qui est mort?

D. Les liens de parenté Quelles sont les relations de parenté entre Catherine Mabille et les autres membres de la famille?

Modèle Suzanne Mabille?
    C'est sa sœur.

1. Guillaume Firket?
2. Benoît Firket?
3. Alain Mabille?
4. Maria Moroni?
5. Annette Dubois?
6. Jacques Dubois?
7. Béatrice Dubois
8. Céline Dubois?
9. Vincent Dubois?
10. François Pinel?

Act. D: This exercise also recycles possessive adjectives. A variant could be to ask how different people are related to others in the family. For example: **Jacques Dubois? C'est le mari de Maria Moroni, c'est le père d'Annette Dubois, c'est le grand-père de Céline Dubois,** etc.

Louis XIV

E. Lire les dates Quelle date va avec quel événement?

1. 1830
2. 1971
3. 1848
4. 1502
5. 1960
6. 1715
7. 1672
8. 1608

a. Abolition de l'esclavage à la Guadeloupe.
b. Indépendance du Sénégal.
c. Joliet et le père Marquette arrivent au Mississipi.
d. Indépendance de la Belgique.
e. Mort de Louis XIV.
f. Samuel de Champlain fonde Québec.
g. Découverte de la Martinique par Christophe Colomb.
h. Le Congo s'appelle maintenant le Zaïre.

F. Les dates de la vie Quand sont-ils nés? Quand sont-ils morts?

Modèle   Alain Mabille
   Il est né en 1951 et il est mort en 1992.

1. Maria Moroni
2. Christine Rasquin
3. Suzanne Mabille
4. Guy Dubois
5. Benoît Firket

TRANSPARENCY:
7-4

G. D'après les images Qu'est-ce qu'ils vont faire?

1.

2.

On y va!   On y va?

3.

Les Nouvelles Galeries

H. La météo

1. Nous sommes en janvier: Quel temps fait-il...
   a. à Montréal?
   b. à San Francisco?
   c. à Algers?
   d. à Dakar (au Sénégal)?
   e. chez vous?
2. Nous sommes en juillet: Quel temps fait-il...
   a. dans la Vallée de la Mort?
   b. à Bruxelles?
   c. à la Réunion?
   d. à St-Pierre-et-Miquelon?
   e. chez vous?

I. Oui ou si? Answer using either **oui, non,** or **si.**

1. Il ne fait pas chaud à Tunis en été?
2. Il ne neige pas à Québec en juillet?
3. Il pleut à Paris au printemps?
4. Il ne fait pas chaud en été à Fort-de-France?
5. Il pleut en hiver à Bruxelles?
6. Il va neiger aujourd'hui?
7. Il n'y a pas de nuages aujourd'hui?
8. Il n'y a pas de vent en hiver à Chicago?

Act. I: CONTINUATION: 1. Vous n'aimez pas parler français? 2. Vous êtes américain(e)? 3. Le professeur ne parle pas français? 4. Vous n'aimez pas faire la cuisine? 5. Vous jouez de la guitare? 6. Vous allez souvent à la bibliothèque? 7. Vous n'avez pas d'amis? 8. Les étudiants à l'université ne sont pas sympathiques?

Mise en pratique

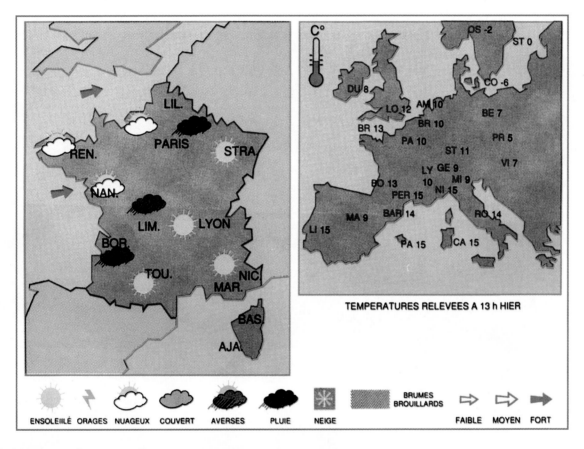

A. La météo en France et en Europe Look at the two maps and answer the following questions. You will have to guess the names of the cities that have been abbreviated.

1. Quel temps fait-il à Paris?
2. Quel temps fait-il à Rennes?
3. Quel temps fait-il à Nice?
4. Où est-ce qu'il y a du vent?
5. Où est-ce qu'il pleut?
6. Où est-ce qu'il y a du soleil?
7. Est-ce qu'il fait chaud à Madrid?
8. Où est-ce qu'il fait bon?
9. Où est-ce qu'il fait frais?
10. Où est-ce qu'il fait froid?
11. Quelle est la saison?

Act. A: This was the weather on December 25, so the season was winter. Early spring or late fall would also be good guesses. ALTERNATIVE ACTIVITY: Have students play meteorologist and present the weather in class. You may also use a national weather map from your area for this activity.

B. La famille d'Alceste Comment est la famille d'Alceste?

1. sa mère
2. son petit frère
3. son grand-père

C. Généalogies célèbres In groups, pick one famous family (real or fictional) and combine your knowledge to say as much as you can about them.

SUGGESTIONS: la famille royale d'Angleterre / la famille royale de Monaco / la famille Kennedy / la famille Simpson

D. La famille de Delphine Voilà des photos de Delphine Cunill (étudiante à l'université d'Orléans) et de sa famille.

Delphine Cunill

Christiane Cunill

De gauche à droite: Laure Cunill, Michel Tournier, Christine Pauzies, Paulette Pauzies, Simone Toussaint, Maria Tournier, Robert Tournier, Christiane Cunill

Laure Cunill

Raymond Cunill

1. À votre avis, qui est Christiane Cunill? Qui est Raymond Cunill? Où est Laure Cunill? Qui est plus âgée, Delphine ou Laure? Quel âge a Delphine? Et Laure?
2. Regardez la photo de la famille en vacances. Où sont-ils? Quel temps fait-il? Combien de personnes est-ce qu'il y a? C'est une grande ou une petite famille? Qui n'est pas sur la photo? Qui sont les autres personnes sur la photo, à votre avis? Comment sont-elles? Qu'est-ce qu'elles aiment? Qu'est-ce qu'elles n'aiment pas?

E. Conversation en français With a partner, find out about each other's families. How many people are there? What is their relationship to you? How old are they? Who is the oldest? The youngest? Where do they live? What are they like?

Structure

▶▶ Le verbe *faire*

The verb **faire** means both *to make* and *to do.* Its conjugation is irregular.

je fais	nous faisons
tu fais	vous faites
il elle } fait	ils elles } font

Faire is used in many expressions referring to the weather. In similar cases, English uses the verb *to be.*

Il **fait** chaud aujourd'hui.   *It's hot today.*

ATTENTION: A question using **faire** does not always require an answer using **faire.**

Question: Qu'est-ce que tu fais?
Réponses possibles: Je travaille. J'étudie. Je parle au téléphone. Je vais en ville. Je fais le ménage. etc.

The imperative or command forms of **faire** are identical with its present tense forms.

—**Fais** la vaisselle!   *"Do the dishes!"*
—Et toi, tu ne fais pas la vaisselle ce soir!?   *"What about you, you're not doing the dishes tonight!?"*

—**Faites** les courses aujourd'hui!   *"Do the shopping today!"*
—Et vous, vous faites les courses demain!   *"And you do the shopping tomorrow!"*

—**Faisons** le ménage.   *"Let's do the housework."*
—Oh non, nous ne faisons pas le ménage le dimanche!   *"Oh no, we don't do housework on Sundays!"*

Vous avez compris?

A. Chez Candide et Alceste
Qui fait quoi? Un X indique la personne qui est responsable du travail.

	faire la cuisine	faire la vaisselle	faire la lessive	faire les courses	ranger	passer l'aspirateur
Candide		X	X			
Alceste	X					X
Les deux				X	X	

1. Candide . . . . .
2. Alceste . . . . .
3. Candide et Alceste . . . . .

B. Les familles et le ménage
Different families divide household tasks up in different ways. Say so, following the model.

Modèle   Martin / le père / la vaisselle
     Dans la famille Martin, le père fait la vaisselle.

1. Grandjean / les filles / le ménage
2. Dellicourt / la grand-mère / les courses
3. Durieux / les enfants / les lits
4. Leclerc / le grand-père / la cuisine

Continuons!

Act. A: FOLLOW-UP: Ask students to make two lists, one for **la famille moderne** and one for **la famille traditionnelle**. Qui sont les membres de ces familles? Qui travaille? Qui fait quoi (vaisselle / courses / etc.). Quel type de famille est-ce qu'ils préfèrent?

A. Chez vous
Et chez vous, qui fait quoi?

Modèle   la cuisine?
     Mon père (fait la cuisine.)

1. la vaisselle?
2. les lits?
3. la cuisine?

4. les courses?
5. le ménage?
6. la lessive?

B. Activités
Qu'est-ce que vous faites... ?

Modèle   le vendredi soir?
     Je travaille, j'étudie, je téléphone à ma sœur, je fais les courses...

1. le vendredi à midi?
2. le dimanche matin?
3. le samedi soir?

4. le mercredi à minuit?
5. le dimanche soir?
6. dans le cours de français?

➤➤ Le verbe *vouloir*

Vouloir means *to want*. Its conjugation is irregular.

je veux	nous voulons
tu veux	vous voulez
il ⎫	ils ⎫
elle ⎭ veut	elles ⎭ veulent

To be more polite, use the following forms:

je **voudrais**	*I would like*
tu **voudrais**	*you would like*
il/elle **voudrait**	*he/she would like*

Vous avez compris?

A. Soyons raisonnable C'est raisonnable, pas raisonnable ou ça dépend?

1. Alceste veut du calme. (Candide parle beaucoup.)
2. Candide veut la clé de la chambre d'Alceste.
3. Cédric Rasquin veut habiter avec son père à Paris. (Ses parents sont divorcés.)
4. Jacques Dubois a un chien. Il veut aussi un chat.
5. Guillaume Firket est un bébé. Il veut manger et dormir!
6. Vous voulez la clé de la voiture de vos parents. (de votre mari / votre femme / votre sœur, etc.)

B. Projets de week-end Qu'est-ce qu'on veut faire ce week-end? Utilisez le verbe **vouloir** au présent.

Modèle   *Virginie **veut** regarder la télévision.*

1. Nous . . . . . aller au cinéma.
2. Marc et Paul . . . . . dormir.
3. Vous . . . . . étudier?
4. Je . . . . . manger dans un restaurant en ville.
5. Tu . . . . . sortir avec des copains?
6. Paulette et Marie-Claude . . . . . nager à la piscine.

C. Et vous? Qu'est-ce que vous voudriez faire ce week-end?

Modèle   lire?
        Oui, je voudrais lire. / Non, je ne voudrais pas lire.

1. sortir?
2. travailler à la bibliothèque?
3. aller au cinéma?
4. aller danser?
5. dormir?
6. étudier?
7. regarder la télévision?
8. parler avec vos parents?
9. passer l'aspirateur?
10. faire la lessive?

The imperative forms of **vouloir** are relatively infrequent. You may want to point out that, although imperative forms exist for almost all verbs, in some cases the use of these forms is semantically implausible. This is the case with **vouloir** where it is difficult to imagine a context where you would tell someone to "want" something. **Veuillez** is used as a polite form (**Veuillez me suivre**) and in letters (**Veuillez agréer mes salutations distinguées**).

Point out that all three forms (**je voudrais, tu voudrais, il/elle voudrait**) sound the same. Teach **vous voudriez, nous voudrions, ils/elles voudraient** for recognition if desired.

DRILL: **On veut sortir!** (je / nous / Candide et Alceste / vous / ma mère / tu)

DRILL: **On ne veut pas travailler!** (je / nous / Candide et Alceste / vous / ma mère / tu)

Act. A: FOLLOW-UP: Ask students to make up more statements. As students read their statements, first react to their reasonableness yourself. Then ask the rest of the class what they think.

Act. C: Ask students, or encourage fellow students to ask follow-up questions. **Pourquoi? Avec qui?** etc.

Continuons!

A. Samedi matin chez les Dubois
Voilà ce que différentes personnes de la famille Dubois font ce matin. Imaginez ce qu'ils veulent faire à la place *(instead)*.

Modèle   Vincent Dubois fait la vaisselle, mais *il veut aller jouer aux cartes avec des copains.*

1. Thérèse Dubois fait les courses, mais . . . . .
2. Céline et Jean-Marc Dubois font leurs devoirs, mais . . . . .
3. Jacques Dubois fait la lessive, mais . . . . .
4. Suzanne Mabille range sa chambre, mais . . . . .

B. Pour mon anniversaire...
In groups, make lists of what different people would like for their birthdays. Report to the class.

Je voudrais...

(Michel) voudrait...

▶▶ Les pronoms d'objet direct

Ask students to give you the *what* or *whom* questions identifying the direct objects: *Who(m) is he watching? What's he looking for?*

Note that noun phrases with indefinite articles (**un arbre, des livres**) are also direct objects. Students will learn how to replace this type of noun phrases in *Leçon 17* where the pronoun **en** is introduced.

Many sentences have a subject, a verb, and a direct object. The direct object is a noun or pronoun that receives the action of the verb. It answers the question *what?* or *whom?* after the verb. A direct object may be either a person or a thing.

Il	regarde	sa fille.	He's	watching	his daughter.
s	v	do	s	v	do

Il	cherche	le parc.	He's	looking for	the park.
s	v	do	s	v	do

Nouns used as subjects and nouns used as direct objects may be replaced by pronouns. The use of pronouns allows speakers and writers to avoid being repetitious and to link ideas across sentences.

Rappel!   You are already familiar with subject pronouns (**je, tu, il, elle, on, nous, vous, ils, elles**) in French. Subject pronouns replace nouns used as subjects.

Suzanne aime les chiens.   *Suzanne likes dogs.*
Elle aime les chats aussi.   *She likes cats, too.*

Here are the forms of direct object pronouns (**les pronoms d'objet direct**) in French.

me	*me*
te	*you (familiar, singular)*
le (l')	*it, him*
la (l')	*it, her*
nous	*us*
vous	*you (formal or plural)*
les	*them*

Direct object pronouns replace nouns used as direct objects. In French, direct object pronouns directly precede the verb they are the object of.

— Tu **m'**aimes?   *"Do you love me?"*
— Oui, je **t'**adore!   *"Yes, I adore you!"*

Study the placement of direct object pronouns in the following sentences. Note the placement of **ne** and **pas** in the negative.

If desired, ask students to give English equivalents. Note that these sentences are purposely fairly decontextualized to help students focus on placement patterns.

1. **Present tense.** The direct object pronoun is placed directly in front of the present tense verb.

   Je déteste les examens.   Je ne déteste pas les examens.
   Je **les** déteste.   Je **ne les** déteste **pas.**

2. **Infinitive constructions.** The direct object pronoun is placed directly in front of the infinitive.

   Je vais chercher mes clés.   Je ne vais pas chercher mes clés!
   Je vais **les** chercher.   Je **ne** vais **pas les** chercher!

3. **With *voici / voilà*.** The direct object pronoun is placed directly in front of **voici** or **voilà.**

   Voilà mes clés!
   Les voilà!

4. **With imperative or command forms.** The direct object pronoun follows the affirmative imperative. It is placed in front of the negative imperative. Note the hyphen that connects the verb form and the pronoun in the affirmative. Note also the use of **moi** and **toi** for **me** and **te** in the affirmative.

   —Mais où sont mes clés?   *"Where are my keys?"*
   —Euh, je ne sais pas, mais   *"Uh, I don't know, but look for*
      cherche-**les** dans la cuisine.   *them in the kitchen. Don't look*
      Ne **les** cherche pas dans   *for them in my bag!"*
      mon sac!

   Regarde-**moi!**   *Look at me!*
   Ne **me** regarde pas!   *Don't look at me!*

Famille, familles...   **175**

Rappel! You are also familiar with stressed pronouns (**moi, toi, lui, elle, nous, vous, eux, elles**). These pronouns replace nouns standing alone, nouns after prepositions, and nouns used after **c'est**.

Qui? **Moi?**

Qui est là? C'est Paul.
Qui est là? C'est **lui.**

Il étudie avec Marc et **moi.**
Il étudie avec **nous.**

Vous avez compris?

Act. A: In some cases, either **aime** or **fait** will be appropriate.

A. On aime ou on fait? Do you *do* or do you *like* each of the following?

Modèle Le printemps? On le . . . . .
On l'aime.

1. Les courses? On les . . . . .
2. Les belles fleurs? On les . . . . .
3. La vaisselle? On la . . . . .
4. Les vacances? On les . . . . .
5. Les lits? On les . . . . .
6. La cuisine? On la . . . . .
7. La piscine? On la . . . . .
8. La lessive? On la . . . . .

B. Oui ou non? For each item, decide which noun the direct object pronoun refers to logically. Opinions may differ.

1. On les aime!   (les examens, les fleurs)
2. On les adore!   (les pique-niques, les devoirs)
3. On la déteste!   (la musique, la bibliothèque)
4. On ne l'aime pas!   (le réveil, la plage)
5. On ne les aime pas! (les cadeaux, les devoirs)

C. L'étourdi Candide has lost his belongings!

Modèle Où sont mes livres?
Les voilà!

1. Où est mon dictionnaire?
2. Où sont mes cahiers?
3. Où sont mes clés?
4. Où est mon chat?
5. Où est ma maison?

D. Les goûts et les couleurs Est-ce que vous les aimez ou est-ce que vous ne les aimez pas?

Act. D: CONTINUATION: le professeur de français / l'été / le printemps / le matin / le soir. Ask students to explain their responses.

Modèle ma sœur
Je l'aime. / Je ne l'aime pas.

1. mes amis
2. les animaux
3. l'hiver
4. la campagne

5. la mer
6. la montagne
7. la neige
8. les vaches

Continuons!

A. Et ce soir? Use direct object pronouns to say what you are going to do or not going to do this evening.

Modèle commencer mes devoirs
Je vais les commencer. / Je ne vais pas les commencer.

1. écouter mes amis
2. étudier le français
3. faire la vaisselle
4. faire la lessive
5. regarder la télévision
6. écouter la radio

Ce soir, est-ce que vous allez regarder la télévision?

B. Trop de noms! Here is a story about Candide and Alceste. Rewrite it replacing some of the nouns with pronouns (subject, direct object, stressed). When you've finished, reread your version to make sure you haven't removed too many nouns. (There is no one right way to do this.)

Candide et Alceste veulent aller en vacances! Mais où? Candide adore les villes et la montagne mais Alceste déteste les villes et la montagne. Alceste aime la campagne et la mer mais Candide n'aime pas la campagne et la mer! C'est un problème! Finalement Candide et Alceste vont rester chez Candide et Alceste!

Découvertes culturelles: La famille: tradition et modernité

➤➤ La famille et l'argent

Act. A: Have students deal with one family group at a time. Encourage them to be specific with purchase decisions if possible. Use to review vocabulary (**livres, hi-fi, disques, rideaux, tapis,** etc.).

Act B: Use the photos to review description of people and rooms:

A. Qui achète? Dans votre famille, qui achète et qui décide d'acheter? Et dans la famille de vos grands-parents? Et pour vous, qui décide? Faites une liste du rôle de chaque personne dans la famille.

Modèle   *Chez mes grands-parents, mon grand-père décide.*

B. Trois générations et un budget.

1. **Les photos.** Qui sont ces gens? Décrivez-les. Quel âge ont-ils? Est-ce qu'ils travaillent? Où? Qui est jeune? riche? heureux? Qui a des problèmes? Qu'est-ce qu'ils aiment? Est-ce qu'ils sont de la même famille? Où sont-ils? Décrivez les pièces.

2. **Les mots clés.** Identifiez pour chaque famille le mot qui définit le mieux les rapports des personnes de la famille entre elles et indiquez la personne qui décide.

	rapports familiaux	personne qui décide
Fiorine et André Thévenet	*une bonne équipe*	*la femme: Ministre des Finances*
Joëlle Thévenet		
Sophie et Richard André		

3. **Mots nouveaux.** Identifiez la signification de ces mots d'après leur contexte.

   régissent-ils = *spend / manage / earn / waste*
   argent = *wallet / checkbook / salary / money*

4. **Le sujet.** Quel est le sujet de cet article? Choisissez les réponses possibles.

   ☐ Le rôle des familles dans les finances de la France.
   ☐ Trois familles, un seul budget.
   ☐ Le budget familial.
   ☐ Les difficultés budgétaires des familles modernes.
   ☐ Qui décide pour le budget dans les familles?
   ☐ Trois familles devant les décisions budgétaires.

Des grands-parents, leur fille et leur petite-fille
Trois générations et un budget

Ils ont près de 80, 50 et 25 ans. Régissent-ils très différemment les uns des autres leur vie quotidienne?

Les grands-parents, Fiorine et André Thévenet

«J'ai toujours eu des rapports très flous avec l'argent» dit André Thévenet, 79 ans, photographe à la retraite. Sa femme n'a jamais travaillé. Mais elle s'est toujours occupée de tout: «Moi, je sais gagner de l'argent, mais je ne sais pas quoi en faire.» Il n'a pas de Carte bleue. Pour ses dépenses personnelles, il paie le plus souvent en liquide. «Chez nous, ce n'était pas l'argent de l'un ou de l'autre. C'était l'argent du ménage. Ensemble, on a formé une bonne équipe», ajoute sa femme.

Leur fille, Joëlle Thévenet

Joëlle a 50 ans, une silhouette de jeune fille et l'esprit d'indépendance. Mariée à 20 ans, divorcée à 26, elle a toujours travaillé: «J'ai toujours pensé qu'une femme devait être autonome.» Responsable de la fabrication dans un groupe de presse, elle gagne près de 20 000 francs par mois, tient seule ses comptes. «Je paie le prix de mon indépendance.»

Leur petite-fille, Sophie André

Bien installés dans leur petit appartement cozy du XXe arrondissement à Paris, voilà Sophie, Richard et leurs deux enfants. Maître nageur, à 8 000 francs par mois, Richard a 32 ans. Sophie, elle, est guide interprète dans une agence de voyages — un job qui lui rapporte de 2 000 à 8 000 francs par mois. «Pour moi, c'est impensable de dépendre de quelqu'un.» Sophie et Richard partagent tout. «Tout ce qu'on a, c'est l'argent de la famille», disent-ils.

Le Nouvel Observateur

C. Analyse culturelle: Le budget, étude de cas. Utilisez **oui** ou **non** pour décrire chaque famille.

	Fiorine et André Thévenet	Joëlle Thévenet	Sophie et Richard André
Les membres de la famille sont indépendants			
Les femmes sont émancipées.			
Les hommes sont autoritaires.			
Les femmes sont autoritaires.			
Les femmes sont dépendantes des hommes.			
Les hommes sont dépendants des femmes.			
La famille est traditionnelle.			
La famille est moderne.			

D. Échanges. C'est l'anniversaire du fils de Sophie et Richard. Ils désirent acheter un tricycle mais ce n'est pas inclu dans leur budget. Imaginez leur conversation

Act. D: Encourage students to be consistent with information given in the article. Have students decide what Sophie and Richard will do. Call their parents? Call their grand-parents? Who will buy the tricycle?

Famille, familles...   **179**

▶▶ La famille wolof

A. Les wolof.

1. **Les ethnies du Sénégal.** Combien de groupes ethniques est-ce qu'il y a dans cette région? Quelle est l'ethnie prédominante?

2. **Les sociétés africaines au Sénégal.** Pour découvrir les sociétés africaines, faites trois questions sur trois aspects différents de la société africaine (aspect économique, familial, social).

B. La famille wolof.

1. **Introduction.** Regardez la première phrase du texte. À quelle question est-ce qu'elle répond?

2. **Le sujet.** Quels mots sont les plus fréquents dans ce texte? Comptez combien de fois ils sont cités dans le texte. D'après ce vocabulaire et la phrase initiale, quel est le sujet du texte?

3. **Les personnes.** Combien de noms sont présentés dans les relations de parenté? Combien de relations familiales sont présentées? Combien de personnes sont inclues dans ces relations?

4. Donnez un titre à ce passage.

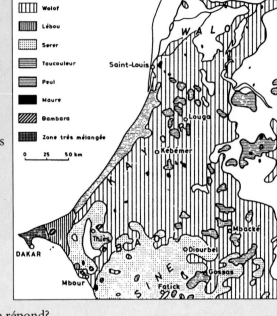

Abdoulaye-Bara Diop

La famille wolof

KARTHALA

Éditions Karthala
2224 boulevard Arago
75013 Paris

La famille wolof

Il n'existe pas de terme propre pour dire parent au sens de père ou mère, L'expression *waa-jur* désigne ces deux personnes à la fois...

Baay englobe le père, ses frères et cousins, plus généralement tout homme de cette génération, à l'exception de l'oncle maternel.
.....
Ndey ou *yaay:* désigne la mère, ses sœurs, cousines et par extension, toute femme de la même génération, exceptée la tante paternelle.
....
Magu-ndey et *rakku-ndey:* désignent, respectivement, la grande sœur et la petite sœur de la mère.
....
Bajjan: sœur du père.., ou sa cousine; plus généralement, toute femme de la génération du père et apparentée à lui.
...
Nijaay: frère de la mère ou cousin de celle-ci; par extension tout homme parent de la mère et de sa génération.

Les collatéraux du même sexe sont désignés par des termes différents, selon qu'ils sont apparentés par le père ou par la mère. Ainsi l'oncle maternel est dénoté par un terme différent de celui d'oncle paternel appelé père. Il en est de même de la tante paternelle par rapport à la tante maternelle assimilée à la mère.

Doom: pour l'homme désigne ses enfants, ceux de ses frères; par extension toute personne de cette génération. Pour la femme, c'est non seulement ses enfants, ceux de ses sœurs mais aussi ceux de ses frères et cousins.

C. Étude culturelle.

1. Chez les Wolof.

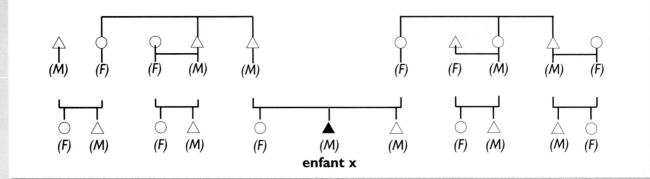

enfant x

- Trouvez l'enfant X sur cet arbre généalogique.
- Soulignez en rouge les personnes qui sont pour lui *Baay;* en bleu, les personnes qui sont *Ndey* ou *Yaay;* en vert, celles qui sont *Magu-ndey;* en jaune, celles qui sont *Bajjan;* en orange, celles qui sont *Nijaay.*
- Comptez combien cet enfant a de *Baay,* de *Ndey,* de *Magu-ndey,* de *Bajjan,* de *Nijaay.*
- Sur la généalogie, écrivez la relation de parenté avec les mots wolof.
- Combien l'enfant a-t-il de pères? de mères?
- Combien l'enfant a-t-il de personnes reliées à lui qui sont différentes des pères et des mères?
- Comment les parents de l'enfant sont-ils groupés? Quelle est l'origine de cette organisation familiale?
- Quelles sont les conséquences de ce vocabulaire sur les rapports de l'enfant avec les membres de sa famille?
- D'après ce vocabulaire, quel type de famille est la famille wolof?

2. Comparaison. Comparez avec votre situation personnelle.

- Combien de personnes appelez-vous pères? Et mères?
- Combien de personnes sont responsables pour vous? Combien s'occupent de vous?
- Qui s'occupe de l'enfant dans votre culture?

D. Échanges: La famille dans les sociétés africaines francophones. Recherches:
Préparez une étude sur la famille dans les sociétés africaines francophones.

- Identifiez le pays et l'ethnie.
- En groupe, identifiez des domaines d'études.
- Choisissez un domaine d'études précis et préparez 10 questions.
- Assemblez vos questions avec celles des autres groupes, et éliminez celles qui sont répétées ou moins importantes, pour avoir quatre groupes de six questions sur des sujets différents.
- Identifiez les éléments constitutifs d'une famille d'après votre optique personnelle. Comment ces questions reflètent-elles vos perspectives personnelles? culturelles?

www explore!
http//voila.heinle.com

*O*rthographe et prononciation

▶▶ Les voyelles en français

Many English vowels are glides or diphthongs: during pronunciation the tongue actually moves. French vowels are simpler sounds with no movement of the tongue involved. Compare the pronunciation of the following:

ENGLISH (diphthongs)	FRENCH (one vowel sound)
lay	les
nay	né
see	si
bow, beau	beau
show	chaud

Activité

Prononcez Repeat after your instructor.

1. la télé
2. un mari
3. c'est la vie
4. difficile
5. joli
6. midi
7. un lavabo
8. un hôtel
9. je vais
10. je ne sais pas
11. une université
12. très bien

*V*ocabulaire de base

TEXT TAPE:
Vocabulaire de base

NOMS

la famille
l'aîné(e) *oldest, first-born (sister or brother in family)*
un cousin, une cousine *cousin*
une famille *family*
une femme *wife, woman*
une fille *daughter, girl*
un fils *son*
une grand-mère *grandmother*
un grand-père *grandfather*
des grands-parents (*m.*) *grandparents*
un mari *husband*
un neveu *nephew*
une nièce *niece*

un oncle *uncle*
des parents (*m.*) *parents, relatives*
un petit-fils *grandson*
une petite-fille *granddaughter*
des petits-enfants (*m.*) *grandchildren*
le (la) plus jeune *youngest*
une tante *aunt*

AUTRES NOMS

une cuisine *kitchen*
une salle de séjour *living room, family room*
le temps *weather*
le vent *wind*

ADJECTIFS

célibataire *single, unmarried*
divorcé(e) *divorced*
marié(e) *married*
mort(e) (en) *dead (in)*
né(e) (en) *born (in)*
veuf, veuve *widower, widow*

ACTIVITÉS

faire les courses *to run errands*
faire la cuisine *to cook*
faire le ménage *to do housework*
faire la vaisselle *to do the dishes*

LE TEMPS

il fait beau *it's nice out*
il fait chaud *it's warm, it's hot*
il fait froid *it's cold*
il fait mauvais *it's nasty out*
il neige *it's snowing*
il pleut *it's raining*
il y a du soleil *it's sunny*
il y a du vent *it's windy*

VERBES

arriver (à) *to arrive (at), to get (to)*
faire *to do, to make*
vouloir *to want, to wish*

DIVERS

après *after, afterwards*
je voudrais, tu voudrais *I would like,
    you would like*
il/elle voudrait *he/she would like*
là *there, here*
Qui...? *Who . . . ?*
si *yes (on the contrary)*

Vocabulaire supplémentaire

NOMS

une femme de ménage *cleaning lady*
la météo *weather forecast*
un nuage *cloud*

VERBES

neiger *to snow*
pleuvoir *to rain*
repasser *to iron*

DIVERS

être en vie *to be alive*
faire la lessive *to do the laundry*
faire les lits *to make the beds*
il fait bon *it's pleasant (mild)*
il fait frais *it's cool*

il fait gris *it's overcast*
il fait lourd *it's hot and humid*
il/elle s'appelle *his/her name is*
il y a des nuages *it's cloudy*
passer l'aspirateur *to vacuum*
Quel temps fait-il? *What's the
    weather like?*
qui *who, that (relative pronoun)*

LE FRANÇAIS TEL QU'ON LE PARLE

Je suis là! *I'm here!*
Qui est là? *Who's there?*
sérieux *trustworthy, reliable,
    responsible*

LE FRANÇAIS FAMILIER

ça caille = il fait très froid

faire du shopping = faire les courses
un frangin = un frère
une frangine = une sœur
mémé, mamie, bonne-maman =
    grand-mère
pépé, bon-papa = grand-père

ON ENTEND PARFOIS...

une avalasse (Louisiane) = beaucoup
    de pluie
il drache (Belgique) = il pleut
    beaucoup
il tombe (Ruanda et Burundi) = il
    pleut
magasiner (Canada) = faire des
    courses
il neigeote (Suisse) = il neige un peu

Vous êtes artiste ou sportif?

En bref

Dans cette leçon...

- Une grande ville: Montréal
- Les vacances: activités et sports
- Les loisirs des jeunes: musique et sports (le verbe **jouer**)
- La possibilité et l'obligation (les verbes **pouvoir** et **devoir**)
- Dire non (suite)
- Quelques expressions au passé

In this lesson...

- A large city: Montréal
- Vacations: sports and activities
- Leisure-time activities for young people: music and sports (the verb **jouer**)
- Possibility and obligation (the verbs **pouvoir** and **devoir**)
- More about saying "no"
- A few expressions in the past

www explore!
http://voila.heinle.com

Develop writing skills with Système-D software!

Practice listening and pronunciation skills with the Text Tape!

Discover the Francophone world!

Build your skills!

INTERNET

SYSTÈME-D

TEXT TAPE

VIDEO TAPE

CD-ROM

Students have an open-ended writing activity in the **Cahier** suitable for use with **Système-D**.

185

Sélectionnez les ingrédients raffinés de l'Ancien Monde, incorporez le savoir-faire du Nouveau. Marinez pendant 350 ans en agitant de temps à autre. Ajoutez-y les saveurs spéciales de plusieurs cultures... voilà Montréal, un étonnant mélange de vitalité et d'humanisme qui aurait enchanté Rabelais, Montaigne ou Bruegel.

Existe-t-il meilleure recette en Amérique?

Troisième site le plus couru en Amérique du Nord par les congrès internationaux (après New York et Washington), Montréal offre davantage pour beaucoup moins.

Montréal et, tout particulièrement, son Palais des Congrès attirent de prestigieux événements mondiaux dont les plus récents sont la Conférence mondiale de l'Énergie, la Ve Conférence internationale sur le SIDA, la réunion du GATT. À l'heure actuelle, la liste des réservations dépasse l'an 2002.

Ses immenses surfaces et sa technologie de pointe font du Palais des Congrès un lieu polyvalent d'une grande flexibilité. Trente et une salles et une superficie de 9 500 m^2 à l'étage des expositions. La salle des congrès permet de recevoir 5 800 personnes pour une conférence et 3 800 convives à un même banquet. Le service du Palais des Congrès de Montréal est hautement réputé.

Ajoutez à ces services un grand nombre d'hôtels de première classe.

Oui, on aime Montréal. Rien d'étonnant à cela. Nous la raffinons depuis trois siècles et demi.

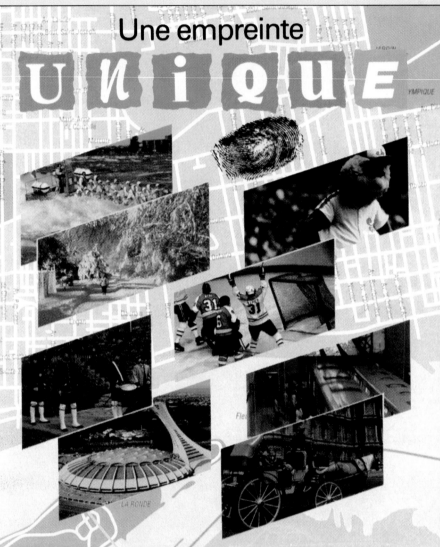

Une empreinte **UNIQUE**

Office des Congrès et du Tourisme du Grand Montréal
Bureau 410
1010, rue Sainte-Catherine ouest
Montréal (Québec) H3B 1G2

Téléphone   (514) 871-1129
Télex   055-60170
Télécopieur   (514) 871-1457

Palais des Congrès de Montréal
201, avenue Viger ouest
Montréal (Québec) H2Z1X7

Téléphone   (514) 871-8122
Télex   055-62429
Télécopieur   (514) 871-1360

Montréal

Photos.
Regardez les photos. Combien de photos représentent...

des activités sportives? ☐	des activités touristiques? ☐
des activités historiques? ☐	des activités urbaines? ☐
des activités commerciales? ☐	des activités nautiques? ☐

Avec un nom et un adjectif, donnez un titre à chaque photo. Choisissez parmi ces mots: culture / théâtre / spectacle / hiver / transport / histoire / sport / musique / traditions / architecture / excitant / amusant / ancien / moderne / blanc / triomphant / intéressant / merveilleux / beau / dynamique

Les activités.
Décrivez les activités de chaque photo:
la scène / les personnes / les activités / le jour / la saison / l'heure

Montréal.
Quels types d'activités caractérisent Montréal? D'après les photos, quelle sorte de ville est Montréal?

Le texte.
Qu'est-ce que le texte décrit? Est-ce que Montréal est une ville appropriée pour organiser une conférence?

You may want to number the photos to help students refer to them. Ask students to quote the number of the photo for each type of activity.

Les activités: You may want to expand with students, reviewing vocabulary: **Est-ce qu'il y a de la musique? Est-ce que les personnes sur la photo sont actives? Est-ce qu'elles jouent? travaillent? marchent? regardent un spectacle? lequel? Est-ce que c'est une scène d'intérieur ou d'extérieur?**

Testez votre potentiel culturel!

Trouvez dans le texte:

- l'âge de Montréal
- le nom d'un peintre flamand
- le nom de deux auteurs français
- trois événements internationaux qui sont célébrés à Montréal
- la surface du Palais des Congrès
- le nombre de personnes que les salles contiennent
- le type de repas *(meal)* qu'on mange au Palais des Congrès
- le type d'hôtels pour les congressistes à Montréal

Vocabulaire

TRANSPARENCY:
8-1

Jacques Dubois announced his arrival
with Paulette in a letter to his son
Vincent in *Leçon 7*.

The **passé composé** of **rencontrer** (part
A.) and **gagner** (part B) are given here
as lexical items since these verbs are
often used in the **passé composé**. The
passé composé with **avoir** will be introduced as a grammar point in *Leçon 10*.

A. Des projets de vacances

Ce soir, Jacques Dubois est là avec son amie Paulette. Il a rencontré Paulette à Nice et maintenant, ils sont chez son fils Vincent. Au dîner, ils parlent des vacances d'été. Jacques voudrait aller en vacances avec ses enfants et petits-enfants, mais c'est difficile parce que tout le monde veut faire des choses différentes. Jacques a envie de faire les musées et de faire de la marche. Il adore marcher, mais son amie Paulette, elle, préfère faire du vélo. Elle adore aussi faire de la photo. Vincent, qui nage très bien, voudrait faire du bateau et de la natation. Thérèse, elle, préfère rester à la plage pour lire mais elle aime aussi faire de la voile. Céline a envie de faire de l'exercice et de la planche à voile. Et Jean-Marc? Comme sa mère, il n'est pas très sportif mais il est artiste: il adore faire de la peinture et du dessin. Et surtout, il ne veut pas partir sans Minou!

- Dans la famille Dubois, qui est artiste? sportif? intellectuel? Qui aime faire des choses fatigantes? Qui n'aime pas faire des choses fatigantes?
- Et vous, vous êtes artiste? Vous aimez les musées? Qui fait de la photo? du dessin? de la peinture?
- Vous faites du sport? Souvent ou parfois? Qui fait de la marche? du vélo? de la natation? de l'exercice? de la voile? de la planche à voile?

B. Maintenant, qu'est-ce qu'ils font?

TRANSPARENCY:
8-2

Qui joue aux cartes? Qui regarde un match de football à la télévision? Qui joue du piano? Qui joue du violon? Qui chante? Mais Thérèse n'est pas là. Est-ce qu'elle est dans la cuisine?

Info plus

Une vieille chanson française.
The song is an Old French song from the seventeenth century. **Une blonde** still means *girlfriend* in Canada today.

Mais non, elle fait une promenade avec les chiens.

- Est-ce que Jacques et Paulette sont heureux? Et Vincent? Pourquoi? Est-ce que Paulette chante bien ou mal? Qui gagne aux cartes? Est-ce que les trois chiens sont à Thérèse?
- Et vous, vous préférez faire du sport ou faire de la musique? Faire de la musique ou écouter de la musique? Faire du sport ou le regarder à la télévision? Faire une promenade ou jouer aux cartes?

Youki is the Dubois' dog. The two others are Jacques and Paulette's (see **Leçon 5)**. If desired, ask students to give them names.

Vous êtes artiste ou sportif? **189**

C. Et les autres membres de la famille?

Après le dîner, Jacques Dubois téléphone aux autres membres de la famille. Qu'est-ce qu'ils veulent faire pendant les vacances? Sylvie veut faire du ski. Elle skie bien pour son âge et elle ne tombe pas souvent. François voudrait jouer au football. À l'école, il est membre d'une équipe qui gagne souvent et un jour, il voudrait être un joueur célèbre! Cédric, lui, a envie de rencontrer des filles. Suzanne voudrait jouer au tennis avec son copain. Elle et Abder ont envie aussi de faire de la plongée sous-marine. Et Béatrice? Elle fait souvent du jogging mais elle adore aussi faire des randonnées à la montagne.

TRANSPARENCY: 8-3

- Dans la famille, qui veut aller à la montagne? Pourquoi? Qui veut aller à la mer? Pourquoi? Et vous, vous préférez la mer, la campagne ou la montagne? Où est-ce que vous ne voulez pas aller en vacances? Pourquoi?
- Pour vous, quel sport est important? merveilleux? horrible? trop fatigant? Est-ce que vous êtes membre d'une équipe de sport à l'université? Est-ce que votre équipe gagne souvent?
- Quel est votre passe-temps préféré à l'université? Et chez vous? Et en vacances? en été? en hiver?

Notes de vocabulaire

1. Mots et expressions utiles.

aller à pied	*to walk to*
à pied	*on foot*
un bateau à voile	*sailboat*
faire du bricolage	*to do odd jobs around the house*
faire du jardinage	*to work in the garden, to garden*
jouer au golf	*to play golf, to golf*
ici	*here*
jouer au basket-ball	*to play basketball*
voici	*here is, here are*

2. Faire une promenade.

Faire une promenade means *to take a walk*. **Faire de la marche** means *to walk for exercise*. **Faire une randonnée** means *to hike*. If you are simply *going someplace on foot (walking there)*, use **aller à pied**.

Tu **fais de la marche?**	*Are you going walking?*
J'aime **faire des promenades.**	*I like to take walks.*
Nous **allons** en classe **à pied.**	*We walk to class.*
Béatrice voudrait **faire une randonnée** à la montagne.	*Béatrice would like to hike in the mountains.*

3. Les jeux et les sports.

When talking about sports or games, the verb **jouer** plus the preposition **à** is generally used to refer to sports or games played by two or more people.

Vous aimez **jouer au** tennis ou vous préférez **jouer aux** cartes?	*Do you like to play tennis or do you prefer playing cards?*

The verb **faire + de la, de l',** or **du** is used to describe participation in a sport or activity. In general, **faire + activité** corresponds to the verb indicating that activity in English.

Il adore **faire du ski** et **faire du jogging** mais il déteste **faire de la marche.**	*He loves to ski and to jog, but he hates walking.*

3: **Faire** can be used for all sports (**faire du football, faire de la natation, faire du golf,** etc.). **Jouer,** however, can only be used for games that are "played," such as tennis or golf, but not swimming or jogging, for example, which tend to be individual activities.

4. La musique.

When talking about playing musical instruments, use the verb **jouer** plus the preposition **de**.

Il **joue du** piano et elle **joue de** la guitare.	*He plays the piano and she plays the guitar.*

5. Avoir envie de + infinitif.

The expression **avoir envie de + *infinitif*** is used to mean *to feel like*.

Tu as envie de faire une promenade?	*Do you feel like taking a walk?*

5: Ask students for other expressions with **avoir** that they already know (**avoir 19 ans, avoir chaud, avoir froid, avoir sommeil**).

If desired, do a brief translation drill to review expressions with **avoir** and with **être:** *I'm hot. He's tired. We're thirsty. He's depressed. Do you feel like taking a walk?*

6. Ce, cet, cette, ces.

Use the adjective **ce** to express the English *this* or *that* and *these* or *those*.

Je n'aime pas **ce** livre. *(masculine singular)*	
Tu n'aimes pas **cet** hôtel? *(masculine singular before a vowel sound)*	
Il n'aime pas **cette** musique. *(feminine singular)*	
Vous n'aimez pas **ces** photos? *(plural)*	

If it is necessary to distinguish between two items, the suffix **-ci** *(here, nearer)* or **-là** *(there, farther)* may be added to the noun.

Tu préfères **cette** voiture**-ci** ou **cette** voiture**-là?**	*Do you prefer this car or that car?*

6: If desired, use the noun pair **ami/amie** to review article and adjective forms before a noun beginning with a vowel (**un ami, une amie; l'ami, l'amie; cet ami, cette amie; quel ami, quelle amie**).

You may want to explain to students that the distinction between **voici/voilà,** **-ci/là,** and **ici/là** in the sense of *this/that* is much stronger in English than in French.

Demonstrative pronouns are treated in the *Appendice de grammaire.*

7: The presentation of past tense forms as lexical items will allow students to become accustomed to such forms before they learn the formal paradigm. Just as small children learning their first language learn verb forms one at a time (rather than learning conjugations or paradigms), so second-language learners can profit from a similar opportunity. If needed or desired, give students additional past tense forms but resist being led into a full-blown discussion of the **passé composé**.

7. Parler au passé.

You will learn how to form the past tense of verbs in French in *Leçons 10, 11,* and *12.* In this lesson, however, you will learn a few past tense forms of selected verbs that are frequently found in the past, for example, **rencontrer** and **gagner**. You have also seen the expression "**j'ai trouvé!**" in *Leçon 6.* For the moment, just learn these forms as vocabulary words.

Jacques **a rencontré** une femme merveilleuse!
Jacques met/has met a marvelous woman!

j'ai rencontré	*I met*
tu as rencontré	*you met*
il/elle a rencontré	*he/she met*

J'ai gagné!   *I won!*

j'ai gagné	*I won*
tu as gagné	*you won*
il/elle a gagné	*he/she won*

8. Les faux amis.

Since French and English share a linguistic history, there are many words that are approximately the same in both languages. These words are known as *cognates.*

8: Cognates are usually easier to recognize in written than in spoken form. Ask students to give the English for the following cognates: **gouvernement / paternel / égalité / justice / changer / double / train / philosophie.**

FRENCH	ENGLISH
animal	*animal*
bleu	*blue*
problème	*problem*

Some French words, however, have evolved differently and have meanings quite different from words they resemble in English. As a result, they may look the same but have very different meanings. Such words are called **faux amis** *(false friends).* Here are some examples:

FRENCH	ENGLISH	RELATED ENGLISH WORD
rester	*to stay*	*to rest*
sympathique	*nice*	*sympathetic*
chambre	*bedroom*	*chamber*
formidable	*great, super*	*formidable*

D'accord?

Act. A: May be done in groups. Have students decide on a few categories before classifying the activities. Compare results with the whole class.

A. Pour qui? Pour quand?

Classez les activités suivantes en catégories:

faire du jardinage / faire de la natation / faire du bateau / faire du ski / faire du vélo / faire les musées / faire de la marche / faire une randonnée / faire du jogging / faire de la photo / faire de la planche à voile / jouer au golf / faire de la plongée sous-marine / jouer au football / jouer au football américain / jouer aux cartes / jouer du piano / jouer de la guitare / jouer du violon / faire de la peinture / faire du bricolage

SUGGESTIONS DE CATÉGORIES: activités pour les jeunes / activités pour les vieux / activités pour l'hiver / activités pour l'été / activités pour le week-end / activités pour la semaine / activités agréables, etc.

B. À mon avis Évaluez ces activités. Utilisez **c'est fatigant, c'est horrible, c'est merveilleux** ou **c'est important.**

Act. B: If desired, remind students about the use of **c'est** + *adjective* to express a general opinion about something. In this case, **ce** does not replace a specific noun but is used in a general sense to refer back to an idea.

Modèle   *Étudier, c'est important!*

1. faire du jogging pendant six heures
2. faire une promenade sur la plage le soir
3. faire la vaisselle pour 20 personnes
4. jouer au football américain
5. faire du sport à 5 heures du matin
6. faire une randonnée à la montagne
7. faire du ski à Chamonix
8. faire de l'exercice pour être en forme
9. aller à pied à la banque quand il fait très froid
10. avoir des professeurs compréhensifs

C. Activités Quel verbe va avec les activités—**gagner, rencontrer, rester** ou **tomber?** Puis évaluez ces activités. C'est agréable ou ce n'est pas agréable?

Modèle   le président
   Rencontrer le président. C'est agréable.

1. chez un ami le week-end
2. un match de football à l'université
3. des personnes importantes
4. dans la neige
5. à la maison le samedi soir
6. à la maison quand il fait froid
7. des garçons ou des filles sympathiques
8. de vélo
9. un match de tennis

D. Personnes célèbres Take turns choosing a famous person and having the other students say what that person does.

Modèle   *—Michael Jordan?*
   —Il joue au basket-ball.

E. Le désir et la réalité Qu'est-ce que vous faites pendant la journée? Faites une liste. Qu'est-ce que vous avez envie de faire maintenant? Faites une liste.

Modèle   *Je mange, j'étudie...*
   Maintenant, j'ai envie de manger. Je n'ai pas envie d'étudier.

F. Le distrait Candide is very absent-minded and is constantly having to ask Alceste what he said. Play the two roles.

Modèle   CANDIDE   Quel livre?
   ALCESTE   *Ce livre!*

1. Quel cadeau?
2. Quelle voiture?
3. Quel homme?
4. Quelle femme?
5. Quel musée?
6. Quels disques?
7. Quel hôtel?
8. Quelles fleurs?

Mise en pratique

A. Les sports et les saisons

Quels sports et quelles activités sont pratiqués chez vous? Quand?

Modèle En hiver?
> *On joue au basketball. On fait du ski. On va au cinéma.*

1. En automne?
2. En hiver?
3. Au printemps?

4. En été?
5. Le week-end?
6. En vacances?

Act. A: FOLLOW-UP: What sports and activities are not common during each season? Why? Have students ask you about sports and activities in the French-speaking world. If you have international students, have them compare these activities with those that are popular in their own country. See also the *Découvertes culturelles* section in this lesson.

B. La famille et les loisirs

Quel est le passe-temps préféré de...

1. votre grand-père?
2. votre grand-mère?
3. votre mère?

4. votre père?
5. vos frères et sœurs?
6. vous?

Act. B: CONTINUATION: Ask what various family members do not do. Have students guess what are your favorite activities.

C. Les Français et les week-ends

Le déjeuner du dimanche en famille

Les week-ends des Français	
«Pour vous, qu'est-ce qui symbolise le plus le week-end?»:	
Le déjeuner en famille	36%
Les moments passés avec les enfants ou les petits-enfants	35%
La promenade à la campagne	30%
Les travaux ménagers, le bricolage, le jardinage	21%
La grasse matinée	19%
La sortie du samedi soir	15%
Les câlins à deux	14%
Les courses du samedi	9%
La messe	8%
Le jogging du matin	3%

Act. C: EXPLICATIONS: **le déjeuner en famille,** c'est quand la famille mange ensemble *(together)* à midi; **la grasse matinée,** c'est quand on reste au lit le matin; **les câlins à deux,** ce sont des gestes tendres.

1. Associez les activités du sondage aux mots appropriés.

aimer quelqu'un *(someone)*	la famille
marcher	le cinéma
manger	l'église
faire de l'exercice	le ménage
le lit	sortir

2. Quelles sont les trois activités les plus importantes du week-end pour les Français? Quelles autres choses font aussi les Français pendant le week-end?
3. Quelles sont les activités qui symbolisent le moins le week-end pour eux?
4. Et dans votre culture, qu'est-ce qui symbolise le week-end? Classez les 10 activités par ordre d'importance dans votre culture. Est-ce qu'il y a d'autres activités à ajouter *(add)*? Est-ce qu'il y a des activités à supprimer *(delete)*?

D. La classe en chiffres

1. Choisissez cinq ou six catégories de loisirs (par exemple, le sport, la musique, les musées, etc.).
2. En groupes de quatre ou cinq, choisissez une catégorie de loisirs et préparez six questions pour vos camarades de classe.
3. Faites votre questionnaire et posez vos questions.
4. Présentez vos résultats à la classe.
5. Quelles sont vos conclusions? (La classe est sportive, n'aime pas beaucoup la musique classique, etc.)

E. Conversation en français
You've gone home for the weekend only to find that your 16-year-old brother has a guest for the weekend, a French teenager who doesn't speak English! Your family, in desperation, enlists your services to find out what their guest likes to do so that they can plan the weekend. Find out the guest's preferences, likes, dislikes, and so forth.

Act. D: This activity could take the whole class period. POSSIBLE PROCEDURE: After the whole class has chosen categories, divide students into as many groups as there are categories. Ask each group to choose a different category and, within that category, to write as many questions as there are members in the group. Each student should then take one of the questions his or her group has generated. Students then circulate in the classroom, asking each other their questions. After a reasonable amount of time, the groups should put their results together to present them to the class either orally, in writing, or both.

TEXT TAPE:
Conversation en français

Structure

CD-ROM:
Build your skills!

▶▶ Les verbes *pouvoir* et *devoir*

Here are the forms of the verbs **pouvoir** *(to be able to, can)* and **devoir** *(to have to, must)*.

pouvoir		devoir	
je peux	nous pouvons	je dois	nous devons
tu peux	vous pouvez	tu dois	vous devez
il } peut elle	ils } peuvent elles	il } doit elle	ils } doivent elles

For all practical purposes, there are no imperative forms of **pouvoir** or **devoir.** If desired, ask students to speculate as to the semantic implausibility of the existence of such forms.

Note that the English equivalent of *should* is the conditional of **devoir.**

Both **pouvoir** and **devoir** may be followed by an infinitive. Note also the various possible English equivalents.

Je ne **peux** pas **parler** maintenant.	*I'm not able to talk now.*
Tu ne **peux** pas **partir**!	*You can't leave!*
Vous **devez téléphoner** à vos parents.	*You've got to call your parents.*
Tu **dois fumer** moins.	*You have to smoke less.*

Vous avez compris?

Act. A: Ask students to justify their answers with examples. **Les étudiants doivent étudier le week-end. Faux. Moi, je n'étudie pas le week-end!** etc. Encourage students to paraphrase and rephrase in order to use the French they know.

A. D'après vous   Vrai ou faux?

1. Un enfant de deux mois peut étudier.
2. Tout le monde doit faire de l'exercice.
3. On peut jouer du piano dans un parc.
4. Les professeurs doivent être sympathiques.
5. Les étudiants doivent étudier le week-end.
6. Un homme de 80 ans peut jouer au football.

Act. B: If desired, explain briefly the use of **le** as a neuter direct object pronoun that replaces a clause.

B. Je dois / je peux   Est-ce que vous **devez** le faire ou est-ce que vous **pouvez** le faire? Peut-être les deux?

Modèle   aller à la bibliothèque
Je peux le faire et je dois le faire!

1. faire de la photo
2. étudier davantage *(more)*
3. faire du jogging
4. jouer de la guitare
5. faire de la natation
6. parler au professeur
7. ranger ma chambre
8. aller à la bibliothèque
9. faire du vélo
10. manger moins

C. Complétez   Use the words in the left-hand column to make sentences. Then, for each one, choose an appropriate continuation from the right-hand column.

1. Mon frère / ne pas / pouvoir aller au cinéma.
2. Tu / ne pas / pouvoir / jouer au tennis.
3. Mlle Durand / devoir / bien parler anglais.
4. Vous / pouvoir / téléphoner à neuf heures.
5. Je / ne pas / pouvoir / aller en classe.
6. Mes parents / ne pas / pouvoir / dormir.
7. M. Brasseur / vouloir / jouer aux cartes tout le temps avec ses amis.

a. Je suis malade.
b. Ils ont beaucoup de problèmes.
c. Sa femme n'est pas contente!
d. Il doit travailler.
e. Il pleut trop.
f. Elle habite Londres.
g. Mais pas après!

Continuons!

A. Associations   Quel verbe—**vouloir, pouvoir** ou **devoir**—associez-vous avec ces activités? Pourquoi?

1. faire ses devoirs
2. être au régime
3. téléphoner à ses parents
4. dormir
5. faire du sport
6. sortir pendant la semaine
7. parler à ses grands-parents
8. faire le ménage

B. Ma vie Faites une liste d'activités pour chaque *(each)* verbe.

1. Je veux. . . (dormir / manger / étudier, etc.)
2. Je peux. . . (nager / faire du vélo, etc.)
3. Je dois. . . (travailler / manger moins / ne pas fumer / ranger, etc.)

▶▶ Les pronoms interrogatifs

Use interrogative pronouns (question words that stand for nouns) to ask about people and things.

Questions about direct objects

1. Use **qui** to ask about *people*.

> **qui + est-ce que + rest of question**

Qui est-ce que Paul aime?	*Who(m) does Paul like?*
Qui est-ce que tu cherches?	*Who(m) are you looking for?*

2. Use **que** to ask about *things*.

> **que (qu') + est-ce que + rest of question**

Qu'est-ce que Jean-Luc regarde?	*What is Jean-Luc watching?*
Qu'est-ce que tu fais?	*What are you doing?*

Questions about subjects

1. Use **qui** to ask about *people*.

> **qui + verb + rest of question**

Here, you do not need **est-ce que.** Note that the third-person singular (the **il**-form) of the verb is used with **qui** as a subject. The **-i** of **qui** is never dropped.

Qui est là?	*Who's there?*
Qui veut manger?	*Who wants to eat?*

2. Use **qu'est-ce qui** to ask about *things*.

> **qu'est-ce-qui + verb + rest of question**

Qu'est-ce qui arrive?	*What's happening (going on)?*
Qu'est-ce qui est important pour toi?	*What's important for you?*

See the **Instructor's Resource Manual** for more information.

If necessary, clarify the terms *subject, direct object,* and *object* of a preposition.

Note that inversion tends to be avoided in the spoken language. Instead, **est-ce que** is used (**Qu'est-ce qu'il fait? Avec qui est-ce que tu parles?**) In informal speech, the interrogative expression is often found at the end of the question (**Il fait quoi? Tu parles avec qui?**). If desired, give other examples of colloquial French (**Tu veux quoi? Il va chez qui?** etc.).

Questions about objects of prepositions

1. After a preposition (**avec, sur, à, de, chez,** etc.), use **qui** to ask about *people.* Unlike English, the question has to start with the preposition.

> preposition + **qui** + **est-ce que** + rest of question

À qui est-ce que tu veux parler?	*Who(m) do you want to talk to?*
Avec qui est-ce qu'elle sort?	*Who's she going out with?*
	(With whom is she goint out?)

If desired, point out that **quoi** is the stressed form of **que**. Like other stressed pronouns, it can be used alone, for emphasis, after **c'est**, and after prepositions (**Quoi? C'est quoi? De quoi est-ce que tu as envie?**).

2. Use **quoi** to ask about *things.* Again, the question will start with the preposition.

> preposition + **quoi** + **est-ce que** + rest of question

De quoi est-ce que vous voulez parler?	*What do you want to talk about?*
Avec quoi est-ce que tu joues?	*What are you playing with?*

Note that **quoi** may be used alone to ask for clarification or to express surprise or indignation. To be a bit more polite, use **comment.**

— Je vais avoir un enfant.	*"I'm going to have a baby."*
— **Quoi?!**	*"What?!"*
— Je m'appelle Émeric Vanderstichele.	*"My name is Émeric Vanderstichele."*
— **Comment?!**	*"Excuse me?!"*

Rappel! You can also use inversion to ask questions such as these:

If desired, give further examples of inversion. (**Qui Paul aime-t-il? Que cherches-tu? Que fais-tu?** etc.). Note that in a **que** question with a noun there is no pronoun duplication as with **qui** (**Qui Paul aime-t-il? Que fait Paul?**).

1. **Qui** aimez-vous?   Chez **qui** vas-tu?
   Que fait-il?   De **quoi** parle-t-il?

Of course, when **qui** is the subject of the question, there is no inversion.

Qui veut jouer au tennis?   **Qui** dort?

2. **Quel** is an adjective. It must be used to modify a noun.

— **Quel chien** est-ce que tu regardes?	*"What dog are you looking at?*
— Je regarde le chien près de l'arbre.	*"I'm looking at the dog next to the tree."*
— **Qu'est-ce que** tu regardes?	*"What are you looking at?"*
— Je regarde le chien près de l'arbre.	*"I'm looking at the dog next to the tree."*

Vous avez compris?

A. Une personne ou une chose? (1) Est-ce que les questions sont sur une personne ou sur un objet? (2) Répondez aux questions selon *(according to)* vos idées sur Malika. (3) Qui est Malika? Comment est-elle?

Act. A: The first question draws students' attention to the distinction made in French between animate (people, animals) and inanimate (inert, not alive) interrogative words, a distinction that interacts with word order in order to help interlocutors keep track of who did what. The second encourages students to act on this distinction by answering the questions. Encourage students to pay attention to coherency between answers. They should be drawing the portrait of one particular person and not answering separate, unrelated questions. If desired, you can bring in a magazine photograph to represent Malika, but this activity works well based simply on student imaginations. The third question encourages students to draw conclusions and to move from the sentence to the paragraph.

1. Qu'est-ce que Malika veut?   4. De quoi est-ce que Malika parle?
2. Qui sort avec Malika?   5. Qui est-ce que Malika cherche?
3. Avec qui est-ce que Malika parle?

B. Des questions Complete using **qui, que,** or **quoi.** Remember to drop the **-e** of **que** in front of a vowel.

Modèle — À *qui* est-ce que vous voulez parler?
— À Madame Renaud, s'il vous plaît.

1. — . . . . . cherche Pierre?
— Moi!

2. — . . . . . est-ce que vous faites?
— Mes devoirs.

3. — De . . . . . est-ce qu'ils parlent?
— Du professeur.

4. — . . . . . regardes-tu?
— Cet homme-là.

5. À . . . . . as-tu envie de jouer?
— Au basket-ball.

6. — . . . . . est-ce que vous voulez?
— Une télévision, une chaîne hi-fi, des vacances,...

Continuons!

A. Et en français Put each sentence into French.

1. *chercher*
   a. What's he looking for?
   b. Who's he looking for?
   c. Who's looking for Pascal?
2. *parler*
   a. Who's he talking to?
   b. What are they talking about?
   c. Who's talking to Pascal?
3. a. What are you doing?
   b. What's happening?
   c. What movie do you feel like watching?

Act. A: Make sure students identify the function of each wh-word (subject? direct object? object of a preposition? adjective?) Then have them decide if the question is about a person or a thing.

B. La famille Martin Read the following paragraph. Make up as many questions as you can about it.

Act. B: Encourage students to ask questions using question words other than interrogative pronouns (**quand, où,** etc.). Students can exchange questions for each other to answer or can ask the instructor their questions.

Les Martin habitent à Genève. Philippe Martin a cinquante ans et sa femme Nadine a quarante-huit ans. Ils ont trois enfants: Luc, vingt-six ans, Isabelle, vingt ans, et Marie-Claude, dix-huit ans. Ils habitent un bel appartement moderne en ville. Philippe Martin est professeur à l'université de Genève. Nadine ne travaille pas, mais elle veut écrire un livre. Luc travaille dans une banque. Il aime beaucoup la campagne et il voudrait avoir beaucoup de chiens et de chats. Mais c'est difficile parce que sa femme n'aime pas les animaux. Isabelle est à l'université où elle étudie l'anglais. Elle va souvent à Londres parce que son petit ami est anglais. Marie-Claude commence l'université. Elle adore sortir avec ses amis et elle parle souvent de politique avec eux.

►► Les expressions négatives

To talk about how people or things are not or what they do not do, or to express ideas such as *never*, *no more*, or *nothing*, you need to learn how to use negative expressions.

1. **In complete sentences.** In complete sentences, negative expressions have two parts: **ne (n')** in front of the conjugated verb and **pas** or another negative word after the verb.

> **ne... pas** *(not)*

Il **ne** chante pas **bien.**   *He doesn't sing well.*

> **ne... jamais** *(never)*

Il **ne** chante **jamais.**   *He never sings.*

> **ne... plus** *(not anymore, no longer)*

Je **n'**habite **plus** chez eux.   *I don't live with them anymore.*

> **ne... rien** *(not anything, nothing)*

Nous **ne** faisons **rien.**   *We're not doing anything.*

Personne can also be the subject of a sentence: **Personne ne veut étudier le samedi soir!**

> **ne... personne** *(no one, nobody)*

Il **n'**y a **personne!**   *There's no one!*

2. **In incomplete sentences.** Frequently the idea of *no* is expressed without using a complete sentence. In these cases, **ne** does not appear. Note the following expressions:

Jamais.	*Never*
Jamais de la vie.	*Not on your life.*
Pas question.	*No way.*
Personne.	*No one.*
Rien.	*Nothing.*
Pas moi.	*Not me. (Not I.)*

— Qui aime travailler?   *"Who likes to work?"*
— **Personne.**   *"Nobody."*

— Qui aime les examens?   *"Who likes tests?"*
— **Pas moi!**   *"Not me!" ("Not I!")*

Toc, toc.   *Knock, knock.*
— Qu'est-ce que c'est?   *"What is it?"*
— **Rien, rien.** Excusez-moi!   *"Nothing, nothing. Excuse me!"*

200   Leçon 8

3. Use **de (d')** (rather than **un, une,** or **des**) after *all* negative expressions.

Il **n'**y a **plus de** fleurs?	*There aren't any more flowers?*
Elle **n'**a **jamais de** stylo!	*She never has a pen!*
Vous **n'**avez **pas d'**animaux dans votre appartement?	*You don't have any animals in your apartment?*

Vous avez compris?

A. Vrai ou faux? Make complete sentences. Then decide if the statement is true or false. If it is false, change it to make it true.

1. Les étudiants / ne jamais / être / fatigués
2. Mes copains et moi, / nous / jouer / aux cartes le dimanche matin
3. Je / rester / à la maison / le week-end
4. Le professeur / ne jamais / être / de mauvaise humeur
5. On / ne rien / faire / dans le cours de français
6. Nous / ne pas / avoir / de problèmes
7. Je / ne plus / regarder / la télévision le samedi matin
8. Les professeurs / ne personne / écouter / en classe

B. Ni ou ni non *(Neither yes nor no)* Answer each question, but *do not* use **oui** or **non.**

Modèle Vous chantez?
Jamais! / Dans ma chambre. / Pas beaucoup.

1. Vous téléphonez à vos parents?
2. Vous sortez le lundi soir?
3. Vous parlez avec vos amis?
4. Vous faites de l'exercice?
5. Vous jouez du piano?
6. Vous gagnez aux cartes?
7. Vous allez à l'université à pied?
8. Vous avez envie d'étudier le samedi soir?
9. Vous voulez être à l'université pendant les vacances de Noël?

Act. B: Brainstorm with students first to establish a list of possible **répliques: pas souvent, une fois par semaine, le dimanche,** etc.

Continuons!

A. Je ne fais jamais... Faites une liste de trois choses que vous ne faites jamais.

Modèle ***Je ne chante jamais.***

B. Je ne vais plus... Faites une liste de trois choses que vous n'allez plus faire.

Modèle ***Je ne vais plus fumer.***

Act. A & B: Make a list for the class for both activities. What five things do people in the class never do? What five things will people in the class not do any more?

C. Jouer au «ni oui ni non» Inventez cinq questions à poser à vos camarades de classe. Ils doivent répondre mais ils ne peuvent pas utiliser le mot **oui** ou le mot **non.**

Modèle — ***Est-ce que tu fumes?***
— ***Jamais, pas beaucoup, etc.***

Act. C: Assign questions for homework or have students work in groups prior to playing the game.

Découvertes culturelles: Sports et loisirs

➤ Quels sports préfèrent-ils?

A. Vos préférences sportives. Utilisez la grille pour exprimer vos préférences.

nom du sport	où	quand
le tennis	*à l'université*	*au printemps*

Act. B: Can be done in groups. Use a transparency to record groups' reports. Ask for several answers for each sport. Provide the time and place for the sports students do not know (**pêche, chasse**, etc.) and have them guess the meaning. VOCABULAIRE UTILE: *usually* = **d'habitude;** *stadium* = **un stade;** *tennis (volleyball, etc.) court* = **un court de tennis (de volley-ball, etc.);** *field, course* = **un terrain (de golf, de sport, de football, d'équitation, de rugby, etc.);** *ice skating rink* = **une patinoire;** *gymnasium* = **un gymnase;** *inside* = **à l'intérieur;** *outside* = **dehors, à l'extérieur**

B. Où et quand? Regardez le tableau de statistiques. Où est-ce qu'on pratique chaque *(each)* sport? Quand?

Modèle alpinisme
> *Dans les montagnes, en Suisse; beaucoup en été, un peu au printemps.*

Act. C: To avoid having students pronounce unfamiliar words, provide a table of the sports and categories and have students complete it (**plongée: sport d'été,** etc.). Can be done in groups.

C. Organisez. Groupez les sports de ce tableau en plusieurs catégories selon *(according to)* leurs caractéristiques communes.

sports violents	sports de campagne	sports gratuits *(free)*
sports de stade	sports d'hiver	sports sans *(without)*
sports d'expertise	sports d'intérieur	équipement
sports d'extérieur	sports lents *(slow)*	sports de nature
sports chers *(expensive)*	sports dangereux	sports d'été
sports avec équipement	sports de détente	sports agressifs
sports de montagne		

Act. D: To avoid having students pronounce unfamiliar words, provide a table of the sports and categories and have students complete (**plongée: le respect,** etc.). Can be done in groups.

D. Caractéristiques socio-psychologiques. Dites à quels sports on associe les caractéristiques suivantes:

la compétition	le plaisir	la dextérité	le respect
l'esprit d'équipe	le développement	l'endurance	l'individualisme

E. Les sports en France. D'après ce tableau, donnez les cinq sports les plus pratiqués des hommes et des femmes. Donnez les moins pratiqués.

La natation d'abord

Taux de pratique sportive en fonction du sexe (1991, en % de la population de 15 ans et plus concernée):

	Occasion-nellement		Réguliè-rement	
	H	F	H	F
• Alpinisme	2,2	1,0	0,6	0,2
• Athlétisme	5,1	2,4	1,8	0,9
• Aviation	1,2	0,6	0,3	0,0
• Basket	4,7	2,7	1,4	1,2
• Bateau à moteur	2,1	0,9	0,4	0,2
• Bateau à voile	2,9	1,7	1,2	0,3
• Planche à voile	3,2	2,3	1,3	0,3
• Boules	15,2	4,7	2,5	0,3
• Cyclisme	17,5	9,7	6,3	2,9
• Chasse	2,8	0,5	3,4	0,1
• Equitation	2,6	2,7	0,6	0,8
• Football	10,1	0,9	6,5	0,2
• Golf	1,6	1,1	0,5	0,3
• Gymnastique	4,2	9,3	2,6	11,4
• Jogging	12,6	8,4	6,5	3,6
• Judo-karaté	1,6	0,9	1,8	0,5
• Natation	20,2	16,7	5,1	6,0
• Patin à glace	3,8	3,1	0,1	0,2
• Pêche en mer	4,6	1,0	1,1	0,2
• Pêche en eau douce	8,6	1,5	4,2	0,2
• Plongée	3,0	1,3	0,9	0,2
• Rugby	2,0	0,2	1,1	0,1
• Randonnée pédestre	11,5	9,3	4,9	4,0
• Ski de fond	8,6	5,9	1,4	1,0
• Ski alpin	13,3	7,9	4,2	2,6
• Ski de randonnée	1,3	1,0	0,4	0,1
• Tennis	15,1	7,8	6,9	2,3
• Volley ball	6,1	2,9	2,1	1,6

Gérard Mermet, *Francoscopie 1995*

F. Pratiques sportives. Choisissez quatre sports différents et dites comment ils sont pratiqués dans votre culture (rarement, fréquemment ou régulièrement). Puis comparez avec les pratiques françaises.

sport	fréquence	où	qui	type d'activité
le football américain	*régulièrement*	*à l'université*	*les étudiants*	*compétitive*

G. Dis-moi quelle activité tu pratiques et je te dirai *(will tell)* qui tu es.

- **Préférences.** Donnez trois activités que vous préférez pratiquer et trois activités que vous détestez pratiquer.
- **Échanges.** Échangez votre feuille avec un de vos camarades de classe et lisez.
- **Conclusions.** Écrivez un rapport sur votre camarades et sa personnalité d'après les activités qu'il aime ou déteste.

Les loisirs des jeunes

Act. A: Do in groups or individually. Have a number of students report while other students take notes. Students taking notes are responsible for (1) reporting on the most frequent activities engaged in by their classmates, and/or (2) asking follow-up questions of the students reporting.

A. Pourquoi est-ce que vous sortez? C'est samedi. Que faites-vous généralement? Complétez la grille.

quand	quoi	avec qui	autres détails
samedi de 14 h à 16 h	*Je / Nous...*		
samedi de 16 h à 18 h			
samedi de 18 h à 20 h			
samedi de 20 h à 22 h			

CULTURE • Comportement

QU'EST-CE QUI VOUS FAIT SORTIR?

C'est au cinéma que vous sortez le plus souvent. Plus qu'aux concerts rock ou en discothèque.

Où sortirez-vous ce week-end? Très probablement, vous irez au cinéma. Sinon, il y a de fortes chances que vous alliez en boîte, ou vous détendre dans un parc de loisirs. Ce sont les tendances générales des sorties des 12–25 ans, selon une enquête du ministère de la Culture sur les habitudes culturelles et de loisirs de cette tranche d'âge.

Après ce viennent les matc concerts du table spectacle fréquent concerts musique et l'opé Vous sou souvent, moins ch c'est le aller/ret plus le dans un régulièr problèm places, r l'éloign loisirs, d transpor

ON PRÉFÈRE SORTIR EN GROUPE!

SURTOUT POUR ALLER VOIR UN MATCH DE FOOT!

C'EST PLUS SÛR!

Dessin de Nikolaz

Les Clés de l'Actualité

B. Pour comprendre.

1. Quel âge ont ces jeunes? Quand est-ce qu'ils sortent?
2. Quelles sont les activités citées dans le sous-titre? le texte? le dessin?
3. Mettez ces activités par ordre de préférence pour les jeunes Français.

C. Comparons. Comparez avec les résultats des activités A et B.

eux	nous
Ils préfèrent...	*Nous préférons...*

D. Invitation. Invitez un(e) ou plusieurs (*several*) camarades de classe à sortir avec vous ce soir. Précisez: pour quelle activité? quand? autres détails?

www explore!
http//voila.heinle.com

Orthographe et prononciation

▶▶ Les voyelles en français (suite)

In English words of several syllables, one syllable is stressed more strongly than the others; for example, the second syllable of *equality*. Vowels in other syllables receive less stress and may even be reduced to an "uh" sound. Compare, for example, the sound of the letter *a-* in *atom* and *atomic*. This system of stressed and unstressed syllables does not occur in French. In French, each syllable is pronounced with approximately the same intensity and vowels are not reduced. Compare the pronunciation of the following words as your instructor pronounces them in English and then in French.

ENGLISH	FRENCH
chocolate	chocolat
animal	animal
salad	salade

Point out the importance of primary stress in English noun-verb pairs such as **ob**ject-ob**ject** and **per**mit-per**mit**.

Point out that the presence of unstressed vowels in English sometimes makes it difficult to spell words like *animal* or *education* where unstressed vowels are reduced.

This explanation deals with syllables in the spoken language.

The father of one of the authors often remarked: «**C'est facile de prononcer l'anglais, il suffit d'enlever toutes les voyelles!**»

Activités

A. Prononcez Repeat the following after your instructor.

1. le cinéma
2. optimiste
3. pessimiste
4. la philosophie
5. un camarade
6. la prononciation
7. un restaurant
8. l'université

B. Des phrases à prononcer Repeat after your instructor.

1. Pierre a une radio mais il n'a pas de télévision.
2. Ça ne va pas! Je suis fatigué, déprimé et malade!
3. Es-tu sportif? courageux? artiste?

Vocabulaire de base

 **TEXT TAPE:**
Vocabulaire de base

Les pronoms interrogatifs (voir pages 197–198)
Les expressions négatives (voir page 200)

NOMS

un bateau, des bateaux *boat*
une chose *thing*
un musée *museum*
un projet *plan, project*
un vélo *bike*

ADJECTIFS

artiste *artist*
autre *(precedes noun) other*
différent(e) *different*
fatigant(e) *tiring*
important(e) *important*

VERBES

devoir *must, to have to*
gagner *to win*
nager *to swim*
pouvoir *can, to be able to*

rencontrer *to meet*
rester *to stay (somewhere)*
skier *to ski*
tomber *to fall*

ACTIVITÉS

faire de la marche *to walk (for exercise)*
faire de la natation *to swim*
faire de l'exercice *to exercise, to get some exercise*
faire du bateau *to go boating*
faire du jogging *to jog*
faire du ski *to ski*
faire du sport *to participate in a sport for exercise*
faire du vélo *to ride a bike, to cycle*
faire les musées *to visit museums*
faire une promenade *to take a walk*
faire une randonnée *to hike*

jouer au football *to play soccer*
jouer au tennis *to play tennis*
jouer aux cartes *to play cards*
jouer de la guitare *to play the guitar*
jouer du piano *to play the piano*
jouer du violon *to play the violin*

DIVERS

à pied *on foot*
avoir envie de + infinitif *to feel like (doing something)*
ce, cet, cette *this, that*
ces *these, those*
ici *here*
mal *badly*
sans *without*
tout le monde *everybody, everyone*
voici *here is, here are*

Vocabulaire supplémentaire

NOMS

le basket-ball *basketball*
un bateau à voile *sailboat*
une carte *card*
le dîner *dinner*
une équipe *team*
le football américain *football*
le golf *golf*
un joueur, une joueuse *player*
un membre *member*
un passe-temps *pastime*

ADJECTIFS

célèbre *famous*
horrible *horrible*
merveilleux, merveilleuse *wonderful, marvelous*

ACTIVITÉS

faire de la musique *to make music*
faire de la peinture *to paint*
faire de la photo *to take photos*
faire de la planche à voile *to windsurf*
faire de la plongée sous-marine *to go scuba diving*
faire de la voile *to go sailing*
faire du bricolage *to do odd jobs around the house*
faire du dessin *to draw*
faire du jardinage *to work in the garden, to garden*
jouer au golf *to play golf*

DIVERS

aller à pied à *to walk to*
être membre (de) *to be a member (of)*
j'ai (tu as, il/elle a) rencontré... *I (you, he/she) met . . .*

LE FRANÇAIS TEL QU'ON LE PARLE

Formidable! *Super! Great!*
J'ai gagné! *I won!*
Pas mal! *Not bad!*
Qu'est-ce qu'ils sont fatigants! *They are so tiring (irritating)!*
Tu es (T'es) sûr(e)? *Are you sure?*

LE FRANÇAIS FAMILIER

le basket = le basket-ball
faire une balade = faire une promenade
faire du footing = faire du jogging
le foot = le football
un truc = une chose

ON ENTEND PARFOIS

le soccer (Canada) = le football
le football (Canada) = le football américain

Magazine francophone

REVUE PÉRIODIQUE

PUBLIÉE À L'AIDE DE
DOCUMENTATIONS INTERNATIONALES

Rédacteur en chef:
Isabelle Kaplan

Rédacteurs adjoints:
L. Kathy Heilenman
Claude Toussaint Tournier

NUMÉRO 2

REVUE EN FRANÇAIS POUR LES ÉTUDIANTS DE «VOILÀ!»

ÉDITORIAL

Pour faire
le portrait d'un pays

Prendre des chiffres, et encore des chiffres.

Faire des additions, des soustractions, des divisions, des multiplications...

Écrire des titres, des questions et faire des colonnes et des listes.

Conclure...

Des chiffres, des statistiques, des faits mathématiques... On regarde une culture et on a l'image d'une réalité culturelle. Pour la population, les modes de vie, les loisirs et les autres catégories, on interroge les chiffres, on regarde les statistiques. Quand partez-vous en vacances? Où allez-vous? Qu'est-ce que vous préférez, le cinéma ou la télévision? Qui fait ceci? Combien font cela? 50 ou 75%? Nous aimons les statistiques, nous adorons les chiffres; ils représentent des informations précises et scientifiques. Nous avons l'illusion de comprendre la culture et nous comparons, nous évaluons, souvent aussi nous jugeons. Mais la culture, est-ce que c'est des chiffres? Et les habitants d'un pays, est-ce que c'est des statistiques? Et les habitants d'un pays, est-ce que c'est des statistiques? Est-ce qu'il est possible d'emprisonner la vie, les émotions dans des paquets chiffrés? Qu'est-ce que les chiffres ne disent pas? À vous de répondre!

TOUT SUR LA FAMILLE

— Au Québec, 25 familles ont plus de 10 enfants. Moins de 1% des familles se rendent à six.

— Une famille sur cinq est monoparentale. Dans 81,9% des cas, les enfants vivent avec la mère.

— Dans les familles biparentales, 86% des couples sont mariés.

— En 1989, le salaire moyen d'une famille biparentale était de 44 213$, alors que celui de la famille monoparentale était de 14 384$.

— 78% des Québécois considèrent qu'on n'accorde pas assez d'importance à la famille dans la société.

— C'est le Québec (49,4%) qui détient le plus haut pourcentage de divorces devant le Canada (38,3%), la Suède (44,1%), le Royaume-Uni (41,7%), la France (31%) et le Danemark (44%).

— Chaque année, quelque 90 000 enfants canadiens vivent un divorce.

Le Québec depuis 1534

1534: Jacques Cartier prend possession de l'actuel Canada pour le roi de France, François 1er.

1608: les Français fondent la ville de Québec qui deviendra aussi le nom d'une province du Canada.

1967: En visite au Québec, le président français Charles de Gaulle encourage l'indépendance de cette province en disant "vive le Québec libre" au cours d'un discours resté célèbre.

1763: Après une guerre entre la France et la Grande-Bretagne, le Canada devient anglais. Mais la Grande-Bretagne permet aux Français de la province de Québec de garder leur langue et leurs coutumes.

1980: Un 1er référendum sur l'indépendance du Québec est organisé. La majorité des Québécois refuse cette indépendance.

Monsieur Dubois, Américain

Il y a 400 ans, sur ordre du roi François 1er, des centaines de personnes originaires de toutes les provinces françaises embarquaient sur des vaisseaux au port de la Rochelle. C'étaient des paysans, des militaires, des artisans et des commerçants, qui partaient s'installer en Nouvelle-France, dans l'actuel Canada. Les lointains petits-enfants de ces pionniers forment aujourd'hui la plus grande partie de la population du Québec. Sur l'autre rive de l'Atlantique vivent donc des Américains qui s'appellent Dubois, Forestier, Langevin, Nadon, Raymond...

Florence Thinard

La famille?
Pas de problème!

Les Canadiens sont heureux de la vie qu'ils mènent, avec leurs enfants et leur conjoint. Mais ils croient que la famille va très très mal...

Les Canadiens — et les Québécois pareillement — sont parfois bizarres: si on les interroge sur leur vie de famille, c'est le bonheur total! Mais si on leur demande s'ils croient que la famille est «en crise», ils s'empressent de dire oui...

Les trois quarts des personnes qui ont répondu à un sondage mené par le Groupe Angus Reid à travers le Canada sur les attitudes face à la famille affirment avoir vécu une enfance heureuse et n'en garder que d'excellents souvenirs. Ils sont vraiment très heureux et satisfaits (à 89%) de leurs relations avec leur conjoint, et de celle qu'ils ont avec leurs enfants (à 90%). Leur famille, «heureuse et remplie d'amour», constitue d'ailleurs la plus grande joie de leur vie.

Sauf que 63% de ces mêmes personnes, dont 70% des Québécois interrogés, croient fermement que la famille vit une crise.

Vous vous sentez proche de...

votre conjoint	**96%**
votre mère	**86%**
vos frères et sœurs	**79%**
votre père	**74%**
votre animal domestique	**69%**
vos beaux-parents	**65%**
vos grands-parents	**52%**

Vous cherchez du soutien moral d'abord auprès de...

un membre de votre famille	**73%**
un ami	**25%**

Êtes-vous d'accord avec les énoncés suivants?

	OUI
La famille canadienne est en crise.	**63%**
Le meilleur modèle est celui où un parent travaille et l'autre prend soin des enfants.	**68%**
Les parents d'aujourd'hui ont plus de difficultés à élever leurs enfants que ceux d'il y a 30 ans.	**74%**
En cas de divorce, la garde des enfants devrait être confiée à la mère.	**30%**
Les adolescentes non mariées devraient être encouragées à donner leur enfant en adoption.	**30%**
Je ne vois rien de mal à ce qu'un couple vive ensemble sans être marié.	**74%**
Le mariage, c'est pour la vie.	**71%**
Je n'ai rien contre l'homosexualité.	**42%**
La religion est très importante dans la vie de tous les jours.	**44%**
Ce n'est pas une bonne époque pour mettre des enfants au monde.	**30%**

La famille canadienne est en crise

	Moins de 40 ans	Plus de 40 ans
D'accord	**26%**	**77%**
En désaccord	**49%**	**10%**
Sans opinion	**26%**	**13%**

Oui, ces changements sont positifs...

Le nombre de familles où les deux parents travaillent à plein temps augmente.	**42%**
Les hommes et les femmes se marient plus tard.	**81%**
Un plus grand nombre de couples «accotés» ont des enfants.	**47%**
Le nombre de familles monoparentales augmente.	**24%**
Les gens qui ne peuvent avoir d'enfants naturellement peuvent maintenant procréer grâce à la technologie.	**71%**
Plus de femmes occupent des postes de direction.	**90%**
Des couples homosexuels élèvent des enfants.	**27%**

Pour élever des enfants, il vaut mieux être mariés.

	Moins de 40 ans	Plus de 40 ans
D'accord	**35%**	**87%**
En désaccord	**51%**	**5%**
Sans opinion	**13%**	**8%**

Portrait de famille

	Moins de 40 ans	Plus de 40 ans
Célibataires	**30%**	**15%**
Veufs, veuves	**1%**	**7%**
Mariés	**46%**	**61%**
Divorcés	**14%**	**16%**
En union de fait	**8%**	**2%**

Regards sur le monde

QUÉBEC

QUÉBEC, PATRIMOINE MONDIAL DE L'UNESCO

Entourée de remparts, dominée par la silhouette familière du château Frontenac, l'hôtel le plus photographié au monde, Québec est plus que la capitale de la province, c'est le berceau de la civilisation française en Amérique.

Des plaines d'Abraham à la Place Royale, les grands moments de l'histoire sont gravés dans chaque pierre. Ville-musée, Québec n'est cependant pas prisonnière du passé. Ses rues grouillent de vie. De la fête nationale le 24 juin, au Carnaval de Québec en février, son carnet de bal est rempli de manifestations culturelles et de réjouissances populaires.

Au-delà de ses remparts, une foule d'activités attendent le visiteur invité à appeler les loups dans la nuit, à descendre des rivières en *rafting*, à escalader des murs de glace, à observer des oies sauvages, à dévaler des pistes en ski ou en vélo de montagne, à faire un voyage nostalgique dans l'île d'Orléans.

ACTIVITÉS

- Sports nautiques
- Bicyclette et vélo de montagne
- Équitation
- Golf
- Chasse et pêche
- Escalade de glace à la chute Montmorency
- Observation de la faune
- Sports d'hiver

Les arts et les lettres

Chanter le français

La chanteuse québécoise Céline Dion a beaucoup de succès au Québec et en France, mais aussi aux États-Unis. Car elle chante en français et en anglais. Comme elle, beaucoup de Québécois sont bilingues: ils sont souvent obligés de parler anglais pour leur travail.

Mais la plupart des Canadiens ne parlent que l'anglais. Même si le français et l'anglais sont les langues officielles du Canada, ils pensent qu'apprendre le français est inutile. C'est pourquoi de nombreux chanteurs du Québec préfèrent chanter uniquement en français pour défendre cette langue.

E. Scorcelletti/Gamma

"De Temps en Temps, Moi, J'ai les Bleus" d'Angèle Arseneault

LE REFRAIN:
De temps en temps, moi, j'ai les bleus
Les bleus royales, les bleus marines,
Les bleus turquoises, les bleus pastels,
Les bleus d'amour,
Les bleus tout court.
C'est pas si mal de temps en temps,
J'en connais qu'ont les bleus tout
  l' temps.

I. D'habitude j'ai d'autres couleurs
    Je me réveille de bonne humeur
    Je m'habille en rouge ou tout en
      blanc.
    Je laisse mes cheveux voler au vent.
    J' mets mes colliers pour déjeuner.

LE REFRAIN

II. Qu'on vienne me voir tôt le matin
    Ou tard le soir ça ne fait rien.
    La porte s'ouvre sans façon.
    La radio chante des chansons.
    Et moi, je ris, j'aime la vie.

LE REFRAIN

III. Je n' me fais jamais de problèmes
    Mes bleus s'en vont et ils reviennent
    Le soleil brille après la pluie.
    C'est toujours comme ça dans la vie.
    On pleure un peu, p'is ça va mieux.

LE REFRAIN

*CLE: l' = le / n' = ne / p'is = puis

D'UNE PAGE À L'AUTRE...

Faites un tableau analytique du *Magazine:* pour chaque article indiquez: (a) le titre de l'article, (b) son sujet, (c) le type d'information et (d) les mots qui justifient vos décisions. Quel est le sujet du *Magazine?* Quels sujets sont absents?

Les arts et les lettres

CHANTER LE FRANÇAIS. Soulignez les phrases de cet article qui se rapportent à Céline Dion. Est-ce qu'il y a un deuxième sujet dans cet article? Lequel?

DE TEMPS EN TEMPS, MOI, J'AI LES BLEUS.

1. Trouvez dans cette chanson les expressions qui s'opposent.
2. Donnez une émotion correspondante à chaque «bleu».

Modèle *Bleus royales: Je suis vraiment déprimé(e).*

3. D'après cette chanson, l'auteur est-elle une personne optimiste ou pessimiste? Pourquoi?

REGARDS SUR LE MONDE

QUÉBEC.

1. Classez toutes les activités présentées d'après leur style (culturelles, sportives, touristiques).
2. Soulignez la phrase qui définit la ville de Québec pour l'auteur.
3. Et pour vous, d'après cette description, Québec, c'est quel type de ville?

À VOTRE AVIS...

RECHERCHES.

1. Dans ce *Magazine,* l'histoire du Canada va jusqu'à 1980. Préparez six questions pour avoir des informations précises et actuelles sur la question de l'indépendance du Québec.
2. Gorée et Québec sont deux sites classés «Patrimoine mondial de l'UNESCO». Dites pourquoi en quatre phrases et comparez les deux villes.

CORRESPONDANCE.

Écrivez une réponse à l'**Éditorial**.

ACTION.

1. **Monsieur et Madame Dubois en 1996.** Faites leur portrait avec les informations des articles du *Magazine.*

Modèle *Les grands-parents de Monsieur et Madame Dubois sont de France, mais eux sont québécois. Ils sont mariés, comme la majorité des couples québécois. etc.*

2. Interviewez Céline Dion. (À faire à deux comme un jeu de rôle.)

À LA LOUPE

L'ÉDITORIAL.

1. Lisez les premières directives de l'*Éditorial* (lignes 1–6). Choisissez quel type de portrait elles présentent: mathématique / humain / subjectif / objectif / général / subtil / succinct / incomplet / précis / suffisant / pauvre / froid / matériel / psychologique.
2. Soulignez les phrases qui expriment une opinion, l'opinion de l'éditorialiste.
3. Choisissez trois phrases différentes dans cet éditorial et dites quels articles illustrent chaque phrase.

LE QUÉBEC DEPUIS 1534.

Dans le texte trouvez trois mots importants pour chaque date:

1534 1967 1763 1980

MONSIEUR DUBOIS, AMÉRICAIN.

Donnez un autre titre à cet article. Soulignez les mots qui indiquent que cet article raconte une histoire passée.

LA FAMILLE? PAS DE PROBLÈME! Trouvez dans le titre, les sous-titres et le texte les phrases qui résument les réponses du questionnaire.

Titre et sous-titres	Texte
Vous vous sentez proche de…	*Ils sont vraiment très heureux et satisfaits de leurs relations avec leur conjoint*

GAGNEZ LE PRIX DES «AMIS DU QUÉBEC»! PARTICIPEZ À NOTRE GRAND JEU-QUIZ !

1er Prix

Répondez en français et calculez vos points. Résultats de votre professeur.

Donnez le nom d'un roi de France.	2 points ___
Donnez le siècle *(century)* de son règne.	4 points ___
Qui est Jacques Cartier?	3 points ___
Donnez trois professions des premiers habitants du Québec.	5 points ___
Donnez le premier nom de la province du Québec.	2 points ___
Donnez la date de l'annexion par la Grande-Bretagne.	3 points ___
Donnez la date du premier référendum.	2 points ___
Quel slogan politique le Général de Gaulle a-t-il créé?	3 points ___
Dites par quel moyen de transports les pionniers français sont arrivés.	4 points ___
Dans quel pays divorce-t-on le plus: le Danemark, la France, le Royaume-Uni, le Canada ou la Suède?	3 points ___
Sur cinq familles combien sont monoparentales au Québec?	4 points ___
Quel pourcentage de Québécois trouvent que la famille est en crise?	4 points ___
Donnez le nom d'un monument célèbre à Québec.	3 points ___
Quelle est la date de la fête nationale?	4 points ___
Pendant quel mois célèbre-t-on le Carnaval de Québec?	2 points ___
Donnez le nom d'une île dans la baie du Saint-Laurent.	4 points ___
Donnez le nom de quatre sports qu'on pratique au Québec.	3 points ___
Donnez le nom de trois chanteurs Québécois.	3 points ___
Pourquoi les chanteurs Québécois chantent-ils en français?	4 points ___

Qu'est-ce qu'on mange?

En bref

Dans cette leçon...

- Le pays thiernois
- Les repas et la nourriture
- Les Français et la nourriture
- Boire et manger
- Les verbes **boire** et **prendre**
- L'article partitif
- L'article partitif après une expression négative
- Le menu d'un restaurant en France
- Un bon plat sénégalais

In this lesson...

- The region of Thiers
- Meals and food
- Eating habits in France
- Drinking and dining
- The verbs **boire** *(to drink)* and **prendre** *(to take)*
- The partitive article **(du, de la, de l')**
- The partitive article following negatives **(de)**
- A French restaurant menu
- A Senegalese dish

www explore!
http://voila.heinle.com

Develop writing skills with Système-D software!

Practice listening and pronunciation skills with the Text Tape!

Discover the Francophone world!

Build your skills!

INTERNET

SYSTÈME-D

TEXT TAPE

VIDEO TAPE

CD-ROM

Students have an open-ended writing activity in the **Cahier** suitable for use with **Système-D**.

Entrée en matière: Produits naturels et régionaux

Les photos: Have students describe the small photographs. Use the photos to recycle previous vocabulary. Offer verbs to select from if students have difficulty: **visiter, regarder, faire une randonnée, faire du bateau, faire du ski, aller au restaurant, aller au musée,** etc.

Have students locate the region of Auvergne and the city of Clermont-Ferrand on a map of France. Thiers is east of Clermont-Ferrand.

Les photos. Voici une brochure un peu comme une page d'album de photos.

Regardez les photos. Décrivez-les. C'est quelle saison? Quelles activités associez-vous avec les photos de cet album?

Cette région s'appelle *Le pays thiernois.* C'est quel type de région?

Quels mots du texte associez-vous avec les photos?

1.	Col de la Charme	a.	plaisir de la table
2.	Aubusson	b.	les musées
3.	(Photo) Fruits, légumes, etc.	c.	le ski de fond
4.	Vollore-Ville	d.	la planche à voile
5.	St-Rémy-sur-Durolle	e.	les châteaux
6.	Lezoux	f.	une petite ville
7.	Maringues	g.	un environnement *Nature*

212

Découvrez un environnement "NATURE"
ainsi qu'Églises, Châteaux, Musées...
Pratiquez le tennis, la planche à voile, la pêche,
la randonnée, le ski de fond...

THIERS

ST-RÉMY S/DUROLLE   LEZOUX

COL DE LA CHARME

AUBUSSON

THIERS

ACCUEIL EN PAYS THIERNOIS
c'est tout cela...
là... où la nature est "nature"
là... où la table reprend son goût.

La brochure. Pour quelles raisons aller en pays thiernois? À quel moment de l'année? En quelle saison? Quel mois? Pourquoi? Pour quoi faire?

Trouvez dans le texte les mots qui indiquent les caractéristiques de cette région. Quels mots s'appliquent aux photos? Quels mots s'appliquent aux produits présentés au bas de la page de publicité?

Regardez les produits au bas de la page. De quelles couleurs sont-ils? Quels produits sont d'origine animale? végétale? D'où viennent-ils? Où sont-ils — dans un magasin? dans un supermarché? ou sur un marché à l'extérieur?

Le message publicitaire. Quelle association y a-t-il entre les produits et les photos? Quand vous regardez cette brochure, quelle impression avez-vous sur le pays thiernois? Quel est le message publicitaire?

Tourisme français. Cette brochure est destinée à des touristes français. Quels sont les éléments importants du tourisme pour les Français? Avec les informations trouvées sur ces pages, faites le portrait des touristes français.

Vocabulaire

TRANSPARENCY:
9-1

The partitive article is presented in the *Structure* section. Exercises in this section do not require the partitive article. Grocery cart = **un chariot**.

Point out that the **-m** in **faim** is not pronounced; it simply nasalizes the vowel. Contrast the pronunciation of **femme** and **faim**. Since students can usually pronounce the word **vin** fairly accurately, point out that **faim** rhymes with **vin**.

Ask students which meal is the most important for them.

If desired, discuss briefly the concept of typical behavior versus individual behavior. In the United States, for example, pizza, is not a typical breakfast food but many people eat it for breakfast.

1. un rôti de bœuf
2. des petits pois *(m.)*
3. des pâtes *(f.)*
4. un pain
5. un croissant
6. une tarte aux pommes
7. un gâteau au chocolat
8. des bonbons *(m.)*

Oh là là, j'ai faim maintenant, moi!

Info plus

Les repas en France.

Traditionally, the noon meal is the most important meal of the day in France. French people take at least an hour to eat and then some time after the meal to drink coffee and read the paper. They will often start the meal with a first course (raw vegetables, **charcuterie**, etc.), followed by the main dish (meat or fish plus vegetable), then a salad, and finally cheese and/or dessert. The evening meal, taken around eight, will be lighter and might consist of soup, **charcuterie**, leftovers, an omelette, or pasta. This is the general pattern, but you will encounter many differences depending on region and family circumstances. Moreover, things are changing, especially in larger cities, where people often have lunch at work or at school. Although lunchtime is shorter, people still often have an appetizer, a main dish, a salad, and cheese or dessert. The evening meal is then considered the main meal.

A. M. Delvaux

«Et pour demain? Pour le petit déjeuner, un pain. Il est très bon ici. Et pour le déjeuner? J'ai un rôti de bœuf, des petits pois, des pâtes. Ça va. Je vais acheter une tarte aux pommes pour le dessert. Et un gâteau au chocolat pour le goûter, à quatre heures. Des bonbons aussi, pour quand j'ai faim entre les repas. Oh là là, j'ai faim maintenant, moi! Je vais prendre un petit quelque chose... un croissant? Bonne idée! Oh, et pour ce soir? Je n'ai pas envie de faire la cuisine. Il y a un bon restaurant chinois pas loin... »

- Comment est M. Delvaux? Qu'est-ce qu'il aime? Est-ce qu'il mange bien ou mal? Pourquoi?
- Et vous, vous aimez les petits pois? Et les pâtes? Vous préférez le rôti de bœuf ou le rôti de porc? Le pain ou les croissants pour le petit déjeuner? Un gâteau au chocolat ou une tarte aux pommes pour le dessert? Les restaurants chinois ou les restaurants français?

B. Mieng Lao

«Bon, pour être en forme, il faut manger des légumes et des fruits... c'est bon pour la santé! Ah, et je voudrais des yaourts et des œufs aussi... Pas de pain, c'est mauvais pour le régime! Et pour être en bonne santé, pas de bonbons et pas de gâteaux! J'ai soif! Je vais acheter un jus de pommes... non, c'est trop sucré. Un jus de pamplemousse, mais sans sucre: c'est meilleur pour la santé.»

1. le jus de pamplemousse
2. l'eau minérale *(f.)*
3. le vin
4. le champagne
5. la bière
6. le thé
7. le café
8. des légumes *(m.)*
9. des fruits *(m.)*
10. un yaourt
11. des œufs *(m.)*

J'ai soif!

TRANSPARENCY: 9-2

- Comment est Mieng Lao? Qu'est-ce qu'elle aime? Elle est en bonne ou en mauvaise santé? Pourquoi?
- Et vous, vous mangez comme Mieng Lao ou comme M. Delvaux? Vous aimez les fruits? les légumes? les yaourts? les œufs? Vous préférez le jus de pommes ou le jus de pamplemousse? Les œufs, c'est bon ou c'est mauvais pour la santé?

C. Mme Baldini

«Est-ce qu'il y a quelque chose à manger pour ce soir? Je vais faire une soupe de tomates. Il y a aussi des restes dans le réfrigérateur et j'ai une pizza dans le congélateur. Ça va, tout le monde adore la cuisine italienne, pas de problème. Est-ce que j'achète des steaks ou un poulet pour dimanche midi? Un poulet! Pour six, c'est plus facile. Avec des haricots verts et des frites... les frites surgelées sont excellentes ici. Ah, il faut aussi deux melons et un jambon. Comme entrée, c'est délicieux, le melon avec le jambon! Il faut un dessert... Voyons... j'ai des fraises et un gâteau, ça va. Ah, je vais aussi acheter des jus de fruit pour les enfants... »

1. des fraises *(f.)*
2. des haricots verts *(m.)*
3. une banane
4. une pêche
5. une pomme
6. une orange
7. un citron
8. la glace à la vanille
9. les frites *(f.)*
10. un poulet
11. un steak
12. un jambon
13. un saucisson

Voyons...j'ai des fraises...

- Comment est Mme Baldini? Est-ce qu'elle habite seule? Combien de personnes est-ce qu'il y a dans sa famille? Qu'est-ce qu'ils vont manger ce soir? Et dimanche?
- Dans votre famille, est-ce qu'on aime le melon comme entrée? Est-ce qu'on l'aime avec le jambon? Est-ce qu'on a un repas de famille le dimanche à midi? Quand est-ce qu'on a un repas de famille?
- Vous préférez le steak ou le poulet? Vous aimez la pizza? Vous l'aimez chaude ou froide? Vous aimez la cuisine italienne?

TRANSPARENCY: 9-3

Explain that the **h-** of **haricots verts** is an aspirate **h** and blocks **élision** and **liaison**. See the *Orthrographe et prononciation* section of this lesson.

Ask students to look at the picture. What meal is this? What time of day is it? Who are these people? What's on the small table? Does this look like a scene that you might find where you live? etc. Ask students: Some friends are invited over for a drink. What time will they arrive? What will be served?

Info plus

L'apéritif.

In France, **l'apéritif** refers both to a drink taken before lunch or dinner and to the convivial time that people share before a meal. When guests are present, **l'apéritif** is served with crackers, chips, nuts, or other snacks. One can be invited for **l'apéritif** by itself, before lunch, or before dinner. In that case, the guest is expected to leave early enough for the family to have time for their meal, especially if it is lunch. Friends can also meet in a café before going home for their meal. **L'apéritif** is then perceived as a transitional time between work and home.

1. des chips *(m.)*
2. une carotte
3. une tomate
4. une laitue
5. un fromage
6. des conserves *(f.)*
7. le beurre
8. le lait

Bon, pour ce soir...

TRANSPARENCY:
9-4

D. Philippe Vandamme

«Bon, pour ce soir... Pour l'apéritif, avant le dîner, des chips. Comme entrée, des crudités: des carottes et des tomates. C'est bien pour Sébastien, qui est au régime. Et surtout pas de mayonnaise pour lui! Une vinaigrette? Oui, mais je vais la faire, c'est meilleur que quand on l'achète. Bon, maintenant, comme plat principal... une omelette, peut-être... avec des champignons. Surtout pas de viande et pas de poisson, avec Anne qui est végétarienne! Après, une salade, deux ou trois fromages... Ah, je n'ai pas de dessert. Il faut acheter un dessert... Voyons, une glace? Oui, bonne idée! Caroline adore la glace au chocolat, et moi aussi. Ça va être un bon petit dîner. Et comme boisson? J'ai des bières dans le réfrigérateur. Tout le monde aime la bière, pas de problème... »

- Comment est Philippe Vandamme? Quel âge a-t-il? Il est étudiant ou il travaille? Il est marié ou célibataire? Pourquoi est-ce qu'il fait les courses? Qui sont Sébastien, Caroline et Anne? Qu'est-ce qu'ils vont manger? Ça va être bon? C'est vrai que tout le monde aime la bière?
- Et vous, vous aimez les crudités? Vous préférez les carottes ou les tomates? Vous préférez la vinaigrette ou la mayonnaise avec les crudités? Vous préférez les fromages français ou les fromages américains? Avec une omelette, vous préférez la bière, le vin ou l'eau? Et avec le fromage?
- Chez qui (Philippe Vandamme, Mme Baldini, etc.) voulez-vous manger ce week-end? Pourquoi?
- Vous préférez manger des choses sucrées ou salées? Quelle est votre boisson préférée? votre légume préféré? votre fruit préféré? votre dessert préféré? Qu'est-ce que vous détestez?

216 *Leçon 9*

E. Et aussi...

La nourriture (Food)

Les légumes:

des asperges (f.)	asparagus
des épinards (m.)	spinach
une pomme de terre	potato
un oignon	onion

La viande:

le bœuf	beef
le porc	pork
le mouton	mutton
la dinde	turkey
la charcuterie	cold cuts
le pâté	pâté
un steak haché	hamburger

Le poisson:

le thon	tuna
le saumon	salmon
une crevette	shrimp

Les fruits:

une poire	pear
une prune	plum
un raisin	grape

Pour le petit déjeuner:

le café au lait	coffee with milk
les céréales	cereals

Pour le goûter:

la confiture	jam
le chocolat	chocolate

Info plus

Le goûter.

Le goûter refers to food eaten in the late afternoon and is the equivalent of British afternoon tea (the French equivalent of the English expression to have a snack is **prendre quelque chose** or **prendre un petit quelque chose**). Since dinner is late in France, French children have a **goûter** when they arrive home from school at four o'clock. Most often, they have bread with jam or chocolate and a cup of hot chocolate or milk. Older children and adults may have a cup of coffee or tea. For their birthday, French children can invite their friends to a **goûter d'anniversaire** featuring cakes and pies.

Pour un pique-nique:

un sandwich (au jambon, au fromage)	(ham, cheese) sandwich
le Coca-Cola, le coca	Coca-Cola, Coke

Et aussi:

le sel	salt
le poivre	pepper
la moutarde	mustard
le riz	rice

- Quelles sont les choses sucrées? salées? Qu'est-ce que vous aimez? Qu'est-ce que vous n'aimez pas?

Remind students to use the definite article after verbs like **aimer**.

Qu'est-ce qu'on mange? **217**

Notes de vocabulaire

1. Mots et expressions utiles.

1: If desired, tell students that there is no feminine singular form of **quelqu'un.**

inviter	*to invite*
japonais(e)	*Japanese*
prendre un verre	*to have a drink*
quelqu'un	*somebody, someone*
une soirée	*party*

2. Bon / mauvais / meilleur. The adjectives **bon** and **mauvais** are placed in front of the noun.

2: A summary of adjective and adverb comparison constructions is in the *Structure* section of *Leçon 15.*

Les professeurs aiment les **bons étudiants,** mais les **mauvais étudiants?**
C'est un problème!

When you want to say that something or someone is better, use **meilleur(e)**
or **meilleur(e)... que.**

Est-ce que les fromages français sont **meilleurs que** les fromages américains?
Are French cheeses better than American cheeses?

Le vin, c'est bon, mais le champagne, c'est **meilleur!**
Wine is good, but champagne is better!

3. Avant / après; devant / derrière. Note the difference in usage of these prepositions.

avant / après = *before / after (in time)*
devant / derrière = *in front of / in back of (in space)*

Est-ce que tu étudies **avant** ou **après** le dîner?	*Do you study before or after dinner?*
Il y a quelqu'un **derrière** toi!	*There's someone behind you!*
Il n'y a personne **devant** moi.	*There's nobody in front of me.*

4. Acheter. The verb **acheter** adds an accent grave over the middle -e- in forms where the ending is silent

j'achète	nous achetons
tu achètes	vous achetez
il elle } achète	ils elles } achètent

5. Il faut. To say that one needs something or has to do something, use **il faut** + *noun* or **il faut** + *verb* in the infinitive.

5: Il faut + subjunctive is treated in *Leçon 20.*

Après le dîner, **il faut un dessert!**
After dinner, one needs dessert!

Pour être en bonne santé, **il faut manger** des légumes.
In order to be healthy, one needs to eat vegetables.

6. J'ai faim! J'ai soif!

6. J'ai faim! J'ai soif! **Avoir faim** and **avoir soif** are expressions with **avoir** similar to **avoir sommeil, avoir chaud,** and **avoir froid.**

Quand M. Delvaux **a faim,** il mange des bonbons.	*When Mr. Delvaux is hungry, he eats candy.*
J'**ai soif!** Je vais boire un Coca-Cola.	*I'm thirsty! I'm going to have a Coke.*

D'accord?

A. Chassez l'intrus Quel mot ne va pas avec les autres à cause du sens *(meaning)?*

1. une pomme de terre / une tomate / le jambon / des haricots verts / une carotte
2. un steak / un rôti / une pomme / un saucisson / un poulet
3. des asperges / une poire / une pêche / une fraise / un pamplemousse
4. le petit déjeuner / le goûter / des crudités / le dîner / le déjeuner
5. le beurre / la confiture / le café au lait / le pain / les épinards
6. une glace / un pâté / des raisins / un gâteau / une tarte
7. le riz / le lait / le thé / la bière / le Coca-Cola
8. des asperges / des petits pois / le sucre / des oignons / des épinards
9. le bœuf / le porc / le mouton / un steak haché / la moutarde
10. la dinde / le saumon / le thon / les crevettes / un poisson

B. Normal ou bizarre? C'est normal ou c'est bizarre?

1. un steak dans un tiroir
2. des épinards dans une salade
3. des bières dans le réfrigérateur
4. le pain dans le réfrigérateur
5. des tomates dans un sac
6. des frites surgelées dans un placard

Act. B: CONTINUATION: des frites avec un steak haché / un yaourt avec des oignons / le lait avec le dîner
Opinions may differ.

C. Qu'en pensez-vous? Est-ce que c'est bon? C'est mauvais? C'est bon pour la santé? C'est mauvais pour la santé? C'est bon pour le régime? C'est mauvais pour le régime?

1. un gâteau au chocolat
2. le lait chaud
3. un steak-frites
4. le café au lait
5. le sucre
6. le fromage
7. le vin
8. le jus d'orange
9. les conserves
10. les épinards
11. la charcuterie
12. une bière chaude

Act. C: You might want to compare French and North American opinions on what is good or not, concerning both health and taste.

D. Quand? Quand est-ce que vous mangez les plats ou vous buvez *(drink)* les boissons suivants? (SUGGESTIONS: au petit déjeuner, à midi, à 16 heures, au dîner, à 21 heures.)

Act. D: CONTINUATION: le fromage? les épinards? le café?

Modèle le café au lait?
> ***Au petit déjeuner, pas au dîner...***

1. une bière?
2. le jambon?
3. une pizza?
4. une glace au chocolat?
5. un sandwich?
6. une omelette?

Act. E: CONTINUATION: Où est/sont...
le jus de pamplemousse? le pain? les
pommes? le jus de pomme? les
restes? etc. Ask students to suggest
other foods and beverages.

E. Dans la cuisine Il est tard *(late)* et vous avez faim et soif. Suivez le modèle.

Modèle Où sont les bananes?...
J'ai faim!

1. Où est le lait?...
2. Où est le jambon?...
3. Où est la pizza?...
4. Où sont les bonbons?...
5. Où est la bière?...

Act. F: CONTINUATION AND
EXPANSION: quand on est triste?
malheureux? fâché? furieux? déprimé?
etc.

F. Des conseils Qu'est-ce qu'il faut faire...

Modèle ... quand on a soif?
Il faut boire!

1. ... quand on a faim?
2. ... quand on a sommeil?
3. ... quand on a chaud?
4. ... quand on a un examen?
5. ... quand on a des problèmes?
6. ... quand on est au régime?

Mise en pratique

Act. A: Answers: 1. le fromage, le vin
2. les tomates, les fraises, etc.
3. le vin 4. les bananes, les poires
5. les petits pois

A. Qu'est-ce que c'est? Voilà des devinettes *(riddles)*. Quelles sont les réponses?

1. Il est bon quand il est un peu vieux. Qu'est-ce que c'est?
2. Elles sont bonnes quand elles sont rouges. Qu'est-ce que c'est?
3. Il est blanc avec le poisson et rouge avec le steak. Qu'est-ce que c'est?
4. Elles sont vertes, jaunes ou brunes. Qu'est-ce que c'est?
5. Ils sont verts et ils sont délicieux quand ils sont très petits. Qu'est-ce que c'est?

B. Les goûts

Act. B: Encourage students to qualify
their answers by using words like
beaucoup or un peu. Expand by having
students organize a class survey or by
having students ask you about your
food/drink preferences.

1. Faites des listes.

| a. les légumes |
| b. la viande et le poisson |
| c. les desserts |
| d. les fruits |
| e. les boissons |

2. Posez des questions pour trouver les préférences de vos camarades de classe.

   Modèle *Tu aimes les haricots verts ou non?*

C. Les Français et la nourriture Regardez ce que mangent les Français dans les années 90 en comparaison des années 70.

Act. C, 2: Avoid the use of the partitive by having students write lists. If desired, teach **plus de** and **moins de**.

EXPLICATIONS: Les volailles, c'est par exemple le poulet, la dinde et le canard *(duck)*.

1. Quels sont les trois aliments préférés des Français en 1970? Et en 1991? Dans le même *(same)* ordre?
2. Faites deux listes: les choses que les Français mangent plus maintenant qu'avant et les choses que les Français mangent moins maintenant. Qu'est-ce qui a beaucoup diminué *(decreased)*? Qu'est-ce qui a beaucoup augmenté *(increased)*? C'est bon ou c'est mauvais pour la santé, à votre avis? Est-ce que les Français mangent mieux maintenant qu'avant? Pourquoi?
3. En groupes, faites une liste des 10 aliments préférés dans votre culture et comparez avec les préférences des Français.

Un an de nourriture

Evolution des quantités consommées par personne et par an (en kg):

	1970	1991
• Pain	80,6	65,0
• Pommes de terre	95,6	64,3
• Légumes frais	70,4	92,3
• Légumes surgelés	0,5	5,5*
• Bœuf	15,6	17,9
• Charcuterie et conserves de viande	9,2	14,6
• Volailles	14,2	22,3
• Œufs	11,5	14,7
• Poissons, coquillages, crustacés	10,8	19,6
• Yaourts	8,6	15,9*
• Huile	8,1	11,8
• Sucre	20,4	9,8

*1989

INSEE

Structure

CD-ROM:
Build your skills!

▶▶ Les verbes *boire* et *prendre*

The verb **boire** means *to drink.* Its conjugation is irregular.

je bois	nous buvons
tu bois	vous buvez
il ⎫ boit elle ⎭	ils ⎫ boivent elles ⎭

DRILL: Alceste ne boit pas le matin. (les enfants / je / tu / Alceste et Candide / nous / vous)

Qu'est-ce qu'**on boit?**   *What's everybody drinking?*

The verb **prendre** means *to take*. Its conjugation is irregular. Note the double **-n-** in the third person plural.

DRILL: Qu'est-ce que tu prends? (elle / nous / Alceste / Alceste et Candide / je / vous)

LISTENING COMPREHENSION: Singulier ou pluriel? Il boit un thé. Elles prennent une orange. Ils ne boivent pas le matin. Elle ne prend pas de petit déjeuner? Elle prend son vélo. Ils prennent la voiture. Elles boivent beaucoup de café. Il boit un thé. Elles prennent un café.

je prends	nous prenons
tu prends	vous prenez
il } prend	ils } prennent
elle	elles

Je sors et **je prends** mon vélo.   *I'm going out and I'm taking my bike.*
Tu vas **prendre** ton dictionnaire   *Are you going to take your dictionary*
   ou pas?   *or not?*

Prendre is also used to express the idea of having a meal or having something to eat or drink.

Point out: **On prend un repas. Manger** is not used with meals.

Students will learn about the usage of the partitive article in the next *Structure* section. Avoid requiring its use here.

À quelle heure est-ce qu'**on prend**   *What time do you eat breakfast at your*
   le petit déjeuner chez toi?   *house?*
Tu prends ton café sans sucre?   *Do you take your coffee without sugar?*
Je prends un croissant, et toi?   *I'll have a croissant. How about you?*

The imperative or command forms of **boire** and **prendre** are identical with their present tense forms.

Bois ton lait!   *Drink your milk!*
Vite, **buvez** votre café, on y va!   *Quick, drink your coffee, we're leaving!*
Il fait chaud. **Buvons** un jus de fruit.   *It's hot. Let's drink a fruit juice.*

Prends ton vélo!   *Take your bike!*
Prenez le bus!   *Take the bus!*
Prenons un café.   *Let's get a cup of coffee.*

Vous avez compris?

Act. A: Redo A asking for complete sentences with direct object pronouns: le lait: On le boit.

A. Ça se boit ou ça se mange? Boire ou manger? Suivez le modèle.

Modèle   le lait
          boire

1. les carottes
2. le fromage
3. les œufs
4. le café
5. le riz
6. la bière
7. le thé
8. l'eau
9. la viande
10. le jus de fruit

222   *Leçon 9*

B. Qu'est-ce qu'on boit? Complétez en utilisant une forme du verbe **boire.**

1. Qu'est-ce que vous ..... ?
2. Ils ..... trop!
3. Marianne ne ..... jamais avec les repas.
4. Qu'est-ce que tu vas ..... ?
5. ..... ton café! Il faut partir!
6. Je ne ..... jamais entre les repas.
7. Vous avez soif? Mais ..... donc votre eau!

C. En famille C'est le matin et la Famille Durieux se prépare *(is getting ready)* à partir. Qu'est-ce qu'ils disent *(are saying)*? Utilisez le verbe **prendre** pour compléter chaque phrase.

Act. C: Ask students to identify which member of the family (**la mère, le père, les enfants**, etc.) might have said each sentence.

Modèle Tu / tes cahiers?
> ***Tu prends tes cahiers?***

1. Je / le sac pour aller au supermarché.
2. Sophie! Paul! Vous / votre vélo?
3. Martine! Ton père / la voiture?
4. Les enfants / leurs livres?
5. Oui, oui maman! Nous / nos sandwichs!

Continuons!

A. Faites des phrases Boire ou prendre? Faites des phrases.

1. Tu / ne rien boire?
2. Elle / aller / prendre / un thé.
3. Est-ce que / il y /avoir / quelque chose à / boire / dans le réfrigérateur?
4. Quand / je / avoir très soif, / je / boire / un jus de fruit.
5. Qu'est-ce que / ils / prendre / au petit déjeuner?
6. M. Pinard / boire / beaucoup de vin rouge / le soir.

B. Un sondage Posez des questions à vos camarades de classe et à votre professeur pour déterminer quand ils prennent leurs repas.

Quand est-ce que tu (vous) prends (prenez)...			
NOM	le petit déjeuner?	le déjeuner?	le dîner?

Practice of the use of the verbs **prendre** and **boire** will continue in exercises following the presentation of the partitive article and the partitive and indefinite articles in the negative.

➡ L'article partitif

To talk about a part of something that you cannot count, use the partitive article.

MASCULINE	FEMININE	BEFORE A VOWEL
du riz	**de la** bière	**de l'**eau
(some) rice	(some) beer	(some) water

Des is considered here only as the plural indefinite article. Point out that the partitive article cannot be dropped, as is sometimes the case in English (Do you want coffee or tea? **Tu veux du café ou du thé?**).

In many cases, the English *some* or *any* can be used to translate the partitive article. Frequently, however, it is omitted.

Est-ce qu'il y a **de la bière** dans le frigo?	*Is there (any) beer in the refrigerator?*
Non, mais il y a **du coca.**	*No, but there's (some) cola.*

If whatever you're talking about is countable, use an indefinite article: **un, une, des.**

Tu veux **un sandwich?**	*Do you want a sandwich?*
Oui, et **des frites,** et après, **une glace** à la fraise! J'ai très faim!	*Yes, and some (French) fries, and then a strawberry ice cream (cone). I'm really hungry!*

Note that some objects can be either counted or not, depending on the context.

Tu veux **du café?**	*You want (some) coffee?*
Tu veux **un café?**	*You want (a cup of) coffee?*
Tu bois **de la bière?**	*Are you drinking beer? (some beer, not all the beer in the world!)*
Je veux **une bière.**	*I want a (can of, bottle of) beer.*
Comme dessert, il y a **une tarte aux pommes.**	*For dessert, there's an apple pie.*
Tu veux **de la tarte?**	*Do you want some pie?*

Vous avez compris?

Act. A: Ask students to speculate about the kinds of people these are, based on their choice of food. FOLLOW-UP QUESTIONS: **Qui est au régime? Qui a faim? Qui n'a pas faim? Qui ne prend pas de viande?**

A. Au restaurant universitaire Qu'est-ce qu'ils mangent aujourd'hui?

Modèle   JEAN-PIERRE: steak, frites, glace au chocolat, eau minérale
Il prend un steak (du steak), des frites, une glace au chocolat (de la glace au chocolat) et de l'eau minérale (une eau minérale).

1. PAULINE: œuf, asperges, fromage
2. MICHEL: jambon, poisson, carottes, pommes de terre, salade, pain, fromage, tarte aux fraises, café
3. FRANÇOIS: crudités, pâtes au fromage, pain, poire, jus de fruit
4. SOLANGE: sandwich au fromage, thé
5. ANNE: poulet, frites, salade, pain, fromage, glace, café

B. Candide fait les courses Candide va au supermarché. Voilà sa liste, mais sans articles! Utilisez des articles (**un, une, des, du, de la** ou **de l'**) pour la compléter.

Act. B: If time permits, ask students to put together possible meals for Candide based on his shopping list.

```
_____ café
_____ vin
_____ gâteau
_____ épinards
_____ rôti de porc
_____ pain
_____ champignons
_____ pommes de terre
_____ tarte aux pommes
_____ œufs
_____ eau minérale
_____ sel
_____ melon
_____ fromage
_____ yaourts
_____ glace
_____ riz
```

Continuons!

A. Dans le frigo Qu'est-ce qu'il y a...

Act. A: Ask students what might be in Alceste's or Candide's refrigerator.

1. dans votre réfrigérateur?
2. dans le réfrigérateur de votre professeur?
3. dans le réfrigérateur à la Maison Blanche?
4. dans le réfrigérateur de...?

B. Boissons typiques Qu'est-ce qu'ils boivent?

Act. B: CONTINUATION: les étudiants quand ils ont des examens? les Français au dîner? les enfants français à table?

1. les Chinois?
2. les Allemands (*Germans*)?
3. les Français?
4. votre grand-mère?
5. vous avec vos amis?
6. vous avec vos parents?

C. Habitudes alimentaires Qu'est-ce qu'ils mangent?

1. les Japonais?
2. les Italiens?
3. les Français au petit déjeuner?
4. les étudiants devant la télévision?
5. votre grand-père?
6. un joueur de football américain?
7. une personne au régime?
8. les enfants français au goûter?

D. La classe et les repas Que prennent vos camarades de classe? Posez des questions.

Modèle   —*Qu'est-ce que tu prends au petit déjeuner?*
      —*Du pain, de la confiture et du café.*

▶ L'article partitif et l'article indéfini après une expression négative

The partitive article, like the indefinite article, is reduced to **de (d')** when it follows a negative expression.

> Qu'est-ce qu'il y a dans le frigo?
> *What's in the fridge?*

> On a **des** pommes mais on **n'**a **pas de** poires. On a **du** vin mais on **n'**a **plus de** lait. On a **de la** confiture mais il **n'**y a **jamais de** beurre.
> *We have (some) apples but we don't have (any) pears. We have (some) wine, but we don't have any more milk. We have (some) jam, but there's never any butter.*

Rappel! Les articles définis, indéfinis et partitifs

	LES ARTICLES DÉFINIS	LES ARTICLES INDÉFINIS	LES ARTICLES PARTITIFS
MASCULIN	le (l')	un	du (de l')
FÉMININ	la (l')	une	de la (de l')
PLURIEL	les	des	

1. Use definite articles:

• *To talk about preferences* (with verbs like **aimer, détester, préférer,** etc).

  J'aime **le thé** mais je préfère **le café.**   *I like tea but I prefer coffee.*

- *To talk about things in general.*

  Les légumes sont bons   *Vegetables are good when*
    quand on est au régime.   *you're on a diet.*

- *To refer to something specified or already mentioned.* English uses definite articles in the same way.

  —On mange une pizza ce soir?   *How about a pizza tonight?*
  —Oui, d'accord.   *Sure, OK.*
  —Bon, alors, qui achète   *Good, who's buying the*
    la pizza, toi ou moi?   *pizza? You or me?*
  —Moi, et toi, tu achètes **le**   *Me, and you're buying*
    coca et **la bière.**   *the cola and the beer.*

  Definite articles do not change after a negative expression.

  Candide n'aime pas **les tomates.**   *Candide doesn't like tomatoes.*

2. Use indefinite articles to refer to unspecified things that you can count. Indefinite articles become **de (d')** after a negative expression.

   —Tu veux **une pomme?**   *Do you want an apple?*
   —Non, je **ne** veux **pas de pomme.**   *No, I don't want an apple.*

3. Use partitive articles to refer to unspecified things that you do not count. Partitive articles become **de (d')** after a negative expression.

   —Est-ce qu'il y a **du fromage?**   *Is there any cheese?*
   —Non, il **n'**y a **pas de fromage**   *No, there isn't any cheese,*
     mais il y a **de la glace.**   *but there's some ice cream.*
   —Je **ne** veux **pas de glace.**   *I don't want ice cream.*
     Est-ce qu'il y a **du yaourt?**   *Is there any yogurt?*
   —Oui, il y a **du yaourt.**   *Yes, there's some yogurt.*

Vous avez compris?

A. Alceste est végétarien mais pas Candide Décidez qui parle, Alceste ou Candide. Ensuite *(Then)*, décidez avec qui vous voulez dîner.

Modèle Je prends du porc.
        C'est Candide.

1. Le matin, j'ai très faim. Je prends du café, du pain, et, de temps en temps, du jambon et des œufs.
2. Je déteste les desserts et je ne prends jamais de glace. Des fruits, ça va mais je ne prends jamais de viande.
3. Un sandwich au fromage et une salade, c'est merveilleux! Un sandwich au jambon, ce n'est pas possible!
4. Le dîner idéal? Euh, un rôti de bœuf, des pommes de terre, des haricots verts, du vin, et, bien sûr, une tarte aux pommes pour terminer.

If desired, ask students to come up with some "rules of thumb" for article use (negative + **de**; **aimer** + **le, la, les,** etc.). Emphasize that these "rules of thumb" will be very helpful in the short term, but that they do not represent descriptive reality. That is, a more complete description of French will include much more information—and exceptions.

Act. A: If desired, have students analyze the use of articles.

B. Chez moi! Chez vous, qu'est-ce qu'on prend et qu'est-ce qu'on ne prend pas pour chaque occasion?

Modèle   au petit déjeuner
des œufs, pas de pizza, du café, pas de glace, etc.

1. au petit déjeuner
2. au déjeuner
3. au dîner
4. à l'anniversaire d'un enfant
5. à la plage
6. pour un pique-nique

Continuons!

A. Le régime de M. Delvaux M. Delvaux est trop gros. Qu'est-ce qu'il doit manger? Qu'est-ce qu'il doit boire? Donnez-lui des conseils *(give him some advice)*.

Modèle   *Mangez des légumes. Ne buvez pas de bière.*

B. Mlle Lao est végétarienne Mlle Lao ne prend pas de viande et elle ne prend pas de poisson. Donnez ses réponses.

Modèle   —Vous prenez des œufs?
—Oui, je prends des œufs.

—Vous prenez du jambon?
—Non, je ne prends pas/jamais de jambon!

1. Vous prenez du pain?
2. Vous prenez du saucisson?
3. Vous prenez des frites?
4. Vous prenez des oranges?
5. Vous prenez du chocolat?
6. Vous prenez du pâté?
7. Vous prenez de la soupe?
8. Vous prenez du thon?

C. Les Français et les repas Voilà comment mangent les Français. Est-ce que c'est comme chez vous? (MOTS UTILES: chez nous aussi; pas chez moi; mais, chez moi, on… ; pas chez nous parce que…)

1. On fait les courses très souvent.
2. Au petit déjeuner:
    a. On prend souvent du café au lait.
    b. On prend souvent du pain avec du beurre et de la confiture.
    c. On prend quelquefois des croissants.

Act. B: Ask students to justify their choice of partitive or indefinite article. Accept any answer that makes sense.

Act. A: Ask students to speculate about what M. Delvaux is going to fix for dinner.

Act. B: Note that direct object pronouns are not possible here. **(Vous prenez du jambon? Oui, j'en prends).** If students are curious, simply tell them that **en** is another kind of pronoun that replaces quantity type words and that they will learn about it later.
For #7, **ça dépend** is a very good answer!
CONTINUATION: **Vous prenez des crevettes? du riz? du poisson? du lait? du poulet? des gâteaux? de la pizza? du fromage?**

Act. C: This is very long if done in a whole class format. SUGGESTION: Divide class into groups and assign parts of the activity. Groups report back to the class and the class reacts to their answers.

Info plus

La famille française et les repas.
Meals are considered important in France. It is a time for the family to be together and for both children and parents to communicate around the table. In some families, however, the television set is in the dining room and meals are taken while watching the news (at one and at eight o'clock).

3. À midi:
    a. On mange souvent à la maison.
    b. On prend du vin avec le repas.
    c. On prend une entrée, un plat principal, un légume, une salade, du fromage et un dessert.
    d. On mange la salade après le plat principal.
    e. On prend le café après le repas.
4. À 4 heures:
    a. Les enfants prennent le goûter (souvent du pain et du chocolat).
    b. Les enfants boivent souvent du chocolat chaud.
    c. Les adultes boivent du café ou du thé.
    d. On prend souvent le goûter à la cuisine.
    e. Les enfants ont des goûters d'anniversaire.
    f. Pour un goûter d'anniversaire, il y a des tartes et des gâteaux.
5. L'apéritif:
    a. On prend parfois l'apéritif dans un café.
    b. On prend l'apéritif avant le déjeuner et avant le dîner quand on a des invités.
    c. On invite souvent des amis à prendre l'apéritif.
6. Le dîner:
    a. On mange toujours en famille.
    b. On mange souvent des restes le soir.
    c. On prend le dîner entre sept heures et neuf heures du soir.
    d. Quand on va à un dîner, on donne des fleurs ou des chocolats.

C'est quel repas? Qu'est-ce qu'ils mangent? Qu'est-ce qu'ils boivent?

Act. D: If students do not have refrigerators, have them imagine one; for example, **le frigo idéal ou le frigo désastre.**

D. Conversation en français Qu'est-ce qu'il y a dans votre réfrigérateur? Pourquoi? Qu'est-ce qu'il n'y a pas dans votre réfrigérateur? Pourquoi?

TEXT TAPE:
Conversation en français

Découvertes culturelles: Cuisine de France et d'ailleurs

▷▷ Manger au restaurant

A. Préparation. Qu'est-ce que vous mangez? Préparez le menu typique des déjeuners d'une semaine typique pour vous.

Modèle *lundi: hamburger/frites...*

Info plus

Rouget, **loup**, and **cabillaud** are fish (red mullet, seabass, and cod respectively).

NOTRE MENU à 110.-

ENTRÉES au CHOIX :   HUITRES (6)
★ La SOUPE de POISSONS   Suppl 30 F
★ SALADE de TOMATES et MOZZARELLA au basilic frais -
★ SALADE de FILETS de ROUGETS au Vinaigre de Framboise -
★ AVOCAT aux CREVETTES

PLATS au CHOIX :
★ FILET de LOUP au Citron et basilic
★ FILET de CABILLAUD au SAFRAN
★ PAVÉ de BOEUF GRILLÉ.
★ LA SUGGESTION du JOUR

L'ASSIETTE de FROMAGES
OU
LES DESSERTS au CHOIX :
CRÈME CARAMEL - MOUSSE au CHOCOLAT -
PATISSERIE MAISON - GLACE 2 boules -

UN VERRE de VIN de PROVENCE

et CAFÉ SEGAFREDO

B. Un menu.

1. Combien de plats est-ce qu'on a pour 110 francs?
2. Qu'est-ce qu'il y a comme boisson?
P Qu'est-ce qu'il y a comme dessert?
4. Si on n'a pas envie de dessert, est-ce qu'il y a autre chose après le plat principal?
5. Devinez ce que c'est *(Guess the meaning):* Avocat? Bœuf grillé? La suggestion du jour? Pâtisserie maison?
6. Qu'est-ce que vous allez prendre?

C. Analyse du menu. Commentez ce menu. Comment est-il? (qualité, équilibre, style de nourriture, etc.)

D. Le restaurant et les clients.

1. Décrivez *(Describe)* le restaurant d'après *(based on)* ce menu.
2. Décrivez trois clients typiques de ce restaurant.

E. Jeu de rôle.

1. Organisez les plats par ordre de préférence et préparez votre commande pour la donner au serveur *(waiter).*
2. Préparez des questions sur le menu pour le serveur.
3. À deux, commandez votre déjeuner (un de vous est le client, l'autre le serveur).

Commande

2236

Act. B: Have students ask you questions about items they don't understand. Keep the exchange in French, as if they were actually in the restaurant. You may also ask students to invent the **suggestion du jour.**

Act. C: Encourage students to make descriptive sentences: **Il y a... , Il est.... , Il n'est pas... , Il n'y a pas assez de... , trop de...** etc.

Act. D: Can be done in groups. Students need to hypothesize. Suggest ideas such as place, decor, service, **Qui est le/la propriétaire? les serveurs?,** and provide initial words: **Il n'est pas... , Il est... / Ils sont... , Ils ne sont pas...**
Note that this menu comes from a beach restaurant in Cannes, which explains why there is so much fish on the menu. Note also that it is more like a bistro type of menu (here, for tourists, but the same kind of menu could as well be for regular customers, such as office or bank workers). The style is simple—good basic menu, not very expensive or fancy.

Act. E: Provide useful words for the waiter by demonstrating with a few students first. Or you may want to quickly pass through class playing waiter with several students. Make the conversation different for each.

La boîte à mots

Le serveur: Vous avez choisi?
Alors vous prenez quoi aujourd'hui?
Et comme boisson?
Ah oui, je le recommande, il est très frais.

Le client: Pour moi, ce sera...
Il est frais ou surgelé votre poisson?
Qu'est-ce que vous recommandez?

➤➤ Un bon plat sénégalais

Act. A: Have students tell you about a dish, identify the ingredients, say when, with whom, where they eat it.

A. Préparation. Aimez-vous la cuisine exotique? Décrivez un plat exotique.

RIZ AU POISSON (Tiébou Dienn)

Repas de grands jours à l'origine, «le Tiébou Dienn» est un des plus célèbres plats sénégalais.

Amélioré, le riz au poisson à la sauce «sous verre» est un délice des yeux et du palais!

Préparation (pour 6 personnes)

Riz: 500 g
Poisson: 450 g
Poisson sec: 300 g
1 chou vert
2 carottes
Potiron: 100 g
1 Oignon ordinaire

2 aubergines
3 diakhatous
1 petit piment
1 navet
4 cuillerées d'huile
1 cuillère concentrée tomate, ail, laurier, sel, poivre

Piler deux gousses d'ail, une feuille de laurier, un demi paquet de persil, du sel, du poivre, un petit morceau de piment.

Nettoyer le poisson, le piquer en 3 ou 4 endroits, et introduire dans les trous, la farce préparée.

Faire chauffer l'huile dans une cocotte, y jeter les oignons émincés puis le concentré de tomates délayé dans un peu d'eau.

Mettre le poisson, ajouter un litre d'eau et les légumes pelés.

Saler, poivrer, laisser cuire une heure.

Quand les légumes sont cuits, les retirer ainsi que le poisson. Les servir dans un plat chaud que l'on maintient encore au chaud.

Dans le bouillon qui reste, jeter le riz lavé, couvrir, laisser cuire 15 minutes au moins.

Servir le riz dans un plat chaud accompagné des légumes et du poisson.

RIZ AU POISSON

Act. B: A **diakhatou** resembles a large, bitter tomato or a small green, very bitter eggplant.

B. Un plat sénégalais. Identifiez les ingrédients de ce plat. Quels ingrédients sont sur la photo? Quel type de plat est-ce? Pour quel repas?

Act. C: Have students underline or otherwise identify these items in the text. Make it a game to see who can find the most items.

C. Une recette sénégalaise–Spécialité wolof.

1. Identifiez les ingrédients exotiques, les épices, les légumes.
2. Identifiez les liquides.
3. Identifiez les actions de préparation.
4. Identifiez l'appareil où on prépare ce plat.

D. Mots nouveaux. Devinez. D'après le contexte, qu'est-ce que c'est?

1. (line 1) piler (dans un mortier) = *mix / crush / slice*
2. (line 4) nettoyer (à l'eau) = *beat / cut / clean*
3. (line 6) jeter (dans la cocotte) = *stir / throw / mix*
4. (line 7) délayé (dans un peu d'eau) = *diluted / sliced / cut*
5. (line 8) mettre (le poisson dans l'huile) = *slice / scrape / place*
6. (line 8) ajouter (un litre d'eau) = *beat / mix / add*
7. (line 11) retirer (les légumes et le poisson) = *mix / take out / add*
8. (line 14) couvrir (le riz) = *cover / remove / cook*

E. Les goûts et les couleurs. Quels ingrédients sont exotiques dans ce plat? Quel aspect de la préparation? Pourquoi une cuisine est-elle exotique? les ingrédients? les actions de préparation? Comment est-ce qu'on mange le plat?

www explore!
http//voila.heinle.com

CUISINE SÉNÉGALAISE
D'HIER ET
D'AUJOURD'HUI

F. Hypothèses. Chaque culture a ses propres goûts et ses propres ingrédients. Préparez une liste des choses que les Français mangent et boivent et qu'on déteste dans votre culture. Préparez une liste des choses qu'on mange et boit dans votre culture et que les Français n'aiment pas.

G. Au restaurant sénégalais. Avant d'aller au restaurant, vous êtes curieux et vous voulez vous préparer à découvrir *(discover)* des plats et des goûts nouveaux. Préparez une liste de questions à poser à un ami sénégalais sur la cuisine sénégalaise.

*O*rthographe et prononciation

See the **Instructor's Resource Manual** for more information.

▶▶ Le *h* aspiré

In general, words beginning with **h-** in French are treated as if they began with a vowel.

> Anne déteste l'hiver. *(élision)*
> Les‿hivers sont froids ici. *(liaison)*
> /z/

A few words, largely of non-French origin, that begin with **h-** are treated as if they began with a consonant. The **h-** is silent, but **élision** and **liaison** do not occur. These words are marked in dictionaries by an asterisk.

*hamburger	Veux-tu des frites avec **le hamburger?**
*haricots verts	Qui aime **les haricots verts?**

Activité

Prononcez et devinez Répétez après votre professeur. Qu'est-ce que c'est en anglais?

1. les hot-dogs
2. faire hara-kiri
3. la Hollande
4. le haschisch

5. le hamac
6. les hamsters
7. le harem
8. les hippies

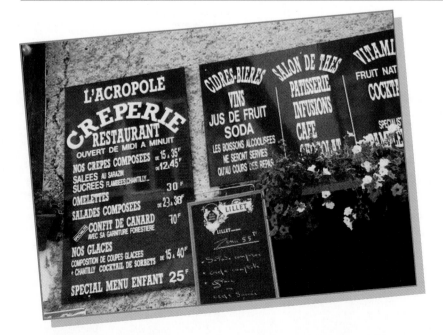

Vocabulaire de base

TEXT TAPE: *Vocabulaire de base*

Quel article? Things that are not usually counted are used in French with either the partitive article (**du beurre, de la glace, de l'eau**) or, in certain cases, with the definite article (**J'aime la glace. Où est le beurre?**). These kinds of nouns will appear in the vocabulary lists with the definite article.

NOMS

une banane *banana*
le beurre *butter*
la bière *beer*
le bœuf *beef*
le café *coffee, café*
une carotte *carrot*
le chocolat *chocolate*
une crevette *shrimp*
la cuisine *cooking, cuisine*
le déjeuner *lunch*
le dessert *dessert*
le dîner *dinner*
l'eau *(f.) water*
une fraise *strawberry*
des frites *(f.) (French) fries*
le fromage *cheese*
un fruit *fruit*
un gâteau (au chocolat) *(chocolate) cake*
la glace (au chocolat, à la vanille, à la fraise) *(chocolate, vanilla, strawberry) ice cream*
des *haricots verts *(m.) green beans*
une idée *idea*
le jambon *ham*
le jus de fruit *fruit juice*
le lait *milk*
un légume *vegetable*
le mouton *mutton*
un œuf *egg*

une orange *orange*
le pain *bread*
une pêche *peach*
le petit déjeuner *breakfast*
des petits pois *(m.) peas*
le poisson *fish*
le poivre *pepper*
une pomme *apple*
une pomme de terre *potato*
le porc *pork*
un poulet *chicken*
un réfrigérateur *refrigerator*
un repas *meal*
le riz *rice*
un rôti *roast*
la salade *salad*
un sandwich (au jambon, au fromage) *(ham, cheese) sandwich*
le saumon *salmon*
le sel *salt*
la soupe (aux tomates) *(tomato) soup*
un steak *steak*
le sucre *sugar*
une tarte (aux pommes) *(apple) pie*
le thé *tea*
le thon *tuna*
une tomate *tomato*
la viande *meat*
le vin *wine*
le yaourt *yogurt*

ADJECTIFS

bon, bonne *(precedes noun) good*
mauvais(e) *(precedes noun) bad*
meilleur(e) *better*

VERBES

acheter *to buy*
boire *to drink*
prendre *to take, to have, to eat, to drink*

DIVERS

avant *before*
avoir faim *to be hungry*
avoir soif *to be thirsty*
entre *between*
être au régime *to be on a diet*
être en bonne/mauvaise santé *to be in good/bad health*
être en forme *to be in shape*
prendre (un petit) quelque chose *to have a snack*
quelque chose *something*
quelqu'un *somebody, someone*
surtout *especially*

Vocabulaire supplémentaire

NOMS

l'apéritif *(m.) a drink (served before a meal)*
des asperges *(f.) asparagus*
une boisson *beverage*

un bonbon *(piece of) candy*
le café au lait *coffee with milk*
des céréales *(f.) cereal*
le champagne *champagne*
un champignon *mushroom*
la charcuterie *cold cuts*

un citron *lemon*
le coca *Coke*
le Coca-Cola *Coca-Cola, cola*
la confiture *jam*
un congélateur *freezer*
des conserves *(f.) canned food*

un croissant *croissant*
des crudités *(f.) raw vegetables*
une dinde *turkey*
l'eau minérale *(f.) mineral water*
l'entrée *(f.) first course (appetizer)*
des épinards *(m.) spinach*
le goûter *light meal eaten in the afternoon*
une laitue *lettuce*
la mayonnaise *mayonnaise*
un melon *melon (cantaloupe)*
la moutarde *mustard*
la nourriture *food*
un oignon *onion*
une omelette (au fromage) *(cheese) omelette*
le plat principal *main dish, main course*
un pamplemousse *grapefruit*
le pâté *pâté*
des pâtes *(f.) pasta, spaghetti, noodles*
une pizza *pizza*
une poire *pear*
une prune *plum*
un raisin *grape*
des restes *(m.) leftovers*
le saucisson *salami*
une soirée *party*
un steak haché *hamburger meat*
la vinaigrette *oil and vinegar dressing*

VERBE

inviter (quelqu'un à faire quelque chose) *to invite (someone to do something)*

ADJECTIFS

chinois(e) *Chinese*
délicieux, délicieuse *delicious*
excellent(e) *excellent*
italien, italienne *Italian*
japonais(e) *Japanese*
salé(e) *salted, salty*
sucré(e) *sweet*
surgelé(e) *frozen*
végétarien(ne) *vegetarian*

DIVERS

c'est bon/mauvais pour la santé *it's healthy/unhealthy (good/bad for your health)*
il faut + noun or infinitive *one needs/we need + noun; / one has to / you have to + infinitive*
prendre un verre *to have a drink*

LE FRANÇAIS TEL QU'ON LE PARLE

À table! *Dinner (Lunch, Breakfast) is ready! Let's eat!*

À la vôtre! *Cheers!*
bon... *all right, OK*
Bon appétit! *Have a nice meal! Enjoy your meal!*
Je n'en peux plus! *I'm full! (also: I'm exhausted!)*
oh là là! *oh la la!*
voyons... *let's see . . .*

LE FRANÇAIS FAMILIER

l'apéro = l'apéritif
les chips = potato chips
le coca = le Coca-Cola
un cracker = cracker
un *hamburger = hamburger
une patate = une pomme de terre
prendre un pot = prendre un verre

ON ENTEND PARFOIS...

un breuvage (Canada) = une boisson
un chien chaud (Canada) = un hot-dog
le déjeuner (Belgique, Canada) = le petit déjeuner
le dîner (Belgique, Canada) = le déjeuner
un pain chargé (Sénégal) = un sandwich
le souper (Belgique, Canada) = le dîner

Point out that the **h-** of **hamburger** is aspirate.

Qu'est-ce que vous portez?

En bref

Dans cette leçon...

- Les vêtements, la mode et la publicité

- Faire et recevoir des compliments

- Les chiffres de 100 à 1.000

- Les verbes comme **finir**

- Le verbe **mettre**

- Raconter au passé: le passé composé avec **avoir**

- Les vêtements et les valeurs: élégance ou confort?

In this lesson...

- Clothing, fashion, advertising

- Giving and receiving compliments

- Numbers from 100 to 1,000

- Verbs like **finir** *(to finish)*

- The verb **mettre** *(to put, place)*

- Talking about what has happened in the past: the **passé composé** with **avoir**

- Clothes and value systems: elegance or comfort?

www explore! http://voila.heinle.com	Develop writing skills with Système-D software!	Practice listening and pronunciation skills with the Text Tape!	Discover the Francophone world!	Build your skills!
INTERNET	**SYSTÈME-D**	**TEXT TAPE**	**VIDEO TAPE**	**CD-ROM**

Students have an open-ended writing activity in the **Cahier** suitable for use with **Système-D**.

Entrée en matière: Des vêtements pour tous

Jet a fait les slips et les tee-shirts, pas le vélo.

Habiller la famille, c'est bien de ne faire que ça

jet

Use this document to recycle vocabulary from previous chapters (describing people and families, food, activities, etc.).

238

La famille.
Comment s'appellent-ils? Quel âge ont-ils? Qui est content? timide? Qui est sérieux?

Ont-ils des personnalités différentes? Décrivez-les.

Le père:	
La mère:	
Le fils:	
La fille:	

Quelles relations existent entre eux? Faites leur portrait.

Les activités.

> Où sont-ils?
>
> Où vont-ils?
>
> C'est quelle saison?
>
> C'est quel jour de la semaine?
>
> Pourquoi font-ils du vélo?
>
> Qu'est-ce qu'il y a dans le panier sur la bicyclette?

Le message publicitaire.

Quelle valeur est à la base de cette réclame publicitaire?

Est-ce que c'est une famille typique? Pourquoi?

Comment est le père? Est-il typique? Et la mère? Et les enfants?

Quelles images de la famille donnent les images publicitaires généralement?

Conversation.
Maintenant faites-les parler.

- La famille est une invention merveilleuse. Utilisez des bulles *(bubbles)* pour écrire des idées optimistes!

- La famille est une invention pénible. Utilisez des bulles pour écrire des idées pessimistes!

Des vêtements ou des sous-vêtements?
Et Jet, qu'est-ce que c'est? Une association sportive? une association pour la protection des animaux? une industrie textile? Que fait la compagnie Jet?

239

Vocabulaire

A. Les chiffres de 100 à 1.000

100	cent	*a hundred*
101	cent un	*a hundred and one*
102	cent deux	*a hundred and two*
200	deux cents	*two hundred*
220	deux cent vingt	*two hundred twenty*
500	cinq cents	*five hundred*
555	cinq cent cinquante-cinq	*five hundred fifty-five*
999	neuf cent quatre-vingt-dix-neuf	*nine hundred ninety-nine*
1.000	mille	*a thousand*

TRANSPARENCY:
10-1

B. Qu'est-ce que vous voulez acheter?

Les vêtements

B. *Le blouson*
259 F

C. *Le chemisier*
149 F

E. *Le pull*
129 F

F. *Le tailleur*
449 F

A. *La robe*
219 F

D. *Le pantalon*
279 F

G. *Le survêtement*
369 F

I. *La parka*
999 F

J. *Les chaussures*
239 F

H. *Les tennis*
399 F

Les sous-vêtements

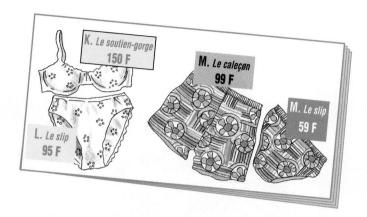

K. Le soutien-gorge
150 F

M. Le caleçon
99 F

M. Le slip
59 F

L. Le slip
95 F

Et les couleurs?

- Le blouson de l'homme est bleu foncé et son pantalon est beige, mais de quelle couleur est son polo? Le pull de l'autre homme est rose. Et son pantalon?
- La femme qui porte le tailleur bleu clair porte une jupe et une veste bleu clair, c'est normal! Mais qu'est-ce qu'elle porte sous la veste? Un tee-shirt jaune. Est-ce que ça va bien avec son tailleur? Quelles couleurs vont bien avec le bleu clair?
- Le survêtement de l'homme est gris foncé avec du bleu foncé, du bleu clair et du violet. Et ses tennis?
- De quelle couleur est la robe?
- De quelle couleur sont le chemisier, le pantalon et le tee-shirt de la femme?
- Quelles sont les couleurs de la parka?
- Quelles sont les couleurs des chaussures?
- Quelles sont les couleurs des sous-vêtements pour femme? Et des sous-vêtements pour homme?
- Quelles couleurs vont bien ensemble, pour des vêtements?

Et les prix?

- La parka coûte 999 francs. Elle coûte cher, n'est-ce pas? Et combien coûte le tailleur? Il coûte cher?
- Quels vêtements sont chers? Quels vêtements ne sont pas chers? Où est-ce que les vêtements sont plus chers, en France ou chez vous?

On the average, one dollar is roughly the equivalent of 5 French francs but you may want to check the current exchange rate.

Comment sont-ils?

- Est-ce qu'il y a des chaussures de sport? des chaussures habillées? Quels sont les vêtements de sport? les vêtements habillés? les vêtements confortables? les vêtements pratiques? les vêtements à la mode? les vêtements démodés?
- Qui est bien habillé? mal habillé? élégant?
- Est-ce que la robe est courte ou longue? Qu'est-ce qui est à la mode pour les femmes maintenant, les robes courtes ou les robes longues? Qu'est-ce que vous préférez, vous?
- Quels vêtements voulez-vous acheter? Quels vêtements ne voulez-vous pas acheter? Pourquoi? Est-ce que vous avez le temps d'acheter beaucoup de vêtements? Combien de fois par semaine (par mois? par an?) est-ce que vous achetez des vêtements?

C. La valise de Claude

TRANSPARENCY: 10-2

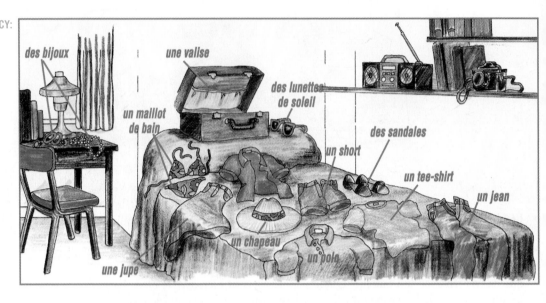

des bijoux

une valise

des lunettes de soleil

un maillot de bain

des sandales

un short

un tee-shirt

un jean

un chapeau

un polo

une jupe

Ask for details: **Quelle est la saison? Quel temps fait-il? Elle va en vacances? Où? (chez ses parents? à la plage? à la montagne? en ville? etc.)**

Regardez les vêtements de Claude. Est-ce que Claude est un garçon ou une fille? Claude a quel âge? Où est Claude? Qu'est-ce que Claude va faire aujourd'hui? De quelle couleur est sa jupe? son tee-shirt? son short? son maillot de bain? son jean?

D. La chambre d'hôtel de M. Lévy

TRANSPARENCY: 10-3

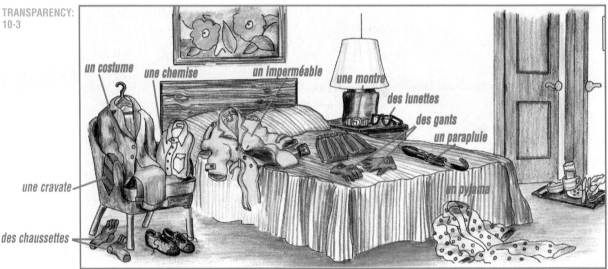

un costume

une chemise

un imperméable

une montre

des lunettes

des gants

un parapluie

une cravate

un pyjama

des chaussettes

FOLLOW-UP: Ask students what city M. Lévy is in and what the weather is probably like.

Voilà la chambre de M. Lévy. Est-ce que c'est un étudiant? Quel âge a M. Lévy? Est-ce qu'il est chez lui? Où est-il? Quelle heure est-il? Qu'est-ce qu'il va faire aujourd'hui? De quelle couleur est son costume? sa cravate? sa chemise? son imperméable? son parapluie?

E. Dans un magasin de chaussures

Paulette a besoin de chaussures pour aller avec son nouveau tailleur. Elle et Jacques vont ensemble dans un magasin de chaussures à Nice.

- Qu'est-ce que Jacques porte aujourd'hui? Et Paulette? Est-ce qu'elle a l'air élégante? De quoi est-ce qu'elle a besoin? Pourquoi? Quelles chaussures est-ce qu'elle va acheter? Et vous, quelles chaussures préférez-vous?

Info plus

Les tailles.

Ask students how sizes of clothing are determined. Are these sizes universal or do they change from one country to another? Ask students for examples.

Tableau comparatif des tailles américaines et françaises.

FEMMES

Robes, manteaux et jupes

Petites tailles

USA	5	7	9	11	13	15		
France	34	36	38	40	42	44		

Tailles normales

USA	6	8	10	12	14	16	18	
France	36	38	40	42	44	46	48	

Chaussures

USA	5 1/2	6	6 1/2	7	7 1/2	8	8 1/2	9
France	36 1/2	37	37 1/2	38	38 1/2	39	39 1/2	40

HOMMES

Costumes

USA	34	36	38	40	42	44
France	44	46	48	50	52	54

Chemises

USA	14 1/2	15	15 1/2	16	16 1/2	17
France	37	38	39	41	42	43

Chaussures

USA	8	9	10	11	12	13
France	41	42	43	44 1/2	46	47

Ask students for their opinions on how appropriate it is to use the word "pretty" to compliment someone on their clothing. (Would you use if for a man? a woman?). How do people respond to a compliment in your students' experience?

Info plus

Quelle jolie robe! Elle te va bien!

Complimenting people on the way they look is a less frequent occurrence in France than in the United States. Should you receive such a compliment, the appropriate response is to pretend modestly that the object is unworthy of notice.

– Quelle jolie robe! *"What a pretty dress!*
  Elle te va bien! *It looks nice on you!"*
– Oh, tu trouves? *"Oh, do you think so?"*

Notes de vocabulaire

1. Mots et expressions utiles.

les affaires *(f. pl.)*	*belongings, stuff*
en solde	*on sale*
une fois	*one time, once*
hier	*yesterday*
un manteau	*coat*
la mode	*fashion*
un voyage	*trip*

2: If desired, teach the adjective **neuf** *(new* in the sense of never used before).

2. Nouveau.
Nouveau means *new*. It is placed in front of the noun it modifies. Here are its forms.

Tu as un **nouveau** stylo? *(masculine singular)*
J'aime bien ta **nouvelle** robe. *(feminine singular)*
J'ai besoin d'un **nouvel** imperméable. *(masculine singular before a vowel sound)*
Où sont les **nouveaux** rideaux? *(masculine plural)*
Voilà mes **nouvelles** lunettes de soleil! *(feminine plural)*

3. Avoir besoin de / avoir l'air (de) / avoir le temps de.
To say that you need something, use the expression **avoir besoin de** + *noun* or *infinitive*.

3: Adjectives used with the expression **avoir l'air** may agree either with the person to whom they refer or with the noun **air**. In this text, they agree with the person referred to.

J'ai besoin de manger quelque chose.	*I need to eat something.*
Paulette **a besoin de** nouvelles **chaussures.**	*Paulette needs new shoes.*

To say what somebody looks like, use the expression **avoir l'air** + *adjective* or **avoir l'air de** + *infinitive*.

Paulette **a l'air élégante** aujourd'hui.	*Paulette looks elegant today.*
Jacques **a l'air d'être** heureux maintenant.	*Jacques seems happy now.*

To say that you have time, use the expression **avoir le temps de** + *infinitive*.

Tu **as le temps de** me **parler?**	*Do you have time to talk to me?*
Je n'**ai** pas **le temps de manger.**	*I don't have time to eat.*

Rappel! Don't forget the other expressions with **avoir** that you already know: **avoir chaud, avoir froid, avoir sommeil, avoir... ans, avoir faim, avoir soif,** and **avoir envie (de).**

4. Fois / temps.
Fois means *time* in the sense of instances or occurrences that you can count. It expresses repetition.

une fois	*one time, once*
deux fois	*two times, twice*
trois fois	*three times*
combien de fois?	*how many times?*
combien de fois par semaine?	*how many times a week?*

Temps refers to *time* as something that is not counted.

> Aujourd'hui je n'ai pas **le temps.**   *Today I don't have (the) time.*

Rappel!

1. Use **heure** in telling time.

   > Quelle **heure** est-il?   *What time is it?*

2. The word **temps** is also used to refer to the weather.

   > Quel **temps** fait-il?   *What's the weather like?*

5. Habillé. Note the meaning of **habillé** in different contexts.

> Il est bien **habillé.**   *He's well dressed.*
> C'est une robe **habillée.**   *It's a formal dress.*

6. Vert foncé / gris clair. Color terms made up of more than one word are invariable.

> J'aime porter ma veste **vert foncé**   *I love to wear my dark green*
>   avec ma jupe **gris clair.**   *jacket with my light gray skirt.*

7. Long, longue. The adjective **long** normally precedes the noun it modifies. In reference to clothing, however, it generally follows the noun.

> une **longue** journée   *a long day*
> une jupe **longue**   *a long skirt*

4: You may want to point out that neither **temps** nor **fois** can be used to say to have a good time. If desired, teach a few expressions with **s'amuser** as lexical items.

D'accord?

A. Chassez l'intrus Quel mot ne va pas avec les autres à cause du sens *(meaning)*?

1. une jupe chaude / un pull / une parka / un maillot de bain
2. un short / des sandales / une cravate / un polo
3. un tailleur / un costume / des tennis / un chemisier
4. un manteau / un imperméable / un pantalon / un blouson
5. un short / des gants / des lunettes de soleil / un tee-shirt
6. des chaussettes / une montre / des chaussures / des sandales
7. une robe / une jupe / un chemisier / un blouson

B. Associations Quels mots ou expressions associez-vous avec les mots suivants:
SUGGESTIONS: Tahiti / il fait frais / la mer / la plage / il fait froid / il pleut / sortir le soir / l'hiver / l'été / il fait chaud / aller danser / aller au théâtre / faire du jogging / jouer au tennis / faire un voyage / travailler dans une banque

1. un manteau et des gants
2. un tailleur et un imperméable
3. une robe et des chaussures élégantes
4. un maillot de bain et des lunettes de soleil
5. un jean et un tee-shirt
6. une valise
7. un survêtement et des tennis
8. un polo blanc et un short
9. un costume et une cravate

C. Vêtements typiques
Est-ce qu'il y a des vêtements typiques? Faites une liste pour chaque catégorie.

1. vêtements de femme
2. vêtements d'homme
3. vêtements d'un(e) étudiant(e) bien habillé(e)
4. vêtements d'un(e) étudiant(e) mal habillé(e)
5. vêtements chers
6. vêtements confortables

D. Vêtements appropriés
Qu'est-ce que vous portez dans les situations suivantes?

Modèle   À New York, le 3 janvier. Vous faites des courses.
Je porte un manteau, des gants...

1. À Montréal, le vendredi 6 octobre. Vous allez au cinéma avec des copains le soir.
2. À Chicago, le lundi 3 décembre. Vous allez en cours le matin.
3. À Londres, le 15 avril à midi. Vous allez au restaurant.
4. À Rome, en juillet. Vous allez au musée.
5. À San Diego, en août. Vous allez à la plage.
6. À Aspen, en février. Vous allez skier.
7. À Dallas, le samedi premier mai. Vous allez danser.
8. À Kansas City, le dimanche 15 octobre. Vous allez dans un club sportif l'après-midi.

E. Vêtements nécessaires
De quoi est-ce que vous avez besoin?

Modèle   Vous allez à la plage.
J'ai besoin d'un maillot de bain, de mes lunettes de soleil...

1. Vous allez chez vos parents pour le week-end.
2. Vous allez en cours.
3. Vous allez étudier chez un copain.

F. Apparences
Utilisez **avoir l'air** + *adjectif* pour décrire les dessins.

Modèle
Elle a l'air élégante.

1.

2.   3.   4.

G. Et eux? Qu'est-ce qu'ils portent? Pourquoi?

Modèle *Madame Vignau porte une robe d'été parce qu'il fait beau et chaud aujourd'hui.*

Act. G: Ask for details: De quelle couleur est sa robe? Où est-ce qu'elle est? Quelle est la saison? Où est-ce qu'ils vont? Quel âge a-t-elle? etc.

Madame Vignau

Dominique Barbier

Olivier et Charlotte Rivière

Magali et Sébastien

Mise en pratique

A. Mes affaires
Faites une liste de dix choses très importantes pour vous. Comparez avec les autres étudiants de la classe.

Modèle *des jeans, mon ordinateur, mon violon...*

B. La mode
Répondez aux questions, puis comparez avec les autres étudiants de la classe.

1. Qu'est-ce qui est à la mode cette année? Qu'est-ce qu'on ne porte plus parce que c'est démodé?
2. Qu'est-ce qu'on porte maintenant pour aller danser en ville? aller à une grande soirée élégante? aller écouter de la musique classique? aller écouter du blues? aller en cours? aller chez des copains le soir?
3. Qu'est-ce que vous achetez souvent en solde? Qu'est-ce que vous n'achetez jamais en solde?

C. Et les Français? Et les Français, quels vêtements est-ce qu'ils aiment acheter? Regardez la liste pour les femmes et pour les hommes et répondez aux questions.

Palmarès 1995 (femmes)

Achats en hausse:
- Caleçons longs: + 65,2%
- Coupe-vent: + 18,9%
- Anoraks et parkas: + 12,7%
- Tailleurs: + 12,3%
- Shorts et bermudas: + 10,7%
- Pantalons et jeans denim: + 9,1%
- Vestes et blazers: + 7,8%
- Jupes: + 4,3%
- Pantalons de ville: + 3,5%

Achats en baisse:
- Robes: - 1,3%
- Imperméables: - 1,4%
- Survêtements: - 1,4%
- Manteaux: - 1,6%
- Jeans velours: - 12,3%

CTCOE

Palmarès 1995 (hommes)

Achats en hausse:
- Coupe-vent: + 17,7%
- Shorts et bermudas: + 8,5%
- Vestes et blazers: + 7,4%
- Anoraks et parkas: + 7,0%
- Pantalons et jeans denim: + 6,6%
- Survêtements: + 4,0%
- Chemises: + 2,1%

Achats en baisse:
- Costumes: - 2,4%
- Pantalons de villes: - 3,1%
- Manteaux: - 6,0%
- Vêtements de travail: - 7,9%
- Imperméables: - 9,7%
- Jeans velours: - 21,8%

CTCOE

EXPLICATIONS: un coupe-vent, c'est un blouson pour quand il fait un peu frais ou pour quand il y a du vent; un caleçon long, c'est un pantalon très collant *(tight)* que les femmes portent souvent avec un long tee-shirt ou un long pull.

1. Qu'est-ce que les femmes françaises achètent plus maintenant qu'avant? Et les hommes? Et qu'est-ce qu'ils achètent moins? Est-ce que les hommes et les femmes achètent les mêmes *(same)* choses?
2. Est-ce que les femmes françaises préfèrent les jupes ou les robes? les jeans ou les jupes? les tailleurs ou les robes? les imperméables ou les parkas? les caleçons longs ou les survêtements?
3. Est-ce que les hommes français préfèrent les costumes ou les vestes? les jeans ou les pantalons habillés? les imperméables ou les coupe-vent?
4. Faites des conclusions sur les Français de maintenant: quels vêtements est-ce qu'ils préfèrent? (élégants? confortables? pratiques? chers? habillés? etc.). Alors *(then)*, comment sont les Français, à votre avis *(in your opinion)*? Quelles activités est-ce qu'ils aiment? Est-ce que c'est comme chez vous maintenant ou est-ce que c'est différent?

D. Un défilé de mode Vous organisez un défilé de mode *(fashion show)* pour étudiants. Décrivez les vêtements pour chaque occasion.

SITUATION	POUR UNE FEMME	POUR UN HOMME
pour aller en cours		
pour une fête habillée		
pour sortir avec des copains		
pour faire du sport		
pour partir en voyage		

E. La tombola Vous venez de gagner *(you have just won)* le grand prix dans un concours *(sweepstakes)* et vous pouvez partir une semaine avec trois amis à Tahiti, à Nice, à Monte-Carlo, à Paris ou à Montréal. Mais il faut organiser votre voyage!

1. Où voulez-vous aller?
2. Quand voulez-vous partir?
3. Où allez-vous rester? (chez des amis? à l'hôtel? dans un appartement?)
4. Qu'est-ce que vous allez faire là-bas *(over there)*?
5. Qu'est-ce que vous avez besoin de prendre avec vous? (Soyez raisonnable et ne prenez pas trop de choses parce que c'est vous qui allez les porter!)

F. Un(e) étudiant(e) à Laval Inventez un(e) étudiant(e), canadien(ne) ou non, qui va à l'université Laval à Québec.

1. **L'étudiant/l'étudiante.** Son nom? Sa nationalité? Description physique?
2. **Caractère et préférences.** Comment est cet(te) étudiant(e)? Qu'est-ce qu'il/elle aime?
3. **Sa chambre.** Comment est sa chambre? Faites une liste ou un plan.
4. **Son placard.** Quels vêtements est-ce qu'il y a dans le placard de cet(te) étudiant(e)? Pourquoi?

G. Conversation en français Un(e) de vos ami(e)s cherche du travail *(work)* et doit aller à un entretien *(interview)*. Qu'est-ce qu'il/elle doit porter? Discutez: C'est pour quel travail? Qu'est-ce qu'il/elle a comme vêtements? Qu'est-ce qu'il/elle doit acheter? etc.

Act. F: POSSIBLE ORGANIZATION: Divide class into at least four groups. Have each group do item 1. Each group passes its description to the next group, which does item 2. The material is then passed on to the next group, which does item 3 and passes all the information along to another group, which does item 4 and then returns the completed activity to the group that originally did item 1. The original group reads and organizes the material for written or oral presentation.

 TEXT TAPE:
Conversation en français

Structure

 CD-ROM:
Build your skills!

▶▶ **Les verbes comme** *finir*

A group of verbs with infinitives ending in **-ir,** such as **finir,** are conjugated in the same way. They are called *second conjugation* or **-ir** verbs. To form the present tense of a verb in this group, remove the infinitive ending (**-ir**) and add the following endings.

finir *to finish*	
je fin**is**	nous fin**issons**
tu fin**is**	vous fin**issez**
il ⎫ elle ⎭ fin**it**	ils ⎫ elles ⎭ fin**issent**

Model pronunciation. Remind students of open syllabification (**fi-nit**).

LISTENING COMPREHENSION:
Singulier ou pluriel? Il grossit. Elles réfléchissent à demain. Ils finissent ou pas? Elle maigrit. Il finit.

DRILL: On réfléchit trop! (nous / je / Candide / tu / Alceste et Candide / vous)

DRILL: Qui choisit? (tu / Alceste / Alceste et Candide / vous / nous / je)

Here are some other verbs in this group.

choisir (de + infinitif)	*to choose (to do something)*
grossir	*to gain weight*
maigrir	*to lose weight*
réfléchir (à)	*to think (about), to reflect*

Elle **réfléchit** trop; elle est pénible.   *She thinks too much; she's a pain.*
Nous **grossissons** en hiver et   *We gain weight in winter and*
   nous **maigrissons** en été!   *we lose weight in the summer!*

The imperative or command forms of verbs conjugated like **finir** are identical to their present tense forms.

Fin**is** vite!   *Finish fast!*
Réfléch**issez!**   *Think!*
Chois**issons** le bleu.   *Let's pick (choose) the blue one.*

Rappel! There are two groups of verbs with infinitives in **-ir:** those like **finir** (**choisir, grossir, maigrir, réfléchir**) and those like **sortir** (**partir, dormir**). They follow two different patterns of conjugation. As you come across other verbs ending in **-ir,** add them to the appropriate list.

Je gross**is.** Je ne dor**s** pas assez.   *I'm gaining weight. I'm not sleeping*
   Je sor**s** trop. Quelle vie!   *enough. I'm going out too much.*
                                        What a life!

Vous avez compris?

A. Associations Quel(s) verbe(s) associez-vous avec:

(VERBES: sortir / partir / dormir / finir / choisir / grossir / maigrir / réfléchir)

1. un lit
2. manger tout le temps
3. avoir des problèmes
4. étudier
5. les copains
6. une université
7. les devoirs
8. faire de l'exercice
9. prendre de la glace ou un gâteau entre les repas

B. Qu'est-ce qu'ils font? Choisissez un des verbes entre parenthèses pour compléter les phrases suivantes.

1. Tu . . . . . . à quelle heure? (grossir / finir)
2. Est-ce que Patrick . . . . . . avec Joëlle ou avec Jacqueline? (sortir / maigrir)
3. Tu manges tout le temps! Tu vas . . . . . . ! (maigrir / grossir)
4. On va . . . . . . un peu. Il y a peut-être une solution. (finir / réfléchir)
5. —Paul et Pierre . . . . . . toujours en classe. (dormir / réfléchir)
   —Oui, et voilà pourquoi ils ne . . . . . . jamais les exercices! (finir / partir)

Continuons!

Et eux? Complétez les phrases avec une forme des verbes **finir, choisir, grossir, maigrir** ou **réfléchir.**

1. —À quoi est-ce que vous ...... ?
   —À mon nouveau jean. Je ...... et il est trop petit!
   —Mais ce n'est pas un problème. Mangez moins et vous allez ......

2. —À quelle heure est-ce qu'ils vont finir?
   —Je ne sais pas. Et toi, tu ...... quand?
   —Je vais ...... à midi. Ça va?
   —Oui, oui, ça va.

3. —Et pour les vacances, qui ...... où vous allez, toi ou ton mari?
   —Nous ...... ensemble où nous allons, mais on ...... toujours par aller
   à la plage!

4. —Patrick! Ça va être le pull bleu ou le polo vert? ...... maintenant!
   Nous partons dans deux minutes!

▶▶ Le verbe *mettre*

Mettre means *to put.* Here is its conjugation in the present tense. Notice the double **t** in the plural forms.

je me**ts**	nous me**ttons**
tu me**ts**	vous me**ttez**
il elle } met	ils elles } me**ttent**

Depending on context, **mettre** can also mean to *put on (clothes).*

Ah non, tu ne **mets** pas de jean
   pour aller chez ta grand-mère!
Je **mets** tes affaires sur la table,
   d'accord?

*Oh no, you're not putting on jeans
   to go to your grandmother's!*
I'm putting your stuff on the table, ok?

The imperative or command forms of **mettre** are identical to the present tense forms.

Mets ton pull! Il fait froid!
Mettez une cravate. C'est un
   restaurant élégant.
Mettons nos lunettes de soleil.
   On va avoir l'air mystérieux!

Put on you sweater! It's cold!
Put on a tie. It's a fancy restaurant.

*Let's put on our sunglasses.
   We'll look mysterious!*

Vous avez compris?

A. Des endroits et des objets Et dans un/une... , qu'est-ce qu'on met?

Modèle   Dans une salle de classe?
   On met des bureaux. On ne met pas de lit.

1. Dans un sac?
2. Sous le lit?
3. Sur une étagère?
4. Dans une cuisine?
5. Dans un tiroir?
6. Dans un réfrigérateur?

B. On sort! Qu'est-ce qu'ils mettent?

1. Alceste / sa cravate
2. Candide / son costume
3. Je / mes chaussures
4. Tu / ton chapeau
5. Vous / votre pantalon
6. Nous / notre manteau

Continuons!

Qu'est-ce qu'on met? On met des vêtements différents pour faire des choses différentes. Utilisez le verbe **mettre** pour expliquer ce qu'on met pour chaque occasion.

Modèle   Il va à l'église. Il ***met un costume.***

1. Vous allez danser. Vous . . . . .
2. Ils vont à la bibliothèque. Ils . . . . .
3. Tu vas faire du jogging. Tu . . . . .
4. Elles vont à l'église. Elles . . . . .
5. Nous allons dans un bon restaurant. Nous . . . . .
6. Il va jouer au tennis. Il . . . . .
7. Je vais nager. Je . . . . .
8. Vous allez faire de la marche. Vous . . . . .

▶▶ Le passé composé avec *avoir*

There are several verbal forms that can be used to talk about the past in French. Of these, the most common is the **passé composé,** or *compound past.* It is called the compound past because it has two parts: a helping or auxiliary verb and a past participle. The majority of verbs in French form their **passé composé** with the helping verb **avoir.**

   Elle **a travaillé** avec moi.   *She worked with me.*
(helping   (past
verb)   participle)

The French **passé composé** may have more than one equivalent in English.

   —Il **a pris** son vélo?   *"Did he take his bike? / Has he taken his bike?"*
   —Oui, il l'**a pris.**   *"Yes, he took it. / Yes, he has taken it."*

Act. A: ALTERNATIVE FORMAT: Ask students to list as many objects as they can. Write all suggestions on the board or an overhead transparency. Then, for each object, ask: **On met . . . dans un sac? Non, alors, dans une cuisine? Oui,** etc.

Act. B: Ask students to speculate as to where each person might be going.

Qu'est-ce qu'on met?: Repeat, but this time ask students what would be bizarre to wear to each place.

Only verbs usually used in the **passé composé** and conjugated with **avoir** are presented in this lesson. Direct object pronoun examples do not require past participle agreement. Students should be encouraged to use the **passé composé** in the limited contexts provided by the exercises and activities of this lesson. This will help to limit premature generalization.

The following lessons will complete the treatment of past time reference in French: verbs conjugated with **être** *(Leçon 11),* the negative and interrogative forms of the **passé composé** *(Leçon 11),* the imperfect *(Leçon 12),* past participle agreement with **avoir** *(Leçon 14),* and the **passé composé** of **être, avoir, vouloir, pouvoir,** and **devoir** *(Leçon 17).*

Past participle of regular verbs

Verbs that belong to the first (-er verbs like **travailler**) and the second (-ir verbs like **finir**) conjugations have regular past participles. The past participle of these verbs is formed by adding endings to the verb stem as illustrated.

INFINITIVE	STEM	ENDING	PAST PARTICIPLE
parler	parl-	**-é**	**parlé**
étudier	étudi-	**-é**	**étudié**
travailler	travaill-	**-é**	**travaillé**
finir	fin-	**-i**	**fini**
choisir	chois-	**-i**	**choisi**
réfléchir	réfléch-	**-i**	**réfléchi**

travailler au passé composé

j'**ai** travaillé	nous **avons** travaillé
tu **as** travaillé	vous **avez** travaillé
il elle } **a** travaillé	ils elles } **ont** travaillé

finir au passé composé

j'**ai** fini	nous **avons** fini
tu **as** fini	vous **avez** fini
il elle } **a** fini	ils elles } **ont** fini

Past participle of irregular verbs conjugated with **avoir**

Some verbs have past participles that do not follow these rules. Of the verbs conjugated with **avoir** that you know, only five have irregular past participles.

boire	**bu**
dormir	**dormi**
faire	**fait**
mettre	**mis**
prendre	**pris**

DRILL: Mettez au passé: Nous parlons à nos parents. Patrick finit ses devoirs. Tu bois un café. Les enfants dorment. Qu'est-ce qu'elle fait? Qu'est-ce que vous prenez comme dessert?

From this point on, verbs with irregular past participles will be indicated as they appear.

NOTE: The verbs **être, avoir, vouloir, pouvoir,** and **devoir** are also conjugated with **avoir** in the **passé composé.** Their use will be studied in *Leçon 17*. Certain other verbs you have studied do not use **avoir** as a helping verb; they use **être** instead. These verbs (for example, **aller, partir,** and **sortir**) will be studied in *Leçon 11*. You will not need to use any of these verbs in the exercises and activities of this lesson.

Direct object pronouns in the passé composé

Direct object pronouns are placed in front of **avoir,** the helping verb. **Le** and **la** become **l'** in front of a vowel.

—Tu as mis **tes gants?**	*"Did you put on your gloves?"*
—Oui, je **les** ai mis.	*"Yes, I put them on."*
—Et tu as aussi mis **ton chapeau?**	*"And did you put your hat on too?"*
—Oui, oui, je **l'**ai mis!	*"Yeah, yeah, I put it on!"*

Vous avez compris?

A. Les problèmes d'Alceste
Alceste a fait la fête hier soir et, ce matin, il y a des conséquences. Regardez les phrases: qu'est-ce qu'il a fait hier soir? Quels sont ses problèmes ce matin? Faites deux listes (hier soir et ce matin) et essayez *(try)* de trouver la cause et l'effet.

Modèle   *(Hier soir) il a trop bu; (ce matin) il est malade.*

1. Il cherche ses clés.
2. Il a dansé pendant des heures.
3. Il a mangé beaucoup de gâteaux.
4. Candide est fâché.
5. Il a porté sa chemise élégante et des lunettes de soleil.
6. Il a mis ses clés sur l'étagère.
7. Il est pauvre.
8. Il n'a pas faim.
9. Il est fatigué.
10. Il a beaucoup parlé avec tout le monde.
11. Il a joué aux cartes.
12. Il a bu trop de vin.
13. Il ne veut plus parler à personne.
14. Il n'a plus ses lunettes de soleil et sa chemise n'est plus élégante.
15. Il a téléphoné à Candide à 3 heures du matin.
16. Il boit de l'eau.

B. Qu'est-ce qu'on a fait?
Choisissez un verbe de la liste pour expliquer ce que tout le monde a fait. Vous pouvez utiliser le même *(same)* verbe plusieurs fois *(more than once).*

trouver / dormir / donner / gagner / jouer / boire / danser / faire / acheter / prendre / mettre

1. Nous avons . . . . . des pommes au supermarché.
2. Qui a . . . . . son café sur la table?
3. Ils ont . . . . . la nuit et ils ont . . . . . le matin.
4. Hier, j'ai . . . . . du ski.
5. Vous avez . . . . . votre chien?
6. Tu as . . . . . au football dimanche? Qui a . . . . . ?
7. Est-ce que vous avez . . . . . vos devoirs?
8. Ils ont . . . . . un sandwich et j'ai . . . . . une bière.

C. Leur week-end

Aujourd'hui, c'est lundi. Qu'est-ce qu'ils ont fait ce week-end? Utilisez les verbes de la liste pour compléter les phrases au passé. Vous pouvez utiliser le même *(same)* verbe plusieurs fois *(more than once)*.

rencontrer / parler / manger / téléphoner / faire / dormir / grossir

1. Hier, je ..... à Suzanne et nous ..... de toi!
2. Candide et Alceste sont au régime, mais ils ..... !
3. Dimanche, nous ..... dans un petit restaurant en ville.
4. Est-ce que vous ..... du sport ou est-ce que vous ..... hier après-midi?
5. Tu ..... une fille merveilleuse au ski dimanche? Mais elle habite loin de chez toi? C'est triste!

Continuons!

A. Hier...

Voilà des activités. Qu'est-ce que vous avez fait hier? Faites une liste et comparez avec les autres étudiants.

ACTIVITÉS POSSIBLES: faire des devoirs / mettre une robe élégante / réfléchir aux examens / donner des fleurs à un ami / jouer aux cartes / dormir / trouver 10 dollars / ranger l'appartement / faire le ménage / faire du sport / acheter du pain / boire un café avec des amis / prendre le dîner avec ses parents, etc.

B. Un jeu!

Faites une liste de trois choses que vous avez faites au moins une fois *(at least once)*. Donnez des détails et soyez original(e)! Comparez avec les autres étudiants: Est-ce que vous avez fait des choses que personne n'a faites dans la classe?

DES VERBES UTILES: jouer / faire / finir / choisir / acheter / donner / regarder / parler / téléphoner / rencontrer / travailler / manger / boire / mettre / prendre

Modèle   *J'ai pris le petit déjeuner avec le président de l'université.*
          J'ai acheté deux jeans velours rouges en solde.

Act. A: Use the list of activities suggested to start a list on the board or on an overhead transparency. Brainstorm with students to add to the list. If students suggest activities that require verbs conjugated with **être** in the **passé composé**, put those activities in parentheses and tell students that they will have to wait to be able to say that. Or, if desired, give students the forms they will need without doing a formal grammar presentation (**sortir, oui, vous dites "je suis sorti" pour les garçons, "je suis sortie" pour les filles**). After establishing a list, ask students to work in pairs or groups to formulate their list of **"activités d'hier."** Do a quick **sondage** to establish the most and least common activities for the class.

Act. B: May be assigned as homework in order to give students an opportunity to reflect.

Découvertes culturelles: Les vêtements: signes et symboles

Chic et propre pour pas cher

Act. A: Provide models: **(1) On est… ou… riche / pauvre / jeune / vieux (vieille) / actif (active) / élégant (élégante) / sale / propre / etc, donc on porte… (2) On aime… / on déteste… / donc on porte… (3) On travaille dans un bureau ou dans une ferme / on aime le confort / on aime le sport, donc on porte…**

Act. B: Have students justify their answers by pointing to words or texts. **(Il n'y a pas de prix, pas de numéro. Il y a des textes, des chiffres avec les photos.)** You may want to ask in English if they can tell what type of article this is as well as what type of magazine it probably came from.

A. Préparation: les styles. Quelles informations donnent les vêtements qu'on porte?

B. Chic et propre pour pas cher. De quoi s'agit-il *(What is it about)?* D'après les photos et le titre, c'est quel type de document? une page de catalogue? le début *(beginning)* d'un article? une photo de famille? une page de journal de mode?

ÉCONOMIE > en couverture

>s'occuper de soi

Chic et propre pour pas cher

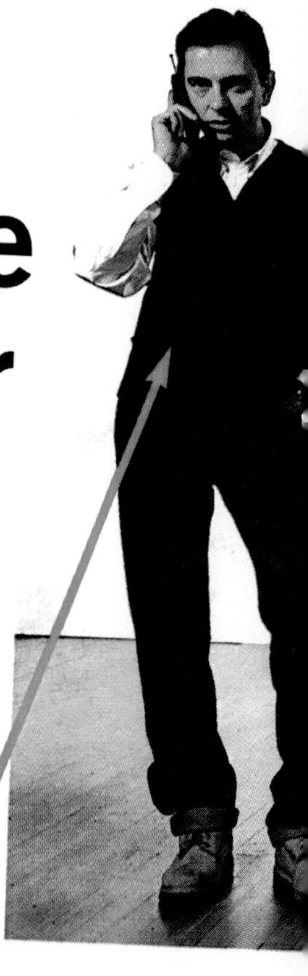

> **Le gilet porté sans cravate sur un jean est un clin d'œil au costume trois pièces des années 60. Finis les uniformes. Chacun personnalise sa tenue.**

L'Express

C. Les personnes. Qui sont ces personnes? Comment sont-elles? Qu'est-ce qu'elles font? Qu'est-ce qu'elles vont faire? Où sont-elles?

D. Des détails. Trouvez dans les textes, les mots qui sont illustrés par la photo.

Modèle *(la photo de l'homme)* **le gilet**

E. Culture. Pouvez-vous placer ces personnes dans une culture spécifique ou une nationalité précise?

F. Les valeurs. Quelles sont les valeurs exprimées par cette photo?

☐ la beauté physique?
☐ la famille?
☐ l'éducation?
☐ l'uniformité sociale?
☐ le matérialisme?

☐ l'élégance?
☐ l'importance de la mode?
☐ les enfants?
☐ l'harmonie dans la famille?
☐ le confort?

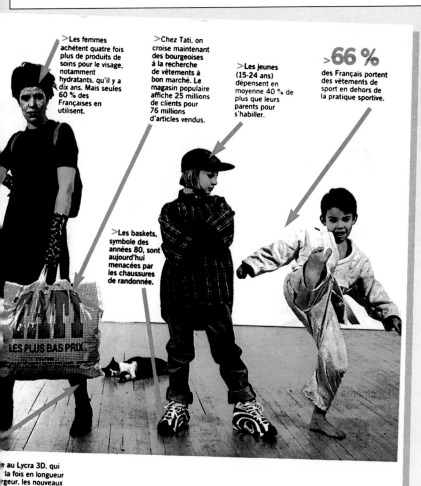

> **Les femmes** achètent quatre fois plus de produits de soins pour le visage, notamment hydratants, qu'il y a dix ans. Mais seules 60 % des Françaises en utilisent.

> **Chez Tati,** on croise maintenant des bourgeoises à la recherche de vêtements à bon marché. Le magasin populaire affiche 25 millions de clients pour 76 millions d'articles vendus.

> **Les jeunes (15-24 ans)** dépensent en moyenne 40 % de plus que leurs parents pour s'habiller.

> **66 %** des Français portent des vêtements de sport en dehors de la pratique sportive.

> **Les baskets,** symbole des années 80, sont aujourd'hui menacées par les chaussures de randonnée.

LES PLUS BAS PRIX

...e au Lycra 3D, qui ...la fois en longueur ...rgeur, les nouveaux ...ements affinent ...es.

G. D'après cette image et ce texte, présentez votre conclusion sur la culture française des années 90.

Modèle *Les Français... ; les hommes... ; les femmes... ; les familles... En France on ne porte plus de...*

▶ Les Français pantouflards

Act. A: Review articles of clothing to prepare students for the word **pantoufle**. Here **sortir** means *to go outside* with no connotation of formality.

A. Pour rester chez moi. C'est un soir d'automne. Faites deux listes: les vêtements que vous mettez chez vous et les vêtements que vous mettez pour sortir.

Une
charentaise

Deux
pyjamas

Les champions de la pantoufle

Les Français achètent chaque année un peu plus d'une paire de pantoufles en moyenne, soit trois fois plus que les Allemands, quatre fois plus que les Danois, sept fois plus que les Italiens, cent fois plus que les Portugais!

Le mauvais temps est un facteur favorable, surtout pour ceux qui habitent dans des maisons et disposent de jardins. Mais il ne saurait expliquer le record national. La «charentaise», née au XVIIe siècle sous Colbert et La Rochefoucauld, reste le symbole d'une nation frileuse, avide de confort et très attachée à son logement. La pantoufle est au pied ce que le foyer est à la vie des Français: un cocon.

FNICF

Une robe de chambre

Gérard Mermet,
Francoscopie 1995

Des
pantoufles

Deux
pyjama

B. Les champions de la pantoufle.

1. **Le sujet du texte.** Trouvez dans le texte les protagonistes de ce match à la pantoufle. Qui achète le plus de pantoufles? Et le moins?

2. **L'architecture du texte.**
   - Quel type de mots trouvez-vous cinq fois dans le premier paragraphe? Donnez un titre à ce paragraphe.
   - Quelles sont les deux références du deuxième paragraphe qui expliquent la popularité de la pantoufle en France? Donnez un titre à ce paragraphe.

3. **Des détails.** Vrai ou faux?

Act B, 3: Have students correct false items.

	vrai	faux	
a.	☐	☐	Les Portugais achètent cent paires de pantoufles par an.
b.	☐	☐	Les Allemands achètent trois fois moins de pantoufles que les Français.
c.	☐	☐	Les Français qui ont un jardin ne portent pas de pantoufles.
d.	☐	☐	Quand il fait mauvais dehors, c'est une bonne idée de mettre des pantoufles dans la maison.
e.	☐	☐	Les pantoufles sont une vieille institution française.
f.	☐	☐	La charentaise symbolise la France.
g.	☐	☐	Les Français aiment beaucoup leur confort et leur maison.
h.	☐	☐	Comme la maison, la pantoufle est un cocon de confort.

4. **À la recherche des significations.** Choisissez les meilleurs synonymes d'après le contexte pour les expressions suivantes.

- il ne saurait expliquer:
  - ☐ il ne peut pas expliquer
  - ☐ il n'aime pas expliquer
  - ☐ il ne veut pas expliquer

- frileux:
  - ☐ quelqu'un qui est nationaliste
  - ☐ quelqu'un qui n'aime pas le froid
  - ☐ quelqu'un qui mange des frites

- les personnes qui disposent de jardins:
  - ☐ les personnes qui refusent les jardins
  - ☐ les personnes qui ont des jardins
  - ☐ les personnes qui tranforment les jardins

- le foyer:
  - ☐ le travail
  - ☐ la maison familiale
  - ☐ la fête de famille

www explore!
http//voila.heinle.com

C. Discussion.

1. **Le mauvais temps.** Décrivez «le mauvais temps». Pourquoi est-il un facteur favorable à la pantoufle? Quels sont les avantages des pantoufles?
2. **Deux scénarios.**
   - Vous habitez dans une maison avec un jardin. Il fait mauvais et vous rentrez chez vous. La maison est très propre. Imaginez les phrases de votre mère (ou de votre père ou de votre mari ou femme).
   - Vous habitez dans un appartement. Comment entrer dans l'appartement quand il fait mauvais temps?

D. Les symboles des Français.

1. **Deux grands hommes de l'histoire.** Colbert et La Rochefoucauld sont deux personnes liées à l'histoire et à la littérature françaises. Préparez des questions pour demander à votre professeur l'identité de ces deux hommes. Quelles personnes sont utilisées comme symbole dans votre culture?
2. **Une nation frileuse.** Qu'est-ce qu'une nation frileuse? Qu'est-ce que les gens de cette nation aiment? Qu'est-ce qu'ils n'aiment pas?

   Modèle   *Ils aiment...*
                   Ils n'aiment pas...
                   Ils sont...
                   Ils ne sont pas...

   Est-ce que vous avez des exemples qui illustrent que la nation française est ou n'est pas frileuse?

E. Comparaisons.

1. Et votre nation, comment est-elle? Est-elle frileuse? Aime-t-elle les cocons ou la grande aventure?
2. Quel vêtement symbolise sa philosophie principale?
3. Décrivez votre nation et donnez des exemples pour illustrer ses caractéristiques principales.

Orthographe et prononciation

▶▶ Les voyelles orales et les voyelles nasales

French has both oral and nasal vowels. Oral vowels are produced mostly within the mouth cavity. Nasals are produced by diverting air into the nose.

ORAL VOWELS	NASAL VOWELS
nos	non
à	an
vert	vend

French has four nasal vowels:

[ã] as in *man*teau, *vête*m*ent*   [ɔ̃] as in *pantal*on, *fon*cé

[ɛ̃] as in *maillot de b*ain, *im*perméable   [œ̃] as in *br*un, un

Point out that English has "nasal-like vowels" (e.g., *sing, impossible*) but that since these sounds are not phonemic, native English speakers are usually unaware of their existence. Tell students to put their fingers lightly along the bridge of their nose when saying *sing* in order to feel the resonance produced by the nasal quality of the vowel in English.

Point out that for many speakers, especially in Paris, **un** is pronounced [ɛ̃] rather than [œ̃].

Activités

A. Prononcez Répétez après votre professeur.

1. C'est quand, ton examen?
2. Elle ne prend jamais de poisson.
3. Il y a vingt et un Américains bruns dans le magasin!

B. Trouvez la règle Regardez les deux listes. Comment est-ce que l'orthographe *(spelling)* indique si une voyelle est nasale ou non?

1. (voyelles orales) brune / semaine / bonne / année / femme / homme
2. (voyelles nasales) brun / humain / bon / an / faim / son

Act. B: Help students formulate rules such as: A vowel followed by one *n* is nasal; a vowel followed by two *n*'s is not.

Vocabulaire de base

🗎 **TEXT TAPE:**
Vocabulaire de base

Les verbes et les prépositions One group of French verbs is followed directly by an infinitive or a noun complement: **Il aime nager. Il aime la glace.** Another group requires that the preposition **à** be inserted: **Je commence à avoir faim. Tu réfléchis à demain?** Still another group requires the preposition **de: Elle a choisi *de* rentrer. Vous avez envie *d'*un café?** Vocabulary lists at the end of each lesson as well as the end vocabulary will give you this information. Here are some of the abbreviations used in dictionaries to indicate this type of information:

A list of verb + preposition + infinitive constructions can be found on p. 547.

inf. = infinitif   qqch. = quelque chose *(something)*   qqn = quelqu'un *(someone)*

Les chiffres de 100 à 1.000 (voir page 240)

NOMS

les affaires *(f. pl.)* belongings, stuff
un chapeau *hat*
une chaussette *sock*
une chaussure *shoe*
une chemise *(man's)* shirt

un chemisier *(woman's)* shirt
un costume *(man's)* suit
une cravate *tie*
un franc *franc*
un gant *glove*
un imperméable *raincoat*

un jean *pair of jeans*
une jupe *skirt*
des lunettes *(f. pl.)* eyeglasses
un maillot de bain *swimsuit, bathing suit*
un manteau *coat*

une montre *wristwatch*
un pantalon *pair of pants*
un parapluie *umbrella*
un prix *price*
un pull *sweater*
une robe *dress*
un short *pair of shorts*
des sous-vêtements *(m. pl.)* *underwear*
un tailleur *(woman's) suit*
une valise *suitcase*
une veste *jacket, sport coat*
des vêtements *(m. pl.) clothes*
un voyage *trip*

VERBES

choisir (de + inf.) *to choose*
finir (de + inf.) *to finish*

grossir *to gain weight*
maigrir *to lose weight*
mettre *to put, to put on, to wear*
porter *to carry, to wear*
réfléchir (à + qqch.) *to think (about), to reflect*

ADJECTIFS

cher, chère *expensive*
clair(e) *light*
confortable *comfortable*
élégant(e) *elegant*
foncé(e) *dark*
habillé(e) *dressed, dressed up, formal*
long, longue *(precedes noun except for clothing) long*
nouveau, nouvel, nouveaux, nouvelle(s) *(precedes noun) new*

pratique *practical*

ADJECTIFS DE COULEUR

beige *beige*
gris(e) *gray*
rose *rose*
violet(te) *purple*

DIVERS

avoir besoin de *to need*
avoir l'air + adj; avoir l'air (de + inf.) *to look like, to seem*
avoir le temps (de + inf.) *to have time (to have the time to + inf.)*
ensemble *together*
hier *yesterday*
une fois *one time, once*

Vocabulaire supplémentaire

NOMS

un bijou, des bijoux *piece of jewelry, jewelry*
un blouson *jacket (aviator-style)*
un caleçon *boxer shorts*
des lunettes de soleil *(f. pl.) sunglasses*
la mode *fashion*
une parka *parka, ski jacket*
un polo *polo shirt*
un pyjama *pair of pajamas*
une sandale *sandal*
un slip *briefs, panties*
un soutien-gorge *bra*
un survêtement *sweatsuit*
un tee-shirt *T-shirt*
des tennis *(m. pl.) sneakers*

VERBE

coûter *to cost*

ADJECTIFS

bien habillé(e) *well dressed*
court(e) *short*
démodé(e) *out of fashion*
mal habillé(e) *badly dressed*

DIVERS

aller bien/mal avec *to go well/badly with*
aller bien/mal ensemble *to go well/badly together*
Combien coûte...? *How much does ...cost?*
combien de fois (par jour, par semaine...) *how many times (a day, a week...)*
coûter cher; ça coûte cher *to be expensive; it's / that's expensive*
en solde *on sale*
être à la mode *to be in fashion*

LE FRANÇAIS TEL QU'ON LE PARLE

—Ça me (te, vous) va bien/mal! *"It fits me (you) well/badly; it looks nice/bad on me (you)."*
—Tu trouves? *"Do you think so?"*
—Quelle taille faites-vous? / Vous faites du combien? *"What's your size?"*
—Je fais du (40, 42...) *"My size is (40, 42 . . .)"*
C'est combien? *How much is it?*

LE FRANÇAIS FAMILIER

un costard = un costume
être bien (mal) fringué(e) = être bien (mal) habillé(e)
être bien (mal) sapé(e) = être bien (mal) habillé(e)
les fringues *(f. pl.)* = les vêtements
une godasse = une chaussure
un imper = un imperméable
un jogging = un survêtement
le look = *stylish appearance*
un sweat *(pronounced "sweet")* = sweatshirt
un training = un survêtement

ON ENTEND PARFOIS...

une mitaine (Canada) = un gant
un sapeur (Congo, Niger, Cameroun, Côte-d'Ivoire) = un homme qui aime être bien habillé

Où est-ce que vous habitez?

En bref

Dans cette leçon...

- Maisons en France: régions, préférences, vacances
- Les maisons, les appartements et les meubles
- Les Dubois, les Mabille et les Rasquin: quelques détails de plus
- Les chiffres supérieurs à 1.000
- Les villes
- Demander des directions
- Encore le passé: le passé composé avec **être**; poser des questions et parler au négatif
- Les verbes comme **vendre**

In this lesson...

- Housing in France: regions, preferences, vacation
- Houses, apartments, and furnishings
- More about the Dubois, Mabille, and Rasquin families
- Numbers above 1,000
- Cities
- Asking for directions
- More about the past: the **passé composé** with **être**, asking questions and saying no in the past
- Verbs like **vendre** *(to sell)*

www explore!
http://voila.heinle.com

Develop writing skills with Système-D software!

Practice listening and pronunciation skills with the Text Tape!

Discover the Francophone world!

Build your skills!

INTERNET

SYSTÈME-D

TEXT TAPE

VIDEO TAPE

CD-ROM

Students have an open-ended writing activity in the **Cahier** suitable for use with **Système-D**.

Les couleurs de la France

LA NORMANDIE

L'ALSACE-LORRAINE

LA PROVENCE

LA BRETAGNE

L'AUVERGNE

LA SAVOIE

Les couleurs de la France. Qu'est-ce que c'est? Choisissez:

☐ un livre de maisons à acheter
☐ des propositions de voyages en France
☐ des propositions de visites touristiques
☐ un inventaire de sites historiques
☐ un livre sur l'habitat régional

Les régions de France. Voici un album de photos des maisons régionales en France. Sur la carte de France (à la fin de votre livre), trouvez les régions de chaque maison et donnez les points de référence correspondants: mer, ville principale, montagne, fleuve, frontière, etc.

sont les couleurs de la vie

LE SUD-OUEST

Les couleurs de la France
Maisons et paysages

Jean Philippe Lenclos
Dominique Lenclos

Éditions
du Moniteur

EDITIONS
LE MONITEUR

17, RUE D'UZES - 75002 PARIS

"Les gens qui sont nés quelque part" ont à cœur de retrouver leurs racines, celles de leur région, de leur ville, de leur village. De revoir les couleurs qui ont marqué de leur empreinte des paysages familiers.

Comme les peintres, les constructeurs ont toujours été influencé par le milieu dans lequel ils évoluent: nature du climat, de la lumière, des matériaux trouvés sur place. Ainsi l'habitat s'est diversifié, créant un style propre à chaque région et donnant à la vie sa coloration spécifique.

Les couleurs de la France:
un livre admirable pour découvrir la diversité régionale et les traditions populaires de l'habitat.

EN VENTE DANS LES LIBRAIRIES
ET PAR CORRESPONDANCE
AU PRIX FRANCO DE 590 F.

Le prix de la plus belle maison régionale.

Organisez un concours pour trouver la plus belle maison de France. Donnez sept points à la maison que vous préférez, puis six à la suivante, etc. Pour chaque *(each)* maison, comptez les points. Dites quelle maison a gagné et donnez les raisons de ce vote.

La France... : Encourage students to provide details using the language they already know. (**Il y a des plages célèbres et historiques. Il pleut souvent comme en Angleterre et la campagne est très verte. Il n'y a pas de montagnes. Les maisons sont vieilles**, etc.)

La France des régions.
Choisissez une de ces régions et, avec la carte géographique, faites une description de cette région: ville, climat, montagnes, etc. Avec les photos du document, décrivez le type de maison de cette région.

Modèle *La Normandie est près de la Bretagne. Elle est en face de l'Angleterre. Les maisons sont vieilles, etc.*

LISTENING ACTIVITY: Have students identify the region corresponding to your sentences.

Modèle:
Teacher: **Il y a des plages.**
Student: **la Bretagne, la Normandie, la Provence**

Il y a des montagnes. / Il fait beau. / Il y a de la neige en hiver. / On fait du ski. / On va à la campagne. / Il y a des villages perchés. / C'est sur la mer Méditerranée. / La ville principale est Marseille. / C'est à côté de l'Italie. / C'est à côté de l'Espagne. etc.

L'habitat régional.

- Dans le texte, identifiez les mots importants qui définissent l'habitat régional.

- Pourquoi l'habitat est-il diversifié?

- Trouvez dans le texte les mots qui indiquent les rapports entre l'habitat et une culture.

Et vous?
Qu'est-ce qu'une maison pour vous?

L'habitat... :
- Help students by providing a few words (**diversifié, un style propre, coloration spécifique**, etc.).
- Point out paragraph two of the text: **nature du climat, de la lumière, des matériaux**, etc.
- **Traditions, histoire, les gens qui sont nés**, etc.

Le prix... : If desired, organize a secret vote and announce the results. Students can debate their choices afterwards.

265

Ask students to reflect on cultural conventions for numbering floors (use of terms such as ground floor, basement, levels, existence of 13th floors, etc.). Are these conventions arbitrary?

Info plus

Le rez-de-chaussée et les étages.
The **rez-de-chaussée** is the ground floor in France. The floor above it (the second floor according to the U.S. system) is then called the first floor or **premier étage,** the next floor (U.S. third floor) the **deuxième étage,** and so on.

TRANSPARENCY: 11-1

*V*ocabulaire

A. 35, rue Minerve, 1060 Bruxelles: la maison des Mabille, en Belgique

C'est une maison de ville, ancienne et agréable. Au sous-sol, il y a une grande cave pratique pour le vin et un garage pour une voiture. Au rez-de-chaussée, il y a trois grandes pièces: un salon qui donne sur le jardin, une cuisine moderne et une salle à manger. Il y a aussi des W.C. Il y a deux étages. Au premier étage, il y a une salle de bains, des W.C. et trois chambres: une pour Annette Mabille, une pour sa fille Sylvie et une pour les amis. Au dernier étage, dans le grenier, il y a la chambre de Suzanne. C'est une chambre assez sombre, mais elle l'adore parce qu'elle est si grande et Suzanne aime être à l'aise! La troisième fille, Catherine, est mariée et n'habite plus chez sa mère.

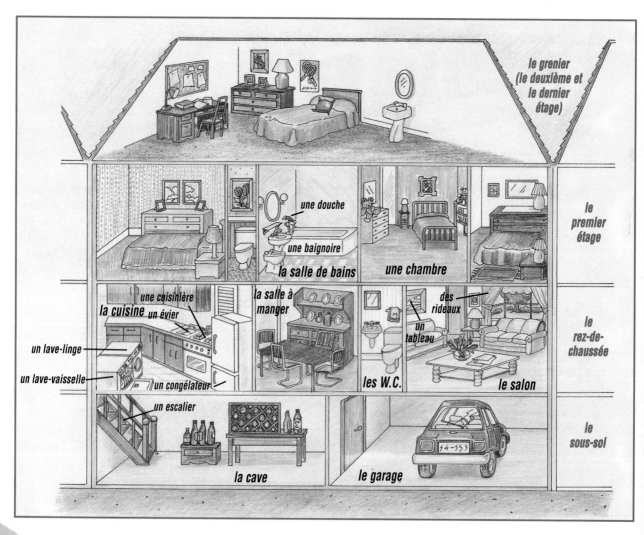

Une maison typique à Bruxelles

Salle de séjour is often used as the equivalent of *living room* in real estate ads. Where there is a separate dining room, however, you often find **salon** used instead of **salle de séjour.**

In France, washing machines can often be found in the kitchen.

Ask students how many English words they can think of to refer to bathrooms (e.g., *ladies' room, john*, etc.). Why are there so many? If desired, discuss briefly what is usually found in bathrooms according to your students' experiences.

Info plus

La salle de bains.

In French homes, **la salle de bains** usually contains a sink, a bathtub (with or without a shower), and a bidet. There is usually no toilet. The toilet is found in **les W.C.** (short for the English *water closet*), which is a separate room. The term **les toilettes** is also used.

- **Leur maison.** Quelle est l'adresse des Mabille? Est-ce qu'ils habitent en France? Est-ce qu'ils ont une maison moderne ou ancienne? Est-ce que c'est une maison confortable, à votre avis? Combien d'étages est-ce qu'il y a? Qu'est-ce qu'il y a au sous-sol? Où est le salon? Et la chambre d'Annette Mabille? Et la chambre de Suzanne?

- **Leurs meubles.** Qu'est-ce qu'il y a dans le salon? dans la salle à manger? dans la cuisine? dans la salle de bains? dans la chambre de Suzanne? Comment est sa chambre?

B. 75, avenue Édith Cavell, 06000 Nice: la maison de Jacques Dubois

un arbre

le toit

des volets (m.)

un mur

la terrasse

la pelouse

Have students speculate about the interior (furniture, colors, etc.).

C'est une maison confortable dans un quartier calme assez loin du centre-ville. À l'intérieur, les pièces sont claires et agréables. En bas, il y a une cuisine et une grande salle de séjour avec un coin salle à manger. Il y a aussi deux chambres et une salle de bains. En haut, il y a une troisième chambre.

À l'extérieur, il y a un garage, une terrasse, une piscine et un grand jardin avec des arbres et des fleurs. Jacques a aussi des légumes dans son jardin, mais ils sont derrière la maison.

Jacques, qui est retraité, aime bien travailler chez lui. Par exemple, l'année dernière, il a mis une piscine pour ses enfants et ses petits-enfants. Et puis, pour entrer chez lui, il faut traverser la pelouse et ce n'est pas très pratique. Alors, il voudrait mettre aussi un chemin qui traverse la pelouse pour aller jusqu'à la rue, mais il ne l'a pas encore fait. Peut-être cet automne, s'il a le temps et l'argent! Ça coûte cher et il ne veut pas devoir de l'argent à la banque.

- Où habite Jacques Dubois? Quelle est son adresse? Il y a combien de pièces dans la maison? Est-ce que vous préférez la maison des Mabille ou la maison de Jacques Dubois? Pourquoi?
- Qu'est-ce que Jacques a déjà fait dans la maison? Qu'est-ce qu'il voudrait faire? Pourquoi?
- À votre avis, quelle est la saison sur la photo? Qui est en vacances chez Jacques Dubois?

C. 23 rue des Taillandiers, 75011 Paris: l'appartement de Jean Rasquin

TRANSPARENCY:
11-3

C'est un trois pièces au quatrième étage d'un immeuble moderne à Paris.

Dans l'appartement de Jean Rasquin il y a une petite cuisine, un grand séjour avec un coin repas, deux chambres et une salle de bains. Il y a aussi une entrée avec des placards, des W.C. et un couloir qui va à la cuisine et au séjour. La cuisine et le séjour donnent sur un grand balcon ensoleillé.

- Où habite Jean Rasquin? Quelle est son adresse? Est-ce que son appartement est grand? Est-ce qu'il est en ordre ou en désordre? Est-ce qu'il est agréable? Pourquoi ou pourquoi pas? À votre avis, est-ce que Jean Rasquin monte en ascenseur ou par l'escalier quand il rentre chez lui? Pourquoi?

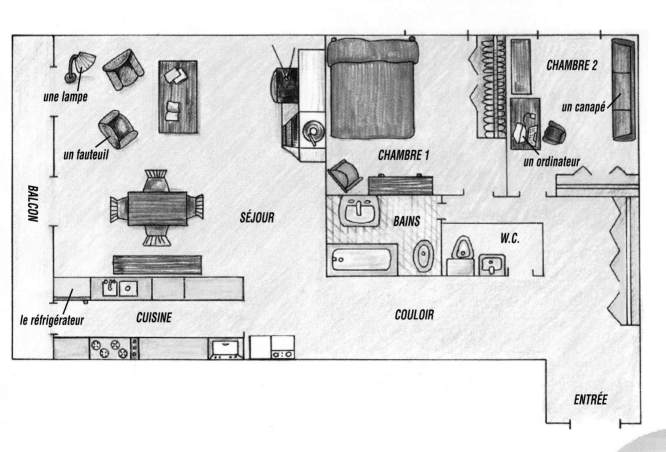

D. Le plan d'une petite ville: Retournons à Cinet, la petite ville française de la leçon 6.

TRANSPARENCIES:
11-4, 11-5, 11-6

Transparencies 11-5 and 11-6 are maps of **Luchon** (a town in the **Pyrénées**) and of **Bruxelles**. These maps are also the basis for activities in the **Cahier d'activités écrites et orales**.

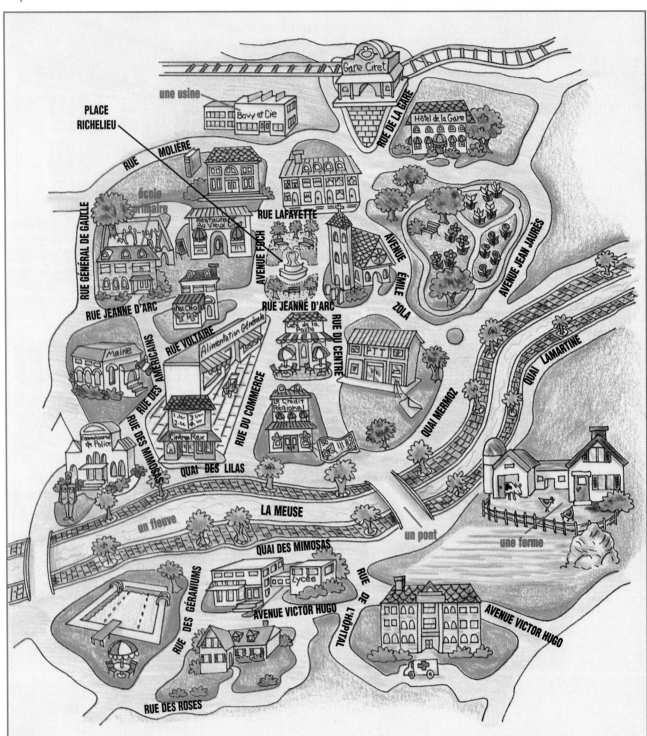

À Cinet, il y a un fleuve, la Meuse, et des ponts. Au centre-ville, il y a une église et, en face de l'église, il y a une place. Il y a aussi une mairie, un commissariat de police, une gare, une banque, une école primaire et un lycée. Et puis, un peu plus loin, il y a un hôpital et une usine, Bovy et Cie. Et parce que Cinet est à la campagne, il y a aussi des fermes.

Si vous êtes à la gare et si vous voulez aller à l'hôpital, il faut traverser le fleuve. Comment? D'abord, vous prenez la rue de la Gare et vous continuez tout droit jusqu'à l'église. À l'église, vous tournez à gauche dans l'avenue Émile Zola. Au bout de l'avenue, vous prenez le quai Mermoz à droite. Ensuite, vous traversez le premier pont à gauche et vous tournez à droite. L'hôpital est au coin de la rue de l'hôpital et de l'avenue Victor Hugo.

- Regardez bien le plan de la ville. Qu'est-ce qu'il y a d'autre à Cinet? Qu'est-ce qu'il n'y a pas à Cinet? Comment allez-vous à l'église si vous êtes à la mairie? Comment allez-vous au commissariat de police si vous êtes au parc? Comment allez-vous à l'école primaire si vous habitez à la ferme?

Section E: As is the case for English, large numbers are seldom written out—except on checks—and it is not uncommon for French speakers to hesitate concerning their orthography. For this reason, many instructors do not require their students to learn their spelling at this level.

Point out that **mil** is an alternate form of **mille** used in dates.

Compare English *one hundred, one thousand* and French **cent, mille** (no number modifier).

The last **Deux-Chevaux** was manufactured in a Citroën factory in Portugal in 1990. This means that all 2CVs for sale today are used cars (**voitures d'occasion**). The red license plate on the Peugeot indicates that this is a tax-free car that belongs or is leased to non-residents of the CE.

E. Les chiffres au-dessus de 1.000

1.000	mille	*a thousand*		2.000	deux mille	*two thousand*
1.001	mille un	*a thousand one*		10.000	dix mille	*ten thousand*
1.100	onze cents,	*eleven hundred,*		100.000	cent mille	*one hundred thousand*
	mille cent	*one thousand one hundred*		1.000.000	un million	*a million*
1.500	quinze cents,	*fifteen hundred,*		1.000.000.000	un milliard	*a billion*
	mille cinq cents	*one thousand five hundred*				

- Combien coûtent ces voitures?
- Quelle voiture préférez-vous? Pourquoi?

Cette Peugeot 106 coûte 73.800 francs français. C'est une petite voiture qui n'est pas très chère.

TRANSPARENCY: 11-7

Cette Deux-Chevaux (2 CV) coûte 16.000 francs français. Elle ne coûte pas très cher parce que c'est une vieille voiture.

Cette Renault Espace coûte 187.500 francs français. C'est une voiture pour sept personnes qui coûte cher mais qui est très pratique pour les grandes familles.

Cette Citroën Xantia coûte 125.200 francs français. C'est une grande voiture qui coûte assez cher.

Notes de vocabulaire

1. Mots et expressions utiles.

un centime	centime ($^1/100$ franc)
aux États-Unis	in the United States
quelquefois	sometimes

2. Les nombres ordinaux. Here are the forms of the ordinal numbers 1–20.

premier, première	1er, 1ère	onzième	11e
deuxième	2e	douzième	12e
troisième	3e	treizième	13e
quatrième	4e	quatorzième	14e
cinquième	5e	quinzième	15e
sixième	6e	seizième	16e
septième	7e	dix-septième	17e
huitième	8e	dix-huitième	18e
neuvième	9e	dix-neuvième	19e
dixième	10e	vingtième	20e

3. Les chiffres et l'argent. In written numbers, French uses a period where English uses a comma, and vice versa.

FRENCH	ENGLISH
12,25 ("douze virgule vingt-cinq")	12.25
3.000 ("trois mille")	3,000

The **franc** is the basic monetary unit in France, Belgium, Luxembourg, and Switzerland. Each **franc** is divided into 100 parts or **centimes.** One Swiss **franc** is worth more than one French **franc,** and one French **franc** is worth more than one Belgian **franc.** Monetary amounts are written like this:

30 F 50 (**"trente francs cinquante"**)   30 francs 50 (centimes)

Beyond 199, the word **cent** (hundred) is written with an **-s** when it is not followed by another number. Otherwise, it has no **-s.** The word **mille** (thousand) never has an **-s.**

100 **cent**   200 **deux cents**   4.000 **quatre mille**

The year may be expressed using either **cent** or **mil.**

1999   **dix-neuf cent quatre-vingt-dix-neuf**
            mil neuf cent quatre-vingt-dix-neuf

4. Jour, semaine et année + dernier. Note the use of **dernier** in these expressions.

dimanche **dernier**	last Sunday
la semaine **dernière**	last week
le mois **dernier**	last month
l'année **dernière**	last year

See the **Instructor's Resource Manual** for more information.

3: Give students, or ask them to research, current dollar values for various monies used in the Francophone world.

3: Note that the *Tolérances grammaticales ou orthographiques* put out by the French Ministry of Education in 1976 admit both **cent** and **cents (deux cent un** or **deux cents un).**

In all other cases, **dernier** precedes its noun.

Il habite au dernier étage.   *He lives on the top floor.*

5. Une pièce.
Une pièce is the generic term for *a room.* **Une salle** is a room used for public functions or a specific purpose (**une salle de classe, une salle de cinéma,** or **une salle à manger,** for example). **Une chambre** is *a bedroom.*

6. Si.
The word **si** has three different equivalents in English.

a. Affirmative response to negative question or statement:

—Tu ne travailles pas assez!   *"You don't work enough!"*
—**Si!** Je travaille trop!   *"I do so! In fact, I work too much!"*

b. **Si** meaning *if* or *whether:*

S'il fait beau, je vais jouer au tennis.   *If it's nice, I'm going to play tennis.*
Je ne sais pas **s'**il va faire   *I don't know whether it will be*
  beau demain.   *nice tomorrow.*

The **-i** of **si** is dropped in front of **il** and **ils** only.

S'ils font la vaisselle, papa va être content!
Si elles font la vaisselle, papa va être content!
Si on ne fait pas la vaisselle, papa ne va pas être content!

c. **Si** meaning *so,* to intensify the meaning of an adjective or an adverb:

Il fait **si** beau aujourd'hui.   *It's so nice out today.*

7. La place des adverbes au passé composé.
In general, short, common adverbs are placed between the helping verb and the past participle in the **passé composé.**

Vous avez **bien** dormi?   *Did you sleep well?*
Vincent a **trop** mangé.   *Vincent ate too much.*
Tu n'as pas **encore** fini?   *You're not finished yet?*

8. Pour demander votre chemin.
When you want to ask for directions, you may say one of the following:

— Pardon, Monsieur (Madame / Mademoiselle), pour aller à la gare (à la poste / à l'hôpital), s'il vous plaît?

— Excusez-moi, Monsieur (Madame / Mademoiselle), pourriez-vous me dire où se trouve la gare (la poste / l'hôpital), s'il vous plaît?

9. Combien est-ce que je vous dois?
The verb **devoir** can also mean *to owe.*

Combien est-ce que je vous **dois?**   *How much do I owe you?*
Mais vous ne me **devez** rien!   *But you don't owe me anything!*

6: *So* as an intensifier is translated by **si** plus an adjective or an adverb (**La chambre de Suzanne est si grande!**). **Alors** expresses a consequence. It is used either alone (**Et alors?**) or followed by a clause (**Nous avons trouvé le film ennuyeux, alors nous sommes partis.**).
  If desired, point out that **l'** may be introduced in front of **on** to facilitate pronunciation (**Si l'on ne fait pas la vaisselle…**).

See the **Instructor's Resource Manual** for more information.

9: Quickly review the conjugation of **devoir.** Add a few personal questions: **Est-ce que vous devez de l'argent à vos amis? à vos parents? Est-ce que vos amis vous doivent de l'argent?** etc.

D'accord?

A. Chassez l'intrus Quel mot ne va pas avec les autres à cause du sens *(meaning)*?

1. le fauteuil / le canapé / le garage / la chaise
2. le fauteuil / la table / le lavabo / le canapé
3. la douche / le lavabo / l'évier / la baignoire
4. les W.C. / le jardin / les arbres / les fleurs
5. l'immeuble / le meuble / la maison / l'appartement
6. l'ascenseur / le sous-sol / le rez-de-chaussée / le premier étage
7. la cuisine / la salle de bains / la terrasse / la salle à manger
8. une cuisinière / un tableau / un lave-vaisselle / un lave-linge

B. Ça va ensemble Avec quel(s) nom(s) de la boîte de gauche vont les adjectifs et les expressions de la boîte de droite?

Modèle un réfrigérateur   *C'est froid, c'est en bas, c'est pratique...*

un jardin	le rez-de-chaussée		sombre	clair
une piscine	le premier étage		froid	à l'extérieur
une terrasse	un couloir		vert	grand
une cave	un balcon	C'est	rouge	à l'intérieur
un arbre	une fenêtre		pratique	en bas
une fleur	une salle de bains		confortable	en haut
un ascenseur	un lave-vaisselle		agréable	calme

Act. C: Ask international students about houses in their country and compare also with "typical" houses in Francophone countries.

FOLLOW-UP: List portable objects in a house (**les objets portatifs**), heavy and/or unmovable objects (**les objets lourds**), furniture usually made of wood (**les meubles en bois**), furniture usually made of plastic (**les meubles en plastique**).

C. Les pièces Faites des listes. Quelles pièces de la maison...

1. sont pour tout le monde?
2. ne sont pas pour tout le monde?
3. sont en haut?
4. sont en bas?
5. ont une télévision?
6. ont un téléphone?
7. ont un lave-linge?

D. Où? Pour vous, où est-ce que ces choses arrivent *(happen)*? Où est-ce qu'elles n'arrivent jamais?

Modèle j'étudie
À la bibliothèque, dans ma chambre, devant la télévision...
Jamais au restaurant, chez mes parents...

1. je parle au téléphone
2. je dors
3. je mange
4. je fais la vaisselle
5. j'étudie
6. j'ai souvent froid
7. j'ai souvent chaud
8. j'ai souvent sommeil

E. Calculons Quelle est la réponse? (+ = plus, – = moins).

Modèle 110 + 5 = ?   *Cent dix plus cinq font cent quinze.*

1. 100 + 120 = ?
2. 330 + 400 = ?
3. 750 + 750 = ?
4. 6.000 + 7.000 = ?

5. 40.500 + 150 = ?
6. 50.000 + 42.000 = ?
7. 250.000 + 300.000 = ?

F. Une course cycliste
Voilà les résultats d'une course cycliste *(bicycle race)* pour hommes en France. Qui est premier? Qui est deuxième? Continuez!

Modèle *Indurain: premier*

Indurain (Esp)	20'23"04	Simon (Fra)	20'25"96
Bugno (Ita)	21'15"59	Theunisse (P-B)	21'26"95
Leblanc (Fra)	21'33"10	Chozas (Esp)	21'35"03
Rondon (Col)	21'48"46	Chiappucci (Ita)	21'49"49
Roux (Fra)	22'07"31	Bruyneel (Bel)	22'10"57
Hampsten (É-U)	22'15"02	Ekimov (Rus)	22'23"40
Camargo (Col)	22'25"12	Ribeiro (Bré)	22'45"12

Act. F: Students do not have to read the times out loud in order to do the exercise. FOLLOW-UP: Ask students to guess the countries (Espagne, Italie, France, Colombie, États-Unis, Pays-Bas, Belgique, Russie, Brésil).

G. Les prix
Combien est-ce que ça coûte, à votre avis *(in your opinion)*?

1. un petit réfrigérateur pour une chambre d'étudiant
2. une maison à Beverly Hills
3. un vélo tout *(all)* terrain (VTT)
4. une petite voiture de sport italienne
5. un studio à New York, près de Central Park
6. une nuit dans un grand hôtel de San Francisco
7. un repas pour deux personnes dans un restaurant très élégant
8. un repas pour deux personnes à McDonald's

Act. G: CONTINUATION: un ordinateur / un Renoir / une petite Renault / une Rolls-Royce / un appartement près de l'université / le livre de français

H. Les directions
La famille Bastin, qui a une ferme près de Cinet, loue *(rents)* des chambres à des touristes en été. Vous passez *(spend)* une semaine dans leur ferme et vous voulez visiter Cinet. Demandez les directions à Monsieur ou à Madame Bastin. Utilisez le plan, page 270, et jouez les deux rôles avec un partenaire.

Modèle VOUS: ***Pourriez-vous me dire où se trouve...***
       M./MME BASTIN: ***C'est facile! Vous prenez...***

Vous voulez aller: à la piscine / à l'église / au parc / au cinéma / au restaurant Au Vieux Cinet.

Act. H: Such a farm is called **un gîte rural.** One can say also that a farmer offers **des chambres d'hôte.**
VARIATION: After having presented the **passé composé avec** *être,* give students a photocopy of Cinet or send a student to the overhead projector and have them write the information you give them on the map so as to guess where you went today (starting from the farm): **D'abord, j'ai traversé le pont et j'ai pris le quai Mermoz à droite...** , etc.

Mise en pratique

A. Nos meubles
Vous venez de déménager *(you have just moved)* dans un nouvel appartement avec deux amis. La cuisine et la salle de bains sont équipées, mais sinon *(otherwise),* il n'y a pas de meubles. En groupes, faites une liste de toutes *(all)* les pièces. Puis, décidez quels meubles vous voulez dans chaque *(each)* pièce. Donnez des détails et les prix approximatifs. Combien est-ce que vous allez dépenser *(spend)*?

B. Et chez vous? En groupes, comparez les endroits *(places)* d'où vous êtes.

SUGGESTIONS: Vous habitez une grande ville, une petite ville, un village? À la mer, près d'un lac, à la montagne... ? Qu'est-ce qu'il y a chez vous? Qu'est-ce qu'il n'y a pas? Est-ce qu'il y a des endroits culturels intéressants? pour faire des courses? pour le sport? Quelles sont les activités préférées des jeunes? etc.

Structure

▶▶ Les verbes comme *vendre*

One group of verbs in French has infinitives that end in **-re.** These verbs are conjugated identically and are grouped together as *third conjugation* or **-re** verbs. To conjugate one of these verbs in the present, drop the infinitive ending (**-re**) and add the endings shown in bold type.

vendre *to sell*	
je vend**s**	nous vend**ons**
tu vend**s**	vous vend**ez**
il / elle } vend *(no ending)*	ils / elles } vend**ent**

Note the following pronunciation points about **-re** verbs:
1. The three singular forms have the same pronunciation.
2. The **-d-** in spelling is not pronounced in the singular. It is pronounced in the plural. Notice especially the difference in pronunciation between **il/elle vend** (no **-d** pronounced) and **ils/elles vendent** (**-d-** pronounced).

Verbs like **vendre** include **descendre** *(to descend* or *to go down; to take down),* **répondre à** *(to answer),* **perdre** *(to lose),* **entendre** *(to hear),* and **attendre** *(to wait* or *to wait for).*

Il n'aime pas **répondre** aux questions.	*He doesn't like to answer questions.*
Nous **descendons.**	*We're coming down.*
J'**attends** dix minutes et c'est tout!	*I'm waiting ten minutes and that's it!*
Elle **perd** ses clés tout le temps.	*She's always losing her keys.*
Tu **entends** quelque chose?	*Do you hear something?*

The imperative or command forms of third conjugation verbs are identical to their present tense forms.

Descend**s** tout de suite!	*Get down here right now!*
Répond**ez,** s'il vous plaît.	*Please answer.*
Attend**ons** cinq minutes!	*Let's wait for five minutes!*

Third conjugation verbs like **vendre** form their past participle in **-u.**

Candide a **vendu** son vélo!	*Candide sold his bike!*
J'ai **attendu** pendant 10 minutes.	*I waited for 10 minutes.*

Vous avez compris?

A. Qu'est-ce qu'on fait? Faites des phrases complètes au présent.

1. Je / descendre / par l'escalier.
2. Ils / perdre / toujours / leurs stylos.
3. Nous / ne pas / répondre / au professeur / en anglais.
4. Tu / attendre / tes copains?
5. Vous / vendre / votre voiture?
6. Anne / attendre / une lettre de son petit ami.
7. Je / ne rien / entendre.

B. Maintenant ou hier? Utilisez une forme des verbes donnés pour compléter les phrases. VERBES: perdre / vendre / attendre / descendre / répondre / entendre

Modèle   Tu as ..... tes clés?   **Tu as *perdu* tes clés?**
               Tu les ..... toujours!   **Tu les *perds* toujours!**

1. Nous ..... notre appartement pour acheter une maison.
2. Patrick ne ..... jamais à mes lettres!
3. Vous avez ..... votre voiture?
4. Alceste a ..... Candide pendant une heure!
5. Tu ..... ? On doit partir!
6. Écoute! Tu as ..... quelque chose—ou quelqu'un?

Continuons!

Bric-à-brac *(rummage sale)* Vous avez fini l'université et vous partez. Vous et vos amis avez décidé de vendre les affaires que vous ne voulez plus parce que c'est trop difficile de les transporter à la maison.

Bric-à-brac: Can be done in groups. Each group sells one thing to the rest of the class.

1. Faites une liste des choses que vous voulez vendre et de leurs prix.
2. Proposez vos affaires à la classe. La classe pose des questions et propose d'acheter ce que vous vendez. Essayez *(try)* d'avoir le meilleur prix possible!

Modèle   VENDEUR: ***Je vends un tapis.***
           ÉTUDIANTS: ***Il est grand? Il est bleu? Combien coûte ton tapis?***
           VENDEUR: ***Qui achète mon tapis?***
           ÉTUDIANTS: ***Moi! Pas moi! Je donne 5 dollars.***

▶▶ Le passé composé avec *être*

A relatively small group of verbs use **être** as a helping or auxiliary verb in the **passé composé** instead of **avoir**.

See the **Instructor's Resource Manual** for more information.

tomber au passé composé	
je suis tombé(e)	nous sommes tombé(e)s
tu es tombé(e)	vous êtes tombé(e)(s)
il est tombé	ils sont tombés
elle est tombée	elles sont tombées

Notice that the past participle of a verb conjugated in the **passé composé** with **être** agrees with its subject.

Marie n'est pas là. Elle est allé**e** à la poste.	*Marie isn't here. She went to the post office.*
Nous sommes sorti**s** hier soir et nous n'avons pas travaillé.	*We went out last night and we didn't work.*
Mes copains sont parti**s** pour New York.	*My friends left for New York.*
Ta grand-mère est descendu**e**?	*Has your grandmother come downstairs?*

Here is a list of the verbs conjugated with **être** that have already been presented.

VERBE	PARTICIPE PASSÉ	VERBE	PARTICIPE PASSÉ
aller	allé	retourner	retourné
arriver	arrivé	rentrer	rentré
descendre	descendu	rester	resté
entrer	entré	sortir	sorti
monter	monté	tomber	tombé
partir	parti		

You can go about learning this list of verbs in several ways.

1. Many **être** verbs fall naturally into pairs of opposites (**arriver–partir, entrer–sortir,** etc.).
2. Verbs conjugated with **être** are always intransitive verbs. That is, they cannot be followed by a direct object. Another way of saying this is that when a verb is followed by a direct object, the auxiliary verb must be **avoir** and not **être.**
3. Many (but not all!) of these verbs have the idea of motion in their meaning.

Vous avez compris?

A. Au passé! Complétez avec **être** ou **avoir.**

1. Mon père ..... mis son manteau et il ..... parti.
2. Ma sœur ..... rentrée à quatre heures du matin.
3. Mes amis ..... allés en ville. Là, ils ..... acheté des jeans et des pulls et ils ..... rencontré des filles. Après, ils ..... sortis ensemble.
4. Vous n'..... pas fini? Mais vous ..... commencé à dix heures!
5. Tu ..... tombé combien de fois?
6. Ma camarade de chambre ..... restée dans sa chambre pour réfléchir à ses problèmes.

B. Hier Utilisez un des verbes de la liste pour dire ce que tout le monde *(everybody)* a fait hier. N'oubliez pas *(do not forget)* l'accord *(agreement)* du participe passé. Vous pouvez utiliser le même *(same)* verbe plusieurs fois *(more than once).*

VERBES: sortir / aller / entrer / descendre / partir / rentrer / arriver / rester / tomber

1. Nous ..... au cinéma, mais nous ..... avant la fin du film.
2. Tu as l'air fatigué. Tu ..... à quelle heure hier soir?
3. Ce n'est pas vrai! Tu ..... dans la chambre de Jean et de Marc!
4. Mes copains ..... danser mais moi, je ..... à la maison.

5. Ils . . . . . avant le cours pour parler au professeur.
6. Mais vous dormez! Est-ce que vous . . . . . hier soir?
7. Les Dumont . . . . . faire du ski.
8. Anne . . . . . dans l'escalier hier soir et elle . . . . . à l'hôpital.

Continuons!

La maison d'Alceste **Quels verbes sont conjugués avec être?** Regardez la maison et utilisez l'illustration pour compléter l'histoire *(story)* d'une journée dans la vie d'Alceste comme il la raconte *(tells)* dans une lettre à Candide.

1. sortir
2. aller
3. arriver
4. rentrer
5. monter
6. tomber
7. descendre
8. entrer
9. rester
10. partir

TRANSPARENCY:
11-9

Cher Candide,

Qu'est-ce que j'ai fait hier? Eh bien, à 10 heures du matin, (1) je . . . . . de la maison avec maman et (2) nous . . . . . au parc. (3) On . . . . . au parc vers *(around)* 10 h 30 et j'ai parlé avec des copains pendant une heure. Puis *(then)* (4) on . . . . . pour le déjeuner à midi. Pour entrer dans la maison, il faut monter un petit escalier. Alors, (5) je . . . . . sans problème mais (6) maman . . . . . Mais pas de problème! (7) Je . . . . . l'aider *(to help her)*. (8) On . . . . . dans la maison et (9) nous . . . . . chez nous pendant tout l'après-midi. Puis, vers six heures, maman et moi, (10) on . . . . . chercher du pain pour le dîner. Et voilà ma journée!

Amicalement,

Alceste

➤ Le passé composé à la forme négative et à la forme interrogative

Remind students that indefinite and partitive articles become **de** after a negative.

DRILL: **Mettez au passé. Je ne réponds pas. Nous n'attendons pas. Suzanne ne part pas. Vous ne faites pas le ménage. Jean-Luc est rentré chez lui. Alceste et Candide ne boivent pas de vin.**

To make a verb in the **passé composé** negative, put the negative expression around **avoir** or **être** (the helping verb). Note that the English equivalent usually requires a helping verb.

Il **n'**a **pas** fait ses devoirs.	*He hasn't done (didn't do) his homework.*
Tu **n'**as **rien** mangé?	*You haven't eaten (didn't eat) anything?*
Candide **n'**a **pas** pris de dessert.	*Candide didn't have (eat) any dessert.*
Je **ne** suis **jamais** allée à Lyon.	*I've never been (gone) to Lyon.*

To ask a question using the **passé composé,** you may use a rising intonation when speaking, or you may use the expression **est-ce que,** or you may invert the helping verb. Again, note that the English equivalent may require a helping verb.

Tu **as** bien **dormi?**	*Did you sleep well?*
Tu n'**as** pas **attendu?**	*You didn't wait?*
Est-ce qu'il **a acheté** le livre?	*Did he buy (has he bought) the book?*
Avez-vous mangé?	*Have you eaten?*
Qu'**est-ce qu'**il **a fait?**	*What did he do?*
Est-ce que Suzanne **est sortie** avec Abder hier?	*Did Suzanne go out with Abder yesterday?*
À quelle heure **êtes-vous rentrés?**	*What time did you get home?*

Vous avez compris?

A. À la forme négative Utilisez l'expression entre parenthèses et mettez les phrases à la forme négative.

1. Tu as trouvé M. Durand? (ne... pas)
2. Il a attendu? (ne... pas)
3. J'ai mangé chez Paulette. (ne... jamais)
4. Ils ont fait la vaisselle. (ne... pas)
5. Vous avez étudié? (ne... pas)
6. La mère de Candide est descendue sans lui! (ne... pas)
7. Il a pris le petit déjeuner? (ne... pas)
8. Tu as mangé du pâté? (ne... jamais)
9. Nous sommes allés aux États-Unis. (ne... jamais)

Act. A, 8: Remind students that **du** changes to **de** after a negative. (**Tu n'as jamais mange de pâté?**)

B. Qu'est-ce qu'ils ont fait hier? Posez des questions pour savoir *(know)* ce que tout le monde a fait hier.

1. Marc / étudier?
2. Vous / sortir / au cinéma?
3. Vous / faire / votre lit?

4. Sabine et Chantal / dormir / chez elles?
5. Tu / perdre / ton cahier?
6. Ils / gagner?
7. Jean-Pierre / manger / chez Nathalie?
8. Tu / partir / pour Denver?

Continuons!

A. La journée de Claudine Voilà les activités de Claudine pour hier. Est-ce que vous avez fait la même *(same)* chose que Claudine?

Modèle   CLAUDINE: J'ai téléphoné à mes parents.
        VOUS: *Je n'ai pas téléphoné à mes parents mais j'ai téléphoné*
                à une amie.

1. J'ai étudié cent pages de philosophie.
2. Je suis allée en ville à 10 heures du matin.
3. J'ai téléphoné à mon professeur d'anglais.
4. Je suis sortie le soir avec des copains.
5. J'ai acheté un disque compact de Mozart.
6. Je suis tombée.
7. J'ai pris le petit déjeuner avec des amis.
8. Je n'ai pas rangé ma chambre.
9. J'ai joué au tennis.
10. J'ai perdu mes clés.
11. Je n'ai pas fait mon lit.
12. Je suis rentrée à minuit.

Act. A: Ask students to first put Claudine's activities in a possible chronological order filling in any gaps they perceive. Then, have students react to each of Claudine's activities in terms of their own lives. Encourage students to add details and to be as specific as possible. Follow up with a survey activity or a writing assignment.

B. L'été de Marie-Claude Voilà une liste des choses que Marie-Claude a faites l'été dernier. Est-ce que vous avez fait les mêmes *(same)* choses ou pas?

Modèle   Elle a nagé dans la mer.
        Moi aussi, j'ai nagé dans la mer. / Moi, je n'ai pas nagé dans la mer. /
        Moi, j'ai nagé dans une piscine.

1. Elle est sortie avec son petit ami.
2. Elle a travaillé dans un restaurant.
3. En juillet, elle est partie en vacances avec sa famille pendant un mois.
4. Elle a grossi un peu.
5. Elle n'a pas joué au tennis.
6. Elle a commencé à fumer.
7. En août, son petit ami est parti en vacances sans elle.
8. Le 10 août, elle a rencontré un bel Espagnol et elle a beaucoup parlé espagnol!

C. Vingt questions pour le professeur Qu'est-ce que le professeur a fait l'été dernier? Posez-lui beaucoup de questions!

Act. C: This activity encourages students to ask questions in the **passé composé** and serves as a listening comprehension activity. Refrain from giving more than minimal information per question to encourage students to formulate additional queries.

Découvertes culturelles: Maison, maisons!

▶▶ Dessine-moi une maison

A. Préparation: Dépenses *(expenses)* familiales. Faites la liste des catégories de dépenses de votre famille, puis organisez cette liste par ordre de priorité décroissante *(in descending order of importance)*.

> se loger

Dessine-moi une maison

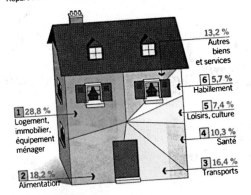

> **La première dépense des ménages**
Répartition en % du budget type des Français

- 13,2 % Autres biens et services
- **6** 5,7 % Habillement
- **5** 7,4 % Loisirs, culture
- **1** 28,8 % Logement, immobilier, équipement ménager
- **4** 10,3 % Santé
- **3** 16,4 % Transports
- **2** 18,2 % Alimentation

En hausse

En baisse

Appareils à fondue, à raclette, pierrade, crêpières, fours compacts, désodorisants parfumants, nettoyeurs à vapeur, tables de cuisson en vitro-céramique, piscines

Baignoires, désodorisants en aérosols, luminaires, moquette, nettoyants ménagers, petit appareillage électrique, vaisselle, végétaux d'intérieur

> **La maison des années de crise**
Surface : 90 m² de plain-pied ; 4 pièces

Le salon-séjour ne comprend plus de cloison : la salle à manger a disparu au profit d'un coin bureau

La cuisine s'agrandit : mieux équipée, elle devient le centre de la vie familiale où l'on prend ses repas

Les chambres rapetissent : elles sont conçues uniquement pour dormir et ranger

Grands placards de rangement

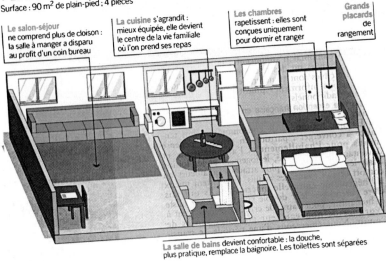

La salle de bains devient confortable : la douche, plus pratique, remplace la baignoire. Les toilettes sont séparées

L'Express

B. Dessine-moi une maison. La première dépense des ménages. Comparez votre liste et la liste des dépenses françaises. Qu'est-ce qui est différent? Qu'est-ce qui est cher en France? Et dans votre pays?

Act. C: If desired, ask students to guess the infinitives of the verb forms **agrandit** and **rapetisse**. Tell students that many **-ir** verbs indicate changes in state (**grandir** = to get bigger, **jaunir** = to get yellow, **blanchir** = to bleach, to make/get white, etc.).

C. Mots nouveaux. Quel adjectif trouvez-vous dans les mots **agrandit, rapetisse?**

D. La maison des Justin. Vous êtes ici chez Monsieur et Madame Justin. C'est quel type de famille? Qui habite avec eux? Imaginez les professions et les goûts des Justin. Qu'est-ce qu'il y a dans les placards de chaque pièce?

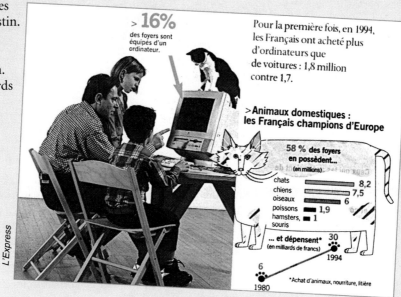

L'Express

E. Une journée typique pour la famille Justin. Choisissez un membre de la famille, parent ou enfant. D'après les informations et les images, décidez ce qu'il ou elle fait heure par heure.

Act. D: Have students recycle vocabulary for clothing, leisure activities, schoolwork, and bedroom furniture.

F. Et le dimanche? Préparez une série de questions pour savoir ce que les Justin font le dimanche.

Modèle *Monsieur Justin, est-ce que vous jouez à la pétanque?*

Act. E: Have students determine a date for their schedules since season will make a difference. Suggest that students use the illustrations as a source of ideas.

G. Les habitudes culturelles. Regardez les statistiques des deux documents. Quelles sont les habitudes françaises d'après ce document? Justifiez votre réponse avec des références précises.

- les types de famille
- la vie familiale
- les habitudes familiales
- les niveaux de vie

Modèle *Les Français font beaucoup de jardinage.*

Act. F: Refer students to previous lessons on leisure activities, food, and clothes to guide their questions.

Act. G: Ask students to develop a sentence for each piece of information. Use to review comparative forms and expressions of quantity such as **beaucoup, un peu, peu de,** etc.

H. Hypothèses. Quelles informations du texte indiquent un changement dans les pratiques de la maison et de la vie de la famille? Quels sont les changements principaux? Faites deux hypothèses sur les causes de ces changements.

Modèle *Il n'y a plus de salle à manger, donc les repas sont moins importants.*

Act. H: Have students cite from the text first and refer to pictures to infer and conclude. Help by focusing attention on one element at a time. Review **ne... plus, donc,** etc.

Une tradition française: la résidence

A. La résidence. Quels aspects de votre résidence sont les plus importants? Organisez cette liste par ordre d'importance pour vous.

le confort / la décoration / l'espace environnant et le quartier / le style / les activités possibles / le modernisme / la lumière / les voisins (les personnes qui habitent à côté) / la proximité de la ville / les transports publics / l'indépendance des membres de la famille / le nombre de pièces / le jardin / la terrasse / le balcon / les volets / les meubles / les plantes / le grenier / la cave

B. Une idée du bonheur.

1. **Pour comprendre.** Soulignez dans le texte les mots qui se réfèrent aux pièces de la maison, à la décoration. aux activités dans la maison. Combien de types de maisons sont cités dans ce texte?

2. **De quoi s'agit-il?** Castorama, qu'est-ce que c'est?

   un agent immobilier / un magasin de meubles / une entreprise de construction / une région / un commerce d'objets pour la maison / une entreprise de jardinage / le nom d'un jardinier / le nom d'une maison / le nom d'un village à la campagne

3. **À la recherche des détails.**

   a. **Mots nouveaux.** Choisissez la meilleure réponse pour ces mots et expressions.
      - la maison de ses rêves:
        ☐ la maison principale ☐ la maison idéale ☐ une maison moderne
      - la pelouse:
        ☐ elle est verte ☐ elle est à l'intérieur de la maison ☐ elle est sur la terrasse
      - aménager (on aménagera le grenier)
        ☐ faire des transformations ☐ décorer ☐ mettre du papier peint sur les murs
      - une demeure:
        ☐ un balcon ☐ une cheminée ☐ une maison
      - retaper:
        ☐ ranger ☐ mettre à neuf (neuf = nouveau) ☐ détruire
      - déménager:
        ☐ partir en voyage ☐ faire des transformations ☐ changer de maison
      - désuets:
        ☐ démodé ☐ neuf ☐ moderne

   b. **Le bonheur.** Quelles lettres du mot **bonheur** sont dans **heureux? malheureux?** Qu'est-ce que le bonheur? Quand est-ce qu'on est heureux ou malheureux?

   c. **Vrai ou faux.** Dans quelles phrases trouvez-vous une explication pour ces phrases? Trouvez les phrases logiques et illogiques.
      - Dans la maison idéale, on peut choisir le papier pour les murs.
      - Dans la maison idéale, tout le monde a sa chambre.
      - Dans la maison idéale, les enfants peuvent faire des dessins sur les murs.
      - Dans la maison idéale, les amis peuvent venir en vacances chez vous.
      - La maison idéale est une vieille maison.
      - Il est impossible d'avoir une deuxième maison.
      - Dans sa maison de campagne, on peut mettre ses vieux meubles.
      - Pour travailler, construire et réparer dans la maison, allez à Castorama.
      - On peut aller à Castorama tous les jours de la semaine.
      - À Castorama, on trouve du matériel pour faire des piscines.

La maison... une certaine idée du bonheur

Une maison. Qui n'a pas eu ce rêve? Un véritable chez soi où tout est à la mesure de ses goûts, de ses gestes, de ses choix?

La couleur du papier peint ou celle des volets; la chambre des enfants, ici celle des parents, la cuisine, le séjour, la terrasse du jardin. Qui n'a pas dessiné la maison de ses rêves, avec de vraies histoires qui vont avec? Un jardin avec une pelouse et des fleurs, une chambre d'amis — "et si on est trop nombreux on aménagera le grenier" —, des petits déjeuners pris dehors et des soirées d'hiver devant la cheminée. La maison... la sienne. Il y en a qui préfèrent acheter de vieilles demeures à retaper. D'autres veulent une maison neuve, conforme à leurs désirs. Il y a (souvenez-vous) ces perpétuels déménagements tous les week-ends ou pour les vacances, lorsqu'on s'en va dans sa maison de campagne. Cette deuxième maison où les objets désuets ou usés trouvent leur place: un meuble ou un lit devenu trop petit. Je crois même qu'une fois devenu adulte, c'est dans les maisons de campagne ou secondaires qu'on retrouve tous les objets du passé, de l'enfance. La maison, musée intime de l'enfance. Le moins adroit envisage d'acheter du matériel pour monter un petit mur, une bordure, installer un rideau ou une véranda... Les enfants vont forcément vouloir aider.

Castorama vous aide à "aller jusqu'au bout de vos projets"

On y trouve tous les articles pour la maison et le jardin. Mais encore, les conseils indispensables; surtout lorsqu'on souhaite faire les choses de ses mains. Creuser une piscine ou semer une pelouse ça n'est pas vraiment sorcier. Encore faut-il avoir à sa disposition les matériels adéquats et les "tuyaux" d'un professionnel. Castorama vous accueille 6 jours sur 7 et s'engage aussi à vous livrer à domicile. Pensez-y.

**CASTORAMA: Centre commercial CAP SUD — Avenue du Roussillon
63170 AUBIERE – Tél. (04) 73 26 00 34**

Texte: Dominique Machabert Photographe: Joël Damase

C. Étude culturelle

1. **Illustration.** Décrivez cette maison. Où est-elle? Quel âge a-t-elle? Quel type de maison est-ce? Comment est-elle? Est-ce la maison idéale? Pourquoi?

2. **Le rêve (*dream*) des Français.** Quelles expressions du texte sont illustrées par cette maison? D'après ce texte et cette illustration, décrivez quelles sortes d'activités, d'habitudes et de loisirs les Français aiment.

Act. C, 2: Have students refer to the text to find useful words and expressions, and make sentences.

Modèle un jardin
> ***Les Français aiment avoir un jardin pour avoir des fleurs et
> des légumes.***

Act. C, 4: Have students use the text to expand into sentences and gradually construct a definition of **la résidence secondaire**.

Hypothèses: Peut-être que... / Ils sont peut-être... / C'est parce que...

Act. E: Have students use one of the three photos. First, brainstorm ideas on the origins of the house, its owners, their story, some events. Provide expressions such as **d'abord, après, ensuite**, etc. Have students list verbs in the infinitive and past participle forms before they write.

TEXT TAPE:
Conversation en français

www explore!
http//voila.heinle.com

3. **La résidence secondaire et les Français.** Qu'est-ce qu'une résidence secondaire? Où est-elle? Comment est-elle? Quelle est sa décoration? Qu'est-ce qu'on fait dans une résidence secondaire? Quand est-ce qu'on va dans cette maison?

4. **Les avantages et les inconvénients de la résidence secondaire.** Considérez une résidence secondaire à la campagne. Faites une liste des avantages et une liste des inconvénients. Vous voulez une résidence secondaire ou pas? Pourquoi?

D. Hypothèses. Pour quelles raisons les Français aiment-ils avoir une résidence secondaire? Formez trois hypothèses avec les éléments sociologiques des leçons précédentes.

E. Avec de vraies histoires... Avec cette phrase le texte fait allusion aux histoires des habitants. Maintenant, une résidence secondaire raconte son histoire et l'histoire de ses habitants. Il y a beaucoup de personnes qui ont habité cette maison. Faites parler la maison au sujet de ses habitants.

F. La maison, musée intime de l'enfance. Pourquoi une maison de campagne est-elle un musée? Quel est le musée de votre enfance? Quels objets? Quelles personnes? Quelles histoires?

G. Conversation en français. Une semaine en France.

1. Vous allez passer une semaine en France avec votre famille pour découvrir la campagne française. Quel est votre budget, voyage inclus? Où est-ce que vous allez? Qu'est-ce que vous allez faire?

2. Décrivez la maison que vous avez louée. Donnez beaucoup de détails sur la maison et ce qu'elle a de bien et de moins bien. Soyez prêt(e) à répondre aux questions qu'on vous demande.

Orthographe et prononciation

➤ Les syllabes

In speech, English syllables tend to end with a consonant sound; French syllables tend to end with a vowel sound. Compare how the two languages divide the following words.

ENGLISH	FRENCH
fin-ish	fi-nir
an-i-mal	a-ni-mal

Activité

Prononcez Répétez après votre professeur.

1. la radio
2. une affiche
3. un réfrigérateur
4. une université
5. commencer
6. vous achetez
7. automne
8. une avenue
9. un hôpital

See the **Instructor's Resource Manual** for more information.

Vocabulaire de base

TEXT TAPE:
Vocabulaire de base

Chiffres au-dessus de 1.000 (voir page 271)
Nombres ordinaux (voir page 272)

NOMS

un arbre *tree*
l'argent *(m.) money*
une baignoire *bathtub*
un balcon *balcony*
une banque *bank*
un canapé *couch*
une cave *basement*
une douche *shower*
une église *church*
un escalier *staircase, stairs*
un étage (premier, deuxième, etc.) *(second, third, etc.) floor*
un fauteuil *armchair*
une ferme *farm*
une gare *train station*
un hôpital *hospital*
un immeuble *apartment house*
un jardin *garden, yard*
une lampe *lamp*

un meuble, des meubles *piece of furniture, furniture*
un mur *wall*
une pièce *room (general term)*
une place *square*
un réfrigérateur *refrigerator*
le rez-de-chaussée *ground floor (American first floor)*
un rideau, des rideaux *curtain, curtains*
une rue *street*
une salle à manger *dining room*
une salle de bains *bathroom*
un salon *living room*
un tableau, des tableaux *painting, paintings*
une terrasse *patio, terrace*
une usine *factory*
les W.C. *(m. pl.) toilet, restroom, water closet*

RAPPEL:
une cuisine *kitchen*
une salle de séjour *living room, family room*

ADJECTIFS

clair(e) *bright, full of light*
dernier, dernière *(precedes noun) last*
sombre *dark*

VERBES

attendre *to wait (for)*
continuer *to continue*
coûter *to cost*
descendre *to go down*
devoir *to owe (also: must, to have to)*
entendre *to hear*
entrer *to go/come in, to enter*
monter *to go up*

perdre *to lose*
rentrer *to go/come home, to go/come back*
répondre (à quelqu'un ou à quelque chose) *to answer (someone), to reply (to someone)*
retourner *to go back, to return*
tourner *to turn*
vendre *to sell*

DIVERS

à droite (de) *to the right (of)*

à gauche (de) *to the left (of)*
à l'extérieur (de) *outside (of)*
à l'intérieur (de) *inside (of)*
alors *so (+ clause)*
assez *quite, sufficiently, enough*
au rez-de-chaussée, au premier étage, etc. *on the first floor, on the second floor, etc.*
Combien coûte... ? *How much does . . . cost?*
coûter cher; ça coûte cher *to be expensive, it's/that's expensive*
d'abord *first (of all)*

déjà *already*
en bas *downstairs*
en désordre *messy*
en *haut *upstairs*
en ordre *straight, neat*
ensuite *next, then*
jusqu'à *until, up to*
pas encore *not yet*
puis, et puis *then, and then*
quelquefois *sometimes*
si *if; so; yes, on the contrary*
tout droit *straight ahead*

Vocabulaire supplémentaire

NOMS

une adresse *address*
un ascenseur *elevator*
une avenue *avenue*
un centime *centime (^{1}/100 franc)*
le centre-ville *center of town, downtown*
le chemin *path, way*
un coin *corner*
un coin repas *breakfast nook, eating area*
un commissariat de police *police station*
un couloir *hall, corridor*
une cuisinière *stove*
une école primaire *elementary school*
une entrée *entranceway*
un évier *kitchen sink*
un fleuve *river*
un garage *garage*
un grenier *attic*
un lave-linge *washing machine*
un lave-vaisselle *dishwasher*
une mairie *city hall*
une pelouse *lawn*
un plan *(town, city) map*
un pont *bridge*
un quartier *neighborhood*
le sous-sol *basement level, underground*

un toit *roof*
des volets *(m.) shutters*

VERBE

traverser *to go across, to cross*

ADJECTIFS

à l'aise *at ease, comfortable (person)*
ancien, ancienne *antique, old*
belge *Belgian*
ensoleillé(e) *sunny*
moderne *modern, contemporary*

DIVERS

au bout (de) *at the end (of)*
à votre avis *according to you*
aux États-Unis *in the United States*
le dernier étage *top floor*
donner sur *to overlook, to have a view of*
en Belgique *in Belgium*
en face (de) *across (from)*
en France *in France*
monter/descendre en ascenseur *to take the elevator (up/down)*
monter/descendre par l'escalier *to take the stairs (up/down)*
pourriez-vous me dire où se trouve... *could you tell me where to find . . .*

LE FRANÇAIS TEL QU'ON LE PARLE

T'as pas 100 balles? *D'ya have (Have you got) 100 francs?*
C'est combien? *How much is it?*
Je vous dois combien? *How much do I owe you?*
excusez-moi / pardon *excuse me*
Où sont les toilettes? *Where's the restroom/bathroom?*

LE FRANÇAIS FAMILIER

une brique = un million d'anciens francs = 10.000 francs
du fric = de l'argent
du pognon = de l'argent
relax(e) = à l'aise
un séjour = une salle de séjour
des sous = de l'argent

ON ENTEND PARFOIS...

la bécosse (Canada) = les W.C.
un char (Canada) = une voiture
la cour, la toilette (Belgique) = les W.C., les toilettes
dispendieux, dispendieuse (Canada) = cher
un galetas (Suisse) = un grenier
un vivoir (Canada) = une salle de séjour

Au travail!

Leçon 12

En bref

Dans cette leçon...

- Les Français au travail
- La vie dans la petite ville de Cinet
- Décrire et raconter au passé: l'imparfait et le passé composé
- Comment relier les phrases: les pronoms relatifs **qui** et **que**
- Patrons et ouvriers
- Les jeunes et l'économie

In this lesson...

- Professions and work
- Life in the small town of Cinet
- How to talk about the way things were and what used to happen in the past: the **passé composé** and the **imparfait**
- How to join sentences: the relative pronouns **qui** and **que**
- Management and labor
- Young entrepreneurs

www explore!
http://voila.heinle.com

Develop writing skills with Système-D software!

Practice listening and pronunciation skills with the Text Tape!

Discover the Francophone world!

Build your skills!

INTERNET

SYSTÈME-D

TEXT TAPE

VIDEO TAPE

CD-ROM

Students have an open-ended writing activity in the **Cahier** suitable for use with **Système-D**.

289

ET DES IDÉES À

Styliste.   Hôtelier.   Architecte.   Attachée de presse.   Chercheur.   Agent immobilier.

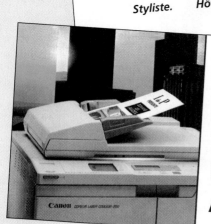

La femme idéale

Vous préférez cette jeune femme? Pourquoi? Qu'est-ce qu'elle porte? Quel âge a-t-elle? Où est-ce qu'elle travaille? Quel est son emploi du temps? Que fait-elle après son travail? Où habite-t-elle? Que fait-elle pendant les week-ends? Est-ce qu'elle est mariée? Est-ce qu'elle a une famille? Est-ce qu'elle aime son travail? Est-ce qu'elle a beaucoup d'argent? Est-ce qu'elle a des problèmes?

Portraits. Que font ces gens? Est-ce qu'ils voyagent? Est-ce qu'ils sont en vacances? Est-ce qu'ils travaillent? Qui est très élégant?

Maintenant, choisissez la personne idéale.

Portraits: Can be group work. Have students read their portraits, and have the others guess which character they are describing.

TOUS LES MÉTIERS.

Financier. Dessinatrice. Entrepreneur. Industriel. Directrice du marketing. Maire.

Identifications. Regardez les images pour trouver les métiers.

Hier, elle a vendu une très belle maison à un jeune couple avec deux enfants. (Elle est styliste? agent immobilier? architecte?)

Il travaille dans un institut et hier il a trouvé une solution possible au problème de la faim dans le monde. (Il est maire? entrepreneur? chercheur?)

Hier, il a travaillé très dur—un dîner pour 150 personnes! (Il est industriel? hôtelier? agent immobilier?)

Hier, elle a fini un projet de publicité pour la photocopieuse Canon. (Elle est dessinatrice? directrice du marketing? attachée de presse?)

This activity recycles past tense forms and the use of **il/elle est + professions.** It can be done in groups with students selecting one person and developing a thorough portrait. An alternative may be to have several students assume the personality of each of these people and have another student interview them about the details of their lives.

OPTIONAL ACTIVITY: Texts that originally appeared under each **métier** are provided in the **Instructor's Resource Manual.** Make copies and ask students to identify the text that refers to each profession.

291

Vocabulaire

Info plus

Le SMIC.

Le SMIC (Salaire Minimum Interprofessionnel de Croissance) is the minimum wage. Beginning May 1, 1996, the SMIC was 6.374,68 F per month (for 169 hours of work) or 37,72 F per hour.

Ask students to give you words they associate with **les travailleurs immigrés.** Ask if there is any difference between refugees, immigrants, and illegal aliens.

Ask students to identify the national origins of refugees, immigrants, and illegal aliens in their areas. Discuss the issues and problems connected with these groups.

Info plus

Les travailleurs immigrés.

Because of a relatively low birth rate over a long period of time, the French have opened their borders at various times to foreign immigration in order to supply their industries, cities, and farms with unskilled workers. These immigrant workers came largely from other French-speaking countries, former French colonies, and neighboring European countries with unemployment problems (Italy, Spain, and Portugal for the most part). Many recent immigrants have come from the countries of the Maghreb (Algeria, Morocco, and Tunisia) and, as a consequence, Islam has become the second most common religion in France. Because of differences in religion, culture, and race, these first- and second-generation immigrants face problems with regard to education and integration into French society.

See *Video Magazine 4: Les immigrés*

Toujours à Cinet

A. Le Crédit Régional

M. Lacroix est banquier: c'est lui le directeur de la banque. Sa secrétaire, Mme Domont, est honnête, responsable et très efficace. Elle tape bien à la machine et elle aime beaucoup son travail et son patron. M. Lionnet et Mlle Caron sont des employés de banque. Mlle Caron gagne le SMIC (6.374,68 F par mois) parce qu'elle a commencé à travailler il y a deux mois, mais M. Lionnet, qui a commencé à travailler à la banque il y a quarante ans, gagne assez bien sa vie. Mme Renglet est juriste et travaille comme cadre à la banque. Elle a un métier intéressant et elle est très bien payée: elle gagne 22.000 F par mois.

- Qu'est-ce que c'est, le Crédit Régional? Que fait M. Lacroix? Qui travaille pour lui? Comment est Mme Domont? Qui gagne beaucoup d'argent? Pourquoi? Qui n'a pas un très bon salaire? Pourquoi? Combien est-ce qu'elle gagne? Est-ce qu'il y a des clients aujourd'hui dans la banque?

B. L'entreprise Bovy

C'est une petite entreprise de 50 personnes où on fait des ordinateurs. M. Bovy est chef d'entreprise. C'est un homme dynamique et toujours très occupé, qui est souvent de mauvaise humeur et qui est assez dur avec ses employés. Pourtant, les affaires marchent bien, mais il a beaucoup de responsabilités et est toujours stressé. M. Saïdi, qui a trente-cinq ans, est un immigré algérien qui est arrivé en France avec ses parents il y a trente ans. Lui et Mlle Jacob sont ingénieurs. Ils sont donc cadres et ce sont eux qui dirigent l'atelier. Alors, ils sont souvent avec les ouvriers et pas souvent dans leur bureau. Mme Collin est une ouvrière qui gagne 50 F l'heure. Elle est mère de famille et voudrait bien rester à la maison et être une femme au foyer, mais elle doit travailler parce que son mari est au chômage.

Explain that **C**^{ie} is the abbreviation for **Compagnie**, which means corporation.

In France, **les entreprises** are divided among **les très petites entreprises** (fewer than 10 employees), **les PME** (petites et moyennes entreprises, between 10 and 499 employees), and **les grandes entreprises** (500 employees and more). The **PME** represent 7% of business and 47% of employment in France, while the **très petites entreprises** represent 93% of business and 21% of employment.

(Source: *Francoscopie 1995*)

To encourage students to think about the issue of sexism in language, ask: What do you visualize when you hear the word "chairman"? When you think of a doctor, an executive, or an engineer, do you picture a man or a woman? Do part or all of this in simple French: **Un cadre, c'est un homme ou une femme? Et un chef d'entreprise?** etc.

- Qui est M. Bovy? Comment est-il ? Est-ce que M. Saïdi est français? À quel âge est-ce qu'il est arrivé en France? Dans l'entreprise Bovy, qui est allé à l'université? Qui a un travail intéressant? Pourquoi? Qui voudrait faire autre chose? Pourquoi? Combien gagne Mme Collin? Ça fait combien par mois si elle travaille 40 heures par semaine? Et par an, ça fait combien? C'est beaucoup ou non, à votre avis?

Info plus

Les femmes et les métiers.

Traditionally in France, as in other countries, women have tended to be found in certain professions and not in others. Today, however, women have gained access to most professions, but the language has not always followed suit. Thus, some professions have only a masculine form, which is used for both men and women.

> **Elle est professeur.**
> **Évelyne est un bon médecin.**
> **Ma mère est cadre dans une grosse entreprise.**
> **Ta sœur veut être ingénieur?**

If the context requires that you differentiate between men and women working in these jobs, you can add the word **femme** in front of the noun.

> **La vie des femmes policiers est quelquefois difficile mais toujours intéressante.**

Note that in Canada, some of these profession names have acquired a feminine form, for example: **une professeure, une ingénieure, une écrivaine.**

See the **Instructor's Resource Manual** for more information.

C. Le Café de la Poste

M. Caron est le gérant du Café de la Poste et Mlle Collin est la serveuse. Il est cinq heures de l'après-midi et il y a beaucoup de clients. M. Bastin est agriculteur et a une ferme près de Cinet. M. Piette, qui parle avec M. Caron, est policier. M. et Mme Ségal sont retraités. Donc, ils ne travaillent plus. M. Meunier ne travaille pas, mais lui, c'est parce qu'il est chômeur. Il a perdu son travail il y a trois mois et il cherche du travail comme ouvrier, mais c'est difficile parce qu'il a cinquante ans. Pourtant, il est fort et en bonne santé et il peut travailler dur.

- Qui est M. Caron? Que fait M. Piette? Et M. Bastin? Et Mlle Collin? Qui ne travaille pas? Pourquoi? Comment est M. Meunier? Comment va-t-il aujourd'hui?

D. Chez Cléo

Mme Renard est commerçante: elle est propriétaire d'un magasin de vêtements, Chez Cléo. Elle a deux employées: une caissière, Mme Derni, et une vendeuse, Mlle Caron, qui travaillent au SMIC. Et Mme Lacroix? C'est une cliente qui cherche une robe pour le mariage de son fils.

- Qu'est-ce qu'on vend dans le magasin? Qui est la patronne? Que fait Mlle Caron? Et son père? Et sa sœur? Est-ce que Mlle Caron gagne bien sa vie? Qui est Mme Derni? Et Mme Lacroix?

E. Et les Dubois?

Info plus

Le baccalauréat.
The **baccalauréat** is a secondary school-leaving exam in France.

Thérèse et Vincent habitent à Cinet aussi. Thérèse est allée à l'université et elle est psychologue. Elle aime vraiment son métier! Et Vincent? Il a toujours vendu des choses. Après le baccalauréat, il a d'abord vendu des voitures et ensuite, trois ans après, il a trouvé du travail chez Bovy pour vendre des ordinateurs. Il a beaucoup voyagé pour eux et après 10 ans, fatigué, il a décidé de prendre des cours pour être agent immobilier. Maintenant, il vend des maisons et il est enfin très heureux de sa vie, lui aussi. Et les enfants? Céline aime les sciences et voudrait être infirmière. Jean-Marc, lui, voudrait être garagiste ou pompier. On verra!

- Qui est allé à l'université dans la famille Dubois? Que fait Vincent? Qu'est-ce qu'il vend maintenant? Et avant? Que veulent faire les enfants? Être pompier, est-ce que c'est dangereux? facile? À votre avis, est-ce que Jean-Marc va vraiment être pompier?

F. Et aussi...

À Cinet, il y a aussi des avocats, des médecins, des dentistes, des cuisiniers, des instituteurs, des coiffeurs et des fonctionnaires.

M. Lacroix, avocat

Mlle Bastin, médecin

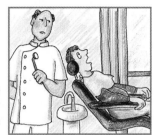
M. Renglet, dentiste

M. Derni, cuisinier

Mme Jacob, institutrice

Mme Meunier, employée de poste

M. Domont, employé de la S.N.C.F.

Mlle Lionnet, employée de mairie

Mlle Meunier, coiffeuse

Mme Meunier, M. Domont et Mlle Lionnet sont fonctionnaires parce qu'ils travaillent pour l'État. Mme Jacob et M. Piette sont aussi fonctionnaires. M. Derni est le cuisinier du restaurant Au Vieux Cinet. C'est un métier dur parce que les journées de travail sont très longues, mais il adore faire la cuisine. Un jour, il voudrait déménager et aller habiter à la mer, où il veut être propriétaire d'un restaurant avec sa femme.

- À votre avis, qui gagne bien sa vie? Qui ne gagne pas bien sa vie?
- Quels métiers sont durs? intéressants? ennuyeux?
- Pour quel(s) métier(s) est-ce qu'il faut être responsable? dynamique? efficace?
- Qui travaille à la gare? Qui travaille à la mairie? Qui travaille avec les enfants? Qui fait du bruit? Qui attend? Qui est heureux? Qui est stressé?
- Qui est le père de M. Lacroix? Où est-ce qu'il travaille? Que fait le père de Mlle Bastin? Où travaille la femme de M. Renglet? Où travaille M. Derni? Et sa femme? Que fait la fille de Mme Jacob? Que fait Mlle Meunier? Et ses parents? Pour qui est-ce que la femme de M. Domont travaille? Que fait le père de Mlle Lionnet?

Info plus

Les fonctionnaires.

Un fonctionnaire is someone who works for the government, for example, a government office employee, a postal worker, or a police officer. Since the public school system is under central government control, teachers are also considered **fonctionnaires**.

TRANSPARENCY: 12-4

Info plus

Les trains en France.

The **S.N.C.F. (Société nationale des chemins de fer français)** is responsible for rail traffic in France. The French rail system allows easy access to all parts of France and has the reputation of being on time. Because of this and because France is much smaller, trains are used much more frequently for travel in France than in the United States.

Notes de vocabulaire

1. Mots et expressions utiles.

aller chez le médecin, chez le dentiste	*to go to the doctor, the dentist*
tout à coup	*all of a sudden*

2. Les affaires.

Affaires can mean *business,* as in u**n homme ou une femme d'affaires** *(businessman, businesswoman)* or **les affaires marchent bien** *(business is good).* It can also mean *belongings,* as in **mes affaires** *(my belongings, my stuff).*

3. Juriste / avocat / notaire.

Un **notaire** is a private lawyer who works for families. **Un notaire** is also a notary public. **Un avocat** is a lawyer who takes cases to trial. **Un juriste** is a general term for people who have law degrees.

4. C'est / Il est + métier.

To say what a person does, use one of the following formulas:

- **Il est (elle est) / ils sont (elles sont)** + *profession (no article)*

Il est dentiste.	*He's a dentist.*
Elles sont étudiantes.	*They're students.*

- **C'est (ce sont)** + **un/une (des)** + *profession*

C'est une secrétaire.	*She's a secretary.*
Ce sont des ingénieurs.	*They're engineers.*

If the word referring to a profession is modified by an article or an adjective, the second formula (**ce** + **être**) has to be used.

C'est l'avocat de mes parents.	*He's my parents' lawyer.*
C'est un avocat intelligent.	*He's an intelligent lawyer.*

D'accord?

A. Associations Quels verbes associez-vous avec...

VERBES: sonner / décider / diriger / entendre / expliquer / gagner / oublier

1. un réveil
2. beaucoup d'argent
3. la grammaire française
4. ses clés
5. du bruit
6. un atelier
7. fumer moins

B. Lieux de travail Qui travaille et qui ne travaille pas dans... ?

1. **une banque:** un avocat / une juriste / un employé / un banquier / un cadre
2. **une usine:** un ingénieur / un instituteur / un chef d'entreprise / une ouvrière / un coiffeur / un directeur
3. **une entreprise:** un juriste / un ouvrier / une commerçante / un cadre / un agriculteur
4. **un hôpital:** un cuisinier / un infirmier / un agent immobilier / un médecin / un avocat
5. **une école:** une institutrice / un dentiste / un ouvrier / une psychologue / un professeur / un garagiste / un gérant
6. **une mairie:** un fonctionnaire / une serveuse / une employée / un pompier / un vendeur

Act B: Opinions may differ depending on students' own experiences. This can lead to an interesting discussion.

C. Les uniformes Qu'est-ce qu'ils portent pour aller travailler?

Modèle Les agriculteurs?
Ils portent des jeans, ils ne portent pas de cravate.

1. Les ouvriers?
2. Les cuisiniers?
3. Les avocats?
4. Les policiers?
5. Les banquiers?
6. Les serveurs?
7. Les serveuses?

D. Des stéréotypes ou non? Comment sont-ils?

SUGGESTIONS: travailleurs / polis / sérieux / bavards / stressés / débrouillards / durs / compréhensifs / sportifs / forts / honnêtes / dynamiques / efficaces

1. les coiffeurs
2. les pompiers
3. les psychologues
4. les pères et les mères de famille
5. les chefs d'entreprise
6. les secrétaires

E. Classer les métiers Faites une liste des métiers pour chaque catégorie.

1. les métiers où on gagne beaucoup d'argent
2. les métiers où on ne gagne pas beaucoup d'argent
3. les métiers où on trouve beaucoup de femmes
4. les métiers où on trouve beaucoup d'hommes
5. les métiers où on a besoin d'un diplôme universitaire
6. les métiers où on n'a pas besoin de diplôme universitaire
7. les métiers où on doit souvent déménager
8. les métiers où on doit beaucoup voyager
9. les métiers où il y a beaucoup de stress
10. les métiers où il n'y a pas beaucoup de stress
11. les métiers où il faut être fort
12. les métiers où on travaille seul

Mise en pratique

A. Et eux? Qui sont-ils? D'où sont-ils? Quel est leur métier? Comment sont-ils?

M. Gomes (Lille)

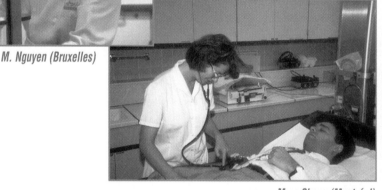

M. Nguyen (Bruxelles)

M. Adibi (Paris)

La famille Pradal (Cahors)

Mme Chang (Montréal)

Pour les jeunes Français, il faut: un travail intéressant (70%), la sécurité de l'emploi (66%), un bon salaire (49%), des perspectives de carrière intéressantes (33%), une bonne ambiance au travail (27%), des responsabilités (19%), un(e) bon(ne) patron(ne) (14%).

Adapté de *Francoscopie 1995*, «Les jeunes et l'emploi» La Tribune/Sofres

B. Le métier idéal Un travail n'est jamais parfait. Quelles sont les trois choses les plus importantes dans un travail, pour vous? Comparez avec les autres étudiants de la classe. Est-ce que vous êtes d'accord *(do you agree)* avec le point de vue des Français?

C. Les rêves du patron M. Lavallée, qui est directeur du personnel d'un grand hôtel touristique, veut trouver la personne parfaite pour chaque position. Faites une liste de ce qu'il veut.

Modèle coiffeur
gentil, ne parle pas trop, beau, a travaillé en Europe, parle espagnol...

1. secrétaire
2. vendeur/vendeuse
3. serveur/serveuse
4. femme de ménage

D. Les boulots d'étudiants

Act. D: If desired, role-play the job interviews.

1. Vous cherchez du travail pour l'été et vous avez trouvé plusieurs *(several)* possibilités. Quel(s) boulot(s) voulez-vous prendre? Pourquoi? Quel(s) boulot(s) ne voulez-vous pas prendre? Pourquoi?

   LES POSSIBILITÉS:
   employé(e) de bureau
   ouvrier/ouvrière dans une usine de boîtes de conserve en Alaska
   vendeur/vendeuse dans un grand magasin
   vendeur/vendeuse dans un magasin de souvenirs à Disney World
   serveur/serveuse dans un restaurant français à New York
   serveur/serveuse dans un restaurant universitaire à Boston
   femme de ménage pour une vieille dame riche à Malibu
   secrétaire pour un(e) avocat(e)
   femme de ménage dans un hôtel américain à Acapulco.

2. Vous avez choisi un travail, mais maintenant, il faut aller parler avec le directeur du personnel. Faites une liste des choses que vous voulez savoir *(know)* avant d'accepter un travail. Faites aussi une liste des questions que vous voulez poser *(ask)*.

E. Le jeu des métiers
En groupes, choisissez un métier et écrivez *(write)* ce qu'on doit faire dans ce métier et les qualités qu'on doit avoir pour ce métier. Les autres étudiants de la classe vont devoir deviner *(guess)* le métier que vous avez choisi à partir de votre description.

Act. E: Tell groups to speak quietly to keep other groups from overhearing.

Structure

CD-ROM:
Build your skills!

▶ Parler au passé: l'imparfait

To talk about how things were in the past or about how things used to be, French uses a verb tense called the **imparfait** *(imperfect)*. The following text tells about a school in Montreal. Can you find the verbs in the **imparfait?**

Have students locate verbs in the **imparfait**. Then, have them give a summary of the text.

«À l'école où j'allais avant, il y avait tellement de bruit dans les classes que je n'arrivais pas à prendre de notes. Les profs étaient dépassés et tout le monde «niaisait». Par exemple, on n'avait pas d'examen le lundi car c'était le premier jour de la semaine; ni le vendredi car c'était le dernier; ni le jeudi car c'était la veille du vendredi... Ici, c'est très différent.»

—Katie Meilleur, diplômée de secondaire 5.

Daniel Pérusse, *Une école pas comme les autres*
Sélection du Reader's Digest

niaiser = *to waste time doing silly things*

Diplômée de secondaire 5 indicates that Katie is a high school graduate.

L'imparfait: formation

1. Take the first person plural form of the present tense and remove the **-ons** ending. This gives you the **imparfait** stem.

PRESENT TENSE FORM	IMPARFAIT STEM
nous **aim**ons	**aim-**
nous **finiss**ons	**finiss-**
nous **vend**ons	**vend-**
nous **dorm**ons	**dorm-**
nous **all**ons	**all-**
nous **av**ons	**av-**
nous **buv**ons	**buv-**
nous **mett**ons	**mett-**
nous **pren**ons	**pren-**
nous **voul**ons	**voul-**
nous **pouv**ons	**pouv-**
nous **dev**ons	**dev-**

2. Add the **imparfait** endings (**-ais, -ais, -ait, -ions, -iez, -aient**) to this stem.

aller à l'imparfait	
j'all**ais**	nous all**ions**
tu all**ais**	vous all**iez**
il / elle } all**ait**	ils / elles } all**aient**

Note that the endings **-ais, -ait,** and **-aient** are pronounced alike.

The verb **être** has an irregular stem. It is the only verb whose **imparfait** forms cannot be derived from the **nous** form of the present tense.

être à l'imparfait	
j'**étais**	nous **étions**
tu **étais**	vous **étiez**
il / elle } **était**	ils / elles } **étaient**

Quand j'**avais** dix ans, je **voulais** être médecin.	*When I was 10, I wanted to be a doctor.*
Ils **étaient** fatigués mais ils ont fini.	*They were tired but they got done.*
Où est-ce que vous **alliez** à l'école avant?	*Where did you go to school before?*

Note the following points:

1. Direct object pronouns function similarly with all one-word verbs, such as the **présent** and the **imparfait.** Note direct object pronoun placement in the following examples:

PRÉSENT
Je **les** attends.   *I'm waiting for them.*
Je ne **les** attends plus!   *I'm not waiting for them any longer!*

IMPARFAIT
Je vous **écoutais.**   *I was listening to you.*
Pardon, je ne vous **écoutais** pas.   *Sorry, I wasn't listening to you.*

Verbs that do not map directly to English are used here to illustrate the problem of direct word-by-word translation. If desired, give students example sentences that are more transparent (**Je la regarde.** / **Je ne la regarde pas.** / **Je la regardais.** / **Je ne la regardais pas.**).

2. Here are the English equivalents of **devoir** and **pouvoir** in the present and the imparfait.

Point out that the exact English equivalents of **devoir** and **pouvoir** depend on context.

	AU PRÉSENT	À L'IMPARFAIT
devoir	must, to have to, to have got to	was supposed to
pouvoir	can, to be able to	could

Tu **dois** moins fumer.   *You have to (must) smoke less.*
Hier soir, je **devais** étudier.   *Last night, I was supposed to study.*
Tu ne **peux** pas sortir!   *You can't go out!*
Je ne **pouvais** rien entendre.   *I couldn't hear anything.*
Quand j'avais quinze ans, je ne   *When I was fifteen, I couldn't go out*
   pouvais pas sortir souvent et je   *often and I was always supposed to*
   devais toujours rentrer avant   *get home before 10:00 in the evening.*
   dix heures du soir.

3. The **imparfait** of **pleuvoir, neiger,** and **il y a.**

Point out that **il y avait** means both *there was* and *there were.*

Il pleut aujourd'hui? Il **pleuvait**   *It's raining today? It was raining*
   hier aussi.   *yesterday too.*
Il **neigeait** quand je suis arrivé.   *It was snowing when I got there.*
Il y avait beaucoup de clients hier. *There were a lot of customers yesterday.*

4. The **imparfait** of verbs like **commencer** and **manger.** Verbs whose infinitives end in -cer add a cedilla to a -c- preceding an ending that begins with -a in order to maintain the /s/ sound. Verbs whose infinitives end in -ger add -e before an ending that begins with -a in order to maintain a soft **g** sound.

imparfait stem: **commenc-**	
je commençais	nous commencions
tu commençais	vous commenciez
il elle } commençait	ils elles } commençaient

imparfait stem: **mang-**	
je mangeais	nous mangions
tu mangeais	vous mangiez
il elle } mangeait	ils elles } mangeaient

5. The **imparfait** of verbs like **préférer** and **acheter.** Although verbs whose infinitives end in -**érer** or -**eter** have a spelling change in the present, they have no spelling change in the **imparfait.**

DRILL: À l'âge de dix ans, qu'est-ce que tu voulais être? (nous / vous / le professeur / Candide et Alceste)

DRILL: Quand il avait seize ans, Candide était beau. (Alceste / laid; Nous / paresseux; Tu / sportif; Je / content; Vous / pénible; Alceste et Candide / heureux)

L'imparfait: usage

The **imparfait** is used:

1. To tell or describe what things were like in the past.

> Il **faisait** beau hier. Les oiseaux **chantaient,** les enfants **jouaient** dans le parc et moi, j'**étais** très content.
> *It was nice out yesterday. The birds were singing, the children were playing in the park, and I was very happy.*

2. To tell how things used to be in the past.

> Quand j'**avais** dix ans, j'**allais** chez mes grands-parents le week-end. Ils **habitaient** une grande maison à la campagne. **Il y avait** un jardin où je **jouais** avec les chiens. Je **mangeais** bien, je **dormais** bien, la vie **était** belle.
> *When I was 10, I used to go to my grandparents' for the weekend. They lived in a big house in the country. There was a yard where I played with the dogs. I ate well, I slept well, and life was grand.*

3. To tell what was going on when something else happened.

> Alceste **prenait** une douche quand le téléphone a sonné.
>
> *Alceste was taking a shower when the telephone rang.*

Vous avez compris?

A. Le bon (?) vieux temps Pour Monsieur Ségal, le monde *(world)* est moins bien maintenant qu'avant. Il préfère le bon(?) vieux temps. Utilisez un verbe à l'imparfait pour compléter les phrases. Puis imaginez ce que la petite-fille de Monsieur Ségal répondrait *(would reply)* à son grand-père. Et vous? Est-ce que vos idées sont comme les idées de Monsieur Ségal ou comme les idées de sa petite-fille?

Modèle   Les femmes ..... à la maison.
   M. SÉGAL: ***Les femmes restaient à la maison.***
   SA PETITE FILLE: ***Oui, mais maintenant, les femmes travaillent—à la maison et à l'université, dans les usines, etc.!***

1. Les jeunes gens ..... polis.
2. Nous ..... en famille le soir.
3. Nous ne ..... pas la télévision.
4. Les jeunes filles ne ..... pas à l'université.
5. Les femmes ..... la cuisine pour leur mari.
6. Les ouvriers ..... bien.
7. Les enfants ne ..... pas le rock.
8. On ..... bien! Ah! La cuisine de ma mère!
9. Les femmes ne ..... pas de pantalon.
10. Les hommes ..... une cravate tous les jours.

B. Souvenirs de mes seize ans Claude se souvient *(remembers)* de ses seize ans. Complétez les phrases avec un verbe de la liste à l'imparfait. Vous pouvez utiliser le même *(same)* verbe plusieurs fois *(more than once)*.

Verbes: avoir / être / aller / commencer / parler / arriver / étudier / vouloir / regarder / aimer / sortir / rentrer / finir / préférer / manger / boire / prendre / travailler / faire

Quand je ..... seize ans, ma sœur et moi, nous ..... au lycée. Je ..... beaucoup parce que je ..... aller à l'université. Ma sœur ne ..... pas le lycée et elle ne ..... jamais. L'école ..... à quatre heures et nous ..... à la maison à quatre heures et demie. Nous ..... une tartine au chocolat et nous ..... un thé et puis, je ..... mes devoirs. Mais ma sœur ..... toujours aller jouer au foot ou écouter des disques. Le soir, toute la famille ..... à huit heures. Après, nous ..... un peu la télévision ou nous ..... dans la salle de séjour. Le week-end, je ..... avec des copains. On ..... quelquefois au cinéma et on ..... parler pendant des heures au café. Mais mes parents ..... sévères et je ..... toujours avant minuit. Et vous, à seize ans, comment ..... -vous?

C. La vie à douze ans Comment était la vie de Jean-Pierre quand il avait douze ans? Complétez l'histoire avec les verbes **devoir** et **pouvoir** à l'imparfait.

Quand j'avais douze ans, je ..... rentrer à la maison après l'école. Je ne ..... pas jouer avec mes copains, parce que je ..... d'abord faire mes devoirs. Ma sœur et moi, nous ..... aussi travailler dans la maison. Nous ..... faire la vaisselle et ranger notre chambre. Après, nous ..... quelquefois regarder la télévision. Mon père, lui, ... regarder la télévision quand il voulait et il ..... aller au lit à minuit! Mais nous, nous ..... aller dormir à neuf heures.

Continuons!

A. Il y a trois ans... Comment était votre vie il y a trois ans?

Modèle *J'avais quinze ans. J'allais à l'école, j'avais beaucoup de copains.*

B. Et vous à douze ans? Qu'est-ce que vous deviez faire à douze ans? Qu'est-ce que vous pouviez faire? Qu'est-ce que vous ne pouviez pas faire? Donnez des détails.

1. Je devais...   2. Je pouvais...   3. Je ne pouvais pas...

Act. B: FOLLOW-UP: Have students ask you about your life three years ago and at the age of 12. Compare student experiences with your own.

➤➤ Parler au passé: l'imparfait et le passé composé

You are now familiar with two ways of talking about the past in French, the **passé composé** and the **imparfait.** The **passé composé** is used to recount events in the past, to say what happened.

Abder a rencontré Suzanne. Ils **ont parlé.** Puis, ils **sont allés** au café.
Abder met Suzanne. They talked. Then they went to the café.

If, however, you want to describe how things were in the past, you must use the **imparfait.**

> Il **faisait** beau hier. Les oiseaux **chantaient,** les enfants **jouaient** dans le parc et moi, j'**étais** très content.
> *It was nice out yesterday. The birds were singing, the children were playing in the park, and I was very happy.*

If the action is to start up again after a description, the **passé composé** must be used.

> Il faisait beau hier. Les oiseaux chantaient, les enfants jouaient dans le parc et moi, j'étais très content. Et puis, tout à coup, il **a commencé** à pleuvoir!
> *It was nice out yesterday. The birds were singing, the children were playing in the park, and I was very happy. And then, all of a sudden, it started to rain!*

The difference in usage between these two past tenses can be summarized as follows:

PASSÉ COMPOSÉ

Tells what happened (recounts, narrates)

Frequently corresponds to the English simple past.

Il **a neigé.**	*It snowed.*

IMPARFAIT

Tells how things were (describes)

Tells how things used to be or what people used to do

Tells what was going on when something else happened

Frequently corresponds to the English progressive past.

Il **neigeait.**	*It was snowing. / It used to snow.*

J'ai oublié!	*I forgot (I've forgotten)!*
Qu'est-ce que tu **as oublié?**	*What did you forget (have you forgotten)?*
Je **dormais** bien quand le réveil a **sonné.**	*I was sleeping well when the alarm clock went off.*
Quand mon frère **avait** cinq ans, il **voulait** être policier.	*When my brother was five, he wanted to be a police officer.*
Avant, je **sortais** beaucoup, mais...	*Before, I used to go out a lot, but...*

Vous avez compris?

A. Mon chat et moi
Regardez l'histoire. Quels verbes sont à l'imparfait? Quels verbes sont au passé composé? Pour chaque verbe, pourquoi est-ce que l'auteur a choisi l'imparfait ou le passé composé?

Act. A: Put students in groups to discuss why they think various verbs concern either action or description in the past. Make sure that students look at the use of language beyond the sentence level.

> C'était un soir d'automne. Il pleuvait et il y avait beaucoup de vent. J'étais à l'intérieur et j'écoutais du Mozart à la radio. Tout à coup, j'ai entendu du bruit dans le jardin... C'était comme quelqu'un qui marchait. J'ai mis mon imperméable et je suis sorti sur la terrasse. Il n'y avait personne. Alors, je suis rentré. Mais deux minutes après, j'ai entendu un plouf et puis beaucoup de bruit. Il y avait quelque chose ou quelqu'un dans la piscine. Alors, je suis retourné dans le jardin et quand je suis arrivé à la piscine, j'ai trouvé un petit chat noir très malheureux qui nageait dans l'eau et qui avait très froid. Et moi, qu'est-ce que j'ai fait? Je suis entré dans l'eau et j'ai pris le petit chat noir avec moi. Voilà comment j'ai rencontré Moïse, mon chat!

B. On n'est jamais tranquille!
Vous pensez *(think)* que tout *(everything)* va bien et puis quelque chose arrive *(happens)!* Voilà des situations typiques. Décidez comment étaient les choses (imparfait) quand quelque chose est arrivé (passé composé).

1. M. Lepropre / être sous la douche / quand / il / entendre le téléphone.
2. Mme Guitton / faire la cuisine / quand / son fils / tomber de la chaise.
3. Nous / sortir / quand / ils / arriver.
4. Je / jouer au tennis / quand / il / commencer / à pleuvoir.
5. Les Pinot / regarder la télévision / quand / ils / entendre un bruit à l'extérieur.

Continuons!

A. Le rêve de Jacqueline
Jacqueline a fait un rêve *(dream)* la nuit dernière et le matin, elle a décidé de l'écrire *(write it down)* pour ne pas l'oublier. Mettez les verbes au passé composé ou à l'imparfait pour raconter *(tell)* son rêve.

> Je (être) seule dans une grande ville sombre. Il (pleuvoir) et je (être) déprimée: je (ne pas avoir) d'amis, pas de métier, pas de famille. Je (réfléchir) à ma vie et je (ne pas regarder) où je (aller). Tout à coup, je (entendre) un bruit. Ce (être) une femme qui (chanter). Je (devoir) rencontrer cette femme! Ce (être) très important! Alors, je (décider) de chercher où elle (être). Je (entrer) dans une vieille maison et je (regarder) dans toutes les pièces. Personne! Je (entrer) dans une église. Je (chercher) à l'intérieur, mais elle (ne pas être) là. Tout à coup, un cheval *(horse)* blanc (arriver) et sur le cheval, il y (avoir) une femme. Ce (être) ma grand-mère! Mais elle (être) jeune, jolie et très heureuse. Ce (être) elle qui (chanter)!

B. Un opéra moderne Un opéra moderne. Mettez les verbes à l'imparfait ou au passé composé pour raconter *(tell)* cette histoire.

Il était une fois *(Once upon a time)* une jolie jeune fille qui (travailler) comme vendeuse dans un petit magasin de chaussures. Elle (ne pas aimer) son patron parce qu'il (être) méchant. Il (adorer) l'argent et, lui, il (gagner) beaucoup d'argent mais les vendeuses qui (travailler) pour lui (ne pas être) bien payées. La jeune fille (ne plus vouloir) travailler pour lui mais elle (ne pas pouvoir) trouver d'autre travail. Alors, elle (décider) de rester dans le magasin de chaussures, mais elle (ne pas être) contente et elle (pleurer) souvent chez elle le soir parce qu'elle (ne pas avoir) assez à manger et parce qu'elle (être) si fatiguée.

Puis, un jour, un beau jeune homme (entrer) dans le magasin. Il (être) très bien habillé et il (avoir) l'air sympathique. Il (ne rien acheter), mais lui et la jeune fille (parler) ensemble et il (inviter) la jeune fille à manger avec lui le soir. Ils (aller) dans un petit restaurant italien où ils (prendre) des spaghetti et du Chianti. Ils (parler beaucoup) et la jeune fille (oublier) l'heure. Puis elle (regarder) sa montre. Il (être) minuit et elle (devoir) être au magasin à sept heures du matin! Elle (expliquer) le problème au jeune homme et ils (partir).

Le matin, elle (sortir) de son lit quand elle (entendre) un bruit. Elle (regarder) par terre et elle (trouver) les clés du jeune homme. Elle (avoir) son numéro de téléphone, alors, elle (téléphoner) chez lui. Et qui (répondre)? Son patron! Le jeune homme (être) le fils de son patron!

C. Histoire en images Voilà l'histoire de la vie de Monsieur Richard. Comment était sa vie quand il était petit? Qu'est-ce qui est arrivé *(happened)*?

1. À dix ans,...

2. À vingt ans,...

3. À quarante ans,...

D. Conversation en français Qu'est-ce que vous avez fait le week-end dernier? Donnez des détails.

▶▶ Les pronoms relatifs *qui* et *que*

Relative pronouns relate or connect two sentences that share the same noun so that speakers and writers can develop an idea or specify what they are referring to. When two sentences are connected by a relative pronoun, each one (now part of the new sentence) is called a clause.

Qui as a relative pronoun was presented as a **Note de vocabulaire** in *Leçon 7*. It is recycled here with the relative pronoun **que**.

The relative pronouns **dont** and **ce dont** are treated in the *Appendice de grammaire*.

J'entends un enfant. L'enfant pleure.

J'entends un enfant **qui** pleure.

I hear a child. The child is crying.

I hear a child who is crying.

C'est le professeur. Tu cherchais ce professeur.

C'est le professeur **que** tu cherchais.

That's the instructor. You were looking for that instructor.

That's the instructor whom you were looking for.

Qui

1. **Qui** is used as a subject. (It is usually followed directly by its verb.)

2. **Qui** may refer to either people or things. The English equivalent of **qui** may be *who*, *that*, or *which*.

   Voilà le professeur **qui** a travaillé avec Janine la semaine dernière.
      (**qui** = person)
   J'ai trouvé une robe **qui** est très belle. (**qui** = thing)

3. The verb following **qui** agrees with the noun that **qui** replaced.

   C'est moi **qui** suis malade!

4. The -**i** of **qui** is never dropped in front of a vowel sound.

Que

1. **Que** is used as a direct object. (It is usually followed by the noun or pronoun that is the subject of the clause.)

2. **Que** may refer to either people or things. The English equivalent of **que** may be *who*, *whom*, *which*, or *that*, or it may even be omitted. **Que** may not be omitted in French.

   C'est l'homme **que** j'ai rencontré hier. (**que** = person)
   C'est le livre **qu'**il a acheté hier. (**que** = thing)

3. The -**e** of **que** is dropped before a vowel sound.

Rappel!   The words **qui** and **que** are also used as interrogative pronouns.

INTERROGATIVE PRONOUNS (AT THE BEGINNING OF A SENTENCE) **qui** = *who?* **que** = *what?*	RELATIVE PRONOUNS (IN THE MIDDLE OF A SENTENCE) **qui** = subject *(who, that, which)* **que** = direct object *(whom, which, that)*

Qui parle? (qui = interrogative pronoun)
C'est le professeur **qui** parle. (**qui** =relative pronoun)

Qu'est-ce que tu cherches? (**que** = interrogative pronoun)
Je cherche le livre **que** j'avais hier. (**que** =relative pronoun)

Vous avez compris?

A. Quelle photo? Choisissez la photo qui va avec la phrase.

Act. A: Have students describe the photos before doing activity A. Rephrase student ideas using relative pronouns whenever possible.

TRANSPARENCY:
12-6

1. Voilà le chien que Stéphanie aime.

    A.    B.

2. Voilà M. Valat qui cherche son fils Julien.

    A.    B.

3. Voilà le chien qui aime Stéphanie.

    A.   B.

4. Voilà Julien qui cherche son père.

    A. 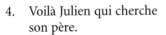   B.

5. Voilà la femme que Candide attend.

A.   B.

6. Voilà la femme qui attend Candide.

A.   B.

B. Arnaud et les femmes Complétez par *(by)* **qui** ou **que**.

—Voilà Arnaud!

—C'est un étudiant . . . . . habite dans notre cité, n'est-ce pas?

—Oui. C'est un homme . . . . . toutes les femmes trouvent beau.

—Et toi?

—Moi, je n'aime pas les hommes . . . . . sont trop beaux, mais j'adore les hommes . . . . . sont intelligents.

—Et Arnaud est intelligent?

—Pas très, non! Mais voilà Aurélie.

—Qui est Aurélie?

—C'est l'étudiante . . . . . sort avec Arnaud. C'est une fille . . . . . je déteste!

Act. B: FOLLOW UP: If time permits, ask students to imagine encounters between Aurélie, Arnaud, and/or another student.

C. Une nouvelle maison Complétez par **qui** ou **que**.

M. Bovy a trouvé une maison: «J'ai trouvé une maison . . . . . j'adore. Il y a un jardin . . . . . est très grand, avec des arbres . . . . . sont très vieux et des fleurs . . . . . ma femme va beaucoup aimer. Il y a des pièces . . . . . sont claires, une cuisine . . . . . j'aime beaucoup, une piscine . . . . . les enfants vont adorer et trois salles de bains . . . . . mes filles vont beaucoup utiliser *(use)!*»

Continuons!

Un peu d'imagination! Complétez ces phrases.

1. Voilà une femme qui . . . . .
2. Voilà un homme que . . . . .
3. J'aime les professeurs qui . . . . .
4. C'est une université qui . . . . .
5. C'est un exercice que . . . . .

Découvertes culturelles: Les Français et le travail

▶▶ La revanche d'un cancre

A. Préparation: Succès scolaire. Est-ce que tout est perdu pour les mauvais étudiants (les cancres)? Quelles sont les possibilités pour plus tard?

Modèle *Ils peuvent faire du cinéma et gagner beaucoup d'argent.*

Entreprise • Création

LA REVANCHE D'UN CANCRE

À 23 ans, cet ex-lycéen indiscipliné crée sa propre collection de T-shirts sur lesquels sont imprimées des antisèches* pour les examens.

À 23 ans, Yankel Tapiro crée sa propre entreprise au nom évocateur: "Antisèche". Installé dans un bureau appartenant à son père, il reçoit une aide de 30 000 francs du fonds départemental pour l'initiative des jeunes. L'idée est de fabriquer et de commercialiser des T-shirts et des sweats sur lesquels sont imprimés... des formules de physique ou de géométrie, des cartes géographiques (l'agriculture aux États-Unis) ou un tableau des verbes irréguliers anglais. Pour les plus jeunes, une table de multiplication ou de conjugaison. Plus rigolo: des bulletins de notes ou des mots d'excuse.■

Pierrick Béquet

Plus de vingt modèles différents.

Les Clés de l'Actualité

*antisèches = solutions à des problèmes d'examen

B. Lire et comprendre.

1. **La photo.** Regardez la photo et décrivez les deux personnes :

	La personne à gauche	La personne à droite
âge		
sexe		
aspects		
expression		
vêtements		

2. **Le sous-titre.** Regardez le sous-titre pour vérifier les informations sur ces deux personnes. Trouvez dans le sous-titre qui est «le cancre» et les mots qui expliquent sa «revanche» *(revenge)*.

3. **Le sujet.** D'après les titres et les sous-titres, quel est le sujet de cet article ?

☐ la difficulté des études au lycée   ☐ l'art des vêtements pour les jeunes

☐ la mode des T-shirts dans les lycées   ☐ la préparation aux examens

☐ le travail des jeunes dans les lycées   ☐ les entreprises créées par les jeunes

4. **Les détails.** Regardez l'article pour trouver...

a. le nom de l'entreprise

b. où est l'entreprise

c. le capital de départ pour l'entreprise en francs

d. l'origine du capital de départ

e. le travail de l'entreprise

f. les décorations et inscriptions sur les T-shirts

5. **Bonne ou mauvaise idée ?** Pourquoi est-ce que l'entreprise a du succès ? Qui n'aime pas ces T-shirts ? Pourquoi ?

C. Acheter et vendre.

1. **Commander.** Vous avez une boutique sur un campus. Quels T-shirts allez-vous commander à Yankel Tapiro ?

2. **Slogan commercial.** Préparez un slogan pour vendre les T-shirts de Tapiro aux étudiants du campus.

3. **Le budget de votre entreprise.** Qu'est-ce que vous allez faire ? Où ? Quand ? Comment ?

- Identifiez vos dépenses et les prix des T-shirts en francs français.
- Calculez à quel prix en francs français vous devez vendre les T-shirts pour faire des bénéfices.
- Préparez une campagne de marketing pour les vendre.

Act. B: You may want to explain to students that **sécher,** in school slang, means to be unable to answer a question on a test. **Une antisèche,** therefore, would be the solution to that problem; in other words, the French equivalent of a "cheat sheet." You can do this in simple French. **Voilà un examen.** (Draw a page from a test, with numbers down the left margin.) **Voilà la question numéro 4.** (Indicate the number 4.) **C'est une question très, très difficile et vous ne savez pas la réponse / ne pouvez pas répondre.** (Put a big X across number 4.) Vous séchez! If desired, discuss briefly the relationship between the literal meaning of **sécher** *(to dry)* and its extension here *(to come up dry, to dry up).*

Act. C, 1: Can be done in groups. Have students decide how many T-shirts and what kinds would sell on their campus.

Act C, 3: If time is short, students can do part of this activity only. Students brainstorm and identify necessary strategies: **faire des affiches / faire des sondages / préparer des annonces à la radio, à la télévision.** Once this is done, ask them to select one marketing device and have them develop it.

➤➤ Le temps perdu

A. Préparation: Le travail et les saisons. Quels jours de l'année n'avez-vous pas envie de travailler? Pourquoi?

B. Le poème.

1. **Le thème.** Trouvez tous les mots associés au travail. Trouvez tous les mots associés au temps qu'il fait. C'est quelle saison? C'est quel jour? C'est quelle heure?
2. **L'architecture.** Quels sont les vers *(lines)* qui font le décor? Lesquels font le dialogue?
3. **Les protagonistes.** Combien de personnes y a-t-il dans le poème? Qui sont-elles?
4. **Les gestes.** Qui fait quoi? Trouvez les actions de chaque personne.
5. **Le dialogue.** Qui parle? À qui? Comment l'appelle-t-il?
6. **Les mots.** Assemblez les mots qui vont avec le soleil et les mots qui vont avec le patron. Quels sont les rapports entre ces personnes—alliances ou oppositions? Quelles associations expliquent le mot «camarade»? Associations religieuses, sociales ou politiques? C'est une référence à quel parti politique?

LE TEMPS PERDU

1   **Devant la porte de l'usine**
    le travailleur soudain s'arrête
    le beau temps l'a tiré par la veste
    et comme il se retourne
5   **et regarde le soleil**
    tout rouge tout rond
    souriant dans son ciel de plomb
    il cligne de l'œil*
    familièrement
10 **Dis donc camarade Soleil**
    tu ne trouves pas
    que c'est plutôt con
    de donner une journée pareille
    à un patron?

Jacques Prévert, *Paroles*
© Editions Gallimard

*œil = e*ye

C. Mots nouveaux. Utilisez le contexte pour comprendre ces mots.

1. un ciel de plomb =
   - ☐ un ciel bleu
   - ☐ un ciel noir
   - ☐ un ciel métallique

2. il cligne de l'œil =
   - ☐ *he shuts his eyes*
   - ☐ *he stares*
   - ☐ *he winks*

3. c'est plutôt con =
   - ☐ utile
   - ☐ sérieux
   - ☐ stupide

4. une journée pareille = ☐ une belle journée comme ça
   - ☐ une journée de travail
   - ☐ une journée de vacances

D. Interprétation. Complétez les phrases suivantes.

1. Les contrastes qu'on trouve dans le poème sont les contrastes entre . . . . .
2. D'après le poète, le travail est . . . . .
3. D'après le poète, les patrons sont . . . . . et ne sont pas . . . . .
4. D'après le poète, l'usine est . . . . . et n'est pas . . . . .
5. D'après le poète, les travailleurs sont . . . . .
6. Le poète pense que . . . . .
7. Le poète est . . . . .

E. Décisions. Écrivez la suite du poème. Que décide le travailleur? Que fait-il?

www explore!
http//voila.heinle.com

Orthographe et prononciation

▶▶ La lettre *r*

The letter r represents the sound [**r**], as in **riz, partez,** and **arrivez.** It sounds nothing like the English **r.** To pronounce the French **r,** first say the word *garage* in English. When you say the **g,** your tongue bunches up toward the back of your mouth. Now, say *garage* again, this time exaggerating the **ga** sound. Leave your tongue bunched up toward the back of your mouth and try to say the word **garage** in French. Keep the tip of your tongue firmly behind your bottom teeth.

Activités

A. Prononcez Répétez après votre professeur.

1. Mes parents ne sont pas raisonnables.
2. Il y a un rat sur la radio.
3. La sœur de Robert va porter une robe rouge mercredi.
4. Les retraités n'ont pas de responsabilités.

B. Trouvez la règle Regardez la liste. Quand est-ce que la lettre **r** n'est pas prononcée en Français?

adorer / avoir / banquier / cours / fruit / porte / métier / cadre

Vocabulaire de base

 TEXT TAPE:
Vocabulaire de base

NOMS

les affaires (*f. pl.*) *business*
un agent immobilier *real estate agent*
un agriculteur *farmer*
un avocat, une avocate *(court) lawyer*

un banquier *banker*
un bruit *noise*
un cadre *executive*
un chef d'entreprise *company head, business owner*
un client, une cliente *client, customer*

un commerçant, une commerçante *shopkeeper, retail store owner*
un/une dentiste *dentist*
un employé, une employée (de bureau) *(office) employee*
une entreprise *firm, business*

une femme au foyer *housewife*
un ingénieur *engineer*
un instituteur, une institutrice *teacher (elementary school)*
un/une juriste *attorney*
un médecin *doctor, physician*
une mère de famille *wife and mother*
un métier *profession, trade*
un ouvrier, une ouvrière *(blue collar) worker*
un patron, une patronne *boss*
un policier *police officer*
un/une propriétaire *owner*
un/une psychologue *psychologist*
un retraité, une retraitée *retired person*
un salaire *salary*
un/une secrétaire *secretary*
un serveur, une serveuse *waiter, waitress*

le travail (un travail) *work (job)*
un vendeur, une vendeuse *salesperson*

dangereux, -euse *dangerous*
dur(e) *hard*
fort(e) *strong*
honnête *honest*
intéressant(e) *interesting*
responsable *responsible*

décider (de + inf.) *to decide (to do something)*
diriger *to manage, to run*
expliquer *to explain*
gagner *to earn, to win*
oublier (de + inf.) *to forget (to do something)*

sonner *to ring*

aller chez le médecin, chez le dentiste *to go to the doctor, the dentist*
avoir des responsabilités *to have responsibilities*
chercher du travail /un travail *to look for work / a job*
enfin *at last, finally*
être bien/mal payé(e) *to be paid well/badly*
il y a *ago*
perdre son travail *to lose one's job*
tout à coup *all of a sudden*
travailler dur *to work hard*
trouver du travail / un travail *to find work / a job*
vraiment *really, truly*

Vocabulaire supplémentaire

un atelier *workshop*
le baccalauréat *French school-leaving exam (secondary level)*
un caissier, une caissière *cashier*
un chômeur, une chômeuse *unemployed person*
un coiffeur, une coiffeuse *hairdresser*
un cuisinier, une cuisinière *cook*
un directeur, une directrice *manager (business, company)*
l'état (m.) *state, nation*
un/une fonctionnaire *civil servant, government worker, state employee*
un garagiste *garage (car repair shop) owner*
un gérant, une gérante *manager (e.g., restaurant, hotel, shop)*
un immigré, une immigrée *immigrant*
un infirmier, une infirmière *nurse*
un pompier *firefighter*
le SMIC *minimum wage*
la S.N.C.F. *French national railway*

algérien, algérienne *Algerian*
dynamique *dynamic*

efficace *efficient*
stressé(e) *stressed*

déménager *to move (from one living place to another)*

les affaires marchent bien *business is good*
être au chômage *to be unemployed*
faire du bruit *to make noise*
gagner sa vie *to earn a living*
gagner ... francs l'heure / par jour / par semaine / par mois *to earn ... francs per hour / per day / per week / per month*
pourtant *however*
taper à la machine *to type*
travailler au SMIC *to work for minimum wage*

Enfin! *At last!*
(Mais) enfin! *For goodness sake!*
Fais / Faites attention! *Pay attention! Watch out!*

Une minute! *Just a minute!*
On verra! *We will (We'll) see!*
Toc toc! *Knock knock!*

le bac = le baccalauréat
un beur, une beurette = jeune né(e) en France de parents du Maghreb *(Algeria, Morocco or Tunisia).* (Not considered pejorative.)
une boîte = une entreprise, une usine, un bureau
bosseur = travailleur
un boulot = un travail *(job)*
le boulot = le travail *(work)*
un flic = un policier
un job = un travail
un smicard = quelqu'un qui gagne le SMIC
le stress *stress*
un toubib = un médecin

une jobine (Canada) = un petit job
un(e) jobiste (Belgique) = un(e) étudiant(e) qui a un job

Magazine francophone

REVUE PÉRIODIQUE
PUBLIÉE À L'AIDE DE
DOCUMENTATIONS INTERNATIONALES

Rédacteur en chef:
Isabelle Kaplan

Rédacteurs adjoints:
L. Kathy Heilenman
Claude Toussaint Tournier

NUMÉRO 3

REVUE EN FRANÇAIS POUR LES ÉTUDIANTS DE «VOILÀ!»

ÉDITORIAL
Numéro spécial

Il était une fois... Tous les pays ont une histoire, et on la lit, on l'apprend à l'école dans les livres, dans les classes. L'histoire, c'est des noms, des chiffres, des dates, des lieux géographiques: champs de bataille, châteaux, cathédrales, montagnes, fleuves et frontières qui changent avec les siècles. Louis XIV, Napoléon, Charles de Gaulle et tous les autres. Étrange! Bizarre, comme cette histoire est toujours l'histoire des hommes: rois, empereurs, généraux, révolutionnaires, imposteurs!... Et les autres? Où sont-ils? Il n'y avait pas de femmes au Moyen Âge? Pendant la Renaissance? Les révolutions?

Il y a une autre histoire, plus modeste et moins connue. L'histoire des femmes, des enfants, des mères, des prostituées, des poétesses, des romancières, les oubliées pendant longtemps.

Maintenant les voilà! Elles sont sorties de l'ombre, de la nuit des temps. Elles arrivent dans la course du XXIᵉ siècle, nombreuses, dynamiques, actives; elles sont partout, avec leur talent, leur imagination, leur patience, leur force et leur ardeur. Elles travaillent, elles chantent, elles écrivent, elles aiment, elles votent, elles gouvernent, elles font le ménage, le jardin, elles pilotent des avions, elles créent des machines, elles font des œuvres d'art. Elles sont les artisans et les artistes du monde de demain. Allez les femmes, à vous la vie, à vous la France, à vous le monde!

Ouvrez ce numéro spécial et découvrez les femmes françaises et les femmes francophones.

Quand ont-elles obtenu le droit de vote?

● En Suède: en 1862 (pour les élections municipales), en 1918 pour les autres scrutins.
● Aux États-Unis: dès 1869, puis 1893 et 1896 dans quatre états de l'Ouest. En 1920 dans tout le pays.
● En Nouvelle-Zélande: en 1893.
● En Norvège: en 1901 (pour les élections municipales), en 1913 pour tous les scrutins.
● En Australie: en 1902.
● En Finlande: en 1907.
● Au Danemark: en 1915.
● En Pologne: en 1917.
● En Grande-Bretagne: en 1918 pour les femmes de plus de 30 ans, en 1928, pour toutes.
● Au Canada: en 1918.
● En Allemagne: en 1918.
● En Russie: en 1918.
● En Islande et aux Pays-Bas: en 1919.
● En Afrique du Sud: en 1930.
● En Espagne, au Portugal et au Brésil: en 1931.
● En France: en 1944.
● En Italie: en 1945.
● En Chine: en 1949.
● En Grèce: en 1954.
● À Monaco: en 1962.
● En Suisse: en 1971.
● Au Liechtenstein: en 1984.

UN COMBAT

a tâche demeure immense. Le combat pour l'égalité entre hommes et femmes est encore loin d'être gagné en cette fin de vingtième siècle. On ne peut que s'en indigner. Certes, des pas ont été franchis, sur lesquels on ne reviendra pas. Notamment dans les pays riches et développés. Mais même dans ce camp-là, la vigilance doit rester de mise si les femmes veulent conserver et transmettre leurs acquis. Restent toutes les autres femmes, la majorité, trop souvent sans droits ni voix. Ce combat pour les droits des femmes est essentiel, car là où la femme est bafouée, règnent l'obscurantisme et ses intégrismes. Ce combat est à la fois un travail de fourmi et de titan, mais il est nécessaire. C'est le combat de la raison, de l'esprit et du cœur. ■

Yann Bouffin

CE QUE LES FEMMES ONT ACQUIS EN FRANCE

● Le droit de vote (depuis 1944).
● L'accès à la contraception (la pilule est autorisée depuis 1967 et remboursée depuis 1973).
● Le droit d'interrompre une grossesse non désirée (loi sur l'Interruption volontaire de grossesse de 1975, remboursée par la Sécurité sociale depuis 1982).
● L'égalité familiale: une femme peut garder son nom de jeune fille, le mari porter le sien accolé à celui de sa femme, les enfants peuvent porter le nom de leur mère mais ne peuvent pas le transmettre (depuis 1985); l'autorité parentale est partagée (1970); la femme mariée signe sa déclaration d'impôt.
● Les droits dans le travail: avec le principe de la non-discrimination sexuelle à l'embauche (1975), l'impossibilité d'être licenciée quand on est enceinte ou en congé maternité (depuis 1980), un salaire théoriquement égal à celui d'un homme (depuis 1972), le droit de ne pas être harcelée sexuellement sur son lieu de travail (1992).

Hommage

Une femme au Panthéon

Le Panthéon est un monument parisien qui abrite les tombeaux de certains hommes célèbres du pays. Marie Curie sera la première femme à reposer au milieu de ces grands hommes.

Quelques hôtes célèbres du Panthéon

Écrivains: **Jean-Jacques Rousseau**; **Voltaire**; **Victor Hugo**.
Hommes politiques: **Jean Jaurès**, député et philosophe; **Jean Moulin**, résistant.
Scientifiques: **Louis Braille**, inventeur de l'écriture pour les aveugles; **Condorcet**, mathématicien et philosophe.

En 1791, les révolutionnaires décident de rassembler les cercueils des grands hommes dans l'église Sainte-Geneviève à Paris. Ils rasent les deux clochers et murent les 42 fenêtres de cette église qui devient le Panthéon. Depuis, 69 hommes célèbres reposent dans ce monument.

Toujours première

La première femme admise au Panthéon sera la scientifique Marie Curie. Pour rendre hommage à son travail, ses cendres et celles de son mari, Pierre Curie, seront déposées là le 20 avril.

Marie Curie a travaillé toute sa vie sur la radioactivité. Elle a découvert le radium, un minerai qui émet des rayons mortels. Elle a été la première femme à recevoir le prix Nobel: d'abord le prix Nobel de physique, avec son mari en 1903. Puis, seule, le prix Nobel de chimie en 1911. Elle a aussi été la première femme professeur à l'université de la Sorbonne, à Paris. En entrant au Panthéon, 61 ans après sa mort, Marie Curie continue d'innover...

Sophie Cindel

Le sais-tu?

 Les femmes représentent la moitié de la population mondiale.

 Elles accomplissent près des $\frac{2}{3}$ du travail effectué dans le monde.

 Sur 100 F de salaire versés dans le monde, les femmes reçoivent 10 F.

 En France, l'école est obligatoire pour les filles depuis 1850.

 En 1944, les Françaises obtiennent le droit de voter et de se présenter aux élections.

Sur 577 députés, l'Assemblée nationale française compte aujourd'hui 35 femmes.

 Depuis 1983, la loi française indique que, dans le travail, hommes et femmes doivent être traités de la même façon.

Regards sur le monde

LANGUE

Les propositions de féminiser la langue répondent au désir du Québec de contribuer à l'enrichissement du français «international». Sentie comme un organisme vivant dans un espace en mouvement, la langue française nord-américaine parviendra-t-elle à ébranler la coutume patriarcale de la langue française?

Masculin et féminin au Québec

L'accession des femmes à des emplois occupés jusque-là par des hommes a provoqué au Québec, au fil des années, une réflexion linguistique étroitement liée à l'évolution sociale, non sans déclencher de vives discussions et un tollé de protestations passionnées.

LE SAVIEZ-VOUS?

Si une majorité choisit de féminiser les titres de fonction, une préférence se dégage pour les formes peu marquées; on peut ainsi comprendre la popularité des formes en -eure (professeure, auteure, ingénieure, superviseure...).

Tous les titres ne peuvent être féminisés; demeurent épicènes chef, commis, mannequin, médecin, substitut, témoin, marin, matelot. L'Office propose toutefois la chef, la commis, etc.

Gazette officielle du Québec

PROFESSIONS, MÉTIERS, TITRES, FONCTIONS ET APPELLATIONS DE PERSONNES AU FÉMININ

Le féminin des noms de professions, de métiers, de fonctions, etc., suit les règles grammaticales de formation du féminin des noms et des adjectifs... (voir le guide *Au féminin* publié par l'Office de la langue française).

Il faut noter que la plupart des noms terminés en -*eur* forment régulièrement leur féminin en -*euse* (c'est notamment le cas pour les noms qui dérivent directement d'un verbe), mais que certains ont une finale en -*eure* que l'usage a retenue. Pour quelques féminins, deux formes sont proposées, les dictionnaires et les guides officiels attestant l'une ou l'autre.

A	
académicien	agent
académicienne	**agente**
acheteur	aide-comptable
acheteuse	**aide-comptable**
acteur	avocat
actrice	**avocate**

À L'AFFICHE MUSIQUE

ZAP MAMA

Des femmes énergiques, drôles, talentueuses qui mêlent les sons empruntés aux quatre coins du monde. Elles sont belges et font découvrir la musique pygmée. Elles chantent, dansent et emportent les salles dans leur enthousiasme.

Elles sont cinq à vouloir mélanger les genres, les traditions musicales, les langues, à bousculer les conventions, à jouer avec les sons, les couleurs, les voix et les rythmes, avec un amour commun pour le chant du monde. Les sons qui nous parviennent sont traversés de rires, de jeux vocaux et bruits d'enfance.

Elles sont belgo-zaïroises, belges et zaïroises et réinventent, recomposent, réinvestissent l'immense potentiel des polyphonies vocales présentes dans toutes les cultures. La beauté essentielle des chants pygmés n'était connue que des initiés, et parfois même de quelques pédants; elle nous est livrée avec toute sa vitalité, sa créativité, cette étonnante symbiose avec l'environnement naturel: bruits d'eau, de vent, d'herbe, chanson de forêts immenses dont l'écho se répercute d'arbre en arbre et porte loin.

Elles vont glaner leur inspiration aux quatre coins du monde: comptines rwandaises, chants populaires zaïrois, rythmes cubains, lamentations syriennes, polyphonies pygmées, mélodies arabo-espagnoles de la renaissance.

déjeuner du matin

Il a mis le café
Dans la tasse
Il a mis le lait
Dans la tasse de café
Il a mis le sucre
Dans le café au lait
Avec la petite cuiller
Il a tourné
Il a bu le café au lait
Et il a reposé la tasse
Sans me parler
Il a allumé
Une cigarette
Il a fait des ronds
Avec la fumée
Il a mis les cendres
Dans le cendrier
Sans me parler
Sans me regarder
Il s'est levé
Il a mis
Son chapeau sur sa tête
Il a mis
Son manteau de pluie
Parce qu'il pleuvait
Et il est parti
Sous la pluie
Sans une parole
Sans me regarder
Et moi j'ai pris
Ma tête dans ma main
Et j'ai pleuré

Jacques Prévert, *Paroles*

© *Éditions Gallimard*

LE BOUQUET

Que faites-vous là petite fille
Avec ces fleurs fraîchement coupées
Que faites-vous là jeune fille
Avec ces fleurs ces fleurs séchées
Que faites-vous là jolie femme
Avec ces fleurs qui se fanent
Que faites-vous là vieille femme
Avec ces fleurs qui meurent

J'attends le vainqueur.

Jacques Prévert,
Paroles

© *Éditions Gallimard*

pour toi mon amour

Je suis allé au marché aux oiseaux
Et j'ai acheté des oiseaux
Pour toi
mon amour
Je suis allé au marché à la ferraille
Et j'ai acheté des chaînes
De lourdes chaînes
Pour toi
mon amour
Et puis je suis allé au marché aux esclaves
Et je t'ai cherchée
Mais je ne t'ai pas trouvée
mon amour

Jacques Prévert, *Paroles*

© *Éditions Gallimard*

D'UNE PAGE À L'AUTRE...

À l'aide des gros titres de ce *Magazine,* cherchez quels articles vous allez lire pour:

- trouver des informations historiques
- trouver des informations internationales
- découvrir l'utilisation d'un grand monument parisien
- identifier des tensions sociales et politiques
- lire un poème sur les marchés
- étudier les rapports entre la grammaire et les préjugés
- découvrir un groupe de musique international

- étudier les relations entre homme et femme
- obtenir des informations sur la langue et le genre des mots
- découvrir des chanteuses francophones
- découvrir une grande chercheuse scientifique
- étudier des innovations législatives québécoises
- lire un poème sur les fleurs

Avez-vous découvert le sujet de ce *Magazine?* Maintenant, choisissez un ordre de lecture pour ces articles.

Les arts et les lettres

ZAP MAMA. Associez chaque phrase du sous-titre avec un paragraphe de cet article. Soulignez les expressions qui indiquent le type de musique que produit Zap Mama.

POÈMES. Pour chaque poème dites qui parle. Dans chaque poème trouvez le mot ou l'expression qui correspond pour former une signification symbolique: petite fille / jeune fille / jolie femme / vieille femme / chaînes / je suis allé / j'ai pleuré.

Modèle *petite fille = fleurs fraîches*

Identifiez les sons et les couleurs de chaque poème. Lequel préférez-vous? Pourquoi?

Modèle *on voit des fleurs*

À LA LOUPE

L'ÉDITORIAL.

1. Trouvez le sujet du premier paragraphe et le sujet du troisième paragraphe. Comparez ces deux sujets.

2. *«Elles sont sorties de l'ombre, de la nuit des temps.»* D'après les autres articles sur cette page, indiquez l'événement essentiel qui est à l'origine du changement? Soulignez les autres événements qui ont contribué au changement. Lesquels sont universels? Lesquels sont spécifiques à la France?

3. Trouvez dans l'*Éditorial* les phrases que chaque article illustre:
   - Une femme au Panthéon
   - Masculin et féminin au Québec
   - Zap Mama
   - pour toi mon amour
   - Déjeuner du matin

UNE FEMME AU PANTHÉON. À l'aide des articles de la première page, faites la liste de ce que les femmes ne pouvaient pas faire quand Marie Curie était professeur et chercheuse à l'université de la Sorbonne?

REGARDS SUR LE MONDE

MASCULIN ET FÉMININ AU QUÉBEC. Complétez ce paragraphe avec des mots extraits de l'article.

Au Québec on veut ___ la langue parce que des professions ___ par des hommes sont maintenant ___ par des femmes. Par exemple, quand une femme est ___ ou ___ on peut dire maintenant ___ , ___ ou ___ . Les Québécois pensent que ces ___ vont contribuer à l'___ de la langue française. Mais la question est de savoir si on peut ___ les traditions patriarcales de la ___ française. L'idée à l'origine de cette loi est que la loi doit refléter les ___ ___ . Mais cette loi provoque aussi beaucoup de ___ et des ___ très ___ .

À VOTRE AVIS...

RECHERCHES.

1. Comparez la place de la France dans la course du XXIe siècle par rapport aux autres pays? Quelle sorte de société était la France traditionnelle? Et maintenant? (Voir aussi page 316, «*Le sais-tu?*»)

2. **Les rapports masculins** Est-ce qu'il y a un élément commun entre les trois poèmes? Lequel?

3. Présentez l'un des **hôtes célèbres** du Panthéon. Donnez ses dates et sa profession, et dites pourquoi il est célèbre.

ACTIONS

1. Préparez un bref discours pour l'arrivée au Panthéon de Marie Curie

2. Débat: pour ou contre la féminisation de la langue française. En groupe, préparez des arguments pour défendre votre point de vue.

CORRESPONDANCE.

1. Écrivez au Président de la république pour recommander de mettre une autre Française au Panthéon.

2. Préparez votre cv pour un des postes offerts dans les *Petites annonces classées.*

3. Écrivez au service immobilier de votre *Magazine* pour obtenir des informations supplémentaires sur les logements offerts. Indiquez la raison de votre recherche.

POUR FINIR.

1. Faites une liste des cinq mots les plus importants de ce *Magazine*.

2. Faites une liste de six mots que vous avez appris sans regarder le dictionnaire.

3. Dites quelles idées sont attachées aux mots **femme, égalité, libération** et **émancipation** pour une Française? Et pour une Québécoise? Et pour vous?

Une invitation chez les Dumas

En bref

Dans cette leçon...

- Les magasins, les restaurants et le marché
- Payer: argent, chèque, carte de crédit et pourboire
- Lire la carte et commander un repas au restaurant
- Les verbes **venir** et **voir**
- Les expressions de quantité
- Invitations et annonces: les pratiques sociales
- La cérémonie du thé au Sénégal

In this lesson...

- Stores, restaurants, and markets
- Paying for things: cash, check, credit card, and tips
- Reading menus and ordering meals
- The verbs **venir** and **voir**
- Quantity expressions
- Invitations and announcements: social practices
- Senegalese tea ceremony

---

www explore!
http://voila.heinle.com

Develop writing skills with Système-D software!

Practice listening and pronunciation skills with the Text Tape!

Discover the Francophone world!

Build your skills!

INTERNET **SYSTÈME-D** **TEXT TAPE** **VIDEO TAPE** **CD-ROM**

Students have an open-ended writing activity in the **Cahier** suitable for use with **Système-D**.

Avec les Compliments
des
Services Culturels
de
l'Ambassade de France

972 Fifth Avenue
New York, N.Y. 10021
(212) 570-4400

Vous êtes cordialement invités à la Fougère
pour la soirée qui suivra la cérémonie

Réponse souhaitée courant Juillet.

Fernand DAVIN
Vice-Président du Conseil Départemental des A.C.V.G.

Vous prie de bien vouloir honorer de votre présence la cérémonie de remise
de la Croix de Chevalier dans l'Ordre National du Mérite qui lui sera faite par

M. Le Batonnier Jean FORISSIER
Officier de la Légion d'Honneur
Officier de l'Ordre National du Mérite

en présence de

Monsieur LE PREFET
Commissaire de la République de la Région Auvergne
Commissaire de la République du Dép. du Puy-de-Dôme
Officier de la Légion d'Honneur
Officier de l'Ordre National du Mérite

et de M. Le Maire de ROYAT
et du Conseil Municipal

Le vendredi 19 Octobre à 18 heures, dans la salle des fêtes, place de Verdun à Royat.

"Les Chabesses" n° **93 B, 63130 ROYAT** - Tél. **04.03.24.18.36**

R.S.V.P.

*Ordre National
du Mérite*

Les annonces.

Voici beaucoup d'annonces. Quelles annonces sont des invitations?

Quelle annonce est la plus personnelle? la moins personnelle?

Quelle annonce est attachée à une autre annonce?

Devinez à quelle sorte d'annonce elle est probablement attachée.

Quelle annonce est triste?

Avec quelle annonce est-ce qu'on va manger? boire?

Quelle annonce demande une réponse?

Quelle annonce présente des vœux pour la Nouvelle année?

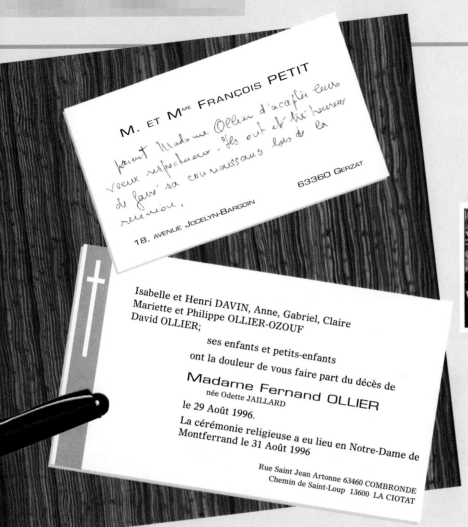

M. ET Mᵐᵉ FRANÇOIS PETIT

*présent Madame Ollier d'accepter leurs
voeux respectueux. Ils ont été très heureux
de faire sa connaissance lors de la
réunion,*

18, AVENUE JOCELYN-BARGOIN

63360 GERZAT

Isabelle et Henri DAVIN, Anne, Gabriel, Claire
Mariette et Philippe OLLIER-OZOUF
David OLLIER;

ses enfants et petits-enfants
ont la douleur de vous faire part du décès de

Madame Fernand OLLIER
née Odette JAILLARD

le 29 Août 1996.

La cérémonie religieuse a eu lieu en Notre-Dame de
Montferrand le 31 Août 1996

Rue Saint Jean Artonne 63460 COMBRONDE
Chemin de Saint-Loup 13600 LA CIOTAT

Info plus

Une annonce.
New Year's wishes can be sent until
mid-January in France.

Les photos.

Quelle photo est triste? À quelle annonce est-elle associée?

Quelle photo est heureuse? À quelle annonce est-elle attachée?

Les relations familiales.
Y a-t-il des personnes de la même famille? Dites comment
elles sont alliées.

Qui est Fernand Davin? Pour qui est la carte de Monsieur et Madame Petit? Quelle
est la date de la carte, à votre avis?

Les villes.
Quelles villes sont dans la même région de France? Quand l'invitation à
la Fougère a-t-elle été envoyée? Pour quelle occasion?

Les décorations.
Quelles décorations honorent les Français? Soulignez ces
décorations. Soulignez les titres. Comment appelle-t-on une personne officielle en
France? Et chez vous?

Les relations familiales: There are no
set answers; students are encouraged to
guess. Useful for review of family
members. Encourage students to
explore all relationships.

Les décorations: La Légion d'Honneur,
created by Napoleon Bonaparte, is a
hierarchized civil military honor awarded
by the President in recognition of
services to the country. (The hierarchies
are: **chevalier, officier, commandeur,
grand croix.**) Other awards are **L'Ordre
National du Mérite** and **Les Palmes
Académiques,** given as cultural and
educational awards to French citizens
and other people in the world.

Vocabulaire

Bon, alors, comme entrée...

Alain et Sophie Dumas ont des invités ce soir: le patron de Sophie et sa femme. C'est une soirée importante pour eux, alors ils sont très occupés tous les deux.

A. D'abord, ils doivent faire les courses.

Alain achète du pain à la boulangerie, des gâteaux à la pâtisserie, un rôti à la boucherie, 500 grammes de pâté et des tranches de jambon à la charcuterie. Il va aussi à l'épicerie pour acheter un litre de lait, deux boîtes de petits pois et deux ou trois fromages. Et pour le vin? Ils veulent ouvrir une ou deux bonnes bouteilles de vin rouge qu'ils ont dans leur cave.

Info plus

Les magasins.

Although the French often do their shopping at a **supermarché** or even an enormous **hypermarché,** many people like to shop at smaller, more specialized stores in their neighborhoods. Here are some examples:

- **une épicerie** *neighborhood grocery store*
- **une boucherie** *beef butcher (also sells mutton)*
- **une charcuterie** *pork butcher (also sells chicken, rabbit, and prepared dishes); ressembles a delicatessen*
- **une boucherie-charcuterie** *combination* **boucherie** *and* **charcuterie**
- **une pâtisserie** *pastry shop (may also sell candy and ice cream)*
- **une boulangerie** *bread bakery (may also sell cakes and chocolates)*
- **une boulangerie-pâtisserie** *combination* **boulangerie** *and* **pâtisserie**

BOULANGERIE

PÂTISSERIE

CHARCUTERIE

EPICERIE FRUITS CREMERIE

ÉPICERIE

BOUCHERIE

Sophie va au marché pour acheter un melon, deux kilos de pommes de terre, un kilo de carottes, un kilo de tomates, des champignons et une grosse laitue.

- Qui est-ce que Sophie et Alain ont invité ce soir? Pourquoi est-ce que c'est une soirée importante, à votre avis? Qu'est-ce qu'Alain achète? Où? Et Sophie? À votre avis, qu'est-ce qu'ils vont préparer pour ce soir? Faites le menu (soupe? entrée? plat principal? après le plat principal? dessert? boissons?).

Ask students: **Quels mots est-ce que vous associez à «un marché»?** If necessary, tell students that a **marché** is an open-air market. The goal is to help students access the schemata of *open-air market* in their culture before discussing the concept of a **marché** in France.

Info plus

Le marché.

The **marché** is a common sight in French cities and towns. **Le marché** takes place at least once a week in a central location. Farmers from neighboring villages come to sell their fresh produce. You can also buy dairy products, **charcuterie,** inexpensive clothing, and various other items. Prices at the market are usually similar to the prices in grocery stores, but the freshness of the produce causes many people to make a special effort to go to the **marché** once or twice a week.

B. Ensuite, ils mettent la table.

TRANSPARENCY:
13-2

Qu'est-ce qu'il y a au milieu de la table? Qu'est-ce qu'il y a à gauche des assiettes? À droite des assiettes? Qu'est-ce qu'il y a devant les verres? Pourquoi est-ce qu'il y a deux fourchettes? deux verres?

C. Malheureusement, dans la cuisine, tout va mal...

La sauce a débordé, le chat a renversé le lait, le chien a pris le fromage et le rôti a brûlé.

- Qu'est-ce qu'il n'y a plus pour ce soir?

D. Au restaurant

- Où est-ce qu'ils mangent ce soir? Pourquoi? Est-ce que les Dumas sont heureux? Pourquoi, à votre avis?

E. Et à deux heures du matin...

> Ce n'était pas un restaurant bon marché!

> Tu parles! Heureusement qu'on avait une carte de crédit!

de la monnaie
l'addition
une carte de crédit
un chéquier
une tasse
une boîte de chocolats

- Qu'est-ce qu'il y a sur la table? Qu'est-ce que les Michaut ont apporté comme cadeau? Et chez vous, qu'est-ce qu'on offre quand on est invité à dîner?
- Regardez bien l'addition. Comment s'appelle le restaurant? Quelle sorte de restaurant est-ce que c'est? Combien a coûté le repas? Ça fait combien en dollars? C'est cher ou c'est bon marché? Est-ce que le service est compris dans l'addition ou est-ce qu'il faut laisser un pourboire? Est-ce que les Dumas ont payé en liquide, par chèque ou avec une carte de crédit?
- Quels sont les plats chauds? les plats froids? Quelles sont les entrées? les plats principaux? les desserts? les boissons? Qu'est-ce que c'est, un Beaujolais?
- À votre avis, qu'est-ce que Madame Michaut a commandé? Et Monsieur Michaut? Qui n'a pas pris de dessert? Est-ce qu'ils ont bu beaucoup de vin?

Le Belvédère

Le 10-4-91
Table C
4 couverts

2 Soupes à l'oignon	80,00
1 Crudités	30,00
1 Pâté maison	40,00
1 Poisson grillé	90,00
1 Steak au poivre vert	110,00
1 Côte d'agneau	110,00
1 Tagliatelle aux champignons	60,00
1 Beaujolais	90,00
1 Eau	20,00
1 Mousse au chocolat	50,00
1 Profiterole	50,00
2 Cafés	30,00
1 Expresso	20,00
1 Thé	15,00
Montant	795,00
Service 18 %	143,00
Total	938,00

TRANSPARENCY: 13-4

Ask students: **Vous êtes invités à dîner chez les parents d'un/une ami/e. Qu'est-ce que vous apportez comme cadeau?**

Info plus

Venez dîner!

French homes are very private places. People do not just "drop by" unannounced, and an invitation to a meal or a visit is a special privilege. It is considered polite to bring a gift if you are invited to eat at someone's home, usually candy (especially chocolates) or flowers. It is also important to thank your host or hostess for an invitation to his or her home when leaving. After a longer stay, a thank-you note will make a good impression.

Ask students: **Est-ce que vous laissez un pourboire quand vous mangez au restaurant? Combien?**

Info plus

Au restaurant.

La carte is a list of the various dishes available in a restaurant. It is the equivalent of the English *menu*. In a French restaurant, **le menu** is a fixed-price meal. You pay one price and get your choice of two or three items in each course listed. It is almost always cheaper to order **le menu** than to order **à la carte**. The words **service compris** or **service inclus** on a menu mean that a service charge (usually between 15 and 20 percent) will automatically be added to your bill. An additional tip (**un pourboire**) is not expected, although you may leave a small amount if you wish. If you want to ask whether a service charge is included or not, ask: **Est-ce que le service est compris?**

Info plus

La pharmacie.

Medicine, cosmetics, and similar products are sold at **une pharmacie**. **Une pharmacie** does not, however, stock the wide variety of merchandise found in an American drugstore. **Le pharmacien** or **la pharmacienne** is frequently consulted about health matters.

F. Dans la salle de bains

- Où sont-ils maintenant? Quelle heure est-il, à votre avis? Qu'est-ce qu'Alain cherche? Pourquoi? Est-ce qu'il y a une pharmacie ouverte la nuit, à votre avis?

G. À table

Notes de vocabulaire

1. Mots et expressions utiles.

combien est-ce que je vous dois?	*how much do I owe you?*
un doigt	*finger*
fermé(e)	*closed*
fermer	*to close*
gratuit(e)	*free (of charge)*
une main	*hand*
utiliser	*to use*

2. Assiette / plat. **Une assiette** is a *plate.* **Un plat** may be either a *serving dish* or the *food* on the serving dish.

2: Ask students what **plat du jour** might mean.

3. Payer. The verb **payer** has a spelling change in the present tense. The -y- changes to -i- in all but the **nous** and **vous** forms.

3: Note that the spelling change for verbs like **payer** is optional (**je paie** or **je paye,** etc.).

je paie	nous payons
tu paies	vous payez
il elle } paie	ils elles } paient

Note that no preposition is used with **payer.**

Qui va **payer** le repas?	*Who's going to pay for the meal?*

4. Tout. The adjective **tout** means *all.* Here are its forms.

	MASCULINE	FEMININE
SINGULAR	tout	toute
PLURAL	tous	toutes

In the following sentences, note the pattern **tout** + *definite article* + *noun.*

Ma sœur étudie **tout le temps.**	*My sister studies all the time.*
Tu as **tous les verres?**	*Do you have all the glasses?*
Le bébé du premier étage a pleuré **toute la nuit.**	*The baby on the second floor cried all night.*
Toutes les filles sont arrivées.	*All the girls have arrived.*

Tout as a pronoun means *all* or *everything.*

Tout va bien?	*Is everything going OK?*
C'est **tout?**	*Is that all? Is that it?*

Here are some common expressions using **tout**.

tout de suite	*right away, at once*
tout le monde	*everyone, everybody*
tout le temps	*all the time*
tous les jours	*every day*
tous les deux	*both*
pas du tout	*not at all*
tout à coup	*suddenly, all of a sudden*
tout à fait	*completely, absolutely*
tout droit	*straight ahead*

5. Je n'ai plus faim. Use the expression **Je n'ai plus faim** to say that you have had enough to eat or that you are full.

6. Non, merci! How do you accept second helpings? And, more importantly, how do you refuse politely?

- To accept, you can say: **Oui, merci** or **Oui, je veux bien, merci (c'est délicieux)**. If you just say **Merci,** in this context, it means *No, thank you*.

- To refuse, you can say: **(Non) merci** or, to be more polite, **(Non) merci, c'est délicieux, mais je n'ai vraiment plus faim.**

7. J'ai mal à la tête! To say that you hurt somewhere, use the expression **avoir mal (à)**.

J'**ai mal!**	*I hurt!*
Tu **as mal à** la tête?	*You have a headache?*
J'**ai mal à** la main.	*My hand hurts.*

8. Les verbes ouvrir et offrir. The verbs **ouvrir** *(to open)* and **offrir** *(to offer, to give)* are irregular. **Offrir** is conjugated like **ouvrir**.

8: Point out that **ouvrir** is conjugated like an **-er** verb although its infinitive ends in **-ir**. Have students redo the conjugation examples of **ouvrir** with **offrir**.

DRILL: **Nous ouvrons la fenêtre.** (vous / Candide et Alceste / tu / je / ma sœur)

DRILL: **Qui a ouvert la fenêtre? C'est Candide! Il a ouvert la fenêtre!** (Alceste / moi, je / vous / toi, tu / nous)

DRILL: **J'offre un beau cadeau** (vous / Thérèse et Vincent / ma mère / tu / nous)

PRÉSENT	j'ouvre	nous ouvrons
	tu ouvres	vous ouvrez
	il elle } ouvre	ils elles } ouvrent
IMPARFAIT	j'ouvrais, etc.	
PASSÉ COMPOSÉ	j'ai ouvert, etc.	
IMPÉRATIF	ouvre! ouvrez! ouvrons!	

D'accord?

A. Magasins Qu'est-ce qu'on vend?

1. **Dans une boulangerie:** du jambon / des lits / des croissants / des chaussures / du pain / des bonbons / du chocolat / des ascenseurs
2. **Dans une charcuterie:** du pâté / du saucisson / des livres / des plantes vertes / des crayons / du jambon
3. **Dans une boucherie:** des cadeaux / des gants / des fraises / un rôti / des ordinateurs / de la viande
4. **Dans une pâtisserie:** des jupes / des gâteaux / des boîtes de chocolats / des tartes / des fauteuils / des pâtisseries / des couteaux / de la glace / des tomates
5. **Dans une épicerie:** du sucre / du café / des chapeaux / du fromage / des légumes / des plats surgelés / des pulls / des tapis / du thé / des boîtes de conserve
6. **Dans une pharmacie:** du café / des stylos / des médicaments / des livres / de l'aspirine

B. Associations Quel mot—**un kilo, une bouteille, une boîte, un morceau** ou **une tranche**—est-ce que vous associez aux produits suivants?

Modèle du saucisson
une tranche, un morceau...

1. du lait
2. des tomates
3. de la soupe
4. du vin
5. du fromage
6. des petits pois
7. des pommes de terre
8. du jambon
9. du pâté
10. des haricots verts

C. Payons Comment est-ce que vous payez?

Modèle Vous achetez une veste.
Je paie en liquide (par chèque, avec une carte de crédit).

1. Vous achetez une glace.
2. Vous achetez une robe élégante.
3. Vous restez une nuit à l'hôtel.
4. Vous prenez un repas dans un restaurant bon marché.
5. Vous achetez un ordinateur.
6. Vous allez au cinéma.
7. Vous achetez un gâteau à la pâtisserie.
8. Vous allez au supermarché.

D. Avec quoi? Qu'est-ce qu'on utilise pour manger...

1. des petits pois?
2. des frites?
3. du poulet?
4. un pamplemousse?
5. une poire?
6. de la salade?
7. une pizza?
8. un sandwich?

Act. D: Ask students: Qu'est-ce que vous n'utilisez pas pour manger...

E. Quel cadeau? Quel cadeau est-ce que vous allez offrir?

Modèle   Vous allez dîner chez votre professeur.
          J'offre une boîte de chocolats.

1. Vous allez dîner chez les parents d'un ami.
2. Vous allez dans une famille où il y a beaucoup d'enfants pour le week-end.
3. Vous allez à une fête chez des copains pour l'anniversaire d'une amie.
4. Vous allez dans une famille française pour le mois de juillet.

F. Qu'est-ce qu'on ouvre? Faites une liste de ce qu'on ouvre.

Modèle   ***On ouvre les fenêtres,...***

Mise en pratique

A. Chez... Vous allez ouvrir un nouveau bistrot français dans votre région.

1. Donnez un nom à votre restaurant.
2. Faites la carte. Est-ce qu'il va y avoir un menu? Des plats à la carte? Combien vont-ils coûter?

B. Au restaurant Hippopotamus à Toulouse

1. Regardez la carte du restaurant Hippopotamus à Toulouse et répondez aux questions.
   • Quand est-ce que le restaurant est ouvert?
   • Qu'est-ce qui est compris dans le prix?
   • Avec quoi est-ce qu'on peut payer?
   • Qu'est-ce qui est moins cher, commander un menu ou commander à la carte?
   • Qu'est-ce qu'on peut avoir pour 62,50 F? Et pour 99,50 F?
   • Qu'est-ce qu'on peut commander avec la viande?
   • Si on prend le menu, qu'est-ce qu'on peut boire?

2. Voilà des personnes qui ont mangé au restaurant Hippopotamus. Qu'est-ce qu'elles ont commandé?
   • **Les Mercier:** M. Mercier, 36 ans, médecin; Mme Mercier, 35 ans, avocate. Ils ont mangé au restaurant Hippopotamus avec leurs deux enfants (4 ans et 6 ans) le dimanche 15 février à midi.
   • **M. et Mme Spalding:** M. Spalding, 70 ans, retraité, était professeur de français dans une université américaine; Mme Spalding, 68 ans, était professeur d'espagnol dans une université américaine. Ils ont déjeuné au restaurant Hippopotamus le mardi 8 juillet. M. Spalding était au régime.
   • **Christophe, Étienne et Brigitte:** des étudiants entre 18 et 20 ans. Ils sont arrivés au restaurant à 22 h 30 (après le cinéma) le samedi 22 avril. Ils avaient très faim.
   • **Alceste et Candide:** Ils sont arrivés au restaurant à 18 heures le vendredi 19 octobre avant d'aller au cinéma. Candide avait très faim. Alceste ne voulait pas passer des heures au restaurant parce que le film commençait à 19 heures.

HIPPOPTAMUS

Les restaurants Hippopotamus sont ouverts tous les jours sans interruption de 11 h 30 à 1 h du matin.

Si vous réglez par chèque, merci de présenter une pièce d'identité. Pour tout paiement, un ticket doit être exigé. Bien sûr, vous pouvez payer par Carte Bleue, Visa et American Express, Eurochèque, Traveller chèque et chèques libellés en Francs Français, ainsi que par titre restaurant. Nous avons le regret de refuser la monnaie étrangère, les chèques sur pays étrangers et les chèques sociétés.

Prix Service Compris (16% / HT).

HIPPO ATOUT
99,50 F

L'Entrée
Œufs pochés à la ciboulette
ou Carpaccio de tomates fraiches
ou Rillettes aux deux saumons
ou Tarama

Le Plat
accompagné de pommes allumettes ou pomme
au four ou haricots verts, servis à volonté.
Bavette
ou Brochette de bœuf
ou Chili con carne
ou Saumon à la plancha

Le Dessert
Mousse au chocolat
ou Crème caramel
ou Ananas en carpaccio
ou Coupe aux trois fraicheurs
ou Coupe délice

La Boisson
Pichet (31 cl) de vin de pays
des Bouches-du-Rhône
ou de Côtes du Lubéron rosé
ou Tourtel Pur Malt (25 cl) sans alcool
ou Bière Gold de Kanterbräu (33 cl)
ou Coca-Cola (33 cl)
ou 1/2 Eau minérale (50 cl)

Les Entrées

Salade de saison	15,00 F
Tarama	34,00 F
Carpaccio de tomates fraîches	28,50 F
Œufs pochés à la ciboulette	26,00 F
Rillettes aux deux saumons	36,00 F
Terrine campagnarde	33,00 F
Cocktail de crevettes	36,00 F
Crottin de chèvre chaud	34,50 F

Les Grillés

Bavette	74,50 F
Hippo Mixed Grill	84,50 F
Entrecôte	88,00 F
T. Bone	99,50 F
Saumon à la Plancha	78,50 F
Chili con carne	63,00 F

Les Sauces
Relevez vos grillés selon votre humeur avec:
une sauce béarnaise,
une sauce roquefort,
une sauce échalotes,
une sauce aux deux poivres,
un beurre maître d'hôtel ou la Spéciale Hippo.

Les Garnitures
Chacun de nos grillés est accompagné, au choix, de pommes allumettes, de pommes au four ou d'haricots verts servis à volonté.

HIPPO MALIN
62,50 F

Le Plat
Accompagné de pommes allumettes
ou pomme au four ou haricots verts,
servis à volonté.

Magic Hamburger
ou Steak Hippo
ou Poulet Super Grill

La Boisson
Un verre (12.5 cl)
de Vin de pays
des Bouches-du-Rhône

ou 1/2 Eau minérale (50 cl)

ou Bière Stella Artois (33 cl)

ou Tourtel Pur Malt (25 cl)
sans alcool

ou Coca-Cola (33 cl)

C. Conversation en français Vous voyagez en Europe pendant l'été. C'est le mois d'août et vous êtes à Toulouse. Il est deux heures de l'après-midi et vous avez très faim mais vous n'êtes pas très riche! Allez au restaurant Hippopotamus, choisissez une table, regardez la carte et commandez un repas.

Structure

▶▶ Le verbe *venir*

The verb **venir** *(to come)* is irregular in the present tense. Notice the double **-n-** in the third person plural form.

je viens	nous venons
tu viens	vous venez
il elle } vient	ils elles } vie**nn**ent

Il **vient** manger chez nous après le film.	*He's coming to eat at our house after the movie.*

Venir is conjugated with **être** in the **passé composé.** The past participle of **venir** is **venu.**

Elle **est venue** le premier février.	*She came on the first of February.*

The **imparfait** of **venir** is regular.

Ils **venaient** toujours à huit heures.	*They always came at eight o'clock.*

The imperative or command forms of **venir** are identical to the present tense forms.

Viens chez moi!	*Come to my house!*
Venez à onze heures!	*Come at eleven!*
Venons à trois heures!	*Let's come at three!*

Venir + **de** + *infinitif* means *to have just* + *verb (past participle)* or the equivalent expression in the simple past.

Je **viens de manger.** Je n'ai plus faim.	*I've just eaten. (I just ate.)* *I'm not hungry anymore.*

Vous avez compris?

A. Une réunion de famille
C'est une réunion de famille chez Thérèse et Vincent Dubois. Utilisez **venir** au présent pour compléter la conversation.

THÉRÈSE: Suzanne ..... avec ses parents?

VINCENT: Non, elle et Abder ..... ensemble.

THÉRÈSE: Bon, d'accord, et ton père, il ..... , n'est-ce pas?

VINCENT: Oui, et Paulette Gilmard ..... avec lui.

THÉRÈSE: Et toi, tu ..... ou non?

VINCENT: Moi, je ne sais pas. Je dois travailler mais, oui, je ..... !

B. Après la réunion de famille
Il y a quelques (some) membres de la famille Dubois qui ne sont pas partis avec les personnes avec qui ils sont arrivés! Utilisez **venir** et **partir** au passé composé pour le dire.

1. Cédric Rasquin ..... avec sa mère et son mari (son beau-père) mais il ..... avec son père.
2. Jacques Dubois et Paulette Gilmard ..... ensemble mais Paulette ..... seule.
3. Suzanne ..... avec Abder mais elle ..... avec ses parents.
4. Jean Rasquin ..... seul mais il ..... avec son fils.

C. Les habitudes
M. Caron, le patron du Café de la Poste, discute des habitudes de ses clients d'il y a des années. Utilisez l'imparfait de **venir** pour le dire.

Modèle M. Ségal (tous les jours pour l'apéritif)
M. Ségal venait tous les jours pour l'apéritif.

1. Mme Ségal (ne jamais)
2. M. Meunier (tout le temps)
3. M. Piette et sa femme (le dimanche)
4. Mme Renard et M. Renglet (quelquefois le samedi)

D. Ce n'est pas vrai!
Candide ne peut pas croire (believe) ce que tout le monde vient de faire. Utilisez **venir de** + *infinif* pour le dire (to say this).

Modèle Mes parents / arriver.
Mes parents viennent d'arriver! Ce n'est pas vrai!

1. Michel et Sandrine / partir / à Tahiti.
2. Il est huit heures du matin et tu / manger / une pizza.
3. Vous / acheter / une voiture de sport!
4. Jean-Pierre / vendre / son ordinateur.
5. Alceste / rire (laugh).

Act A & B: These activities go together and are suitable for encouraging students to speculate about what might have happened. One strategy is to treat the two activities as simple fill-in-the-blank verb exercises (students will tend to pay little if any attention to meaning). Then go back and re-read them, making a list on the board or a transparency of who came with whom and with whom they left (e.g., **Jacques Dubois et Paulette Gilmard sont venus ensemble mais Paulette est partie seule. Pourquoi? Un problème entre elle et Jacques? Jacques voulait rester et Paulette était fatiguée**, etc.).

Act. B: Remind students that **partir** is conjugated with **être** in the **passé composé.**

Act. C: The people in this activity were presented in *Leçon 12.* If desired, ask students what they remember about them before doing the activity.

Continuons!

A. Mais pourquoi? Qu'est-ce qu'ils viennent de faire?

Modèle Tu n'as plus soif.
> *C'est parce que tu viens de boire un Coca-Cola.*

1. Abder a soif.
2. Nous sommes fatigués.
3. Nous n'avons plus d'argent.
4. Les Dubois sont malades.

5. J'ai très froid.
6. Céline a très chaud.
7. Thérèse est contente.
8. Alceste est très triste.

B. D'où venez-vous? Utilisez ces questions pour trouver d'où vient tout le monde.

De quelle ville...

1. ... vient votre père?
2. ... viennent vos grands-parents?

3. ... vient votre professeur de français?
4. ... venez-vous?

➤ Les expressions de quantité

Expressions of quantity are followed by **de** + *noun*. There is no article. Expressions of quantity may be either nouns (**un verre de lait**) or adverbs (**trop de lait**). In both cases, the pattern is *quantity expression* + **de (d')** + *noun*.

> Tu veux **un morceau de fromage?** *Do you want a piece of cheese?*
> Il mange **trop de chocolat.** *He eats too much chocolate.*

Here is a list of quantity expressions that you already know.

assez de	enough (of)
une assiette de	a plate of
beaucoup de	a lot of
une boîte de	a box of
une bouteille de	a bottle of
un kilo de	one kilo of
un morceau de	a piece of
un peu de	a little, a little bit of
une tasse de	a cup of
une tranche de	a slice of
trop de	too much of, too many of
un verre de	a glass of

Rappel!

1. When talking in general and after verbs such as **aimer** and **détester**, use **le, la, l',** or **les** (definite articles).

> Je n'**aime** pas **les** petits pois! *I don't like peas.*
> **Les** petits pois sont bons pour toi. *Peas are good for your health.*

Act. A: The reverse chronology of this activity may prove difficult for some students. If desired, recast it: *Tu viens de boire un Coca-Cola, donc tu n'as plus soif.*

Act. B: If desired, give the name of countries as needed. Model answers by first going through the activity and giving answers for yourself. (**Mon père vient de Californie mais mes grands-parents viennent de Belgique. Moi, je viens aussi de Californie.**) If desired, ask students to produce similar brief monologs.

The *Rappel* section reviews concepts first presented in *Leçons 1, 3,* and *9.*

2. When you are not talking in general, use either the indefinite article or the partitive article.

   a. If you are talking about things you can count, use **un, une,** or **des** (indefinite article).

   Tu veux **des** petits pois?   *Do you want (some) peas?*
   Mangeons **une** pomme!   *Let's eat an apple!*

   b. If you are talking about things that you cannot count, use **du, de la,** or **de l'** (partitive article).

   Tu veux **du** lait?   *Do you want (some) milk?*

3. After expressions of quantity, use **de** followed directly by a noun (no article).

   Tu veux **un verre de** lait?   *Do you want a glass of milk?*
   Il boit **beaucoup de** lait.   *He drinks a lot of milk.*
   Vous mangez **trop de** frites.   *You eat too many French fries.*

4. After negative expressions, **un, une, du, de la, de l',** and **des** all become **de (d').** **Le, la, l',** and **les** remain the same.

   Lui, il aime **les** vieilles maisons mais elle n'aime pas **les** vieilles maisons. Elle préfère **les** appartements modernes. Alors, il a **une** vieille maison mais elle **n'**a **pas de** maison du tout.

   Il **n'**y a **plus de** lait dans le frigo.
   Candide **ne** boit **jamais de** vin.

Vous avez compris?

A. Normal ou pas? Est-ce que c'est normal ou pas normal, ou est-ce que ça dépend?

1. une tasse de bière	7. une boîte de petits pois
2. un kilo de pommes de terre	8. un kilo de Coca-Cola
3. un morceau de lait	9. une tranche de jambon
4. une tranche de glace	10. un verre de jus d'orange
5. un morceau de fromage	11. une boîte de frites
6. une tasse de thé	12. une bouteille de sucre

B. Des quantités Soyez logique pour compléter les expressions.

Modèle   une tasse
    une tasse de thé, une tasse de café, etc.

1. une assiette
2. un kilo
3. une tasse
4. un verre
5. une tranche
6. une bouteille

Continuons!

A. Combien? Utilisez une expression de quantité pour compléter les phrases.

1. Patrick a bu ..... vin: il est malade.
2. Je n'ai pas ..... argent: je dois aller à la banque.
3. Les Lange ont ..... travail: ils ont huit enfants, deux chiens et une grande maison.
4. J'ai ..... argent, mais pas assez pour acheter une glace.
5. Est-ce que vous prenez ..... sucre dans votre café?
6. Bonjour, Madame. Je voudrais ..... haricots verts, ... lait, ... saucisson, ... soupe aux tomates, ... fromage et ..... vin blanc, s'il vous plaît.

Act. B: There may be more than one possible choice depending on interpretation (e.g., **une salade / de la salade**).

B. Le frigo de Mlle Piggy Complétez avec **un, une, d', des, le, la, l', les, du, de la, de l', ou de.)**

Mlle Piggy aime Kermit la grenouille (*frog*) et elle aime aussi manger! Elle aime ..... gâteaux au chocolat, ... glace et ..... bonbons. Elle aime aussi ..... tarte aux pommes et ..... pâtisseries. Maintenant, la pauvre Mlle Piggy est au régime parce que Kermit trouve qu'elle est trop grosse. Alors, dans son frigo, il y a beaucoup ..... légumes et ..... fruits. C'est tout. Le matin, elle prend ..... tasse ..... thé et ..... morceau ..... pain. À midi, elle prend ..... yaourt ou ..... assiette ..... crudités. Le soir, elle prend ..... salade avec ..... verre ..... lait. Elle ne mange jamais ..... frites et elle ne boit plus ..... bière. Mais elle peut prendre un peu ..... vin. Mais, même (*even*) quand Mlle Piggy est mince et n'est pas au régime, il n'y a pas ..... jambon dans son frigo! Et est-ce qu'il y a ..... cuisses de grenouille (*frog legs*)? Mais non, il n'y a pas ..... cuisses de grenouille! Quelle horreur!

▶▶ Le verbe *voir*

If desired, tell students that the imperative or command forms of **voir** are identical with the present tense forms. However, these forms are rarely used in the literal sense because of semantic implausibility. The infinitive, on the other hand, is frequently used with imperative force (for example, **voir la page 121**). The first person plural imperative form is frequently used idiomatically to express encouragement, often with an undertone of displeasure (**un peu de silence, voyons**), or to express some hesitation (**voyons, comme entrée...**).

DRILL: **Je ne vois rien. (tu / Candide / je / Candide et Alceste / nous)**

The present tense of the verb **voir** (*to see*) is irregular.

je vois	nous voyons
tu vois	vous voyez
il } elle } voit	ils } elles } voient

Qu'est-ce que tu **vois?**   *What do you see?*
Je ne **vois** rien.   *I don't see anything.*

Voir is regular in the **imparfait.**

Quand j'avais quinze ans, j'avais un petit ami que je **voyais** tous les jours.
When I was 15, I had a boyfriend that I saw every day.

The **passé composé** of **voir** is conjugated with **avoir**. The past participle of **voir** is **vu**.

Tu n'**as** pas **vu** mon chien?   *You haven't seen my dog?*

DRILL: Je n'ai rien vu. (tu / Candide / je / Candide et Alceste / nous)

Vous avez compris?

A. De la fenêtre... Voilà ce que tout le monde voit de sa fenêtre. Utilisez le verbe **voir** au présent pour le dire *(to say this)*.

1. Candide / des arbres.
2. Tu / un mur!
3. Daniel et Guy / des voitures.
4. Nous / la rue.
5. Je / des personnes qui marchent dans la rue.
6. Vous / la fenêtre du couple qui habite en face.

Act. A: FOLLOW-UP: Ask students what they can see from their windows, from the classroom windows, or from their favorite vantage point.

B. Dans les rêves Voilà ce que différentes personnes ont vu dans leur rêve *(dream)* la nuit dernière. Utilisez le verbe **voir** au passé composé pour le dire *(to say this)*.

1. Je . . . . . un chien orange.
2. Candide . . . . . un chat vert qui parlait espagnol.
3. Alceste . . . . . un homme qui portait cinq chapeaux.
4. Nous . . . . . un monstre qui nous a demandé de venir avec lui.
5. Tu . . . . . le professeur qui marchait avec un grand chien noir?
6. Mes petites sœurs . . . . . une belle femme habillée en blanc.
7. Vous . . . . . une voiture qui était grande comme une maison!

Act. B: Ask students to rank the dreams from most to least bizarre. Ask them to make up other dream sightings.

Continuons!

Les contacts perdus Il y a des personnes qu'on voyait avant mais qu'on ne voit plus maintenant. Utilisez le verbe **voir** à l'imparfait pour le dire *(to say this)*.

Modèle En été, Claudine / sa tante Irène tout le temps, mais maintenant, elle...
En été, Claudine voyait sa tante Irène tout le temps, mais maintenant, elle ne la voit plus.

1. Avant, tu / tes cousins tout le temps, mais maintenant, tu...
2. L'année dernière, mon mari et moi, nous / les Dumont tout le temps, mais maintenant, nous...
3. Quand vous aviez dix ans, vous / vos grands-parents tout le temps, mais maintenant, vous...
4. Pendant l'hiver, Alceste / ses copains au café tout le temps, mais maintenant, il...
5. Quand elles étaient jeunes, Anne et Claire / leur père tout le temps, mais maintenant, elles...
6. À l'université, je / Jean-Luc tout le temps, mais maintenant, je...

Les contacts perdus: Given the complexity and length of the responses, this activity works best as a written exercise.
   FOLLOW-UP: Ask students for possible reasons why these people no longer see each other.

Découvertes culturelles: La vie en société

⇒ Pour un beau dîner

A. Préparation. Qu'est-ce qu'il faut pour mettre la table (mettre le couvert) pour un dîner élégant?

Modèle *Il faut des verres, des fourchettes, etc.*

Act. B: Help students pronounce and understand the names of objects: **fourchette à poisson, fourchette à rôti, la petite cuillère,** etc. Make a transparency or copy of the picture and have students write the names of objects with an arrow for each. Review **à gauche, à droite, devant, de l'autre côté, à côté de,** etc., prior to doing this activity.

B. Mettre le couvert.

1. Regardez le texte et nommez les objets qui sont sur la table. Indiquez leur place sur la table par rapport aux autres objets.

   Modèle *Il y a deux fourchettes, la fourchette à poisson, qui est...*

2. Nommez les objets de décoration sur la table.

Savez-vous mettre le couvert?

Règle d'or d'un couvert agréable à regarder: l'alignement et la symétrie des éléments.

Vous disposez les couverts dans l'ordre de leur usage: si l'on doit commencer par du poisson, les couverts à poisson se trouveront à droite du couvert à rôti.

Les verres sont alignés par ordre de taille: verre à eau, verre à vin rouge, verre à vin blanc (le plus petit). La coupe à champagne, légèrement en retrait sur cette photo, peut également être alignée à gauche du verre à eau, ou ne pas figurer sur la table: de nos jours, on boit souvent le champagne en apéritif et non plus au dessert.

La serviette se trouve à droite, le pain à gauche. La cruche à eau et la salière sont à disposition des convives. Le vin, servi en carafe ou dans sa bouteille, est apporté au dernier moment. Les couverts à dessert n'apparaissent qu'avec le dernier changement d'assiettes.

Mettre le couvert peut être une opération sophistiquée, mais il suffit d'un rien pour lui donner un air de fête: une jolie nappe, un bouquet, un bougeoir, des petits pains dorés, et voilà! Bon appétit!

C. Le repas.

1. Imaginez le menu qui va être servi et présentez-le avec tous les plats et leurs noms. N'oubliez pas les boissons.
2. Comparez cette table avec une table de cérémonie dans votre culture. Quelles sont les occasions pour un beau dîner? Quelles sont les différences? les similarités?

> **Modèle** *Chez moi, on prépare une belle table pour... , avec...*
> *On décore avec...*

Act C, 1: Could be drawn and designed as if it were to be placed on a card next to the plate of each guest. Refer students to the menu in *Leçon 9* and have them present their menu with the occasion indicated, date, place, etc.

D. L'apéritif.

1. À quelle cérémonie associez-vous le champagne? À quel moment du dîner vient le champagne traditionnellement? Trouvez dans le texte la nouvelle pratique du champagne.
2. **Étude ethnologique.** Pour découvrir la pratique française de l'apéritif, imaginez que vous êtes ethnologue et préparez cinq questions que vous allez poser à votre professeur.

Act. D: You may want to ask students to also investigate the topic of champagne. The www would be one good source.

TDC pour l'élève

Un joli couvert

➤ Une tradition sénégalaise

A. Préparation. Dans quelles cultures est-ce qu'on boit du thé? Quand? Avec qui? Est-ce qu'il y a des cérémonies?

Act. B: Refer students to the text— a professor's **Journal de voyage.** The tea ceremony takes a long time, since the stove does not heat the water fast.

B. La cérémonie du thé.

1. Regardez la photo à la page 341. Qui prépare le thé? Où? Avec quoi? Cherchez dans le **Journal de voyage** le nom des objets employés par la jeune fille. Quels sont les ingrédients employés pour faire le thé?
2. La cérémonie du thé compte combien de tasses de thé? Pourquoi est-ce qu'on appelle le moment du thé une cérémonie?
3. Pouvez-vous évaluer combien de temps dure la préparation du thé?
4. Quel est le pays d'origine de la cérémonie du thé? Dans les objets nécessaires pour préparer le thé, il y a un objet qui vient de Madagascar. Pouvez-vous trouver lequel?

C. Mots nouveaux.

1. Trouvez sur la page du **Journal de voyage** un synonyme de **boire**, de **appréciées**, de **différent**.
2. Trouvez d'autres mots pour dire **une petite boule** et **couper très fin**.

Act. D: Ask students to produce a few sentences. They will have to infer this from information in the text. Suggest that they use expressions from the **Journal de voyage**.

D. Rituels et cérémonies. Identifiez quels aspects de la culture sénégalaise cette cérémonie décrit.

1. Le point de vue des jeunes filles qui préparent le thé.

   Modèle *Le temps du thé c'est un moment pour...*

2. Le point de vue des personnes qui boivent le thé.

   Modèle *Le temps du thé c'est un moment pour...*

3. Quelles connotations avez-vous pour l'expression **cérémonie du thé** après la lecture de ce **Journal de voyage**?

La CÉRÉMONIE DU THÉ AU SÉNÉGAL

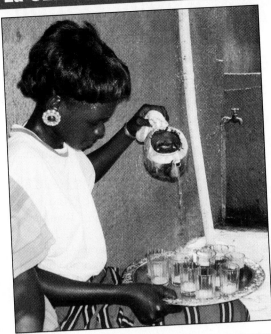

Au Sénégal, après les repas de midi et du soir, on reste assis ensemble pour déguster du thé et se reposer avant de reprendre les activités de travail. C'est toute une cérémonie qui se déroule autour de cette boisson. On l'appelle «attaya» et elle vient de la Mauritanie.

Au Sénégal, les thés préférés sont le «Gun Power», qui est très fort et qui se présente en toutes petites boulettes de feuilles de thé, et le «thé vert de Chine», aussi très apprécié, qui est plus fin.

Qu'est-ce qu'il faut?

On utilise le matériel traditionnel qui est simple et peu cher.
- une théière (25/40cl)
- de petits verres transparents et assez épais
- un plateau pour déposer les verres et la théière
- un petit fourneau malgache avec du charbon de bois, pour faire bouillir l'eau

Chaque personne reçoit trois tasses de thé au goût distinct.
- La première s'appelle «lewel» et elle n'est pas très sucrée.
- La deuxième s'appelle «niarel». Elle est plus sucrée que la première et elle contient un peu de menthe fraîche.
- La troisième s'appelle «niétel». C'est la plus sucrée et elle contient aussi de la menthe fraîche.

Aujourd'hui, visite chez les parents d'Aminata. Plat traditionnel, que nous avons pris assis au sol, en cercle autour d'un grand plat. Il faisait très chaud, mais nous avions faim, et une brise légère passait sur la terrasse. Puis on attend le thé. Moment délicieux, il fait bon, on n'a plus faim, repos et paix après la fatigue du voyage. Deux des jeunes sœurs d'Aminata, assises sur des tabourets bas autour d'un petit fourneau faisaient chauffer de l'eau. Elles parlaient et riaient doucement entre elles. Quand l'eau a bouilli, elles ont mis le thé dans la théière, et elles ont versé le thé d'une théière dans une autre plusieurs fois, de très haut. Le thé fumait et faisait des bulles en remplissant la théière.

—Pourquoi faites-vous cela?, je leur ai demandé.

—Pour le faire mousser.

—Est-ce qu'il n'est pas plus facile de le fouetter avec deux fourchettes?

—Peut-être, m'ont-elles répondu, mais alors nous n'avons plus le temps de bavarder... Et elles ont éclaté de rire. Pendant ce temps-là, les autres parlaient ou dormaient sur la terrasse, en attendant le thé. C'était le moment d'aller chasser l'image et de saisir les membres de la famille d'Aminata dans leurs habitudes et leurs gestes traditionnels.

Journal de voyage — Institut d'Été, Dakar 1996.

www explore!
http//voila.heinle.com

Orthographe et prononciation

➤➤ L'alphabet et les sons

It is true that in both English and French, the relationship between sounds and how they are written is far from straightforward. In English, for example, the sound represented by the letter **f-** in the word *full* can also be spelled **-ff** *(puff)*, **-gh** *(tough)*, **-ph-** *(telephone)*, and even **-lf** *(half)!* To make matters even more complicated, a letter combination like **-gh-** may represent more than one sound *(laugh, daughter, ghost, through).*

Likewise, in French, the sound represented by the letter **k-** in a word like **kilo** may also be spelled **c-** (**cours, combien**), **-cc-** (**d'accord**), **-q** (**cinq**), or even **qu-** (**qui, quoi**). Similarly, the letter **-s-** may represent more than one sound (**disque, disent, trois**).

In spite of this seemingly chaotic state of affairs, considerable regularity can be found in both the French and English spelling systems. Can you find the regularity underlying the spellings of the words in the English pairs below?

mad	made
not	note
bit	bite
met	meet
set	seat
fed	feed
bet	beat

Activité

Trouvez la règle Look at the list of words below. How many ways can you find to spell the sound **é** as in **étudiant**?

écouter

vous ouvrez

elle a acheté

mes

manger

les

boulanger

chez

See the **Instructor's Resource Manual** for more information.

Vocabulaire de base

TEXT TAPE:
Vocabulaire de base

NOMS

l'addition (f.) *restaurant bill, check*
une aspirine *aspirin*
une assiette (de) *plate (of)*
une boisson *beverage, drink*
une boîte (de) *can (of), box (of)*
une bouteille (de) *bottle (of)*
une boucherie *butcher shop*
une boulangerie *bakery*
la carte *restaurant menu*
une carte de crédit *credit card*
une charcuterie *pork shop,
    delicatessen*
un chèque *check*
un couteau *knife*
une cuillère *spoon*
une cuillère à soupe *soup spoon,
    tablespoon*
un doigt *finger*
une entrée *appetizer*
une épicerie *grocery store*
une fourchette *fork*
un(e) invité(e) *guest*
un kilo (de) *one kilogram (of)*
une liste (de) *list (of)*
une main *hand*
un marché *market*
un médicament *medicine*

un morceau (de) *piece (of)*
une pâtisserie *pastry shop, pastry*
une petite cuillère *teaspoon*
une pharmacie *pharmacy*
un pharmacien/une pharmacienne
    pharmacist
une plante verte *houseplant*
un plat *serving dish, dish of food*
le plat principal *main dish, main
    course*
une serviette *napkin*
une soirée *party, evening*
une tasse (de) *cup (of)*
une tranche (de) *slice (of)*
un verre (de) *glass (of)*

ADJECTIFS

bon marché *(invar.) cheap,
    inexpensive*
délicieux, délicieuse *delicious*
excellent(e) *excellent*
fermé(e) *closed*
ouvert(e) *open*
tout, tous, toute, toutes *all*

VERBES

apporter *to bring*

commander *to order*
fermer *to close*
inviter *to invite*
offrir *to offer, give*
ouvrir *to open*
payer *to pay*
utiliser *to use*
venir *to come (conj. with **être**)*
venir de *to have just*
voir *to see*

DIVERS

assez (de) *enough (of)*
au milieu (de) *in the middle (of)*
Combien est-ce que je vous dois?
    How much do I owe you?
heureusement *happily, luckily*
malheureusement *unhappily,
    unluckily*
pas du tout *not at all*
Quelle sorte de...? *What kind
    of . . . ? What sort of . . . ?*
tous les deux, toutes les deux *both*
tous les jours *every day*
tout à fait *absolutely, completely*
tout de suite *right away, at once*
trop (de) *too much (of)*

Vocabulaire supplémentaire

NOMS

une assiette à soupe *soup plate*
une boîte de chocolats *box of
    chocolates*
une boulangerie-pâtisserie *bakery
    that also sells pastries*
un chéquier *checkbook*
un couvert *silverware, place setting*
un gramme (de) *one gram (of)*

un litre (de) *one liter (of)*
le menu (à... francs) *fixed-price meal
    (for . . . francs)*
la monnaie *change, coins*
une nappe *tablecloth*
une sauce *sauce, gravy*

ADJECTIFS

gratuit(e) *free (of charge)*

VERBES

brûler *to burn*
déborder *to spill over*
préparer *to prepare*
renverser *to knock over*

DIVERS

à la carte *à la carte*

avoir mal *to hurt*
avoir mal à la tête *to have a headache*
laisser un pourboire *to leave a tip*
mettre la table *to set the table*
payer avec une carte de crédit *to pay by credit card*
payer en liquide *to pay cash*
payer par chèque *to pay by check*
service compris *tip included*

LE FRANÇAIS TEL QU'ON LE PARLE

heureusement que (nous avions une carte de crédit!) *thank goodness (we had a credit card!)*
J'abandonne! *I give up!*
J'en ai assez! *I've had it! I've had enough! I'm fed up!*
Mais qu'est-ce qu'on va faire? *But what are we going to do?*
Tu parles! *You bet! You're telling me!*
'y a pas = il n'y a pas

Pour offrir de payer quand on invite à boire un verre ou quand on invite au restaurant:
c'est moi qui invite *it's my treat, I'm paying*

Au restaurant:
Est-ce que je pourrais avoir l'addition, s'il vous plaît? *Could I have the bill, please?*
Est-ce que le service est compris? *Is the tip included?*
Vous avez choisi? *Are you ready to order?*

À table:
Servez-vous! *Help yourself!*
Encore un peu de vin? *Some more wine?*
Merci. (Non, merci.) *No, thank you.*
Oui, je veux bien, merci. *Yes, please.*
Je n'ai plus faim! *I'm full!*

LE FRANÇAIS FAMILIER

j'en ai marre = j'en ai assez
j'en ai ras le bol = j'en ai assez

ON ENTEND PARFOIS...

un dépanneur (Canada) = *neighborhood grocery store with late hours*
donner une bonne-main (Suisse) = donner un pourboire
donner une dringuelle (Belgique) = donner un pourboire
gréyer la table (Canada) = mettre la table
un légumier (Belgique) = quelqu'un qui vend des légumes
payer (Afrique) = acheter
une praline (Belgique) = un chocolat

Info plus

C'est moi qui invite.

When you hear **C'est moi qui invite,** you can be sure that the person who said it will pay for the drink or meal. Although **C'est moi qui invite** literally means *I'm the one inviting,* it is really the equivalent of the English expression *It's my treat.* It is generally considered polite then for you to offer to pay the next time you are together. However, French students do tend to split the bill when they go out together. Similarly, if you take out a pack of cigarettes or something to eat when in the company of French people, you are expected to offer it around.

Que faire un jour de pluie?

En bref

Dans cette leçon...

- Journaux et magazines en France
- Pour communiquer: écrire, téléphoner, aller à la poste, utiliser le Minitel
- Les verbes **dire, lire** et **écrire**
- Les pronoms d'objet indirect
- L'accord du participe passé

In this lesson...

- Newspapers and magazines in France
- Communicating: writing, using the telephone, going to the post office, using the Minitel
- The verbs **dire, lire,** and **écrire**
- Indirect object pronouns
- Past participle agreement

www explore!
http://voila.heinle.com

Develop writing skills with Système-D software!

Practice listening and pronunciation skills with the Text Tape!

Discover the Francophone world!

Build your skills!

INTERNET

SYSTÈME-D

TEXT TAPE

VIDEO TAPE

CD-ROM

Students have an open-ended writing activity in the **Cahier** suitable for use with **Système-D**.

Entrée en matière: Pour communiquer

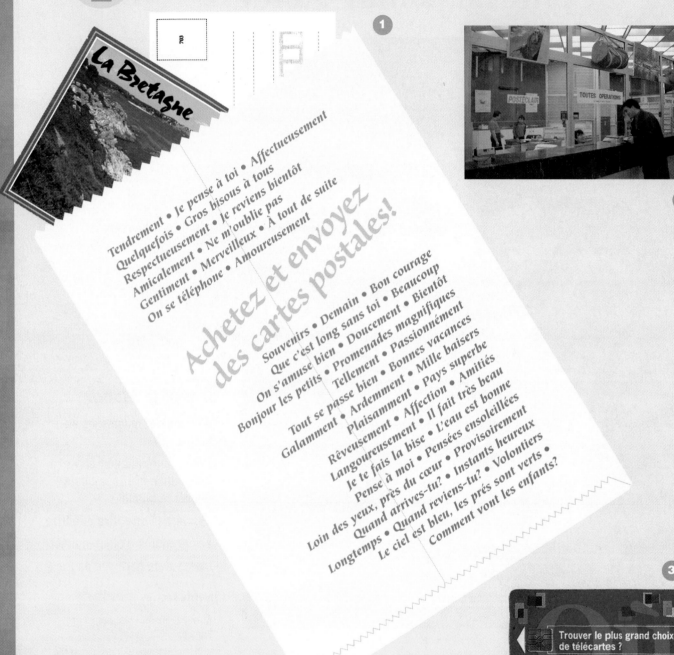

La Bretagne

Tendrement • Je pense à toi • Affectueusement
Quelquefois • Gros bisous à tous
Respectueusement • Je reviens bientôt
Amicalement • Ne m'oublie pas
Gentiment • Merveilleux • À tout de suite
On se téléphone • Amoureusement

Achetez et envoyez des cartes postales!

Souvenirs • Demain • Bon courage
Que c'est long sans toi • Beaucoup
On s'amuse bien • Doucement • Bientôt
Bonjour les petits • Promenades magnifiques
Tellement • Passionnément
Tout se passe bien • Bonnes vacances
Galamment • Ardemment • Mille baisers
Plaisamment • Pays superbe
Rêveusement • Affection • Amitiés
Langoureusement • Il fait très beau
Je te fais la bise • L'eau est bonne
Pense à moi • Pensées ensoleillées
Loin des yeux, près du cœur • Provisoirement
Quand arrives-tu? • Instants heureux
Longtemps • Quand reviens-tu? • Volontiers •
Le ciel est bleu, les prés sont verts •
Comment vont les enfants?

Trouver le plus grand choix
de télécartes ?

Télécarte 120

Les illustrations. Since students will
not yet be able to identify the various
items, have them use the numbers to
make two lists, one for **téléphone** and
one for **lettres et cartes postales**. If
desired and if students are curious,
give them the appropriate words
(**numéro 6, oui, c'est un téléphone,
c'est une cabine téléphonique**, etc.).

Les illustrations. Regardez les illustrations et les différentes façons de
communiquer. Dites quelles formes de communication sont représentées.
Lesquelles sont orales? Lesquelles sont écrites?

Les cartes postales.

Pourquoi et quand les cartes postales sont-elles utiles? Quelles formules est-ce qu'on utilise pour les cartes postales? Regardez les notices sur l'enveloppe de cartes postales pour trouver une formule pour...

parler du temps

parler des activités

parler de l'environnement

exprimer l'affection

terminer

parler à quelqu'un qu'on aime

parler à un(e) ami(e)

donner un message important

À vos stylos!

Choisissez une photo dans une leçon de *VOILÀ!* et imaginez que c'est une carte postale. Pour qui est-elle? Quel texte mettez-vous? Quelle formule choisissez-vous pour commencer? Pour finir?

The conjugation of **lire**, **dire**, and **écrire** is in the *Structure* section of this lesson.

Vocabulaire

nord

ouest ← → est

sud

Paris

• La Baule

Additional questions: **Est-ce que Stéphane, Béatrice, Michel et Nathalie sont français? D'où est-ce qu'ils viennent? Qu'est-ce qu'ils étudient? Qu'est-ce qu'ils ont fait en juin? Et vous, quand est-ce que vous avez des examens?**

TRANSPARENCY: 14-1

Stéphane (étudiant en droit), Béatrice (étudiante en médecine), Michel (étudiant en littérature anglaise et américaine) et Nathalie (étudiante en sciences économiques) sont des étudiants suisses qui viennent de Lausanne. Ils ont passé leurs examens en juin et les ont réussis. Maintenant, ils sont en vacances à La Baule, en Bretagne, où ils font du camping.

Aujourd'hui, il pleut. Alors, ils ont décidé d'écrire des lettres et de lire des journaux et des magazines. Stéphane veut aussi téléphoner chez lui parce que c'est l'anniversaire de sa mère, et Nathalie voudrait téléphoner à un ami qui habite à La Baule, mais elle n'a pas son numéro de téléphone.

• La Baule, c'est au nord, au sud, à l'ouest ou à l'est de la France? Pourquoi est-ce qu'on va en vacances à La Baule? La Baule, c'est comme Lausanne? Pourquoi? Est-ce que c'est facile pour Stéphane, Béatrice, Michel et Nathalie de parler avec les personnes qui habitent à La Baule? Pourquoi?

• Qu'est-ce qu'ils font à La Baule? Quel temps fait-il aujourd'hui? Qu'est-ce que vous faites quand il pleut en juillet? Et eux? Est-ce que Stéphane veut ou doit téléphoner à sa mère? Pourquoi? Et Nathalie, est-ce qu'elle veut ou doit téléphoner?

A. À la poste

Stéphane   Béatrice

Trouver le plus grand choix de télécartes?

Télécarte 120

une télécarte

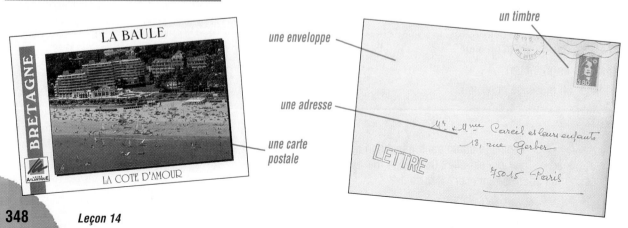

LA BAULE

BRETAGNE

une enveloppe

un timbre

une adresse

LETTRE

Mr & Mme Careil et leurs enfants
18, rue Gerber
75015 Paris

une carte postale

LA COTE D'AMOUR

À la poste, Stéphane vient d'acheter une télécarte. Il n'a pas téléphoné de la poste parce qu'il y avait trop de personnes qui attendaient. Alors, il va téléphoner d'une cabine téléphonique. Et Béatrice? Elle a acheté 10 timbres pour cartes postales et deux timbres pour lettres.

- Qu'est-ce que Stéphane a fait à la poste? Et Béatrice?

une boîte aux lettres

B. Dans une cabine téléphonique

Stéphane téléphone à Lausanne. Nathalie cherche le numéro de téléphone de son ami dans l'annuaire. Il y avait des Minitels à la poste, mais ils étaient tous occupés et elle ne voulait pas attendre.

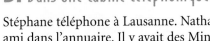

Là, regarde!

Oui, c'est ça!

Alors, ça y est?

Nathalie   Michel

un annuaire

- Où est-ce que Stéphane téléphone? Que fait Nathalie? Pourquoi est-ce qu'elle n'a pas utilisé le Minitel à la poste?

le Minitel

Ask students: **Qu'est-ce qu'on peut faire à la poste?**

Info plus

La poste.

The post office in France is run by the government and is known as **les P. et T.** (postes et télécommunications), or simply **le bureau de poste** or **la poste** *(the post office).* This is where you go to mail letters, buy stamps, send telegrams, make phone calls, and even do your banking. You can also buy stamps at tobacco shops **(bureaux de tabac)** and mail letters in any yellow mailbox **(la boîte aux lettres),** which you will probably find nearby. Note that telegrams and telephone service are part of the postal system in France.

TRANSPARENCY: 14-2

Brief phone conversations appear in the *Notes de vocabulaire* section of this lesson.

Ask students: **Comment est-ce qu'on peut payer dans une cabine téléphonique?**

Info plus

Téléphoner en France.

Telephone service in France was greatly modernized in the 1980s. Telephone booths are numerous and easy to use. Some are coin-operated, but most now require a telephone card, **une télécarte,** that can be purchased at the post office or in a **bureau de tabac.** Telephone directories and many other services have been computerized and can be accessed through minicomputers **(les Minitels)** available on loan to home subscribers or in the larger post offices. **Minitels** can also be used to reserve train or plane seats, to reserve theater tickets, and to place other kinds of orders. See the *Découvertes culturelles* section for this lesson.

Que faire un jour de pluie?   **349**

C. Au bureau de tabac

Ask students: **Où est-ce qu'on peut acheter des cigarettes, des cartes postales, des journaux?**

Info plus

Le bureau de tabac.

Un bureau de tabac, or **un tabac**, is a small store where cigarettes, stamps, postcards, newspapers, magazines, comic books, matches, telephone cards, and candy can be bought. The French government has a monopoly on tobacco products and matches. These items can only be bought in a **bureau de tabac** that is duly licensed by the government. This is not necessarily the case in other parts of the world where French is spoken. In Belgium, for example, tobacco products and matches are commonly sold in grocery stores.

Point out that, in France, you cannot buy cigarettes or matches in supermarkets or gas stations.

Au bureau de tabac, ils achètent des cartes postales, des enveloppes, des bonbons, des journaux et des magazines. Michel voudrait aussi acheter des cigarettes mais les autres détestent les cigarettes et ne sont pas contents quand Michel fume!

un journal

un magazine

des cartes postales

- Où sont-ils? Qu'est-ce qu'on vend dans ce magasin? Qui va souvent dans ce magasin? Et chez vous, où est-ce qu'on achète des journaux? des timbres? des cigarettes? Qu'est-ce que Nathalie et Stéphane sont en train de lire?

D. Dans un café

Parts of newspapers and magazines: **le sommaire, une rubrique, un titre (les gros titres), un article, la première page, la publicité, les petites annonces.** You may want to bring French magazines and newspapers to class.

Explain to students that **culturel** in French means *intellectual* in this context.

Michel est en train de lire *Paris-Match* parce qu'il adore les photos de ce magazine et parce qu'il aime les articles sur les célébrités. En vacances, il déteste les choses culturelles. Et puis, toute l'année, il doit lire de la littérature, alors... Béatrice fait son courrier: elle veut envoyer des cartes postales à tous ses amis en Suisse. Stéphane est en train de lire *Ouest-France.* Il aime lire les titres, la page des sports, les bandes dessinées et les dessins humoristiques. Mais surtout, il veut lire la météo pour demain! Nathalie, elle, aime bien lire *L'Express* parce qu'elle aime la politique et veut être au courant des événements importants de la semaine. Elle aime aussi les rubriques scientifiques et littéraires et elle est en train de lire un article sur le nouveau roman de l'écrivain Jean-Marie Le Clézio. C'est un beau roman d'amour et elle voudrait bien aller l'acheter dans une librairie pour pouvoir le lire s'il continue à pleuvoir.

- Quel magazine américain ou canadien est comme *Paris-Match*? Qui aime lire ces magazines? *Ouest-France*, c'est un journal pour toute la France? Quelles nouvelles est-ce qu'il y a dans la presse aujourd'hui? Est-ce que ce sont des nouvelles importantes, à votre avis? Quelle est la météo de demain pour La Baule? Où est-ce qu'il va faire beau? Où est-ce qu'il va faire mauvais? Et vous, qu'est-ce que vous aimez lire en vacances? Où est-ce qu'on peut lire les nouvelles sportives? les nouvelles politiques? Où est-ce qu'on trouve des bandes dessinées et des dessins humoristiques? Qui aime les lire? Pourquoi?

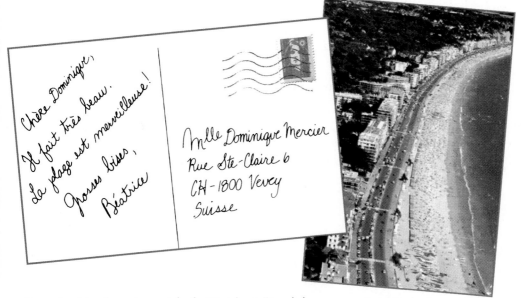

Additional questions:
Qu'est-ce que Michel aime dans *Paris-Match*?
Pourquoi est-ce qu'il n'aime pas lire des choses culturelles en vacances?
Que fait Béatrice? Qu'est-ce que Stéphane aime lire dans le journal? Pourquoi est-ce que Nathalie aime lire *L'Express*?

A **mini-lexique** for letter writing appears in the **Notes de vocabulaire** section of this lesson.

TRANSPARENCY: 14-3

- Regardez bien la carte postale de Béatrice à Dominique.
  Dominique, c'est un homme ou une femme? C'est vrai qu'il faisait beau à La Baule ce jour-là? Et vous, est-ce que vous aimez écrire des cartes postales quand vous êtes en vacances? Et des lettres? Sur vos cartes postales de vacances, est-ce que vous voulez toujours dire la vérité? Quand est-ce que vous ne voulez pas la dire?
- Qu'est-ce que vous aimez faire quand il pleut?
- Quels magazines préférez-vous? Pourquoi? (SUGGESTIONS: les magazines d'information, les magazines sur les célébrités, les magazines de sport, les magazines sur les ordinateurs, les magazines féminins, les magazines littéraires, les magazines scientifiques, les magazines sur les maisons et les jardins, les magazines de mode, les magazines sur la santé, les magazines de cuisine, les magazines sur les voyages, les magazines de photos, les magazines de cinéma, etc.)
- Dans le journal, vous préférez la politique ou le sport? la publicité ou la météo? les petites annonces ou les dessins humoristiques? Quels renseignements est-ce qu'on peut trouver dans les petites annonces?
- Quel est votre écrivain préféré? Votre journaliste préféré(e) à la télévision? Vous préférez les romans ou les poèmes?

Notes de vocabulaire

1. Mots et expressions utiles.

demander (qqch. à qqn)	to ask (someone for something)
une dissertation	paper (written for a class)
un facteur	mail carrier
masculin(e)	masculine
mettre une lettre à la poste	to mail a letter
passé(e): la semaine passée, le mois passé	last (week, month)
poser une question (à qqn)	to ask (someone) a question
un sommaire	table of contents (of a magazine)

2. Cher.
The adjective **cher, chère** has two meanings in English. Placed before the noun, it means *dear;* after the noun, it means *expensive.*

Cher John,...	*Dear John, . . .*
La BMW est une voiture **chère**.	*The BMW is an expensive car.*

3. Envoyer.
The -**y**- in the stem of the verb **envoyer** changes to -**i**- in the present tense when the ending following it is silent. This is the same pattern you learned for the verb **payer** (**je paie, nous payons**).

3: Regular verbs with spelling changes will be treated as *Notes de vocabulaire* as they occur. Note that the spelling change for **envoyer** is obligatory; for **payer** it is not.

j'envoie	nous envoyons
tu envoies	vous envoyez
il elle } envoie	ils elles } envoient

4. Au téléphone.
Allô is how you say *hello* on the telephone. Read the following short phone conversations and try to find an English equivalent for each sentence.

4: Telephone vocabulary is presented for recognition only.

—Allô!

—Allô, je suis bien chez Cédric Rasquin? C'est Jean-François Jolivet.

—Ah, bonjour, Jean-François! C'est sa maman à l'appareil! Je te le passe, hein! (Cédric! Jean-François au téléphone!)

—Allô, Bovy et Compagnie, bonjour!

—Oui, bonjour Madame, ici Vincent Dubois. Est-ce que je pourrais parler à Monsieur Bovy, s'il vous plaît?

—Monsieur Bovy n'est pas ici ce matin. Pouvez-vous rappeler après deux heures?

—Allô!

—Bonjour, chérie!

—Mais qui est à l'appareil?

—C'est moi, Jean!

—Jean? Jean qui?

—C'est bien le 05 61 48 95 45 à Toulouse?

—Ah non, c'est le 05 61 46 95 45.

—Oh, excusez-moi, Madame, j'ai fait un faux numéro!

—Office du Tourisme, bonjour!

—Bonjour, Monsieur, ici Jacques Dubois. Je voudrais parler à Madame Benoît, s'il vous plaît.

—C'est à quel sujet?

—Je voudrais un renseignement sur le concert de ce soir, Place Massena.

—Ne quittez pas, je vous la passe.

5. Pour écrire.

When you write in French, it is important to know how to start and finish your letter.

- Informal letters to people you know well:

Cher Paul,	*Dear Paul,*
Mon chéri, Ma chérie, (Mon amour,)	*Darling, My love,*
Amicalement, (Très amicalement, Bien amicalement,)	*Cordially,*
Grosses bises, (Gros bisous,)	*Love,*
Je t'embrasse,	*Hugs and kisses,*

- Formal letters:

Monsieur (Madame, Mademoiselle),	*Dear Sir (Madam, Miss),*
Je vous prie d'agréer, Monsieur (Madame, Mademoiselle), l'expression de mes sentiments les meilleurs.	*Very truly yours, Sincerely,*

Info plus

Les numéros de téléphone.
In order to accommodate increasing telephone use, French telephone numbers became ten-digit instead of eight-digit numbers on October 18, 1996. The telephone number 05 61 48 95 45 indicates that the location involved is in the southwest of France (05) and in the department of **la Haute Garonne** (61). See the *Découvertes culturelles* section of this lesson.

5: Letter-writing vocabulary is presented for recognition and reference only.
Ask students to guess the meaning of **chéri.** Ask them to think of an English cognate (e.g., *cherish*).
If desired, warn students not to use the verb **baiser** to translate *to kiss.* Although they will find that meaning in a dictionary, this verb is commonly used in France today with the meaning *to make love.*

D'accord?

A. Chassez l'intrus
Quel mot ne va pas avec les autres à cause du sens *(meaning)*?

1. enveloppe / courrier / timbre / article / facteur
2. bureau de tabac / annuaire / cabine téléphonique / téléphone
3. journal / magazine / courrier / article / publicité
4. écrivain / événement / littérature / roman
5. petite annonce / titre / article / facteur
6. ensoleillé / littéraire / couvert / nuageux
7. droit / météo / médecine / sciences économiques / littérature

Act. A: Chassez l'intrus (gender).
1. **facteur / timbre / cabine téléphonique / courrier**
2. **enveloppe / carte postale / adresse / numéro de téléphone.**
3. **facteur / boîte aux lettres / petites annonces / librairie**
4. **page / politique / publicité / magazine**
5. **renseignement / écrivain / vérité / journal**

B. Trouvez la suite Qu'est-ce qui va ensemble?

1. Où est l'annuaire?
2. Tu dois acheter le journal d'aujourd'hui.
3. Combien coûtent les timbres pour le Canada?
4. Où est-ce qu'on peut téléphoner, s'il vous plaît?
5. Où est la cabine téléphonique?
6. Est-ce qu'il y a un bureau de tabac près de l'hôtel?
7. Je cherche un appartement pour l'été.

a. Il y a un article sur toi.
b. Pour une lettre ou pour une carte postale?
c. Je voudrais acheter un journal et des cigarettes.
d. Regarde dans les petites annonces du *Figaro*.
e. J'ai besoin d'un numéro de téléphone.
f. Mais à la poste, Monsieur!
g. Tout près du supermarché, à droite.

Act. C: Ask students to make a list of activities from most to least preferred.

C. Moi, je préfère! Qu'est-ce que vous préférez? Qu'est-ce que vous aimez beaucoup? un peu? pas du tout?

lire le journal
lire des magazines
lire des lettres
écrire des lettres
écrire des cartes postales
écouter la radio
regarder la télévision
lire des magazines d'information
lire les nouvelles politiques dans le journal
lire des magazines qui ont des photos

lire des magazines féminins
lire des magazines spécialisés
lire des romans
écrire des romans
écrire des poèmes
lire des essais philosophiques
lire des bandes dessinées
lire de la littérature classique
lire de la littérature moderne

Act. D: FOLLOW-UP: Ask students to correct false statements.

D. Les médias C'est vrai ou c'est faux?

1. Les nouvelles importantes sont à la première page du journal.
2. Il y a des articles sur les enfants dans les magazines féminins.
3. Il y a des adresses dans les petites annonces.
4. Les petites annonces sont très faciles à lire.
5. On parle de littérature sur la page des sports.
6. Vous devez lire les petites annonces pour trouver un appartement.
7. La météo n'est jamais dans le journal.
8. Pour trouver le numéro de téléphone de mes amis, je regarde dans les petites annonces.
9. Dans les magazines, les photos sont en couleurs.
10. Il y a des articles sur la cuisine dans les magazines scientifiques.
11. Dans l'annuaire, il n'y a pas d'adresses.
12. En France, les boîtes aux lettres sont jaunes.
13. Les bureaux de tabac ne vendent pas de timbres.
14. En France, on peut téléphoner à la poste.

Mise en pratique

A. La météo

1. Avec une carte de France, trouvez le nom d'une région ou d'une ville qui correspond à la météo du jour.

Act. A: Students have not yet seen all the weather expressions used here. Have them guess from context.

> Temps pluvieux sur la moitié ouest du pays.
>
> Brume matinale sur le nord et les côtes de la Manche.
>
> Temps chaud et nuageux sur le centre.
>
> Vent persistant sur le midi de la France.
>
> Beau temps sur les côtes de la Méditerranée.
>
> Temps lourd et orageux sur les montagnes du centre.
>
> Temps frais et ensoleillé sur les montagnes du sud, avec vent léger.
>
> Temps nuageux sur la capitale le matin et l'après-midi.

2. Quel temps préférez-vous? Quel temps n'aimez-vous pas? Alors, où est-ce que vous avez envie d'aller pour vos vacances de printemps en France?
3. Qu'est-ce que vous allez faire? Pour chaque annonce de météo, choisissez des vêtements appropriés au temps et une activité pour cette journée.

B. Le voyage d'une carte postale
Quelles sont les étapes *(steps)* et les aventures du voyage d'une carte postale? (Où est-ce qu'on la vend? Pourquoi est-ce qu'on l'achète? Qui l'écrit? Où est-ce qu'elle arrive? Qui la lit?)

Act. B: Suitable for group work. Have students explain what has happened to a postcard (use one of your own, invent one, or use the one on page 351) from its departure to its final destination. Ask for details: **Elle est dans le sac pendant trois jours. Elle va dans la boîte aux lettres un soir d'été,** etc. Students can use **elle, on,** or **je** to talk about or as the postcard.

C. Où, quand, qui, à qui?
Choisissez une profession. Qu'est-ce qu'une personne de cette profession aime lire et écrire? déteste lire et écrire?

Act. C: Review professions. Ask students to make simple sentences.

D. Journaux et magazines
Qu'est-ce qu'ils cherchent dans un journal? Et dans un magazine?

Act. D: Provide some ideas to help students get started: **des articles amusants, les films de la semaine,** etc. Bring magazines and newspapers and let students leaf through them to generate ideas.

une directrice d'école	un avocat
un cuisinier	une femme médecin
une mère de famille	un chômeur
une étudiante	un commerçant
un agriculteur	un cadre
une pianiste	une adolescente
un professeur	un secrétaire
un infirmier	un garagiste

E. Des magazines Pour chaque (each) magazine, répondez aux questions suivantes.

1. Quelle sorte de magazine est-ce?
2. Qu'est-ce qu'il y a sur la couverture (cover)?
3. De quoi est-ce qu'on parle probablement dans ce magazine?
4. Qui va le lire? Pourquoi?
5. Et vous? Quel magazine voulez-vous lire? Quel magazine ne voulez-vous pas lire?

A.

B.

C.

D.

E.

F.

G.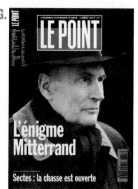

H.

I.

J.

K.

L.

F. Conversation en français Il fait beau aujourd'hui et vous avez décidé d'aller
travailler dehors, dans un parc. Là, vous voyez quelqu'un qui est en train de lire
L'Express. Comme vous n'avez plus envie d'étudier et que vous avez envie de parler
français, vous décidez de parler avec cette personne. Essayez d'avoir une
conversation de deux ou trois minutes.

Structure

▶▶ Les verbes de communication: *dire, lire, écrire*

Dire (to say, tell)

Note the **vous** form, **vous dites.**

Point out that two other verbs have the ending **-tes** in the second person plural (vous êtes, vous faites)

je dis	nous disons
tu dis	vous di**tes**
il elle } dit	ils elles } disent

Pourquoi est-ce que vous **dites** ça?   *Why do you say that?*

The imperative or command forms of **dire** are the same as the present tense forms.

Non, non, non, ne le **dis** pas!   *NO, don't say it!*
Dites toujours la vérité.   *Always tell the truth.*
Disons, quoi, six heures. Ça te va?   *Let's say, what, six? How does that suit you?*

The past participle of **dire** is **dit. Dire** is conjugated with **avoir** in the **passé composé.**

DRILL: Qu'est-ce que tu as dit? (il / Candide et Alceste, vous / nous / je)

Qu'est-ce qu'il **a dit?**   *What did he say?*

The **imparfait** of **dire** is regular.

Qu'est-ce qu'il **disait?**   *What was he saying?*

Note the formula **dire quelque chose à quelqu'un** *(to say something to someone).*

François, **dis** merci **à** M. Laporte.   *François, say thank you to Mr. Laporte.*
Est-ce que vous **avez dit** la vérité   *Did you tell your parents the truth?*
   à vos parents?

The verb **dire** is used in two idiomatic expressions.

1. To ask for the French equivalent of a word in English:

    Comment **dit**-on *then* en français?   *How do you say "then" in French?*

2. To find out what a word means:

    Que **veut dire** *poche?*   *What does "poche" mean?*
    Qu'est-ce que ça **veut dire?**   *What does that mean?*

Écrire (to write)

j'écris	nous écrivons
tu écris	vous écrivez
il elle } écrit	ils elles } écrivent

DRILL: **Les étudiants n'écrivent pas de lettres.** (je / vous / Alceste / tu / nous)

Les étudiants n'**écrivent** pas souvent à leurs parents; ils préfèrent téléphoner! — *Students don't write to their parents often; they'd rather phone!*

The imperative or command forms of **écrire** are the same as the present tense forms.

Écris une lettre à ta grand-mère tout de suite! — *Write a letter to your grandmother right away!*

Écrivez votre nom, s'il vous plaît. — *Write your name, please.*

Écrivons un roman! — *Let's write a novel!*

The past participle of **écrire** is **écrit. Écrire** is conjugated with avoir in the **passé composé.**

J'**ai écrit** deux lettres hier. — *I wrote two letters yesterday.*

The **imparfait** of **écrire** is regular.

Elle **écrivait** une carte postale. quand je suis entré. — *She was writing a postcard when I came in.*

The verb **décrire** (to describe) is conjugated like **écrire.**

Lire (to read)

je lis	nous lisons
tu lis	vous lisez
il elle } lit	ils elles } lisent

DRILL: **Alceste lit le journal le matin.** (tu / les étudiants / je / nous / vous)

Vous **lisez** beaucoup? — *Do you read a lot?*

Ma mère **lit** toujours le journal le matin. — *My mother always reads the newspaper in the morning.*

The imperative or command forms of **lire** are the same as the present tense forms.

Lis cet article avant demain. — *Read this article before tomorrow.*

Ne **lisez** pas ce roman! — *Don't read that novel!*

Lisons Le Rouge et le noir cet été. — *Let's read The Red and the Black this summer.*

The past participle of **lire** is **lu. Lire** is conjugated with avoir in the **passé composé.**

Est-ce que tu **as lu** ce roman? — *Have you read this novel?*

The imparfait of **lire** is regular.

Avant, je **lisais** beaucoup, mais
maintenant je n'ai plus le temps.

*I used to read a lot, but now I don't have
(the) time.*

Vous avez compris?

A. Activités du week-end
Utilisez les verbes entre parenthèses pour dire ce que tout le monde fait ce week-end.

Act. A: FOLLOW-UP: Ask students to characterize the people in this activity.

1. Aline ..... un roman de Hawthorne. (lire)
2. Jacques et Alain ..... des dissertations. (écrire)
3. Nous ..... un article sur la politique dans un magazine très sérieux. (lire)
4. Tu ..... une lettre à ta sœur? (écrire)
5. Je ..... à un ami et je ..... ma vie à l'université. (écrire / décrire)

B. Activités du week-end, suite
Maintenant, utilisez le passé composé pour dire ce qu'on n'a pas fait ce week-end.

1. Aline ..... le roman de Hawthorne. Elle ..... un roman d'amour!
   (ne pas lire / lire)
2. Jacques et Alain ..... leurs dissertations. Ils ..... des poèmes pour leurs petites amies! (ne pas écrire / écrire)
3. Nous ..... l'article sur la politique. Nous ..... un article sur les sports!
   (ne pas lire / lire)
4. Tu ..... de lettre à ta sœur! Tu ..... une carte postale à toute la famille!
   (ne pas écrire / écrire)
5. Je ..... à mon ami; je ..... ma vie à l'université au téléphone!
   (ne pas écrire / décrire)

C. La vie était belle à dix ans!
La vie était plus facile avant. Utilisez les verbes à l'imparfait pour le dire.

1. Les professeurs ..... quand nous ..... des bandes dessinées. (ne rien dire / lire)
2. Je ..... de dissertations. (ne pas écrire)
3. Je ..... de livres sérieux. (ne pas lire)
4. Nous ..... des petits poèmes pour notre mère. Elle était très contente! (écrire)

Continuons!

Parlons un peu

1. Est-ce que vous écrivez des lettres? À qui?
2. Quels magazines est-ce que vous lisez? Quels magazines est-ce que vous ne lisez jamais? Pourquoi?
3. À qui est-ce que vous dites toujours la vérité? À qui est-ce que vous ne dites jamais la vérité?
4. Qu'est-ce que vous lisez à la plage?
5. Est-ce que vous voulez être journaliste? écrivain? Pourquoi ou pourquoi pas?
6. Est-ce que vous aimez lire des poèmes? écrire des poèmes?
7. Qu'est-ce que vous lisez maintenant?

Parlons un peu: This exercise is designed to use the verbs presented in this lesson. Note that direct object pronouns are not possible in items 1 or 6.

▶ Les pronoms d'object indirect

Indirect objects indicate the person to whom something is given, shown, said, and so forth.

> I talked *to my father* yesterday. *(to my father* is the indirect object)

With verbs that have both a direct and an indirect object, English permits two different word orders. In these two sentences, *Joel* is the indirect object.

> He gave the book to *Joel.*   He gave *Joel* the book.

In French, the preposition **à** appears in front of a noun used as an indirect object.

> Il a donné le livre **à Joël.**   *He gave Joel the book. (He gave the book to Joel.)*

Indirect object pronouns (**les pronoms d'objet indirect**) replace nouns used as indirect objects.

me	*(to) me*
te	*(to) you (familiar, singular)*
lui	*(to) him, (to) her*
nous	*(to) us*
vous	*(to) you (formal or plural)*
leur	*(to) them*

Note that **lui** can mean either *(to) him* or *(to) her*. The context almost always indicates which is meant.

Indirect object pronouns follow the same placement rules as direct object pronouns.

1. In front of a one-word verb.

> Il **me** parle pendant des heures.   *He talks to me for hours.*
> Je **leur** disais que...   *I was telling them that...*

2. In front of the infinitive in a verb + infinitive combination.

> Tu vas **lui** parler demain?   *Are you going to talk to him/her tomorrow?*
> Non, je ne peux pas **lui** parler demain.   *No, I can't talk to him/her tomorrow.*

3. In front of the helping verb in the **passé composé.**

> Martin **lui** a donné le livre.   *Martin gave him/her the book (gave the book to him/her).*
> Céline ne **leur** a pas écrit.   *Céline didn't write (to) them.*

4. With imperative or command forms. Indirect object pronouns, like direct object pronouns, follow affirmative imperatives and precede negative imperatives. Note that **me** and **te** become **moi** and **toi** when they follow the verb form.

> Parlez-**moi** d'amour!   *Talk to me about love!*
> Ne **lui** donne pas ce cadeau!   *Don't give him/her that present!*

Rappel!

1. The indirect object pronoun **leur** is already plural. Do not add **-s.** The possessive adjective **leur** *(their)* does take **-s** when it modifies a plural noun.

> —Il a parlé aux étudiants de **leurs** devoirs?
> *Did he talk to the students about their assignments?*
> —Oui, il **leur** a parlé de **leurs** devoirs!
> *Yes, he talked to them about their assignments.*

2. A few verbs that are followed by direct objects in English are followed by indirect objects in French. Here are the ones you have already learned.

- téléphoner **à**
  Il a téléphoné **à** ses parents.   *He called his parents.*
  Il **leur** a téléphoné.   *He called them.*

- répondre **à**
  Il n'a pas répondu **à** sa sœur.   *He didn't answer his sister.*
  Il ne **lui** a pas répondu.   *He didn't answer her.*

- demander **à**
  Il a demandé de l'argent **à** Paul.   *He asked Paul for some money.*
  Il **lui** a demandé de l'argent.   *He asked for some money.*

Encourage students to start a list of verbs that take an indirect object for themselves.

Vous avez compris?

A. Cédric et son père
Voilà des idées de Cédric sur son père. La mère et le père de Cédric sont divorcés et Cédric habite avec sa mère. Son père, Jean Rasquin, habite à Paris. Est-ce que Cédric aime son père? Est-ce que son père aime Cédric?

1. Je ne le vois jamais.
2. Il me téléphone le week-end.
3. Il m'offre des cadeaux.
4. Je n'aime pas les cadeaux qu'il m'offre.
5. Il m'a acheté un vélo.
6. Il m'invite à venir le voir à Paris l'été.
7. Je lui envoie des photos de moi et de ma mère.
8. Il me dit qu'il m'aime.
9. Quand il est en vacances, il m'écrit des cartes postales.
10. Quand je suis à Paris avec lui, il me dit qu'il est très occupé.

*Act. A: Do in steps. First ask students whether Cédric's statements are positive or negative. (**C'est positif/négatif?**) Ask students why Cédric loves/hates his father. Make two lists. Finally, ask students to draw a conclusion (**Cédric aime/déteste son père.**) and support their opinon. If desired, ask students to add to the lists using other structures. (**Son père n'est pas sérieux, Cédric est égoïste**, etc.)*

B. Parler avec des pronoms
Remplacez les mots en italique par des pronoms d'objet indirect.

Modèle   Je n'écris plus *à mes parents;* je téléphone *à mes parents.*
    Je ne leur écris plus; je leur téléphone.

1. Le professeur n'a pas dit la date de l'examen *aux étudiants.*
2. Candide a apporté des fleurs *à sa mère.*
3. Roméo a chanté une chanson *à Juliette.*
4. Nous n'allons pas téléphoner *à nos parents* ce soir.
5. Patrick a décrit sa sœur *à ses copains.*
6. Le professeur veut écrire une lettre *à sa fille.*

Act. B: CONTINUATION: Qu'est-ce que tu vas envoyer à ton père pour son anniversaire? Je vends mon vélo à Charles. Tu n'écris pas à Martine? À quelle heure est-ce que vous parlez à M. Moreau? J'écris à Marc.

C. Répondez avec des pronoms Répondez aux questions avec un pronom d'objet indirect.

Modèle   Tu vas envoyer ce cadeau *à ta sœur?* (oui)
Oui, je vais lui envoyer ce cadeau.

1. Tu ne donnes pas cette robe *à Claudine?* (si)
2. Est-ce que vous allez téléphoner *à vos parents* ce soir? (non)
3. Est-ce que tu as écrit *à ta grand-mère?* (oui)
4. Ton mari ne *t'*apporte plus de cadeaux? (non)
5. Tu as parlé *au professeur?* (non)

Continuons!

Act. A: Use **cette semaine** or **ce week-end** depending on which is most appropriate (**cette semaine** at the beginning of the week and **ce week-end** at the end, for example).

A. Je vais... Utilisez des pronoms d'objet direct et indirect pour dire ce que vous allez faire cette semaine ou ce week-end.

Modèles   perdre mes clés   ***Non, je ne vais pas les perdre.***
parler à mes parents   ***Oui, je vais leur parler.***

1. écrire à un(e) ami(e)
2. écouter mes amis
3. perdre mes affaires
4. parler au président de l'université
5. dire la vérité tout le temps
6. payer les repas de mes copains
7. envoyer douze roses au professeur de français
8. faire mon lit
9. lire les romans de Tolstoï
10. trouver la vérité

B. Histoire d'amour Voilà la triste histoire d'amour de David, mais il y a trop de noms. Écrivez-la de nouveau avec des pronoms sujets *(subject pronouns),* des pronoms disjoints *(stressed pronouns),* des pronoms d'objet direct et des pronoms d'objet indirect. Mais faites attention: pour comprendre l'histoire, il ne faut pas remplacer tous les noms!

David aime Claudine mais Claudine n'aime pas David. David cherche Claudine toute la journée. David va à la bibliothèque. À la bibliothèque, David trouve Charles et Monique et David parle à Charles et Monique, mais David ne trouve pas Claudine. David va au restaurant universitaire. Devant le restaurant, David voit une étudiante. Est-ce que c'est Claudine? Non, ce n'est pas Claudine; c'est sa copine Mireille.

David rentre dans sa chambre où David téléphone à Claudine pour inviter Claudine au cinéma, mais Claudine ne répond pas. David ne peut pas trouver Claudine! Enfin, à onze heures du soir, David trouve Claudine. Mais Claudine n'est pas seule—Claudine est avec Robert!

Après, le pauvre David trouve Claudine partout. David va à la bibliothèque. Voilà Claudine—mais avec Robert! David trouve Claudine et Robert au restaurant universitaire. David trouve Claudine et Robert au cinéma. Claudine regarde Robert tout le temps et Claudine parle à Robert avec beaucoup d'enthousiasme! David n'est pas content. David commence vraiment à détester Claudine et Robert! Alors, David décide de téléphoner à la copine de Claudine—Mireille. Si David va au cinéma avec Mireille, Mireille va peut-être aimer David. Mireille va peut-être parler à David avec beaucoup d'enthousiasme. David rêve beaucoup!

➤➤ L'accord du participe passé

You have already learned that the past participle of verbs conjugated with **être** in the **passé composé** agrees with the subject of the sentence.

See the **Instructor's Resource Manual** for more information.

Martine est rentrée chez elle et
  elle a regardé la télévision.

*Martine came home and
  she watched television.*

The past participle of verbs conjugated with **avoir** in the **passé composé** agrees instead with a direct object when the direct object precedes the verb. This occurs in three instances.

1. When a direct object pronoun precedes the verb.

   —Les Lemont ont vendu **leur maison?**

   Have the Lemonts sold their house?

   —Oui, ils l'ont vendue la semaine passée.

   Yes, they sold it last week.

   —Tu as envoyé **les cartes** de Noël?

   Did you send the Christmas cards?

   —Oui, je **les** ai envoyées hier.

   Yes, I sent them yesterday.

2. In a question using **quel.**

   Quelle chemise est-ce que Paul a achetée?

   Which shirt did Paul buy?

   Quels magazines est-ce que tu as achetés?

   Which magazines did you buy?

3. In a sentence containing the relative pronoun **que.** In this case, **que** functions as a preceding direct object. The past participle agrees with the noun that **que** has replaced.

   C'est **la lettre que** j'ai écrite hier.

   That's the letter (that) I wrote yesterday.

   Où sont **les magazines que** tu as lus?

   Where are the magazines that you read?

   Note that past participles agree only with preceding direct objects, not with indirect objects.

   Martin **leur** a donné les fleurs.

   Martin gave them the flowers.

   Les fleurs? Martin **les** a données à ses parents.

   The flowers? Martin gave them to his parents.

As with verbs conjugated with **être** in the **passé composé,** past participle agreement in verbs conjugated with **avoir** in the **passé composé** is primarily a written phenomenon. There are only a few verbs where this agreement is reflected in pronunciation.

1. For verbs with a past participle that ends in a consonant, the addition of **-e** because of a preceding feminine direct object causes the final consonant to be pronounced.

—Où est-ce que tu as **mis** mes chaussettes?	*Where did you put my socks?*
—Je les ai **mises** dans le tiroir.	*I put them in the drawer.*
—Tu as **ouvert** la fenêtre?	*Did you open the window?*
—Oui, je l'ai **ouverte.**	*Yes, I opened it.*
—Tu as **écrit** la lettre à Marc?	*Did you write the letter to Marc?*
—Oui, je l'ai **écrite** hier.	*Yes, I wrote it yesterday.*

2. As is the case for adjectives, past participles ending in **-s** are identical in the masculine singular and plural.

—Est-ce que Michel a **pris** ses gants?	*Did Michael take his gloves?*
—Non, il ne les a pas **pris.** Les voilà, sur la table.	*No, he didn't take them. There they are, on the table.*

Vous avez compris?

A. Faire les accords Est-ce qu'il y a accord du participe passé *(past participle agreement)?* Faites les accords quand c'est nécessaire.

1. Ma robe? Oui, je l'ai pris___ .
2. Quelle voiture est-ce que tu as acheté___ ?
3. Nous sommes rentré___ tard hier soir.
4. Est-ce qu'elles sont descendu___ ?
5. Mes devoirs? Tu les as donné___ au professeur?
6. Les pommes! Qui les a mangé___ ?
7. Quelles fleurs est-ce que tu as mis___ sur la table?
8. Ils sont entré___ par la porte du garage.
9. Mais ils sont sorti___ quand ils ont rencontré___ deux gros chiens méchants.
10. Où est mon parapluie? Tu ne l'as pas pris___ ?
11. Il n'y a plus de tomates! Elles ont mangé___ toutes les tomates?
12. —Et la porte?! Qui l'a ouvert___ ?
    —Pas moi, j'ai ouvert___ la fenêtre mais pas la porte.

B. Les préparatifs de fête Il y a une fête ce soir et voilà ce que tout le monde a fait:

- Patrick a acheté les fleurs et le vin.
- Aline a fait le ménage.
- Jean-Michel a fait la cuisine.
- Patrice a mis la table.
- Daniel est allé au supermarché pour acheter le fromage, les légumes et les jus de fruit.
- Véronique est allée chercher le pain à la boulangerie.
- Luc est allé chercher les tartes et le gâteau à la pâtisserie.
- Bruno a fait les crudités.
- Diane a fait la sangria.

Mais Roger veut être sûr que tout est vraiment prêt *(ready)*. Répondez aux questions de Roger.

Modèle   On a fait la cuisine?
Oui, Jean-Michel l'a faite.

1. On a acheté le fromage?
2. On a mis la table?
3. On a acheté le gâteau?
4. On a fait le ménage?

5. On a acheté le pain?
6. On a acheté les jus de fruit?
7. On a fait les crudités?
8. On a fait la sangria?

Continuons!

A. Des vacances à Barcelone   Pierre et Ingrid sont allés en vacances à Barcelone l'été passé. Mais il y a trop de noms dans leur histoire. Écrivez de nouveau l'histoire avec des pronoms, mais faites attention: il ne faut pas remplacer tous les noms par des pronoms si on veut comprendre l'histoire! Quand vous avez fini, lisez votre texte pour être sûr qu'on va vous comprendre.

Pierre et Ingrid sont allés à Barcelone l'été passé. Ingrid a fait les valises. Pierre a choisi ses vêtements. Pierre a mis ses vêtements sur le lit et Ingrid a mis les vêtements de Pierre dans une valise. Ingrid a pris aussi sa jupe bleue et sa robe orange. Ingrid a mis sa jupe bleue et sa robe orange dans la valise.

À Barcelone, Pierre et Ingrid ont trouvé un hôtel pas cher. Pierre a aimé l'hôtel mais Ingrid n'a pas aimé l'hôtel parce qu'Ingrid aime les grandes chambres claires. Dans cet hôtel, Pierre et Ingrid ont parlé avec une Espagnole sympathique. L'Espagnole sympathique s'appelait Mercedes. Pierre et Ingrid ont invité Mercedes à Paris. Mercedes va aller chez Pierre et Ingrid pour les vacances de Noël. Pierre et Ingrid vont acheter un cadeau pour Mercedes parce que Mercedes a invité Pierre et Ingrid chez Mercedes à Ségovie.

Pierre et Ingrid ont fait un beau voyage.

B. Les vacances de Dominique   Dominique (une femme) et Dominique (un homme) ont fait chacun *(each)* un voyage intéressant, mais qui a fait quoi? (SUGGESTIONS: D'abord, décidez si on parle de Dominique la femme, de Dominique l'homme ou si c'est impossible à dire et faites trois listes. Ensuite, mettez les phrases *(sentences)* ensemble pour décrire chaque voyage.

Dominique a gagné un million à la loterie. Dominique a mangé du poisson. Dominique a fait de la natation. Dominique a envoyé beaucoup de cartes postales de la plage. Dominique est partie à Nairobi (Kenya). Dominique est resté sur la plage. Dominique a acheté du poisson. Dominique est restée un mois. Dominique est allé au casino. Dominique est parti en été. Dominique a acheté des masques africains. Dominique a fait un safari-photo. Dominique est allé à Nice. Dominique est rentrée en Concorde à Paris. Dominique est resté quinze jours. Dominique a perdu son argent. Dominique est arrivée en hiver. Dominique est rentré à Paris en auto-stop *(hitchhiking)*. Dominique est parti en train avec ses amis. Dominique est sorti tous les soirs. Dominique est descendue dans un hôtel près d'un parc. Dominique est descendu dans un hôtel bon marché. Dominique est montée sur un éléphant. Dominique a dansé dans les discothèques. Dominique a pris beaucoup de photos de lions.

Découvertes culturelles: Systèmes de communication

➤➤ Le Minitel

A. Préparation.

1. **Regardez.** Où sommes-nous? Qu'est-ce qu'il y a sur la photo?
2. **Imaginez.** Quelle heure est-il? Qui travaille à ce bureau? (Un homme ou une femme?) Quel est son travail? Où est cette personne en ce moment? Que fait-elle?

Minitel 10
Tous les avantages d'un super téléphone. Un accès plus facile aux services Télétel.

Voici le Minitel 10, un Minitel* encore plus performant pour communiquer encore plus facilement. Aussi simple à utiliser qu'un Minitel 1, le Minitel 10 apporte en plus tous les avantages d'un super téléphone: vous allez découvrir une nouvelle manière de communiquer, plus rapide et plus pratique, que ce soit avec un correspondant ou avec un service Télétel.

*Minitel : marque déposée

Avec le Minitel 10, tout est plus simple. Plus besoin de décrocher: appuyez sur une touche, et la ligne est à vous. Appuyez sur une autre touche, et le Minitel 10 composera automatiquement l'un des vingt numéros de téléphone ou de services Télétel mis en mémoire dans son répertoire.

La ligne est occupée? Pas de problème! Avec la touche Bis, le Minitel 10 se chargera de rappeler votre correspondant et vous ne décrocherez que lorsqu'il sera au bout du fil.

Il n'y a plus de temps mort avec le Minitel 10. Ainsi, lorsque vous aurez trouvé le numéro de téléphone de votre correspondant grâce à l'Annuaire Électronique, le Minitel 10 pourra composer directement le numéro.

Même la communication avec votre entourage est facilitée! Grâce à l'écoute collective, vous pouvez organiser une conférence autour de votre Minitel 10, et si vous avez quelque chose à dire à votre entourage, appuyez sur la touche Secret: vous pourrez parler sans interrompre votre correspondant et sans qu'il vous entende.

B. Le Minitel 10, qu'est-ce que c'est? Où est le Minitel sur la photo?

Modèle   *Il est devant la fenêtre...*

Act. B: Use these questions to review prepositions of location: **à côté de, à gauche de, à droite de, derrière, près de, loin de,** etc.

C. Le langage de la communication. Quels mots du texte s'appliquent à la communication par Minitel? Trouvez dans le texte les équivalents des mots suivants:

1. la personne avec qui on communique
2. prendre le téléphone
3. taper un chiffre
4. faire un numéro de téléphone entièrement
5. faire un numéro de téléphone une seconde fois
6. une liste de numéros
7. conserver des informations
8. parler avec deux ou trois personnes en même temps

D. Les usages du Minitel.

Act. D, 1: Ask students to find the words in the text that relate to each topic. This will help them understand the text.

1. **Les usages du Minitel.** Trouvez dans le texte les informations nécessaires pour compléter ces colonnes.

Les qualités du Minitel	Pour contacter qui	Méthode d'utilisation

2. D'après la photo et le texte, donnez une définition du Minitel et de ses usages.

Modèle   *Le Minitel c'est pour...*

E. Renseignements supplémentaires. Comment avoir accès à un Minitel? Préparez cinq questions sur le Minitel pour avoir des informations sur la distribution et l'usage du Minitel: prix, achat ou location, services, usage personnel, professionnel, etc.

Act. E: Brainstorm with students to suggest question topics: cost, other functions of the Minitel, where to obtain it, other technological needs, types of services one can obtain, etc. Students can use their questions to ask the instructor for further information.

F. Moi et mon Minitel. Vous êtes en France et vous voulez avoir accès à un Minitel.

1. Pourquoi êtes-vous en France? des raisons personnelles? touristiques? d'affaires?
2. Pourquoi est-ce que vous employez votre Minitel? Soyez spécifique.

Modèle   *Je suis... Je travaille pour... Aujourd'hui je vais... parce que...*

Act. F, 1: Have students come up with a specific plan. Could be group work.

Act. F, 2: Use to introduce business French: renting a car, organizing a business trip, reserving a room, finding out the cost of merchandise, obtaining information on real estate, etc. Students may use the www to do research on various topics.

➡️ La numérotation à 10 chiffres

Act. A: Have students brainstorm to find these numbers. Alternatively, you may want to assign this for homework so that students can look up the numbers they don't know.

A. Quel numéro?

1. Chez vous, quel numéro faites-vous quand vous voulez...
   - obtenir un numéro que vous ne savez pas?
   - appeler les pompiers?
   - appeler une ambulance?
   - appeler un service sans payer la communication?
   - appeler la police?
   - appeler un numéro en France de votre pays?

2. Combien de chiffres ont les numéros de téléphone dans votre pays? Est-ce qu'il y a aussi un numéro pour votre état ou pour votre province?

France Telecom

Vendredi 18 octobre 1996 à 23 h., he française (soit 21 h. UTC), la France a changé numérotation téléphonique. Cette évolution accompagne et surtout anticipe le développement cesse croissant des télécommunications (nouveau services, télécopieurs, mobiles, etc.). Elle crée une ressource de numéros pour plusieurs dizaines d'ar et s'inscrit dans une perspective d'harmonisation européenne et internationale.

La Nouvelle Numérotation Téléphonique concerne tou vos correspondants en France et est intervenue pour le 18 octobre 1996. Elle vise à simplifier et à unifier le système français (notamment par la suppression du 1

De l'étranger, vous joindrez tous vos **correspondant** avec un numéro à 9 chiffres, après **l'indicatif** 33.

Comment appeler tous vos correspondants en France ?

▶ **Pour un correspondant en Ile-de-France (Paris et région parisienne) :**

il n'y a aucun changement. Les numéros ont 9 chiffre et commencent par le 1.

Nouvelle numérotation téléphonique française

vendredi 18 octobre 1996 à 21h. UTC

9 chiffres pour appeler tous vos correspondants en France

Pas de changement pour les numéros dont les trois premiers chiffres sont :		
1 30	1 43	1 49
1 34	1 44	1 53
1 39	1 45	1 55
1 40	1 46	1 60
1 41	1 47	1 64
1 42	1 48	1 69

Tout savoir sur la Nouvelle Numérotation Téléphonique Française

B. La carte de France. En combien de zones téléphoniques est divisée la France pour cette nouvelle numérotation?

1. Où est la région de l'Île de France? C'est la région de quelle ville?
2. Quelles zones téléphoniques sont pour la province?
3. Quelle zone téléphonique a la Corse?

C. Changements. Trouvez la date du changement des numéros de téléphone en France. Combien de chiffres est-ce qu'il y avait avant cette date? Combien est-ce qu'il y a de chiffres maintenant?

D. Les villes de France. Dites les zones téléphoniques des villes suivantes d'après la carte: Bordeaux, Toulouse, Marseille, Nice, Strasbourg, Lyon.

Act. D: Students can say **la zone 3, la zone 4,** etc. Students can also give geographic location (**sud-est, nord-est,** etc.) in order to identify city locations.

r un correspondant en province
s régions) :

uterez simplement selon sa localisation, le 2,
4 ou le 5 en tête de son numéro actuel qui ne
pas.

nnaître le chiffre à
reportez-vous à la
contre ou consultez
u ci-dessous.

▶ **Pour les services mobiles :**
il suffira d'ajouter le 6 en tête des numéros actuels.

Faites précéder de :	Le numéro actuel commençant par :	Faites précéder de :	Le numéro actuel commençant par :
6	01	6	07
6	02	6	08
6	03	6	09
6	06		

▶ **Pour les services nationaux (Vidéotex, Audiotex,...) :**
il suffira d'ajouter le 8 en tête des numéros à 8 chiffres commençant par 36.

▶ **Pour les départements et les territoires d'Outre-Mer (DOM-TOM) :**
il n'y a aucun changement. Vous composez l'indicatif à 3 chiffres du DOM ou du TOM suivi du numéro à 6 chiffres du correspondant.

Le numéro actuel commençant par :	Faites précéder de :	Le numéro actuel commençant par :	Faites précéder de :	Le numéro actuel commençant par :
20	2	48	4	76
21	5	49	4	77
22	4	50	4	78
23	2	51	4	79
24	5	53	3	80
25	2	54	3	81
26	5	55	3	82
27	5	56	3	83
28	5	57	3	84
29	5	58	3	85
31	5	59	3	86
32	3	60	3	87
33	5	61	3	88
34	5	62	3	89
35	5	63	4	90
37	5	65	4	91
38	4	66	4	92
39	4	67	4	93
40	4	68	4	94
41	4	69	4	95
42	4	70	2	96
43	4	71	2	97
44	4	72	2	98
45	4	73	2	99
46	4	74		
47	4	75		

Liste établie au 31 mars 1995

La numérotation en France

En France, la Nouvelle Numérotation se traduit pour tous les abonnés par le passage de leur numéro actuel à un numéro à 10 chiffres, commençant par un 0 qui n'est pas composé à l'international: on ajoute le 01 pour l'Île de France, le 02 pour le Nord-Ouest, le 03 pour le Nord-Est, le 04 pour le Sud-Est, le 05 pour le Sud-Ouest et le 06 pour les mobiles.

Tous les appels se font en composant ces 10 chiffres; le 16 disparaît.
Île-de-France ↔ Province: 10 chiffres
D'une région à une autre région: 10 chiffres
À l'intérieur d'une même région: 10 chiffres

Pour appeler l'étranger, le 00 remplace le 19.

 **France Telecom**

France Télécom Réseaux et Services Internationaux
246 rue de Bercy 75584 Paris Cedex 12

RCS Paris B 380 129 866

Réservation et renseignements

Mais ce n'est pas tout !

Si vous êtes détenteur de la carte Passeport "Senior" ou "Famille", vous bénéficiez d'un avantage supplémentaire :

10% de remise

sur les tarifs Bleus des hôtels du "Passeport" Air Inter Europe.

Centres de réservations Hertz :

Paris : (1) 39 38 38 38

Autres villes : 05 05 33 11 (appel gratuit)

3615 code HERTZ

Centres de réservations Air Inter Europe :

Paris : (1) 45 46 90 00

Bordeaux : 56 13 10 10	Nice : 93 14 84 84
Lyon : 72 11 56 56	Strasbourg : 88 61 49 12
Marseille : 91 39 36 36	Toulouse : 61 30 68 68

3615 code AIRINTER

ou votre Agence de Voyages

Hertz loue des Ford et d'autres grandes marques.

3615 code HERTZ and 3615 code AIRINTER are the access numbers on the Minitel.

E. Pour appeler Hertz. Vous travaillez dans une agence de voyage à Montréal et vous voulez changer les numéros de téléphone de la compagnie Hertz et de l'agence Air Inter sur votre ordinateur. Quels vont être les nouveaux numéros?

l'agence Hertz de Paris	
le numéro gratuit pour les autres villes	
le Centre de réservations Air Inter Europe... de Paris	
de Bordeaux	
de Lyon	
de Marseille	
de Nice	
de Strasbourg	
de Toulouse	

Act. F: Have students first focus on the paragraph **Vendredi 18 octobre 1996 à 23 h., heure française** and hypothesize why these numbers are changing and if there will be consequences. Since France Télécom is a public service, some answers will be evident: no change in price, changing information in phone booths, move to 10 numbers to make it possible to expand the telephone system and its services, need to reprint telephone books, etc.

www explore!
http//voila.heinle.com

F. Pourquoi? Travaillez par deux. Préparez chacun *(each)* cinq questions sur ce changement de numérotation. Puis passez vos questions à votre partenaire et essayez de répondre à ses questions pendant qu'il/elle répond à vos questions.

*O*rthographe et prononciation

▶▶ Homonymes

Homonyms are words that have the same pronunciation but whose spelling and meaning differ. English has many homonyms.

dew, due, do   aisle, isle, I'll

French also has various sets of homonyms.

a / à *(have / to)*   peu / peux / peut *(little / can / can)*
ces / ses *(those / his* or *her)*   son / sont *(his* or *her / are)*
la / là *(the / there)*   vin / vingt *(wine / twenty)*
où / ou *(where / or)*

For some French speakers, the words **et** and **est** may be homonyms.

Activité

Homonymes Trouvez le mot juste.

1. Patrick est (à / a) New York avec (sont / son) frère.
2. (Où / Ou) est-ce que je (peut / peu / peux) mettre le (vingt / vin)?
3. (Ces / Ses) enfants sont (ces / ses) enfants?
4. (On / Ont) dit qu'ils (on / ont) fini.

*V*ocabulaire de base

TEXT TAPE:
Vocabulaire de base

NOMS

une adresse *address*
un article *article*
une bande dessinée *comic strip, comic book*
une boîte aux lettres *mailbox*
une cabine téléphonique *telephone booth*
une carte postale *postcard*
le courrier *mail, correspondence*
une dissertation *paper (written for class)*
le droit *law*
un écrivain *writer*
une enveloppe *envelope*

un facteur *mail carrier*
un journal, des journaux *newspaper*
un(e) journaliste *journalist, reporter*
une lettre *letter*
une librairie *bookstore*
la littérature *literature*
un magazine *magazine*
la médecine *medicine (studies, science)*
la météo *weather forecast*
un numéro (de téléphone) *(telephone) number*
une page *page*
une petite annonce *classified ad*
la pluie *rain*
la politique *politics*

la publicité *advertising*
une question *question*
un renseignement *piece of information*
les sciences économiques *(f. pl.) economics*
un timbre *stamp*
la vérité *truth*

ADJECTIFS

cher, chère *(precedes noun) dear*
cher, chère *(follows noun) expensive*
ensoleillé(e) *sunny*
passé(e) *last (day, month, etc.)*

VERBES

décrire *to describe*

demander (qqch. à qqn) *to ask (someone for something)*

dire (qqch. à qqn) *to say, to tell (something to someone)*

écrire (qqch. à qqn) *to write (something to someone)*

envoyer (qqch. à qqn) *to send (something to someone)*

lire *to read*

réussir à + inf. (conj. like finir) *to succeed to + inf.*

réussir (un examen) (conj. like finir) *to pass (a test), to succeed*

DIVERS

être au courant de + nom *to be informed, to know about*

être en train de + inf. *to be in the middle of (doing something)*

être étudiant en (droit, médecine...) *to study (law, medicine. . .)*

poser une question (à qqn) *to ask (someone) a question*

Quel temps fait-il? *What's the weather like?*

vouloir dire *to mean*

Vocabulaire supplémentaire

NOMS

l'amour *(m.)* love

un annuaire (des téléphones) *telephone book*

un bureau de tabac *tobacco shop*

une célébrité *celebrity*

un dessin humoristique *cartoon (in a newspaper or magazine)*

l'est *(m.)* east

un événement *event*

le Minitel *Minitel*

le nord *north*

une nouvelle *piece of news*

l'ouest *(m.)* west

un poème *poem*

la presse *press, (news)papers*

un roman *novel*

une rubrique *section, column (in a periodical)*

le sommaire *table of contents of a magazine*

le sud *south*

un titre *title*

ADJECTIFS

culturel, culturelle *cultural*

féminin(e) *feminine*

littéraire *literary*

masculin(e) *masculine*

scientifique *scientific*

suisse *Swiss*

un temps...

   couvert *overcast*

   nuageux *cloudy*

DIVERS

en Bretagne *in Brittany*

en Suisse *in Switzerland*

mettre une lettre à la poste *to mail a letter*

faire du camping *to go camping, to camp*

passer un examen *to take a test*

POUR ÉCRIRE DES LETTRES

- INFORMAL LETTERS TO PEOPLE YOU KNOW WELL:

Cher Paul, *Dear Paul,*

Mon chéri, Ma chérie, (Mon amour,) *Darling, My love,*

Amicalement, (Très amicalement, Bien amicalement,) *Cordially,*

Grosses bises, (Gros bisous,) *Love,*

Je t'embrasse, *Hugs and kisses,*

- FORMAL LETTERS:

Monsieur, (Madame, Mademoiselle,) *Dear Sir (Madam, Miss),*

Je vous prie d'agréer, Monsieur, (Madame, Mademoiselle,) l'expression de mes sentiments les meilleurs *Very truly yours, Sincerely,*

LE FRANÇAIS TEL QU'ON LE PARLE

- AU TÉLÉPHONE:

Allô! *Hello!*

Ici Stéphane Martin. *This is Stéphane Martin. (formal)*

C'est Stéphane! *This is Stéphane. (informal)*

Qui est à l'appareil? *Who is it?*

C'est à quel sujet? *What is it about?*

Pouvez-vous rappeler? *Can you call back?*

Quel est votre numéro de téléphone? *What's your (tele)phone number?*

Excusez-moi, j'ai fait un faux numéro. *Excuse me, I dialed a/the wrong number.*

Ne quittez pas. *Could you hold? Don't hang up. Stay on the line.*

Je vous le/la passe. *I am putting you through to him/her.*

C'est ça. *That's it. (depends on context)*

Tiens! *Ah! (to express surprise)*

LE FRANÇAIS FAMILIER

une dissert = une dissertation

donner un coup de fil = téléphoner

une pub = une annonce publicitaire, une publicité

ON ENTEND PARFOIS...

les annonces classées (Canada) = les petites annonces

une carte-vue (Belgique) = une carte postale

le postillon (Canada) = le facteur

une tabagie (Canada) = un bureau de tabac

Chez les Hanin

En bref

Dans cette leçon...
- Habitudes quotidiennes
- Le corps
- La vie de famille
- La santé
- Les verbes réfléchis
- Faire des comparaisons
- Le travail: temps et espace
- Les crèches

In this lesson...
- Daily routines
- The body
- Family life
- Health
- Reflexive verbs
- Making comparisons
- Work: time and space
- Daycare

www explore!
http://voila.heinle.com

Develop writing skills with Système-D software!

Practice listening and pronunciation skills with the Text Tape!

Discover the Francophone world!

Build your skills!

INTERNET

SYSTÈME-D

TEXT TAPE

VIDEO TAPE

CD-ROM

Students have an open-ended writing activity in the **Cahier** suitable for use with **Système-D**.

Entrée en matière: Être père

La paternité en question.

Depuis quelques années, l'évolution des modes de vie et des sciences biologiques a abouti au développement de formes nouvelles de paternité.... Ces récentes évolutions ont fait éclater la fonction paternelle en trois fonctions; le géniteur, le père affectif et l'éducateur...

Gérard Mermet, Francoscopie 1995

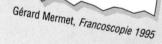

Les nouveaux pères: You may want to expand on this topic and have students list the specific characteristics of each type of father.

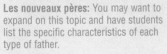 Décrivez ces pères. Comment sont-ils? Que font-ils? Où sont-ils? Quelle heure est-il? Quel temps fait-il? Que fait la mère?

374

Bien sec avec *Babysek*

Babysek.

La serviette qui aide les papas à sécher les bébés.

Comme elle est douce la peau de nos bébés! Quel plaisir de les bichonner, de les bouchonner, de les pouponner. Mais pour protéger cette douceur, quelques bons principes à l'heure du bain: une serviette plus grande, plus épaisse, plus douce. Et l'heure du bain est un plaisir pour les papas comme pour les bébés! Avec ses nouvelles fibres de coton pur et son nouveau tissage élastique, mœlleux et léger . . . voilà votre bébé sec et heureux! Et son papa bien soulagé! Achetez Babysek, la serviette qui sèche en douceur la peau douce de nos bébés!

En vente dans tous les grand magasins.

La photo. Où se passe cette scène? Qui est là? C'est dans quelle pièce de la maison? Décrivez la pièce. Quels objets y a-t-il dans la pièce? De quelle couleur sont-ils? Et l'enfant, quel âge a-t-il? Décrivez-le. Qui est cet homme? un docteur? un infirmier? Est-ce qu'il habite dans cette maison? Pourquoi est-ce qu'il est avec cet enfant? Décrivez cet homme, ce qu'il porte et ses qualités. Regardez le texte «La paternité en question» et dites quel type de père il est probablement.

Le produit. Est-ce que c'est un produit français ou international? En quoi consiste ce produit? Quelles sont les qualités du produit? Trouvez les adjectifs qui se rapportent à la serviette. Trouvez les expressions qui se rapportent au bébé. Trouvez les verbes qui se rapportent aux soins du bébé. Quel est l'élément exploité ici pour vendre ce produit?

Vocabulaire

A. C'est le soir chez les Hanin.

Julie et son frère Nicolas viennent de prendre un bain et vont aller au lit. Nicolas, neuf mois, est tout nu sur la table. Il a les cheveux châtains et les yeux marron. C'est un bébé sage qui ne pleure pas souvent. Julie, trois ans, est en train de se sécher. Rousse et frisée, c'est une petite fille adorable, mais elle fait beaucoup de bêtises parce qu'elle est énergique et têtue. Elle ne s'ennuie jamais! Les deux enfants sont en bonne santé: ils n'ont pas souvent de rhume et ils n'ont jamais la grippe.

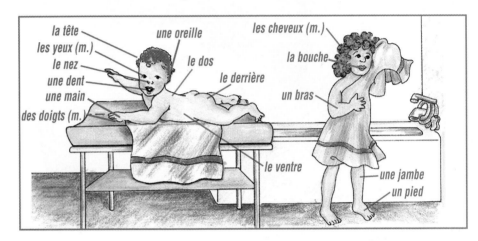

- C'est quelle pièce? Quelle heure est-il? Qui n'est pas dans la pièce? Pourquoi? Qui sont les enfants? Quel âge ont-ils? Est-ce qu'ils sont faciles ou difficiles? Pourquoi?
- Où est Nicolas? Et Julie? Comment sont-ils?

B. Et maintenant, c'est le matin.

Le réveil sonne et Bruno Hanin se réveille. C'est le père de Julie et de Nicolas. Il est seul aujourd'hui parce que sa femme, Véronique, est en voyage d'affaires à San Francisco. C'est dur de se lever ce matin parce qu'il tousse et il a un peu mal à la gorge. Il faudrait se soigner, mais il n'a pas le temps!

Il va dans la salle de bains pour se préparer.

D'abord, il prend une douche et se lave les cheveux.

Ensuite, il se brosse les dents, se rase et se peigne.

Et finalement, il s'habille.

une brosse à cheveux

- À quelle heure est-ce que le réveil sonne? C'est tôt ou c'est tard? Est-ce que Bruno habite seul? Où est sa femme? Est-ce que Bruno est en forme ce matin? Qu'est-ce que Bruno fait dans la salle de bain le matin? Comment est-ce qu'il s'habille? Quelle heure est-il maintenant? Faites une description de Bruno: Est-il grand ou petit? Est-il brun, blond ou roux? Est-il chauve? Est-il barbu (est-ce qu'il a une barbe)?
- Quels articles de toilette voyez-vous dans la salle de bains des Hanin? Qu'est-ce qu'il y a dans leur chambre? Qu'est-ce qu'on utilise pour se réveiller? se laver? se sécher? se peigner? se brosser les dents? se raser?
- À votre avis, combien de fois par jour est-ce qu'il faut se brosser les dents? Combien de fois par semaine est-ce qu'il faut se laver les cheveux? Est-ce que vous aimez mieux prendre un bain ou une douche? Le matin ou le soir? Quel shampooing utilisez-vous? Utilisez-vous un séchoir à cheveux ou non?

C. Et maintenant, les enfants.

D'habitude, la femme de Bruno l'aide le matin avec les enfants, mais cette semaine, il est tout seul et c'est beaucoup plus difficile.

TRANSPARENCY:
15-3

Nicolas et Julie partagent une chambre. Nicolas est réveillé mais Julie dort encore et est en train de rêver d'un grand chien noir. Bruno la réveille.

Bruno change et lave Nicolas. Bien sûr, comme d'habitude, Julie veut se laver toute seule et elle met de l'eau partout.

If desired, teach **collant(e)** as an adjective.

Bruno habille Nicolas, mais Julie veut s'habiller et se coiffer toute seule.

- Est-ce que Nicolas est matinal? Et Julie? Que fait Bruno? Que fait Julie? Est-ce qu'elle est sage? Qu'est-ce qu'elle va mettre?

D. Enfin, les enfants sont propres et habillés.

TRANSPARENCY: 15-4

Bruno a préparé le petit déjeuner et maintenant, il est en train de boire son café et de lire son journal. Enfin, il essaie, parce que Nicolas s'amuse à manger et Julie n'a pas faim. Bruno commence à s'énerver.

- Décrivez le petit déjeuner chez les Hanin. Est-ce que c'est un petit déjeuner calme ou énervant pour Bruno? Pourquoi est-ce que Julie ne veut pas manger?

E. Finalement...

Bruno emmène Nicolas à la crèche et Julie à l'école maternelle.

- Où vont les enfants? Pourquoi?
- Et maintenant, rêvons un peu avec Bruno. Décrivez une matinée idéale pour lui, à votre avis? Et pour vous?

Les crèches and other child-care arrangements in France are the subject of a *Découvertes culturelles* section later in this lesson.

 See also **Vidéo Magazine 3** for further treatment of **les crèches** and other child-care arrangements in France.

Notes de vocabulaire

1. Mots et expressions utiles.

un corps	*body*
un collant	*tights, pantyhose*
du déodorant	*deodorant*
faire la sieste	*to take a nap*
un rêve	*dream*
sale	*dirty*

2: Student explanations deliberately skirt the complex issue of terminology (**pronominal / réfléchi**) with verbs such as **se lever**, **se parler**, and **se dépêcher**. This text divides the category of pronominal verbs into reflexive verbs (this lesson), reciprocal verbs *(Leçon 16)*, and idiomatic reflexive verbs *(Leçon 16)*.

2. Les verbes réfléchis.

A *reflexive verb* is a verb whose action is reflected onto the person concerned. French has many verbs like this. You can identify them by the reflexive pronoun that precedes the infinitive (*se laver*). English has a few verbs that act in this way (for example, *to cut oneself*), but frequently the *yourself* is implied or optional. Look at the following examples of a verb used nonreflexively and reflexively.

Bruno **habille** les enfants.	*Bruno's dressing the children.*
Bruno **s'habille.**	*Bruno's getting (himself) dressed.*

In the first sentence, Bruno is dressing someone else; in the second sentence, the reflexive pronoun **se (s')** indicates that he is dressing himself. The use of these verbs will be described in more detail in the **Structure** section of this lesson.

3: Point out the difference in pronunciation between **cheveux** and **chevaux**. (If desired, point out that French speakers have similar problems with words like *angry* and *hungry*.)

3. Les cheveux.

Note that the word **cheveux** *(hair)* is plural in French. The singular is **un cheveu. Mon cheveu,** then, would mean *my one hair!*

4. Comment décrire les personnes?

Here are some possible ways to describe people. Bruno, for example, might describe his children as follows:

Julie a trois ans. Elle est petite, rousse et frisée. Elle a les yeux verts et elle a un petit nez adorable.
Nicolas a neuf mois. Il a les cheveux châtains et les yeux marron.

5. Les dents/ses dents.

In certain cases where possession is obvious, French tends to use a definite article (**le, la, les**) where English would use a possessive adjective (*my, your, his, her,* etc.).

Il va se laver **les** cheveux.	*He's going to wash his hair.*
Elle se brosse **les** dents trois fois par jour.	*She brushes her teeth three times a day.*

6: Like **payer**, the spelling change for **essayer** is actually optional (j'essaie/j'essaye.)

6. Essayer et emmener.

The verb **essayer** is conjugated like **payer.**

j'essaie	nous essayons
tu essaies	vous essayez
il elle } essaie	ils elles } essaient

If followed by an infinitive, it takes the preposition **de.**

Bruno **essaie d'**habiller les enfants.	*Bruno tries to get the children dressed.*
Je vais **essayer de** partir tôt.	*I'm going to try to leave early.*

The verb **emmener** is conjugated like **acheter**.

j'emmène	nous emmenons
tu emmènes	vous emmenez
il }\ elle } emmène	ils }\ elles } emmènent

Je t'emmène? *Can I take you?*
Emmenons le chien avec nous! *Let's take the dog with us!*

D'accord?

A. Le corps C'est pour quoi faire?

Modèle les pieds
C'est pour porter le corps, c'est pour marcher, etc.

1. les yeux
2. les oreilles
3. la bouche
4. les dents
5. les jambes

B. Toujours le corps On en a combien?

1. On a deux yeux, deux... , deux...
2. On a un(e)... , un(e)...
3. On a dix...
4. On a beaucoup de...

C. Énigme Quelle partie du corps est-ce que vous utilisez pour...

1. nager?
2. jouer du violon?
3. téléphoner?
4. pleurer?
5. jouer au football?

D. À quoi ça sert? Sur quelle partie du corps est-ce que vous mettez ces choses?

1. des lunettes de soleil?
2. du dentifrice?
3. des chaussettes?
4. des gants?
5. un chapeau?
6. du shampooing?

Act. D: If desired, ask students to justify their answers.

E. Normal ou bizarre? C'est normal ou c'est bizarre pour vous?

Modèle   Henri se lave les dents, puis il prend le petit déjeuner.
C'est bizarre. / C'est normal. / Ça dépend.

1. Alceste sort, puis il s'habille.
2. Jeanne se lève, puis elle prend une douche.
3. Bruno se sèche, puis il prend un bain.
4. Jacqueline se lève, puis elle se réveille.
5. Candide s'habille, puis il se lève.
6. Patricia se coiffe, puis elle se lave les cheveux.
7. Patrick se lave le visage, puis il descend.
8. Cédric s'amuse, puis il étudie.

F. Réaction! Choisissez une réaction pour les activités suivantes.

Ça m'amuse. / Ça m'énerve. / Ça m'ennuie.

1. regarder la télévision à midi quand je suis en train de manger
2. étudier à la bibliothèque le samedi soir
3. aller en classe à huit heures du matin
4. partir en voyage à huit heures du matin
5. emmener mon petit frère et ma petite sœur au cinéma
6. lire le journal au lit le dimanche matin
7. lire un article sur la politique américaine dans un magazine sérieux
8. faire les magasins pour trouver des vêtements
9. partir en vacances avec mes parents
10. mettre des vêtements élégants pour aller dans un restaurant élégant avec mes parents et leurs amis
11. ouvrir un cadeau d'un(e) ami(e)
12. offrir un cadeau à un(e) ami(e)

G. Conseils Qu'est-ce qu'il faut faire? Qu'est-ce qu'il ne faut pas faire?

Act. G: Accept both reflexive and non-reflexive verbs. For example: **Pour avoir des bonnes dents, il faut se brosser les dents, il ne faut pas manger trop de sucre, il faut aller chez le dentiste,** etc. Ask for details: **Combien de fois par jour est-ce qu'il faut se brosser les dents? Combien de fois par an est-ce qu'il faut aller chez le dentiste?**

1. Pour avoir des bonnes dents, il faut / il ne faut pas...
2. Pour avoir des beaux cheveux, il faut / il ne faut pas...
3. Pour être propre, il faut / il ne faut pas...
4. Pour aller travailler le matin, il faut / il ne faut pas...
5. Quand on est tout nu, il faut / il ne faut pas...
6. Quand on est en vacances, il faut / il ne faut pas...
7. Quand on a la grippe, il faut / il ne faut pas...

H. Problèmes Où est-ce que vous avez mal?

1. Vous avez la grippe.
2. Vous avez un gros rhume.
3. Vous êtes tombé de vélo.
4. Vous avez trop mangé.
5. Vous avez trop bu.
6. Vous avez trop parlé.
7. Vous êtes tombé dans les escaliers.
8. Votre camarade de chambre a écouté de la musique rock toute la journée.

Mise en pratique

A. Portraits Décrivez ces personnes.

1. votre sœur ou votre frère (ou un[e] cousin[e] si vous n'avez pas de frères et sœurs)
2. votre père ou votre mère
3. un de vos professeurs
4. un de vos amis ou une de vos amies
5. Candide ou Alceste

B. Ressemblances Dans votre famille, qui est comme qui? Qui n'est pas comme qui? Pourquoi? Et vous, vous êtes comme qui?

Modèle *Mon père n'est pas comme ma mère parce qu'il a les cheveux blonds et ma mère a les cheveux châtains...*

Act. B: Give students a few moments to reflect or assign as homework to be prepared before class.

C. Rêvons! Qu'est-ce que vous rêvez de faire?

Modèle le vendredi soir?
Je rêve d'aller au cinéma avec un(e) ami(e).

1. le dimanche matin?
2. le lundi matin?
3. le samedi soir?
4. pendant les vacances de printemps?
5. pendant l'été?

Act. C: Suitable for pair work. What are the most common **rêves**?

D. Un monstre pour Hollywood! On vous a demandé de créer un monstre pour un film d'horreur. Dessinez *(draw)* le monstre que vous proposez et indiquez les différentes parties de son corps. Vous allez devoir décrire et défendre votre création.

Act. D: LISTENING COMPREHENSION: Describe a monster for students to draw. Allow students to ask questions. Ask students to illustrate their monsters. Suitable for group work. Other possibilities: Have student or instructor at board or overhead drawing while other students describe their monster. Have a contest for **le meilleur monstre**.

E. La santé Voilà ce que pensent les Français de la santé:

> Pour les Français, être en bonne santé, c'est d'abord prendre plaisir à la vie (88%), pouvoir faire ce que l'on veut (80%), ne pas être malade (63%), vivre vieux (60%), ne pas souffrir (56%), ne pas avoir besoin de consulter un médecin (40%).

Gérard Mermet, *Francoscopie 1995*

1. Et pour vous, c'est quoi la santé? Trouvez cinq choses et comparez-les avec vos camarades de classe. Est-ce que vous pensez comme les Français? (Prendre plaisir à la vie, c'est aimer la vie; souffrir, c'est avoir mal.)
2. Que faut-il faire pour être en bonne santé? Trouvez dix choses à faire ou à ne pas faire et comparez-les avec la classe.

Structure

▶▶ Les verbes réfléchis

Reflexive verbs are verbs whose action reflects onto their subjects. There are a few verbs like this in English.

I cut *myself.*   She's looking at *herself* in the mirror.

In French, such verbs are called **verbes réfléchis.** They are listed in vocabulary lists and dictionaries with the reflexive pronoun **se** in front of the infinitive (for example, **se lever** = *to get up*). This reflexive pronoun will change as the verb is conjugated. Reflexive pronouns follow the same rules for placement as direct and indirect object pronouns.

Reflexive verbs are conjugated as follows:

se laver *to wash (oneself)*	
je me lave	nous nous lavons
tu te laves	vous vous lavez
il elle } se lave	ils elles } se lavent

To negate a reflexive verb, place **ne** in front of the reflexive pronoun. Place **pas** after the verb.

je ne me lave pas	nous ne nous lavons pas
tu ne te laves pas	vous ne vous lavez pas
il elle } ne se lave pas	ils elles } ne se lavent pas

To form questions with reflexive verbs, use intonation, put **est-ce que** in front of the sentence, or use inversion.

Tu te lèves tôt?   *Do you get up early?*
Est-ce que **tu te laves** les cheveux   *Do you wash your hair every day?*
   tous les jours?
À quelle heure **te lèves-tu?**   *What time do you get up?*

In the infinitive form, the reflexive pronoun is placed directly before the infinitive. This pronoun must agree with the subject of the sentence.

Nous allons **nous** habiller maintenant.   *We're going to get dressed now.*
Je ne veux pas **m'**habiller.   *I don't want to get dressed.*

Note that many verbs that are used reflexively in French can also be used nonreflexively. In this case, the action is directed toward someone or something else. Look at the following examples:

Point out to students that the difference between reflexive and nonreflexive use in French may be reflected in verb choice in English.

A discussion of the function of **se** as either a direct or indirect object is provided in **Leçon 16**.

Bruno **se réveille** à six heures et demie.	*Bruno wakes up at 6:30.*
Bruno **réveille** les enfants à sept heures.	*Bruno wakes the children up (gets the children up) at 7:00.*
Nicolas **s'amuse** à manger.	*Nicolas is having a good time eating.*
Ça n'**amuse** pas son père!	*That doesn't amuse his father!*
Comment **vous appelez**-vous?	*What's your name?*
Appelle ton frère!	*Call your brother!*
Bruno **couche** les enfants et puis il **se couche.**	*Bruno puts the children to bed and then he goes to bed.*
Paulette n'aime pas **se promener** toute seule mais elle adore **promener** son chien.	*Paulette doesn't like to take walks by herself but she loves to walk her dog.*

Here are some additional verbs that may be used both reflexively and nonreflexively:

arrêter / s'arrêter	*to stop, to stop (oneself)*
changer / se changer	*to change, to change one's clothes*
déshabiller / se déshabiller	*to undress (someone else), to get undressed*
ennuyer / s'ennuyer	*to bore (someone else), to get bored*
maquiller / se maquiller	*to make up (someone else), to put makeup on (oneself)*
soigner / se soigner	*to take care of (someone else), to take care of (oneself) (in the case of illness)*

Rappel!   Several verbs in this lesson have spelling changes in the present tense.

1. **appeler / s'appeler.** Doubles the letter -l- in front of silent endings:

    tu t'appelles (BUT vous vous appelez)

2. **changer / se changer.** Like **manger:**

    nous nous changeons

3. **ennuyer / s'ennuyer.** Like **envoyer:**

    je m'ennuie (BUT nous nous ennuyons)

4. **lever / se lever; promener / se promener.** Like **acheter:**

    il se lève (BUT vous vous levez)
    il se promène (but vous vous promenez)

5. **sécher / se sécher.** Like **préférer:**

    tu te sèches (BUT vous vous séchez)

Vous avez compris?

A. Quand?
Normalement, quand est-ce qu'on fait ces activités? Complétez la grille. (Un verbe peut figurer dans plusieurs cases.)

VERBES: se changer / se déshabiller / s'amuser / se brosser les dents / se coucher / se laver / se lever / se promener / se réveiller / se raser

le matin	à midi	l'après-midi	le soir	n'importe quand (no matter when)

Act. A: Have students compare their perceptions. Vote to establish what is "normal" for the class. Ask students to add activities within each category.

B. Et vous?
Voilà ce que font différentes personnes à différents moments de la journée. Et vous?

Modèle Jean-François se lève à six heures du matin. Et vous?
Moi aussi, je me lève à six heures. / Moi, je ne me lève pas à six heures.

1. Janine se lave les cheveux le matin. Et vous?
2. Magali se maquille tous les jours. Et vous?
3. Marc se rase tous les jours. Et vous?
4. Candide se promène l'après-midi. Et vous?
5. Alceste se regarde souvent dans le miroir. Et vous?
6. Mohammed se brosse les dents après tous les repas. Et vous?
7. Sylvie se réveille à dix heures du matin. Et vous?
8. Sandrine s'habille après le petit déjeuner. Et vous?

C. La vie n'est pas facile
Voilà ce que différentes personnes doivent faire, mais ce n'est pas ce qu'elles veulent faire! Utilisez les suggestions entre parenthèses pour dire ce que ces personnes veulent vraiment faire.

Act. C: Personne is a feminine noun, thus the use of **elles** in the direction line.

Modèle Nous nous réveillons à cinq heures du matin. (midi)
Mais nous voulons nous réveiller à midi.

1. Mes frères se rasent deux fois par jour. (une fois par jour)
2. Ma petite sœur s'appelle Linda. (Mary)
3. Mon petit frère se couche à huit heures. (dix heures)
4. Candide se promène seul. (avec un copain)
5. Tu te lèves à sept heures. (neuf heures)
6. Nous nous arrêtons à sept heures. (cinq heures)
7. Vous vous préparez pour aller à la bibliothèque. (au restaurant)

D. Réfléchi ou non? Complétez les phrases suivantes avec le verbe réfléchi ou le verbe non-réfléchi.

1. Je ne . . . . . pas à l'école! (amuser / s'amuser)
2. Bruno . . . . . les cheveux de Julie tous les matins. (brosser / se brosser)
3. Véronique . . . . . le matin. (maquiller / se maquiller)
4. Tu me . . . . . ! (énerver / s'énerver)
5. Vous n'allez pas sortir en short! Vous allez . . . . . ! (changer / se changer)
6. Qu'est-ce que vous . . . . . ? (regarder / se regarder)
7. Le soleil me . . . . . le matin. (réveiller / se réveiller)
8. Je dois . . . . . tôt ce soir. (coucher / se coucher)
9. Cet exercice me . . . . . ! (ennuyer / s'ennuyer)

Continuons!

A. Un jour dans la vie de X Choisissez un(e) étudiant(e) de la classe ou votre professeur et répondez aux questions suivantes. Attention! Il faut deviner (*guess*), pas demander! Après, vérifiez avec la personne que vous avez choisie. Est-ce que vous avez bien deviné?

1. Comment est-ce qu'il/elle s'appelle?
2. À quelle heure est-ce qu'il/elle se réveille?
3. Est-ce qu'il/elle se maquille?
4. À quelle heure est-ce qu'il/elle se lève?
5. Est-ce qu'il/elle prend une douche ou un bain?
6. Est-ce qu'il/elle se lave les cheveux tous les jours? Quand?
7. Est-ce qu'il/elle se regarde souvent dans le miroir?
8. Combien de fois par jour est-ce qu'il/elle se brosse les dents? Avec quel dentifrice?
9. Est-ce qu'il/elle aime se promener? Où? Avec qui?

Act. A: Depending on your class and the person chosen, you may want to add or delete questions.
  CONTINUATION: **Est-ce qu'il/elle s'ennuie souvent? Quand? Où? Est-ce qu'il/elle fait la sieste l'après-midi? À quelle heure est-ce qu'il/elle se couche?**

B. La journée de Candide Voilà la journée de Candide... mais en désordre et pas complète! Remettez les éléments de sa journée en ordre chronologique (il y a plusieurs possibilités!). Rajoutez les éléments qui manquent (*missing*).

1. Il se couche.
2. Il se lave.
3. Il se rase.
4. Il prend une douche.
5. Il se lève.
6. Il se sèche.
7. Il va dans la salle de bains.
8. Il se peigne.
9. Il s'habille.
10. Il boit du café.
11. Il retourne chez lui.
12. Il met son manteau.
13. Il sort de la maison.
14. Il arrive au bureau.
15. Il dit au revoir à Alceste.
16. Il sort au restaurant avec un ami.
17. Il rentre au bureau.
18. Il dit bonjour à Alceste.
19. Il se réveille.
20. Il boit un verre de vin.
21. Il prépare le dîner.
22. Il fait la vaisselle.
23. Il se couche.
24. Il prend une aspirine.

Act B: First, have students establish a chronological order they find satisfactory (students should add to and/or modify the list suggested). Then ask students to add details, rewrite sentences, and so forth. The final assignment can be a composition.

C. Un sondage En groupes de trois ou quatre, préparez des questions à poser à vos camarades de classe sur leurs habitudes de tous les jours (une question par personne de votre groupe). Choisissez une des questions de votre groupe et promenez-vous dans la classe pour la poser à tout le monde. Quand vous avez fini, retournez dans votre groupe et organisez les résultats pour les présenter à la classe.

D. Voilà Georges... ou est-ce que c'est Georgette?

1. C'est à vous de décider. C'est Georges ou Georgette? Comment est-il/elle? Où habite-t-il/elle?
2. Décrivez une journée typique de Georges/Georgette?

TEXT TAPE:
Conversation en français

E. Conversation en français Vous interviewez une célébrité locale pour le journal de votre université. Posez des questions à cette personne sur sa vie, ses habitudes quotidiennes *(daily)*, etc.

▶▶ Les verbes réfléchis à l'impératif

The negative imperative of reflexive verbs is formed by putting **ne** in front of the reflexive pronoun and **pas** after the verb.

Ne t'énerve **pas.**	*Don't get annoyed.*
Ne vous déshabillez **pas!**	*Don't get undressed!*
Ne nous levons **pas** ce matin.	*Let's not get up this morning.*

The affirmative imperative of reflexive verbs is formed by adding the stressed form of the reflexive pronoun (**toi, vous,** or **nous**) after the verb, connected by a hyphen.

Lève-**toi!**	*Get up!*
Soignez-**vous!**	*Take care of yourself!*
Changeons-**nous** et allons en ville.	*Let's get changed and go downtown.*

Vous avez compris?

A. Combattre le stress! Voilà des idées pour combattre le stress. Ce sont de mauvaises ou de bonnes idées?

1. Couchez-vous tôt le soir.
2. Levez-vous tard le dimanche.
3. Sortez le week-end et amusez-vous bien.
4. Énervez-vous tout le temps.
5. Ne vous promenez pas.
6. Arrêtez-vous de travailler à deux heures du matin.

B. Le mauvais exemple M. Rivière dit à ses deux filles de ne pas être comme leur frère Paul.

Modèles Paul ne se lave pas.
Lavez-vous!

Paul s'énerve tout le temps.
Ne vous énervez pas!

1. Paul fume.
2. Paul se lève tard.
3. Paul boit trop.
4. Paul rentre tard le soir.
5. Paul s'amuse toute la nuit.
6. Paul n'est pas gentil avec les autres.
7. Paul se couche tard.
8. Paul demande la voiture le week-end.

Continuons!

Marie-Claire a un problème! Les parents de Marie-Claire arrivent dans une heure. Voilà la liste de tout ce qu'elle doit faire avant leur arrivée. Aidez-la. Qu'est-ce qu'elle doit faire d'abord? Est-ce qu'il y a d'autres choses qu'elle a oubliées?

Modèle *Écoute, Marie-Claire, d'abord, lave-toi les cheveux, puis...*

**LA LISTE
DE
MARIE-CLAIRE**

- ranger ma chambre
- mettre une robe
- trouver la photo de mes parents
- faire la vaisselle
- me brosser les dents
- me coiffer
- me sécher les cheveux
- cacher les photos de mes petits amis
- me laver les cheveux
- faire mon lit

La comparaison des adjectifs et des adverbes

Use the following expressions to compare people or things.

plus (... que)	*more (. . . than)*
aussi (... que)	*as (. . . as)*
moins (... que)	*less (. . . than)*

A noun or a stressed pronoun is used after **que.** Note the various English equivalents possible.

Marie est **plus** belle **que moi,** mais je suis plus intelligente.
Marie is prettier than I (am), but I'm smarter.

Georges n'est pas **aussi** grand **que Jérôme,** mais il est plus fort.
Georges isn't as tall as Jérôme, but he's stronger.

Stéphane est **moins** têtu **que Marc.**
Stéphane is less stubborn than Marc.

Mon chien est **plus** intelligent **que mon chat.**
My dog is more intelligent than my cat.

Mon frère sort **plus** souvent **que moi.**
My brother goes out more (often) than I.

Est-ce que les professeurs travaillent **moins que les étudiants?**
Do teachers work less than students?

Bon / meilleur; bien / mieux

Bon *(good)* and **meilleur** *(better)* are adjectives. They agree with the nouns they modify.

Beth est une **bonne** étudiante. Elle est **meilleure** que sa copine Anne.
Beth is a good student. She's better than her friend Anne.

Bien *(well)* and **mieux** *(better)* are adverbs. They modify verbs. They are invariable.

Beth travaille **bien.** Elle travaille **mieux** que sa copine Anne.
Beth works well. She works better than her friend Anne.

Mauvais / mal

Mauvais *(bad)* is an adjective and, like **bon,** agrees with the noun it modifies. To say *worse* as an adjective, use **plus mauvais.**

—Il fait **mauvais** aujourd'hui.   *"It's nasty out today."*
—Oui, mais il faisait **plus mauvais** hier.   *"Yes, but yesterday it was worse."*

Mal *(badly)* is an adverb. Like **bien,** it modifies a verb. To say *worse* as an adverb, use **plus mal.**

—Elle joue **mal** aujourd'hui.   *"She's playing badly today."*
—Oui, mais hier elle a joué **plus mal.**   *"Yes, but yesterday she played worse."*

Vous avez compris?

A. L'égocentrisme Voilà une liste que Sandrine a faite pour se comparer à ses camarades de classe, à sa famille et à ses amis. Elle a utilisé les symboles +, – et = pour indiquer ses opinions. Interprétez sa liste.

Modèle   intelligent(e): Martine +, Gauthier –
Martine est plus intelligente que moi. Gauthier est moins intelligent que moi. (Je suis plus intelligente que Gauthier.)

1. beau (belle): Colette =, Danielle +, Valérie –
2. travailleur (travailleuse): mes frères –, ma mère =
3. riche: Bertrand +, Christophe –
4. fort(e) en maths: Annick +, Pierre –

B. Et les enfants? M. et Mme N'Somwé parlent de leurs enfants. Utilisez **bon, bien, meilleur(e)** ou **mieux** pour compléter ce qu'ils disent.

—Jacqueline est . . . . . en maths qu'Évelyne.
—Oui, mais Évelyne travaille . . . . . que Jacqueline. Jacqueline est un peu paresseuse, tu sais.
—Peut-être. Mais elle est . . . . . en langues que son frère.
—Oui, mais lui, il travaille assez . . . . . Et il est . . . . . que ses sœurs en sciences.

Continuons!

A. Comparez Faites les comparaisons suivantes:

1. les chats et les chiens
2. les étudiants et les professeurs
3. les hommes et les femmes
4. la ville et la campagne
5. Los Angeles et New York
6. Alceste et Candide
7. Julie et Nicolas Hanin

B. La décision de Marie-Laure Deux jeunes gens ont invité Marie-Laure au Bal du printemps. Elle ne peut pas décider quelle invitation elle va accepter.

1. Marie-Laure compare. Lisez la liste et comparez Marc à Antoine.

   Marc: intelligent / sérieux / gentil / bien équilibré / très grand / sportif / membre du club de foot / ne parle pas beaucoup / paie toujours / a une voiture de sport.

   Antoine: intellectuel / artiste / branché / adore le rock / assez petit mais très beau / adore parler de politique / aime s'amuser / a beaucoup d'amis / n'a jamais d'argent / fume

   Modèle   Marc est plus sérieux qu'Antoine, mais Antoine adore parler de politique.

2. La décision. Quelle invitation est-ce que Marie-Laure doit accepter? Pourquoi?

Act. B: FOLLOW-UP: Ask students which invitation they would choose. You can also give students a choice between the "twin" sisters of Marc (Martine) and Antoine (Antoinette).

Découvertes culturelles: Le travail: temps et espace

▶ Crèches et haltes-garderies

Act. A: Use to review question forms, vocabulary pertaining to daily life and routines, adjectives of description, etc.

A. Préparation. Quelles sont les questions que les parents ont avant de placer leur enfant dans une crèche?

Modèle *À quelle heure commencez-vous?*

B. Les crèches.

1. **Renseignements généraux sur les crèches.** Quelles questions correspondent aux questions que vous avez trouvées pour l'activité A?

2. Donnez les informations concernant les catégories suivantes:

Le nom des endroits qui gardent les enfants:	
Les papiers nécessaires pour l'inscription:	
Le lieu du bureau d'inscription:	
Les personnes pour qui les crèches existent:	
Les prix par mois:	
Les personnes avec prix spéciaux:	

3. **Renseignements généraux sur les haltes-garderies.** Donnez les informations concernant les catégories suivantes et citez la partie du texte qui contient cette information:

L'âge minimum de l'enfant:	
L'âge maximum de l'enfant:	
Les types d'accueil:	
Le prix horaire normal:	
Le prix horaire réduit:	

4. **Vrai ou faux?**

vrai	faux	
☐	☐	a. Les parents qui habitent Clermont peuvent utiliser les crèches clermontoises.
☐	☐	b. Les parents qui travaillent peuvent utiliser les crèches clermontoises.
☐	☐	c. Les enfants qui ont moins de quatre ans peuvent aller dans une halte-garderie.

LES CRÈCHES

Pour garder vos enfants en bas âge

La Ville offre aux Clermontois trois possibilités pour la garde de leurs enfants en bas âge: les crèches collectives, les crèches familiales et les haltes-garderies. Ces trois formules par leur caractère spécifique répondent aux besoins et aux désirs des parents. Les crèches collectives permettent à l'enfant de s'habituer très tôt à la vie en société.

Les crèches familiales assurent le placement des nourrissons auprès des assistantes maternelles. Les enfants y retrouvent un milieu familial bénéfique. Les haltes-garderies, au fonctionnement très souple, reçoivent les enfants de 3 mois à 4 ans pendant la journée de façon discontinue.

Qui peut inscrire son enfant dans les crèches municipales?
Les parents clermontois qui travaillent et dont le domicile est situé à l'intérieur du secteur géographique de la crèche choisie. En cas de domiciliation hors commune, une demande de dérogation doit être adressée à M. le Maire.

Et dans les haltes-garderies municipales?
Tous les enfants peuvent être accueillis, soit occasionnellement, soit régulièrement à temps partiel (sur réservation).

Où et comment inscrire?
Sur place dans l'établissement concerné. Se munir du livret de famille et du carnet de santé de l'enfant.

Quels sont les tarifs dans les crèches?

Tarif normal: 850 à 3 160F par mois selon les revenus.
Tarif réduit Clermontois: de 500 à 1 600 F (selon le quotient familial).
Tarif à mi-temps: de 705 à 1 045 F.

Dans les haltes-garderies	
Tarif normal : 6,00 F à 19,00 F 1ère heure : 6,00 F 2e heure : 8,50 F 3e heure : 12,00 F 4e heure et au-delà : 19,00 F	**Tarif "temps partiel" :** De 55,00 F à 130,00 F par jour
Tarif réduit: pour les Clermontois: 1ère heure : 5,20 F 4e heure : 11,50F 2e heure : 6,00 F 5e heure 3e heure : 8,50 F et au-delà : 19,00F	

	vrai	faux	
d.	☐	☐	Les enfants qui ont quatre mois peuvent aller dans une halte-garderie.
e.	☐	☐	Les haltes-garderies gardent les enfants quelques heures par jour.
f.	☐	☐	On paie les haltes-garderies au mois seulement.
g.	☐	☐	Les crèches ont des tarifs préférentiels pour les habitants de la ville.
h.	☐	☐	Il est nécessaire de réserver avant de déposer un enfant à la halte-garderie.
i.	☐	☐	Le livret de famille est indispensable pour s'inscrire dans une crèche.
j.	☐	☐	Si l'enfant n'a pas de bulletin de santé, il ne peut pas être inscrit.

5. **Informations versus interprétation.** Trouvez dans le texte d'introduction les phrases qui ne sont pas objectives. Êtes-vous d'accord avec ces interprétations?

Act. B, 5: Can be done as a reading activity or as listening comprehension.

Devenez assistante maternelle

Tout en continuant à s'occuper de leurs propres enfants, certaines mères au foyer peuvent augmenter leur budget familial en devenant assistantes maternelles. Elles bénéficient:
– des congés payés.
– d'un salaire versé directement par la ville (aucun rapport financier avec les parents tant au niveau du montant du prix de journée que de la régularité des paiements).

– du gros matériel (lit complet, parc, baby-relax, etc.) fourni par la ville de Clermont-Ferrand.
En cas de problèmes, la directrice de la crèche est à la disposition de l'assistante maternelle pour lui apporter aide et conseils.
Les personnes intéressées doivent prendre contact directement avec la directrice de la crèche familiale la plus proche de leur domicile.

C. Les assistantes maternelles. Vrai ou faux?

	vrai	faux	
a.	☐	☐	Les assistantes maternelles travaillent dans des crèches municipales.
b.	☐	☐	Les femmes qui ne travaillent pas peuvent devenir assistantes maternelles.
c.	☐	☐	Les assistantes maternelles restent chez elle pour s'occuper d'autres enfants.
d.	☐	☐	Les parents paient les assistantes maternelles directement.
e.	☐	☐	Les assistantes doivent acheter des lits d'enfants, des parcs et des baby-relax.
f.	☐	☐	L'assistante maternelle est sous le contrôle d'une directrice de crèche de quartier.
g.	☐	☐	L'assistante maternelle n'est pas payée pendant les vacances.
h.	☐	☐	Il est nécessaire de faire des études pour devenir assistante maternelle.

D. Étude culturelle.

1. **Évaluation.** Utilisez ce document pour comparer le système des crèches et de haltes-garderies en France et chez vous. Faites une phrase pour chaque sujet.

	organisation	financement	horaires	accès
en France				
chez nous				

2. **Le livret de famille.** Préparez une lettre pour obtenir des explications sur le livret de famille. Quels sont vos sujets? Dans quel ordre allez-vous organiser votre lettre?

☐ le format du livret	☐ les raisons	☐ l'utilisation
☐ les remerciements	☐ le contenu	☐ le motif de votre lettre

Act. D, 1: Can be done in groups and handed in, or can be done in brainstorming fashion by the whole class. Have students make two sets of sentences, one for each country per topic. This will help students as they prepare their comparisons. Once the sentences are written, help students generate comparisons. **Le système français (leur système) est plus… moins… aussi… Il y a plus de… moins de… autant de…** If time permits, have students infer some of the reasons, e.g., **système socialisé, système d'entreprise privée,** etc.
CONTINUATION: Have students prepare a list of questions that would provide information that is not addressed in the brochure. For example: **Comment est-ce qu'on appelle les personnes qui travaillent dans les crèches?**

Act. D, 2: Use to review letter writing with official formulas. Have students brainstorm topics of questions, using the model from activity E, 2.

Voilà! See **Video Magazine 3** for additional information on **crèches** and **haltes-garderies.**

Les parents au travail

A. Les mots du travail. Comment est défini le travail pour vous? Pour chaque catégorie, trouvez les mots correspondants.

Act. A: Can be group work while serving as a review of vocabulary relating to work.

• le local du travail	*le bureau, ...*
• le type de travail	
• les personnes qui travaillent	
• les problèmes du travail	

MODE DE VIE ●

Travailler à temps partiel

Même s'il faut jongler financièrement, même si les patrons ont du mal à s'y faire, vous n'êtes manifestement pas prêts à y renoncer! Moins d'argent, mais plus de temps pour les enfants... c'est payant!

Galère ou solution miracle?
Vous témoignez...

" *L'équilibre familial passe avant tout*

Angèle, 33 ans.

" Ma demande a été accueillie plutôt fraîchement

Natalie, 31 ans.

" *J'ai mis un an à obtenir un accord*

Hélène, 40 ans.

" *Si j'avais su, je m'y serais mise plus tôt*

Corinne, 34 ans.

" *C'est un peu duraille financièrement*

Marie-Christine, 39 ans.

" *Venant d'un homme, ça les a surpris!*

Claude, 35 ans.

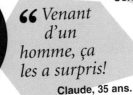

B. Le temps partiel.

1. Quel est le titre de cet article? Sous quelle forme est-il présenté? Où sont les réponses à la question? Qui est **vous** dans la phrase, «Vous témoignez...»?
2. Dans l'introduction, trouvez les mots qui identifient les problèmes du travail à temps partiel. Ensuite, trouvez les mots qui identifient les avantages. Quelle est la réponse principale de l'article? Le temps partiel est-il galère ou solution miracle?

C. Les travailleurs à temps partiel.

1. D'après cette introduction, qui sont-ils? Faites leur portrait.
2. D'après cet article, qui aime le travail à temps partiel? Pourquoi? Qui trouve le temps partiel difficile? Pourquoi? Qui a des regrets? des difficultés?

D. Le travail à temps partiel. Qu'est-ce que c'est?

1. Donnez une définition du travail à temps partiel.
2. Faites une liste des raisons pour lesquelles on veut travailler à temps partiel.
3. Faites une liste des avantages du travail à temps partiel qui sont différents des réponses trouvées dans les citations (*quotes*) du point de vue des patrons et des employés.
4. Faites une liste des inconvénients du travail à temps partiel pour les patrons et dites pourquoi. Faites une liste des problèmes pour les travailleurs et dites pourquoi.

E. Elles parlent / Il parle au patron.

Choisissez une de ces personnes. Dites sa profession et sa situation familiale. Faites-la parler et donner les raisons pour lesquelles elle/il veut travailler à temps partiel.

Modèle *Je veux retourner à l'université et faire des études. Je veux être libre pour...*

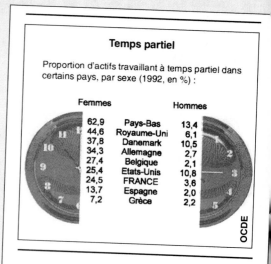

Temps partiel

Proportion d'actifs travaillant à temps partiel dans certains pays, par sexe (1992, en %) :

Femmes		Hommes
62,9	Pays-Bas	13,4
44,6	Royaume-Uni	6,1
37,8	Danemark	10,5
34,3	Allemagne	2,7
27,4	Belgique	2,1
25,4	Etats-Unis	10,8
24,5	FRANCE	3,6
13,7	Espagne	2,0
7,2	Grèce	2,2

OCDE

3 millions de personnes travaillent à temps partiel, soit 13,7 % de la population active. Ce travail s'est beaucoup développé depuis une dizaine d'années. Il concerne 26% des femmes actives, contre 4% des hommes.

Gérard Mermet, *Francoscopie 1995*

Orthographe et prononciation

➤➤ Les lettres *-ti-* et *-th-*

In French, **-ti-** (as in **action**) is pronounced like an **s**. There is no **sh** sound. In addition, **-th-** is pronounced like a **t**. There is no **th** sound.

Activité

Prononcez Répétez après votre professeur.

1. Fais attention!
2. Je n'ai plus de patience.
3. Où est le dictionnaire?

4. Il n'est pas très enthousiaste.
5. Allons au théâtre ce soir!

Vocabulaire de base

TEXT TAPE:
Vocabulaire de base

NOMS

un bébé *baby*
une bouche *mouth*
un bras *arm*
une brosse à dents *toothbrush*
un cheveu, des cheveux *hair*
un corps *body*
une dent *tooth*
un dos *back*
une jambe *leg*
un nez *nose*
un œil, des yeux *eye, eyes*
une oreille *ear*
un pied *foot*
une tête *head*

RAPPEL DE VOCABULAIRE
un doigt *finger*
une main *hand*

VERBES

aider (qqn à + inf.) *to help (someone do something)*
amuser *to amuse (someone)*
   s'amuser *to have a good time, to play*
appeler *to call*
   s'appeler *to be named*

arrêter *to stop*
   s'arrêter *to stop (oneself)*
brosser *to brush*
   se brosser (les cheveux, par ex.)
      to brush (one's hair, for example)
coucher *to put to bed*
   se coucher *to go to bed*
emmener (conjugué comme acheter)
   to take (somebody somewhere)
énerver *to irritate, to annoy (someone)*
   s'énerver *to get irritated, annoyed*
ennuyer (conjugué comme envoyer)
   to bore
   s'ennuyer *to be bored*
essayer (de + inf.) *to try (to)*
habiller *to dress (someone else)*
   s'habiller *to get dressed*
laver *to wash (something, someone else)*
   se laver *to wash (oneself)*
lever (conjugué comme acheter) *to lift, raise*
   se lever *to get up*
partager *to share*
pleurer *to cry*
promener (un chien, par ex.)
   (conjugué comme acheter) *to take for a walk (a dog, for example)*
   se promener *to take a walk*

regarder *to look at*
   se regarder *to look at oneself*
réveiller *to wake (someone else) up*
   se réveiller *to wake up (oneself)*
rêver (de) *to dream (about, of)*

ADJECTIFS

marron *(invar.) brown (eyes)*
roux, rousse *red (hair)*
têtu(e) *stubborn*

DIVERS

avoir mal *to hurt*
avoir mal à la tête, à la gorge, au dos
   to have a headache, a sore throat, a backache
bien sûr *of course*
combien de fois (par jour/mois/an...)
   how many times (a day/month/year)
d'habitude *usually*
encore *still, again*
finalement *finally*
mieux *better (adv.)*
partout *everywhere*
prendre une douche *to take a shower*
tard *late*
tôt *early*
tout(e) seul(e) *all alone, all by oneself*

Vocabulaire supplémentaire

NOMS

un article de toilette *toilet article*
une barbe *beard*
un collant *tights, pantyhose*
une crèche *day-care center, nursery*
le dentifrice *toothpaste*
le déodorant *deodorant*
un derrière *rear end*
une école maternelle *nursery school, kindergarten*
un gant de toilette *washcloth*
une moustache *moustache*
un peigne *comb*
un rasoir *razor*
un rêve *dream*
le savon *soap*
un séchoir (à cheveux) *(hair) dryer*
une serviette de bain *bath towel*
le shampooing *shampoo*
un ventre *stomach, abdomen*
un visage *face*

VERBES

changer *to change*
    se changer *to change one's clothes*
coiffer *to fix someone's hair*
    se coiffer *to fix one's own hair*
déshabiller *to undress (someone else)*
    se déshabiller *to get undressed*
maquiller *to make up (someone else)*
    se maquiller *to put makeup on (oneself)*
peigner *to comb (someone else)*
    se peigner (les cheveux, par ex.) *to comb (one's own hair, for example)*
se préparer *to get (oneself) ready*
raser *to shave (someone else)*
    se raser *to shave (oneself)*
sécher (conjugué comme préférer) *to dry off (someone, something)*
    se sécher (conjugué comme préférer) *to dry off (oneself)*

soigner *to treat (illness), to look after*
    se soigner *to treat oneself, to take care of oneself*
tousser *to cough*

ADJECTIFS

adorable *adorable*
barbu(e) *bearded*
châtain(e) *light brown (hair)*
chauve *bald*
énervant(e) *annoying*
frisé(e) *curly*
matinal(e) *early riser, morning person*
nu(e) *naked*
propre *clean*
réveillé(e) *awake*
sale *dirty*

DIVERS

avoir la grippe *to have the flu*
avoir un rhume *to have a cold*
faire des bêtises *to do dumb things*
faire la sieste *to take a nap*
il faudrait (+ inf.) *one should (+ inf.)*
prendre un bain *to take a bath*
tout nu(e) *stark naked*

LE FRANÇAIS TEL QU'ON LE PARLE

Allez! *Come on!*
mon chéri, ma chérie *darling, my love*
mon chou *darling, my love (literally: my cream puff or my cabbage)*
mon grand, ma grande *darling, my love (to one's child)*
Il est temps! *It's time!*
Voyons! *Come on now! For goodness sake!*

DES EXPRESSIONS AVEC LES PARTIES DU CORPS

arriver comme un cheveu dans la soupe = arriver à un mauvais moment
être bête comme ses pieds = être très bête
se lever du pied gauche = se lever de mauvaise humeur
il me casse les pieds = il m'ennuie beaucoup
jouer comme un pied = jouer très mal
avoir une bonne tête = avoir l'air sympathique
faire la tête = ne pas être content *(to make a face)*
à l'œil = gratis *(free)*
Mon œil! *My foot!*
coûter les yeux de la tête = coûter très cher
dormir sur les deux oreilles = très bien dormir

LE FRANÇAIS FAMILIER

se barber = s'ennuyer
se débarbouiller = se laver (le visage)
s'éclater = s'amuser
Quelle barbe! *What a bore!*

ON ENTEND PARFOIS...

avoir le temps long (Belgique) = s'ennuyer
crollé(e) (Belgique) = frisé(e)
une débarbouillette (Canada) = un gant de toilette
une lavette (Suisse) = un gant de toilette
un linge de bain (Suisse) = une serviette de bain
siester (Afrique) = faire la sieste

Une histoire d'amour

En bref

Dans cette leçon...

- L'amour et le mariage
- Le couple et le travail ménager
- Les vacances: Le Club Med à Marrakesh
- Raconter des histoires
- Les verbes réciproques
- Les verbes réfléchis et réciproques au passé
- Les verbes **savoir** et **connaître**
- Préposition ou conjonction?

In this lesson...

- Love and marriage
- Couples and housework
- Vacations: the Marrakesh Club Med
- Narrating and describing
- Reciprocal verbs
- Reflexive and reciprocal verbs in the past
- The verbs **savoir** and **connaître**
- Preposition or conjunction?

www explore!
http://voila.heinle.com

Develop writing skills with Système-D software!

Practice listening and pronunciation skills with the Text Tape!

Discover the Francophone world!

Build your skills!

INTERNET　　**SYSTÈME-D**　　**TEXT TAPE**　　**VIDEO TAPE**　　**CD-ROM**

Students have an open-ended writing activity in the **Cahier** suitable for use with **Système-D**.

Entrée en matière: Je t'aime un peu, beaucoup, pas du tout...

La photo: Have students focus on the picture alone, not the text, so that the text can be used to provide more specific information later. Students may want to give the two people in the photo names to make it easier to talk about them. Let students invent freely.

La photo.

Les données
l'endroit
la saison
le jour de la semaine
l'heure
le temps qu'il fait
les objets

Le couple
l'âge
l'apparence physique
la profession
les vêtements
les préférences
les loisirs

D'après quels indices avez-vous décidé vos réponses?

La scène. Décrivez la scène. Qui voyez-vous dans cette scène? Que font les personnages? Pourquoi est-ce qu'il y a des hommes dans un bateau? Qui sont-ils?

Le pique-nique. Quel est ce repas? Qu'est-ce que ce couple mange? Quelle est la boisson? Qu'est-ce qu'il y a sur la nappe? à côté de l'arbre? dans le sac?

Le texte: Direct students to scan the text in order to find information.

Le texte. Maintenant, regardez le texte et donnez des informations supplémentaires sur le couple. Quelle est leur nationalité?

La réclame publicitaire. Sur quelle partie de cette illustration porte la publicité? Nommez les objets qui représentent ce produit.

Le message publicitaire. Quelles sont les qualités de ce produit? Soulignez dans le texte les mots qui se réfèrent au produit. Est-ce que ces mots se réfèrent aussi à la photo?

Quel est le message du texte? Quel est le message de la photo? Comparez-les. Quel est le message le plus fort? Pourquoi? Quels sont les messages visuels souvent employés pour vendre un produit?

À votre avis, dans quelle sorte de magazine peut-on trouver cette publicité?

Un scénario: Can be done in groups. Students can present as a dialogue, as a short story, or they can adopt one of the characters and write a short (auto)biography. Alternative: Have students tell the story of the day in the photo from either person's point of view.

Un scénario. Imaginez les événements avant la scène, et ce qui va se passer après.

AVANT

C'était en...

Il était...

Elle avait...

400

**Entente cordiale:
Baguette parisienne et Philadelphia cheese,
musique cajun à la radio,
langage commun de Chipie
et du coton d'Amérique.**

Il parlait un peu français. Elle parlait un peu anglais. Mais ils avaient en commun cette même passion pour les vêtements Chipie en coton d'Amérique. Très cool et très confort.

Vous avez le choix entre un coton délicieusement souple et chaud, ou sec et frais, résistant pour un usage intensif, ou doux comme le velours.

Mais ce sera toujours un coton de grand confort. Quelle que soit la marque de ce que vous aurez choisi, vous saurez d'avance que vous vous y sentirez bien. A condition qu'y figure le Label Cotton USA.

CHIPIE

LE COTON D'EXCELLENCE.

APRÈS

Et puis...	Elle n'est pas... , mais elle a...	Et ils sont... / ils ont...

TRANSPARENCY:
16-1

Vocabulaire

A. Un jour d'été à Marrakech

Ask students: **Est-ce que vous aimez voyager seul? En groupe? Avec un(e) ami(e)? Quels sont les avantages et les inconvénients?**

Info plus

Le Club Med.

Le Club Méditerranée was created in 1950 as a response to the need for organized vacations in postwar France. From its beginnings as a small vacation club, Club Med has gone on to become a large enterprise with resorts in many countries around the world. The democratic atmosphere that it promotes (informal dress, meals at group tables, etc.) and its relatively inexpensive prices have made travel abroad more widely available.

Have students compare Valérie and Christophe's life styles. Will they be compatible?

Valérie Tremblay, 30 ans, est une journaliste qui vient de Montréal mais qui habite toute seule à Paris à cause de son travail. Elle est en vacances au Club Med à Marrakech, au Maroc.

- Où est Valérie Tremblay maintenant? C'est loin de chez elle? C'est où, chez elle? Que fait-elle à Paris? Pourquoi est-elle venue au Maroc? Décrivez Valérie.

- Et Christophe Delcourt, que fait-il maintenant? C'est où, chez lui? Que fait-il dans la vie? Décrivez Christophe.

Christophe Delcourt, 27 ans, est un médecin qui habite à Lyon avec ses parents et ses frères et sœurs. Lui aussi est en vacances au Club Med à Marrakech.

B. La rencontre

C'est dans la rue qu'ils se rencontrent pour la première fois. Elle se promène pour prendre des photos pendant que lui, il cherche un tapis pour ses parents. Et qu'est-ce qui se passe? Ils se voient, ils s'arrêtent, ils se regardent et... c'est le coup de foudre, ils tombent amoureux!

- Où est-ce qu'ils se rencontrent pour la première fois? Qu'est-ce qu'elle faisait? Et lui? Qu'est-ce qu'il pense quand il la voit? Et qu'est-ce qu'elle pense quand elle le voit? Et vous, est-ce que vous pensez qu'ils vont bien ensemble? Ou bien vous pensez qu'ils se trompent?

C'est lui!

C'est elle!

C. Une soirée à la Mamounia

Have students create short sentences for each character: **Ah, elle est si belle, elle est si élégante, elle a l'air si intelligent, je l'aime**, etc.

Ne me quitte pas!

Mon chéri, je t'aime!

Ce soir, ils sortent ensemble à la Mamounia, l'hôtel célèbre de Marrakech. Ils se parlent pendant des heures et se racontent leur vie. Ils sont amoureux, ils s'entendent bien... La vie est belle! Mais ils ont seulement un jour ensemble: Christophe vient d'arriver et c'est le dernier jour de vacances de Valérie. Demain, elle doit rentrer à Paris.

- Où sont-ils? Qu'est-ce qu'ils portent ce soir? Quelle heure est-il, à votre avis? Qu'est-ce qu'ils font? Est-ce que Christophe va pouvoir sortir avec Valérie longtemps?

D. La fin des vacances de Valérie

Ils doivent se séparer, mais ils ne veulent pas se quitter. Il la serre dans ses bras, ils s'embrassent longtemps, ils se disent qu'ils s'aiment et qu'ils vont se retrouver un jour. Mais maintenant, Valérie doit se dépêcher...

- Où va Valérie? Et Christophe? Qu'est-ce qu'ils font? Qu'est-ce qu'ils se disent?
- Et après les vacances, qui va appeler le premier, à votre avis? Qu'est-ce qu'ils vont se dire? Qu'est-ce qui va se passer?

Ask students to imagine Valérie and Christophe's first conversation on the phone after their vacation.

«Je t'aime!» Ask students: Qui le dit? Quand? Où? À qui?

Info plus

Amour! Amour!

Romantic love has a long literary tradition in France and is reflected in popular songs and films as well as in novels and plays. This influences relationships between the sexes and is behind the ideal of **l'amour-passion** or **le grand amour,** which is viewed as an event overriding more mundane social conventions.

E. Le mariage

C'est le grand amour! En automne, ils se retrouvent souvent à Paris ou à Lyon. En décembre, ils se fiancent. À Noël, Valérie emmène son fiancé à Montréal, où il rencontre sa famille. Et en juin, ils se marient.

- À votre avis, où est-ce qu'ils se marient? Où vont-ils en lune de miel ? Et où va habiter le nouveau ménage?

F. La vie de couple

'en ai assez, moi!

Ils veulent fonder une famille et en octobre, Valérie est enceinte. Ils attendent le bébé avec impatience et ils ont un petit garçon en juillet. Tous les deux adorent l'enfant. Mais Valérie, qui déteste le ménage, s'ennuie à la maison. Et puis, c'est toujours elle qui prépare les repas, qui passe l'aspirateur, qui fait la lessive, qui repasse... Elle n'a jamais le temps de se reposer. Christophe a bon caractère, c'est un homme sérieux et honnête, mais il ne fait rien dans la maison et il n'a jamais le temps de s'occuper de l'enfant. Si seulement il pouvait l'aider! Elle est déçue de sa vie et commence à penser à son travail... Pourtant, elle se souvient aussi de Marrakech, de leur amour, de leur mariage, de leur première année ensemble... Est-elle heureuse? Parfois elle pense que oui, parfois elle pense que non... Elle ne sait pas quoi penser!

- Qu'est-ce qui se passe en octobre? en juillet? Est-ce que c'est un couple heureux? Quand Christophe rentre le soir, que dit Valérie? Que répond Christophe? Quelles sont les idées de Valérie? Qu'est-ce qui va se passer?
- Et vous, que pensez-vous de Christophe? Et de Valérie?

G. La crise

Après un an, Valérie n'a plus de patience. Elle veut faire quelque chose d'autre dans la vie et elle a décidé de retourner travailler, mais Christophe n'est pas d'accord. Il pense que sa femme a mauvais caractère, qu'elle n'est jamais contente, qu'elle n'est pas assez patiente, qu'il gagne assez d'argent pour deux et que l'enfant a encore besoin d'elle. Et puis, il est un peu jaloux et se demande si Valérie n'a pas envie de le tromper, si elle lui est vraiment fidèle. Elle lui cache peut-être quelque chose? Elle a peut-être rencontré quelqu'un d'autre? Valérie et Christophe sont en crise et se disputent souvent. Est-ce que c'est la fin de leur histoire?

S'il te plaît!

Je m'en vais!

- Que veut faire Valérie? Que pense Christophe de cette idée? Comment est-ce qu'il trouve sa femme? Qu'est-ce qu'il se demande? Comment va le ménage maintenant?
- À votre avis, où va Valérie? Pourquoi?
- À votre avis, qu'est-ce qui va se passer? Est-ce qu'ils vont se réconcilier? se quitter? divorcer?

Ask students: **Comment est la vie typique d'un homme? d'une femme?**

Info plus

Liberté, égalité, fraternité?!
Traditionally, the role of women in French society was limited by religious beliefs, social taboos, and strict legislation that made women legally dependent on their husbands. Now, with the lessening influence of the Catholic Church and the repeal of repressive legislation, women share much more equally in French society.

Voilà! See **Video Magazine 3** for further treatment of women in Francophone countries.

TRANSPARENCY: 16-4

You may wish to point out that Christophe would be considered "traditional" and not up-to-date by many French young people.

Obviously, there will be differences of opinion as to whether Valérie's opinions and feelings are "right." This is a real issue that you may want to work into class or small group discussion. One idea would be to have students work in groups, listing the pros and cons (**Je suis / Je ne suis pas d'accord avec Valérie parce que...**).

Ask students to imagine the dialogue between Christophe and Valérie when he returns from the office in the evening.

Notes de vocabulaire

1. Mots et expressions utiles.

le divorce	*divorce*
s'endormir	*to fall asleep*
faire attention	*to be careful, to pay attention*
infidèle	*unfaithful*

2. Les verbes réciproques.

In French, the reflexive pronoun is also used to express the idea of reciprocity (**se regarder** = *to look at oneself* or *to look at each other*).

Ils **se** parlent souvent.   *They often talk (to each other).*

This is discussed further in the **Structure** section of this lesson.

3. Les verbes réfléchis et réciproques idiomatiques.

A small group of reflexive and reciprocal verbs are idiomatic. Their meaning and use must be learned individually.

se demander	*to wonder*
se dépêcher	*to hurry*
se disputer	*to argue, to fight*
s'entendre bien / mal (avec)	*to get along well / badly (with)*
se marier (avec)	*to marry, to get married*
s'occuper de	*to take care of*
se reposer	*to rest*
se retrouver	*to get together, to meet (again)*
se souvenir de	*to remember*
se tromper	*to be wrong, to make a mistake*

Ma camarade de chambre et moi, **nous nous entendons bien.**	*My roommate and I get along well.*
Je **m'entends avec** tout le monde.	*I get along with everybody.*
Christophe et Valérie **se marient** en juin.	*Christophe and Valérie are getting married in June.*
Tu **te maries avec** Marc?	*You're marrying Marc?*
On va **se retrouver** après le film?	*Shall we get together after the film?*
Tu **te souviens de** nos vacances à Marrakech?	*Do you remember our vacation in Marrakech?*
Vous devez **vous reposer.**	*You've got to rest.*

Note that although **se marier** is a reflexive verb, **divorcer** is not. Also, unlike English, **divorcer** is never followed by a direct object.

Je **divorce!**	*I'm getting a divorce!*
Jean et Béatrice ont **divorcé** en 1990.	*Jean and Béatrice got divorced in 1990.*
Est-ce que Valérie et Christophe vont **divorcer?**	*Are Valérie and Christophe getting divorced?*

2: To avoid involving students in an overly complex discussion of the types of pronominal verbs in French, the term *reflexive pronoun* is used in this text to refer to the pronoun that indicates reflexivity (**elle se lève**), reciprocity (**elles se regardent**), idiomatic or intrinsic pronominality (**je m'en souviens**), and passive or middle voice (**le français se parle ici**). Strictly speaking, it is not accurate to say that the reflexive pronoun can be used to express the idea of reciprocity.

3: If desired, point out to students that **se souvenir** exists only in the reflexive form.

3: Although **divorcer** is never followed by a direct object, it is possible to say **divorcer d'avec quelqu'un** or **divorcer de quelqu'un: Est-ce que Valérie va divorcer d'avec Christophe / de Christophe?**

 See the **Instructor's Resource Manual** for more information.

4. Que: conjonction. In the following sentence, **que** is used as a subordinating conjunction to link two clauses.

> Christophe dit **qu'**il a des problèmes.   *Christophe says (that) he has problems.*

4: The idea of **que** as a subordinating conjunction is usually obvious for students since the same pattern exists in English.

5. Quelqu'un de + adjectif / quelque chose de + adjectif. The adjective following **quelqu'un de** and **quelque chose de** is always masculine singular.

> Ta sœur est **quelqu'un d'important?**   *Is your sister someone important?*

6. Quitter / partir / sortir. **Quitter** means *to leave someone* or *something*. It must be followed by a direct object.

> Vous n'allez pas **quitter l'université?!**   *You're not going to leave school?!*

6: If desired, point out that **sortir** is often followed by the preposition **de** and **entrer** by the preposition **dans**. (Il *est entré dans* la salle de classe. Elle *est sortie de* la salle de classe.)

Sortir means *to go out.* It is the opposite of **entrer** *(to enter, to go in, to come in).* **Partir** means *to leave.* It is the opposite of **arriver** *(to arrive).* Both **sortir** and **partir** are intransitive verbs. They may be followed by a prepositional phrase or an adverb. They are never followed by a direct object.

> Valérie **est sortie** hier soir.   *Valérie went out last evening.*
> Christophe **part** pour Paris demain. *Christophe is leaving for Paris tomorrow.*

7. Préposition ou conjonction? Sometimes English words have more than one equivalent in French. Note these differences in usage.

- preposition + noun / pronoun
  > Il vient **à cause de toi.**   *He's coming because of you.*
  > Il est resté là **pendant une heure.**   *He stayed there for an hour.*

- conjunction + subject + verb
  > Il vient **parce qu'il veut** te rencontrer.   *He's coming because he wants to meet you.*
  > Il est resté là **pendant que je travaillais.**   *He stayed there while I was working.*

7: Stress that **parce que** and **pendant que** must be followed by subject + verb.

D'accord?

A. Chassez l'intrus Quel mot ne va pas avec les autres à cause du sens?

1. s'aimer / se séparer / se disputer / divorcer
2. sortir ensemble / se détester / se marier / se fiancer
3. s'entendre / s'embrasser / tomber amoureux / se quitter
4. amour / coup de foudre / divorce / lune de miel
5. repasser / se reposer / passer l'aspirateur / faire la lessive

B. Les contraires Trouvez le contraire.

1. se marier
2. travailler
3. se détester
4. s'ennuyer
5. s'entendre bien
6. se réveiller
7. oublier
8. se réconcilier
9. se quitter

C. Choisissez Complétez avec **que, pendant que, parce que, pendant** ou **à cause de**.

1. La sœur de mon fiancé nous a raconté . . . . . elle allait divorcer.
2. J'ai lu votre article . . . . . je mangeais et je l'ai trouvé intéressant.
3. Ils se séparent . . . . . ses chats: elle n'aime pas les chats et lui, il les adore.
4. J'ai rencontré mon mari . . . . . les vacances.
5. Candide et Alceste disent . . . . . ils vont partir à Montréal.
6. Solange veut quitter son petit ami . . . . . il est infidèle.
7. Je voudrais habiter à Nice, mais nous devons habiter à Paris . . . . . le travail de ma femme.

D. Problèmes de couple Choisissez le bon verbe et mettez-le à l'imparfait ou à l'infinitif dans la phrase.

1. Quand il . . . . . (arriver / sortir) à la maison le soir, Christophe était si fatigué qu'il ne voulait pas . . . . . (sortir / quitter)! Mais Valérie, elle, s'ennuyait et elle voulait . . . . . (partir / quitter) de la maison pour s'amuser un peu.
2. Christophe, lui, ... (se demander / demander) si Valérie était fidèle ou si elle . . . . . (se tromper / le tromper).
3. Un matin, Valérie a décidé de . . . . . (quitter / partir) de la maison. Est-ce qu'elle voulait . . . . . (quitter / divorcer) Christophe ou est-ce qu'elle voulait . . . . . (partir/quitter) travailler?
4. Et vous, vous pensez vraiment que Valérie va . . . . . (quitter / partir) Christophe? Ou bien vous pensez que le couple va . . . . . (se disputer / se réconcilier)?

E. Conseils Qu'est-ce qu'il faut faire? Qu'est-ce qu'il ne faut pas faire?

Modèle ... quand on veut s'amuser le soir?
Il faut sortir avec un(e) ami(e), il ne faut pas se reposer.

1. ... quand on rencontre quelqu'un d'intéressant?
2. ... quand on s'ennuie?
3. ... quand on sort tard la nuit?
4. ... quand on retrouve quelqu'un de sa famille après des années?
5. ... quand on s'aime?
6. ... quand son mari ou sa femme est infidèle?
7. ... quand on a des enfants?
8. ... quand on a un mari jaloux ou une femme jalouse?

Mise en pratique

A. Le couple idéal, la famille idéale Qu'est-ce que c'est pour vous, le couple idéal? Et la famille idéale? Écrivez vos idées en groupes de deux ou trois et puis comparez-les avec les idées des autres groupes.

1. Le mari idéal: Il est sérieux? Il est amusant? ...
2. La femme idéale: Elle est sérieuse? Elle est amusante? ...
3. La rencontre idéale: Où? Quand? ...

4. La demande en mariage: Qui? Où? Quand? …
5. Le mariage idéal: Où? Quand? À quel âge? …
6. La lune de miel idéale: Où? Pourquoi? …
7. Le couple idéal: Qui fait quoi? Qui décide quoi? Comment sont-ils ensemble? …
8. La famille idéale: Combien d'enfants? Quand? Où? …

B. Chez le conseiller conjugal

Christophe et Valérie ont décidé d'essayer de s'entendre et ils vont chez le conseiller conjugal *(marriage counselor)*. En groupes:

1. Faites une liste des choses qui ne vont pas, du point de vue de Valérie (Il ne fait rien à la maison, je m'ennuie, etc.).
2. Faites une liste des choses qui ne vont pas, du point de vue de Christophe (Elle n'est jamais contente, etc.).
3. Essayez de trouver des solutions.

C. L'histoire de Christophe et de Valérie

Finissez l'histoire de Christophe et de Valérie.

1. Où est-ce qu'ils habitent, à Lyon, à Paris ou à Montréal? Pourquoi?
2. Ils ont un enfant. Comment s'appelle-t-il? Comment est-il?
3. Est-ce qu'ils vont avoir d'autres enfants? Pourquoi ou pourquoi pas?
4. Qu'est-ce que Valérie pense de Christophe et qu'est-ce que Christophe pense de Valérie?
5. Quels sont les problèmes du couple?
6. Racontez la fin de l'histoire. Est-ce qu'ils vont rester ensemble ou est-ce qu'ils vont divorcer?

Act. B: One way to organize this activity would be to divide the class into two, half of the class writing Valérie's point of view and half of the class writing Christophe's point of view. Then, have both sides face each other and express their grievances: **Tu ne fais jamais rien à la maison, tu n'es jamais contente, je m'ennuie toute la journée, tu ne m'aides jamais,** etc. Let the other side answer while you play the moderator, until a compromise is reached (if at all possible). At the end, decide with the whole class if this marriage can be saved or not.

Act. C: This can be written as a semi-guided composition.

Structure

 CD-ROM:
Build your skills!

▶▶ Les verbes réciproques

Reciprocal verbs (**les verbes réciproques**) indicate reciprocal action. In English, this is expressed by the use of a reciprocal pronoun or prepositional phrase: *(to) each other* or *(to) one another*. In French, the reflexive pronouns (**nous, vous, se,**…) serve this purpose.

Candide et Alceste **se** parlent.	*Candide and Alceste are talking to each other.*
Vous ne **vous** parlez plus?	*You're not speaking (to each other) anymore?*

Note that many verbs can be used both reflexively and reciprocally. In French, this is ambiguous, and speakers must depend on context to distinguish between these meanings. In English, no such ambiguity exists.

Ils **se** parlent.	*They're talking to themselves / They're talking to each other.*

DRILL: **Christophe et Valérie ne se parlent plus.** (nous / vous / Candide et Alceste / leurs parents)

DRILL: **Christophe et Valérie se disputent.** (nous / vous / Candide et Alceste)

Vous avez compris?

A. Bonne nouvelle / mauvaise nouvelle? Décidez si c'est une bonne ou une mauvaise nouvelle.

1. Candide et Alceste ne se parlent plus.
2. Valérie et Christophe se réconcilient.
3. Vincent et Thérèse Dubois se séparent.
4. Vous vous disputez avec un(e) ami(e).
5. Alceste et sa mère se téléphonent tous les jours.

B. Choisissez Complétez les phrases avec un des verbes entre parenthèses au présent. C'est bien ou c'est mauvais?

1. Christophe et Valérie ..... (aimer / s'aimer) et ils ..... (écrire / s'écrire) tous les jours.
2. Alceste ..... (téléphoner / se téléphoner) souvent à sa mère et ils ..... (parler / se parler) pendant des heures.
3. Adrien ..... (tromper / se tromper) sa femme avec une secrétaire de vingt ans.
4. Martine ..... (voir / se voir) souvent sa copine Mireille et elles ..... (raconter / se raconter) tous leurs problèmes.
5. Monsieur et Madame Renglet ..... (séparer / se séparer) après vingt ans de mariage parce qu'ils ne ..... (entendre / s'entendre) plus.

Continuons!

Des nouvelles de Cinet: Have students propose reasons for each event (M. Lionnet and Mlle Caron sont tombés amoureux, etc.).

Des nouvelles de Cinet Voilà les dernières nouvelles de Cinet. Faites des phrases complètes.

1. Monsieur Lionnet et Mademoiselle Caron / se marier.
2. Monsieur Bovy et Monsieur Saïdi / ne plus se parler.
3. Monsieur et Madame Ségal / se disputer / tout le temps.
4. Monsieur et Madame Domont / ne pas s'entendre. Ils vont divorcer.
5. Madame Renard et Monsieur Renglet / se retrouver / au café le soir.

▶▶ Les verbes réfléchis et réciproques au passé

Reflexive and reciprocal verbs follow the usual rules for formation of the **imparfait.**

> À seize ans, je ne **m'entendais** pas **bien** avec mes parents.
> *When I was 16, I didn't get along well with my parents.*

> Nous **nous reposions** quand le téléphone a sonné.
> *We were resting when the telephone rang.*

DRILL: On s'est bien amusé. (les filles / nous / Candide / vous / tu)

Reflexive and reciprocal verbs are always conjugated with **être** in the **passé composé.** The past participle of these verbs will in most cases agree with the subject of the verb.

Ma sœur s'est marié**e** l'année passée.	*My sister got married last year.*
Nous nous sommes amusé**s.**	*We had a good time.*
Ils se sont rencontré**s** à Paris.	*They met in Paris.*

The rules governing past participle agreement with reflexive and reciprocal verbs are complex. Although such verbs use **être** as a helping verb, their past participles really agree with a preceding direct object (if one exists). Since the reflexive or reciprocal pronoun usually represents a direct object, this means that the past participle agrees with both the preceding direct object (the reflexive pronoun) and the subject.

Sometimes the reflexive or reciprocal pronoun represents an indirect object rather than a direct object. In these cases, there is no past participle agreement. This will happen with two specific types of verbs.

If desired, have students compare: Jacques parle à Paulette. Il lui parle. / Paulette parle à Jacques. Elle lui parle. / Jacques parle à Paulette et Paulette parle à Jacques. Ils se parlent.

1. Verbs with indirect objects (no past participle agreement):

se dire	se parler	s'écrire	se donner
se raconter	se téléphoner	se demander	

   Les deux sœurs **se sont téléphoné** et elles **se sont parlé** pendant des heures.
   The two sisters called each other and talked for hours.

2. Reflexive verbs having reference to a part of the body (no past participle agreement):

   Marie **s'est lavé** les mains.   *Marie washed her hands.*

Have students compare: Elle a lavé la voiture. Elle l'a lavée. Elle s'est lavée. Elle s'est lavé les mains.

In this sentence, **mains** is the direct object, and **se** is the indirect object, telling to whom the hands belong.

Vous avez compris?

A. Mariages Avec qui est-ce qu'ils se sont mariés? Choisissez parmi:

Martha / Napoléon / Marie-Antoinette / mon grand-père / Franklin / Anne Boleyn / Joe DiMaggio.

Modèle   Marilyn Monroe
          Elle s'est mariée avec Joe DiMaggio.

1. George Washington
2. Henri VIII
3. Eleanor Roosevelt
4. ma grand-mère
5. Joséphine
6. Louis XVI

B. Qu'est-ce qu'ils ont fait? Soyez logique.

Modèle   Philippe a utilisé une serviette de bain.
          Il s'est séché.

Act. B: To practice the use of these verbs in the infinitive, redo the exercise using **pour** + *verb* (Philippe a utilisé une serviette de bain pour se sécher.).

1. Marguerite a utilisé du savon.
2. Richard a utilisé une brosse à dents.
3. Charles a mis une chemise, un costume, une cravate et des chaussures.
4. Donna a entendu le réveil.
5. Alceste et Candide ont utilisé une brosse à cheveux.

C. Qu'est-ce qu'ils ont fait? Accordez les participes passés quand c'est nécessaire.

1. Paulette s'est couché___ tôt hier soir.
2. Est-ce que Candide et Alceste se sont brossé___ les cheveux?
3. Martine et Valérie se sont retrouvé___ au café. Elles se sont parlé___ pendant une heure, et puis elles sont parti___ ensemble.
4. Ils se sont rasé___ la tête! Mais pourquoi?
5. Nous nous sommes bien amusé___ hier soir.
6. Christophe et Valérie se sont vu___ et c'était le coup de foudre.
7. Valérie s'est demandé___ si elle allait divorcer.

D. Les souvenirs d'un vieux couple Monsieur et Madame Ségal sont mariés depuis longtemps et ils se souviennent de leur vie pendant les premières années de leur mariage. Complétez le dialogue avec les verbes entre parenthèses à l'imparfait.

—Tu te souviens quand tu me ..... (apporter) le café au lit le matin?

—Oh, oui, tu ..... (ne jamais se lever) avant huit heures.

—Oui, mais je ..... (se coucher) toujours tard parce que je ..... (s'occuper) du ménage le soir.

—C'est vrai, et moi, je ..... (se coucher) tard aussi parce que je ..... (vouloir) rester avec toi.

—Nous ..... (s'entendre) si bien!

—Oui, nous ..... (ne jamais se disputer).

Continuons!

A. Rencontre sur la plage C'est l'été. Catherine et Olivier se sont rencontrés à la plage. Racontez leur histoire.

SUGGESTIONS: se voir / se regarder / se parler / sortir ensemble / s'embrasser / se disputer / se séparer / se rencontrer / se retrouver / s'amuser / se téléphoner / s'écrire / se dire au revoir / s'entendre bien (avec).

B. Racontez l'histoire Imaginez que vous êtes une des personnes suivantes. Racontez votre histoire.

1. Béatrice Dubois: 37 ans, divorcée, remariée avec Paul Pinel
   Jean Rasquin: 45 ans, divorcé, premier mari de Béatrice Dubois
2. Jacques Dubois: 68 ans, retraité, veuf (sa femme est morte)
   Paulette Gilmard: 66 ans, retraitée, a rencontré Jacques Dubois à Nice
3. M. Ségal: 69 ans, retraité, marié, se dispute tout le temps avec sa femme
   Mme Ségal: 67 ans, retraitée, mariée, se dispute tout le temps avec son mari
4. M. Domont: 40 ans, employé de la S.N.C.F., marié
   Mme Domont: 40 ans, secrétaire, mariée mais veut divorcer
5. M. Renglet: 50 ans, dentiste, marié, retrouve Madame Renard au café le soir
   Mme Renglet: 45 ans, cadre dans une banque, mariée.
6. Bruno Hanin: 29 ans, écrivain, marié, deux enfants, s'occupe beaucoup de ses enfants
   Véronique Hanin: 27 ans, ingénieur, mariée, deux enfants, voyage beaucoup pour son travail

Act. A & B: Stories can be written from various points of view and in various time frames.

Act. B: Couples have appeared in earlier lessons: Dubois-Rasquin, Dubois-Gilmard, *Leçons 5* and *7;* Ségal, Domont, Renglet, *Leçon 12;* Hanin, *Leçon 15.*

If time is limited, choose only one or two couples to discuss.

GROUP FORMAT 1: Divide class into groups and assign one couple per group.

GROUP FORMAT 2: Divide class into groups. Assign half of each couple to a group. After preparing, the group (or one member of the group) plays the role of one of the partners.

FOLLOW-UP: Play marriage counselor and listen to both stories. Your advice can be reasonable or off-the-wall.

C. Conversation en français Quel âge aviez-vous la première fois que vous êtes tombé(e) amoureux(-euse)? Comment était la personne que vous aimiez? Comment est-ce que vous vous êtes rencontrés? Racontez toute l'histoire.

TEXT TAPE:
Conversation en français

Act. C: Students may invent a story of their first love if they wish.

⏩ Les verbes *savoir* et *connaître*

Savoir means *to know a fact* or *to know how to;* **connaître** means *to know* in the sense of *to be acquainted with.* Here are the forms of the verbs **connaître** and **savoir** in the present tense.

connaître	
je connais	nous connaissons
tu connais	vous connaissez
il } connaît elle }	ils } connaissent elles }

Vous **connaissez** Christophe?   *Do you know Christophe?*
Oui, je le **connais.**   *Yes, I know him.*

Tell students that the **i** in **connaître** has a circumflex only when it is followed by a **t.**

The imperative forms of **connaître** are regular (**connais, connaissez, connaissons**) but they are not widely used (**connais-toi toi-même** is one example of this usage).

savoir	
je sais	nous savons
tu sais	vous savez
il } sait elle }	ils } savent elles }

Vous **savez** pourquoi Valérie est partie?   *Do you know why Valérie left?*
Non, je ne **sais** pas.   *No, I don't know.*

The imperative forms of **savoir** are irregular (**sache, sachez, sachons**) and are also relatively uncommon. For many speakers, the imperative forms of **savoir** are avoided insofar as they belong to an elevated register and may sound somewhat pompous (**Sache que tout est fini entre nous!**).

Savoir et *connaître* au passé

Both **savoir** and **connaître** are regular in the **imparfait.**

Quand elle avait vingt ans, Valérie **connaissait** bien Montréal et elle **savait** où aller pour s'amuser.
When she was 20, Valérie knew Montreal well and she knew where to go to have a good time.

Both **savoir** and **connaître** are conjugated with **avoir** in the **passé composé.** The past participle of **connaître** is **connu.** The past participle of **savoir** is **su.**

   The **passé composé** of **connaître** can have the meaning *to have met.* The **passé composé** of **savoir** can mean *to have found out* as well as *to have learned.*

Valérie **a connu** Christophe à Marrakech.
Valérie met Christophe in Marrakech.

J'**ai su** la vérité quand je lui ai parlé.
I found out (learned) the truth when I talked to him / her.

This explanation foreshadows a discussion of the **imparfait / passé composé** distinction among similar verbs (**vouloir, pouvoir, devoir, être,** and **avoir**) in *Leçon 17.* If desired, introduce the expression **faire la connaissance de quelqu'un.**

Une histoire d'amour   **413**

Savoir ou connaître?

Both **connaître** and **savoir** can be translated by the English verb *to know*. They are not, however, interchangeable.

To help students understand the difference between **savoir** and **connaître**, tell them that **savoir** means *to know by fact* while **connaître** means *to know by familiarity.*

DRILL: **Est-ce que tu connais Candide?** (les étudiants / vous / Alceste / nous)

- **connaître**

1. Means *to know* in the sense of knowing a person or being familiar with a place or a situation.
2. Must have a direct object.
3. Cannot be followed by a **que** clause.

Est-ce que vous **connaissez** Paul? Il **connaît** très bien la France.	*Do you know Paul? He knows (is well acquainted with) France very well.*
Quand j'avais vingt ans, je **connaissais** toutes les boîtes de Toulouse.	*When I was 20, I knew (was familiar with) all the nightclubs in Toulouse.*
Il l'**a connue** chez moi.	*He met her at my place.*

- **savoir**

DRILL: **Vous ne savez pas nager!** (Candide / nous / tu / Candide et Alceste)

DRILL: **Je ne le savais pas.** (tu / Candide et Alceste / vous / le professeur)

DRILL: **On l'a su hier** (Candide et Alceste / le professeur / nous / je / tu / vous)

1. Means *to know* by fact or learning.
2. When followed by an infinitive, means *to know how to.*
3. May be used with or without a direct object.
4. May be followed by a clause beginning with **que** (*to know that*), **pourquoi** (*to know why*), **quand** (*to know when*), etc.

—Tu **sais** quand il vient?	*"Do you know when he's coming?"*
—Non, je ne **sais** pas.	*"No, I don't."*
Tu ne **sais** pas **nager?**	*You don't know how to swim?*
Je **sais qu'**il est allé à Montréal.	*I know (that) he went to Montreal.*
Tu ne **savais** pas ça?	*You didn't know (weren't aware of) that?*
Quand est-ce que vous l'**avez su?**	*When did you find out about it?*

Vous avez compris?

A. Savoir ou connaître? Lisez les phrases suivantes et décidez si les verbes anglais (*know, met, find out*) correspondent au verbe **savoir** ou au verbe **connaître** en français. Ne traduisez pas! *(Don't translate!)*

1. Do you *know* the Joneses?
2. Yes, I *met* them in New York.
3. *Did* you *know* that Mary got married last weekend?
4. No! How *did* you *find out*?
5. Who *knows* how this works?
6. Paul *knows,* but I don't *know* where he is.
7. Do you *know* where the Art Institute is?
8. No, I'm sorry. I just moved here and I don't *know* the city very well yet.

B. Connaissances Qui connaît qui?

Modèle   Il connaît Jeanne? Oui, il . . . . .
          Oui, il *la connaît.*

1. Elle connaît Paul? Oui, elle . . . . .
2. Tu connais les Durand? Non, je . . . . .
3. Vous connaissez mon père? Non, nous . . . . .
4. Tes parents connaissent ton camarade de chambre? Oui, ils . . . . .
5. Candide connaît Alceste? Oui, il . . . . .

C. Les métiers et le savoir-faire Qu'est-ce qu'ils savent faire? Suivez *(follow)* le modèle.

Modèle   Christophe est médecin.
        Il sait soigner.

1. Valérie est journaliste.
2. M. Hécan est professeur.
3. Mlle Verdier et M. Dupont sont secrétaires.
4. Janine est femme au foyer.
5. Patrick and Jean-Paul sont cuisiniers.
6. Nous sommes étudiants.

Continuons!

A. Un voyage à Montréal Complétez le dialogue avec **connaître** ou **savoir** au présent.

—Est-ce que tu . . . . . que nous allons à Montréal cet été?
—C'est vrai? Tu . . . . . la ville?
—Moi, non. Mais ma femme la . . . . . un peu et nous . . . . . des Canadiens.
   Ils vont nous montrer des choses intéressantes.
—Vous . . . . . où vous allez dormir?
—Oui, dans un petit hôtel pas cher, rue Saint-Denis.
—Je . . . . . un bon restaurant rue Saint-Denis. Ils . . . . . faire des frites comme à
   Bruxelles.
—C'est vrai? C'est quel numéro, rue Saint-Denis?
—Je ne . . . . . pas, mais c'est facile à trouver.

B. La femme de Monsieur Vilar Un ami de Monsieur Vilar lui a demandé comment il a rencontré sa femme. Complétez le dialogue avec **savoir** ou **connaître** au passé composé ou à l'imparfait.

—Comment est-ce que tu . . . . . ta femme?
—Eh bien, j'avais vingt ans et j'étais étudiant à Montpellier. Je n'étais pas de
   Montpellier et je ne . . . . . pas beaucoup d'autres étudiants. Je ne . . . . . même
   pas comment leur parler. J'étais très seul et très timide. Mais un jour, je . . . . .
   qu'il y avait une maison pour étudiants étrangers et un soir, pendant que j'étais
   là, une jolie jeune fille anglaise est entrée. Nous nous sommes parlé et je . . . . .
   que ses parents venaient souvent en vacances près de chez moi et qu'ils . . . . .
   mes parents! Alors, on est sorti et... mais tu connais la fin de l'histoire!

Découvertes culturelles: À la maison et en vacances

▶ Les travaux ménagers

A. Préparation: Les travaux ménagers. Traditionnellement, on a divisé les travaux ménagers selon les sexes. Comment est-ce que ces travaux se divisent dans votre culture?

travaux masculins	travaux féminins	les deux

B. Répartition des tâches.

1. **Mots clés.** Quel est le mot clé dans le titre du premier paragraphe? du deuxième paragraphe? du troisième paragraphe?
2. **Idées majeures.**
   a. Quels mots du premier paragraphe correspondent au mot **redéfinition**?
   b. Quels mots du deuxième paragraphe correspondent au mot **égalitaire**?
   c. Quels mots du troisième paragraphe correspondent au mot **spécialisée**?
3. **Quelques détails.** Complétez le tableau suivant avec les informations données dans le texte.

Travaux	hommes?	femmes?	% des couples
laver le linge	*non*	*oui*	*97%*

C. Comparaisons. Comparez cette liste de travaux avec la liste des travaux énumérés dans l'activité A.

1. Quels travaux ne sont pas sur la liste des travaux accomplis par les couples français?
2. Quels travaux sont communs aux deux cultures mais faits par une personne différente du couple?
3. Pour chaque tâche, devinez un pourcentage approximatif d'hommes ou de femmes qui font cette tâche dans votre culture.

D. Dialogue. Un couple français dialogue dans la cuisine.

1. Choisissez l'heure et le sujet.
2. Préparez les reproches de la jeune femme d'après ces statistiques.
3. Préparez les arguments du jeune homme d'après ces statistiques.
4. Écrivez un dialogue qui part d'un point chaud, et finit par un dénouement.

RÉPARTITION DES TÂCHES

L'évolution de la condition féminine a entraîné une redéfinition de la vie de couple.
Très longtemps, les femmes s'étaient contentées de leur condition de mère et d'épouse. Aujourd'hui, plus d'une femme sur trois est active et le modèle du couple biactif est majoritaire. Entre ces deux conceptions, il s'est produit une révolution, celle du féminisme.

La répartition des tâches est plus égalitaire...
Les femmes ont aujourd'hui moins de temps, mais aussi moins de goût pour les tâches domestiques. Les contributions masculines sont un peu plus fréquentes, mais le déséquilibre reste important: 4 h 38 par jour en moyenne pour les femmes, 2 h 41 pour les hommes. Les salariés (en particulier les cadres supérieurs) sont en général mieux disposés que les indépendants, commerçants, chefs d'entreprise, professions libérales ou les agriculteurs.

... mais elle reste spécialisée.
Une nouvelle répartition des tâches et des décisions est amorcée entre les sexes. Mais c'est encore la femme qui, le plus souvent, lave le linge (dans 97% des couples), fait la cuisine (84%), passe l'aspirateur (75%), lave la vaisselle (73%), fait les courses (67%). Les tâches principalement masculines sont plus limitées: porter du bois, du charbon ou du mazout et laver la voiture. Plus de 70% des hommes les prennent en charge et plus de 80% y participent.

Il existe enfin des tâches «négociables» entre les époux: faire la cuisine; laver les vitres; passer l'aspirateur ou le balai; laver la vaisselle; faire les courses; mettre le couvert. Les hommes les prennent en charge dans 10 à 20% des couples et les autres y participent assez largement. Ils s'y prêtent d'autant plus que leur compagne exerce une activité professionnelle. Les hommes continuent d'avoir chaque jour près d'une heure de temps libre de plus que les femmes (3 h 40 contre 2 h 50).

Gérard Mermet, *Francoscopie 1995*

➡️ Vacances à Marrakech

Act. A: Students can brainstorm or in groups select a foreign country and say what they would do if they were visiting there.

A. Préparation: Des vacances de rêve. Quelles activités préférez-vous quand vous êtes en vacances dans un pays étranger?

B. L'Hôtel Oasis

1. **L'hôtel.** Décrivez l'Hôtel Oasis d'après les photos et le texte.
   Est-ce que c'est un hôtel traditionnel?
   Où est-il situé?
   Quels sont les avantages de cet hôtel?
   Qui descend dans cet hôtel? Pendant combien de temps?
   C'est quel type d'hôtel?
2. **Les activités.** Quelles sont les activités offertes? Quelles sont les activités que vous aimez et les activités que vous ne pouvez pas faire?
3. **Mots nouveaux.** Complétez à l'aide des mots du texte.
   a. Une forêt de palmiers s'appelle une . . . . .
   b. Le contraire du travail c'est la . . . . .
   c. L'hôtel est situé sur une . . . . . célèbre.
   d. Pour aller de l'hôtel à la palmeraie il y a une . . . . .
   e. Les jeunes qui s'occupent des enfants s'appellent des . . . . .
   f. Autour de la vieille ville il y a des . . . . .

Act. B, 4: You may want to have students describe the persons, their origins, interests, tastes, professions etc. Then explain why they selected these activities for them.

4. **L'organisation de l'hôtel.** Faites le programme d'une journée typique à l'Hôtel Oasis.

• Un adulte: • Un enfant:

LE CLUB MED

Le Club Med est un club de vacances qui offre des structures de vacances en groupe. Créé par Serge Trigano, le Club existe depuis plus de quarante-cinq ans. Au commencement, un club amical plus qu'une entreprise commerciale, il offrait des prix réduits, des logements simples et l'occasion de pratiquer des sports jusque là réservés aux gens riches. Son organisation démocratique l'ouvrait à tous. Installés dans des lieux intéressants et exotiques, il était devenu le lieu de vacances préféré des jeunes familles. Avec la démocratisation des vacances, le Club n'a plus le même magnétisme; sa clientèle est devenue internationale et ses séjours plus chers. Le Club Med a un village de vacances à Marrakech.

Le personnel du Club est jeune, entre 20 et 25 ans, et on les appelle des G.O., «gentils organisateurs». Les touristes s'appellent des G.M., «Gentils Membres».

C. Le Club Med, commerce et culture.

1. **Qu'est-ce que le Club Med?** Pour mieux comprendre ce qu'est le Club Med, préparez des questions.
   • Identifiez des sujets.
   • Préparez trois questions par sujet.
   • Mettez vos questions sur le www.
2. **Le Club Med, aventure commerciale.** Lisez l'extrait sur le Club Med et répondez aux questions.
   a. Donnez l'âge du Club et le nom de ses employés.
   b. Soulignez les mots qui donnent les caractéristiques du Club.
   c. Quelle est la différence entre le Club et une agence de tourisme?
   d. Quelles étaient les caractéristiques du Club à l'origine?
   e. Que signifie la démocratisation des vacances?
   f. Où sont placées les familles moyennes dans la hiérarchie sociale?
   g. Pourquoi les étrangers aiment-ils le Club Med?

MARRAKECH

Maroc

Dans notre *Hôtel Oasis*, vous êtes chez vous!

VOTRE HÔTEL

De vos fenêtres, admirez la place traditionnelle et ses monuments aux ornementations mauresques, les remparts de la vieille ville.

Pour votre confort: chambres à deux lits climatisées avec salle de bains voûtée. Ligne téléphonique et télévision dans chaque chambre. Aussi chambres individuelles sur demande.

Pour vous régaler: 2 restaurants, l'un est spécialisé en cuisine marocaine.

Pour vous distraire: un hammam, des boutiques multiples, des films étrangers dans la salle de télévision et sauna ouvert 24 heures sur 24. Pour le soir, night club, disco, dîner aux chandelles sur la terrasse.

Pour vos excursions: *Loca voiture*, agence de location de voitures sur place. Enfin une navette pour toutes vos promenades dans la superbe palmeraie (5 hectares) où vous trouverez activités sportives, restaurants, terrains de jeu, table de pique-nique et barbecue. Garderie pour vos enfants 6 ans et plus avec moniteurs sportifs.

VOS ACTIVITÉS SPORTIVES

Deux piscines olympiques: une à l'hôtel, l'autre dans la palmeraie. 5 courts de tennis, avec leçons, moniteurs et tournois organisés chaque semaine. Autres activités au choix: volley-ball, pétanque, golf, aérobic, culture physique et tir à l'arc.

Vacances à Marrakech! Heureux voyages, heureux séjours!

- De la fenêtre de votre hôtel, vue sur la place la plus célèbre au monde
- Sport de détente à tous moments: tennis, équitation, golf et, pourquoi pas, sieste dans un hamac dans une palmeraie géante
- Les couleurs, l'animation des souks et leurs trésors pour vos achats
- Pour un voyage vers le grand Sud, prenez la route des kasbahs
- Et le soir, fêtes où rivalisent les danseurs, les acrobates, les costumes et les parfums violents

VISITE DU MAROC

Des excursions vous sont proposées pendant votre séjour.

À la demi-journée.
Visite des souks.
Visite de Marrakech en voiture ouverte.
Visite guidée de la ville et des monuments.

Tél.: 212.4.048.16
Fax: 212.4.064.74

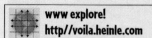

www explore!
http//voila.heinle.com

D. Travailler au Club Med.

1. Choisissez l'endroit du Club où vous voulez travailler.
2. Préparez un curriculum vitae pour offrir vos services au Club.
3. Préparez une lettre à envoyer avec votre c.v.
4. Passez une interview.

E. Le rêve.
Ça y est, vous passez l'été au Club Med comme G.O. (Gentil Organisateur). Votre journée a été dure, vous êtes mort(e) de fatigue et vous vous endormez. Votre nuit est agitée par un rêve extraordinaire. Racontez votre rêve.

Orthographe et prononciation

➤ Les lettres qu-

In French **qu-** is always pronounced as **k.** It never has a **w** sound as in English.

Activité

Prononcez Répétez après votre professeur.

1. Quelle est la question?
2. Quand? Avant le quinze?
3. Vous avez dit quatre ou quatorze?

Vocabulaire de base

NOMS

l'amour *(m.)* *love*
le couple *couple*
le divorce *divorce*
la fin *end*
une histoire *story*

VERBES

connaître *to know (be familiar with)*
se demander *to wonder*
se dépêcher *to hurry (up)*
se disputer (avec) *to argue (with)*
divorcer *to divorce*
embrasser *to kiss, to embrace*
s'endormir (conjugué comme dormir)
　to fall asleep
s'entendre (bien / mal) (avec qqn) *to
　get along (well / badly) (with
　someone)*
se marier (avec) *to marry, to get
　married (to)*
s'occuper (de) *to take care (of)*
penser (à / de) *to think (about / of)*
penser (que) *to think (that)*
quitter *to leave (someone, someplace)*
raconter *to tell (a story)*
repasser *to iron*
se reposer *to rest*
se retrouver *to get together, to meet
　(again)*
savoir *to know*
se souvenir de (conjugué comme venir)
　to remember
se tromper (de) *to be wrong, to make a
　mistake*

ADJECTIFS

amoureux, amoureuse (de) *in love
　(with)*
jaloux, jalouse *jealous*
patient(e) *patient*

DIVERS

à cause de *because of*
faire attention *to pay attention, to be
　careful*
faire la lessive *to do the laundry*
longtemps *a long time*
passer l'aspirateur *to vacuum*
pendant que *while*
que *that*
quelque chose (d'intéressant, d'autre...)
　something (interesting, else . . .)
quelqu'un (d'intéressant, d'autre...)
　someone (interesting, else . . .)
Qu'est-ce qui se passe? *What's
　happening?*
seulement *only*
tomber amoureux, amoureuse (de) *to
　fall in love (with)*

*Un mariage dans la cathédrale
d'Elne (Pyrénées-Orientales)*

Vocabulaire supplémentaire

NOMS

un coup de foudre *love at first sight*
une crise *crisis*
un(e) fiancé(e) *fiancé(e)*
la lune de miel *honeymoon*
un ménage *household, couple*
la patience *patience*
une rencontre *encounter, meeting*

VERBES

cacher *to hide*
se fiancer *to get engaged*
se réconcilier *to make up*
se séparer *to separate, to break up*
tromper *to fool, to cheat*

ADJECTIFS

déçu(e) *disappointed*
enceinte *pregnant*
fidèle (à) *faithful (to)*
infidèle *unfaithful*

DIVERS

attendre quelque chose avec impatience
*to be excited about something, not to
be able to wait for something*
au Maroc *in Morocco*
avoir bon / mauvais caractère *to be
easy / hard to get along with*
avoir de la patience *to be patient, have
patience*
être en crise *to be in a crisis*
fonder une famille *to start a family*
serrer quelqu'un dans ses bras *to hug
somebody*
sortir avec *to go out with, to date*
sortir ensemble *to go out together, to
date*

LE FRANÇAIS TEL QU'ON LE PARLE

Je m'en vais! *I'm leaving!*
je ne sais pas quoi penser *I don't know
what to think*
je pense que non *I don't think so*
je pense que oui *I think so*
C'est promis! *I promise!*
Mon amour! *My love!*

LE FRANÇAIS FAMILIER

draguer *to be looking for action*
un dragueur *guy who's always after girls*
faire gaffe = faire attention
Génial! *Great! Super!*
Super! *Great! Super!*

ON ENTEND PARFOIS...

attendre famille (Belgique) = être
enceinte
avoir un coup de soleil (pour) (Haïti)
= avoir un coup de foudre (pour)
être en famille (Canada) = être enceinte
tomber en amour (Canada) = tomber
amoureux

Magazine francophone

REVUE PÉRIODIQUE
PUBLIÉE À L'AIDE DE DOCUMENTATIONS INTERNATIONALES

Rédacteur en chef:
Isabelle Kaplan

Rédacteurs adjoints:
L. Kathy Heilenman
Claude Toussaint Tournier

NUMÉRO 4

REVUE EN FRANÇAIS POUR LES ÉTUDIANTS DE «VOILÀ!»

ÉDITORIAL

Cultures en conflit, conflits culturels

Ils vivent en France, vont à l'école française, travaillent dans les usines et sur les routes de France, dans les bureaux et dans les hôpitaux, ils ont des diplômes français, la sécurité sociale, les allocations familiales, et s'ils sont français ils sont élus maires, députés. Parfois aussi, ils sont en prison, devant les tribunaux, battus par la police, alphabétisés par des volontaires. On les trouve sur les scènes des théâtres, dans les magasins de disques, dans les maisons et les appartements où les sons de leur musique nouvelle et exotique rythment la vie quotidienne.

Qui sont-ils? Les immigrés.

Venus de tous les coins du monde, à des moments différents de l'histoire, pour des raisons différentes, ils font de la France un pays multiculturel où leurs modes de vie et leurs problèmes confrontent les habitudes traditionnelles, changent les optiques, réveillent parfois les vieux instincts racistes, la violence qui refuse. Leur vie et leur présence forcent l'évolution d'une culture ancienne qui n'aime pas toujours les changements, la nouveauté. Mais les confrontations dans un pays républicain et socialiste sont aussi dialectiques et l'assimilation dans un monde où les frontières disparaissent promet un avenir de liberté et de fraternité.

À l'avenir de prouver l'idéologie démocratique d'une nation qui vient de célébrer le bicentenaire de sa Révolution!

Ouvrez ce **DOSSIER IMMIGRATION** et faites connaissance avec les nouveaux immigrés, leur vie, leurs problèmes et leur rencontre avec leur pays d'adoption.

Khalid El Quandili

31 ans. Président de l'association Sport Insertion Jeunes

Khalid El Quandili devrait être secrétaire d'État chargé des banlieues. Fils de maçon, arrivé de Rabat à 6 mois avec ses parents, il a grandi dans les bidonvilles de Nanterre, vécu aux Bosquets de Montfermeil, et dans les cités chaudes d'Argenteuil, de Gennevilliers ou de Meaux. Parcours qui l'a poussé à créer en 1984 l'association Sport Insertion Jeunes. Sa réussite, Khalid la doit à sa ténacité et surtout à son image de grand sportif. À 14 ans, il se passionne pour le karaté puis pour le full-contact (mélange de boxe et de karaté), au point de devenir champion de France (1979), puis champion du monde (de 1986 à 1992) de full-contact. Il devient l'idole des jeunes. Et leur médiateur auprès des hommes politiques. François Mitterrand le reçoit en décembre 1991, lui demande ce dont il a besoin. *«Nous organisons une Nuit des Troph*ées *pour récompenser des sportifs qui s'occupent de jeunes dans les cités,* lui répond-il. *Si vous pouvez venir, ce serait formidable.»* Mitterand accepte. En 1992, il se rend à Épinay-sur-Seine. En juin 1993, à l'Institut du Monde arabe et, cette fois, accompagné de Simone Veil. *«Le plus beau jour de ma vie»,* confie Khalid...

Khalid El Quandili

Djamel Attala
«Je me sens plus algérien que français»

Farouk Sekkaî
«Les Français n'ont pas confiance en nous»

Bouzid
«Je rêve de créer un territoire pour les exclus»

A. RAMEY

Près de 100 000 personnes originaires d'Asie du sud-est sont arrivées en France à la fin des années 70, fuyant leur pays pour des raisons politiques.

■ Jeunes immigrés

En 1990, le nombre de jeunes de moins de 16 ans vivant dans une famille dont le chef est immigré était de 1,7 million, soit 14% de l'ensemble de cette tranche d'âge. Pour les 16/22 ans, des inégalités se manifestent au niveau de la scolarisation: à 20 ans, 46% d'entre eux sont encore scolarisés, contre 50% pour la moyenne nationale. Et en ce qui concerne le travail, 30% sont touchés par le chômage (40 à 50% pour les jeunes d'origine maghrébine), contre 24% en moyenne.

Les Asiatiques d'Ici

Texte: Lam Van Be

Qui sont-ils? Pourquoi ont-ils quitté leur pays d'origine?
Est-ce qu'ils s'adaptent bien à leur terre d'accueil?

La population du pays a beaucoup changé au cours des vingt dernières années.

Si, dans les années d'après-guerre, le Canada et le Québec ont accueilli des vagues d'immigrants relativement homogènes composées principalement d'Européens, l'immigration des dernières années leur a par contre amené une population plus diversifiée. Cette diversification se manifeste tant au niveau de la langue, de la culture que du pays d'origine.

LES ASIATIQUES AU CANADA

Bien que l'immigration asiatique au Canada date du début du siècle, la présence asiatique au pays n'est vraiment importante que depuis les vingt dernières années. Au Québec, contrairement à la plupart des immigrés de l'après-guerre qui y sont venus après la Seconde Guerre mondiale et qui se sont anglicisés, ces nouveaux arrivants s'intègrent à la société québécoise francophone.

Aussi, dans cette même période, l'implantation de plusieurs usines de fabrication d'autos, de matériel électronique tant au Québec qu'en Ontario a ouvert la grande porte aux immigrants-investisseurs venant de la Corée du Sud, du Japon, de Taïwan et de Hong Kong.

Quelques définitions

groupes ethniques, communautés ethniques: Ces termes, dans le langage courant, désignent les personnes d'origine autre que française ou britannique.

allophone: personne dont la langue maternelle n'est ni le français ni l'anglais (francophone ou anglophone).

minorités visibles: les communautés culturelles de race noire, les Asiatiques et les Latino-Américains.

immigrant: personne qui entre dans un pays étranger pour s'y établir.
Si la personne a quitté son pays pour des raisons politiques ou de détresse, on l'appelle *réfugié*.

Au Canada, depuis quelque temps, un bon nombre de gens entrent au pays pour demander ensuite le statut de réfugié. Ce sont des *revendicateurs du statut de réfugié*.

diaspora: l'ensemble de la population vivant à l'extérieur de leur pays natal forme une diaspora.

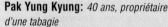

Lê Phuong Mai: *25 ans, étudiante.*

«Mon nom de famille est Lê. On m'appelle ici indifféremment Lê, Phuong ou Mai. Je suis arrivée à Montréal en 1975 avec mes parents à l'âge de 6 ans. Je termine mes études en médecine cette année.

Je me trouve plus chanceuse que mes parents car je n'ai pas vécu la terrible guerre du Viêtnam. J'ai ainsi évité toutes les souffrances que mes cousines ont dû endurer sous le régime communiste.

Même avec toute ma gratitude à l'égard de mes parents, j'éprouve cependant certains malaises dans ma relation avec eux, à cause de la différence entre la culture-mère et la culture de la société où j'ai grandi.»

Pak Yung Kyung: *40 ans, propriétaire d'une tabagie*

«Je suis arrivé au Québec l'année dernière comme immigrant-investisseur. J'ai acheté cette tabagie il y a seulement trois mois.

Il faut que j'apprenne vite le français car mes clients sont presque tous francophones. Les gens ici me prennent pour un Chinois. Pour leur expliquer que je suis Coréen, il faut que je leur dise: Hyundai.»

Yam Sann: *19 ans, étudiant*

«Je suis Cambodgien. Je suis arrivé au Québec en 1985 avec mes parents après avoir passé trois ans dans le camp de réfugiés de Khao I Dang en Thaïlande.

J'étudie présentement la technique en informatique au cégep de Saint-Laurent. J'habite avec mes parents comme le veut la tradition cambodgienne, mais je trouve que la vie est difficile à cause de la discipline excessive imposée par mes parents.

Je ne peux pas porter les vêtements qu'ils détestent, ni rencontrer mon amie qui n'est pas d'origine cambodgienne, ni sortir les fins de semaine sans leur autorisation. Je songe à quitter la maison, que mes parents le veuillent ou non.»

Les vacances de Simon
Une nouvelle inédite par Angèle Kingué

Cameroun

Les aéroports sont des lieux de prédilection par excellence pour les curieux désireux d'observer les émotions humaines à l'œuvre. Valises, cartons, sacs, larmes, sanglots, cris de joie, rires, courses affolées, regards nerveux, mines défaites, c'est cela les aéroports! Les aéroports de Douala ou d'Abidjan ne sont pas différents. Mais ce qui frappe lorsqu'on arrive à l'aéroport de Douala, après l'humidité et la chaleur, c'est la horde de chauffeurs de taxi et de porteurs qui se ruent vers vous pour solliciter votre clientèle. C'est aussi la longue heure d'attente qu'il faut passer aux bagages avant de voir arriver votre valise cahin-caha.

Je n'oublierai jamais l'arrivée de mon frère Simon. C'étaient les grandes vacances de 1974. J'avais alors 16 ans, le visage rond et luisant, assez potelé, «bien nourri» comme dirait mon père, moi je préfère dire que j'étais de taille et de corpulence moyennes. Cela faisait 5 ans que mon frère était parti en France faire des études de Droit et de Commerce. Son retour était donc une grande célébration familiale. On se demandait tous s'il avait changé, on n'aurait pas dit d'après les lettres qu'il nous écrivait. Elles étaient très affectueuses, pleines de conseils, et d'encouragement. Mais nous nous demandions quand même s'il était toujours aussi beau, aussi bavard et aussi amusant qu'avant, ou alors s'il aurait les gestes affectés, et l'air arrogant et indifférent de beaucoup de «revenants». Mon ami Yomkil m'avait raconté que son frère Matip ne savait plus parler le Bassa, sa langue maternelle, après un bref séjour en France et pire même n'arrivait plus à manger les mets locaux.

La maison de Natyk

s'asseoir
comme un inconnu
poser les mains
sur la table

du regard
simplement
demander asile
et permission

user du pain
et du feu
qu'on n'a pas faits
soi-même

remasser les miettes
à la fin
pour les porter
aux oiseaux

ne dire
qui l'on est
d'où l'on vient
ni pour quoi

réserver la parole
à autre chose
et mettre sa chaise
à la fenêtre

Mohammed Dib,

J'avais hâte de voir mon frère mais en même temps, j'étais habitée d'une espèce d'anxiété et d'appréhension. Il était prestigieux d'avoir un membre de la famille en France surtout à cette époque. Malheureusement, plusieurs revenants tombaient dans le culte de soi. J'entendis quelqu'un annoncer que la porte venait de s'ouvrir, et que les passagers descendaient de l'avion. Il apparut soudain, vêtu d'une veste de daim, avec ce même sourire de charmeur, et l'œil vif. Je lui sautai au cou, en criant son nom, il m'embrassa sans prononcer mon nom, embrassa mes parents, mon frère, mes sœurs et tout le reste de la famille! Il se rappelait de tout le monde, et appelait chacun par son nom. «Mais comment se fait-il qu'il ne m'ait pas encore appelée par mon nom?» me demandai-je. Ça y était, mon frère m'avait oubliée. C'est alors que je l'entendis demander: «Mais où est Angèle?»

«Mais tu l'as saluée la première!»

«Mon Dieu! Joli bébé, tu as grandi, tu es une vraie femme. Je ne t'avais pas reconnue, tourne-toi que je te regarde. Comme tu es belle!»

La chanteuse franco-tunisienne, que l'on a pu voir dans "La nuit sacrée", nous parle tendances, musique et code de la nationalité.

Les Clés: Une de vos chansons, *"Yanari",* évoque des problèmes très actuels...

Amina: C'est l'histoire d'un "sans papiers" renvoyé dans son pays. On lui demande ce qu'il a vu à Paris. Il dit que, là-bas, les gens mangent tous les jours, mais que, dans le pays de l'abondance, on ne partage pas.

J'avais un gros paquet de sucre dans le cœur. Je souris, fis une virevolte et lui sautai au cou. Après le dîner, il se rappelait des plats traditionnels et les mangea avec appétit, il nous raconta les histoires du Mans et de Toulouse, les deux villes dans lesquelles il avait étudié. Il parlait beaucoup de ses amis martiniquais et marocains. «Là-bas», nous disait-il, «si quelqu'un vous dit: «on va prendre un pot?» vous devez payer votre part.»

«Mais pourquoi?» disions-nous.

«Là-bas les bus sont silencieux: on lit ou on dort, on ne crie pas fort, on ne parle pas au voisin, et on ne connaît pas toujours ses voisins. On marche très vite, il y a de grands bâtiments qui s'étendent à perte de vue...»

Le lendemain, je me précipitai chez Yomkil lui raconter que mon frère n'avait pas attrapé la maladie des revenants lui, qu'il mangeait tout, parlait encore très bien le Mbang.

Bref, mon frère était un vrai gars, UN VRAI AFRICAIN.

Immigration. Quelles connotations a pour vous le mot **immigration**? À quoi et à qui pensez-vous quand vous entendez ce mot?

Nationalités. Cherchez dans les articles toutes les nationalités qui sont mentionnées. Combien sont représentées? Comment pouvez-vous les grouper?

Noms et prénoms. Cherchez les noms et les prénoms qui sont cités dans ces articles. De quel pays viennent les personnes mentionnées? Est-ce que ce sont des noms traditionnellement français?

Titres et sous-titres. Identifiez les sujets du *Magazine* d'après les titres et les sous-titres. Dans ce *Magazine,* on parle des immigrés dans quels pays?

Informations ou opinions? D'après le format, les titres et les illustrations, décidez quels articles vont être des articles d'informations objectives, des articles d'opinion et des faits divers.

Les arts et les lettres

AMINA, LA MÉTISSE. D'après le sujet de ses chansons, et celle de «Yanari», quel type de chansons chante Amina? Pourquoi?

LES VACANCES DE SIMON. Identifiez où se passe la scène, les personnages et les circonstances.

Comment la nouvelle est-elle construite? Trouvez les moments importants et soulignez les phrases qui marque les moments de la narration.

Tracez la vie de Simon et faites son portrait d'après cette nouvelle.

Faites le portrait de l'auteur d'après cette nouvelle: son enfance, sa famille, ses sentiments, ses émotions.

Avec ce que décrit cette nouvelle, qu'est-ce que vous avez appris sur la culture africaine?

LA MAISON DE NATYK. Que fait et que dit la personne dans ce poème? Pourquoi cette personne est-elle dans cette maison? Comment est la maison idéale pour cette personne?

Comparez comment on reçoit un inconnu dans votre culture et dans celle du poète. Quelles actions paraissent négatives, quelles actions paraissent agréables?

À LA LOUPE

L'ÉDITORIAL.

1. D'après les premiers mots de chaque paragraphe, dites dans quel paragraphe on parle des sujets suivants: les origines des immigrés / les perspectives pour le futur / les activités professionnelles.
2. Identifiez les professions que font les immigrés d'après cet éditorial.
3. Soulignez dans le troisième paragraphe les expressions et les phrases qui illustrent le titre de l'éditorial. Quels problèmes existent probablement dans la France contemporaine? L'éditorial est-il optimiste ou pessimiste?

LES PROBLÈMES. Soulignez dans chaque article du *Magazine* les mots qui font allusion à des problèmes et faites la liste de ces problèmes en deux catégories: problèmes sociaux et problèmes économiques. Lesquels de ces problèmes vous paraissent universels? spécifiques à la France? spécifiques au Québec?

FRANCE/QUÉBEC. Comparez les articles des pages 423 et 424. Faites une liste des caractéristiques de l'immigration en France: origine des immigrés, professions, langue, traditions et culture. D'après l'article de la page 424, faites la liste des caractéristiques de l'immigration au Québec.

Comparez l'immigration en France et au Québec. Quelles sont les différences? Comment les immigrés sont-ils différents? Comment leur situation est-elle différente? Justifiez vos conclusions.

Quels articles sont plus objectifs? Quels articles sont plus neutres?

À VOTRE AVIS...

RECHERCHES.

1. Avec tous les articles de ce *Magazine,* présentez la situation des immigrés en France en sept phrases: trois phrases pour les faits, trois pour les problèmes et une pour conclure.
2. Choisissez une des trois phrases tirées de l'*Éditorial* et préparez 10 questions pour rechercher le sujet qu'elle présente.

Leurs modes de vie confrontent les habitudes traditionnelles.

Ils réveillent parfois les vieux instincts racistes.

Leur vie et leur présence forcent l'évolution d'une culture ancienne.

ACTIONS.

1. Vous allez interviewer Khalid El Quandili à la radio. Préparez douze questions pour votre interview, puis faites l'interview avec un(e) camarade qui joue le rôle de Khalid.
2. «Réserver la parole à autre chose» dit le poète Mohammed Dib. Imaginez le dialogue qui a lieu entre le poète et son hôte.

CORRESPONDANCE.

1. Sur le modèle des récits de Lê Phuong Mai, Samn Yam et Pak Yung Kyung, page 424, faites parler Djamel Attala, Farouk Sekkai et Bouzid (page 423 en haut à droite).
2. De France, Simon écrit à Angèle. Écrivez sa lettre, donnant des détails sur sa vie, son logement, ses activités, ses amis, ses problèmes et ses aspirations.

POUR FINIR.

1. D'après les articles que vous avez lus, quelles connotations ont les mots suivants en France? et au Québec?
   immigrés / intégration / conflits / terre d'accueil / métisse / hospitalité
2. D'après tous les articles de ce *Magazine*, donnez trois faits que vous avez appris sur l'immigration en général, sur l'immigration en France et sur l'immigration au Québec.
3. Donnez cinq mots que vous avez appris sans utiliser de liste de vocabulaire. Faites une phrase avec chaque mot.

Une soirée devant la télévision

En bref

Dans cette leçon...

- La télévision en France et au Québec: les programmes et les téléspectateurs
- Parler de films et de romans
- La radio et les jeunes
- Le pronom **en**
- Certains verbes au passé: les verbes **être, avoir, devoir, pouvoir** et **vouloir**
- Les verbes **croire, vivre** et **suivre**

In this lesson...

- Television in France and Quebec: TV schedules and the television audience
- Talking about movies and novels
- Radio and youth
- The pronoun **en**
- Some verbs in the past: **être, avoir, devoir, pouvoir,** and **vouloir**
- The verbs **croire, vivre,** and **suivre**

www explore!
http://voila.heinle.com

Develop writing skills with Système-D software!

Practice listening and pronunciation skills with the Text Tape!

Discover the Francophone world!

Build your skills!

INTERNET

SYSTÈME-D

TEXT TAPE

VIDEO TAPE

CD-ROM

Students have an open-ended writing activity in the **Cahier** suitable for use with **Système-D**.

Entrée en matière: Devant la télévision

Possible warm-up questions: **Dans quelle pièce sommes-nous? Quels sont les meubles? Quel âge ont les enfants? Comment est leur famille? Où sont les parents? C'est une sœur et un frère? Qu'est-ce qu'ils regardent?** etc.

Observez et devinez. À quelle scène appartiennent ces descriptions: 1, 2, 3 ou 4? Quelles phrases sont dites? Quelles phrases sont descriptives?

Il entre sans faire de bruit.

Il porte un pantalon mais pas de chemise.

Un avion descend du ciel.

Tiens, c'est comme le 14 juillet!

Un nuage radioactif monte dans le ciel.

Il y a des explosions.

Tu as vu l'avion qui tombe?

Ils ne sont pas surpris.

Maman, maman!

C'est minuit.

Il porte un vieux chapeau.

Ils sont assis sur le canapé.

Il est devant la maison.

Regarde, c'est rouge, et jaune et noir!

Il y a beaucoup de bruit.

L'air est dangereux.

Tu as vu le grand couteau?

Qu'est-ce qu'elle lit?

Au secours, Maman, c'est le loup *(wolf)*!

Ils appellent leur mère.

Ils regardent avec grande attention.

Il porte un costume noir.

Un avion brûle dans le ciel.

Le bruit est extraordinaire.

C'est le soir.

Oh, regarde comme c'est beau!

Tu as vu, ce gros nuage gris et blanc?

Il y a un petit nuage dans le ciel.

Alors, il se lève.

Elle est horrifiée!

Elle n'a rien entendu.

Il y a une petite lampe sur la commode.

Des bombes tombent du ciel.

Une pollution mortelle s'élève dans le ciel.

Dans cinq minutes elle sera morte.

Elle est seule dans la maison.

1   2

L'histoire. Trouvez l'histoire!

L'histoire: Encourage students to use words and expressions from *Observez et devinez.*

	Quelle est l'histoire à la télévision?	Que font les enfants?	Que disent les enfants?
Dessin 1			
Dessin 2			
Dessin 3			
Dessin 4			

You may want to make a transparency of the cartoon and draw in bubbles to fill in **Que disent les enfants?** The words put into bubbles can either be taken from *Observez et devinez* or can be invented by students.

Le message de l'humoriste. Quel est le message de l'humoriste qui a fait ce dessin? Quelle est la morale de cette histoire?

Le message de l'humoriste: Have students give a title to the story that indicates the moral.

Sempé, *La Grande Panique*

429

Vocabulaire

A. À la télévision ce soir

18.45 TOM ET JERRY
Dessin animé.
18.55 LA ROUE DE LA FORTUNE
Jeu animé par Olivier Chiabodo et Frédérique Le Calvez.
19.25 PREMIERS BAISERS
Série française. Quand il revient de voyage, Luc apprend que Svetlana sort avec un autre.
20.00 LE JOURNAL
Avec LA MÉTÉO.
20.45 POULET FERMIER
Téléfilm français de Philippe Triboit avec Francis Perrin et Annie Cordy. **Comédie policière.** On a trouvé le corps d'un notaire dans un champ près d'un village. L'inspecteur Médeuze est envoyé de Paris pour faire une enquête sur le meurtre. Comme tout le village détestait la victime, il y a beaucoup de suspects, comme par exemple, la fermière propriétaire du champ, lieu du crime... Le meurtrier est-il du village?
22.20 SACRÉE SOIRÉE
Variétés. Hommage à Jacques Brel.

19.00 CANAILLE PELUCHE
Émission pour enfants.
19.35 LES SIMPSON
20.00 C'EST PAS LE 20 HEURES
20.35 ÉLÉPHANTS D'AFRIQUE
Documentaire.
21.30 LA CRISE
Film français de Coline Serreau avec Vincent Lindon et Patrik Timsit (1992). **Comédie dramatique.** Un homme perd son travail le jour où sa femme le quitte. Il essaie de parler avec sa famille et ses amis, mais personne ne l'écoute.

19.15 FLASH INFO
19.20 COUSTEAU
La pollution en mer.
20.00 JOURNAL et MÉTÉO
20.50 LES GENS DE MOGADOR
Feuilleton français en 6 épisodes. À la mort de sa mère, Frédéric et sa femme Ludivine deviennent les propriétaires du domaine de Mogador. Mais il y a des problèmes dans le couple.
22.40 ENVOYÉ SPECIAL
Magazine. Les gardiennes de prison aux États-Unis; la France de la corruption; Tibétains en exil, avec une interview du Dalai Lama.

19.00 VOYAGE EN TUNISIE
Documentaire.
19.45 VIVRE À HIROSHIMA AUJOURD'HUI
Reportage.
20.30 8 1/2 JOURNAL
20.40 HIROSHIMA, MON AMOUR
Film français d'Alain Resnais, avec Emmanuelle Riva (Elle), Eiji Okada (Lui) et Bernard Fresson (l'Allemand) (1958). **Drame.** Une actrice française va à Hiroshima pour participer à un film. Là-bas, elle rencontre et aime un Japonais. Cet amour lui rappelle un autre amour qu'elle a vécu pendant la guerre de 40, avec un Allemand.
22.10 LE MISANTHROPE
Pièce de théâtre en cinq actes de Molière. **Comédie.** Alceste déteste la société mais il est amoureux de Célimène, une jeune veuve coquette et mondaine.

19.00 LE 19–20 DE L'INFO
20.05 FOOTBALL
Bordeaux-Montpellier
22.45 FAUT PAS RÊVER
Magazine.
Mexique, Madagascar, France

19.00 DOCTEUR QUINN, FEMME MÉDECIN
Série américaine avec Jane Seymour.
19.54 6 MINUTES et Météo
20.00 MADAME EST SERVIE
Série américaine avec Judith Light et Danza. La famille de Tony arrive d'Italie et Tony essaie d'apprendre l'Italien à Angela.
20.45 LA GLOIRE DE MON PÈRE
Film français d'Yves Robert d'après les **Souvenirs d'enfance** de Marcel Pag (1990). **Comédie.** Marcel est né en Provence à fin du dix-neuvième siècle. Son père, Joseph, instituteur à Marseille et sa mère, Augustin couturière. La famille, accompagnée de la Rose et de l'oncle Jules, passe ses vacances d'été dans une petite maison de campagne près d'un village provençal.

B. Vingt heures

Ask students: CNN, ESPN, AE, HBO, c'est quoi? Et CBS, NBC, ABC? Quelle est la différence? Pourquoi regarder la télévision?

Aujourd'hui, c'est le 6 août et il est vingt heures.

- Qu'est-ce qu'on fait au rez-de-chaussée? Est-ce qu'on fait autre chose en même temps? Et au premier étage, qu'est-ce qu'on fait? Et au deuxième étage? Où habite le chien? Est-ce qu'il y a des enfants dans l'immeuble? Où?

Info plus

La télévision en France.

There are seven television stations in France: **Télévision Française 1 (TF1)**, **France 2**, **France 3**, **Canal Plus (Canal +)**, **Arte**, **Modulation 6 (M6)**, and **La Cinquième**. **Arte** and **La Cinquième** are cultural channels, **La Cinquième** offering programs only during the daytime while **Arte** offers them only in the evening. **TF1** and **M6** are private channels, while **France 2** and **France 3** are government-run. **Canal +** is a special channel that has to be paid for separately.

French television used to be regulated by the government. With the privatization of some French television channels, French programming has become more varied, but a significant amount of French television originates in the United States. Thus, many of the perceptions that the French have of North America are colored by the way people are depicted on American TV.

Information correct as of publication. The situation in other countries varies. For example, Belgian television stations are government-run, but there is cable access to a wide range of programming from other European countries.

TRANSPARENCY: 17-2

Au premier étage, on a déjà regardé un dessin animé pour enfants, un jeu télévisé et une série française sur TF1. Maintenant, on regarde une série américaine, *Madame est servie,* sur M6. Ils aiment bien l'acteur Tony Danza! Mais après, ils vont changer de chaîne et regarder du football sur France 3... Ils ne vont pas voir le début, mais ce n'est pas grave, ils vont voir la fin!

- Regardez le programme de télévision. Comment s'appelle le dessin animé? Il est français ou américain? C'est à quelle heure? Comment s'appelle le jeu télévisé? Est-ce qu'il y a le même jeu chez vous? À votre avis, qu'est-ce qui est différent? Comment s'appelle la série à dix-neuf heures vingt-cinq? C'est une série française ou américaine? Et la série à vingt heures? C'est une nouvelle ou une vieille série? Qu'est-ce qu'ils vont regarder après? Pourquoi est-ce qu'ils ne vont pas voir le début?

Ask students: **Quel est votre feuilleton préféré? Votre série préférée? Pourquoi? Est-ce que c'est une bonne idée de passer des feuilletons et des séries américains à la télévision française? Qu'est-ce que les Français vont penser des Américains à cause de cela?**

Info plus

Un feuilleton ou une série?

Un feuilleton is a continuing story (with or without a set number of episodes) like the American **feuilletons** *Dallas, Santa Barbara,* and *Dynastie,* all of which are seen on French television. **Une série** is a half-hour or an hour show like *Deux Flics à Miami* (Miami Vice), *Melrose Place, Alerte à Malibu* (Baywatch), or *Roseanne* (all on French television also). Many American series are shown on French television, even though the French also have their own series, such as, *Hélène et les garçons, Premiers baisers,* and *Les Nouvelles filles d'à côté.*

Où est-ce qu'on va!

Ça fait peur!

C'est une soirée France 2 au rez-de-chaussée! Maintenant, on regarde les informations, comme tous les jours. Elles durent une demi-heure, mais après, il y a la météo et la publicité. Avant le journal, télévisé, on a regardé un documentaire de Cousteau et après, on va regarder *Les Gens de Mogador,* le feuilleton de l'été. On va finir la soirée avec *Envoyé Spécial,* un magazine d'information avec des reportages souvent intéressants.

• Comment sont les personnes du rez-de-chaussée? Qu'est-ce qu'elles aiment? Regardez le programme. De quoi va-t-on parler dans l'émission de Cousteau? C'est à quelle heure? Comment s'appellent les informations? Combien de temps durent-elles? Est-ce que les nouvelles sont bonnes aujourd'hui, à votre avis? Qu'est-ce que c'est, *Les Gens de Mogador*? À quelle heure est-ce que ça commence? Qu'est-ce que c'est, *Envoyé Spécial*? Qu'est-ce qu'il y a au programme d'*Envoyé Spécial* aujourd'hui? Il y a une interview de qui? C'est intéressant, à votre avis?

C. Et au deuxième étage?

Il est maintenant vingt-deux heures. Qu'est-ce qui se passe au deuxième étage? Pendant le dîner, ils ont écouté un concert de musique classique à la radio. Maintenant, ils vont regarder le programme pour voir s'il y a quelque chose à la télévision. S'ils ne trouvent rien d'intéressant, ils vont regarder un film sur leur magnétoscope parce qu'ils adorent le cinéma. Il y avait des beaux films ce soir à la télévision, mais il est trop tard maintenant. Sur TF1, il y a une émission de variétés qui commence dans vingt minutes. D'habitude, ils n'aiment pas beaucoup les vedettes de la chanson, mais aujourd'hui, c'est une émission sur Jacques Brel, le célèbre chanteur belge mort en 1978. Sur Arte, il y a une pièce de Molière avec des bons acteurs, et ils aiment bien rire. Mais ils aiment bien avoir peur aussi, alors ils vont peut-être regarder un film d'horreur qu'ils ont en cassette vidéo.

- Qui habite au deuxième étage? Où sont les deux hommes maintenant? Où sont les deux autres personnes? Pourquoi, à votre avis? Qu'est-ce qu'ils ont fait pendant le dîner? Qu'est-ce qu'ils vont faire maintenant? Comment s'appelle l'émission de variétés? Et la pièce de Molière? Et vous, est-ce que vous préférez l'émission sur Jacques Brel, la comédie de Molière ou un film d'horreur?

- Vous pouvez choisir: est-ce qu'il y a quelque chose d'intéressant à la télévision pour vous ce soir? Qu'est-ce que vous avez envie de regarder? Qu'est-ce que vous n'avez pas envie de regarder? Pourquoi? Avec quelle famille est-ce que vous voulez passer la soirée? Pourquoi?

TRANSPARENCY: 17-4

Passer is used in this lesson in the sense of *to spend*. **Passer** in the sense of *to go by* is presented in **Leçon 18**.

D. Pour parler de films

Est-ce que vous préférez les comédies ou les drames? Les comédies sont des films comiques (par exemple, les films de Laurel et Hardy ou encore le film pour enfants *Madame Doubtfire*) et les drames sont des films sérieux où on n'a pas envie de rire (par exemple, *La Liste de Schindler*). Mais une comédie peut aussi être dramatique quand le film est en même temps amusant et sérieux (par exemple, *Forrest Gump* ou encore *Beignets de tomates vertes*) ou bien romantique quand c'est une histoire d'amour amusante (par exemple, *Quand Harry rencontre Sally*).

Préférez-vous les films d'amour (par exemple, *Sur la route de Madison*, avec Clint Eastwood et Meryl Streep)? les films d'aventures (par exemple, les films qui racontent les aventures d'Indiana Jones)? les films d'horreur qui font peur (par exemple, *L'Exorciste* ou encore *Le Vendredi treize*)? les westerns (par exemple, les films avec John Wayne)? les films d'espionnage (comme les James Bond)? les films de science-fiction (comme *Star Trek*)? les dessins animés *(Le Roi lion* ou *Cendrillon*, par exemple)? Ou bien encore les films policiers (par exemple: *La Firme* avec Tom Cruise ou encore *Le Fugitif* avec Harrison Ford)?

- Regardez le programme de télévision du 6 août. Quels sont les films aujourd'hui? Est-ce que ce sont des films français ou des films étrangers (pour les Français)? Est-ce qu'il y a des comédies? des drames? Qu'est-ce que c'est, un téléfilm? Quel film voulez-vous voir? Quel film ne voulez-vous pas voir? Pourquoi?

Discuss the scene. **Qui est la victime? Où sont-ils? Qui est derrière le rideau?** etc.

E. Pour parler de films policiers

Dans un film policier, d'habitude, il y a un meurtre et il y a souvent les mêmes personnages: un meurtrier ou une meurtrière (appelé aussi un tueur ou une tueuse), une victime, des suspects, un ou des témoins et un inspecteur de police. Le meurtrier tue la victime et l'inspecteur fait une enquête pour apprendre la vérité. Il interroge les suspects et les témoins, il vérifie le lieu du crime et il cherche l'arme du crime (par exemple un revolver ou un couteau).

- Regardez le programme. Il y a aujourd'hui une comédie policière sur TF1, *Poulet fermier*. Qui est la victime? Qui est Médeuze? Où est le lieu du crime? Qui est suspect? Pourquoi? Est-ce que *Poulet fermier* est un téléfilm violent, à votre avis?

Notes de vocabulaire

1. Mots et expressions utiles.

annoncer (conjugué comme commencer)	*to announce*
comprendre (conjugué comme prendre)	*to understand*
danseur, danseuse	*dancer*
devenir (conjugué comme venir)	*to become*
en effet	*indeed, in fact*
ennuyeux, ennuyeuse	*boring*
le goût	*taste*
international(e), internationaux, internationales	*international*
les médias	*media*
montrer	*to show*
un musicien, une musicienne	*musician*
national(e), nationaux, nationales	*national*

permettre (de) (conjugué comme mettre)	to allow, to permit
pourtant	however
promettre (qqch. à qqn) (conjugué comme mettre)	to promise (something to someone)
un reporter	reporter
une station (de radio)	(radio) station
revenir (conjugué comme venir)	to come back
surprendre (conjugué comme prendre)	to surprise
une télécommande	remote control

2. Ne... rien de / ne... personne de.
As was the case with adjectives following the expressions **quelque chose de** and **quelqu'un de,** the adjective following **ne... rien de** and **ne... personne de** is always masculine singular.

Il y a **quelque chose d'intéressant** ici?	Is there anything interesting here?
Non, il **n'**y a **rien d'intéressant** ici.	No, there's nothing interesting here.
Il y a **quelqu'un d'intéressant** ici?	Is there someone/anybody interesting here?
Non, il **n'**y a **personne d'intéressant** ici.	No, there's no one/nobody interesting here.

3. À la télé / à la radio.
To talk about what is on television or on the radio, use **à la télévision** or **à la radio.**

Qu'est-ce qu'il y a **à la télévision** ce soir?	What's on television tonight?

4. Un programme / une émission.
Le programme refers to the television schedule. To refer to an individual television program, use **une émission.**

J'ai vu dans **le programme** qu'il y a **une émission** sur les éléphants ce soir.	I saw in the schedule that there's a program on elephants tonight.

5. Même.
The word **même** can mean *same* or *even*. Here are some expressions using **même.**

c'est la **même** chose	it's the same thing, it's all the same
quand **même**	all the same, even so, nevertheless
c'est toujours la **même** chose	it's always the same old story
même pas moi	not even me
en **même** temps	at the same time
Personne n'a aimé le repas, **même** pas moi!	Nobody liked the meal, not even me!
J'ai beaucoup de travail, mais j'ai quand **même** le temps de m'amuser.	I have a lot of work, but I have time to have fun even so.

The adjective **même** changes meaning according to whether it is placed before or after the noun it modifies. See the *Appendice de grammaire.*

6. Victime. The word **une victime** is always feminine in gender, even if it refers to a man, while the word **un témoin** is always masculine in gender even if it refers to a woman.

7. Les familles de verbes: les verbes composés. A verb family consists of verbs that have a common base form and are conjugated similarly but have different meanings.

- Les verbes comme **mettre** *(to put)*

permettre (de)	*to permit, to allow*
promettre (de)	*to promise*

—Je veux sortir ce soir!	*"I want to go out tonight!"*
—Je ne vais pas te **permettre de** le faire.	*"I'm not going to let you do it."*
—Mais tu m'as **promis!**	*"But you promised me!"*

- Les verbes comme **prendre** *(to take)*

apprendre (à)	*to learn*
comprendre	*to understand*
surprendre	*to surprise*

Jacques **apprenait** à skier quand il est tombé.	*Jacques was learning to ski when he fell.*
Je n'**ai** rien **compris.**	*I didn't understand anything.*

- Les verbes comme **venir** *(to come)*

revenir	*to come back*
devenir	*to become*

Quand est-ce que vous **revenez?**	*When are you coming back?*
Elle **est devenue** toute rouge, puis elle est sortie.	*She got all red and then she left.*

D'accord?

A. Chassez l'intrus Quel mot ne va pas avec les autres à cause du sens?

1. dramatique / violent / grave / comique
2. un documentaire / un acteur / le journal télévisé / les informations
3. un chanteur / un reporter / un jeu / une vedette de la télévision
4. un magnétoscope / un programme / une émission / une chaîne
5. une émission amusante / une pièce comique / un drame / une comédie

B. La télévision chez vous Vrai ou faux?

1. On annonce la météo pendant le journal télévisé.
2. Il n'y a pas de publicité à la télé.
3. Il y a beaucoup de séries.
4. Il y a beaucoup de sport le week-end.
5. Le journal télévisé dure toujours entre trente et quarante minutes.
6. Il y a beaucoup d'émissions de variétés avant Noël.

Act. B: CONTINUATION: Il y a un journal télévisé à vingt heures. Il y a des dessins animés le samedi matin.

C. Les émissions de télévision Quelle sorte d'émission est-ce?

Modèle Premiers baisers
C'est une série française.

Act. C: CONTINUATION: Le Tour de France; Itinéraires: Brésil; Astro, le petit robot; Champs-Élysées: Spécial chanson française; Télé foot 1; Théâtre, Cycle Shakespeare: «La Comédie des erreurs»; Les jeux de 20 heures.
    Ask students to decide on Candide and Alceste's favorite television programs.

Les émissions de télévision du 6 août

1. Docteur Quinn, femme médecin
2. Éléphants d'Afrique
3. La roue de la fortune
4. Flash infos
5. Les Simpson
6. Faut pas rêver
7. Voyage en Tunisie
8. Vivre à Hiroshima aujourd'hui
9. Poulet fermier
10. Sacrée soirée

Les autres émissions de la semaine

1. Barenboim joue Beethoven
2. Football américain: Super Bowl
3. Salut, les 60! Avec Johnny Halliday, Claude François, Elvis Presley, Simon et Garfunkel, Aretha Franklin, les Beatles et Sylvie Vartan
4. Le Mariage de Figaro
5. Le Juste Prix
6. Astérix et Cléopâtre
7. Melrose Place

D. La télévision et les âges

1. Quelle sorte d'émissions est-ce que vous regardiez à cinq ans? à douze ans? à seize ans?
2. Et maintenant? Quelle sorte d'émissions est-ce que les enfants regardent? et les étudiants? et les professeurs?
3. Quelle sorte d'émissions est-ce que les enfants ne regardent pas? et les personnes âgées? et vous?

E. J'ai peur! J'ai peur! Dites de quoi vous avez le plus peur.

1. Vous marchez seul dans la rue tard le soir et il n'y a personne.
2. Vous voyez un gros chien méchant quand vous faites du jogging.
3. Vous regardez le film **Psycho** tard le soir.
4. Vous entendez le téléphone à trois heures du matin.
5. C'est la nuit et vous entendez un bruit bizarre. Vous cherchez mais vous ne trouvez rien.
6. Vous faites du camping et un gros animal entre sous la tente pendant que vous dormez.
7. Quelqu'un arrête sa voiture à côté de vous et vous propose de vous emmener là où vous voulez aller.

De quoi d'autre est-ce que vous avez peur? En groupes, faites une liste et comparez avec les autres étudiants de la classe.

F. Associations Quels verbes est-ce que vous associez avec les idées suivantes?

1. le français
2. l'anglais
3. être sage
4. les vacances
5. un cadeau
6. la vie

G. Méli-mélo *(mish-mash)* Répondez aux questions.

1. Qu'est-ce que vos parents ne vous permettaient pas de faire quand vous aviez dix ans?
2. Quand est-ce que vous devenez tout rouge?
3. Si vous ne comprenez pas quelque chose, qu'est-ce que vous faites?
4. Qu'est-ce que vous voulez apprendre à faire?
5. Qu'est-ce que vous avez promis de faire et que vous n'avez pas fait?
6. Qu'est-ce qui vous a surpris(e) quand vous êtes arrivé(e) à l'université?

Mise en pratique

A. Le film typique En groupes, décidez du film qui représente pour vous les catégories suivantes:

- la comédie
- la comédie romantique
- le film d'amour
- le film policier
- le film de science-fiction
- le film d'horreur
- le film d'aventures

Comparez avec les autres étudiants.

B. Quelle sorte de film est-ce?

Lisez les descriptions des films et répondez aux questions.

1 LA VIE EST BELLE.
Amér., noir et blanc (1946), de Frank Capra: La veille de Noël, un ange sauve un désespéré du suicide et lui montre l'importance de la vie. Avec James Stewart, Donna Reed, Lionel Barrymore.

2 CYRANO DE BERGERAC.
Franç., coul. (1989), de Jean-Paul Rappeneau: Au XVIIe siècle, Cyrano de Bergerac, qui a un très grand nez, est amoureux de sa cousine Roxane mais n'ose pas le lui dire. Avec Gérard Depardieu et Anne Brochet.

3 TINTIN ET LE TEMPLE DU SOLEIL.
Franco-belge, coul. (1969), dessin animé de Raymond Leblanc, d'après la B.D. d'Hergé. Tintin, Milou et le Capitaine Haddock partent en Amérique du Sud pour retrouver le Professeur Tournesol.

4 TROIS COULEURS: BLEU
Franç., coul. (1992), de Krzysztof Kieslowski: Une jeune femme, qui a perdu son mari (un compositeur célèbre) et son enfant dans un accident de voiture, décide de tout quitter pour vivre autrement. Avec Juliette Binoche et Benoit Régent.

5 LE SILENCE DES AGNEAUX.
Amér., coul. (1990), de Jonathan Demme: À la recherche d'un tueur en série, une jeune femme qui travaille pour le FBI se fait aider par un autre tueur, un psychiatre très intelligent mais cannibale. Avec Jodie Foster et Anthony Hopkins.

6 QUATRE MARIAGES ET UN ENTERREMENT.
Brit., coul. (1994), de Mike Newel: Charles, célibataire endurci, rencontre une belle Américaine. Va-t-il pouvoir résister? Avec Hugh Grant et Andie MacDowell.

7 LES MISÉRABLES.
Franç., coul. (1994), de Claude Lelouch: Un fils de prisonnier aide une famille juive pendant la guerre. Avec Jean-Paul Belmondo, Michel Boujenah, Alessandra Martinez, Salomé, Annie Girardot.

8 NIKITA.
Franç., coul. (1989), de Luc Besson: Une jeune femme, condamnée à la prison à vie pour le meurtre d'un policier, devient tueuse pour les services secrets français. Avec Anne Parillaud et Jean-Hughes Anglade.

Quelle sorte de films sont sur la liste? Quels sont les films américains? français? autres? Quels sont les vieux films? Quel film n'est pas en couleurs? Pourquoi? Quels films ne sont pas pour les enfants, d'après vous? Quels films sont pour les enfants? Quels sont les films violents? dramatiques? comiques? romantiques? Quels films avez-vous vus? Quels films avez-vous aimés? détestés? Pourquoi? Quel(s) film(s) voulez-vous voir? Quel film ne voulez-vous pas voir? Pourquoi?

Act. B: FOLLOW-UP: Ask students what kinds of movies they like and hate.

C. La télévision française

Lisez les informations suivantes sur la télévision française. Est-ce que c'est comme la télévision chez vous?

1. Il y a des chaînes qui n'ont pas d'émissions la nuit.
2. Il y a des informations à une heure de l'après-midi.
3. Il y a toujours des informations à huit heures du soir.
4. Les dernières informations sont entre dix heures et demie et une heure du matin.
5. On donne la météo après les informations.
6. Il y a des séries américaines à la télévision.
7. Il y a des séries françaises à la télévision.
8. Les émissions ne commencent pas exactement à l'heure ou à la demie heure.

D. Nouvelles d'un soir à la télévision

Vous êtes le directeur des informations à la télévision et c'est vous qui êtes responsable du journal télévisé de vingt heures. Voilà une liste des nouvelles de la journée. Lisez-la et décidez quelles sont les cinq ou six nouvelles les plus importantes à présenter ce soir. Faites attention: votre journal télévisé doit être équilibré.

- Le président a parlé à la télévision.
- Un millionnaire a acheté un tableau de Van Gogh.
- Le nouveau film de Spielberg est sorti à Los Angeles.
- Le chanteur canadien Robert Charlebois donne un concert à Paris.
- Le président va aller à Montréal au mois d'août.
- Un accident de voiture a fait douze morts.
- Scandale et drogue dans le monde du football français.
- Des médecins suédois vont aller à Harvard travailler sur un projet biogénétique.
- Le prix de la viande diminue.
- La police a trouvé 100 kilos de cocaïne à Miami.
- Trois gangsters sont entrés dans une banque la nuit et ont pris dix millions de francs.
- Trois astronautes sont partis pour Mars.
- Coupe du monde de football ce soir: Cameroun-Belgique.
- Monica Seles a gagné à Roland-Garros.
- Le franc français a diminué sur le marché international.

TEXT TAPE:
Conversation en français

E. Conversation en français

Vous êtes en France cet été pour apprendre le français et vous habitez avec une famille française. Nous sommes le six août et il est vingt heures trente. Regardez le programme de télévision à la page 430 et discutez de ce que vous voulez regarder avec les autres membres de la famille.

Structure

▶▶ Le pronom *en*

En is a personal pronoun that replaces nouns referring to persons and things in the following cases.

Quantité

The pronoun **en** may express the idea of quantity in the following cases (note that it is not always possible to translate **en** directly into English).

1. With a number expression (including **un/une**):

Il a trois livres?	*Does he have three books?*
Oui, il **en** a trois.	*Yes, he has three (of them).*

Vous avez une voiture?	*Do you have a car?*
Oui, j'**en** ai une.	*Yes, I have one.*

   > You may want to point out to students that if there is one of something, the word **un** or **une** must be expressed in the affirmative: **j'en ai un**, but **je n'en ai pas**.

2. With an adverb of quantity:

Tu as **beaucoup de** travail?	*Do you have a lot of work?*
Non, je n'**en** ai pas **beaucoup.**	*No, I don't have a lot (of it).*

3. As a replacement for a partitive construction:

Il y a **du fromage?**	*Is there any cheese?*
Bien sûr, il y **en** a.	*Of course there is (some).*

Tu as **de l'argent?**	*Do you have (any) money?*
Oui, j'**en** ai.	*Yes, I do (have some).*

Il n'y a plus **de lait?**	*There isn't any more milk?*
Non, il n'y **en** a plus.	*No there isn't any more.*

   > En can refer to people only when replacing a partitive or indefinite article or a number (J'ai *des* frères. / J'*en* ai. J'ai *trois frères.* / J'*en* ai trois. In other cases, **de** + *person* is replaced by **de** + **pronoun tonique** (J'ai peur *de lui*. Il a besoin *de toi.*).

4. As a replacement for the plural indefinite article **des** + *a noun:*

Il y a **des pommes?**	*Are there any apples?*
Oui, oui, il y **en** a.	*Yes, there are (some).*

Il n'y a plus **d'oranges?**	*There aren't any more oranges?*
Non, il n'y **en** a plus.	*No, there aren't any more.*

De + nom

En may replace **de** + *noun* referring to an object or place.

Tu as peur **des chiens?**	*Are you afraid of dogs?*
Non, je n'**en** ai pas peur.	*No, I'm not afraid of them.*

Il a besoin **d'amour.**	*He needs (some) love.*
Oui, et moi aussi, j'**en** ai besoin.	*Yes, and I need it (some of it) too.*

Où placer le pronom **en?**

En follows the placement rules you already know for direct and indirect object pronouns. There is no past participle agreement with the pronoun **en.**

> Il **en** demande trois.
> Il **en** demandait trois.
> Il va **en** demander trois.
> Il **en** a demandé trois.
> Il n'**en** a pas demandé trois.

Note that **en** always follows **y** in the expression **il y a.**

Est-ce qu'il **y en** a?	*Are (Is) there any?*
Il **y en** a.	*There are (is) some.*
Il n'**y en** a pas.	*There aren't (isn't) any.*

As was the case with direct and indirect object pronouns, **en** precedes a negative imperative form and follows an affirmative one. Note that first-conjugation verbs add an **-s** to the second-person singular form of the imperative when the pronoun **en** follows. This serves to facilitate pronunciation.

Parle-lui!	*Talk to him!*
BUT	
Parle**s-en!**	*Talk about that!*

Vous avez compris?

A. Devinez Mais de quoi est-ce qu'on parle?

Modèle   J'en ai mangé une.
            J'ai mangé une pomme.

1. Il y en a dans mon frigo.
2. Je n'en ai pas.
3. J'en veux beaucoup.
4. J'en ai un.
5. Les étudiants n'en ont pas beaucoup.
6. Les étudiants en boivent trop.

B. Dans votre chambre Qu'est-ce que vous avez dans votre chambre?

Modèles   une télévision?
             Oui, j'en ai une. / Non, je n'en ai pas.

             des chaises?
             Oui, j'en ai. / Non, je n'en ai pas.

1.	un bureau?	4.	un grand lit?
2.	un ordinateur?	5.	un réveil?
3.	des rideaux?	6.	un chat?

Ask students to restate the rules for pronoun placement. If desired, in order to focus attention on differences between English and French word order, ask students to translate the examples.

Act. A: CONTINUATION: Le professeur en a une. Les étudiants en mangent beaucoup. J'en ai peur. Les professeurs en ont besoin.

Act. B: CONTINUATION: des affiches de Frank Sinatra / des bouteilles de vin / un téléphone / un magnétoscope / un éléphant rouge

C. Dans le frigo   Dans le frigo idéal, qu'est-ce qu'il y a?

Modèle   du jus de fruit?
   Oui, il y en a. / Non, il n'y en a pas.

1. du lait?
2. de la bière?
3. du Coca-Cola?
4. du thé glacé *(iced)?*
5. de l'eau?
6. des tomates?

Act. C: CONTINUATION: **des bananes / de la viande / du poisson / des épinards**

D. En veux-tu, en voilà...   Utilisez le pronom **en** pour refaire les phrases.

Modèle   Tu as acheté cinq chemises?
   Tu en as acheté cinq?

1. Je voudrais acheter une voiture.
2. Tu as assez d'argent?
3. Non, mais je vais gagner beaucoup d'argent.
4. Paul a peur des chats noirs.
5. Jeanne ne mange jamais de viande.
6. Nous avons bu trop de vin hier soir.

Act. D: CONTINUATION: **Nous avons mangé une pizza hier. Est-ce qu'il y a de la bière dans votre frigo? Non, il n'y a plus de bière.**

Continuons!

Chez Georges   Voilà où Georges (le monstre que vous avez rencontré à la ***Leçon 15***) habite. Remplacez les noms par des pronoms quand vous pensez que c'est nécessaire. Utilisez des pronoms sujets, des pronoms toniques, des pronoms d'object direct, des pronoms d'objet indirect ou le pronom **en**.

Georges habite une chambre chez les Dupont. Georges aime beaucoup les Dupont parce que les Dupont sont très gentils avec Georges, mais Georges déteste sa chambre. Sa chambre a une grande fenêtre mais il n'y a pas de rideaux et Georges a besoin de rideaux. Georges n'a pas de bureau et Georges voudrait un bureau pour écrire sa biographie. Georges voudrait aussi avoir beaucoup d'étagères. Il y a une étagère, mais l'étagère est trop petite. Georges a parlé aux Dupont de la chambre et Georges a demandé aux Dupont d'acheter à Georges un bureau, des étagères et des rideaux. Les Dupont ont promis à Georges d'acheter une étagère, mais Georges veut deux étagères. Les Dupont ont dit à Georges que les Dupont allaient acheter un bureau aussi. Mais si Georges veut des rideaux, c'est Georges qui doit acheter les rideaux. Alors, Georges ne sait pas si Georges va rester chez les Dupont ou si Georges va quitter les Dupont pour chercher une autre chambre où il y a des rideaux. Les rideaux sont très importants pour Georges parce que Georges ne veut pas qu'on regarde Georges pendant que Georges est en train de travailler à son livre. C'est un monstre très timide!

▶▶ Les verbes *vouloir, pouvoir, devoir, avoir* et *être* au passé composé

These verbs are often found in the **imparfait** rather than the **passé composé** since they tend to refer to states in the past (how things were).

In the **passé composé,** they express a change of state (an event, something that happened). Their exact English equivalent will depend on the context. Note the form of the past participles of these verbs in the examples that follow:

- **vouloir (voulu)**

  M. Smith **voulait** aller au match de football mais Mme Smith n'**a** pas **voulu.** Donc, ils sont restés à la maison.
  Mr. Smith wanted (felt like = state of mind) to go to the football game, but Mrs. Smith didn't want to (she said no, decided not to go = something that happened). So they stayed home.

- **pouvoir (pu)**

  Vincent a bu trop de café et il n'**a** pas **pu** dormir.
  Vincent drank too much coffee and he couldn't sleep (what happened as a result of drinking too much coffee).

  Quand j'**avais** dix-huit ans, je ne **pouvais** pas sortir en boîte parce que mes parents **étaient** vieux jeu.
  When I was 18 (how things were), I couldn't go out to clubs to dance (wasn't allowed to = how things were) because my parents were old-fashioned.

- **devoir (dû)**

  Paul **devait** arriver à cinq heures et il n'est toujours pas là. Il **a dû** manquer le train.
  Paul was supposed to be here at 5 o'clock (how things were) and he's not here yet. He must have missed the train (something that happened).

- **avoir (eu)**

  Michel n'**avait** pas peur des chiens mais quand il a vu Oscar, il **a eu** peur...
  Michel didn't used to be afraid of dogs (how things were), but when he saw Oscar, he got afraid... (became afraid, got frightened = something happened to make him afraid).

- **être (été)**

  Après ce long voyage, j'**étais** fatigué et j'**ai été** content quand le train est arrivé.
  After that long trip, I was tired (how things were), and I was happy (change in how things were = I became happy) when the train arrived.

Vous avez compris?

A. En anglais Traduisez le paragraphe en anglais idiomatique. Pour chaque verbe, décidez pourquoi on a choisi le passé composé ou l'imparfait.

Hier, j'ai invité ma famille au restaurant pour célébrer l'anniversaire de mariage de mes parents. Je voulais aller dans un restaurant italien parce que je voulais manger des pâtes. Mais mes parents n'ont pas voulu et ils ont choisi un restaurant grec *(Greek)*. Ils voulaient manger de la moussaka. Le restaurant était plein *(crowded)* et nous avons dû attendre. Heureusement, ce soir-là, je ne devais pas étudier.

Il y avait beaucoup de choses nouvelles sur le menu et on ne pouvait pas choisir. Alors, on a décidé de commander des plats différents et de partager. J'ai beaucoup mangé parce que j'avais très faim, mais après le dîner— catastrophe! Je n'ai pas pu payer parce que je n'avais pas mon sac! Alors, c'est Papa qui a dû payer. Et où était mon sac? Quand nous sommes rentrés, je l'ai vu sur la table; alors j'ai été contente et j'ai pu aller dormir.

B. Histoire de fantôme Complétez cette histoire de fantôme par des verbes au passé composé ou à l'imparfait.

Anne et Jacques ..... (habiter) dans un ranch en Amérique du Sud. Ils ..... (avoir) beaucoup d'animaux et ils ..... (être) heureux dans un pays *(country)* où il ..... (faire) toujours beau et chaud. Le soir, ils ..... (aller) dormir de bonne heure et ils ..... (dormir) toujours très bien parce que la maison ..... (être) très calme.

Une nuit, Anne ..... (aller) dans la cuisine pour prendre un verre d'eau et elle ..... (voir) un homme dans le salon. Alors, elle ..... (avoir) peur. Elle ..... (retourner) dans la chambre et elle ..... (dire) à son mari qu'il y ..... (avoir) un homme dans la maison. Jacques ..... (prendre) son revolver et il ..... (aller) dans le salon. Quand il ..... (arriver), l'homme le ..... (regarder), et puis il ..... (sortir) à travers *(through)* le mur. Ce ..... (être) un fantôme. Cette nuit-là, Anne et Jacques ..... (ne pas pouvoir) bien dormir!

Continuons!

You may begin using the CD-ROM/Internet activity **"Un Meurtre à Cinet"** here, and continue using it through *Leçon 20.*

A. Un crime à Cinet? Est-ce qu'il y a eu un crime à Cinet? Mettez les verbes entre parenthèses au passé composé ou à l'imparfait pour reconstituer l'histoire.

À cinq heures, hier soir, il y ..... (avoir) beaucoup de monde *(a lot of people)* au Café de la Poste. M. Meunier ..... (parler) avec M. Bastin. Les Ségal ..... (boire) du thé. Tout ..... (être) calme. Puis, tout à coup, la porte s'est ouverte *(opened)* et M. Piette est apparu, l'air très sérieux. Il ..... (regarder) les gens pendant une ou deux minutes. Puis il ..... (aller) parler à M. Caron, le propriétaire.

—Où est Mlle Collin? Elle est serveuse ici, non?

—Oui, oui, mais elle ..... (finir) il y a deux heures et elle ..... (partir) juste après. Pourquoi? Il y a un problème?

—Peut-être. Ses parents ..... (téléphoner). Elle ..... (ne jamais arriver) chez elle!

Tout à coup, M. Caron ..... (avoir) très peur. Et puis, il ..... (se souvenir) que Mlle Collin ..... (avoir l'air) bizarre aujourd'hui. Elle ..... (regarder) sa montre tout le temps et elle ..... (ne rien écouter).

M. Piette ..... (demander) à tous les clients du café s'ils ..... (connaître) Mlle Collin et s'ils avaient vu *(had seen)* quelque chose ou quelqu'un quand Mlle Collin ..... (partir). Alors, M. Ségal ..... (vouloir) parler seul avec M. Piette. Il lui ..... (dire) qu'il ..... (ne pas bien connaître) Mlle Collin, mais qu'il ..... (connaître) bien le fils du banquier, Jacques Lacroix, qui ..... (aller) se marier dans deux semaines avec une pharmacienne. Eh bien, à trois heures de l'après-midi, Monsieur et Madame Ségal ..... (se promener) dans la rue quand tout à coup, ils ..... (voir) Jacques Lacroix dans sa voiture au coin de la rue du Café de la Poste. Mlle Collin ..... (être) avec lui et ils ..... (s'embrasser)!

Alors, M. Piette ..... (téléphoner) aux parents de Jacques Lacroix et il ..... (apprendre) que personne dans la famille Lacroix ne ..... (savoir) où Jacques ..... (être). Alors, qu'est-ce qui ..... (se passer), à votre avis?

B. Histoire-squelette Voilà le squelette *(skeleton)* d'une histoire. Donnez des détails pour l'étoffer *(to flesh it out)*. Souvenez-vous d'utiliser l'imparfait pour dire comment étaient les choses *(description)* et le passé composé pour dire ce qui s'est passé *(narration)*.

Modèle *Il était onze heures du soir. Je regardais la télé quand, tout à coup, j'ai entendu du bruit...* (Continuez à raconter l'histoire.)

J'ai entendu du bruit.
J'ai eu peur.
J'ai mis mon imperméable.
J'ai pris une lampe.
Je suis sorti de la maison.

Je suis allé voir.
J'ai vu quelque chose.
Je suis rentré.
Je suis allé dormir.

▶▶ Les verbes *croire, suivre* et *vivre*

The verbs **croire** *(to believe)*, **suivre** *(to follow)*, and **vivre** *(to live)* are irregular.

Le verbe **croire**

PRÉSENT	je crois	nous croyons
	tu crois	vous croyez
	il / elle } croit	ils / elles } croient

IMPARFAIT	je croyais, etc. ...
PASSÉ COMPOSÉ	j'ai cru, etc. ...
IMPÉRATIF	crois! croyons! croyez!

Point out to students that **croire à** is generally used to mean *to believe in* in the sense of *to have faith or confidence in*. **Croire en** is used with God.

Crois-moi! C'est la vérité!　　*Believe me! It's the truth!*
Je ne te **crois** pas!　　*I don't believe you!*
Quand nous avions 12 ans, nous　　*When we were 12, we didn't*
　ne **croyions** plus aux histoires　　　*believe our parents' stories anymore.*
　de nos parents.
On l'**a cru** mort!　　*We thought he was dead!*

DRILL: **Alceste ne croit pas au père Noël. (tu / je / Candide / les professeurs / vous / nous)**

Expressions avec **croire**

- **croire + que** = *to believe that*

    Vous **croyez qu**'il se trompe?　　*Do you think that he's wrong?*

- **croire + à** = *to believe in*

    Tu **crois au** père Noël?　　*Do you believe in Santa Claus?*

- **croire en Dieu** = *to believe in God*

- **croire que oui / non** = *to believe so/not to believe so*

Le verbe **suivre**

PRÉSENT	je suis	nous suivons
	tu suis	vous suivez
	il / elle } suit	ils / elles } suivent

IMPARFAIT	je suivais, etc. ...
PASSÉ COMPOSÉ	j'ai suivi, etc. ...
IMPÉRATIF	suis! suivons! suivez!

DRILL: Tu nous as suivis! (Candide / vous / Candide et Alceste)

Tu **suis** cette rue jusqu'à la poste, et puis...	You take (follow) this road as far as the post office and then . . .
Quand il était petit, mon frère me **suivait** partout!	When he was little, my brother used to follow me everywhere!
Tu nous **as suivis** et nous voulions être seuls!	You followed us and we wanted to be alone!
Suis-moi!	Follow me!
Suivez le guide!	This way, please (in a museum, for example).

Expressions avec **suivre**

• **suivre** + **cours** = *to take a class/course*

Elle **suit trois cours** ce trimestre.	*She's taking three courses this quarter.*

Le verbe **vivre**

PRÉSENT	je vis	nous vivons
	tu vis	vous vivez
	il } elle } vit	ils } elles } vivent
IMPARFAIT	je vivais, etc. ...	
PASSÉ COMPOSÉ	j'ai vécu, etc	
IMPÉRATIF	vis! vivons! vivez!	

Point out to students that **vivre** can be used to mean *to be alive* as well as *to live*. **Habiter** refers only to one's residence. **Je vis à Bruxelles / J'habite à Bruxelles** but **Je vis bien** (habiter is not possible) / **Jeanne Calment a 120 ans et elle vit encore?**

DRILL: Candide vit bien. (vous / les professeurs / je / tu / vous)

If desired, give students the expression "Vive le.... "

Nous **vivons** bien maintenant que j'ai trouvé du travail.	We live well (we're doing fine) now that I've found a job.
Il **vivait** à Londres quand il l'a su.	He was living in London when he found out.
Vous **avez vécu** à Paris pendant cinq ans?	You lived in Paris for five years?
Vivons ensemble. C'est moins cher.	Let's move in (live) together. It's less expensive.

Expression avec **vivre**

• **être facile / difficile à vivre** = *to be easy / difficult to get along with*

Ma sœur a 12 ans et elle n'**est** pas **facile à vivre.**	*My sister is 12 and she is not easy to get along with.*

Vous avez compris?

A. Qu'est-ce que vous croyez? Utilisez **je crois que oui** ou **je crois que non** pour exprimer vos opinions.

Act. A: Have students guess meanings of cognates if necessary.

1. Il est plus important d'avoir un métier que vous aimez que d'avoir un métier où vous gagnez beaucoup d'argent.
2. C'est très important d'avoir un diplôme d'université.
3. Les hommes et les femmes doivent aller à l'armée pendant un an.
4. La pollution est un grand problème.
5. Tout le monde doit parler anglais.

B. La réponse est non! Répondez à la forme négative.

Modèle   Elle te croit?
Non, elle ne me croit pas.

1. Vous croyez qu'il se trompe?
2. Il vous suit?
3. Tu vis là?
4. Vous suivez un cours de mathématiques?
5. Ils vivent ensemble?

C. Et maintenant... Tout change avec l'âge.

Modèle   Vous croyez les professeurs?
Non, je les croyais avant, mais je ne les crois plus!

1. Tes parents te croient?
2. Patrick vit avec Georges?
3. On suit des cours de latin au lycée?
4. Les étudiants vivent bien à l'université?
5. Tu vis avec tes parents?

Continuons!

Méli-mélo Répondez aux questions.

1. Est-ce que vous croyez à la chance *(luck)*?
2. Est-ce que vous croyiez au père Noël quand vous aviez six ans?
3. Est-ce que vous croyez que la vie est juste *(fair)*? Donnez un exemple.
4. Combien de cours est-ce que vous suivez à l'université?
5. S'il y a quelqu'un qui vous suit le soir, qu'est-ce que vous faites?
6. Est-ce que vous vivez bien à l'université?
7. Est-ce que vous êtes facile ou difficile à vivre? Pourquoi?

Découvertes culturelles: Les médias

▶ La télévision

Act. A: Make sure students focus on **ce soir**, or give them different days of the week and/or times of the day (**matinée, après-midi**). The goal is to have students use their knowledge of television programming within their own culture to draw up an evening's schedule. May be done in groups and each group's reconstruction compared.

A. Préparation: Quel est le programme?

Votre soirée est libre. Vous avez décidé de regarder la télévision et vous regardez le programme. Quel type d'émissions allez-vous probablement trouver ce soir? À quelle heure? Combien de temps vont-elles durer?

Modèle   *Une série (nom de la série), à 19 heures 30, pendant une demi-heure.*

B. Un programme de télévision.

1. **L'origine.** En quelles langues est ce programme? Où sommes-nous? en France?
   a. Trouvez quatre émissions qui sont certainement en français.
   b. Quelles émissions viennent des États-Unis?
   c. Combien d'émissions au total sont en français? combien en anglais? Quelle est la langue la plus représentée?

MERCREDI 4 JANVIER

MERCREDI 17:55 / 19:30

SOIR

18:00 [SRC] **2 7 11 CE SOIR** / Information (1h).
3h   [TQS] **2 4 16 30 35** LA GUERRE DES CLANS / Jeu
3 NEWS (1h).
[TVA] **4** LE TVA, EDITION QUEBEC
5 6 NEWSWATCH (1h).
5 22 NEWS
5 6 7 8 9 10 11 LE TVA, EDITION 18 HEURES
8 NEWS
8 NEWSLINE (1h).
9 12 13 CE SOIR / Information
12 PULSE / Information (1h).
15 17 24 45 VIVE L'AMERIQUE DE CHARLIE BROWN / Dessins animés
33 THE MacNEIL/LEHRER NEWSHOUR (1h).
57 ITN WORLD NEWS
[TV5] DES CHIFFRES ET DES LETTRES / Jeu

18:30 [TQS] **2 4 16 30 35** SONIA BENEZRA
Talk-show
Inv.: Les BB, Stéphane Rousseau et Dominique Michel. (1h). REPRISE.
[TVA] **4 5 6 7 8 9 10 11** PIMENT FORT / Jeu
Inv.: Dominique Lévesque, Chantal Francke et Dany Turcotte. REPRISE.
5 8 22 NEWS
9 13 AUJOURD'HUI / Information
12 LA COUR EN DIRECT
15 17 24 45 CINE-CADEAU

DESSINS ANIMÉS   G

(4) "ASTERIX CHEZ LES BRETONS", Fr. 1986. Dessins animés de P. Van Lams-

weerde. — Deux Gaulois vont prêter main-forte à un village d'Angleterre qui résiste toujours aux troupes d'invasion romaines. — Adaptation plus ou moins réussie d'une bande dessinée. Dessins fidèles à la conception originale. Passages amusants. (1h 30).

57 THE NIGHTLY BUSINESS REPORT
[TV5] LA CUISINE DES MOUSQUETAIRES
Cuisine
Pot au feu du braconnier.

18:45 [TV5] VISIONS D'AMERIQUE / Magazine
19:00 **2 7 9 11 12 13**
7h   RBO HEBDO / Comédie
Nouvelle case horaire. (2e de 3). Les meilleurs moments de la première moitié de la saison de cette série humoristique mettant en vedette André Ducharme, Bruno Landry, Guy A. Lepage et Yves Pelletier.

3 NEWS
[TVA] **4 5 6 7 8 9 10 11** LA POULE AUX OEUFS D'OR / Jeu
Jeu télévisé de Loto-Québec qui regroupe huit concurrents qui courent la chance de gagner jusqu'à 250 000 $.

5 6 ADRIENNE CLARKSON PRESENTS
Documentaire sur le retour des patineurs artistiques britanniques Jayne Torvill et Christopher Dean et sur leur entraînement pour les Jeux olympiques d'hiver de Lillehammer en 1994. (1h).
5 JEOPARDY! / Jeu
8 8 WHEEL OF FORTUNE / Jeu
12 ENTERTAINMENT TONIGHT
Magazine
22 STAR TREK: THE NEXT GENERATION / Science-fiction
d'une mission sur la planète Minos pour retrouver un vaisseau spatial. (1h). REPRISE.
33 THE NIGHTLY BUSINESS REPORT

57 THE MacNEIL/LEHRER NEWSHOUR (1h).
[TV5] JOURNAL TELEVISE DE F2
19:30 [SRC] **2 7 9 11 12 13** SANTA MARIA
Nouvelle case hraire. Richard et Maria (Patrice L'Ecuyer, Rita Lafontaine) ont droit à de nombreuses surprises lorsqu'ils sont de garde au centre la veille du jour de l'an. Elyse: Christine Séguin.

[TQS] **2 4 16 30 35** L'EPICERIE EN FOLIE-METRO / Jeu
3 ENTERTAINMENT TONIGHT
Magazine
[TVA] **4 5 6 7 8 9 10 11** CINEMA DES FETES

DRAME DE MOEURS   G

(3) "WALL STREET", E.-U. 1987. Drame de moeurs de O. Stone avec Charlie Sheen, Michael Douglas et Daryl Hannah. — Un important spéculateur s'intéresse à un courtier ambitieux qu'il mêle à quelques-unes de ses affaires aventureuses. — Vision privilégiée du milieu des affaires. Récit nerveux et complexe. Réalisation contrôlée et souvent inventive. Interprétation solide de M. Douglas. (2h 30).

5 WHEEL OF FORTUNE / Jeu
8 8 JEOPARDY! / Jeu
12 ELLEN / Comédie
Ellen (Ellen DeGeneres) fait la rencontre d'un professeur de collège lors d'une visite dans un musée. Roger: Gregory Martin. Joe: David Anthony Higgins.
33 DESIGN CLASSICS
La popularité qu'a connue la Volkswagen conçue par Ferdinand Porsche en 1933 à la demande d'Hitler.

2. **Émissions et horaires.** Quels sont les types d'émissions les plus fréquentes entre 18 et 19 heures? 19 et 20 heures? 20 et 21 heures? 21 et 22 heures?

3. **Les informations.** À quelle heure sont-elles? Dans quelle langue? Sur quelles chaînes?

4. **Les films.** Quels sont les films de la soirée? Dans quelle langue? Sur quelles chaînes? Quelle sorte de films est-ce?

5. **Les documentaires.** Combien y a-t-il de documentaires? Classez-les par ordre d'intérêt pour vous.

6. **Les feuilletons et les séries.** Quelles émissions sont probablement des feuilletons ou des séries? Comment le savez-vous? Dans quelle langue sont-elles? D'où viennent beaucoup de séries?

Act. B, 6: Have students give a name to each category: **documentaire historique, politique,** etc.

7. **Ce soir.** Est-ce qu'il y a des jeux? des émissions de musique? des émissions de cuisine? des émissions sur les vedettes de la télévision et du cinéma?

C. Évaluations.

1. **Comment sont-elles?** Trouvez les mots qui donnent une évaluation pour: *Astérix chez les Bretons, Wall Street* et *La Cavalière.* Quelle émission a une évaluation positive? Quelle émission a une évaluation négative?

2. **Quel public?** Pour chaque type d'émission, dites quel public va probablement choisir de la regarder.

Act. C, 2: Point out the style of these evaluations. Guide students to reproduce them in a similar vein.

Act. C, 3: Ask for specific details about the audience: age, professions, why they are watching, who is not watching and why not. This should be an opportunity to recycle much language, verbs in particular, from previous chapters.

Modèle *Les dessins animés à 18 heures 30: les enfants de 3 à 6 ans, avant d'aller se coucher, mais pas les parents.*

MERCREDI

TV5 ENVOYE SPECIAL / Information
Témoignages d'hommes et de femmes après leur apparition dans l'un des reportages diffusés depuis cinq ans. (1h 30).

SE ZOOM / Magazine
SRC 2 7 9 11 12 13 SOUS UN CIEL VARIABLE
Camille et Allan (Patricia Nolin, Robert Toupin) prennent leurs distances à la suite d'une maladresse. Kathleen (Ginette Morin) demande des explications à Camille. Lisette se fait du souci pour Léon qui est déprimé. (1h).

TQS 2 4 16 30 35 CINEMA

COMÉDIE   G

PRIMEUR. (4) "ASSOCIES, INC" (Company Business), E.-U. 1991. Comédie de N. Meyer avec Gene Hackman, Mikhaïl Baryshnikov et Kurtwood Smith. — Un agent de la CIA sympathise avec un espion soviétique qu'il doit escorter jusqu'à Berlin pour l'échanger contre un collègue retenu par le KGB. — Intrigue d'espionnage compliquée à plaisir. Traitement désinvolte. Suspense assez efficace. Scène finale bien orchestrée. Jeu plein d'aisance de G. Hackman. (2h).

3 WOMEN OF THE HOUSE PREMIERE. (1h).

5 6 THE NANNY / Comédie
Voir 3B, lundi 20h.

5 THE COSBY MYSTERIES / Drame (1h).

8 22 SISTER, SISTER / Comédie

8 HOME IMPROVEMENT / Comédie
Tim (Tim Allen) commet une grosse erreur lorsqu'il rate le souper romantique que Jill a organisé. Brad et Jennifer (Zachery Ty Bryan, Jessica Wesson) échangent un premier baiser. REPRISE.

12 BEVERLY HILLS, 90210
Téléroman (1h).

15 17 24 45 AVOIR 16 ANS
L'histoire d'un adolescent qui a été confié aux moines bouddhistes à l'âge de huit ans. (1h). REPRISE.

33 GESTAPO
Des documents d'archives rendus publics depuis la chute du mur de Berlin illustrent en partie ce documentaire sur la création, le développement et les activités de la Gestapo dans les années 30 et 40. (1h).

57 JIHAD IN AMERICA
Documentaire sur les activités des mouvements islamistes radicaux aux Etats-Unis. Discussion sur la question des libertés civiques dans une société face au terrorisme. (1h).

SE HEROS
(Hero). Comédie dramatique. (2h).

20:30 5 6 EMPTY NEST / Comédie
Afin d'aider Harry (Richard Mulligan) à surmonter l'annonce des fiançailles de son ex-amie, Carol lui organise un rendez-vous avec une chanteuse de boîte de nuit (Carol Kane). Leonard: Kevin Cooney. REPRISE.

8 22 ALL AMERICAN GIRL
Comédie

8 ELLEN / Comédie
Voir 12, 19h 30.

21:00 SRC 2 7 9 11 12 13 ENJEUX
9h Documentaire sur l'espionnage industriel et sur la protection que le système judiciaire, la police, les avocats, les lois et les tribunaux offrent contre ce type de vol. (1h).

3 DOUBLE RUSH
PREMIERE.

5 6 TOUCHED BY AN ANGEL
Drame (1h).

5 DATELINE NBC / Information (1h).

8 12 22 ROSEANNE / Comédie

8 MODELS INC. / Drame (1h).

15 17 24 45 POIROT / Policier
Poirot (David Suchet) rencontre lady Millicent (Frances Barber) qui affirme être victime de chantage de la part d'un dénommé Lavington (Terence Harvey). (1h). REPRISE.

33 MYSTERY!
"A DARK ADAPTED EYE" (1re de 2). Pendant la Deuxième Guerre mondiale, Faith (Helena Bonham-Carter) quitte Londres pour aller vivre avec ses tantes Vera et Eden (Celia Imrie, Sophie Ward) dans un petit village du Suffolk. (1h 30).

57 GREAT PERFORMANCES
Portrait du trompettiste de jazz Miles Davis décédé en 1991. Présentation d'extraits de documentaires, de spectacles et d'interviews avec des musiciens de jazz. (2h). REPRISE.

TV5 CINEMA

MÉLODRAME   NC

(6) "LA CAVALIERE" (2e de 2), Fr. 1992. Mélodrame de P. Monnier avec Ilaria Borrelli, Jean-Pierre Bouvier et Daniela Poggi. — Deux femmes, qui ont aimé successivement le même homme, se disputent après sa mort la propriété où elles ont toutes deux vécu leur amour. — Téléfilm au goût prononcé pour la sensiblerie facile. Illustration façon carte postale. Dialogues indigents. Interprétation peu crédible. (1h 30).

21:30 3 LOVE & WAR / Comédie
Nouvelle case horaire.

8 22 ELLEN / Comédie
Voir 12, 19h 30.

12 GRACE UNDER FIRE / Comédie
Voir 22B, mardi 21h 30.

22:00 SRC 2 7 9 11 12 13
10h **LE TELEJOURNAL**

MERCREDI 19:30/22:00

➤➤ Les jeunes choisissent

Act. A: To help students organize their thoughts, make a grid with two columns: **avantages et inconvénients;** and three rows: **radio, presse écrite,** and **télévision.** Put the grid on the board or a transparency and fill it in as students discuss this issue, or have students work in groups to complete it.

A. Préparation: Vos préférences. Pour avoir des informations sur l'actualité préférez-vous la radio, la presse écrite (les journaux) ou la télévision? Pourquoi?

SOCIÉTÉ • Médias

▶ LES JEUNES PRÉFÈRENT LA RADIO

Les Français se méfient de plus en plus des informations diffusées par la télévision. Le taux de confiance dans la presse écrite reste stable, et la radio gagne de l'audience, spécialement auprès des 18–24 ans.

Pour la septième année consécutive, un sondage, réalisé à la demande de trois journaux nationaux, mesure le degré de confiance des Français dans leurs médias. La question principale était: les informations diffusées par la télévision, la radio et la presse écrite vous paraissent-elles plutôt proches ou plutôt éloignées des faits réels? ■

Évolution des indices de crédibilité chez les 18...

Radio 43 % 42 %

Presse écrite 30 % 20 %

Télévision 45 % 7 %

1989 1993

Les Clés de l'Actualité

B. Les jeunes préfèrent la radio.

1. **L'illustration annonce le sujet.** Regardez l'illustration et faites une phrase qui résume les résultats.
2. **Le sous-titre.** Soulignez dans le sous-titre les mots et expressions qui font référence à l'illustration. Qu'est-ce que vous apprenez sur la télévision? la presse écrite? la radio?
3. **L'article.** Trouvez dans l'article les mots et expressions qui annoncent le sujet de cet article.

Act. B, 3: Encourage students to identify words even if they do not understand exactly what they mean.

C. Mots nouveaux.

1. **"Se méfient."** D'après le contexte et l'illustration, le verbe **se méfient,** indique-t-il une idée positive ou négative? **Se méfient** signifie **ne croient pas, préfèrent** ou **détestent?** Trouvez un mot dans le texte qui exprime le contraire de **se méfient.**
2. **"Le taux."** C'est une référence aux calculs, à un objet ou à des personnes?
3. **"Auprès de."** Donnez un synonyme pour **auprès de.**
4. **"Éloignées."** Si on peut trouver le mot **près** dans le mot **proche,** quel mot retrouvez-vous dans le mot **éloignées?**

D. Pratique. Complétez à l'aide de ces mots: **se méfier / taux / auprès / éloignés.**

> Pour être bien informés, les Français préfèrent la radio à la télévision parce qu'ils n'ont pas confiance en la télévision. La télévision est si visuelle qu'on est obligé de _____ _____ des informations qu'elle donne. Très souvent, les faits sont très _____ de la présentation à la télévision. Les sondages révèlent des _____ d'audience de moins en moins nombreux pour les informations à la télévision. Ces sondages sont faits _____ des gens qui regardent la télévision et écoutent la radio.

E. Un sondage. En groupes de deux ou trois, trouvez cinq questions qu'on a posées pour ce sondage.

-
-
-
-

Act. E: If time permits, have students use their questions to interview one another and to then compare their answers with the results of the French opinion poll.

Act. F, 1: Refer students to activity A, above.

Act. F, 2: Can be done in groups. You may want to have students identify what is specific to each medium first. Students will hypothesize using what they know of television, and what they know of French television. You may find it useful to review verbs such as **dire** and **présenter.**

F. Faut-il se méfier de la télévision?

1. Quelles sont les caractéristiques de la télévision? de la presse écrite? de la radio?
2. À votre avis, pour quelles raisons les jeunes Français se méfient-ils beaucoup plus de la télévision maintenant qu'en 1989?

Modèle *Les journalistes de la télévision choisissent des images violentes, etc.*

www explore!
http//voila.heinle.com

*O*rthographe et prononciation

➤➤ Les lettres -s- et -ss-

The letter **-s-** may be pronounced as an **s** or as a **z,** or it may be silent.

1. At the beginning of a word, or next to a consonant, the letter **-s-** is pronounced as an **s.**

    sur
    sous
    disque

2. Between two vowels, the letter **-s-** is pronounced **z.**

    rose
    grise
    ils disent
    organisation

3. At the end of a word, the letter **-s** is silent.

    dos
    tu fais
    les chats

4. The letter combination **-ss-** is always pronounced **s.**

    passer
    un dossier
    grosse
    une adresse

Point out adjectives that follow the pattern **-ais/-aise (français, mauvais, anglais).** Also remind students that the **-s** of **tennis** is pronounced.

Point out other spellings of the sound **s:** **-ç- (garçon), -ce- (Alceste), -ci- (pharmacien), -ti- (patient, attention),** and **-x (dix, six).**

Activité

Prononcez Répétez après votre professeur.

1. Sa sœur a sommeil.
2. C'est un cours impossible.
3. Elle s'est brossé les cheveux.
4. Isabelle et Élisabeth lisent beaucoup.

Vocabulaire de base

TEXT TAPE:
Vocabulaire de base

NOMS

un acteur, une actrice *actor, actress*
une chaîne (de télévision) *(television) station, channel*
une chanson *song*
un chanteur, une chanteuse *singer*
une comédie *comedy (movie, play)*
un concert *concert*
le début *beginning*
un dessin animé *(animated) cartoon*
un documentaire (sur) *documentary (on)*
un drame *drama*
une émission *program*
un film d'amour *romantic movie*
un film d'aventures *adventure movie*
un film de science-fiction *science fiction movie*
un film d'horreur *horror movie*
un film policier *detective/police movie*
les informations (f. pl.) *news*
une interview *interview*
un jeu (télévisé) *game show*
le journal (télévisé) *(television) news*
une pièce (de théâtre) *play*
un reportage *(news) report, (news) story*
une série *series*
une station *(radio) station*
un téléfilm *made-for-television movie*
une vedette (de la télévision, de cinéma...) *(television, movie, etc.) celebrity*
un western *western (movie)*

ADJECTIFS

célèbre *famous*
comique *funny, amusing, comic*

dramatique *dramatic*
ennuyeux, ennuyeuse *boring*
étranger, étrangère *foreign*
grave *serious*
même *same; even*
violent(e) *violent*

VERBES

apprendre (à) *to learn (to)*
comprendre *to understand*
croire (à / que) *to believe (in / that)*
devenir (conjugué avec être) *to become*
durer *to last*
montrer *to show*
passer *to spend*
permettre (de) *to allow, to permit*
promettre (qqch. à qqn) *to promise (something to someone)*
revenir (conjugué avec être) *to come back*
suivre *to follow*
surprendre *to surprise*
vivre *to live, to be alive*

DIVERS

à la radio *on the radio*
à la télévision *on television*
avoir peur (de) *to be afraid (of)*
croire que oui *to believe / think so*
croire que non *not to believe / to think not*
être facile / difficile à vivre *to be easy / difficult to get along with*
pourtant *however*
suivre un cours *to take a class / course*

Vocabulaire supplémentaire

NOMS

une cassette vidéo *video cassette*
un danseur, une danseuse *dancer*
une émission de variétés *variety show*
un feuilleton *soap opera*
un film d'espionnage *spy movie*
le goût *taste*
un magazine (littéraire,
    d'information...) *TV magazine*
un magnétoscope *video cassette recorder*
les médias *media*
un musicien, une musicienne *musician*
un programme *television / radio
    schedule*
un reporter *reporter*
une télécommande *remote control*

ADJECTIFS

international(e), internationaux,
    internationales *international*
national(e), nationaux, nationales
    national
romantique *romantic*

VERBE

annoncer (conjugué comme
    commencer) *to announce*

DIVERS

ça me fait peur *that scares me*
croire au Père Noël *to believe in Santa
    Claus*
croire en Dieu *to believe in God*
en effet *indeed, in fact*
en même temps *at the same time*
faire peur (à) *to scare*
ne... personne (de sympathique...) *no
    one (nice, etc.)*
ne... rien (de comique...) *nothing
    (funny, etc.)*
quand même *all the same, even so*

LE FRANÇAIS TEL QU'ON LE PARLE

Ça m'est égal! *I don't mind/care! It's all
    the same to me!*
On change? *Shall we switch?*
Où est-ce qu'on va! *Where are we going?*
Ça fait peur! *It/that's scary!*
suivez le guide *this way, please (lit.
    follow the guide)*

POUR PARLER DES FILMS ET DES ROMANS POLICIERS

l'arme du crime (f.) *crime weapon,
    murder weapon*
un crime *crime*
le lieu du crime *crime scene*
un meurtre *murder*
les personnages *characters*
    le meurtrier, la meurtrière (le tueur,
        la tueuse) *murderer (killer)*
    la victime *victim*
    le suspect, la suspecte *suspect*
    le témoin *witness*
    l'inspecteur, l'inspectrice (de police)
        (police) inspector
un revolver *revolver, gun*
faire une enquête *to hold / run an
    investigation*
interroger *to question, interrogate*
tuer *to kill*
vérifier *to check, verify*

LE FRANÇAIS FAMILIER

avoir la trouille = avoir peur
avoir la frousse = avoir peur
un poulet = un policier
un thriller = adventure story
zapper = changer souvent de chaîne télé

ON ENTEND PARFOIS...

frousser (Zaïre) = avoir peur

Remind students that **victime** is always
feminine in gender and **temoin** is always
masculine, regardless of the actual sex
of the person referred to.

Le tour du monde en 365 jours

En bref

Dans cette leçon...

- Les pays du monde
- Les moyens de transport
- Les vacances des Français
- Voyages à l'étranger
- Faire des projets (le futur)
- Le pronom **y**
- Les pronoms personnels: récapitulation

In this lesson...

- Countries of the world
- Ways of getting around
- Vacations in France
- Traveling in other countries
- Making plans (the future)
- The pronoun **y**
- Personal pronouns: review

www.explore!
http://voila.heinle.com

Develop writing skills with Système-D software!

Practice listening and pronunciation skills with the Text Tape!

Discover the Francophone world!

Build your skills!

INTERNET

SYSTÈME-D

TEXT TAPE

VIDEO TAPE

CD-ROM

Students have an open-ended writing activity in the **Cahier** suitable for use with **Système-D**.

457

3615 Fnac is a
Minitel reference.

Un objet spatial. Qu'est-ce que cette image représente? Est-ce un OVNI (objet volant non identifié) des années 70? une soucoupe *(saucer)* volante des années 50?

Le CD-Rom. Comment utiliser **Voyageur 1?** Qu'allez-vous voir? Qu'allez-vous entendre? Qu'est-ce que vous allez faire encore?

Pour qui est fait ce CD-Rom? Avec quelles intentions? À quoi ressemble-t-il sur cette image? Quels mots du slogan expliquent son aspect?

Une agence. Quelle agence propose ce produit? Comment s'appelle-t-elle? Où est-elle située? Quel est le travail de cette agence?

Info plus

La Fnac.
La Fnac (Fédération nationale d'achats) is a chain of stores with outlets in major French cities. Founded as a bookstore, it now also sells magazines as well as audio visual, photographic, and electronic equipment. It is the favorite store of young people and bookworms.

Acheter Voyageur 1. Comment pouvez-vous commander le CD-Rom **Voyageur 1?** Appelez ou écrivez à **Fnac Voyages** pour le commander.

Avec un partenaire, préparez ce dialogue:
• L'agent de voyage demande votre destination, votre budget, etc.
• Vous répondez et vous posez des questions sur les autres services de la Fnac.

Vocabulaire

A. Un grand voyage

Jean-Pierre et Anne se sont mariés le cinq septembre et, comme ils adorent voyager à l'étranger, ils ont décidé de faire le tour du monde pendant un an. Ils sont tous les deux professeurs dans un lycée de Bruxelles et ils ne sont pas très riches, mais ils ont fait des économies et ils ne vont pas aller dans des hôtels de luxe, bien sûr. Ils détestent les voyages organisés parce que c'est trop cher et ils n'aiment pas voyager en groupe. Donc, ils vont partir seuls, avec un sac à dos. Ils veulent traverser l'Europe, l'Asie, l'Australie, l'Amérique et l'Afrique et ils vont visiter beaucoup de pays en train, en avion, en voiture, en autocar, en bateau et même en vélo.

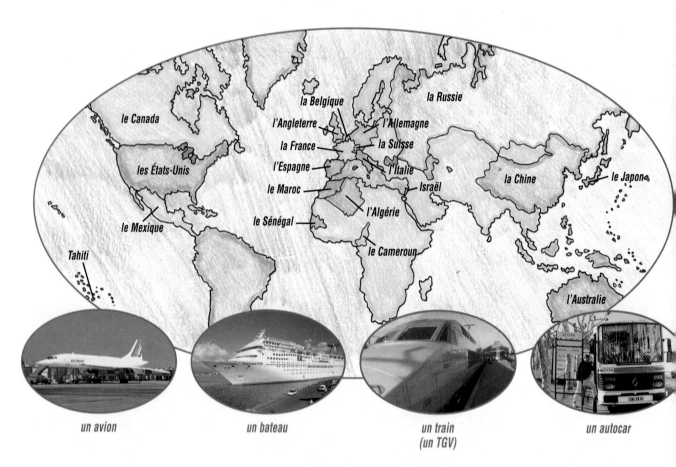

un avion   un bateau   un train (un TGV)   un autocar

- Qui sont Jean-Pierre et Anne? Qu'est-ce qu'ils vont faire pendant leur lune de miel? Comment vont-ils voyager? Pourquoi? Qu'est-ce qu'ils vont voir? Quels moyens de transport vont-ils utiliser?

Anne a essayé d'écrire leur voyage, mais il y avait trop de choses à faire... Alors, elle a écrit seulement un résumé. Le voilà:

B. Bruxelles, 7 septembre

Voilà, c'est la veille du grand départ! Quel voyage nous allons faire! On a réservé les premières nuits d'hôtel et on a fait nos bagages. Nous emportons deux sacs à dos, un autre petit sac, nos passeports, les billets d'avion et de train (pour le bateau, on verra), les chèques de voyage, nos permis de conduire, les cartes, les plans, les appareils-photo, le caméscope... On est raisonnable: les sacs ne sont pas trop lourds. J'espère que nous n'avons rien oublié!

Première étape: l'Europe en train... Nous allons d'abord traverser la France en TGV. Ça va plus vite et comme on la connaît bien, la France, on ne va pas s'arrêter cette fois. Mais on veut visiter la Suisse et l'Italie plus lentement: faire des randonnées à la montagne, faire les musées, se promener dans les vieux quartiers des villes italiennes... Mais pas question de faire les magasins: il n'y a pas de place dans les sacs!

À notre voyage!

- Qu'est-ce qu'ils emportent avec eux? Et comme vêtements? Est-ce qu'ils oublient quelque chose, à votre avis? Est-ce que leurs bagages sont lourds ou légers? Et vous, qu'est-ce que vous emportez quand vous partez en voyage?

- Quels endroits d'Europe est-ce qu'ils vont visiter? Pourquoi? Quels pays d'Europe ne vont-ils pas visiter?

en Suisse

If desired, give students further information about train travel in France. Explain that train tickets can be bought in advance, but that the ticket must be **composté** (punched or otherwise marked, usually by a machine at the train station) the day of the trip. Point out that it is necessary to reserve a seat on the TGV. You may also indicate www sites dealing with train travel.

C. Dans le train, Milan–Florence, 20 septembre

Quels problèmes à Milan! Hier, notre taxi est arrivé en retard à l'hôtel. À la gare, nous nous sommes trompés de quai et nous avons vu notre train qui partait de l'autre quai. Bien sûr, nous l'avons manqué. Alors, nous sommes retournés au guichet pour changer nos billets, mais il n'y avait plus de train et nous avons dû attendre le lendemain. Malheureusement, aujourd'hui, tous les compartiments étaient pleins et il n'y avait plus de place assise. Alors, voilà, nous sommes debout dans le couloir. Ce n'est pas facile d'écrire et je m'arrête.

- Quels problèmes ont-ils eus à Milan? Où étaient-ils quand le train est parti? Qu'est-ce qu'ils ont dû faire? Où ont-ils passé la nuit, à votre avis? Quel est le problème aujourd'hui?

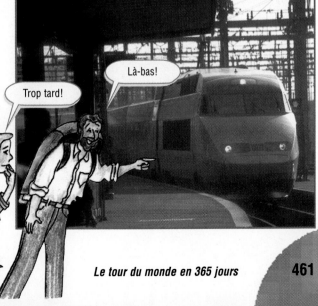

Là-bas!

Trop tard!

Le tour du monde en 365 jours **461**

TRANSPARENCY:
18-3

D. Dans l'avion, Pékin-Tokyo, 27 décembre

Découvrir la Chine, c'était merveilleux! Hong Kong d'abord, et puis Guilin et ses montagnes, Hangzhou et son lac, Shanghai la moderne et Pékin bien sûr, avec la Grande Muraille et la Cité Interdite... Quel pays magnifique! Et nous avons trouvé les habitants vraiment gentils. Mais on a souvent eu peur pendant les vols intérieurs surtout quand c'étaient des vieux avions russes! C'était horrible! Et puis, à l'aéroport de Pékin, quelle affaire! Nous étions en avance et l'avion était à l'heure, mais on nous a dit que nos billets n'étaient pas bons et que nous devions en acheter d'autres. Mais avec quel argent? Finalement, ils les ont acceptés, mais alors, nous étions en retard! À la douane, heureusement, on n'a pas eu de problème: les douaniers ne nous ont rien demandé. Nous sommes arrivés à la porte quand on la fermait, mais enfin, on n'a pas manqué l'avion et nous voilà! L'avion est presque vide, le pilote vient de dire qu'il fait un temps magnifique à Tokyo, les hôtesses de l'air sont en train d'apporter des apéritifs aux passagers... Je crois que le vol va être agréable, cette fois.

Et maintenant, le Japon...

• Quand sont-ils arrivés en Chine à votre avis? Combien de temps sont-ils restés dans ce pays? Qu'est-ce qu'ils en pensent? Qu'est-ce qui s'est passé à l'aéroport? Où vont-ils passer le Nouvel An?

en Chine

au Japon

E. Dans le bateau, Tahiti–Bora Bora, 9 avril

Après le désert, les îles... Temps chaud et ensoleillé tous les jours... Quel climat! Et la mer est d'un bleu, mais d'un bleu! Et puis, voyager en bateau, mon rêve de toujours! C'est beaucoup moins rapide que l'avion, c'est même très lent, mais la vie en mer est si agréable. Bien sûr, ce n'est pas une croisière. Il n'y a pas de piscine et le restaurant n'est pas élégant. Mais après l'Australie que nous avons traversée en autocar...

- Où sont-ils allés après le Japon? Comment est l'Australie? Comment ont-ils voyagé dans ce pays? Où sont-ils maintenant? Est-ce qu'Anne est contente? Expliquez.

en Australie
(Sydney et son opéra)

à Tahiti

F. Carmel, 2 mai

TRANSPARENCY: 18-5

Et nous voilà en Californie, aux États-Unis. Nous avons décidé de louer une voiture à Los Angeles parce que nous avons découvert que Los Angeles sans voiture, c'est difficile: pas de métro, peu d'autobus! Et puis, c'est si facile de conduire ici! Les routes sont bonnes et il y a beaucoup d'autoroutes. L'Amérique, c'est vraiment le pays de l'avion et de la voiture. Les autres moyens de transport ne sont pas très pratiques, même s'il y a des autocars et des trains qui traversent le pays. Comme nous avons deux mois et que nous voulons voir du pays, ça va donc être la voiture

l'Amérique en voiture

Première étape: Los Angeles–San Francisco. Mais nous sommes tombés amoureux de Carmel et nous avons décidé de rester une semaine. Quel endroit merveilleux! Nous allons louer des vélos pour faire des promenades.
Deuxième étape: San Francisco–Reno–Salt Lake City.
Troisième étape: Yellowstone.
Quatrième étape: Mount Rushmore.
Cinquième étape: Chicago (rendre visite à Frédéric).
Sixième étape: Montréal et Québec.
Septième étape: New York.

Je voulais voir la Louisiane et la Floride et Jean-Pierre voulait passer par le Texas et le Mexique, mais c'est vraiment impossible. Il faudrait six mois!

Carmel

la ville de Québec

Voilà! You may want to show **Video Magazine 2:** *Documentaire: Le Québec et ses habitants.*

- Qu'est-ce qu'ils ont décidé de voir aux États-Unis? Pourquoi? Et au Canada, pourquoi ont-ils choisi Montréal et Québec?
- Qui est Frédéric, à votre avis?
- Deux mois pour voir les États-Unis et le Canada, c'est assez, à votre avis? Qu'est-ce qu'il faut voir aux États-Unis et au Canada?

G. Madrid, 2 septembre

Nous avons passé un mois au Cameroun et au Sénégal. Il faisait très chaud et, en plus, c'était la saison des pluies, mais c'était vraiment intéressant. Au Cameroun, nous avons vécu huit jours chez Évelyne, qui passait l'été chez ses parents à Douala, près de la mer. C'était merveilleux de faire la connaissance d'une famille africaine et de pouvoir partager leur vie. Après le Cameroun et le Sénégal, on est allé quinze jours au Maroc, puis nous sommes partis pour l'Espagne. Et nous voilà! On est très fatigué et on n'a plus d'argent. Alors, on fait de l'auto-stop. On est arrivé à Madrid en camion et on espère partir demain, mais comment?

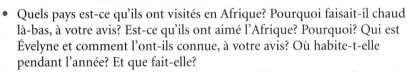

TRANSPARENCY: 18-6

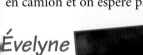
Évelyne

au Sénégal (la Grande Mosquée, Dakar)

- Quels pays est-ce qu'ils ont visités en Afrique? Pourquoi faisait-il chaud là-bas, à votre avis? Est-ce qu'ils ont aimé l'Afrique? Pourquoi? Qui est Évelyne et comment l'ont-ils connue, à votre avis? Où habite-t-elle pendant l'année? Et que fait-elle?
- Où sont-ils maintenant? Comment est-ce qu'ils vont rentrer chez eux?

Notes de vocabulaire

1. Mots et expressions utiles.

changer (de train, d'avion...)	*to change (trains, planes, etc.)*
un continent	*continent*
être à	*to belong to*
un souvenir	*souvenir*
une station de métro	*subway station*
un steward	*cabin attendant, steward*
un ticket	*ticket (bus or subway)*

Voilà! You may want to show the video segments on Sénégal (**Video Magazine 1:** *Documentaire: Le Sénégal*) and on Cameroun (**Video Magazine 6:** *Documentaire: Le Cameroun*).

Point out to students that **passer** is conjugated with **avoir** when it is transitive (has a direct object) but with **être** when it is intransitive.

Tell students that **huit jours** is *a week*, while **quinze jours** is *two weeks*.

2. Les continents, les pays et leurs habitants.

l'Afrique *(f.)*	africain, africaine
l'Algérie *(f.)*	algérien, algérienne
l'Allemagne *(f.) (Germany)*	allemand, allemande
l'Amérique *(f.)*	américain, américaine
l'Angleterre *(f.) (England)*	anglais, anglaise
l'Asie *(f.)*	asiatique
l'Australie *(f.)*	australien, australienne
la Belgique	belge
le Cameroun	camerounais, camerounaise
le Canada	canadien, canadienne
la Chine	chinois, chinoise
l'Espagne *(f.) (Spain)*	espagnol, espagnole
les États-Unis *(m. pl.)*	américain, américaine
l'Europe *(f.)*	européen, européenne
Israël *(m.)*	israélien, israélienne
l'Italie *(f.)*	italien, italienne
le Japon	japonais, japonaise
le Maroc	marocain, marocaine
le Mexique	mexicain, mexicaine
la Russie	russe
le Sénégal	sénégalais, sénégalaise
la Suisse *(Switzerland)*	suisse
Tahiti *(f.)*	tahitien, tahitienne

3. Les prépositions et les pays. Here is how to express *to* or *in* with the name of a country.

> **en** + *feminine country* (country whose name ends in **-e**)
> **en** + *country beginning with a vowel* (masculine or feminine)
> **au** + *masculine country* (except countries beginning with a vowel)

Il va **en France** en été.	*He's going to France in the summer.*
Namur est **en Belgique?**	*Namur is in Belgium?*
Vous allez **en Israël?**	*Are you going to Israel?*
Il fait beau **en Espagne** en mai.	*The weather is nice in Spain in May.*
Il est allé **au Canada.**	*He went to Canada.*

Note the following:

a. Use **aux** with **États-Unis** because it is masculine plural.

Aux États-Unis, on aime beaucoup le Coca-Cola.	*In the United States, people like cola a lot.*

b. Although **Mexique** *(Mexico)* ends in **-e,** it is masculine. Use **au.**

On parle espagnol **au Mexique.**	*Spanish is spoken in Mexico.*

c. Generally, states in the United States and provinces in Canada follow the rules for countries. Except for a few states and provinces, however, usage is not yet firmly fixed. But you will always hear **en Californie, en Floride, en Louisiane, au Québec,** and **au Texas.**

d. Although usage may vary, in general, you can use **à** for small islands: **à Tahiti, à la Martinique, à Saint-Martin, à la Guadeloupe.** Note that, for some islands, the definite article is also needed.

4. À l'heure / en retard / en avance / tôt / tard / à bientôt.
If you are **à l'heure,** you are *on time.* If you are **en avance,** you are *early,* and if you are **en retard,** you are *late!* It all depends on what time you were supposed to be there.

    Tôt *(early)* and **tard** *(late),* by contrast, are general terms. Remember that **à bientôt** means *see you soon.*

Il est huit heures dix et le film commence à huit heures. Nous sommes **en retard.**	*It's 8:10 and the movie starts at 8:00. We're late.*
J'arrive toujours **en avance** parce que je ne veux pas manquer le train.	*I always get there early because I don't want to miss the train.*
Le docteur Martin a beaucoup de travail. Il part **tôt** le matin et il rentre **tard** le soir.	*Dr. Martin has a lot of work. He leaves early in the morning and gets home late at night.*
Trop **tard!**	*Too late!*
Allez! Salut! **À bientôt!**	*Ok. 'Bye. See you soon.*

5. Visiter / rendre visite à.
Use **visiter** to express the idea of *visiting a place.* Use **rendre visite à** to express the idea of *paying a visit to a person.*

On va **visiter** Paris!	*We're going to visit Paris!*
Je vais **rendre visite à** Frédéric.	*I'm going to visit Frédéric.*

6. Ce (adjectif démonstratif) et quel (adjectif interrogatif).
You studied **ce** and **quel** in *Leçons 6* and *8.* Review their forms and meanings.

- **Ce, cet, cette, ces.** The demonstrative adjective **ce** means either *this* or *that.*

Ce passeport français est à qui?	*Whose French passport is this?*
Cette carte est à vous?	*Is this map yours?*
Cet appareil-photo est à lui.	*That (This) camera is his.*
Ces valises sont à moi.	*These (Those) suitcases are mine.*

- **Quel, quelle, quels, quelles.** The interrogative adjective **quel** means *which* or *what.* The noun it modifies may either immediately follow **quel** or be separated from it by the verb **être.**

Quel aéroport cherchez-vous?	*What airport are you looking for?*
Quels pays est-ce que tu as visités?	*What countries did you visit?*
Tu étais à **quelle** station?	*What station were you at?*
Quelles robes est-ce qu'elle a prises?	*What dresses did she take?*
Quelle est ton adresse?	*What's your address?*

3: Which preposition to use in front of the names of islands is far from standardized. In general, it is probably best to ask students to simply memorize the most common ones.

See the **Instructor's Resource Manual** for more information.

Remind students that **à / de** is used in front of a city. If desired, teach the patterns of **de** + *feminine country* or *masculine country* beginning with a vowel; **du** + *masculine country;* **des** + **États-Unis.** Personalized questions: Ask students: **De quel(s) pays sont venus vos parents? vos grands-parents?**

5: The expression **aller voir** is also used to mean *to visit someone.*

6: Ce and **quel** were introduced for recognition and limited use in *Notes de vocabulaire, Leçons 6* (quel) and *8* (ce). Review briefly here.

Demonstrative and interrogative pronouns are treated briefly in the *Appendice de grammaire.*

Remind students that **-ci** and **-là** can be used to differentiate between *this* (ci) and *that* (là) if necessary.

Draw students' attention to the fact that **quel** + *noun* in a sentence in the **passé composé** may require past participle agreement.

TRANSLATION EXERCISE: Ask students how they would ask the following questions in French: What time is it? What's the weather like? How old are you? What countries have you visited? What time do you go to bed? What time do you get up?

A form of **quel** may be placed in front of a noun to express a reaction.

Quelle affaire!   *What a deal!*
Quel voyage!   *What a trip!*

7. En avion / en voiture / à pied. To talk about how you get places, use one of the following expressions.

aller à pied	*to walk, to go on foot*
aller en autobus, en autocar	*to take the bus, to go by bus*
aller en avion	*to fly, to go by air*
aller en bateau	*to take the boat, to go by boat*
aller en métro	*to take the subway, to go by subway*
aller en train	*to take the train, to go by train*
aller en vélo	*to bicycle, to go by bicycle*
aller en voiture	*to drive, to go by car*

Est-ce que tu **vas** à Nice **en avion, en voiture** ou **en train**?   *Are you flying, driving, or taking the train to Nice?*
Je **vais** à la bibliothèque **à pied**.   *I'm walking to the library.*

8. Conduire. The verb **conduire** *(to drive)* refers to the physical act of driving. Its conjugation is irregular.

PRÉSENT:	je conduis	nous conduisons
	tu conduis	vous conduisez
	il elle } conduit	ils elles } conduisent
IMPARFAIT :	je conduisais, etc. ...	
PASSÉ COMPOSÉ:	j'ai conduit, etc. ...	

J'adore **conduire**. Je vais partout en voiture.   *I love driving. I drive everywhere.*

9. Place. The French word **place** can mean *square, seat,* or *room (space).*

À Cinet, il y a une église sur la **place**.   *In Cinet, there is a church on the square.*
Est-ce qu'il y a une **place** près de la fenêtre?   *Is there a seat near the window?*
Est-ce qu'il y a de la **place**?   *Is there (any) room?*

10. Rapide / vite. **Rapide** is an adjective. Use it to modify nouns. **Vite** is an adverb. Use it to modify verbs.

Elle a une voiture **rapide**.   *She has a fast car.*
Elle conduit **vite**.   *She drives fast.*

7: Either **à vélo** or **en vélo** may be used.

8: **Conduire** is presented here only in the sense of *to drive a car* (no indication of a change in location), an expression that students ask for. Point out that *to drive somewhere* = **aller quelque part en voiture**. *To drive someone somewhere* = **accompagner** or **emmener quelqu'un à...** If desired, tell students that **traduire** is conjugated like **conduire**.

9: Remind students that **endroit** = *place*, in the sense of *location*.

11. **Espérer.** The verb **espérer** changes the **-é** to **-è** in front of a silent ending. (**Préférer** and **sécher** are conjugated like **espérer**).

J'**espère** que tu vas bien. *I hope that you're fine.*
Nous **espérons** partir à huit heures. *We hope to leave at eight o'clock.*

12. **Découvrir.** The verb **découvrir** is conjugated like **ouvrir.**

Nous **avons découvert** un petit restaurant sympathique. *We discovered a nice little restaurant.*
J'**ouvre** la boîte et qu'est-ce que je **découvre?** Un petit chien blanc! *I open the box and what do I find? A white puppy!*

13. **Passer.** **Passer** is conjugated with **avoir** when it is transitive (has a direct object) but with **être** when it is intransitive.

Jean-Pierre et Anne **ont passé** la nuit à Milan. *Jean-Pierre and Anne spent the night in Milan.*
Ils **sont passés** par la Suisse. *They went through Switzerland.*

D'accord?

A. Chassez l'intrus Trouvez les mots qui ne vont pas.

1. compartiment / quai / vol / train / TGV
2. autobus / taxi / croisière / métro
3. être en avance / être assis / être à l'heure / être en retard
4. hôtesse de l'air / allemand / pilote / steward
5. merveilleux / magnifique / horrible / délicieux
6. avion / camion / route / autoroute

Act. A: CONTINUATION (gender):
(1) **billet / avion / île / taxi;** (2) **place / voiture / carte / pays;** (3) **Japon / France / Espagne / Allemagne**

B. En voyage Quelles phrases vont ensemble? Il peut y avoir plus d'une possibilité.

1. Est-ce que le train est à l'heure?
2. L'avion de Paris est arrivé?
3. À quelle heure part l'avion pour Rome, s'il vous plaît?
4. Est-ce que tu es allé à la banque?
5. Est-ce que je dois changer de train?
6. Est-ce qu'il y a un autre vol pour New York?
7. C'est la saison des vacances.
8. Comment est-ce que je peux aller à l'hôtel?

a. J'ai manqué mon avion.
b. Non, Madame, il est en retard.
c. En taxi ou en métro.
d. Non, Mademoiselle, il va arriver dans cinq minutes.
e. À 15 h 25, porte numéro 35.
f. Oui, à Lyon.
g. Oui, j'ai acheté des chèques de voyage.
h. Tu dois acheter ton billet à l'avance si tu veux une place assise.

C. Les déplacements *(Getting around)* Vous passez un an à Paris. Voici une liste de ce que vous voulez voir. Choisissez un moyen de transport pour aller...

1. à Rome
2. à la tour Eiffel
3. à Big Ben
4. aux plages de la Côte d'Azur
5. au Mont Blanc (en Suisse)
6. voir les pyramides d'Égypte

D. Les moyens de transport

1. Quels sont les moyens de transport lents? rapides? chers? bon marché? agréables? pas agréables?
2. Quels sont les moyens de transport pratiques et pas pratiques...
   a. pour une famille de sept personnes?
   b. pour un chef d'entreprise?
   c. pour un étudiant pauvre?
   d. en hiver à Montréal?
   e. en été à Los Angeles?
3. Pour vous, quels sont les moyens de transport pratiques et pas pratiques...
   a. sur votre campus?
   b. où vous habitez?
   c. pour rentrer chez vous?
   d. pour aller en vacances en Floride ou en Californie?

E. La vie et les voitures Répondez aux questions.

1. À quel âge est-ce que vous pouvez avoir un permis de conduire dans votre pays?
2. Quand avez-vous appris à conduire? Avec qui?
3. Est-ce que vous avez une voiture à l'université? Pourquoi ou pourquoi pas?
4. Quelle sorte de voiture est-ce que vous préférez?
5. Est-ce que vous préférez conduire sur les petites routes de campagne ou sur les autoroutes? Pourquoi?
6. Quand est-ce que vous conduisez?
7. Est-ce que vous conduisez bien? vite?
8. Quand est-ce que vous ne devez pas conduire?
9. Est-ce que vous connaissez quelqu'un qui conduit mal? Qui?

F. Associations Quels pays est-ce que vous associez avec...

1. le champagne?
2. le caviar?
3. les pâtes?
4. la bière?
5. le Coca-Cola?
6. les voitures de sport?
7. la mode?
8. le soleil, les plages, les vacances?
9. l'art?
10. la nature?

G. Leçon de géographie Dans quel pays sont ces villes?

Modèle Paris
   en France (en Europe)

1. Madrid
2. Toronto
3. Casablanca
4. Acapulco
5. Hiroshima
6. Guilin
7. Lausanne
8. Toulouse
9. Dakar

H. Des touristes naïfs!

Les touristes sont parfois surpris par les choses qu'ils ne connaissent pas. Jouez le rôle d'un touriste naïf qui voyage en France et dites aux personnes qui voyagent avec vous de regarder ce que vous venez de voir.

Act H: FOLLOW-UP: Ask students if they find the pictures unusual and why.

Modèle   Regardez ..... sandwich!
            Regardez *ce* sandwich!

TRANSPARENCY: 18-7

1. Regardez ..... pain!   2. Regardez ..... viande!   3. Regardez ..... gâteaux!   4. Regardez ..... chien!

I. Des touristes français

Maintenant, écoutez un groupe de touristes français qui disent ce qu'ils trouvent bizarre en Amérique du Nord. Utilisez une forme de **quel** pour compléter chaque phrase.

Act I: If desired, discuss stereotypes and cross-cultural behavior.

Modèle   ..... sandwich!
            Quel sandwich!

TRANSPARENCY: 18-8

1. ..... chaussures! Des tennis avec un tailleur!   2. ..... petit déjeuner! Ils mangent tout ça?   3. ..... gros frigos! Mais qu'est-ce qu'ils mettent dedans?   4. ..... pain! C'est comme du coton!

J. Rapide ou vite? Complétez par **rapide** ou **vite.**

1. Je ne comprends rien. Tu parles trop .....
2. Vous avez fini? Vous êtes ..... !
3. Ne marche pas si ..... !
4. Le train est moins ..... que l'avion.
5. M. Bovy aime les employés ..... qui travaillent .....
6. ..... ! Dépêchez-vous!

Mise en pratique

Act. A: Could also be done with Cameroon and/or Senegal after viewing the video.

A. Là-bas! Qu'est-ce qu'il y a là-bas? Quel temps fait-il? Quelle est la meilleure saison pour voyager? Qu'est-ce qu'il faut visiter? Qu'est-ce qu'on peut faire?

1. en Italie
2. en Israël
3. en Australie
4. au Japon

TRANSPARENCY: 18-9

B. Retours de voyage Voilà des photos de personnes qui viennent de rentrer de voyage. Pour chaque illustration, décidez où elles sont allées, pourquoi, comment elles ont voyagé et ce qui s'est passé. Puis écrivez un paragraphe pour chacune des illustrations.

Act. C: Do in small groups. Compare the questions produced by various groups and have students vote to decide on the five or ten "most essential" questions.

Act. D: If no students have traveled outside of North America, ask for students who have traveled to other parts of North America.

C. Dix questions utiles quand on voyage Vous faites un voyage dans un pays francophone. Quelles sont les dix questions les plus importantes et les plus utiles?

D. Devinez le pays

1. Trouvez un ou plusieurs étudiants qui ont voyagé hors de (outside of) l'Amérique du Nord. Posez-leur des questions pour deviner (guess) quels pays ils ont visités.
2. Posez des questions à votre professeur sur ses voyages hors de l'Amérique du Nord. Devinez quels pays il/elle a visités.

E. Un horaire de trains Voilà l'horaire des trains Paris-Bordeaux.

TRANSPARENCY:
18-10

Numéro de train		4011	4011	8311	8311	7800/1	8515	97087	8417	8419	8521	8519	8521	14013	98361	4837/6	8525	8433	6964/5	97269
Notes à consulter		41	22	23	15	24	25	26	27	28	29	30	31	32	19	2	33	34	35	36
				TGV	TGV	TGV	TGV		TGV	TGV	TGV	TGV	TGV				TGV	TGV		
Paris-Montparnasse	D			08.30	09.00		**10.00**		10.45	10.45	11.05	11.15	11.15				12.45	13.55		
Paris-Austerliz	D	07.33	07.33																	
Les Aubrais-Orléans	D	08.32	08.32																	
St-Pierre-des-Corps	D	09.29	09.37	09.32	09.56	10.23			11.43	11.43								14.54		
Poitiers	D	10.42	10.51	10.20	10.43	11.13			12.31	12.31							14.21	15.45		
Angoulême	D	11.42	11.50			12.01		**12.30**	13.16	13.16							15.06			
Bordeaux-St-Jean	A	13.12	13.16			12.58	**13.08**	**13.50**	14.15	14.15	14.26	14.18	14.26	14.26	14.20	15.03	16.02			**16.46**

15. Circule : jusqu'au 10 juil : les sam et dim, à partir du 11 juil : tous les jours- 🍷

19. Circule : tous les jours sauf les dim et fêtes

20. Circule : tous les jours sauf les dim et fêtes- 2ᵉ CL- AUTOCAR

21. Circule : jusqu'au 10 juil : les sam et dim, à partir du 11 juil : tous les jours- 🛏 - ♿

22. Circule : jusqu'au 8 juil : tous les jours sauf les sam et dim- 🛏 - ♿

23. Circule : jusqu'au 8 juil : tous les jours sauf les sam et dim- 🍷 - ♿

24. Circule : du 2 juil au 10 sept : les sam- 🍷 - ♿

25. 🍱 1ʳᵉ CL assuré certains jours- 🍷 - ♿

26. 🚲

27. Circule : jusqu'au 1ᵉʳ juil et à partir du 29 août : tous les jours- 🍱 1ʳᵉ CL assuré certains jours- 🍷 - ♿

28. Circule : du 2 juil au 28 août : tous les jours- 🍷 - ♿

29. Circule : du 27 juin au 8 juil : tous les jours sauf les sam et dim- 🍱 1ʳᵉ CL- 🍷 - ♿

30. Circule : jusqu'au 10 juil : les sam et dim, à partir du 11 juil : tous les jours- 🍱 1ʳᵉ CL- 🍷 - ♿

31. Circule : du 25 juin au 10 juil : les sam et dim, du 11 juil au 28 août : tous les jours- 🍱 1ʳᵉ CL- 🍷 - ♿

32. Circule : jusqu'au 24 juin et à partir du 29 août : tous les jours

33. Circule : les sam et le 14 juil- 🍷 - ♿

34. Circule : les ven et le 13 juil- 🍷 - ♿

35. ♿

36. Circule : jusqu'au 2 juil : les sam, du 3 juil au 3 sept : les sam, dim et fêtes les 10, 17 et 24 sept

Symboles						
A	Arrivée	🛏	Couchettes	♿	Facilités handicapés	
D	Départ	🛏	Voiture-lits			
		✕	Voiture-restaurant			
TGV	Réservation obligatoire	⊗	Grill-express	🚲	Vélo : Transport gratuit	
		🍱	Restauration à la place			
		🍷	Bar			
⇄	Cabine 8	🛒	Vente ambulante			

Remarques — **Les trains circulant tous les jours ont leurs horaires indiqués en gras.**

Tous les trains offrent des places assises en 1ʳᵉ et 2ᵉ classe sauf indication contraire dans les notes.

Certains trains circulent rarement ne sont pas repris dans cette fiche.

«Source SNCF»

1. Regardez les symboles, en bas de l'horaire. Pouvez-vous deviner *(guess)* ce qu'ils veulent dire? Expliquez avec vos propres mots *(explain in your own words)*.
2. Quels trains sont des TGV (dites le numéro des trains)? Combien d'heures est-ce qu'il faut pour aller de Paris à Bordeaux en TGV? Et avec un train normal?
3. Regardez le train numéro 8515. À quelle heure est-ce qu'il part de Paris? À quelle heure est-ce qu'il arrive à Bordeaux? Est-ce qu'il s'arrête dans d'autres villes? Est-ce qu'on peut manger dans ce train? et boire? Est-ce qu'il y a un train tous les jours?
4. Vous voulez aller à Angoulême. Regardez bien l'horaire. Est-ce que tous les TGV s'arrêtent à Angoulême? Si vous ne prenez pas le TGV, dans quelle gare devez-vous partir de Paris? Combien de temps faut-il pour aller à Angoulême avec un train normal? Et avec le TGV? Si vous voulez prendre le TGV et vous voulez arriver à Angoulême vers midi, qu'est-ce que vous devez faire à Poitiers? Est-ce que vous pouvez prendre ce train toute l'année? Tous les jours?
5. Vous êtes à Paris et vous devez être à Bordeaux le samedi 6 juillet dans l'après-midi. Vous devez réserver votre place à l'avance parce que vous voulez prendre le TGV. À la gare, vous demandez l'heure des trains, combien de temps il faut pour aller à Bordeaux, le prix, etc. Finalement, vous faites la réservation et vous achetez un billet.

Act. E, 1: TGV information: Seat reservation is obligatory for all TGV's. If you travel first class (**en première classe**), you may also reserve a meal served at your seat on most TGVs if the trip takes over an hour. Otherwise, the bar sells beverages, breakfast, and light meals as well as items such as magazines and **télécartes** for both first and second class passengers.

Act. E, 5: A dialogue illustrating item 5 is found in the **Instructor's Resource Manual** for this lesson.

Structure

See the **Instructor's Resource Manual** for more information.

➤➤ Le futur

Formation du futur

You already know how to talk about things in the future by using the verb **aller** + *infinitive*. **Aller** + *infinitive* is called the **futur proche** or *near future*. It is the equivalent of the English *to be going to do something.*

> Je **vais étudier** demain.   *I'm going to study tomorrow.*

French also has a future tense. It corresponds to the English *will + verb.* To form the future tense in French, add the following endings to the infinitive form of the verb (for verbs ending in **-re,** drop the **-e** first).

Emphasize that the majority of verbs form the future tense in a regular fashion. Give examples from verbs that are irregular in the present but regular in the future (e.g. **mettre, prendre, boire, suivre, dire, ouvrir,** etc.).

The **futur antérieur** is treated briefly in the *Appendice de grammaire.*

manger	
je manger**ai**	nous manger**ons**
tu manger**as**	vous manger**ez**
il / elle } manger**a**	ils / elles } manger**ont**

choisir	
je choisir**ai**	nous choisir**ons**
tu choisir**as**	vous choisir**ez**
il / elle } choisir**a**	ils / elles } choisir**ont**

attendre	
j'attendr**ai**	nous attendr**ons**
tu attendr**as**	vous attendr**ez**
il / elle } attendr**a**	ils / elles } attendr**ont**

Je t'**attendrai** et nous **mangerons** en ville.	*I'll wait for you and we'll eat downtown.*
Va dormir, on **parlera** demain.	*Go to bed, we'll talk tomorrow.*
À quelle heure est-ce que vous **partirez?**	*What time will you leave?*
J'espère que tu te **coucheras** tôt.	*I hope (that) you'll go to bed early.*

Certain verbs have irregular future stems.

aller	ir-	Qui **ira** pour nous?	*Who'll go for us?*
avoir	aur-	Je l'**aurai** demain.	*I'll have it tomorrow.*
devoir	devr-	Tu **devras** partir.	*You'll have to go.*
envoyer	enverr-	Qui l'**enverra**?	*Who'll send it?*
être	ser-	Je **serai** ici.	*I'll be here.*
faire	fer-	Tu le **feras**?	*You'll do it?*
pouvoir	pourr-	Ils **pourront** venir.	*They'll be able to come.*
savoir	saur-	Tu le **sauras**!	*You'll find out!*
venir	viendr-	Nous **viendrons**.	*We'll come.*
voir	verr-	On **verra**.	*We'll see.*
vouloir	voudr-	Il **voudra** le savoir.	*He'll want to know it.*

DRILL: **Demain, tout le monde sera content!** (Candide / nous / tu / les étudiants / je)

DRILL: **Alceste fera la vaisselle. Nous / la cuisine; Tu / les courses; Candide et son amie / le ménage; Je / ne rien)**

Note the use of the future to indicate what will happen if something else occurs.

- **si + présent / futur**

> S'il **fait** mauvais demain,
>   nous **irons** au cinéma.

> *If it's bad out tomorrow,*
>   *we'll go to the movies.*

The use of **si** clauses is treated more fully in *Leçon 19*.

Les changements d'orthographe au futur

1. Verbs such as **lever** change the -e- to -è- in all forms of the future. Note that **appeler** changes the single -l- to -ll- in all forms of the future.

2. Verbs such as **ennuyer** change the -y- to -i- in all forms of the future. Note that **envoyer** has an irregular future stem (**enverr-**).

3. Verbs such as **espérer** and **préférer** retain the -é- in all forms of the future.

Refer students to the *Appendice de verbes*, beginning on page 552.

> Nous l'**appellerons** Minou.
> Il **s'ennuiera**.
> Nous **achèterons** le journal demain.
> Tu **préféreras** cela.

> *We'll call it Minou.*
> *He'll be bored.*
> *We'll buy the paper tomorrow.*
> *You'll prefer that.*

L'emploi du futur

In most cases, the use of the future in French parallels that of English. However, note the following:

1. The future tense is used after **quand** in French when the action is expected to occur in the future. In English, the present is used.

> Je te **téléphonerai** quand **j'arriverai**.   *I'll call you when I get there.*

2. The present tense is often used instead of the future when the context is clear. English usage is similar.

> Demain soir, nous **mangeons**
>   chez les Dumont.
> L'année prochaine, je **vais** en France.

> *Tomorrow evening we're eating*
>   *at the Dumonts'.*
> *Next year, I'm going to France.*

Vous avez compris?

A. Hier ou demain? Complétez en utilisant **hier** ou **demain**.

1. —Tu prendras ta voiture ..... ?
   —Non, je l'ai vendue .....
2. —Tu as écrit à ton frère ..... ?
   —Non, mais je lui écrirai .....
3. —Vous ferez la vaisselle ..... , non?
   —Oui, c'est vous qui l'avez faite ..... et il n'y en a pas aujourd'hui!
4. —Elle est allée en ville ..... ?
   —Oui, et elle ira en ville ..... !
5. —On se parlera ..... ?
   —Non, non et non! On s'est déjà trop parlé .....

Act. B: CONTINUATION: Quand je vais en ville, j'achète une chemise. Vous comprenez les informations? Qui finit ses devoirs avant minuit? Je ne m'ennuie pas. Vous pouvez voir votre examen lundi. Ces enfants ne voient pas souvent leurs parents. Je sais la vérité.

B. Au futur! Écrivez les phrases suivantes au futur.

1. Tu prends ta voiture quand tu pars pour Lyon?
2. Vous pouvez partir avec vos amis.
3. Nous voulons leur parler quand ils arrivent.
4. Mon petit frère fait la vaisselle.
5. Après un an à Paris, tu connais la ville.
6. Tu m'attends devant l'épicerie.
7. Quand je suis à Paris, je vois mes amis.
8. Nous écrivons à nos amis français.

C. Les plaintes de Julien Julien voudrait être grand (*grown-up*). Voilà ce qu'il doit faire maintenant. Dites ce qu'il fera quand il sera grand.

Modèle   Je me réveille à sept heures. (à midi)
   Quand je serai grand, je me réveillerai à midi!

1. Je me lève à sept heures et demie. (à dix heures)
2. Je me couche à huit heures. (quand je voudrai)
3. Je prends une douche le soir. (ne pas prendre de douche)
4. Je mange des légumes. (ne pas manger de légumes)
5. Je bois du lait. (du Coca-Cola)
6. Je ne comprends pas les adultes. (comprendre les adultes)
7. Je ne peux pas regarder la télévision le soir. (pouvoir regarder la télévision le soir)
8. Je ne suis pas heureux! (être heureux)

Continuons!

A. Parlons un peu!

Act. A: Make sure students understand that they do not have to answer a question truthfully! Help students find ways to respond to questions that they don't want to answer—a helpful strategy in any language (e.g., **Oh, je ne sais pas, peut-être, on verra bien.**).

1. En été, ...
   a. où est-ce que vous serez?
   b. est-ce que vous travaillerez? Qu'est-ce que vous ferez?
   c. est-ce que vous voyagerez? Où? Avec qui? Comment?

2. Après l'université, ...
   a. quel sera votre métier?
   b. où est-ce que vous habiterez?
   c. combien d'argent est-ce que vous gagnerez?
   d. est-ce que vous aurez des enfants? Combien? Quels seront leurs noms?
   e. quelle sorte de maison est-ce que vous aurez?
   f. est-ce que vous vous marierez? Avec qui?

B. La voyante *(Play fortune-teller)* Qui dans la classe...

1. aura dix enfants? n'aura pas d'enfants?
2. vendra des voitures pour gagner sa vie?
3. se mariera à l'âge de 22 ans? ne se mariera pas?
4. sera coiffeur / coiffeuse?
5. sera très riche? ne sera pas très riche?
6. sera pompier? sera avocat(e)? sera joueur / joueuse de football?
7. . . . . .

Act. B: Personne is a possible answer. Ask students to continue to make predictions for their classmates.

C. Prévision Écrivez quatre prédictions (au futur, bien sûr) pour un(e) autre étudiant(e) de la classe. Échangez vos prédictions, lisez ce qu'on a écrit sur vous et réagissez. (Je pense que oui/non. J'espère que oui/non. Je ne pense pas. Je ne sais pas. Pas question! ...)

Act. C: ALTERNATIVE FORMAT: Distribute index cards with students' names on them. Have each student make four predictions for the person whose name is on his or her card. Collect the cards and read them aloud, eliciting reactions.

D. L'avenir du professeur Et votre professeur? Écrivez quatre ou cinq prédictions pour votre professeur. Permettez-lui de réagir!

E. Conversation en français Qu'est-ce que vous allez faire cet été? Et après l'université? Avec un camarade de classe ou votre professeur, passez deux ou trois minutes à parler du futur. Ne monopolisez pas la conversation et n'oubliez pas de poser des questions à votre partenaire aussi.

TEXT TAPE:
Conversation en français

Act. E: Point out that it is not necessary to use only the future tense to talk about the future.

▶▶ Le pronom *y*

The pronoun **y** always refers to things. It varies in meaning according to its use.

1. **Il y a. Y** is part of a fixed expression. It has no independent meaning.

Est-ce qu'**il y a** de la confiture?	*Is there any jam?*
Non, **il** n'**y a** pas de confiture, mais **il y a** du beurre.	*No, there isn't any jam, but there's (some) butter.*

2. **Y** replaces **à** + *thing*. **Y** functions as a sort of indirect object pronoun for things.

Je ne veux pas répondre **à votre question.**	*I don't want to answer your question.*
Je ne veux pas **y** répondre.	*I don't want to answer it.*

3. **Y** is an adverb meaning *here / there*. **Y** replaces prepositional phrases indicating place (**à, dans, sous, sur, en...** + *place*).

Il va **au cinéma.**	*He's going to the movies.*
Il **y** va.	*He's going there.*
Je pense qu'il est **en Italie.**	*I think he's in Italy.*
Je pense qu'il **y** est.	*I think he's there.*
Tu ne vas pas mettre le lait **dans le frigo?**	*You're not going to put the milk in the refrigerator?*
Tu ne vas pas **y** mettre le lait?	*You're not going to put the milk there?*

Note that the pronoun **y** follows the placement rules you already know for direct and indirect object pronouns: in front of a one-word verb or a command form in the negative, in back of a command form in the affirmative, in front of the infinitive in a sentence with an infinitive, and in front of the helping verb in the **passé composé.** Note the spelling change in the **tu** form of **-er** (first-conjugation) verbs and the verb **aller** when followed by **y.**

Tu **y** vas?	*Are you going (there)?*
N'**y** va pas!	*Don't go there!*
Il ne veut pas **y** aller.	*He doesn't want to go (there).*
Nous n'**y** sommes jamais allés.	*We never went (there).*
Vas-**y!**	*Go ahead! (Go there!)*

If desired, tell students *stressed pronouns* rather than *indirect object pronouns* are used with **penser à** + *person* (Je pense à Marc. Je pense à lui.).

Rappel! When the noun following the preposition **à** is a person, replace it with an indirect object pronoun. If the noun following **à** is a thing, replace it with the pronoun **y.** Compare:

Je réponds **aux questions.**	J'**y** réponds.
Je réponds **au professeur.**	Je **lui** réponds.

Vous avez compris?

A. Devinez Mais où sont-ils?

Modèle   Le livre y est.
   Le livre est sur la table.

1. Mes parents y habitent.
2. Le professeur y va souvent.
3. Je n'y vais jamais.
4. Mes clés y sont.
5. J'y suis.
6. J'y reste pendant des heures.

Act. A, 5: Point out that **j'y suis** may also mean *I've got it,* in the sense of *I understand now.*

B. Allez-y! Remplacez les mots en italique par le pronom **y**.

Modèle   Il est allé *en ville.*
          Il y est allé.

1. Je travaille toujours *dans ma chambre.*
2. Nous n'allons jamais *à la bibliothèque.*
3. Tu n'aimes pas dormir *sur la plage?*
4. Je vais *au restaurant* ce soir.
5. Elle est restée quinze jours *à Rome.*
6. Vous n'êtes pas allés *en Belgique?*
7. Je verrai mes amis *au café.*
8. Quand il avait seize ans, il habitait *au Japon.*

Continuons!

Une lettre de Jean-Pierre C'est le 20 août et Jean-Pierre vient de finir une lettre à son ami Patrick. Il lui raconte le voyage qu'Anne et lui sont en train de faire mais il a mis trop de noms. Remplacez les noms par des pronoms quand c'est nécessaire.

Cher Patrick,

Comment vas-tu? Tu as passé de bonnes vacances en Italie? Maman nous a écrit que ta sœur se mariait en octobre. Dis à ta sœur que nous sommes très contents pour ta sœur.

Tout va bien pour nous. Quel voyage, mon vieux! Nous sommes maintenant au Maroc. Nous restons quinze jours au Maroc et puis nous rentrons en Belgique par l'Espagne et la France. Anne est à la piscine, mais il faisait trop chaud à la piscine, alors je ne suis pas resté avec Anne et je suis rentré dans notre chambre. Il fait frais dans notre chambre et c'est très agréable.

J'ai adoré l'Australie et la Chine, mais Anne a préféré Tahiti. C'est parce qu'on a fait beaucoup de bateau à Tahiti. On a vu Frédéric à Chicago. Frédéric va très bien, mais Frédéric dit que Frédéric est très seul. Écris une lettre à Frédéric si tu as le temps... Je pense que Frédéric a besoin de lettres. Frédéric aime Chicago, mais Frédéric trouve que les hivers sont trop froids à Chicago. Savais-tu que la Belgique était plus petite que le lac Michigan?!

On pense rentrer à la fin de ce mois ou début septembre. On t'invitera pour te montrer les photos et les films. On a beaucoup de photos et de films!

À bientôt et bien amicalement,

⏩ Récapitulation: Les pronoms personnels

French has several kinds of personal pronouns. These pronouns are used to refer to people or things and they serve to help speakers and writers avoid repetition and link discourse across sentences. You have already studied several different kinds of pronouns. In each of the example sentences, try to explain how the pronouns both avoid repetition and ensure discourse cohesion (tie sentences and phrases together through a sort of cross-referencing).

Personal pronouns

If desired, ask students to give English equivalents of examples. These examples are simple and transparent in order to help students recognize how pronouns are used in discourse. If desired, ask students to think of other kinds of pronouns they know (e.g., relative, interrogative).

Some grammarians group **y** and **en** among the personal pronouns; others do not. We have chosen to do so here for reasons of simplicity of presentation. **Y** and **en** are not included in the table since they are invariable. You may want to ask students to review the more extensive explanations found earlier (subject pronouns, *Leçon 2;* stressed or tonic pronouns, *Leçon 5;* direct object pronouns, *Leçon 7;* indirect object pronouns, *Leçon 14;* reflexive / reciprocal pronouns, *Leçons 15* and *16).*

The use of more than one personal pronoun (double object pronouns) is treated briefly in the *Appendice de grammaire.*

- subject   Voilà Paul. **Il** vient d'arriver.
- direct object   Voilà Paul! Tu ne **l'**as pas vu?
- indirect object   Voilà Paul! Tu veux **lui** parler, non?
- reflexive   Voilà Paul. Il vient de **se** lever!
- stressed   C'est Paul? Non, ce n'est pas **lui,** c'est son frère.
- **y**   Paul va en ville? Non, il n'**y** va pas. Il rentre chez lui.
- **en**   Paul a trois frères? Non, il **en** a deux.

Here is a chart showing personal pronoun forms.

SUJET	OBJET DIRECT	OBJET INDIRECT	RÉFLÉCHIS	TONIQUES
je	me/m'	me/m'	me/m'	moi
tu	te/t'	te/t'	te/t'	toi
il	le/l'	lui	se/s'	lui
elle	la/l'	lui	se/s'	elle
nous	nous	nous	nous	nous
vous	vous	vous	vous	vous
ils	les	leur	se/s'	eux
elles	les	leur	se/s'	elles

Only stressed or tonic pronouns can stand alone, without a verb. Stressed pronouns refer to people.

> —Qui est là?
> —**Moi.**

Ask students to find the nouns that the pronouns refer to. Note that the example sentences can be read as a "story" about Monsieur and Madame Renglet from the village of Cinet. If desired, ask students to reconstruct and flesh out the story.

Subject pronouns represent the person or thing that is the subject of the verb. The subject and the verb agree with one another.

> Monsieur Renglet est de Lille.
> Madame Renglet est de Strasbourg.
> **Ils** se sont rencontrés à Paris et **ils** habitent à Cinet.

Direct object pronouns represent the person or thing that receives the action of a verb. Verbs that take direct objects in French are not followed by a preposition. Verbs that require a preposition will be found in constructions with indirect object pronouns or with the pronouns **y** or **en** (see below).

> Madame Renglet n'aime pas Monsieur Renglet... elle **le** déteste!

Indirect object pronouns are used after verbs that are followed by the preposition **à** (**parler à, répondre à, donner quelque chose à, téléphoner à,** etc.). Indirect object pronouns refer only to people.

> Quand Madame Renglet parle à Monsieur Renglet, il ne **lui** répond pas.

Reflexive pronouns are used when the subject and the object of a verb are the same person or persons. They are also used when a verb has reciprocal force.

> Pourquoi est-ce que Madame Renglet déteste Monsieur Renglet? C'est simple. Monsieur Renglet ne **s'**occupe jamais de Madame Renglet. Quand il **se** lève, il prend le petit déjeuner, il lit son journal et puis il sort. Il rentre très tard le soir et il **se** couche. Ils ne **se** parlent pas et Madame Renglet ne **s'**amuse pas!

The pronoun **y** is generally used to refer to a location or place.

> Madame Renglet décide d'aller en ville pour faire des courses. Mais quand elle **y** est, elle découvre Monsieur Renglet au café de la Poste avec Madame Renard. Alors, elle va chez le pharmacien pour **y** acheter des médicaments.

The pronoun **en** is used to refer to a quantity or to replace **de** + *noun*. It can refer to people or things.

> Le pharmacien demande à Madame Renglet pourquoi elle a besoin de ces médicaments. Ce sont des médicaments dangereux! Madame Renglet lui répond qu'elle **en** a besoin pour son mari!

The unstressed personal pronouns (subject, direct object, indirect object, reflexive, **y,** and **en**) must be accompanied by a verb form.

- **One-word conjugated verbs:** pronoun in front of conjugated verb.

> Le pharmacien regarde Madame Renglet. Madame Renglet **le** regarde aussi.

- **Conjugated verb + infinitive:** pronoun in front of infinitive.

> Madame Renglet a les médicaments qu'elle a achetés. Est-ce qu'elle va **les** donner à son mari ou est-ce qu'elle ne va pas **les** donner à son mari?

- **Auxiliary (helping) verb + past participle:** pronoun in front of helping verb.

> Madame Renglet est allée dans la cuisine. Elle **y** est allée chercher un verre d'eau pour son mari. Est-ce que Madame Renglet a mis les médicaments dans le verre ou non? Oui, elle **les** a mis dans le verre d'eau!

- **Imperative or command structures:** pronoun precedes verb in negative imperatives and follows verb in affirmative imperatives.

> —Voilà de l'eau. Bois-**en!**
> (Monsieur Renglet commence à boire.)
> —Non, non, arrête, ne **la** bois pas!

Vous avez compris?

A. Une grand-mère Trouvez et soulignez les pronoms utilisés dans ce texte. Trouvez le(s) nom(s) qu'ils représentent?

JANINE SUTTO

Tous les dimanches

Comédienne, grand-mère de Félix, trois ans, et de Sophie, un an, les enfants de sa fille Mireille Deyglun, comédienne elle aussi, et du journaliste Jean-François Lépine.

«Les brunchs du dimanche sont devenus une institution: je les passe toujours en compagnie de mes petits-enfants, Félix et Sophie. Mireille et moi avons toutes deux des horaires très chargés, mais je m'arrange pour voir les petits au moins une fois par semaine. Leur présence m'est indispensable.

Depuis que Félix sait parler, nous avons régulièrement des conversations au téléphone. Les enfants aiment qu'on leur parle, qu'on les écoute. Il me raconte sa journée, ce qu'il a appris. Il chante aussi, il adore ça. Il m'appelle "nonna", ce qui veut dire grand-maman en italien. C'est comme cela qu'on appelait ma grand-mère italienne. Je l'ai peu connue mais mon frère, de neuf ans mon aîné, m'a beaucoup parlé d'elle. Et je me souviens de ma grande tristesse lorsque j'ai dû la quitter pour venir au Canada, à l'âge de neuf ans. Ce fut une rupture difficile, douloureuse.

Je veux être très présente pour Félix et Sophie. Mais je ne les gâte pas trop. Un bonbon ou un petit jouet leur suffit; c'est la surprise qui les amuse. Je n'interviens pas dans leur éducation. Leurs parents doivent faire ça tous seuls. Mais je serai toujours là pour leur donner des conseils.»

L'Actualité

B. Un grand-père Lisez le texte et choisissez le pronom entre parenthèses qui convient dans chaque cas.

VAN DUONG NGO

Le choc des cultures

Retraité vietnamien. Onze petits-enfants. Vit avec sa fille Maï et sa petite-fille Anh, 13 ans.

« Mes petits-enfants sont éparpillés un peu partout dans le monde: en Californie, en Allemagne, en Australie et ici, au Canada. Forcément, il y a des différences culturelles entre (eux / vous / moi), mais tous parlent assez bien vietnamien pour que nous puissions communiquer.

Ma petite-fille Anh m'est la plus proche, puisque (elle / je / il) vis avec elle. Lorsque (vous / ils / nous) sommes arrivés à Montréal il y a huit ans, ma fille s'est rapidement trouvé un emploi et je (me / te / se) suis beaucoup occupé d'Anh. Je (la / l' / le) emmenais au parc, je l'accompagnais jusqu'à l'autobus d'écoliers. Nous étions toujours ensemble. Et encore aujourd'hui, c'est (lui / nous / moi) qui vais (les / le / la) chercher le soir, après ses cours de natation. Je (leur / lui / la) ai appris à lire sa langue maternelle et à jouer des instruments de musique traditionelle...

Ma relation avec mes grands-parents, au Viêt-Nam, était très différente. Par exemple, il m'était impossible de regarder mon grand-père dans les yeux, de (le / leur / lui) parler directement. Nos rapports étaient distants, très hiérarchisés. C'est beaucoup plus ouvert maintenant. Mais il y a des choses qui (me / te / le) choquent. Le fait que ma petite-fille regarde des émissions à la télévision que (moi / je / nous) peux difficilement supporter, par exemple. Je trouve ça trop permissif, trop... sexy. Je (te / se / me) considère comme plus sévère que la plupart des grands-parents québécois, qui entretiennent souvent une relation presque égalitaire avec leurs petits-enfants. »

L'Actualité

Continuons!

Et vos grands-parents? Comment sont vos rapports avec vos grands-parents? Écrivez un paragraphe pour les décrire.

Et vos grands-parents?: Do in steps. First, brainstorm with students about relationships between grandparents and grandchildren. Mine the two texts used above for expressions, ideas, and wording. Discuss possible organizations (first person narrative or description / third person narrative or description / dialogue / etc.). Have students write first drafts without looking up words or worrying too much about accuracy of language. Students work in groups (if desired, each group can choose the best draft to develop further). Final steps should include a check of appropriate pronoun usage as well as proofreading.

Découvertes culturelles: Les Français à l'étranger

▶ Les voyages à l'étranger

Act. A: Ask for details, where they go, for how long, why, etc.

A. Les voyages à l'étranger. Quel type de personnes dans votre culture voyage dans des pays étrangers? Pourquoi?

B. Les Français à l'étranger.

Act. B, 1: Have students scan the text to identify these elements. Ask each time for words that justify the answers given.

1. **Paragraphes.** Dans quel paragraphe trouvez-vous des indications sur les pourcentages de voyages faits l'été? les voyages de visite à la famille? les professions des vacanciers? les voyages des immigrés? les nouvelles destinations? les destinations les plus fréquentes? les destinations des immigrés?

Act. B, 2: Ask for justifications.

2. Vrai ou faux?

	vrai	faux	
a.	☐	☐	Les Français vont de plus en plus à l'étranger.
b.	☐	☐	Les jeunes préfèrent les voyages de visite en famille.
c.	☐	☐	15% représente le vrai taux des départs à l'étranger.
d.	☐	☐	En France, les ouvriers non qualifiés ne partent pas à l'étranger.
e.	☐	☐	40% des Français voyagent à l'étranger pour leurs vacances.
f.	☐	☐	On ne peut pas inclure 40% des séjours à l'étranger dans les statistiques parce que ce sont des voyages pour rendre visite à la famille.
g.	☐	☐	Les immigrés vont à l'étranger pour des visites touristiques.
h.	☐	☐	En été, les habitants des pays du sud voyagent vers le nord.
i.	☐	☐	On va plus en Italie qu'avant.
j.	☐	☐	Les Français abandonnent l'Espagne et le Portugal pour leurs vacances.
k.	☐	☐	La majeure partie des voyageurs qui vont en Afrique du Nord sont des touristes.
l.	☐	☐	Les immigrés qui travaillent en France rentrent chez eux pendant les vacances.
m.	☐	☐	L'Amérique du Nord est un pôle d'attraction pour la majorité des touristes français.
n.	☐	☐	Peu de touristes français vont en Slovaquie et en Hongrie.
o.	☐	☐	Depuis les changements de régime politique, les pays de l'Est attirent des touristes.

12% des Français sont partis à l'étranger au cours de l'été 1993.

Après avoir atteint un maximum de 13,4% en 1980, la proportion de Français partant à l'étranger a baissé.

Les taux les plus forts concernent les jeunes de moins de 30 ans, les Parisiens, les cadres et les patrons. La proportion très élevée parmi les ouvriers non qualifiés s'explique par les voyages d'immigrés dans leurs pays d'origine. 40% des séjours à l'étranger avaient pour but de rendre visite à des parents ou amis, de sorte que la proportion de départs à l'étranger, en dehors de ces cas, n'est que de 13% (au lieu de 21% pour l'ensemble des séjours).

70% des séjours à l'étranger ont eu lieu en Europe, dont près de la moitié dans la péninsule Ibérique.

3   La quête du soleil explique que les grands courants de migration se produisent dans le sens nord-sud. Près du tiers des séjours à l'étranger se sont déroulés en Espagne et au Portugal. On constate depuis quelques années une diminution importante de la place de l'Italie: 9% des séjours en 1993 contre 15,4% en 1979.

4   Hors d'Europe, c'est toujours l'Afrique du Nord qui reste la destination la plus fréquente, mais les chiffres sont faussés par le nombre des voyages effectués par des immigrés travaillant en France (65% des séjours).

5   Les pays plus lointains (États-Unis, Canada, Asie, Amérique latine…) concernent une minorité de vacanciers: 9% dont plus de la moitié en Amérique du Nord. L'attirance des pays de l'Est, plus accessibles depuis leur début de libéralisation, devrait se faire sentir au cours des prochaines années; ceux-ci ne représentent cependant qu'une faible proportion des séjours.

Gérard Mermet, *Francoscopie 1995*

C. Étude culturelle. Avec ce que vous avez appris sur les Français, faites ces activités.

1. **Comprendre.** Pourquoi les taux les plus forts de voyages à l'étranger concernent-t-ils les jeunes? les Parisiens? les cadres et les patrons? les ouvriers non qualifiés?

2. **Les voyages.** Pour chaque groupe dites comment ils vont voyager et ce qu'ils vont faire à votre avis.
   a. les jeunes
   c. les cadres et les patrons
   b. les Parisiens
   d. les immigrés

3. **Les immigrés.** D'après les informations du texte, faites le portrait des immigrés.

a.	origine nationale:
b.	profession et lieu de travail:
c.	style de vie:

4. **La baisse des voyages à l'étranger.**
   a. Pouvez-vous imaginer les raisons de la baisse des voyages?
   b. **Jeu de rôle.** Préparez des questions pour faire un sondage sur ces raisons. Faites ce sondage à deux: une personne fait l'enquête, l'autre prend la personnalité d'un Français décrit dans ce texte pour répondre.

Act. C, 1: Students will have to infer from information given. Have students find several reasons: money: **ils sont plus riches**, etc. education, time, escape, family, etc.

Act. C, 2: Ask for details about various trips. In what ways will these trips be alike? different?

Act. C, 3: Ask for details. Students will need to infer. Guide their guesses and provide some facts as appropriate. **Les immigrés viennent d'Algérie, du Maroc, de Tunisie et du Portugal essentiellement. Tous les salariés français ont droit à 5 semaines de congés payés. Les ouvriers ont tendance à prendre ces 5 semaines en bloc alors que les cadres les étalent sur plusieurs périodes de vacances au cours de l'année.**

Voilà!   See **Video Magazine 4:** *Les immigrés.* You may want to use the *Interview* with Maria here.

⮞ Un voyage autour du monde

A. Préparation: Les grands voyages. Quelles difficultés présentent les grands voyages? Quelles solutions avez-vous?

Modèle   PROBLÈMES   *Ils sont très chers.*
            SOLUTIONS   *Travailler pendant l'année pour avoir assez d'argent, etc.*

B. Opération Rev' d'été.

1. **Rev'Vacances, qu'est-ce que c'est ?** Regardez la première et la dernière photo et utilisez les mots de la deuxième colonne pour déterminer ce que les mots de la première colonne veulent dire.

Colonne 1	Colonne 2
6 080 F	le logement et les repas
Paris/Paris	la durée du voyage
9 jours	le nom du pays
Ch+ pt. déj.	le prix du voyage
Martinique	une carte annuelle à Rev'Vacances
Carte Fidélité	la ville de départ

2. **Qu'est-ce que Rev'Vacances offre?** À l'aide des photos et du texte, faites la liste des offres de cette organisation.

Modèle   *des prix spéciaux, une carte...*

Opération Rev' d'Été **REV'** VACANCES **50 à 100 % gratui[t]**

Partez en amoureux : pour une personne payante, la deuxième règle 50 %

ou Partez en famille : pour deux adultes payants, un enfant (–12 ans) gratuit

*De mai à octobre, avec REV'VACANCES, pour certaines destinations, à des dates définies et selon les conditions de l'OPÉRATION REV' D'ÉTÉ. Quand vous partez à 4, seules 3 personnes payent leur voyage. Quand vous partez à 2, la 2ème personne ne règle que 50% du prix du voyage. Quand vous partez en couple accompagné d'un enfant de moins de 12 ans, celui-ci bénéficie de la gratuité totale, avion compris.

MARTINIQUE 6 080 F*
9 jours Paris/Paris - Ch. + pt. déj.

L'île aux fleurs, et aux plages de rêve. Nous vous proposons un choix de 3 hôtels de classe : Novotel Diamant~~~, Sofitel Bakoua~~~~~, La Batelière~~~~~.

GUADELOUPE 6 13[0
9 jours Paris/Paris - Ch. + p[t.]

Coucher de soleil flamboya[nt] émeraude, doux alizés et [...] dans des hôtels de qualité, Novotel Fleur d'Epée~~~ Plantation Ste Marthe~~~~[~]

3. Où aller? Si vous voulez faire les choses suivantes, quel voyage choisirez-vous?

Act. B, 3: Ask students to justify their answers using the photos and the text and focusing on words they know.

a. passer mes journées sur la plage
b. vivre en petite colonie de vacanciers
c. découvrir le charme des petits hôtels locaux
d. profiter d'un climat doux et de l'air de la mer
e. apprécier le confort des grands hôtels modernes
f. faire une croisière culturelle

g. admirer des paysages magnifiques
h. passer mes soirées à regarder le soleil se coucher
i. photographier des animaux sauvages
j. parler français avec la population locale
k. passer presque deux semaines à l'étranger
l. voyager de l'autre côté de la terre

4. Conditions de voyages.

a. Trouvez toutes les expressions qui se rapportent aux avantages financiers proposés par Rev'Vacances.

b. **Des pays et des chiffres.** Écoutez les prix des voyages et dites de quel voyage on parle.

c. Vrai ou faux?

Act. B, 4b: Use to review large numbers. Say one of the costs and have students identify the country. Speak at natural speed.

Act. B, 4c: Have students correct the statements if possible.

	vrai	faux	
1.	☐	☐	Un voyageur qui fait partie d'un groupe de quatre personnes ne paie pas.
2.	☐	☐	Les enfants de 10 ans ne paient pas leur voyage s'ils sont avec leurs parents.
3.	☐	☐	Les couples paient 75% du prix du voyage.
4.	☐	☐	Ces conditions sont valables toute l'année.
5.	☐	☐	Les bébés ne paient pas l'avion.
6.	☐	☐	Si vous voyagez plus d'une fois avec Rev'Vacances, vous avez des réductions la deuxième fois.
7.	☐	☐	Il est plus avantageux de voyager à quatre adultes que de voyager avec un enfant.

KENYA 6 550 F*
9 jours Paris/Paris

Safari Kilimandjaro / Océan Indien. Visitez la magnifique réserve d'Amboseli et le Parc National de Tsavo, puis prélassez-vous à Mombasa au bord de l'Océan Indien.

ILE MAURICE 10 160 F*
10 jours Paris/Paris - 1/2 pens.

Rêve entre ciel et mer dans le dernier né des hôtels de la prestigieuse chaîne Beachcomber : Le Victoria~~~~.

REUNION 7 700 F*
10 jours Paris/Paris - Ch. + pt. déj.

Un hôtel plein de charme dans l'île à grand spectacle. Hôtel Archipel ~~~ situé dans une oasis tropicale.

Avec REV'VACANCES, vous entrez dans un monde de privilèges.

EGYPTE 5 990 F*
12 jours Paris/Paris - Pens. complète

« Tous les Trésors de la Vallée du Nil. » Une fabuleuse croisière au Pays des Pharaons. Visites, pension complète, bateau et hôtels ~~~~.

SENEGAL 4 950 F*
8 jours Paris/Paris -Demi-pens.

Entre océan et lagune, dans un domaine de 5 hectares, à 80 km au sud de Dakar, les 100 bungalows du Village Hôtel Club du Baobab sont répartis sur la belle plage de la Somone.

Dès votre 2e voyage, vous bénéficierez de facilités de paiement, des réductions fidélité et parrainage jusqu'à 4 400 F ainsi que de nombreux autres avantages.

C. Mots nouveaux. Trouvez le mot pour exprimer:

1. le point d'arrivée du voyage
2. payer (le prix du voyage)
3. voyager avec quelqu'un
4. se reposer sur une plage
5. rouge et orange comme le feu
6. le prix inclut les trois repas et la chambre d'hôtel

D. Pour mieux voyager Complétez à l'aide des mots trouvés dans l'activité C.

1. Ne descendez pas, nous ne sommes pas encore arrivés à notre ..... , nous sommes en transit dans cette gare.
2. Les vacances, ce n'est pas fait pour travailler, mais plutôt pour ..... au soleil, sur la plage, à la piscine, dans son jardin ou sur son balcon.
3. Les hôtels français offrent des séjours de vacances qui donnent les prix pour la ..... complète ou la demi ..... , si on ne prend pas le déjeuner de midi.
4. Excusez-moi, Monsieur, mais vous ne pouvez pas partir, vous n'avez pas ..... le prix de votre chambre.
5. Les Français voyagent surtout en famille, ils sont toujours .... de leurs enfants.
6. Il est impossible de ..... sur la terrasse, il y a trop de vacanciers qui occupent tous les fauteuils et font beaucoup de bruit.
7. Monsieur, apportez-moi la note, je voudrais ..... l'addition.
8. Je suis désolé, je ne peux pas vous ..... à l'aéroport, ma voiture ne marche pas.

E. Voyage dans la francophonie.

1. Où sont ces pays? Donnez les coordonnées géographiques de ces pays, et dites ce que vous savez sur eux.
2. Quels autres pays francophones connaissez-vous? Dites où ils sont d'après une carte du monde.
3. **Votre voyage francophone.** En groupe vous avez décidé de mettre en usage votre français. Vous allez organiser un voyage autour du monde, mais seulement en descendant dans des pays francophones.
   a. Choisissez votre point de départ.
   b. Dites comment vous voyagez et avec qui.
   c. Que faites-vous pour vous préparer à ce voyage?
   d. Décrivez votre itinéraire, pays par pays.
   e. Une rencontre par pays. Qui rencontrez-vous en voyage?
   f. Dites deux choses que vous ferez dans chaque pays.
   g. Dites ce que vous achèterez comme cadeau pour rapporter.
4. **Vos cartes postales.** Dans chaque pays où vous descendez, vous écrivez une carte postale pour votre professeur de français qui fait une collection. Choisissez une carte postale par pays et rédigez le texte. Parlez de ce que vous faites, de ce que vous avez vu et de qui vous avez rencontré.

Act. D: Answers: 1. destination, 2. se prélasser, 3. pension, pension, 4. réglé, 5. accompagnés, 6. se prélasser, 7. régler, 8. accompagner

Act. E, 1 & 2: Put students in pairs and have each pair select one of these countries and, with the help of a map, locate the country. Review direction words (**au nord de, au sud de,** etc.) along with prepositions with countries.

Act. E, 3: Assign as much as students can do without becoming bored. Students will need to research these countries. The Internet is useful for this.

Act. E, 3: Ask students to look at the text **12% des Français voyagent à l'étranger for details.** Students should come up with a travel philosophy: sports, comfort and relaxation, cultural exploration, etc.

Act. E, 3c: Use to review verbs: **lire des guides de voyage, apprendre une langue, consulter le Minitel, trouver des renseignements sur l'Internet,** etc.

Act. E, 3d: Ask for time frame: duration of travel, duration of stay in each country, etc.

Act. E, 3e: Refer students to the previous text to identify some French travel companions and their life styles, etc.

Act. E, 4: Review correspondance and letter-writing activities in **Leçon 14.** Briefly review past tenses since students will need them here.

www explore!
http//voila.heinle.com

Orthographe et prononciation

▶▶ Orthographe anglaise ou orthographe française?

People who know both French and English are often prone to spelling mistakes caused by the fact that many words in French have an English counterpart whose spelling differs only slightly. Here are some examples of words commonly misspelled in both French and English.

ENGLISH	FRENCH
apartment	appartement
address	adresse
terrace	terrasse
carrot	carotte
personality	personnalité
literature	littérature

Activités

A. En anglais Trouvez et corrigez *(correct)* les fautes d'orthographe *(spelling mistakes)* dans ces phrases en anglais.

1. You can't go to Japon with an enfant only a few weeks old!
2. You're not being reasonnable.
3. She has a new apartement, but I don't know her addresse.

B. En français Trouvez et corrigez les fautes d'orthographes dans ces phrases en français.

1. Philippe est une personalité de la télévision.
2. Pour maigrir, je fais des exercises et je mange des carrottes.
3. On dance sur la terrace tous les soirs.

Vocabulaire de base

TEXT TAPE:
Vocabulaire de base

Les pays et les continents (voir page 466)

NOMS

un aéroport *airport*
un appareil-photo *camera*
un autobus *bus (city)*
un autocar *bus (between cities)*
une autoroute *highway, expressway, freeway*
un avion *airplane*

des bagages *(m.pl.) luggage*
un billet (simple, aller-retour) *ticket (one-way, round-trip)*
une carte *map*
un endroit *place, spot*
une île *island*
le métro *subway*
le monde *world*

un passeport *passport*
un pays *country*
une place *seat, room, square (town)*
un quartier *neighborhood*
une route *road*
un taxi *taxi*
un ticket *ticket (bus or subway)*
un train *train*

VERBES

conduire *to drive*

découvrir (conjugué comme ouvrir) *to discover*

emporter *to take, to carry (away)*

espérer (que) *to hope*

louer *to rent*

manquer (un train, un avion) *to miss (a train, a plane)*

passer (conjugué avec être) *to go by, to stop by, to pass*

rendre visite à *to visit (a person), to pay a visit to*

traverser *to go across, to cross*

visiter *to visit (a place)*

ADJECTIFS

assis(e) *seated, sitting down*

horrible *horrible*

léger, légère *light (weight)*

lent(e) *slow*

lourd(e) *heavy*

merveilleux, merveilleuse *marvelous, wonderful*

rapide *fast*

vide *empty*

DIVERS

aller à pied *to walk*

aller en avion *to fly*

aller en vélo *to ride a bicycle*

aller en voiture *to drive*

être à l'heure *to be on time*

être à *to belong to*

être debout *to be standing (up)*

être en avance *to be early*

être en retard *to be late*

faire la connaissance de (qqn) *to meet (someone for the first time)*

faire un voyage *to take a trip*

là-bas *over there*

lentement *slowly, slow*

On verra! *We will see!*

par *by, through*

Qu'est-ce qui s'est passé? *What happened?*

vite *fast, rapidly*

COMMENT S'APPELLENT-ILS?

algérien(ne) *Algerian*

belge *Belgian*

chinois(e) *Chinese*

italien(ne) *Italian*

japonais(e) *Japanese*

marocain(e) *Moroccan*

sénégalais(e) *Senegalese*

suisse *Swiss*

Vocabulaire supplémentaire

NOMS

un caméscope *camcorder*

un camion *truck*

un chèque de voyage *traveler's check*

le climat *climate*

un compartiment *(train) compartment*

un continent *continent*

une croisière *cruise*

un départ *departure*

la douane *customs*

un douanier *customs officer*

un désert *desert*

une étape *step, stage, stop*

un guichet *ticket window*

un habitant, une habitante *native, inhabitant*

une hôtesse de l'air *stewardess*

un journal *diary*

le lendemain *the day after*

un moyen de transport *means of transportation*

un passager, une passagère *passenger*

un permis de conduire *driver's license*

une porte *gate*

un pilote *pilot*

un quai *platform*

un sac à dos *backpack*

la saison des pluies *rainy season*

un souvenir *souvenir, memory*

une station de métro *subway station*

un steward *cabin attendant, steward*

le TGV (train à grande vitesse) *very rapid French train*

la veille *the day before*

un vol *flight*

un voyage organisé *(package) tour*

ADJECTIFS

magnifique *magnificent, superb*

plein(e) *full, crowded*

quelque *few, some*

VERBES

changer (de train, d'avion...) *to change (train, planes, etc.)*

réserver *to reserve*

DIVERS

à l'étranger *abroad*

de luxe *luxurious*

en groupe *as a group*

faire de l'auto-stop *to hitchhike*

faire des économies *to save money*

faire le tour du monde *to go around the world*

faire les (ses) bagages *to pack*

faire les magasins *to go shopping*

presque *almost*

LE FRANÇAIS FAMILIER

un bus = un autobus

un car = un autocar

COMMENT S'APPELLENT-ILS?

africain(e) *African*

allemand(e) *German*

anglais(e) *British*

asiatique *Asian*

australien, australienne *Australian*

camerounais(e) *Cameroonian*

européen, européenne *European*

israélien, israélienne *Israeli*

mexicain(e) *Mexican*

russe *Russian*

tahitien(ne) *Tahitian*

LE FRANÇAIS TEL QU'ON LE PARLE

Il y a de la place? *Is there any room?*

Quelle affaire! *What a deal! What a mess! (depends on context)*

Trop tard! *Too late!*

Le Tour de France

Leçon

19

En bref

Dans cette leçon...

- La France: les régions et le patrimoine français
- Le Tour de France
- S'orienter
- Une grande ville: Strasbourg
- Souhaits et demandes: le conditionnel
- Faire des hypothèses
- Les pronoms relatifs **ce qui** et **ce que**

In this lesson...

- France: regions and the French heritage
- The Tour de France
- Directions
- Strasbourg, an important city
- Wishes and requests: the conditional
- Talking about "what if"
- The relative pronouns **ce qui** and **ce que**

---

www explore! http://voila.heinle.com	Develop writing skills with Système-D software!	Practice listening and pronunciation skills with the Text Tape!	Discover the Francophone world!	Build your skills!
INTERNET	**SYSTÈME-D**	**TEXT TAPE**	**VIDEO TAPE**	**CD-ROM**

Students have an open-ended writing activity in the **Cahier** suitable for use with **Système-D**.

Entrée en matière: Tourisme en France

Premier coup d'œil: Have students describe each photo and identify the **tourisme** expression in order to match each with its photo.
Answers: **Tourisme vert, Tourisme culturel, Tourisme sportif**

Premier coup d'œil. Regardez les photos qui illustrent cette annonce. Imaginez que vous êtes en vacances en France. Complétez.

Le type de vacances	
Photo 1	
Photo 2	
Photo 3	

Trouvez dans le texte comment les Français appellent ces trois types de vacances.

Coup d'œil sur le texte. Complétez ce tableau avec les activités proposées dans le texte.

Les activités sportives:	
Les activités culturelles:	
Les activités vertes:	

Info plus

Le salon.

A **salon** is a yearly exhibit of same-line products that have been brought together to introduce new models to merchants and the general public. Two that take place in Paris and draw large crowds are the **Salon de l'automobile** and the **Salon des arts ménagers**.

Renseignements. Qu'est-ce que l'affiche annonce? Qui a organisé cet événement? En quelle saison se passe-t-il? Combien d'heures par jour est-il ouvert? Pourquoi ne ferme-t-il pas tous les jours à la même heure?

Le salon. Est-ce qu'il y a un salon semblable chez vous? Comment avoir des renseignements supplémentaires pour aller à ce salon? À quelle condition pouvez-vous avoir ces renseignements?

En France. D'après ce que vous savez de la France, où irez-vous découvrir le tourisme sportif? le tourisme culturel? le tourisme vert? Lequel de ces tourismes préférez-vous en France? Pourquoi?

1er SALON DES VACANCES EN FRANCE

MAUCE RC LYON 327 398 222 PHOTOS A. PERIER

Le tour de France des idées vacances.

A pied, en famille, à l'hôtel, en VTT, au bord de la mer, au printemps,
en autocar, un week-end, à la montagne, entre amis, sous la tente,
en visite, en calèche, au fil de l'eau, dans un gîte, ...
300 exposants pour faire découvrir une France à votre goût,
pour choisir et préparer vos vacances... au meilleur prix.

TOURISME VERT - TOURISME CULTUREL - TOURISME SPORTIF

Pour préparer votre visite, connaître les exposants,
les nouveautés, les animations, les séjours à gagner...
tapez 36 15 VLV, comme Vive Les Vacances
(Métronome 2,23 F la minute)

Le Salon des Vacances en France

16.17.18 FÉVRIER - PARC DES EXPOSITIONS
PORTE DE VERSAILLES - PARIS

de 10h à 19h - Nocturne vendredi 16 février jusqu'à 22h.

FRANCE info 105.5

Vocabulaire

A. La France et ses régions

La France est entourée de mers et de pays. Quel(s) pays sont au nord? à l'est? au sud? à l'ouest? Comment s'appellent les mers? Où sont-elles? Quelle est la différence entre la mer et l'océan?

En France, il y a des montagnes. Comment s'appellent-elles? Où sont-elles? Quelles sont les montagnes les plus hautes? En France, il y a aussi des fleuves, comme par exemple la Seine, qui passe à Paris (c'est pourquoi il y a beaucoup de ponts à Paris). Quels autres fleuves sont indiqués sur la carte? Par quelles villes passent-ils? En France, il y a aussi, bien sûr, des forêts, des collines (plus petites que les montagnes), des rivières (plus petites que les fleuves) et des grandes plages de sable.

Regardez bien la carte. On fait du cheval en Camargue et on fait du surf sur la Côte Atlantique près de Biarritz. Qu'est-ce qu'il y a à faire sur la Côte d'Azur à votre avis (la côte entre Saint-Tropez et Nice)? Et dans les Pyrénées? Et en Normandie? Qu'est-ce qui s'est passé sur les plages de Normandie? Savez-vous en quelle année c'était?

En France, chaque région a ses spécialités. Pouvez-vous trouver où on fait du vin sur la carte? Qu'est-ce qu'on fait en Normandie? Il y a beaucoup de cathédrales partout en France. Pouvez-vous en trouver deux sur la carte? Près de la Loire, il y a aussi beaucoup de châteaux magnifiques, comme par exemple Chenonceaux, qui se trouve sur l'eau. En connaissez-vous d'autres? En Provence, il y a des monuments romains, comme par exemple le Pont du Gard. Quel monument célèbre du dix-neuvième siècle se trouve aussi sur la carte?

• Dans quelle région voulez-vous passer des vacances? Pourquoi?

Info plus

Histoire et géographie.

Until the French Revolution (1789), France was divided into 34 **provinces**. These **provinces** represented more or less natural physical divisions of France. Today France is divided into 95 **départements,** which are in turn regrouped into 22 **régions.** These **régions** are roughly identical to the old **provinces. Départements** serve administrative functions (postal codes, license plates, telephone numbers, records, elections, etc.). The **régions** serve to link the local **départements** to the central, national government.

   Although the **départements** and **régions** have officially replaced the **provinces** as administrative divisions, the French still tend to talk about their country in terms of the geographic and historical regions represented by **les provinces.**

   Each **province** has its own historical tradition and special identity. **La Normandie** (Normandy), for example, is associated with certain foods (apples, cider, calvados, butter, camembert, cream), countryside (cows in pastures, orchards, farms, beaches), architecture, traditions, and history (Vikings, the Norman Conquest, World War II).

En Normandie:

Le cimetière américain

Le Mont-Saint-Michel

Deauville

B. Le Tour de France

Tous les ans, en juillet, il y a une grande course cycliste en France qui s'appelle le Tour de France. En voilà des commentaires à la télévision.

Info plus

Le Tour de France.

The **Tour de France** presented here is imaginary and schematic. There are rest days **(jours de repos)** and the number of days differs from year to year. Racers may take the train or fly between two cities on a rest day. The **Tour de France** may also start outside France and go through neighboring countries.

A map of the 1996 **Tour de France** can be found in the *Cahier d'activités écrites et orales* and in the **Instructor's Resource Manual.**

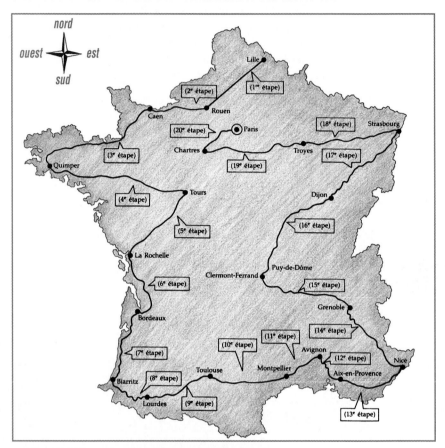

29 juin: Départ.

Et voilà, ils sont partis pour 3.250 km! Première étape: Lille-Rouen... Pays plat mais étape difficile à cause des routes... Au bord de la route, des groupes de gens regardent passer les coureurs. Aujourd'hui, il fait beau et chaud. C'est rare dans le nord, région de nuages, de ciel gris et de temps frais, même en été.

30 juin: Deuxième étape, Rouen-Caen.

C'est vraiment la campagne, la Normandie, avec ses villages, ses fermes, ses vaches, son calme...

À Caen, malgré la pluie, les habitants sont tous au centre-ville pour voir l'arrivée des coureurs.

Info plus

La campagne.

Distances between the borders of France are never more than about 800 miles. Yet within this relatively small country, the variety of landscapes, climates, and vegetation is as great as the variety of the architecture, traditions, and lifestyles embodied in each of the old provinces. Further, the French countryside still bears the mark of a long agricultural tradition, and many French feel a strong attachment to the countryside. For them, **la campagne** represents a refuge from the polluted air and the noise of modern cities. In contrast to the stress and aggravation of the city, **la campagne** offers the urban dweller picturesque, pastoral landscapes for small trips, summer homes, and weekend outings.

TRANSPARENCY:
19-3

1ᵉʳ juillet: Troisième étape, Caen-Quimper.

L'ouest: la Bretagne, avec ses forêts, sa côte et ses ports... Beaucoup d'étrangers là-bas cette année. Mais qu'est-ce qui se passe? Il y a eu un accident... Oh là là, c'est terrible! Un coureur est tombé! Non, non, ce n'est pas grave, ça va. Il a de la chance! Tant mieux!

Allez Richard! Vas-y!

7 juillet: Huitième étape, Biarritz-Lourdes...

Étape de montagne, fatigante et difficile. Il fait très lourd; il y aura peut-être des orages l'après-midi. Beaucoup de touristes dans les Pyrénées! Et voilà Richard Virenque qui passe... La foule est enthousiaste!

Richard Virenque: Richard Virenque was born in Casablanca (Morocco) in 1969. He has been part of the Tour de France since 1992, and was third in the 1996 Tour de France.

You might want to ask students if they know the only American to have won the Tour de France, Greg Lemond, who won three times (1986, 1989, and 1990).

10 juillet: Onzième étape, Montpellier-Avignon...

La Provence, terre de vacances, avec ses paysages pleins de soleil, ses platanes, ses monuments historiques... C'est le sud, où la vie est plus calme. Il n'y a pas beaucoup de monde aujourd'hui au bord des routes... Mais où sont donc les gens? Attendent-ils les coureurs à Avignon? Ou bien sont-ils tous sur les plages?

TRANSPARENCY: 19-4

Info plus

La Provence.

Platanes *(plane trees)* are found everywhere in **Provence,** where they give shade in the streets, roads, and squares. Along with the climate, the regional accent, the regional cuisine, and the game of **pétanque, platanes** are associated by the French with **Provence** and the south of France.

Le Pont du Gard

17 juillet: Seizième étape, au centre de la France...
Course contre la montre au Puy-de-Dôme! À 1.465 mètres, ce n'est pas une montagne comme dans les Alpes ou dans les Pyrénées, mais ce n'est plus vraiment une colline! Dur, dur pour les coureurs. Pour mieux voir, les gens sont sur la route, beaucoup trop près des coureurs. Dangereux, ça!

Le Puy-de-Dôme

la Cathédrale de Chartres

23 juillet: Dernière étape, Chartres-Paris...
Étape courte et très rapide. La cathédrale est déjà loin. Il y a foule sur les Champs-Élysées pour voir l'arrivée. Aujourd'hui, enfin, on saura qui va gagner!

Questions
1. Quand est-ce que les coureurs sont au nord de la France? à l'ouest? au sud? à l'est? au centre?
2. Comment est la Normandie? Où est-ce qu'elle se trouve?
3. Qu'est-ce qu'il y a en Bretagne? Où est-ce qu'elle se trouve?
4. Comment est la Provence? Où est-ce qu'elle se trouve?
5. Où se trouve le Puy-de-Dôme? Qu'est-ce que c'est?
6. Où se trouvent les Champs-Élysées?

TRANSPARENCY:
19-5

The arrival of the Tour de France takes place traditionally on the Champs-Élysées in Paris.

Notes de vocabulaire

1. Mots et expressions utiles.

à ta (votre) place	in your place, if it were me
chasser	to hunt
une étoile	star
pêcher	to fish
un zoo	zoo

2. Orientation. Note the following ways of indicating directions.

à l'est de	to the east of
à l'ouest de	to the west of
au bord de	at the side of, on the edge of, on the shore of, on the bank of
au centre de	in the center of
au nord de	to the north of
au sud de	to the south of
à 20 km de*	20 kilometers from
sur la côte	on the coast

3. Les gens. There are various ways to express the meaning of the English word *people* in French.

a. **Les gens** *(m. pl.)* = *people* in a collective, indefinite sense.

J'ai rencontré des **gens** sympathiques pendant mes vacances.	I met some nice people during my vacation.

b. **Une personne (des personnes)** = *person (people)* when referring to specific people. The word can be either singular or plural but it is always feminine, even when referring to males.

Chez les Berthier, j'ai rencontré **une personne** très sympathique.	At the Berthiers', I met a very nice person.

c. **On** = *people* or *they* in a collective, general sense.

On conduit à gauche en Australie.	People (they) drive on the left in Australia.
On dit qu'il va pleuvoir ce soir.	They say that it's going to rain this evening.

d. **Monde** *(m. sing.)* = *people* in certain idiomatic expressions. It is always masculine singular.

Il n'y a pas beaucoup de **monde.**	There aren't many people.
Il y a **du monde** sur la Côte d'Azur en été.	There are a lot of people (It's crowded) on the French Riviera in the summer.

3a: Les gens: If desired, teach **le peuple** = *people* in the sense of a social class or a nation.

3b: Une personne: Remind students that as a pronoun, **personne** means *no one*. In this case it is masculine.

3d: Monde: If desired, teach the expression **un monde fou**.

*Un kilomètre (km) = *1.609 miles;* un mètre = *approx. 1 yard (3 feet) (1 yard = 0.91 mètres)*

4. Le superlatif.
The following constructions are used to say that something or some action is the "most extreme" compared with others.

Adjectives that precede the noun	Definite article + **plus / moins** + (noun) (**de ...**) Paris est **la plus grande ville de France.** Alceste est **le moins beau de sa famille.**
Adjectives that follow the noun	Definite article+ noun + definite article + **plus / moins**+ adjective (**de ...**) C'est **la ville la plus intéressante du monde.** C'est **la personne la moins sportive du groupe.**
With verbs (as adverbs)	Verb + **le plus / le moins** C'est lui qui **travaille le plus** mais qui **gagne le moins.**
Bon	Definite article + **meilleur** + noun (**de ...**) C'est **le meilleur étudiant de la classe.**
Bien	Verb + **le mieux** (**de ...**) Vous **chantez le mieux** de la classe.

The **superlatif** is presented here for recognition and limited use. If desired, ask students to give English equivalent in order to compare how English and French encode this meaning.

D'accord?

A. Réagissez
Quelle est votre réaction? SUGGESTIONS: j'aime / je déteste / c'est agréable / ce n'est pas agréable / c'est ennuyeux / c'est intéressant / c'est horrible / c'est terrible / c'est merveilleux / c'est dangereux / ça dépend...

1. faire du surf à Biarritz
2. aller au Québec en hiver
3. passer ses vacances sur la Côte d'Azur au mois d'août
4. se promener dans une grande forêt
5. faire du cheval
6. pêcher dans une rivière
7. aller au zoo
8. s'embrasser sous les étoiles
9. chasser en Alaska
10. visiter un château du seizième siècle
11. regarder passer le Tour de France
12. être coureur cycliste

Chassez l'intrus *(gender):* (1) nuage / château / côte / étranger; (2) région / calme / étoile / forêt; (3) sable / groupe / vache / village; (4) terre / pont / foule / colline

Chassez l'intrus *(meaning):* (1) pluie / village / nuage / orage; (2) château / terre / monument / cathédrale; (3) forêt / colline / rivière / foule; (4) gens / touriste / habitant / vache; (5) pont / rivière / fleuve / étoile; (6) nord / zoo / sud / est / ouest

B. La chance
Est-ce qu'ils ont de la chance? Utilisez **il/elle a de la chance** ou **il/elle n'a pas de chance** pour réagir.

1. Candide a trouvé cent francs dans la rue.
2. Alceste a perdu son passeport.
3. La sœur de Candide va travailler comme femme de ménage dans un hôtel à Cannes cet été.
4. Alceste a fait la connaissance d'une fille à la plage pendant les vacances.
5. Candide va dans les Alpes avec sa famille cet été.

C. Qu'est-ce qui est... ? À quoi ou à qui est-ce que vous pensez quand vous entendez ces adjectifs?

Modèle merveilleux
un voyage en Afrique, le film Le Roi Lion, *l'actrice Catherine Deneuve, avoir un A en philosophie, passer ses vacances en France, regarder les étoiles la nuit...*

1. extraordinaire
2. historique
3. amusant
4. calme
5. dangereux
6. rare

D. Où se trouve... ? Ghislaine est une étudiante française dans votre université. Pendant les vacances, elle veut rendre visite à des amis qui habitent les États-Unis. Mais elle ne sait pas où se trouvent les villes où ils habitent. Dites-lui où se trouvent ces villes.

Modèle Long Beach, Californie
C'est sur la côte ouest, au sud de Los Angeles.

1. Milwaukee, Wisconsin
2. Ft. Lauderdale, Floride
3. Boulder, Colorado
4. Berkeley, Californie
5. Atlantic City, New Jersey

Act. D: Possible answers: (1) au nord des États-Unis, au nord de Chicago, au bord du lac Michigan; (2) en Floride, au sud, sur la côte est, au bord de la mer, au nord de Miami; (3) au nord et à l'ouest de Denver; (4) sur la côte ouest, à l'est de San Francisco; (5) sur la côte est, au sud de New York, au bord de l'océan...

E. Vacances! Vos amis ont passé leurs vacances dans des endroits différents et vous racontent leurs souvenirs de voyage. Où sont-ils allés? Quand? Combien de temps? Quel temps faisait-il? Qu'est-ce qu'ils ont fait là-bas? C'étaient des bonnes vacances ou pas? Pourquoi?

À Montréal

À la Guadeloupe

En Suisse

F. Des questions. À votre avis...

1. Quelle est la meilleure voiture: la Mercedes, la Cadillac ou la BMW?
2. Quelle est la moins grande ville: Paris, Lyon ou Lille?
3. Quelle est la plus belle ville: Boston, San Francisco ou Toronto?
4. Quel est l'animal le plus intelligent: le chien, le chat ou le dauphin?
5. Quel est le métier le plus dangereux: pompier, policier ou militaire?

Act. F: CONTINUATION: Quel est le métier le plus intéressant: chef d'entreprise ou médecin? Quelle est la plus belle ville du monde? Quel est le métier le plus intéressant? Quel est l'homme le plus important du monde? Quelle est la femme la plus importante du monde? Quel est le meilleur livre du monde? Quel est le meilleur film du monde?

Mise en pratique

A. Les vacances dans votre pays Comment sont les vacances dans votre pays?

1. Combien de semaines de vacances est-ce qu'on a par an?
2. Quand est-ce qu'on prend ses vacances? Où?
3. Est-ce qu'on passe ses vacances en famille? avec des copains?
4. Est-ce qu'on voyage beaucoup en voiture? en train? en avion?
5. Est-ce qu'on aime les voyages organisés quand on va à l'étranger? Est-ce que les jeunes aiment partir en vacances à l'étranger avec un sac à dos?
6. Est-ce que les jeunes vont à l'étranger pour apprendre les langues étrangères?

B. Un beau voyage Quelle chance! Vous et des amis allez faire un voyage cet été dans un pays où on parle français. Vous avez votre billet d'avion mais vous devez organiser tout le voyage. Vous partez le 24 juin et revenez le premier août. Décidez:

1. Où irez-vous?
2. Votre itinéraire. Faites une carte avec votre itinéraire *(itinerary)*.
3. Les moyens de transport. Comment allez-vous voyager?
4. Le logement. Dormirez-vous à l'hôtel? Dans des hôtels de luxe ou des petits hôtels pas chers? Ferez-vous du camping?
5. Les étapes. Combien de temps allez-vous rester à chaque étape? Qu'est-ce que vous ferez là-bas?

Act. B: May be done in groups, assigned for preparation at home, or done in class. If done in groups, you may ask each group to present their trip to the class either on a transparency or on a poster.

C. Conversation en français Racontez le meilleur voyage que vous avez jamais fait *(the best trip you ever took)*. Où? Quand? Combien de temps? Avec qui? Comment avez-vous voyagé? Qu'est-ce que vous avez fait? Donnez des détails et soyez prêts *(ready)* à répondre à des questions.

TEXT TAPE:
Conversation en français

Act. C: Have students vote for the best trip.

CD-ROM:
Build your skills!

Le conditionnel

You already know two expressions in the conditional.

| je **voudrais** | *I would like* |
| il **faudrait** | *one should* |

In general, the conditional is a French verb form that corresponds to the English *would + infinitive (he would go, we would listen).*

Formation

The **conditionnel passé** is treated briefly in the *Appendice de grammaire*.

The conditional is formed by using the infinitive as the stem and then adding the following endings: **-ais, -ais, -ait, -ions, -iez, -aient.** The final **-e** of **-re** verbs is dropped before the endings are added. Another way to look at this is to say that the conditional is formed by using the future stem plus the **imparfait** endings.

manger	
je manger**ais**	nous manger**ions**
tu manger**ais**	vous manger**iez**
il elle } manger**ait**	ils elles } manger**aient**

choisir	
je choisir**ais**	nous choisir**ions**
tu choisir**ais**	vous choisir**iez**
il elle } choisir**ait**	ils elles } choisir**aient**

vendre	
je vendr**ais**	nous vendr**ions**
tu vendr**ais**	vous vendr**iez**
il elle } vendr**ait**	ils elles } vendr**aient**

DRILL: **Candide devrait travailler.** (je / vous / les étudiants / tu / nous)

Verbs with irregular stems in the future use the same stem to form the conditional. Verbs with spelling changes in the future have identical changes in the conditional.

À ta place, je **dirais** la vérité.	*In your place (If I were you), I'd tell the truth.*
Est-ce que je **pourrais** venir te parler?	*Could I come talk to you?*
Est-ce que vous **auriez** un dollar?	*Would you have a dollar?*
J'**achèterais** ce manteau-là si j'avais l'argent.	*I'd buy that coat if I had the money.*

Usage

The conditional can be used to express wishes or requests. It lends a tone of deference or politeness that makes a request seem less abrupt. Compare the following:

Je **veux** un bonbon.	*I want a piece of candy.*
Je **voudrais** un bonbon.	*I would like a piece of candy.*
Il **faut** étudier!	*You have to study! / We have to study! / One has to study!*
Il **faudrait** étudier!	*You should study! / We should study! / One should study!*

504   *Leçon 19*

Note that the verb **pouvoir** in the conditional corresponds to the English
could + infinitive and that the verb **devoir** in the conditional corresponds to
the English *should + infinitive.*

Pouvez-vous me donner un renseignement?	*Can you give me some information?*
Pourriez-vous me donner un renseignement?	*Could you give me some information?*
Tu **dois** travailler!	*You must work!*
Tu **devrais** travailler!	*You should work!*

The conditional can also be used to express something that depends on a condition
that may or may not come true.

Si j'avais le temps, je **jouerais** au tennis.	*If I had the time, I would play tennis.*

Note that in French, you use the **imparfait** in the **si** or *if* clause, never the conditional.

Si tu **allais** à Paris, tu verrais la tour Eiffel.	*If you went to Paris, you would see the Eiffel Tower.*

Rappel! *Would* has two meanings in English. One corresponds to the French conditional, the other to the French **imparfait.** Compare these two sentences.

Quand j'étais en France, je **me levais** toujours à neuf heures.	*When I was in France, I would always get up at nine o'clock.*
(*Would* = habitual action in the past = **imparfait**)	
À votre place, je **prendrais** l'avion.	*In your place (If I were you), I would take the plane.*
(*Would* = if possible = conditional)	

Vous avez compris?

A. La politesse Voilà des situations de communication avec des suggestions. Dans
quelles circonstances est-ce qu'on utiliserait chacune *(each one)?* Laquelle est la plus
polie?

1. Demander des informations:
   a. Madame, où se trouve la banque s'il vous plaît?
   b. Pardon, Madame, pourriez-vous me dire où se trouve la banque?
   c. Et la banque?
2. Demander à quelqu'un de faire quelque chose:
   a. Passe-moi le sel s'il te plaît!
   b. Voudriez-vous me passer le sel s'il vous plaît?
   c. Auriez-vous la gentillesse de me passer le sel s'il vous plaît?
3. Demander à quelqu'un de faire quelque chose:
   a. Chut! Pas si fort!
   b. S'il vous plaît, ne parlez pas si fort!
   c. Excusez-moi, Monsieur, est-ce que vous pourriez parler un peu moins fort?
4. Demander de répéter:
   a. Répétez, s'il vous plaît.
   b. Quoi?
   c. Pourriez-vous répéter?

Act. A: Set up three categories, **à un ami / poli / très poli**, and ask students to choose in which category each statement belongs. If desired, briefly discuss the nuances involved and elicit similar nuances from students for their own native languages.

B. On est poli Utilisez **pouvoir** au conditionnel pour demander quelque chose poliment.

Modèle   M. Gaudin à Mme Gaudin / faire la cuisine ce soir
Est-ce que tu pourrais faire la cuisine ce soir?

1. Un(e) étudiant(e) à son/sa camarade de chambre / faire ton lit
2. Une patronne à une secrétaire / taper cette lettre
3. Un professeur à un(e) étudiant(e) / répondre à ma question
4. Une mère à son fils / acheter des pommes au supermarché
5. Mme Gaudin à ses enfants / attendre deux minutes

C. Complétez Complétez par le conditionnel. Puis traduisez chaque phrase en anglais idiomatique.

1. Si j'avais assez d'argent, je . . . . . (acheter) une voiture de sport.
2. Si tu avais le temps et l'argent, où est-ce que tu . . . . . (aller)?
3. Si nous étions malades, nous . . . . . (ne pas être) en classe.
4. Si vous travailliez, vous . . . . . (ne pas avoir) de problème avec ces exercices.
5. S'ils gagnaient le match, ils . . . . . (être) heureux.
6. Tu . . . . . (arriver) à l'heure si tu partais plus tôt.
7. S'il t'aimait, il te le . . . . . (dire).

Continuons!

Imaginez Qu'est-ce que vous feriez dans chaque cas?

1. Si j'avais faim à minuit, je...
2. Si mon ami(e) était malade, je...
3. Si j'habitais à New York, je...
4. Si j'invitais un(e) ami(e) à dîner, je...
5. Si j'allais en France, je...
6. Si je gagnais un million à la loterie, je...
7. Si je perdais mon passeport à Marseille, je...
8. Si je manquais mon avion, je...

➤➤ Les phrases avec *si*

Use **si** to talk about "what if," to make suggestions, or to express a wish.

a. **If...** To talk about what will probably happen if a certain condition is fulfilled, use **si** with a verb in the present tense (**si tu veux**) followed by a clause with a verb in the future (**je le ferai**). Note that **si** can be either in the first or second part of the sentence (the first or second clause).

S'il **fait** beau demain, il y **aura** beaucoup de monde à la plage.
Nous **mangerons** dans le jardin s'il ne **pleut** pas.

If it's nice out tomorrow, there'll be a lot of people at the beach.
We'll eat in the yard if it doesn't rain.

To talk about *what might happen if,* use **si** with a verb in the **imparfait** followed by a clause with a verb in the **conditionnel.** Again, **si + imparfait** may be in either clause.

Si j'avais assez d'argent, j'**achèterais** ce livre.	*If I had enough money, I'd buy that book.*
Tu ne **serais** pas si fatigué **si** tu ne **sortais** pas le soir.	*You wouldn't be so tired if you didn't go out at night.*

Remind students that the verb in the **si** clause must be in the **présent** or the **imparfait**.

TABLEAU RÉCAPITULATIF	
si CLAUSE	RESULT CLAUSE
présent	futur
imparfait	conditionnel

b. **Pour suggérer.** Use **si + imparfait** to suggest a course of action.

—J'ai faim.	*"I'm hungry."*
—Moi aussi. **Si** on **allait** au restaurant?	*"Me, too. How about going out to dinner?"*
—D'accord.	*"OK."*

c. **Pour exprimer un souhait ou un regret.** Use **si + imparfait** to express a wish or regret.

—Ah! Si nous **étions** riches!	*"If only we were rich!"*
—Tu rêves! On ne sera jamais riche!	*"You're dreaming. We'll never be rich!"*

Vous avez compris?

A. Dans la foule Voilà ce qu'on a entendu au Tour de France cette année. Utilisez le présent et le futur pour faire des phrases complètes.

Modèle   si / tu / avoir soif / je / aller chercher / quelque chose à boire
  Si tu as soif, j'irai chercher quelque chose à boire.

1. si / ils / ne pas faire attention / il y a / un accident
2. je / ne pas avoir / mon parapluie. // Si / il / commencer à / pleuvoir / je / rentrer
3. Virenque / gagner / si / il / continuer / comme ça
4. il y avoir / un accident / si / cet enfant / rester / si près de la route

B. Faites des suggestions Alceste a des problèmes et Candide voudrait l'aider. Jouez le rôle de Candide et faites des suggestions à Alceste.

Modèle   ALCESTE: J'ai soif.
  CANDIDE: ***Si on allait au café? Si tu buvais de l'eau?***

1. J'ai faim.
2. Je suis fatigué.
3. Je m'ennuie.
4. Je ne veux pas travailler.

Continuons!

A. Faire des phrases
Faites des phrases logiques avec les éléments des deux colonnes.

Modèle   *Si j'étais riche, j'achèterais une voiture.*

1. avoir le temps
2. être fatigué
3. avoir des vacances
4. être le professeur
5. avoir faim
6. être riche
7. dormir mal

a. me coucher
b. acheter une voiture
c. donner des A
d. faire du sport
e. regarder la télévision
f. aller en Australie
g. prendre quelque chose

B. La vie serait belle!
Tout le monde a des problèmes, et vous, vous voulez aider tout le monde. Faites des suggestions à chacun *(to each one)*.

Modèle   —Ma fille est paresseuse.
   —*Alors, si elle travaillait?!*

1. —Je suis pauvre.
2. —Mon camarade de chambre est toujours pessimiste.
3. —Je n'ai pas de voiture.
4. —Je n'ai pas d'amis.
5. —Nous travaillons tout le temps.
6. —Nous n'avons pas de vacances.

C. La vie est belle!
Imaginez que les personnes suivantes obtiennent *(get)* ce qu'elles veulent. Quelles pourraient être les conséquences? Qu'est-ce qu'elles pourraient faire?

Modèle   PATRICK: Oh, si j'avais une voiture... ou un vélo.
   Si Patrick avait une voiture ou un vélo, il pourrait arriver à l'université à l'heure!

1. CARINE: Si j'avais un petit ami!
2. DAVID: Si j'étais grand... et beau!
3. VALÉRIE: Si j'avais deux mois de vacances!
4. CHRISTOPHE: Si j'étais sportif!

➤ Les pronoms relatifs *ce qui* et *ce que*

The relative pronouns **dont** and **ce dont** are treated briefly in the *Appendice de grammaire*.

The relative pronouns **ce qui** and **ce que** are the equivalent of the English *what* in sentences such as *I don't know what happened* or *I don't know what you want*.

Ce qui functions as the subject of its clause (part of the sentence).

Je ne sais pas **ce qui** s'est passé.	*I don't know what happened.*

Ce que functions as the direct object of its clause.

Je ne comprends pas **ce que** tu veux.	*I don't understand what you want.*

The word **tout** can be placed in front of both **ce qui** and **ce que**.

J'aime **tout ce qui** est beau.	*I like everything (that is) beautiful.*
Je vais te dire **tout ce que** je sais.	*I'm going to tell you everything (all) that I know.*

Rappel! The word *what* has three possible equivalents in French.
The one used depends on the function of *what* in the sentence.

1. *What* = interrogative adjective. Use **quel.**

   Quel homme?   *What man?*
   Quelle est la date?   *What's the date?*

2. *What* = interrogative pronoun. Use **qu'est-ce qui** *(subject)* or **qu'est-ce que** *(direct object).*

   Qu'est-ce qui se passe?   *What's going on?*
   Qu'est-ce que tu veux?   *What do you want?*

3. *What* = relative pronoun. Use **ce qui** *(subject)* or **ce que** *(direct object).*

   Je ne sais pas **ce qui** se passe.   *I don't know what's going on.*
   Tu ne comprends pas **ce que**   *You don't understand what I mean?*
   je veux dire?

Vous avez compris?

A. Ce qui ou ce que? Complétez par **ce qui** ou **ce que.**

—Tu ne sais pas ..... s'est passé?
—Non, j'étais à la bibliothèque et tout ..... je sais, c'est que j'ai trois examens et...
—Ah, oui, c'est terrible, ça. Mais ..... s'est passé ici, c'est qu'il y a eu un orage et
on n'a pas eu d'électricité pendant trois heures! Nous nous sommes bien amusés!
Tu veux savoir ..... on a fait?
—Non, non et non! Je ne veux pas savoir ..... vous avez fait!
—Bon, si c'est comme ça, tout ..... je vais te dire, c'est que tu dois regarder .....
se trouve dans ton lit et...

B. Quel, qu'est-ce qui, qu'est-ce que, ce qui ou ce que? Complétez avec **quel, qu'est-ce qui, qu'est-ce que, ce qui** ou **ce que.**

1. ..... est bon?
2. ..... pays avez-vous visités?
3. ..... tu as dit?
4. Je n'aime pas ..... tu as fait!
5. Est-ce que tu sais ..... se trouve dans la boîte?

Act. B: Brainstorm first with students, then ask individuals for their opinions.

Continuons!

A. Réactions Qu'est-ce qui...

Modèle ... vous amuse?
   Ce qui m'amuse: sortir avec des amis, etc.

1. ... vous amuse?
2. ... vous endort?
3. ... vous ennuie?
4. ... vous énerve?

Act. A: Do this activity as lists. If complete sentences are desired, tell students that a *de* is needed (Ce qui m'amuse, c'est *de* sortir avec des amis).

B. Goûts et obligations Et les autres? Complétez les phrases.

1. Ce que le professeur doit faire, c'est...
2. Ce que les étudiants aiment faire, c'est...
3. Ce que mes amis détestent faire, c'est...

Découvertes culturelles: Le patrimoine français

▶ Les sites touristiques en France

SI VOUS AVEZ PEU DE TEMPS, JE VOUS CONSEILLE DE COMMEN- CER PAR BEAUBOURG. VERSAILLES, C'EST CONSTRUIT POUR DURER.

A. Si vous avez peu de temps.

1. **Des gens.** Qui sont ces personnes? Qui parle? De quelle nationalité est-il? Comment le savez-vous? Et les deux autres personnes? Que font-elles? D'où viennent-elles? Décrivez-les.
2. **Une ville.** Où se passe cette scène? Comment le savez-vous?
3. **Pour rire un peu!** Quel est l'élément comique du texte? du dessin? De qui et de quoi le dessinateur se moque-t-il *(make fun)*?

B. Vos connaissances culturelles. Nommez tous les monuments présentés sur ces images et dites où ils se trouvent sur la carte de France à l'aide des points cardinaux (le nord, le sud, l'est, l'ouest) et des régions que vous connaissez (en Provence, etc.).

Act. B: Do this as a game. Starting with the Eiffel Tower, number the monuments clockwise. Divide the class into two groups and ask groups to nominate a team reporter. Give students the number of points for each monument. Teams take turn identifying monuments and attempting to identify them. Here are the numbers and suggested points (based on familiarity to most students) for each monument: 1. Tour Eiffel (1 point); 2. Beaubourg (3 points) 3. Notre-Dame (2 points) 4. Le Louvre (2 points) 5. Mont Blanc (4 points) 6. Saint-Tropez (3 points) 7. Chenonceaux (3 points) 8. Fontainebleau (5 points) 9. Mont St-Michel (2 points) 10. Palais du Luxembourg (5 points). After the game, refer students to the map of France, page 494 and the map of Paris, page 68.

CE QU'ILS VISITENT LE PLUS CHEZ NOUS

PAR JEAN CREISER

La France, terre bénie du tourisme? C'est toujours une évidence pour les voyageurs étrangers qui visitent notre pays. Mais cela ne semble pas l'être encore pour les Français eux mêmes qui font toujours trop peu d'efforts pour comprendre ou aider leurs hôtes. Conclusion: les étrangers aiment bien la France... mais parfois un peu moins les Français. La France reste pourtant la destination touristique préférée de la plupart de nos voisins européens: les Anglais, les Belges, les Hollandais, les Italiens, les Espagnols... C'est la quatrième destination des Allemands après l'Italie, l'Espagne et l'Autriche et la cinquième des Américains. Que recherchent chez nous les touristes étrangers? C'est souvent, tout simplement, le soleil et la mer, surtout pour les peuples du Nord. Mais c'est aussi notre art de vivre, notre culture, notre cuisine, notre patrimoine historique et artistique. C'est tout cela que reflètent assez bien les dix sites et monuments français que préfèrent nos hôtes.

C. Qui sont «ils»?

1. Trouvez dans le texte toutes les expressions qui se rapportent *(refer)* au «ils» du titre.
2. Étudiez leurs destinations et les raisons de leur voyage. Où vont-ils? Que vont-ils visiter? Pourquoi viennent-ils en France?
3. Trouvez les expressions qui se rapportent *(refer)* aux sentiments positifs et négatifs des étrangers pour la France et pour les Français.

D. Un Tour de France culturel.

1. **Identification.** Quels dessins représentent des sites célèbres? Quels sites sont naturels? Quels sites ont un élément culturel? Lequel?
2. **Comparaisons.** Quel type de site est plus fréquent chez vous: les sites géographiques ou les sites à élément culturel? Et en France? Pourquoi?
3. **Choix et décisions.** Pourquoi les étrangers choisissent-ils ces monuments?

E. Patrimoine et tourisme.
Le patrimoine, c'est la richesse d'un pays, passé de génération en génération.

1. Regardez la carte de France. Qu'est-ce que vous observez sur la distribution des monuments les plus visités? Expliquez cette distribution des sites de visite.

2. **Une visite chez le Ministre du Tourisme.** Vous allez rencontrer Madame le Ministre pour l'interroger sur la valeur économique du patrimoine français. Référez-vous au texte et préparez six questions sur un des thèmes suivants:
   - le tourisme dans l'économie nationale
   - les infrastructures pour les touristes
   - les problèmes à l'arrivée des touristes étrangers
   - les incitations à mieux recevoir *(welcome)* les touristes étrangers
   - le tourisme des Français en France (saison, dates)

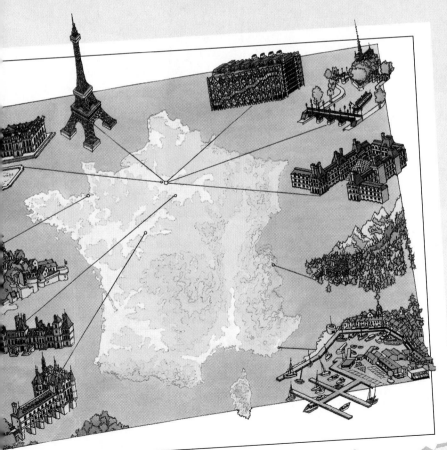

Figaro Magazine

➤ Une grande ville: Strasbourg

A. Où est Strasbourg?

1. **En France.** Quelles sont les indications sur cette page de guide pour trouver Strasbourg sur la carte de France? Qu'est-ce que le paragraphe d'introduction vous apprend sur la situation géographique de Strasbourg? Soulignez dans le paragraphe d'introduction les références géographiques, historiques, touristiques, religieuses et architecturales.

2. **La ville.** Où trouvez-vous des renseignements sur la ville elle-même? Quels sont ces renseignements? Pour qui sont-ils notés?

B. Le plan.

1. **La ville.** D'après ce plan, quelle sorte de ville est Strasbourg? Décrivez-la. Quels types d'installations offre-t-elle? Où? Pour qui ce plan a-t-il été préparé?

2. **Les rues.** Comment sont les rues? Organisez les rues selon leurs noms. Pourquoi ces noms? Quels noms sont célèbres? Quels noms sont traditionnels? Quelle date de l'histoire ces noms évoquent-ils? Quelles personnes célèbres?

3. **Les monuments.** Trouvez sur la carte les monuments représentés par des photos. Identifiez leur adresse. Quels monuments ont un paragraphe descriptif? Pourquoi?

Act. A, 1: **Le Nord et l'Est** refers to **les Régions,** current French administrative subdivisions. **Lorraine et Alsace** refers to the **provinces,** a reference to pre-revolutionary subdivisons. **Provinces** have their own culture, languages, traditions, etc. and are still felt to be legitimate, if not official, regions of France.

Strasbourg ⑯

À mi-chemin entre Paris et Prague, Strasbourg mérite bien son surnom de « carrefour de l'Europe » ; et, en 1977, la capitale de l'Alsace a affirmé sans complexe sa vocation internationale en construisant le très moderne Palais de l'Europe, siège du Parlement européen, à proximité immédiate de son centre historique. Un des moyens pour découvrir la capitale de l'Alsace est d'effectuer une promenade en bateau, au départ du palais Rohan. Vous verrez les ponts couverts et leurs tours de guets médiévales qui gardent toujours l'accès des quatre canaux de la Petite France, l'ancien quartier des tanneurs aux quais bordés de moulins et de maisons à colombage et à encorbellements, qui s'étend presque jusqu'à l'église Saint-Thomas, la « cathédrale des protestants », où se trouve le fameux mausolée du maréchal de Saxe.

Statue de la cathédrale

Bateau-promenade sur le canal *Parking*

Le portail central de la façade occidentale de la cathédrale

🔒 **Cathédrale Notre-Dame**
La construction de ce magnifique édifice de grès rose des Vosges, commencée en 1015, ne se termina qu'en 1439 par l'achèvement de sa façade occidentale aux portails ornés, sous la rosace délicate, de nombreuses sculptures. Notamment, le portail de droite est flanqué dans les embrasures des statues des Vierges sages et des Vierges folles.

Le portail latéral sud, consacré à la Vierge, est encadré des étonnantes figures de l'Église et la Synagogue ; à l'intérieur du transept, le pilier des Anges, chef-d'œuvre gothique, se trouve près de l'horloge astronomique qui, tous les jours à 12 h 30, fait mouvoir le défilé de ses automates sur la musique d'un carillon. Autres spectacles : depuis la plate-forme panoramique de la tour, la vue sur la ville, la Forêt-Noire et les Vosges ; et, le soir, le son et lumière en allemand et en français.

La place de la cathédrale est entourée de belles demeures, comme la pharmacie du Cerf (12 maison Kammerzell (1 1589) aux façades rich sculptées.

🏛 **Musée de l'Œuvr Notre-Dame**
3, place du Château. **⚡** &
Ouv. t.l.j. **Fermé** 1er janv., 1er mai, 1er nov., 25 déc. 🔞
Ses collections retrac moyen de document sculptures déposées de la cathédrale et o d'orfèvrerie, l'histoir de la cathédrale du x

Palais de l'Europe se dresse à proximité du centre de la ville

MODE D'EMPLOI

Bas-Rhin. 🚶 250 000. ✈ 12 km
au sud-ouest de Strasbourg. 🚌
place de la Gare (88 22 50 50).
place des Halles (88 77 70 09). 🛈
17, place de la Cathédrale (88 52
28 28). 🚇 du lun. au sam. 🎭
Festival de musique classique (juin) ;
festival de jazz (juil.) ; Musica,
festival de musique contemporaine
(de mi-sept. à déb. oct.).

ce grand palais classique abrite
trois musées : archéologique,
Beaux-Arts, Arts décoratifs.
Les Grands Appartements
comportent une luxueuse
décoration rocaille et un
riche mobilier. Dans l'aile
des Écuries est exposée
l'une des plus belles
collections de faïences et
de porcelaines de France.
Non loin, dans
l'Ancienne Douane, le
musée d'Art moderne
présente des œuvres
de l'impressionnisme
à nos jours.

🏛 Musée historique
3, place de la Grande Boucherie.
📞 88 52 50 00. **Fermé** pour
restauration jusqu'au printemps
1995. 📷 ♿
Dans la Grande Boucherie du
XVIe siècle, est évoqué le passé
militaire, économique et
politique de la ville.

🏛 Musée alsacien
23, quai St-Nicolas. 📞 88 35 55 36.
Ouv. du mer. au lun. **Fermé** 1er janv,
Ven. Saint, 1er mai, 1er nov, 25 déc. 📷
Dans trois maisons des XVIIe et
XVIIIe siècles, il retrace l'histoire
des arts populaires de la
région, notamment par des
reconstitutions d'intérieurs.

au
XVIIe siècle.
Une exposition
présente, en outre,
des peintures alsaciennes
du Moyen Âge
et de la Renaissance.

🏛 Palais Rohan
2, pl du Château. 📞 88 52 50 00. **Ouv.**
du mer. au lun. **Musée d'Art moderne**,
5, rue du Château **ouv.** t.l.j. **Musées
fermés** 1er janv., Ven. Saint, 1er mai, 1er
et 11 nov, 25 déc. 📷 ♿
Dessiné en 1730 par le premier
architecte du roi, Robert de
Cotte, pour les cardinaux-
princes-évêques de Strasbourg,

STRASBOURG : LE CENTRE VILLE

Cathédrale Notre-Dame ④
Maison Kammerzell ③
Musée alsacien ⑦
Musée de l'Œuvre
  de Notre-Dame ⑤
Palais Rohan ⑥
Petite France ②
Ponts couverts ①

0   250 m

LÉGENDE

🚏 Embarcadère

🅿 Parc de stationnement

🛈 Information touristique

✝ Église

**Les ponts couverts et leurs tours
médiévales**

---

4. **Les références.** Dans chaque
texte, trouvez les références
architecturales, historiques,
artistiques et religieuses. Où
aller...
   - pour trouver des objets
     traditionnels alsaciens?
   - pour voir des objets sacrés et
     précieux?
   - pour voir des peintures
     impressionnistes?
   - pour voir des chambres et des
     cuisines typiquement
     alsaciennes?
   - pour avoir une vue sur la ville
     et la campagne alsacienne?
   - pour voir le mausolée du
     Maréchal de Saxe?
   - pour voir des assiettes et des
     plats français anciens?
   - pour voir des sculptures
     religieuses?
5. **Strasbourg, patrimoine
   français.** Cherchez dans le texte
   tous les mots qui insistent sur la
   valeur de Strasbourg. Quelle est
   leur connotation?

Voilà! See **Video Magazine 6**

Guides Voir: France

Act. C: If desired, assign students to research and present French cities other than Strasbourg.

Act. C, 1: This can be done in small groups. Refer students to the Heinle & Heinle WWW page for supplementary information on Strasbourg. Have students prepare a written report in the form of a schedule.
LISTENING COMPREHENSION ACTIVITY: Choose a starting point and describe a possible itinerary that would allow someone to visit certain monuments and sites. Ask students to note the monuments on the itinerary. ALTERNATIVE: Provide students with beginning and end points and have them give you a possible route.

Act. C, 2: You may want to have different groups of students select different cities in France if they have access to tools to do research: guide books, the Internet, etc.
Review formulas for official letters. Refer students to **Leçon 14.**

Act. C, 2b: Could be judged by a jury of students who will decide the best guide/visit.

Act. D: Students can either select a French city in groups of two and share the research and the report, or all can select the same city and divide the research topics. The report can take the form of a tour offering, a one-day visit using illustrations, etc. When students are done, you may want to ask them to compare their city to Strasbourg.

C. Visite de Strasbourg. Vous êtes de passage à Strasbourg.

1. Préparez une visite intéressante et donnez un horaire détaillé de cette visite.

La durée de votre visite (un, deux ou trois jours)?
Où allez-vous?
Qu'est-ce que vous allez visiter?
Qu'est-ce que vous allez faire?
Pendant combien de temps?
Dans quel ordre?

2. Vous avez envie de passer l'été à Strasbourg comme guide pour les touristes anglophones.
   a. Écrivez au directeur du Syndicat d'Initiative pour lui proposer vos services. Mettez un curriculum vitae dans votre lettre.
   b. Présentez oralement votre programme de visite, avec tout ce que vous avez projeté (explications des sites que vous visiterez, pauses, etc.) pour votre interview avec le directeur.

D. Villes et tourisme. Choisissez une ville française que vous aimeriez visiter. Préparez des recherches sur cette ville. Utilisez le www aussi. Trouvez:

- ses données démographiques
- son histoire
- sa région
- ses monuments
- ses hommes et femmes célèbres
- son économie
- son rôle administratif
- ses infrastructures

Présentez votre ville à vos camarades.

www explore!
http//voila.heinle.com

Orthographe et prononciation

▶▶ Mots apparentés

Many French and English words are similar in spelling and meaning. These are called *cognates* in English, **mots apparentés** in French.

1. French **-té** becomes English *-ty:*

   université   universi*ty*
   socié**té**   socie*ty*

2. French **-re** becomes English *-er:*

   théâ**tre**   theat*er*
   memb**re**   memb*er*

3. French **-iste** becomes English *-istic:*

   optim**iste**   optim*istic*
   réal**iste**   real*istic*

4. French **-ique** becomes English *-ical:*

   log**ique**   log*ical*
   phys**ique**   phys*ical*

Activité

Trouvez l'anglais Trouvez le mot anglais apparenté au mot français.

1. beauté
2. historique
3. pessimiste
4. nécessité
5. octobre
6. comique
7. liberté
8. égalité
9. fraternité
10. idéaliste
11. centre
12. cynique

Vocabulaire de base

 **TEXT TAPE:**
Vocabulaire de base

NOMS

l'arrivée *(f.)* *arrival*
le calme *calm, peace and quiet*
le centre *center*
le centre-ville *downtown*
un château, des châteaux *castle, mansion*
une colline *hill*
la côte *coast*
le départ *departure*
l'est *(m.)* *east*
une étoile *star*
un étranger, une étrangère *foreigner, stranger*
un fleuve *river (major)*

une forêt *forest*
une foule *crowd*
les gens *(m. pl.)* *people*
un groupe *group*
un(e) habitant(e) *native, inhabitant*
le nord *north*
un nuage *cloud*
l'ouest *(m.)* *west*
un pont *bridge*
une région *region, area*
le sable *sand*
le sud *south*
la terre *earth, ground*
un(e) touriste *tourist*
une vache *cow*

ADJECTIFS

plat(e) *flat*
terrible *terrible*

VERBES

se trouver *to be located*

DIVERS

à ta (votre) place *in your place, if it were me*
au bord de *at the side of, on the edge of, on the shore of, on the bank of*
avoir de la chance *to be lucky*

Vocabulaire supplémentaire

NOMS

un accident *accident*
les Alpes *(f. pl.)* *the Alps*
la Bretagne *Brittany*
une cathédrale *cathedral*
les Champs-Élysées *Champs-Élysées (main street in Paris)*
un commentaire *comment, remark*
la Côte d'Azur *French Riviera*
un coureur (cycliste) *cyclist*
une course (cycliste) *race (bicycle)*
un kilomètre (km) *kilometer*
un mètre *meter*
un monument *monument*
la Normandie *Normandy*
l'océan *(m.)* *ocean*
un orage *thunderstorm*
un paysage *landscape, scenery*
une spécialité *speciality*
un platane *plane tree*
un port *port*
la Provence *Provence (south of France)*

les Pyrénées *(f. pl.)* *Pyrenees*
une rivière *river, stream*
un siècle *century*
un zoo *zoo*

ADJECTIFS

historique *historical*
rare *rare*
romain(e) *Roman*

VERBES

chasser *to hunt*
indiquer *to indicate*
pêcher *to fish*

DIVERS

chaque *each*
contre la montre *against the clock, timed race*
être entouré(e) (de) *to be surrounded (by)*

être indiqué(e) *to be indicated*
faire du cheval *to go horseback riding*
faire du surf *to go surfing*
il y a beaucoup de monde *there are a lot of people, it's crowded*
malgré *in spite of, despite*
Qu'est-ce qu'il y a à faire? *What is there to do?*

LE FRANÇAIS TEL QU'ON LE PARLE

Tant mieux! *So much the better! Good!*

LE FRANÇAIS FAMILIER

terrible *terrific*
avoir de la veine = avoir de la chance

ON ENTEND PARFOIS

un morne (Antilles) = une colline
le temps bleu (Louisiane) = un orage

Leçon 20

Le bonheur, qu'est-ce que c'est?

En bref

Dans cette leçon...

- Le bonheur, qu'est-ce que c'est? Différents points de vue
- La politique et les problèmes sociaux
- La vie, ses plaisirs et ses problèmes
- Idées, émotions et points de vue: le subjonctif
- Les valeurs des jeunes

In this lesson...

- What it means to be happy: various viewpoints
- Politics and social problems
- Life, its pleasures and problems
- Ideas, emotions, and points of view: the subjunctive
- Values among young people

517

DOSSIER

Une grande enquête "le Nouvel Observateur"-Sofres

*Pourquoi 88%
des Français se déclarent*

HEUREUX

PAR JOSETTE ALIA

Comment le bonheur de chacun peut-il résister? Crise et chômage au-dedans, guerre et fanatisme au-dehors: les nuages sont noirs. Et pourtant, la joie de vivre n'a pas disparu. Nous l'avions testée en 1973, puis en 1983. Nous venons de refaire l'enquête.

Qui n'est pas inquiet? La crise est là. La Bosnie agonise. Le sida sera la peste du troisième millénaire. La croissance ne crée plus d'emplois. La couche d'ozone est trouée. L'islamisme tue. La purification ethnique se poursuit. Les saisons elles-mêmes ne sont plus ce qu'elles étaient. Pourtant, réfléchissez. Ou plutôt ne réfléchissez pas. Fermez les yeux, posez-vous la question: suis-je heureux? Comme neuf Français sur dix, vous répondrez oui. Mais sans oser le dire trop fort, et avec un arrière-goût amer dans la bouche. N'y a-t-il pas quelque impudence à se reconnaître heureux aujourd'hui?

Bonheur frileux, bonheur minimaliste, bonheur en creux. Bonheur quand même.

Le Nouvel Observateur

Une photo: If students have difficulty, help them out with the following: C'est une onde intérieure, la famille est comme un cocon, comme un bain de vie, mais intérieur. La réalité est extérieure, on la fuit, on n'y vit pas.

Une photo. Que font-ils? C'est quelle saison? Où sont-ils? Pourquoi sont-ils dans l'eau? Qu'est-ce qu'ils portent?

Est-ce que le photographe les a placés intentionnellement dans l'eau? Est-ce que c'est un endroit symbolique? Pourquoi ne sont-ils pas à l'air libre, à l'extérieur? Pourquoi sont-ils ensemble?

Heureux! Ces gens sont-ils heureux? Pourquoi sont-ils heureux? Est-il naturel d'être heureux pour ces trois Français? Pour eux, qu'est-ce que c'est le bonheur?

Les mots. Soulignez les mots associés au bonheur, puis soulignez les mots opposés au bonheur.

See **Video Magazine V:** *Éditorial: Qu'est-ce que le bonheur?*

Le texte. Comment le bonheur peut-il résister? Qu'est-ce qui s'oppose au bonheur selon l'auteur de cet article? À quels phénomènes et à quels événements du monde contemporain pensez-vous avec les mots **crise, chômage, guerre, fanatisme?** Quels sont les nuages noirs qui dominent vos journées? et celles des Français? Comment l'auteur de cet article définit-elle le bonheur des Français? Par rapport à quoi? Sur quelles bases ses définitions du bonheur sont-elles construites?

Le texte: Explain the meaning of **guerre: C'est quand des pays ou des peuples ne s'entendent pas et utilisent des armes les uns contre les autres.**

Et vous? Êtes-vous heureux? Quand? Pourquoi? Et les gens de votre pays, sont-ils heureux? Qu'est-ce qui s'oppose au bonheur dans votre pays? Qu'est-ce que c'est, le bonheur, dans votre pays? Quelle photo pourrait illustrer ce bonheur dans votre culture?

Le bonheur. Est-il naturel d'être heureux? Qu'est-ce qui fait le bonheur? Et où est le bonheur, en moi ou extérieur à moi? Est-ce que le bonheur change de définition suivant les époques historiques? Le bonheur est-il possible dans la vie contemporaine? Qu'est-ce que ce sondage va révéler?

519

Vocabulaire

Ask students to describe what is going on in each picture.

TRANSPARENCY:
20-1

Chaque personne a une opinion différente sur le bonheur. Voilà ce que pensent quelques membres de la famille Dubois.

A. Vincent Dubois

C'est un optimiste qui aime profiter de la vie. Il a beaucoup d'amis et il adore sortir. Ses activités préférées? Manger, boire et bavarder. Il apprécie beaucoup l'argent, le confort matériel et les voitures. Il est donc assez matérialiste. Son grand rêve? Prendre la retraite à cinquante-cinq ans. Les grands problèmes du monde ne l'intéressent pas. Il ne s'occupe pas de politique et il se méfie des gens qui en font, mais il est pour l'ordre et l'autorité. Il dit qu'il est contre le racisme et l'intolérance, mais il pense qu'il y a un problème d'immigration en France et il se méfie des étrangers. À son avis, il y aurait sûrement moins de chômage, de pauvreté, de drogue et de terrorisme si la police était plus sévère avec les immigrés. Pour lui, le bonheur, c'est les sorties, les loisirs, l'amitié et l'argent.

B. Thérèse Dubois

Ce qui est important pour elle, c'est la vie privée. Elle est individualiste et très indépendante, mais elle a quelques amis qu'elle voit souvent. Elle est assez pessimiste et elle est toujours inquiète pour ses enfants et pour Vincent. Elle a peur de la violence, des accidents de voiture, des maladies, surtout du cancer et du sida, et bien sûr de la mort. Comme Vincent, elle ne s'intéresse pas aux grands problèmes sociaux actuels sauf quand ils concernent sa vie personnelle. Pour elle, le bonheur, c'est sa famille, son travail, les voyages et les vacances.

C. Jacques Dubois

Il a besoin de sécurité et il n'aime pas les changements. Il vit dans une maison agréable au sud de la France et il n'a pas de soucis financiers. Il déteste la solitude et il a beaucoup souffert de la mort de sa femme avant de rencontrer Paulette. Ses passe-temps préférés? Faire du jardinage, faire du bricolage et faire de la musique avec Paulette. C'est un réaliste qui n'a pas beaucoup d'illusions. Il est conscient des problèmes du monde et il sait que la vie peut être injuste, mais il pense qu'il ne peut rien faire pour aider. La spiritualité est importante pour lui et il croit en Dieu, mais il sait bien qu'on n'a pas toujours raison dans la vie. Alors, il respecte la liberté des autres et il n'essaie pas d'imposer ses opinions. Pour lui, le bonheur, c'est la sécurité, la santé et l'amour.

TRANSPARENCY: 20-2

D. Suzanne Mabille

Elle est idéaliste. Ce ne sont pas la richesse et le confort qui l'intéressent, mais tous les grands problèmes du monde. Elle est contre la guerre, la pauvreté, l'injustice, le racisme et l'intolérance. Elle s'intéresse aussi à la recherche sur le sida et à la protection de l'environnement... À son avis, la pollution sera un des grands problèmes de l'avenir et c'est pourquoi elle est pour l'écologie. Elle critique beaucoup le gouvernement et la société actuelle. Elle pense qu'il faut agir et elle a beaucoup de projets pour l'avenir. Elle veut faire de la politique et espère avoir un jour le pouvoir de changer le monde. Elle ne comprend pas son oncle Vincent et elle discute souvent

avec lui. Elle le trouve égoïste et il la trouve naïve. Son grand-père Jacques pense qu'elle perdra sûrement ses illusions quand elle devra gagner sa vie après l'université. Évidemment, Suzanne pense qu'il a tort. Elle refuse d'accepter ces idées traditionnelles et elle veut montrer à toute sa famille qu'on peut changer les choses quand on le veut vraiment! Pour elle, le bonheur, ce serait une société juste où il y aurait l'égalité entre les gens, la liberté pour tout le monde et la paix dans le monde.

Info plus

La politique.

Because the system of centralized government does not allow for much involvement in local decision making, the French tend to be fascinated by national politics. Politics is taken very seriously, and elections are watched closely. Politics are discussed everywhere, and arguments, often quite theoretical, are common. Young people, high school and university students in particular, spend long hours in cafés talking politics, sometimes taking action in political demonstrations (des manifestations). In the 90s, however, high school and university students' demands have tended to be of a more pragmatic nature. Afraid of unemployment and unhappy about the lack of subsidies for universities and the subsequent sorry state of buildings and studying conditions, students are asking for more money, more teachers, and a better employment outlook for young people.

TRANSPARENCY: 20-3

E. Abder Hafid

C'est le copain de Suzanne. Venu du Maroc pour étudier la médecine à Bruxelles, il a rencontré Suzanne pendant une fête à la maison des étudiants étrangers. Il ne s'occupe pas de politique et il n'est pas actif dans les groupes d'étudiants parce qu'il a beaucoup de travail et il veut réussir. Et puis, sa famille n'est pas riche et il n'aura plus d'argent du gouvernement marocain s'il ne réussit pas ses examens chaque année. Cependant, comme Suzanne, il est idéaliste. Son rêve? Travailler pour Médecins sans frontières ou Médecins du monde et aller partout dans le monde où on a besoin de médecins. Il sait que c'est très difficile et souvent dangereux, et qu'il ne pourra probablement pas faire ça toute sa vie, mais il voudrait vraiment le faire quelques années avant de se marier et d'avoir des enfants.

F. Cédric Rasquin

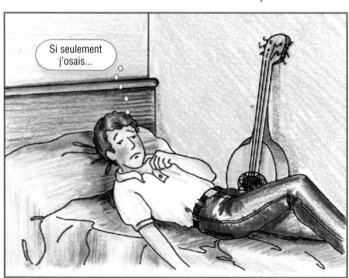

Si seulement j'osais...

Il n'est pas du tout satisfait de sa vie. Il a eu un grand malheur quand il avait dix ans: ses parents ont divorcé. Maintenant, il vit avec sa mère et son beau-père à Toulouse et il lui est très difficile de s'adapter à sa nouvelle vie. Il adore son père mais il ne le voit pas souvent, malheureusement, parce qu'il habite Paris. Cédric souffre beaucoup de la solitude et il trouve sa vie quotidienne ennuyeuse. Il voudrait avoir un groupe de copains et s'amuser comme les autres. Il voudrait aussi trouver le grand amour, mais il n'ose pas parler aux filles et il est toujours déçu. Alors, il rêve pour oublier la réalité... Pour lui, le bonheur, ce serait des parents qui s'entendraient bien, un père qui s'occuperait de lui et une petite amie qui le comprendrait.

G. Guillaume Firket

Coucou, mon lapin!

Il est très actif et plein de vie! Il a quelques besoins très simples: manger, boire, dormir, être aimé. Il adore quand on l'embrasse et quand on le prend dans les bras. Il n'a pas de soucis et il ne se pose pas de questions... Mais il n'est pas toujours heureux. Il fait des cauchemars la nuit et il pleure quand il se réveille tout seul dans sa chambre. Pour lui, le bonheur, c'est être tout le temps près de ses parents et avoir tout ce qu'il veut.

Questions

1. Comme qui est-ce que vous êtes? Pourquoi?
2. Comme qui est-ce que vous n'êtes pas du tout? Pourquoi?
3. Comme qui est-ce que vous voudriez être? Pourquoi?
4. Comme qui est-ce que vous ne voudriez pas être? Pourquoi?

Ask students which person they like most, least, and why.

Notes de vocabulaire

1. Mots et expressions utiles.

se droguer	*to take drugs*
un(e) drogué(e)	*drug addict*
un préservatif	*condom*
séropositif, séropositive	*HIV positive*

2. S'intéresser à / intéresser. Use **s'intéresser à** to say that you *are interested in* or *are not interested in* something.

Je **m'intéresse à** la politique.   *I'm interested in politics.*

Use **intéresser** to say that something *interests* or *does not interest* you.

La politique ne m'**intéresse** pas.   *Politics doesn't interest me.*

Le bonheur, qu'est-ce que c'est?

3. Avoir raison / avoir tort. Use **avoir raison** to say that someone *is right*. Use **avoir tort** to say that someone *is wrong*.

C'est vrai. Tu **as raison.**   *That's true. You're right.*
Ce n'est pas vrai. Tu **as tort!**   *That's not true. You're wrong!*

4. Souffrir. The verb **souffrir** is conjugated like **ouvrir.**

On **souffre** quand on a faim.   *You suffer when you're hungry.*
Jacques **a** beaucoup **souffert.**   *Jacques has suffered a lot.*
N'aie pas peur. Tu ne **souffriras** pas!   *Don't be afraid. It won't hurt.*

D'accord?

Act. A: Chassez l'intrus (gender): (1) immigration / santé / pouvoir / amitié; (2) avenir / paix / accident / malheur; (3) sortie / mort / santé / rêve; (4) solitude / bonheur / guerre / société
    Chassez l'intrus (meaning): (1) injustice / racisme / pauvreté / égalité; (2) loisirs / guerre / accident / maladie; (3) amitié / santé / confort / malheur; (4) apprécier / refuser / accepter / respecter

A. Associations Indiquez le verbe de la liste de droite que vous associez à chaque terme de la liste de gauche.

1. les copains	a. critiquer
2. la politique	b. refuser
3. l'autorité	c. bavarder
4. le confort	d. discuter
5. les parents	e. souffrir
6. les examens	f. se méfier
7. la vie à l'université	g. respecter
8. faire le tour du monde seul avec un sac à dos	h. s'adapter
	i. oser
9. le gouvernement	j. apprécier
10. la solitude	

Act. B: FOLLOW-UP: Ask students what would be a dream or nightmare for them.

B. Un rêve ou un cauchemar? Pour eux, ce serait un rêve ou un cauchemar?

1. Suzanne Mabille: habiter dans une petite maison à la campagne
2. Thérèse Dubois: une sortie avec les copains de Vincent
3. Jacques Dubois: faire de la musique avec Paulette
4. Guillaume Firket: être avec ses parents
5. Cédric Rasquin: sortir avec son père
6. Vincent Dubois: être au régime
7. Abder Hafid: partir avec Médecins du monde

C. Comment sont-ils? Trouvez l'adjectif.

1. Anne n'a pas d'illusions. Elle est . . . . .
2. Paul adore l'argent. Il est . . . . .
3. Patrick est très content de sa vie. Il est . . . . .

4. Monique n'aime pas les maisons modernes. Elle aime les maisons . . . . .
5. Daniel est . . . . . parce qu'il pense qu'il n'a pas réussi un examen important.
6. Dominique n'invite pas beaucoup de monde chez elle. Elle veut avoir une vie . . . . .
7. Béatrice pense que le monde peut devenir meilleur. Elle est . . . . .
8. Mohammed Temkit vient d'Algérie, mais il habite et travaille en France. C'est un . . . . .

D. On a tort! On a raison! Choisissez!

1. Il faut avoir des loisirs pour être équilibré.
2. Il n'y a pas trop de violence à la télévision.
3. Notre société est trop matérialiste.
4. Il faut profiter de la vie.
5. La liberté est une illusion.
6. Le sida est un des plus grands problèmes actuels.
7. Il faut s'intéresser à la politique.
8. La richesse est plus importante que la santé.

Act. D: Use as a listening comprehension activity. Read each item and give your own opinion. Students react to your opinion using **vous avez tort** or **vous avez raison**.

E. Pour ou contre? Est-ce que vous êtes pour ou contre...

1. la guerre?
2. la violence?
3. l'amitié?
4. la paix?
5. le gouvernement?
6. le confort matériel?
7. l'autorité?
8. l'écologie?
9. le changement?
10. le terrorisme?
11. la retraite à 55 ans?

Act. E: Add items as appropriate for your class.

F. Comment êtes-vous?

1. Je suis...
2. Je ne suis pas...
3. Dans dix ans, je serai...
4. Il y a cinq ans, j'étais...

G. Complétez

1. Malheureusement...
2. Évidemment...
3. Je vais probablement...
4. Je vais sûrement...
5. Mes parents sont pour...
6. Mes parents sont contre...
7. Je souffre quand...
8. Je refuse de...

Mise en pratique

A. Une vie de rêve ou... un cauchemar? Imaginez une vie de rêve ou une vie de cauchemar pour chaque personne. Où est-ce qu'ils vivraient? Avec qui? Qu'est-ce qu'ils feraient? Pourquoi?

1. votre professeur
2. vos parents
3. un(e) camarade de classe
4. vous

Act. B: Students may refer to the first part of the lesson for ideas.
FOLLOW-UP/ALTERNATIVE: Ask students to describe a wonderful day for each person.

B. Un jour horrible chez les Dubois
Hier, tout allait mal dans la famille Dubois. Choisissez une personne. Utilisez votre imagination et ce que vous connaissez de cette personne pour raconter cette journée horrible.

Jacques Dubois   Suzanne Mabille   Guillaume Firket   Abder Hafid
Thérèse Dubois   Vincent Dubois   Cédric Rasquin

C. Discutons

1. De quoi est-ce que vous discutez souvent avec vos amis? avec votre famille?
2. Qui doit s'occuper des enfants dans une famille?
3. À quel âge faut-il prendre la retraite?
4. De qui ou de quoi doit-on se méfier?
5. Est-ce que vous faites des cauchemars? Est-ce que vous faisiez des cauchemars quand vous étiez plus jeune? Est-ce que vous vous en souvenez?
6. Est-ce que vous vous êtes adapté(e) vite à la vie à l'université? Pourquoi ou pourquoi pas?

Act. D: Ask students to make a list of **soucis** for the class. Rank them from most to least important. Then, ask students to specify what they do about their concerns (demonstrate, join groups, worry, etc.).

D. Les grandes causes
Quels sont les grands problèmes actuels? Voilà ce que pensent les Français de 18 à 24 ans.

◆ Les grandes causes ◆

Les causes qui paraissent les plus importantes aux jeunes de 18 à 24 ans:

- la prévention du sida (79%);
- la prévention de la drogue (69%);
- l'aide aux malades et aux handicapés (49%);
- la défense de l'environnement (49%);
- les causes humanitaires en France (48%);
- la prévention de la délinquance (47%);
- les droits des jeunes (45%);
- les causes humanitaires dans le monde (40%);
- la lutte contre le racisme (40%);
- l'action en faveur du tiers-monde (31%);
- l'action en faveur des banlieues (23%);
- l'intégration des immigrés (18%);
- l'aide aux réfugiés politiques (8%).

Ministère de la Jeunesse et des Sports
Sofres, avril 1993

---

1. Quel est le problème actuel le plus important pour les jeunes Français? le moins important?
2. En groupes: décidez! Est-ce qu'il y a des causes importantes pour les jeunes Français qui ne seraient pas importantes pour vous? Est-ce qu'il y a des causes qui manquent sur la liste? Faites une liste des 10 causes les plus importantes pour vous et mettez-les par ordre d'importance.
3. Est-ce que les grandes causes que vous avez écrites concernent des problèmes dans le monde ou des problèmes dans votre pays? Quel est pour vous le plus grand problème du monde maintenant? Et le plus grand problème dans votre pays?

E. Les valeurs Quelles valeurs sont importantes pour vous? Voilà une comparaison des valeurs dans la société française selon l'âge.

1. Quelle est la valeur la plus importante pour les jeunes entre 15 et 20 ans? pour les gens entre 21 et 49 ans? pour les gens de plus de 50 ans? Et quelle est la valeur la moins importante pour chaque groupe?
2. En groupes: mettez les valeurs par ordre d'importance pour vous, pour vos parents et pour vos grands-parents. Est-ce qu'il y a une grande différence entre les générations dans votre pays? Est-ce que la société française est comme la société dans votre pays?

En hausse

	Plus de 50 ans	21-49 ans	15-20 ans
La tolérance, le respect des autres	33%	45%	46%
Le respect de l'environnement et de la nature	19%	28%	32%
La générosité	20%	24%	25%
La solidarité avec les gens, avec les peuples	16%	21%	19%

	Plus de 50 ans	21-49 ans	15-20 ans
Le goût de l'effort et du travail	47%	34%	21%
Le sens de la famille	29%	30%	17%
Le courage	21%	20%	15%
La fidélité, la loyauté	20%	20%	13%
Le sens du devoir	18%	7%	7%
Le sens de la justice	16%	18%	10%
Le civisme, le respect du bien commun	9%	8%	3%
L'attachement à la patrie	7%	2%	4%

En baisse

Infographie: WaG

F. Bonheur et malheur

1. Qu'est-ce qui est important pour votre bonheur? Pensez à cinq choses.
2. De quoi est-ce que vous avez peur? Pensez à cinq choses.
3. Comparez avec vos camarades de classes. Qu'est-ce que c'est que le bonheur pour eux? Est-ce que c'est un bonheur privé? Est-ce que le bonheur concerne aussi le pays et le monde? De quoi est-ce qu'ils ont peur? Est-ce que ça concerne la vie privée ou le monde?

 See **Video Magazine 5** for further treatment of **le bonheur.**

Act. F: Have students first identify words, then insert them in sentences; e.g., **Pour moi, le bonheur c'est…** May be converted to a survey format.

G. L'immeuble de Jean Rasquin à Paris
Regardez l'immeuble de Jean Rasquin à Paris (*Leçon 11*, page 269). Qui d'autre habite cet immeuble? Des familles? Des couples? Des enfants? Comment sont ces gens? Qu'est-ce qu'ils font? Qu'est-ce qu'ils aiment? Qu'est-ce qu'ils mangent? Qu'est-ce qu'ils portent? Comment sont leurs appartements? C'est à vous de décider!

1. Choisissez un appartement. Qui habite cet appartement? Un couple? Une famille? Comment est-ce qu'ils s'appellent? Quel âge ont-ils? Est-ce qu'ils travaillent? Quel est leur métier?
2. Leurs habitudes. Qu'est-ce qu'ils font pendant la journée? le soir?
3. Leurs idées et leurs valeurs. Qu'est-ce qu'ils pensent? Quelles sont leurs idées politiques? Comment trouvent-ils la société actuelle?
4. Interviewez les habitants d'un des autres appartements. Quelles questions allez-vous leur poser?

Act. G, 4: VARIATION: Have each student wear a slip of paper identifying his or her apartment. The entire class circulates and tries to find out as much as possible about the other people living in the apartment building. If time permits, have students write a summary of their findings.

H. Conversation en français
Qu'est-ce qui vous rend *(makes you)* heureux? malheureux? Donnez des exemples.

TEXT TAPE:
Conversation en français

Le bonheur, qu'est-ce que c'est? **527**

Structure

▶▶ Le subjonctif, qu'est-ce que c'est?

The subjunctive is a mood, not a tense. Moods mark how a speaker considers an event. A mood may contain tenses, which deal with time. You have already used several moods in French.

1. The *indicative mood* deals with events as facts. Tenses refer to the different time periods in which events happen.

   présent: what is happening   Il **fait** beau.
   passé composé: what did happen   Il **a fait** beau hier.
   imparfait: what was happening   Il **faisait** beau quand tu es arrivée.
   futur: what will happen   Il **fera** beau demain.

2. The *conditional mood* deals with "what would happen if."

   S'il faisait beau, nous **irions** à la plage.

3. The *imperative mood* gives direct commands.

   Fais tes devoirs!

4. The *subjunctive mood* deals with how one feels about an event.

   Je suis contente qu'il **fasse** beau.

Vous avez compris?

Identifiez le mode Identifiez le mode *(mood)* de chaque verbe en italique. Si le verbe est à l'indicatif, donnez le temps *(tense)*. Expliquez votre choix.

1. Ne me *regarde* pas comme ça!
2. Si Paul pouvait, il *serait* à la plage avec ses copains.
3. Je ne lui *ai* pas encore *parlé*.
4. Nous le *ferons* demain.
5. Il ne veut pas que je le *fasse*.
6. Il *faisait* beau quand nous sommes sortis.
7. Nous sommes contents que tu *puisses* venir.

▶▶ Formation du subjonctif: les verbes à une racine

Although the subjunctive mood, like the indicative mood, actually does contain several tenses, only the *present subjunctive* and *past subjunctive* are in general use. In this book, you will deal only with the *present subjunctive*. From now on, when we refer to the subjunctive, we mean the present subjunctive.

The majority of French verbs have only one stem in the subjunctive. It is derived from the third person plural (**ils**) form of the present tense of the indicative mood.

Point out that using the third-person plural of the present as the stem for the subjunctive works for many verbs. Ask students to find the subjunctive stem of a few more verbs (**ouvrir, dire,** etc.)

PRESENT TENSE (INDICATIVE)	SUBJUNCTIVE STEM
ils parlent	**parl-**
ils étudient	**étudi-**
ils finissent	**finiss-**
ils vendent	**vend-**
ils sortent	**sort-**
ils écrivent	**écriv-**
ils mettent	**mett-**
ils suivent	**suiv-**
ils vivent	**viv-**

The subjunctive endings are added to this stem.

SUBJUNCTIVE ENDINGS			
je	**-e**	nous	**-ions**
tu	**-es**	vous	**-iez**
il / elle	**-e**	ils / elles	**-ent**

---

lire au subjonctif

(que) je lise	(que) nous lisions
(que) tu lises	(que) vous lisiez
(qu')il / (qu')elle } lise	(qu')ils / (qu')elles } lisent

étudier au subjonctif

(que) j'étudie	(que) nous étudiions
(que) tu étudies	(que) vous étudiiez
(qu')il / (qu')elle } étudie	(qu')ils / (qu')elles } étudient

There are three irregular verbs in this group of verbs with one stem in the subjunctive.

VERB	SUBJUNCTIVE STEM
faire	**fass-**
savoir	**sach-**
pouvoir	**puiss-**

---

faire au subjonctif

(que) je fasse	(que) nous fassions
(que) tu fasses	(que) vous fassiez
(qu')il / (qu')elle } fasse	(qu' ils / (qu')elles } fassent

Ask students to locate forms that are similar.

It is probably unrealistic to expect students to spontaneously produce utterances with subjunctives except for a few memorized phrases. Not only are the subjunctive forms new, use of the subjunctive entails using a two-clause sentence, which also increases the cognitive load. For this reason, activities in *VOILÀ!* ask for only limited production of subjunctive forms. Once students have become familiar with the idea behind the subjunctive and are familiar with its forms, they should be able to continue to acquire its uses as they gain experience with French.

DRILL: **Alceste veut que Candide.** (vendre sa voiture / partir en vacances / lire des livres sérieux / faire son lit le matin)

Mettez au subjonctif: Have students generate ideas as to why the subjunctive is required. Accept all ideas. As further examples are seen, students will narrow down their hypotheses by themselves. This will help make the concept of subjunctive seem somewhat less foreign.
CONTINUATION: **Il faut que vous . . . ménage (faire); Je veux que tu . . . la vérité (dire); Nous ne sommes pas contents que vous . . . (ne jamais étudier); Vous êtes triste que nous . . . , mais vous m'oublierez (se séparer); Je suis content que tu . . . avec ma sœur (sortir).**

Note that some forms of the present indicative and imperfect are spelled the same as corresponding forms of the present subjunctive.

INDICATIVE PRESENT

je parle	nous parlons
tu parles	vous parlez
il elle } parle	ils elles } parlent

INDICATIVE IMPERFECT

je parlais	nous parlions
tu parlais	vous parliez
il elle } parlait	ils elles } parlaient

SUBJUNCTIVE PRESENT

(que) je parle	(que) nous parlions
(que) tu parles	(que) vous parliez
(qu')il (qu')elle } parle	(qu')ils (qu')elles } parlent

Vous avez compris?

Mettez au subjonctif Mettez les verbes entre parenthèses au subjonctif. Puis traduisez *(translate)* chaque phrase en anglais idiomatique. Pouvez-vous deviner *(guess)* pourquoi le subjonctif est utilisé dans ces phrases?

1. Il faut que tu . . . . . : ton chien ou moi. (choisir)
2. Elle est triste qu'ils . . . . . sans elle. (partir)
3. Il fait froid. Je veux que tu . . . . . ton manteau. (mettre)
4. Nous partirons avant qu'elles . . . . . (arriver)
5. Ma grand-mère veut que je lui . . . . . à Noël. (rendre visite)
6. Je ne vous parle plus pour que vous . . . . . étudier dans le calme. (pouvoir)

➤ Formation du subjonctif: les verbes à deux racines

Several verbs have two stems in the subjunctive, one for the singular and third person plural forms, the other for the **nous** and **vous** forms. The first stem of these verbs is derived as described earlier. The second stem comes from the **nous** form of the present indicative. The regular subjunctive endings are used.

VERB	STEM 1 (je, tu, il, elle, ils, elles)	STEM 2 (nous, vous)
boire	**boiv-**	**buv-**
croire	**croi-**	**croy-**
devoir	**doiv-**	**dev-**
lever	**lèv-**	**lev-**
prendre	**prenn-**	**pren-**
venir	**vienn-**	**ven-**
voir	**voi-**	**voy-**

Tell students that spelling-change verbs such as **acheter, promener, emmener, appeler, préférer, espérer, sécher, envoyer, essayer, payer,** and **ennuyer** also have two stems in the subjunctive. Help students conjugate a few of these. They can check their work by referring to the verb tables in the *Appendice de verbes.*

boire au subjonctif

(que) je boive
(que) tu boives
(qu')il }
(qu')elle } boive

(que) nous buvions
(que) vous buviez
(qu')ils }
(qu')elles } boivent

DRILL: Candide veut qu'Alceste... (boire un verre avec lui / le prendre au sérieux / venir en vacances avec lui)

DRILL: Il faut que vous... (boire beaucoup d'eau / vous lever tôt / voir que j'ai raison)

There are two irregular verbs in this group.

VERB	STEM 1	STEM 2
aller	**aill-**	**all-**
vouloir	**veuill-**	**voul-**

Il faut **que tu ailles** en ville.   *You have to go to town.*
Il faut **que vous alliez** en ville.

Mes parents sont contents **que je**
   veuille continuer mes études.

My parents are happy that I
   want to continue my studies.

Vos parents ne sont pas contents
  que vous vouliez continuer
vos études?

Your parents aren't happy that you
   want to continue your studies?

▶ Formation du subjonctif: Les verbes *être* et *avoir* au subjonctif

The verbs **être** and **avoir** are totally irregular in the subjunctive. They must be memorized.

être au subjonctif

(que) je sois
(que) tu sois
(qu')il }
(qu')elle } soit

(que) nous soyons
(que) vous soyez
(qu')ils }
(qu')elles } soient

DRILL: Je suis heureux que tu sois content. (le professeur / les étudiants / vous)

avoir au subjonctif	
(que) j'aie	(que) nous ayons
(que) tu aies	(que) vous ayez
(qu')il ⎫	(qu')ils ⎫
(qu')elle ⎭ ait	(qu')elles ⎭ aient

Vous avez compris?

A. Mettez au subjonctif Mettez les verbes entre parenthèses au subjonctif. Puis traduisez *(translate)* chaque phrase en anglais idiomatique. Pouvez-vous deviner *(guess)* pourquoi le subjonctif est utilisé dans ces phrases?

1. Marie, il faut que tu ..... ; tu vas être en retard. (se lever)
2. Nous sommes tristes que vous ..... avec nous à la soirée chez les Dumont. (ne pas venir)
3. Mon médecin voudrait que je ..... des vacances mais je n'ai pas le temps. (prendre)
4. Je ne veux pas que tu ..... du vin le matin. (boire)
5. Nous ne sommes pas contents qu'ils ..... rester chez nous tout l'été. (vouloir)
6. Il faut que tu ..... le professeur. (voir)
7. Je suis content qu'elle ..... partir. (ne pas devoir)
8. Je ne veux pas que tu ..... à la fête chez Éric. (aller)
9. Il faut qu'elle nous ..... ! (croire)
10. Il faut que les Dubois ..... une nouvelle voiture. (acheter)

B. Mettez au subjonctif Mettez les verbes entre parenthèses au subjonctif. Puis traduisez *(translate)* chaque phrase en anglais idiomatique. Pouvez-vous deviner *(guess)* pourquoi le subjonctif est utilisé dans ces phrases?

1. Je ne veux pas que vous ..... peur. (avoir)
2. Il ne faut pas qu'ils ..... froid. (avoir)
3. Je suis triste que tu ..... malade. (être)
4. Il n'est pas content que nous ..... raison. (avoir)
5. Je vais lui donner des gants pour qu'elle ..... froid. (ne pas avoir)
6. Je ne veux pas que vous ..... en colère contre moi. (être)

▶ Usage du subjonctif

1. **En général.** The subjunctive is the second conjugated verb in a two-verb sentence. It follows the word **que.**

   Il faut **que tu sois** à l'heure.   *You have to be on time.*

2. **Il faut que + subjonctif / il faut + infinitif.** You already know the expression **il faut (il faudrait).** The subjunctive is used after **il faut que (il faudrait que)** when the subject is specified. If no subject is specified, **il faut (il faudrait) + infinitif** is used. Compare:

Il faut qu'il **travaille.**	*He has to work.* (A particular specific person has to work.)
Il faut travailler.	*You have to work.* (Nobody in particular; a general truth: one has to work.)
Il faudrait téléphoner.	*We (someone/unspecific) should call.*
Il faudrait que tu **téléphones.**	*You (someone specific) should call.*

3. **Vouloir que / vouloir + infinitif.** The subjunctive is used after **vouloir que** when there is a change of subjects in the two parts of the sentence. **Vouloir que + subjonctif** is the only way to say an English sentence such as *I want you to be happy.* If there is no change of subject, **vouloir + infinitif** is used. Compare:

Je **veux que** vous **soyez** content.	*I want you to be happy.* (change of subject = subjunctive)
Je **veux être** content.	*I want to be happy.* (no change of subject = infinitive)

4. **Être content (triste) que + subjonctif / être content (triste) de + infinitif.** The subjunctive is used after the expressions **être content que** and **être triste que** when there is a change of subject. If there is no change of subject, the expression **être content (triste) de + infinitif** is used. Compare:

Je **suis content que** tu **sois** ici.	*I'm happy (that) you're here.* (change of subject = subjunctive)
Je **suis content d'être** ici.	*I'm happy to be here.* (no change of subject = **de** + infinitive)

5. **Pour que (avant que) + subjonctif / pour (avant de) + infinitif.** The subjunctive is used in clauses introduced by **pour que** and **avant que** when there is a change of subject. If there is no change of subject, the expression **pour + infinitif** or **avant de + infinitif** is used. Compare:

If desired, teach **jusqu'à / jusqu'à ce que.**

For reading purposes, you may want to explain the use of pleonastic **ne** with **avant que.**

Je veux te parler **avant que** tu **partes.**	*I want to talk to you before you leave.* (change of subject = subjunctive)
Je veux te parler **avant de partir.**	*I want to talk to you before I leave.* (no change of subject = infinitive)
Je le fais **pour que** tu t'**amuses.**	*I'm doing it so that you'll have a good time.* (change of subject = subjunctive)
Je le fais **pour** m'**amuser.**	*I'm doing it (in order) to have a good time.* (no change of subject = infinitive)

Rappel! Although verbs in the subjunctive are usually found in **que** clauses, not every **que** clause has a subjunctive! For example, the following expressions are followed by the indicative:

dire que	*to say that*
savoir que	*to know that*
espérer que	*to hope that*
parce que	*because*

Elle m'**a dit qu'**elle venait.	*She told me she was coming.*
Je **sais qu'**il **est parti.**	*I know (that) he left.*
J'**espère qu'**elle **comprendra.**	*I hope (that) she'll understand.*
Parce que c'**est** comme ça!	*Because that's the way it is!*

Vous avez compris?

Act. A: CONTINUATION: Je veux te parler avant que tu . . . (se coucher); Il faut . . . des fruits (manger)

A. Subjonctif ou infinitif? Mettez les verbes au subjonctif ou à l'infinitif.

1. Je veux . . . . . en France. (aller)
2. Il ne veut pas que vous . . . . . trop de gâteau. (manger)
3. Ils sont tristes de . . . . . d'appartement. (changer)
4. Il faut que tu . . . . . à la banque. (aller)
5. Je vais à la bibliothèque pour . . . . . (étudier)
6. Ils ne sont pas contents que nous ne leur . . . . . jamais. (écrire)
7. Je vais boire un verre de lait avant de . . . . . dormir. (aller)
8. Je vais écrire ma lettre maintenant pour qu'elle . . . . . ce soir. (partir)

Act. B: CONTINUATION: il fera beau demain; je travaille

B. Complétez Complétez les phrases par une des expressions suivantes: je veux que / je sais que / je suis content(e) que / j'espère que / je suis triste que / il faut que.

Modèles vous soyez à l'heure
Il faut que vous soyez à l'heure.

vous serez à l'heure
J'espère que vous serez à l'heure.

1. tu ne vas pas te tromper
2. la vie n'est pas facile
3. tu sois malade
4. il a eu un accident en Suisse
5. nous soyons sérieux
6. nous arrivions à l'heure
7. tu as trop bu hier soir
8. il fasse beau aujourd'hui
9. tu suives un cours de maths
10. vous vous couchiez plus tôt

C. Indicatif, subjonctif ou infinitif? Mettez les verbes au subjonctif, à l'infinitif ou à l'indicatif.

1. Je vais en ville pour ..... une robe longue. (chercher)
2. Je sais que tu ..... parce que moi, je ..... toujours raison!
   (se tromper; avoir)
3. Christiane est contente de ..... en vacances. (être)
4. Il faut que nous ..... la vérité. (savoir)
5. Mes amis ne savent pas que je ..... au Japon. (partir)
6. Il faut ..... les dents trois fois par jour. (se brosser)
7. J'espère qu'ils ..... (s'aimer)
8. Il va partir avant que je ..... lui parler. (pouvoir)

Continuons!

A. Avant de partir au bal
Les sœurs de Cendrillon partent pour le bal. Mais avant de partir, elles lui ont parlé. Qu'est-ce qu'elles lui ont dit de faire? (Par exemple: faire la vaisselle / faire les lits / laver les murs / travailler dans le jardin / préparer le café...)

Modèle   *Nous voulons que tu laves la salle de bains.*

B. Le cauchemar du professeur
Le professeur Parfait a fait un cauchemar la nuit dernière. Il a rêvé qu'un étudiant dirigeait l'université et faisait la loi *(was laying down the law)* pour les professeurs. Qu'est-ce que vous pensez que l'étudiant disait? Suivez le modèle.

Modèle   *Il faut que vous ayez des heures de bureau le samedi!*

C. Chez le conseiller conjugal
Monsieur et Madame Bataille ont des problèmes dans leur couple et sont allés voir un conseiller conjugal *(a marriage counselor)*. Il leur a demandé de faire une liste des changements qu'ils voudraient voir dans l'autre. Faites les deux listes.

Modèle   *Je voudrais que tu ne sortes plus avec tes copains le soir.*

D. Et en français? Traduisez *(translate)* en français.

1. I want you to leave.
2. I want to leave.
3. He is happy to be here.
4. He is happy she is here.
5. He is sad she must work Saturday night.
6. He is sad he has to work Saturday night.
7. He is sad because she has to work Saturday night.
8. What do you want me to do?
9. I want you to be happy.
10. I don't want to be happy!

Act. D: This translation exercise will serve to focus students' attention on the patterns they have just learned and on how those patterns contrast with English.

Découvertes culturelles: Le bonheur à la française

▶ Plus ça change...

Français, comme vous avez changé !

Les Français sont formidables.

On les disait passifs, étranglés par la crise, affolés par l'avenir, tétanisés par la peur de voir s'envoler leur petit bonheur précaire dans un monde incertain. Et les voilà qui font la grève par procuration, pas mécontents de balancer un pied de nez aux élites et de tisser d'inédites solidarités. On les disait individualistes et déprimés, n'écoutant qu'eux-mêmes une fois la télé éteinte, incapables de voir la vie en rose et de s'adapter.

1 On ne consomme plus pour paraître, mais p[...] être mieux dans sa peau.

Plus serei[...]

2 On mange moins, plus équilibré, et l'on se passionne pour sa santé.

Plus équilibr[...]

3 On a un peu peur des autres et de l'avenir: o[...] veut du confort et de la sécurité.

En sécurité

4 On refuse de passer pour un pigeon: on veut être consulté, informé et consommer actif.

Mieux informé

5 On ne veut plus perdre son temps: on se réserve des loisirs et une vie privée.

Plus de plaisir

6 Face aux produits, on exige le droit à l'infidéli[...] zappeuse, par éclectisme et par curiosité.

Moins de modes

7 On ne croit plus à la rédemption par l'argent. On préfère le solide, le durable, l'authentique: le sens.

Plus de sens

8 On veut de l'éthique en politique, de la transparence en affaires.

Plus d'honnêteté

9 On fait fructifier son capital humain, on espère sauvegarder l'environnement, on aime communier avec la nature.

Plus d'authenticité

10 Le plaisir passe par la convivialité en tribu et par la solidarité en société.

Plus de solidarité

Act. A, 1: First, draw students' attention to clothes and accessories. Then ask them to draw conclusions (**pas de cravate, pas de veste, téléphone, vêtements décontractés, casquette américaine, veste en jean**, etc. CONCLUSIONS: **plus décontractés, plus internationaux, américanisés, aiment les sports, la technologie**, etc.). If necessary, give students additional examples (**Madame, vos vêtements sont simples et confortables, le confort est plus important que la mode. Monsieur, vous ne portez pas de cravate, vous êtes décontracté** *(relaxed)*. **Monsieur et Madame, vos enfants n'ont pas de noms traditionnels, vous avez des enfants modernes. Alexis, tu as une casquette comme un enfant américain, tu es très international**, etc.).

Act. A, 2: Refer students to previous lessons for cultural and linguistic information and ideas. Can be group work, each group taking a different person.

A. Les nouveaux Français.

1. **Quatre Français.** Voilà Monsieur et Madame Toulemonde et leurs deux enfants, Océane et Alexis. Décrivez ces quatre personnes dans leur état actuel comme si vous leur parliez et concluez sur ce changement.

   Modèle *Monsieur, vous avez un téléphone mobile, donc vous aimez la technologie!*

2. **Une famille moderne.** D'après cette photo, imaginez une journée typique de chaque membre de la famille. Pour chaque personne, dites ce qu'ils font ce jour-là (profession, loisirs, vacances, maison ou appartement, sports, problèmes, etc.).

B. Les Français sont formidables.

1. **Les Français d'avant et de maintenant.** Complétez ce tableau d'après les indications du texte.

Act. B, 1: Ask for several details and justification from information in the text.

Avant, les Français étaient...	Maintenant, les Français sont...

2. Associez une phrase ou une expression de ce texte à une des phrases numérotées du texte qui l'accompagne.

Act. B, 2: Have students link words from the article to the summary in the shaded box.

3. **Mots nouveaux.**
   a. Trouvez dans le texte de gauche un mot qui signifie: angoissés / immobilisés / créer des relations.
   b. **Faire la grève** signifie: refuser de travailler / être très sérieux / écrire des lettres.
   c. **Balancer un pied de nez aux élites** signifie: rire de / se battre contre / attaquer.
   d. **Une fois la télévision éteinte** signifie: après avoir arrêté la télévision / regarder la télévision rarement / refuser de regarder la télévision.
   e. **Et les voilà qui...** Que représente **les** dans cette expression?

Act. B, 3a: Help students by identifying sentences containing words. Students may need to use dictionaries. Réponses: **affolés, tétanisés, tisser.**

4. **Les anciens stéréotypes.** Choisissez dans le texte trois adjectifs qui caractérisent les Français d'avant et expliquez ce que ces adjectifs veulent dire. Que faisaient probablement les Français? Qu'est-ce qu'ils ne faisaient pas?

   Modèle *Ils étaient passifs: ils ne prenaient pas de décision...*

Act. B, 4: Can be group work. Use to review **imparfait** and previous vocabulary. Students should focus on very concrete activities and events. At the end have groups compare their sentences when you recapitulate. See if everyone agrees.

5. **Les nouveaux Français.** De même, choisissez trois choses que les Français font maintenant et donnez des exemples qui illustrent cette notion.

   Modèle *Ils balancent un pied de nez aux élites. Ils ne respectent pas la hiérarchie, etc.*

C. Portrait des nouveaux Français.

Dans le texte ombré *(shaded)*, chaque phrase est résumée en un adjectif ou une expression. À l'aide de ces expressions, faites le portrait des nouveaux Français en l'illustrant d'exemples concrets, tirés des exercices B4 et B5. Référez-vous aux éléments culturels que vous avez découverts dans les leçons précédentes et dans les *Magazines francophones*.

Modèle *Les nouveaux Français: Les Français des années 90 sont plus sereins...*

Act. C: Could be a composition topic. Use also to review vocabulary and cultural information gleaned throughout *VOILÀ!* Provide cohesive devices (**mais, de plus, finalement, par exemple, cependant, pourtant,** etc.) to link ideas and help students construct a few short paragraphs where ideas are linked, or contrasted.

D. Changements culturels.

1. Et chez vous? Les gens ont-ils changé? Comment étaient-ils avant et comment sont-ils maintenant?
2. Écrivez une lettre à vos compatriotes, sur le modèle du premier paragraphe de cet article et qui indique les changements de votre société. Adressez-vous directement à eux.

Chers compatriotes,

   Comme vous avez changé...

See **Video Magazine 5** for further treatment of **le bonheur**.

▶▶ Les jeunes et le bonheur

SOCIÉTÉ ■ Jeunes
VIE MOROSE OU VIE EN ROSE?

Selon un sondage récent, les jeunes veulent rompre avec l'esprit morose ambiant.

Un sondage réalisé par l'institut Louis-Harris (pour Martini Bianco) en mai 1995 auprès de 500 jeunes sur le thème de la "morosité" révèle que les 18–24 ans désirent échapper aux humeurs chagrines. Cette étude fait apparaître une classe d'âge optimiste et battante, puisque 80% d'entre eux disent "non à la morosité".

Lorsqu'ils se réveillent moroses, et pour combattre cet état d'esprit, 55% des 18–24 ans s'habillent avec un jogging et des baskets, 18% avec une robe de chambre et des charentaises* à carreaux, 16% avec une chemise à fleurs et un chapeau de paille.

Pour sortir de cet état d'esprit, la plupart des personnes interrogées cherchent à s'évader et rêvent d'un "ailleurs": 41% pensent que l'objet idéal anti-morosité (selon des réponses suggérées) est un billet d'avion éternellement valable, tandis que 26% préféreraient une machine à voyager dans le temps. Pour les obtenir, la carte de crédit à débit différé de 50 ans serait bienvenue.

▲ L'importance de l'argent ▼

Quand on leur demande ce qui pourrait modifier une réalité parfois tristounette, l'épaisseur de leur portefeuille recueille 43% des réponses, devant leur look (18%), et la taille de leur appartement (13%). ■

JE VOIS LA VIE EN NOIR!

CHANGE DE LUNETTES MON VIEUX!

Dessin de NIKOLAZ

NIKOLAZ 95

Les Clés de l'Actualité

* une chaussure d'intérieur, symbole du cocon familial

A. La vie en rose.

1. **Dessin humoristique.** Décrivez ces deux jeunes garçons. Comment est celui qui est assis sur le banc? Qu'est-ce qu'il porte? Et celui qui est debout? Qu'est-ce qu'il porte? Quelle est la différence entre ces deux garçons?
2. **Identification.** Et vous, vous êtes comme lequel de ces deux jeunes? Pourquoi?

B. Vie morose ou vie en rose?

1. Le sujet de l'article. Quels mots ou expressions des titres et sous-titres de cet article annoncent...

Act. B, 1: Use the cartoon to help students guess the meaning of **rompre**.

• les personnes que cet article concerne?
• l'origine de cet article?
• le sujet de l'article?
• une réponse à la question du titre?

2. Des chiffres. Complétez avec des chiffres du texte:

Âge des personnes considérées:
Nombre de personnes consultées:
Nombre de personnes qui sont moroses:
Nombre de personnes qui voient la vie en rose:
Pourcentage de personnes pour qui les jeans sont signes d'optimisme:
Pourcentage de personnes qui rêvent de voyager:
Pourcentage de personnes qui rêvent d'avoir beaucoup d'argent:

3. Vie morose et vie en rose. Quels mots ou expressions du texte se réfèrent à...

La vie morose	La vie en rose

C. Et chez vous? Comment est-on dans votre culture?

1. La vie en rose, la vie morose. Quels événements dans le monde et dans votre culture sont responsables des attitudes des jeunes de votre culture?

La vie en rose	La vie morose

2. Comment voyez-vous la vie? Êtes-vous morose ou voyez-vous la vie en rose? Dites pourquoi.

Je vois la vie en rose	Je suis morose
Je pense...	parce que...
Je crois...	parce que...
Je sais ...	parce que...
Je voudrais...	parce que...

www explore!
http//voila.heinle.com

Orthographe et prononciation

▶ Du français de tous les jours à l'anglais cultivé

The English language contains two layers of words, those that are more commonly found in everyday speech and those that are characteristic of the written language and formal speech.

EVERYDAY ENGLISH	FORMAL, LEARNED ENGLISH
Keep on going.	You may continue.
Everybody was happy.	There was general rejoicing.

In many cases, words belonging in the more formal, learned layer of English have entered English directly from Latin or indirectly via French from Latin. As a result, English often has two words to express the same idea, one belonging to the everyday vocabulary and the other related to a French word.

EVERYDAY ENGLISH	FRENCH	FORMAL, LEARNED ENGLISH
start	**commencer**	commence
think about	**réfléchir**	reflect on
food	**nourriture**	nourishment

Activités

A. Français-anglais Pour chaque verbe français, trouvez deux verbes anglais qui correspondent, un verbe formel et un verbe de l'anglais de tous les jours.

Modèle commencer
to commence, to start

1. regarder
2. chercher
3. préparer
4. entrer
5. monter
6. partir
7. raconter
8. regretter

B. Trouvez les mots français Voilà des phrases écrites en anglais formel. Pouvez-vous trouver des mots français qui correspondent aux mots en italique? Pouvez-vous traduire *(translate)* l'anglais formel en anglais de tous les jours?

1. She *descended* the staircase wearing an elegant dress and a disdainful smile.
2. His *primary* concern was to *reconcile* their differences before *autumn*.
3. The *interior* is white and the *exterior* is green.

See the **Instructor's Resource Manual** for more information.

Vocabulaire de base

NOMS

un accident *accident, crash*
l'amitié *(f.) friendship*
l'avenir *(m.) future*
le bonheur *happiness*
le chômage *unemployment*
l'environnement *(m.) environment*
l'immigration *(f.) immigration*
un(e) immigré(e) *immigrant*
une guerre *war*
une maladie *sickness, illness*
le malheur *misfortune*
la mort *death*
la paix *peace*
un passe-temps *pastime*
le pouvoir *power*
le racisme *racism*
un rêve *dream*
la santé *health*
la société *society*
la solitude *solitude*
une sortie *outing, evening/night out*
la violence *violence*

ADJECTIFS

actif, active *active*
chaque *each*
déçu(e) *disappointed*
idéaliste *idealistic*
indépendant(e) *independent*
individualiste *individualistic*
injuste *unfair*
inquiet, inquiète *worried*
juste *fair, just, right*
matérialiste *materialistic*
optimiste *optimistic*
pessimiste *pessimistic*
privé(e) *private*

quelque *few, some*
réaliste *realistic*
satisfait(e) (de) *satisfied (with)*
social, sociale, sociaux, sociales *social*
traditionnel, traditionnelle *traditional*

VERBES

agir *to act*
critiquer *to criticize*
discuter (de) *to discuss*
intéresser *to interest*
s'intéresser à *to be interested in*
refuser (de + infinitif) *to refuse (to do something)*
respecter *to respect*

DIVERS

à mon (ton, son, etc.) avis *in my (your, his, her) opinion*
avant de + infinitif *before*
avant que *before*
avoir raison *to be right*
avoir tort *to be wrong*
cependant *nevertheless, however*
être contre *to be against*
être pour *to be for*
évidemment *obviously, of course*
faire de la musique *to make music*
faire du bricolage *to do odd jobs around the house*
faire du jardinage *to do gardening*
il faut (que) *one has to, it is necessary that*
pour (que) *so that, in order to*
probablement *probably*
sauf *except*
sûrement *certainly*

Vocabulaire supplémentaire

NOMS

une activité *activity*
l'autorité *(f.) authority*
un besoin *need*
le cancer *cancer*
un cauchemar *nightmare*
un changement *change*
le confort *comfort*
Dieu *God*
la drogue *drug (illegal)*
l'écologie *(f.) ecology*
l'égalité *(f.) equality*
un gouvernement *government*
une illusion *illusion*
l'injustice *(f.) injustice*
l'intolérance *(f.) intolerance*
la liberté *freedom*
les loisirs *(m. pl.) leisure (spare time) activities*
une opinion *opinion*
l'ordre *(m.) order*
la pauvreté *poverty*
la pollution *pollution*
un préservatif *condom*
la protection *protection*
la réalité *reality*
la recherche (sur) *research*
la richesse *wealth*
la sécurité *feeling of security, safety*
le sida *AIDS*
la spiritualité *spirituality*
le terrorisme *terrorism*

Since the advent of the slogan **Touche pas à mon pote,** the meaning of **pote** has been taken to mean **un copain d'une autre race.**

ADJECTIFS

actuel, actuelle *present, current*
drogué(e) *drug addict*
financier, financière *financial*
matériel, matérielle *material*
personnel, personnelle *personal*
séropositif, séropositive *HIV positive*
simple *simple*

VERBES

accepter (de + inf.) *to accept*
s'adapter à *to adapt to*

apprécier *to appreciate*
bavarder *to chat*
concerner *to concern*
se droguer *to take (illegal) drugs*
imposer *to impose*
se méfier de *to mistrust, not to trust*
oser *to dare*
souffrir (conjugué comme ouvrir) *to suffer*

DIVERS

avoir des illusions *to have illusions*
avoir des soucis *to have worries*
être conscient(e) de *to be aware of*
faire de la politique *to be involved in politics*
prendre la retraite *to retire*
profiter de la vie *to make the most of life*
se poser des questions *to wonder, to have doubts*
la vie quotidienne *daily life*

LE FRANÇAIS FAMILIER

la came = la drogue
ce n'est pas la mer à boire *it's not the end of the world, it's not asking the impossible*
un leader *leader*
tchatcher = bavarder, parler pour ne rien dire
avoir de la tchatche = parler beaucoup, être bavard
un pote = un copain

LE FRANÇAIS TEL QU'ON LE PARLE

Coucou! *Peek-a-boo!*
mon lapin *sweetheart, my love (like mon chou or mon chéri)*

ON ENTEND PARFOIS...

avoir de la jasette (Canada) = être bavard
babiner (Canada) = bavarder
barjaquer (Suisse) = bavarder

Appendice de grammaire

- **Les temps composés**
- **Le passé simple**
- **Le participe présent**
- **L'infinitif**
- **Les pronoms relatifs** *dont* et *ce dont*
- **Les pronoms démonstratifs**
- **Les pronoms possessifs**
- **L'ordre des pronoms d'objet,** *y* et *en*
- **La place des adjectifs**

These grammar points are included to help adapt instruction to individual contexts. Activities to accompany this section can be found in the **Cahier d'activités écrites et orales.**

▶▶ Les temps composés

See the **Instructor's Resource Manual** for more information.

A compound tense (**un temps composé**) has two parts: a helping verb and a past participle. The **passé composé,** for example, is a compound tense (present tense of **avoir/être** + past participle). The **passé composé** refers to an event in the past, to something that happened or has happened.

Ils **ont pris** ma radio!   *They took my radio!*
Sa mère **est allée** à Londres.   *His mother went/has gone to London.*
Mon oncle **a** déjà **lu** le journal.   *My uncle already read/has already read the newspaper.*

Nous nous **sommes regardés.**   *We looked at each other.*

Three other compound tenses besides the **passé composé** are in common use. These tenses are used to date events chronologically in a narration in the past or in the future. Each one is formed by using a form of **avoir** or **être** as a helping verb plus a past participle.

Le plus-que-parfait: avoir/être à l'imparfait + participe passé

The **plus-que-parfait** refers to an event in the past that happened before another event in the past, that is, to something that had happened before something else.

Il **avait** déjà **mangé** quand je suis arrivé.	*He had already eaten when I got there.*
Elle **était** déjà **partie** quand je lui ai téléphoné.	*She had already left when I called her.*
Je m'**étais** déjà **couché** quand l'inspecteur m'a téléphoné.	*I had already gone to bed when the police inspector called me.*

Le futur antérieur: avoir/être au futur + participe passé

The **futur antérieur** refers to an event in the future that will happen before another event in the future, that is, to something that will have happened before something else.

Mon père **aura mangé** avant que j'arrive.	*My father will have eaten before I get there.*
J'espère que Marie **sera rentrée** quand ses parents téléphoneront.	*I hope Mary will have gotten back by the time that (when) her parents call.*
Je me **serai lavé** les cheveux avant que tu arrives.	*I will have washed my hair before you get here.*

Le conditionnel passé: avoir/être au conditionnel + participe passé

The **conditionnel passé** refers to an event that would have happened if something else had happened.

Il t'**aurait dit** la vérité si tu lui avais parlé.	*He would have told you the truth if you had talked to him.*
Elle **serait partie** s'il y avait eu un train.	*She would have left if there had been a train.*
Tu te **serais souvenu** d'elle si tu l'avais vue.	*You would have remembered her if you had seen her.*

Note that past participles agree in all compound tenses as they do for the **passé composé.**

C'est elle la fille que j'avais rencontré**e** il y a deux ans!
Nous serons arrivé**s** avant 18 heures demain.
Ils se seraient couché**s** de bonne heure, mais il y avait des examens et...

See the *Appendice de verbes* for examples of verbs conjugated in these tenses.

See the **Instructor's Resource Manual** for more information.

▸▸ Le passé simple

The **passé simple** *(simple past tense)* in French is found in written narration where it is basically the equivalent of the **passé composé.** To read French narration such as that found in novels, fairy tales, or detective stories, you will need to be able to recognize verb forms in the **passé simple.**

1. The **passé simple** of regular -**er** verbs like **parler** is formed by adding the endings -**ai**, -**as**, -**a**, -**âmes**, -**âtes**, -**èrent** to the infinitive stem (**parl-**).

je parl**ai**	nous parl**âmes**
tu parl**as**	vous parl**âtes**
il elle } parl**a**	ils elles } parl**èrent**

2. The passé simple of regular -**ir** and -**re** verbs like **finir, partir,** and **vendre** is formed by adding the endings -**is**, -**is**, -**it**, -**îmes**, -**îtes**, -**irent** to the infinitive stem (**fin-, part-, vend-**).

je fin**is**	nous fin**îmes**	je vend**is**	nous vend**îmes**	je part**is**	nous part**îmes**
tu fin**is**	vous fin**îtes**	tu vend**is**	vous vend**îtes**	tu part**is**	vous part**îtes**
il elle } fin**it**	ils elles } fin**irent**	il elle } vend**it**	ils elles } vend**irent**	il elle } part**it**	ils elles } part**irent**

3. Other verbs. Many verbs have irregular **passé simple** forms. Frequently, but not always, the stem of the **passé simple** is based on the past participle. All verbs in this category take the same set of endings: -**s**, -**s**, -**t**, -**^mes**, -**^tes**, -**rent**.

VERB	STEM	
avoir	eu-	il **eut**
boire	bu-	elles **burent**
connaître	connu-	il **connut**
courir	couru-	elle **courut**
croire	cru-	il **crut**
devoir	du-	ils **durent**
dire	di-	elle **dit**
être	fu-	elle **fut**
faire	fi-	elles **firent**
falloir	fallu-	il **fallut**
lire	lu-	il **lut**
mettre	mi-	elles **mirent**
pouvoir	pu-	elle **put**
prendre	pri-	il **prit**
recevoir	reçu-	il **reçut**
rire	ri-	elles **rirent**
savoir	su-	elle **sut**
suivre	suivi-	il **suivit**
venir	vin-	il **vint**
vivre	vécu-	elle **vécut**
voir	vi-	ils **virent**
vouloir	voulu-	elle **voulut**

▶▶ Le participe présent

The present participle is a verbal form ending in **-ant.** A present participle may be used either as an adjective or as a verb.

Formation

The present participle is formed by removing the **-ons** ending from the **nous** form of the present tense and adding **-ant.**

chanter	**chantant**
finir	**finissant**
attendre	**attendant**
sortir	**sortant**
prendre	**prenant**

Avoir, être, and **savoir** have irregular present participle forms.

être **étant**	avoir **ayant**	savoir **sachant**

1. Present participles used as adjectives agree with the noun they modify.

Nous avons vu **un film amusant** à la télévision hier.	*We saw a funny (amusing) film on television last night.*
Vous avez **des idées surprenantes.**	*You have surprising ideas.*

2. **En** followed by a present participle may be translated by a variety of English words *(by, in, on, as,* etc.). It explains how something is done.

Il a appris à faire la cuisine **en regardant** sa mère.	*He learned to cook by watching his mother.*

3. The phrase **tout en** + present participle expresses the idea of two actions going on at the same time. **Tout** does not always have an English equivalent.

Continue. Je peux t'écouter **tout en travaillant.**	*Keep going. I can listen to you while I work.*

ATTENTION! Verb forms in *-ing* are very common in English. They are only rarely, however, the equivalent of the French present participle. Compare the following:

Nous avons commencé **à étudier.**	*We started studying.*
Elle était **assise.**	*She was sitting down.*
Voilà la femme **de ménage.**	*There's the cleaning lady.*

Rappel! The English progressive tenses have no direct equivalent in French.

He is singing. = Il **chante.**
She was singing. = Elle **chantait.**

▶▶ L'infinitif

The infinitive of a verb is the form found in a vocabulary list or in the dictionary. Infinitives in French end in **-er (parler, aller, espérer)**, **-ir (finir, sortir, ouvrir)**, **-re (vendre, prendre, être)**, or **-oir (vouloir, devoir, avoir).**

You have already seen infinitives used in a number of ways.

1. As the equivalent of the English *to + verb:*

Il ne veut pas **nager.**	*He doesn't want to swim.*
Vous ne m'avez pas dit de **faire** la vaisselle!!	*You didn't tell me to do the dishes!!*

2. As the equivalent of the English *verb + -ing:*

Il est parti sans **manger.**	*He left without eating.*
Qui a envie de **jouer** au tennis?	*Who feels like playing tennis?*

3. As part of a compound noun:

une salle à **manger**	*a dining room*
une machine à **écrire**	*a typewriter*

Verbe + infinitif

Verbs in French may be followed directly by an infinitive or may require the insertion of **à** or **de** in front of the infinitive.

Tu aimes **étudier?**	*You like to study?*
J'essaie **de** t'**aider.**	*I'm trying to help you.*
Elle a commencé **à étudier.**	*She's started to study.*

Here are two lists of verbs, one that inserts the preposition **à** before an infinitive and one that inserts the preposition **de.** These lists represent the verbs presented in *VOILÀ!* and so are not complete. You should continue to add to these lists as you study French.

VERBE + **à** + INFINITIF	VERBE + **de** + INFINITIF
aider qqn à	accepter de
apprendre à	choisir de
chercher à	décider de
commencer à	demander à qqn de
continuer à	dire à qqn de
inviter qqn à	essayer de
passer (du temps) à	finir de
réussir à	offrir de
s'amuser à	oublier de
se préparer à	permettre de
	promettre à qqn de
	refuser de
	rêver de
	venir de *(to have just)*

►► Les pronoms relatifs *dont* et *ce dont*

Dont

The relative pronoun **dont** connects two sentences sharing the same noun just as do the relative pronouns **qui** and **que. Dont,** however, indicates that the shared word is preceded by the preposition **de** in one of the sentences. In other words, **dont** replaces **de** plus the following word. The English equivalent is *of whom, of which, about whom, about which,* or *whose.* Although English allows some of these relative pronouns to be deleted, French does not.

> C'est **le professeur.** + Je connais le fils **de ce professeur.** =
>   C'est le professeur **dont** je connais le fils.
>   *That's the instructor. + I know that instructor's son (the son of that instructor). =*
>   *That's the instructor whose son I know.*

> J'ai vu **les étudiants.** + Tu m'as parlé **de ces étudiants.** =
>   J'ai vu les étudiants **dont** tu m'as parlé.
>   *I saw the students. + You talked to me about those students. =*
>   *I saw the students you talked to me about.*

> Voilà **le crayon.** + J'ai besoin **de ce crayon.** =
>   Voilà le crayon **dont** j'ai besoin.
>   *There's the pencil. + I need that pencil.*
>   *There's the pencil I need (of which I have need).*

Ce dont

Ce dont, like **ce qui** and **ce que,** means *what* and refers to something indefinite. It is used with expressions incorporating **de** such as **avoir besoin de, avoir peur de, se souvenir de,** etc.

> **Ce dont** j'ai besoin, c'est de paix! *What I need is some peace!*
> Je ne sais pas **ce dont** j'ai envie. *I don't know what I feel like having.*

►► Les pronoms démonstratifs: *celui, celle, ceux, celles*

You have already learned the forms and use of the demonstrative adjective **ce.**

> Tu veux **cette** pomme? *Do you want this/that apple?*
> Vous voyez **cet** homme et *Do you see that man and those women?*
>   **ces** femmes?

A demonstrative pronoun replaces a demonstrative adjective and its noun. Here are some examples.

Tu veux cette pomme-ci ou **celle-là?**   *Do you want this apple or that one?*
  (**celle-là = cette pomme-là**)

—Vous voyez cet homme?   *"Do you see that man?"*
—Quel homme?   *"What man?"*
—**Celui** qui est derrière la table.   *"The one behind the table."*
(**celui qui est derrière la table = cet homme qui est derrière la table**)

Demonstrative pronouns cannot stand alone. They must be followed by one of three structures:

1. **-ci** or **-là:**

    —Prenez une pomme.   *"Take an apple."*
    —**Celle-ci** ou **celle-là?**   *"This one or that one?"*

See the **Instructor's Resource Manual** for more information.

2. A prepositional phrase:

    —Tu veux ces livres-ci ou   *Do you want these books or Marc's?*
    ceux de Marc?

3. A relative clause:

    —Tu veux un magazine?   *"Do you want a magazine?"*
    —Oui, mais je veux **celui que**   *"Yes, but I want the one you're reading!"*
    tu lis!

▶▶ Les pronoms possessifs

You have already learned the forms and use of possessive adjectives.

—C'est **ton** livre?   *"Is this your book?"*
—Non, c'est **leur** livre.   *"No, it's their book."*

A possessive pronoun replaces a possessive adjective and its noun.

—C'est **le tien?**   *"Is this yours?"*
—Non, c'est **le leur.**   *"No, it's theirs."*

Here are the forms of the possessive pronouns.

MINE	YOURS *(familiar)*	HIS, HERS, ITS
le mien	le tien	le sien
la mienne	la tienne	la sienne
les miens	les tiens	les siens
les miennes	les tiennes	les siennes
OURS	YOURS *(formal, pl.)*	THEIRS
le nôtre	le vôtre	le leur
la nôtre	la vôtre	la leur
les nôtres	les vôtres	les leurs

Possessive pronouns agree in number and gender with the noun they replace.

Voilà mon affiche et voilà **la vôtre.**   *Here's my poster and here's yours.*
  (**la vôtre=votre affiche**)

David a pris tes clés et **les miennes!**   *David took your keys and mine!*
  (**les miennes = mes clés**)

—On prend ta voiture ou   *"Shall we take your car or mine?"*
  la mienne?
—Prenons **la tienne,** elle est   *"Let's take yours; it's less dirty."*
  moins sale.
  (**la mienne = ma voiture, la tienne = ta voiture**)

See the **Instructor's
Resource Manual** for
more information.

▶ L'ordre des pronoms d'objet, *y* et *en*

When more than one object pronoun is used, certain rules of order apply. For all cases except affirmative commands, Table 1 applies. Use Table 2 for affirmative commands.

TABLE 1. BEFORE THE VERB

me te se nous vous	BEFORE	le la les	BEFORE	lui leur	BEFORE	y	BEFORE	en

---

TABLE 2. AFFIRMATIVE COMMANDS (AFTER THE VERB)

le la nous	BEFORE	moi (m') toi (t') lui nous vous leur	BEFORE	y	BEFORE	en

---

Fatima donne **des fleurs à sa mère.**	Fatima **lui en** donne.
La mère de Fatima donne **les fleurs à sa mère!**	Elle **les lui** donne!
Donne **ces fleurs à ton père.**	Donne-**les-lui.**
On ne va plus parler **de cela aux enfants!**	On ne va plus **leur en** parler!
On **m'**a donné **des fleurs** hier.	On **m'en** a donné hier.
Donnez-**moi ce crayon.**	Donnez-**le-moi.**
Donnez-**moi des crayons.**	Donnez-**m'en.**
Il **y** a **des crayons?**	Il **y en** a?

▶▶ La place des adjectifs

As you have already learned, the majority of adjectives in French follow the noun they modify.

> Candide n'aime pas les films **violents.** *Candide doesn't like violent movies.*

A small group of adjectives, however, precede the noun they modify.

beau, (bel) belle, beaux, belles	Jacques Dubois a une **belle** maison.
bon, bonne	J'ai une **bonne** idée.
grand, grande	Suzanne a une **grande** chambre.
gros, grosse	Quel **gros** chien!
jeune	François est un **jeune** enfant.
joli, jolie	Sylvie a une **jolie** chambre.
long, longue	Quelle **longue** journée!
mauvais, mauvaise	Ça, c'est une **mauvaise** idée.
nouveau, (nouvel) nouvelle, nouveaux, nouvelles	J'ai une **nouvelle** robe.
pauvre	La **pauvre** femme!
petit, petite	Tu vois le **petit** chat?
vieux (vieil), vieille, vieux, vieilles	M. Martin est un **vieil** homme.

Some adjectives may be found either before or after the noun they modify. These adjectives change meaning according to their position.

ADJECTIF	AVANT LE NOM	DERRIÈRE LE NOM
dernier, dernière	*last of a series, final* le **dernier** jour de la semaine le **dernier** étage	*last, most recent* (for **semaine, mois, année**) la semaine **dernière**
cher, chère	*dear, beloved* **Chère** Aline, Je t'écris pour...	*expensive* La Mercédès est une voiture **chère.**
grand, grande	*great, important* (refers to people) On dit que Napoléon était un **grand** homme.	*tall* (refers to people) Mais on ne dit pas que c'était un homme **grand!**
même	*same* C'est la **même** chose.	*very, even, itself* Elle, c'est la bonté (*goodness*) **même.**
pauvre	*unfortunate, pitiful* Le **pauvre** garçon, il a tout perdu.	*without money* C'est un garçon **pauvre** mais intelligent.
propre	*own* C'est ma **propre** idée.	*clean* Tu as les mains **propres?**

Appendice de verbes

▶ A. Verbs *être* and *avoir*

avoir (to have)

INFINITIF: **avoir** (to have)
PARTICIPE PRÉSENT: ayant
PARTICIPE PASSÉ: eu

INDICATIF

PRÉSENT	IMPARFAIT	PASSÉ SIMPLE	FUTUR
ai	avais	eus	aurai
as	avais	eus	auras
a	avait	eut	aura
avons	avions	eûmes	aurons
avez	aviez	eûtes	aurez
ont	avaient	eurent	auront

PASSÉ COMPOSÉ	PLUS-QUE-PARFAIT	FUTUR ANTÉRIEUR
ai eu	avais eu	aurai eu
as eu	avais eu	auras eu
a eu	avait eu	aura eu
avons eu	avions eu	aurons eu
avez eu	aviez eu	aurez eu
ont eu	avaient eu	auront eu

CONDITIONNEL

PRÉSENT DU CONDITIONNEL	CONDITIONNEL PASSÉ
aurais	aurais eu
aurais	aurais eu
aurait	aurait eu
aurions	aurions eu
auriez	auriez eu
auraient	auraient eu

SUBJONCTIF

PRÉSENT DU SUBJONCTIF
que j' aie
que tu aies
qu'il/elle ait
que nous ayons
que vous ayez
qu'ils/elles aient

IMPÉRATIF
aie
ayons
ayez

être (to be)

INFINITIF: **être** (to be)
PARTICIPE PRÉSENT: étant
PARTICIPE PASSÉ: été

INDICATIF

PRÉSENT	IMPARFAIT	PASSÉ SIMPLE	FUTUR
suis	étais	fus	serai
es	étais	fus	seras
est	était	fut	sera
sommes	étions	fûmes	serons
êtes	étiez	fûtes	serez
sont	étaient	furent	seront

PASSÉ COMPOSÉ	PLUS-QUE-PARFAIT	FUTUR ANTÉRIEUR
ai été	avais été	aurai été
as été	avais été	auras été
a été	avait été	aura été
avons été	avions été	aurons été
avez été	aviez été	aurez été
ont été	avaient été	auront été

CONDITIONNEL

PRÉSENT DU CONDITIONNEL	CONDITIONNEL PASSÉ
serais	aurais été
serais	aurais été
serait	aurait été
serions	aurions été
seriez	auriez été
seraient	auraient été

SUBJONCTIF

PRÉSENT DU SUBJONCTIF
sois
sois
soit
soyons
soyez
soient

IMPÉRATIF
sois
soyons
soyez

▶ B. Regular verbs

-er verbs

INFINITIF: parler (to speak)
PARTICIPE PRÉSENT: parlant
PARTICIPE PASSÉ: parlé

INDICATIF

PRÉSENT	IMPARFAIT	PASSÉ SIMPLE	FUTUR
parle	parlais	parlai	parlerai
parles	parlais	parlas	parleras
parle	parlait	parla	parlera
parlons	parlions	parlâmes	parlerons
parlez	parliez	parlâtes	parlerez
parlent	parlaient	parlèrent	parleront

PASSÉ COMPOSÉ	PLUS-QUE-PARFAIT	FUTUR ANTÉRIEUR
ai parlé	avais parlé	aurai parlé
as parlé	avais parlé	auras parlé
a parlé	avait parlé	aura parlé
avons parlé	avions parlé	aurons parlé
avez parlé	aviez parlé	aurez parlé
ont parlé	avaient parlé	auront parlé

CONDITIONNEL

CONDITIONNEL	CONDITIONNEL PASSÉ
parlerais	aurais parlé
parlerais	aurais parlé
parlerait	aurait parlé
parlerions	aurions parlé
parleriez	auriez parlé
parleraient	auraient parlé

SUBJONCTIF

PRÉSENT DU SUBJONCTIF: parle, parles, parle, parlions, parliez, parlent

IMPÉRATIF

parle, parlons, parlez

-ir verbs

INFINITIF: dormir* (to sleep)
PARTICIPE PRÉSENT: dormant
PARTICIPE PASSÉ: dormi

INDICATIF

PRÉSENT	IMPARFAIT	PASSÉ SIMPLE	FUTUR
dors	dormais	dormis	dormirai
dors	dormais	dormis	dormiras
dort	dormait	dormit	dormira
dormons	dormions	dormîmes	dormirons
dormez	dormiez	dormîtes	dormirez
dorment	dormaient	dormirent	dormiront

PASSÉ COMPOSÉ	PLUS-QUE-PARFAIT	FUTUR ANTÉRIEUR
ai dormi	avais dormi	aurai dormi
as dormi	avais dormi	auras dormi
a dormi	avait dormi	aura dormi
avons dormi	avions dormi	aurons dormi
avez dormi	aviez dormi	aurez dormi
ont dormi	avaient dormi	auront dormi

CONDITIONNEL

CONDITIONNEL	CONDITIONNEL PASSÉ
dormirais	aurais dormi
dormirais	aurais dormi
dormirait	aurait dormi
dormirions	aurions dormi
dormiriez	auriez dormi
dormiraient	auraient dormi

SUBJONCTIF

PRÉSENT DU SUBJONCTIF: dorme, dormes, dorme, dormions, dormiez, dorment

IMPÉRATIF

dors, dormons, dormez

---

*Other verbs like **dormir** are **mentir, partir, sortir, s'endormir**. Note that **partir, sortir**, and **s'endormir** are conjugated with **être** in the *passé composé*.

VERBE: -ir verbs
INFINITIF: finir* (to finish)
PARTICIPE PRÉSENT: finissant
PARTICIPE PASSÉ: fini

INDICATIF				CONDITIONNEL	SUBJONCTIF	IMPÉRATIF
PRÉSENT	IMPARFAIT	PASSÉ SIMPLE	FUTUR	CONDITIONNEL	PRÉSENT DU SUBJONCTIF	
finis	finissais	finis	finirai	finirais	finisse	
finis	finissais	finis	finiras	finirais	finisses	finis
finit	finissait	finit	finira	finirait	finisse	
finissons	finissions	finîmes	finirons	finirions	finissions	finissons
finissez	finissiez	finîtes	finirez	finiriez	finissiez	finissez
finissent	finissaient	finirent	finiront	finiraient	finissent	
PASSÉ COMPOSÉ	PLUS-QUE-PARFAIT		FUTUR ANTÉRIEUR	CONDITIONNEL PASSÉ		
ai fini	avais fini		aurai fini	aurais fini		
as fini	avais fini		auras fini	aurais fini		
a fini	avait fini		aura fini	aurait fini		
avons fini	avions fini		aurons fini	aurions fini		
avez fini	aviez fini		aurez fini	auriez fini		
ont fini	avaient fini		auront fini	auraient fini		

VERBE: -re verbs
INFINITIF: vendre† (to sell)
PARTICIPE PRÉSENT: vendant
PARTICIPE PASSÉ: vendu

INDICATIF				CONDITIONNEL	SUBJONCTIF	IMPÉRATIF
PRÉSENT	IMPARFAIT	PASSÉ SIMPLE	FUTUR	CONDITIONNEL	PRÉSENT DU SUBJONCTIF	
vends	vendais	vendis	vendrai	vendrais	vende	
vends	vendais	vendis	vendras	vendrais	vendes	vends
vend	vendait	vendit	vendra	vendrait	vende	
vendons	vendions	vendîmes	vendrons	vendrions	vendions	vendons
vendez	vendiez	vendîtes	vendrez	vendriez	vendiez	vendez
vendent	vendaient	vendirent	vendront	vendraient	vendent	
PASSÉ COMPOSÉ	PLUS-QUE-PARFAIT		FUTUR ANTÉRIEUR	CONDITIONNEL PASSÉ		
ai vendu	avais vendu		aurai vendu	aurais vendu		
as vendu	avais vendu		auras vendu	aurais vendu		
a vendu	avait vendu		aura vendu	aurait vendu		
avons vendu	avions vendu		aurons vendu	aurions vendu		
avez vendu	aviez vendu		aurez vendu	auriez vendu		
ont vendu	avaient vendu		auront vendu	auraient vendu		

*Other verbs like **finir** are **agir, choisir, grossir, maigrir, réfléchir, réussir.**
†Other verbs like **vendre** are **attendre, descendre, perdre, rendre, répondre.** Note that **descendre** is conjugated with **être** in the *passé composé.*

▲ C. Reflexive verbs

VERBE

INFINITIF **se laver** (to wash oneself)
PARTICIPE PRÉSENT se lavant
PARTICIPE PASSÉ lavé

INDICATIF

PRÉSENT	IMPARFAIT	PASSÉ SIMPLE	FUTUR
me lave	me lavais	me lavai	me laverai
te laves	te lavais	te lavas	te laveras
se lave	se lavait	se lava	se lavera
nous lavons	nous lavions	nous lavâmes	nous laverons
vous lavez	vous laviez	vous lavâtes	vous laverez
se lavent	se lavaient	se lavèrent	se laveront

PASSÉ COMPOSÉ	PLUS-QUE-PARFAIT	FUTUR ANTÉRIEUR
me suis lavé(e)	m'étais lavé(e)	me serai lavé(e)
t'es lavé(e)	t'étais lavé(e)	te seras lavé(e)
s'est lavé(e)	s'était lavé(e)	se sera lavé(e)
nous sommes lavé(e)s	nous étions lavé(e)s	nous serons lavé(e)s
vous êtes lavé(e)(s)	vous étiez lavé(e)(s)	vous serez lavé(e)(s)
se sont lavé(e)s	s'étaient lavé(e)s	se seront lavé(e)s

CONDITIONNEL

CONDITIONNEL	CONDITIONNEL PASSÉ
me laverais	me serais lavé(e)
te laverais	te serais lavé(e)
se laverait	se serait lavé(e)
nous laverions	nous serions lavé(e)s
vous laveriez	vous seriez lavé(e)(s)
se laveraient	se seraient lavé(e)s

SUBJONCTIF

PRÉSENT DU SUBJONCTIF

me lave
te laves
se lave
nous lavions
vous laviez
se lavent

IMPÉRATIF

lave-toi
lavons-nous
lavez-vous

▲ D. Verbs with spelling changes

VERBE	PRÉSENT	IMPARFAIT	PASSÉ COMPOSÉ	PASSÉ SIMPLE	FUTUR	CONDITIONNEL	PRÉSENT DU SUBJONCTIF	IMPÉRATIF
manger* (to eat)	mange	mangeais	ai mangé	mangeai	mangerai	mangerais	mange	
	manges	mangeais	as mangé	mangeas	mangeras	mangerais	manges	mange
mangeant	mange	mangeait	a mangé	mangea	mangera	mangerait	mange	
mangé	mangeons	mangions	avons mangé	mangeâmes	mangerons	mangerions	mangions	mangeons
	mangez	mangiez	avez mangé	mangeâtes	mangerez	mangeriez	mangiez	mangez
	mangent	mangeaient	ont mangé	mangèrent	mangeront	mangeraient	mangent	

*Other verbs like **manger** are **bouger, changer, déménager, diriger, interroger, loger, nager, neiger, partager, ranger, voyager.**

VERBE	PRÉSENT	IMPARFAIT	PASSÉ COMPOSÉ	PASSÉ SIMPLE	FUTUR	CONDITIONNEL	PRÉSENT DU SUBJONCTIF	IMPÉRATIF
commencer*	commence	commençais	ai commencé	commençai	commencerai	commencerais	commence	
(to begin)	commences	commençais	as commencé	commenças	commenceras	commencerais	commences	commence
commençant	commence	commençait	a commencé	commença	commencera	commencerait	commence	
commencé	commençons	commencions	avons commencé	commençâmes	commencerons	commencerions	commencions	commençons
	commencez	commenciez	avez commencé	commençâtes	commencerez	commenceriez	commenciez	commencez
	commencent	commençaient	ont commencé	commencèrent	commenceront	commenceraient	commencent	
essayer†	essaie	essayais	ai essayé	essayai	essaierai	essaierais	essaie	
(to try)	essaies	essayais	as essayé	essayas	essaieras	essaierais	essaies	essaie
essayant	essaie	essayait	a essayé	essaya	essaiera	essaierait	essaie	
essayé	essayons	essayions	avons essayé	essayâmes	essaierons	essaierions	essayions	essayons
	essayez	essayiez	avez essayé	essayâtes	essaierez	essaieriez	essayiez	essayez
	essaient	essayaient	ont essayé	essayèrent	essaieront	essaieraient	essaient	
acheter‡	achète	achetais	ai acheté	achetai	achèterai	achèterais	achète	
(to buy)	achètes	achetais	as acheté	achetas	achèteras	achèterais	achètes	achète
achetant	achète	achetait	a acheté	acheta	achètera	achèterait	achète	
acheté	achetons	achetions	avons acheté	achetâmes	achèterons	achèterions	achetions	achetons
	achetez	achetiez	avez acheté	achetâtes	achèterez	achèteriez	achetiez	achetez
	achètent	achetaient	ont acheté	achetèrent	achèteront	achèteraient	achètent	
préférer§	préfère	préférais	ai préféré	préférai	préférerai	préférerais	préfère	
(to prefer)	préfères	préférais	as préféré	préféras	préféreras	préférerais	préfères	préfère
préférant	préfère	préférait	a préféré	préféra	préférera	préférerait	préfère	
préféré	préférons	préférions	avons préféré	préférâmes	préférerons	préférerions	préférions	préférons
	préférez	préfériez	avez préféré	préférâtes	préférerez	préféreriez	préfériez	préférez
	préfèrent	préféraient	ont préféré	préférèrent	préféreront	préféreraient	préfèrent	
appeler	appelle	appelais	ai appelé	appelai	appellerai	appellerais	appelle	
(to call)	appelles	appelais	as appelé	appelas	appelleras	appellerais	appelles	appelle
appelant	appelle	appelait	a appelé	appela	appellera	appellerait	appelle	
appelé	appelons	appelions	avons appelé	appelâmes	appellerons	appellerions	appelions	appelons
	appelez	appeliez	avez appelé	appelâtes	appellerez	appelleriez	appeliez	appelez
	appellent	appelaient	ont appelé	appelèrent	appelleront	appelleraient	appellent	

*Other verbs like **commencer** are **divorcer, se fiancer, menacer.**
†Other verbs like **essayer** are **employer, (s')ennuyer, payer.**
‡Other verbs like **acheter** are **emmener, (se) lever, (se) promener.**
§Other verbs like **préférer** are **espérer, (se) sécher.**

▶ E. Irregular verbs

VERBE	PRÉSENT	IMPARFAIT	PASSÉ COMPOSÉ	PASSÉ SIMPLE	FUTUR	CONDITIONNEL	PRÉSENT DU SUBJONCTIF	IMPÉRATIF
aller	vais	allais	suis allé(e)	allai	irai	irais	aille	
(*to go*)	vas	allais	es allé(e)	allas	iras	irais	ailles	va
allant	va	allait	est allé(e)	alla	ira	irait	aille	
allé	allons	allions	sommes allé(e)s	allâmes	irons	irions	allions	allons
	allez	alliez	êtes allé(e)(s)	allâtes	irez	iriez	alliez	allez
	vont	allaient	sont allé(e)s	allèrent	iront	iraient	aillent	
boire	bois	buvais	ai bu	bus	boirai	boirais	boive	
(*to drink*)	bois	buvais	as bu	bus	boiras	boirais	boives	bois
buvant	boit	buvait	a bu	but	boira	boirait	boive	
bu	buvons	buvions	avons bu	bûmes	boirons	boirions	buvions	buvons
	buvez	buviez	avez bu	bûtes	boirez	boiriez	buviez	buvez
	boivent	buvaient	ont bu	burent	boiront	boiraient	boivent	
conduire	conduis	conduisais	ai conduit	conduisis	conduirai	conduirais	conduise	
(*to lead,*	conduis	conduisais	as conduit	conduisis	conduiras	conduirais	conduises	conduis
to drive)	conduit	conduisait	a conduit	conduisit	conduira	conduirait	conduise	
conduisant	conduisons	conduisions	avons conduit	conduisîmes	conduirons	conduirions	conduisions	conduisons
conduit	conduisez	conduisiez	avez conduit	conduisites	conduirez	conduiriez	conduisiez	conduisez
	conduisent	conduisaient	ont conduit	conduisirent	conduiront	conduiraient	conduisent	
connaître	connais	connaissais	ai connu	connus	connaîtrai	connaîtrais	connaisse	
(*to know*)	connais	connaissais	as connu	connus	connaîtras	connaîtrais	connaisses	connais
connaissant	connaît	connaissait	a connu	connut	connaîtra	connaîtrait	connaisse	
connu	connaissons	connaissions	avons connu	connûmes	connaîtrons	connaîtrions	connaissions	connaissons
	connaissez	connaissiez	avez connu	connûtes	connaîtrez	connaîtriez	connaissiez	connaissez
	connaissent	connaissaient	ont connu	connurent	connaîtront	connaîtraient	connaissent	
courir	cours	courais	ai couru	courus	courrai	courrais	coure	
(*to run*)	cours	courais	as couru	courus	courras	courrais	coures	cours
courant	court	courait	a couru	courut	courra	courrait	coure	
couru	courons	courions	avons couru	courûmes	courrons	courrions	courions	courons
	courez	couriez	avez couru	courûtes	courrez	courriez	couriez	courez
	courent	couraient	ont couru	coururent	courront	courraient	courent	
croire	crois	croyais	ai cru	crus	croirai	croirais	croie	
(*to believe*)	crois	croyais	as cru	crus	croiras	croirais	croies	crois
croyant	croit	croyait	a cru	crut	croira	croirait	croie	
cru	croyons	croyions	avons cru	crûmes	croirons	croirions	croyions	croyons
	croyez	croyiez	avez cru	crûtes	croirez	croiriez	croyiez	croyez
	croient	croyaient	ont cru	crurent	croiront	croiraient	croient	

VERBE	PRÉSENT	IMPARFAIT	PASSÉ COMPOSÉ	PASSÉ SIMPLE	FUTUR	CONDITIONNEL	PRÉSENT DU SUBJONCTIF	IMPÉRATIF
devoir (to have to, to owe) devant dû	dois dois doit devons devez doivent	devais devais devait devions deviez devaient	ai dû as dû a dû avons dû avez dû ont dû	dus dus dut dûmes dûtes durent	devrai devras devra devrons devrez devront	devrais devrais devrait devrions devriez devraient	doive doives doive devions deviez doivent	dois devons devez
dire (to say, to tell) disant dit	dis dis dit disons dites disent	disais disais disait disions disiez disaient	ai dit as dit a dit avons dit avez dit ont dit	dis dis dit dîmes dîtes dirent	dirai diras dira dirons direz diront	dirais dirais dirait dirions diriez diraient	dise dises dise disions disiez disent	dis disons dites
écrire* (to write) écrivant écrit	écris écris écrit écrivons écrivez écrivent	écrivais écrivais écrivait écrivions écriviez écrivaient	ai écrit as écrit a écrit avons écrit avez écrit ont écrit	écrivis écrivis écrivit écrivîmes écrivîtes écrivirent	écrirai écriras écrira écrirons écrirez écriront	écrirais écrirais écrirait écririons écririez écriraient	écrive écrives écrive écrivions écriviez écrivent	écris écrivons écrivez
envoyer (to send) envoyant envoyé	envoie envoies envoie envoyons envoyez envoient	envoyais envoyais envoyait envoyions envoyiez envoyaient	ai envoyé as envoyé a envoyé avons envoyé avez envoyé ont envoyé	envoyai envoyas envoya envoyâmes envoyâtes envoyèrent	enverrai enverras enverra enverrons enverrez enverront	enverrais enverrais enverrait enverrions enverriez enverraient	envoie envoies envoie envoyions envoyiez envoient	envoie envoyons envoyez
faire (to do, to make) faisant fait	fais fais fait faisons faites font	faisais faisais faisait faisions faisiez faisaient	ai fait as fait a fait avons fait avez fait ont fait	fis fis fit fîmes fîtes firent	ferai feras fera ferons ferez feront	ferais ferais ferait ferions feriez feraient	fasse fasses fasse fassions fassiez fassent	fais faisons faites
falloir (to be necessary) fallu	il faut	il fallait	il a fallu	il fallut	il faudra	il faudrait	il faille	

*Other verb conjugated like **écrire: décrire.**

VERBE	PRÉSENT	IMPARFAIT	PASSÉ COMPOSÉ	PASSÉ SIMPLE	FUTUR	CONDITIONNEL	PRÉSENT DU SUBJONCTIF	IMPÉRATIF
lire (to read) lisant lu	lis lis lit lisons lisez lisent	lisais lisais lisait lisions lisiez lisaient	ai lu as lu a lu avons lu avez lu ont lu	lus lus lut lûmes lûtes lurent	lirai liras lira lirons lirez liront	lirais lirais lirait lirions liriez liraient	lise lises lise lisions lisiez lisent	lis lisons lisez
mettre* (to put) mettant mis	mets mets met mettons mettez mettent	mettais mettais mettait mettions mettiez mettaient	ai mis as mis a mis avons mis avez mis ont mis	mis mis mit mîmes mîtes mirent	mettrai mettras mettra mettrons mettrez mettront	mettrais mettrais mettrait mettrions mettriez mettraient	mette mettes mette mettions mettiez mettent	mets mettons mettez
ouvrir† (to open) ouvrant ouvert	ouvre ouvres ouvre ouvrons ouvrez ouvrent	ouvrais ouvrais ouvrait ouvrions ouvriez ouvraient	ai ouvert as ouvert a ouvert avons ouvert avez ouvert ont ouvert	ouvris ouvris ouvrit ouvrîmes ouvrîtes ouvrirent	ouvrirai ouvriras ouvrira ouvrirons ouvrirez ouvriront	ouvrirais ouvrirais ouvrirait ouvririons ouvririez ouvriraient	ouvre ouvres ouvre ouvrions ouvriez ouvrent	ouvre ouvrons ouvrez
pleuvoir (to rain) pleuvant plu	il pleut	il pleuvait	il a plu	il plut	il pleuvra	il pleuvrait	il pleuve	
pouvoir (to be able) pouvant pu	peux peux peut pouvons pouvez peuvent	pouvais pouvais pouvait pouvions pouviez pouvaient	ai pu as pu a pu avons pu avez pu ont pu	pus pus put pûmes pûtes purent	pourrai pourras pourra pourrons pourrez pourront	pourrais pourrais pourrait pourrions pourriez pourraient	puisse puisses puisse puissions puissiez puissent	
prendre‡ (to take) prenant pris	prends prends prend prenons prenez prennent	prenais prenais prenait prenions preniez prenaient	ai pris as pris a pris avons pris avez pris ont pris	pris pris prit prîmes prîtes prirent	prendrai prendras prendra prendrons prendrez prendront	prendrais prendrais prendrait prendrions prendriez prendraient	prenne prennes prenne prenions preniez prennent	prends prenons prenez

*Other verbs conjugated like **mettre: permettre, promettre.**
†Other verbs conjugated like **ouvrir: découvrir, offrir, souffrir.**
‡Other verbs conjugated like **prendre: apprendre, comprendre, surprendre.**

VERBE	PRÉSENT	IMPARFAIT	PASSÉ COMPOSÉ	PASSÉ SIMPLE	FUTUR	CONDITIONNEL	PRÉSENT DU SUBJONCTIF	IMPÉRATIF
recevoir	reçois	recevais	ai reçu	reçus	recevrai	recevrais	reçoive	
(to receive)	reçois	recevais	as reçu	reçus	recevras	recevrais	reçoives	reçois
recevant	reçoit	recevait	a reçu	reçut	recevra	recevrait	reçoive	
reçu	recevons	recevions	avons reçu	reçûmes	recevrons	recevrions	recevions	recevons
	recevez	receviez	avez reçu	reçûtes	recevrez	recevriez	receviez	recevez
	reçoivent	recevaient	ont reçu	reçurent	recevront	recevraient	reçoivent	
rire*	ris	riais	ai ri	ris	rirai	rirais	rie	
(to laugh)	ris	riais	as ri	ris	riras	rirais	ries	ris
riant	rit	riait	a ri	rit	rira	rirait	rie	
ri	rions	riions	avons ri	rîmes	rirons	ririons	riions	rions
	riez	riiez	avez ri	rîtes	rirez	ririez	riiez	riez
	rient	riaient	ont ri	rirent	riront	riraient	rient	
savoir	sais	savais	ai su	sus	saurai	saurais	sache	
(to know)	sais	savais	as su	sus	sauras	saurais	saches	sache
sachant	sait	savait	a su	sut	saura	saurait	sache	
su	savons	savions	avons su	sûmes	saurons	saurions	sachions	sachons
	savez	saviez	avez su	sûtes	saurez	sauriez	sachiez	sachez
	savent	savaient	ont su	surent	sauront	sauraient	sachent	
suivre	suis	suivais	ai suivi	suivis	suivrai	suivrais	suive	
(to follow)	suis	suivais	as suivi	suivis	suivras	suivrais	suives	suis
suivant	suit	suivait	a suivi	suivit	suivra	suivrait	suive	
suivi	suivons	suivions	avons suivi	suivîmes	suivrons	suivrions	suivions	suivons
	suivez	suiviez	avez suivi	suivîtes	suivrez	suivriez	suiviez	suivez
	suivent	suivaient	ont suivi	suivirent	suivront	suivraient	suivent	
venir†	viens	venais	suis venu(e)	vins	viendrai	viendrais	vienne	
(to come)	viens	venais	es venu(e)	vins	viendras	viendrais	viennes	viens
venant	vient	venait	est venu(e)	vint	viendra	viendrait	vienne	
venu	venons	venions	sommes venu(e)s	vînmes	viendrons	viendrions	venions	venons
	venez	veniez	êtes venu(e)(s)	vîntes	viendrez	viendriez	veniez	venez
	viennent	venaient	sont venu(e)s	vinrent	viendront	viendraient	viennent	
vivre	vis	vivais	ai vécu	vécus	vivrai	vivrais	vive	
(to live)	vis	vivais	as vécu	vécus	vivras	vivrais	vives	vis
vivant	vit	vivait	a vécu	vécut	vivra	vivrait	vive	
vécu	vivons	vivions	avons vécu	vécûmes	vivrons	vivrions	vivions	vivons
	vivez	viviez	avez vécu	vécûtes	vivrez	vivriez	viviez	vivez
	vivent	vivaient	ont vécu	vécurent	vivront	vivraient	vivent	

*Other verb conjugated like **rire: sourire.**

VERBE	PRÉSENT	IMPARFAIT	PASSÉ COMPOSÉ	PASSÉ SIMPLE	FUTUR	CONDITIONNEL	PRÉSENT DU SUBJONCTIF	IMPÉRATIF
voir	vois	voyais	ai vu	vis	verrai	verrais	voie	
(to see)	vois	voyais	as vu	vis	verras	verrais	voies	vois
voyant	voit	voyait	a vu	vit	verra	verrait	voie	
vu	voyons	voyions	avons vu	vîmes	verrons	verrions	voyions	voyons
	voyez	voyiez	avez vu	vîtes	verrez	verriez	voyiez	voyez
	voient	voyaient	ont vu	virent	verront	verraient	voient	
vouloir	veux	voulais	ai voulu	voulus	voudrai	voudrais	veuille	
(to wish,	veux	voulais	as voulu	voulus	voudras	voudrais	veuilles	veuille
to want)	veut	voulait	a voulu	voulut	voudra	voudrait	veuille	
voulant	voulons	voulions	avons voulu	voulûmes	voudrons	voudrions	voulions	veuillons
voulu	voulez	vouliez	avez voulu	voulûtes	voudrez	voudriez	vouliez	veuillez
	veulent	voulaient	ont voulu	voulurent	voudront	voudraient	veuillent	

Lexique

This list contains words and expressions found in the *Vocabulaires de base* and *Vocabulaires supplémentaires.* Words and expressions included in *Le français familier, Le français tel qu'on le parle,* the *On entend parfois* sections, the *Mini-lexiques de téléphone et de correspondance* (Lesson 14), and the *Expressions avec les parties du corps* section (Lesson 15) are not included. The number following each entry indicates the lesson in which a particular word appears as *Vocabulaire de base* (B) or as *Vocabulaire supplémentaire* (S). Additional information about the use of certain words and expressions may be found in the lesson vocabulary lists as well as in the lesson(s) where they appear.

ABRÉVIATIONS

adj.	adjectif	inf.	infinitif	qqch.	quelque chose
adv.	adverbe	invar.	invariable	qqn	quelqu'un
f.	féminin	m.	masculin	v.	verbe
fam.	familier	pl.	pluriel	*	**h** aspiré

➤ Français-Anglais

A

à in, at, to (5B); — **bientôt** see you soon (1B); — **cause de** because of (16B); — **côté de** next to, beside (5B); — **demain** see you tomorrow (1B); — **droite (de)** to the right (of) (11B); — **gauche (de)** to/on the left (of) (11B); — **l'aise** at ease, comfortable (person) (11S); — **l'extérieur (de)** outside (of) (11B); — **l'intérieur (de)** inside (of) (11B); — **l'étranger** abroad (18S); — **la carte** à la carte (13S); — **la radio** on the radio (17B); — **la télévision** on television (17B); — **mon avis** in my opinion (20B); — **pied** on foot (8B); — **quelle heure?** at what time? (6B); — **ta (votre) place** in your place, if it were me (19B); — **votre avis** according to you (11S); — **... heure(s)** at . . . o'clock (6B)

accepter (de + inf.) to accept (20S)
accident *(m.)* accident (19S/20B)
acheter to buy (9B)
acteur *(m.)*, **actrice** *(f.)* actor, actress (17B)
actif, active active (5S/20B)
activité *(f.)* activity (20S)

actuel, actuelle present, current (20S)
(s')adapter à to adapt to (20S)
addition *(f.)* restaurant bill, check (13B)
adjectif *(m.)* adjective
adolescent *(m.)*, **adolescente** *(f.)* adolescent, teenager (5S)
adorable adorable (15S)
adorer to love (4B)
adresse *(f.)* address (11S/14B)
adulte *(m.)* adult (5B)
aéroport *(m.)* airport (18B)
affaires *(f.pl.)* belongings, stuff (10B); business (12B); **les affaires marchent bien** business is good (12S)
affiche *(f.)* poster (1S/3B)
Afrique *(f.)* Africa (18B)
africain(e) African (18S)
âgé(e) old, elderly (2S/5B)
agent immobilier *(m.)* real estate agent (4S/12B)
agir to act (20B)
agréable agreeable, nice, pleasant (3B)
agriculteur *(m.)* farmer (12B)
aider (qqn à + inf.) to help (15B)
aimer to like, to love (4B); — **mieux (que)** to like better (than); to prefer (4B)
aîné(e) *(m. ou f.)* oldest (person in family) (7B)

actuel, actuelle present, current (20S)
Algérie *(f.)* Algeria (18B)
algérien, algérienne Algerian (12S/18B)
Allemagne *(f.)* Germany (18B)
allemand(e) German (18S)
aller to go (6B); — **à pied** to walk to (8S/18B); — **chez le médecin** to go to the doctor (12B); — **en avion** to fly (18B); — **en vélo** to ride a bicycle (18B); — **en voiture** to drive (18B); **alors** so (+ clause) (11B)
Alpes *(f.pl.)* Alps (19S)
américain(e) American (2B)
Amérique *(f.)* America (18B)
ami *(m.)*, **amie** *(f.)* friend (4B)
amitié *(f.)* friendship (20B)
amour *(m.)* love (14S/16B)
amoureux, amoureuse (de) in love (with) (16B)
amusant(e) fun (2S/4B)
amuser to amuse (someone) (15B); **s'amuser** to have a good time, play (15B)
an *(m.)* year (5B)
ancien, ancienne antique, old (11S)
anglais *(m.)* English (language) (4B)
anglais(e) British (18S)
Angleterre *(f.)* England (18B)
animal *(m.)*, **animaux** *(pl.)* animal (4B)
année *(f.)* year (1S/6B)

anniversaire *(m.)* birthday (1S)
annoncer to announce (17S)
annuaire (des téléphones) *(m.)* (telephone) book (14S)
août *(m.)* August (1B)
apéritif *(m.)* drink (served before a meal) (9S)
appareil-photo *(m.)* camera (18B)
appartement *(m.)* apartment (6B)
appeler to call (15B); **s'appeler** to be named (15B)
apporter to bring (13B)
apprécier to appreciate (20S)
apprendre (à) to learn (to) (17B)
après after, afterwards (7B)
après-midi *(m.)* afternoon (6B)
arbre *(m.)* tree (6S/11B)
argent *(m.)* money (11B)
arme du crime *(f.)* crime weapon (17S)
armoire *(f.)* wardrobe (3S)
arrêter to stop (15B); **s'arrêter (de + inf.)** to stop oneself (15B)
arrivée *(f.)* arrival (19B)
arriver (à + inf.) to arrive (at), get (to) (7B)
article *(m.)* article (14B); **— de toilette** *(m.)* toilet article (15S)
artiste *(m. ou f.)* artist (8B)
ascenseur *(m.)* elevator (11S)
Asie *(f.)* Asia (18B)
asiatique Asian (18S)
asperges *(f.pl.)* asparagus (9S)
aspirine *(f.)* aspirin (13B)
assez quite, sufficiently, enough (11B); **— (de)** enough (of) (13B)
assiette (de) *(f.)* plate (of) (13B)
assiette à soupe *(f.)* soup plate (13S)
assis(e) seated, sitting down (18B)
atelier *(m.)* workshop (12S)
attendre to wait (for) (11B); **— qqch. avec impatience** to be excited about something, to not be able to wait for something (16S)
au bord de at the side of (19B)
au bout (de) at the end (of) (11S)
aujourd'hui today (1S/6B)
au milieu (de) in the middle (of) (13B)
au premier étage on the second floor (11B)
au revoir good-bye (1B)
au rez-de-chaussée on the first floor (11B)
aussi also (1B); **aussi... que** as . . . as (2B)
Australie *(f.)* Australia (18B)
australien, australienne Australian (18S)
autobus *(m.)* bus (city) (18B)
autocar *(m.)* bus (between cities) (18B)
auto-stop *(m.)* hitchhiking (18S)
automne *(m.)* autumn (1B)
autorité *(f.)* authority (20S)
autoroute *(f.)* highway, expressway (18B)

autre other (8B)
avant before (9B)
avant de + inf. before (20B)
avant que + subjonctif before (20B)
avec with (1B)
avenir *(m.)* future (20B)
avenue *(f.)* avenue (11S)
avion *(m.)* airplane (18B)
avocat *(m.)*, **avocate** *(f.)* (court) lawyer (12B)
avoir to have (3B); **— ... ans** to be . . . years old (5B); **— besoin de** to need (10B); **— bon/mauvais caractère** to be easy/hard to get along with (16S); **— chaud** to be hot (6B); **— de la chance** to be lucky (19B); **— de la patience/ne pas avoir de patience** to have patience/ to not have patience (16S); **— des illusions** to have illusions (20S); **— des responsabilités** to have responsibilities (12B); **— des soucis** to have worries (20S); **— envie de (+ inf.)** to feel like (+ inf.) (8B); **— faim** to be hungry (9B); **— froid** to be cold (6B); **— l'air (+ adj.)** to look like, to seem (10B); **— l'air (de + inf.)** to look like, to seem (10B); **— la/une grippe** to have the flu (15S); **— le temps (de + inf.)** to have time to (+ inf.) (10B); **— avoir mal** to hurt (13S/15B); **— mal à la tête** to have a headache (13S/15B); **— mal à la gorge** to have a sore throat (15B); **— mal au dos** to have a backache (15B); **— peur (de)** to be afraid (of) (17S); **— raison** to be right (20B); **— soif** to be thirsty (9B); **— sommeil** to be sleepy (6B); **— tort** to be wrong (20B); **— un rhume** to have a cold (15S)
avril *(m.)* April (1B)

B

baccalauréat *(m.)* secondary school-leaving exam (12S)
bagages *(m.pl.)* luggage (18B)
baignoire *(f.)* bathtub (11B)
baladeur *(m.)* walkman (3S)
balcon *(m.)* balcony (11B)
banane *(f.)* banana (9B)
banc *(m.)* bench (5S)
bande dessinée *(f.)* comic strip, comic book (5S/14B)
banque *(f.)* bank (6S/11B)
banquier *(m.)* banker (12B)
barbe *(f.)* beard (15S)
barbu(e) bearded (15S)
basket-ball *(m.)* basketball (8S)
bateau *(m.)*, **bateaux** *(pl.)* boat (6S/8B); **— à voile** *(m.)* sailboat (8S)

bavard(e) talkative (5B)
bavarder to chat (20S)
beau (bel), belle, beaux, belles beautiful, handsome (2B)
beaucoup a lot, much (4B); **— de** a lot of, many (4B)
bébé *(m.)* baby (5S/15B)
beige beige (10B)
belge Belgian (11S/18S)
Belgique *(f.)* Belgium (11S/18S)
besoin *(m.)* need (20S)
bête dumb, stupid (2B)
bêtise *(f.)* dumb thing (15S)
beurre *(m.)* butter (9B)
bibliothèque *(f.)* library (6B)
bien fine, good, well (1B); **— élevé(e)** well-mannered (5S); **— habillé(e)** well-dressed (10S); **— payé** well paid (12B); **— sûr** of course (15B)
bière *(f.)* beer (9B)
bijou *(m.)*, **bijoux** *(pl.)* piece of jewelry, jewelry (10S)
billet (aller-retour, simple) *(m.)* ticket (round trip, one way) (18B)
bizarre weird, strange, odd (2B)
blanc, blanche white (3B)
bleu(e) blue (3B)
blond(e) blond (2B)
blouson *(m.)* jacket (aviator) (10S)
bœuf *(m.)* beef (9B)
boire to drink (4S/9B)
boisson *(f.)* beverage (9S/13B)
boîte (de) *(f.)* can (of), box (of) (13B); **— aux lettres** *(f.)* mailbox (14B); **— de chocolats** *(f.)* box of chocolates (13S)
bon, bonne good (9B); **bon marché** *(invar.)* cheap, inexpensive (13B); **bon week-end!** have a nice weekend! (1S)
bonbon *(m.)* (piece of) candy (9S)
bonheur *(m.)* happiness (20B)
bonjour hello (1B)
bouche *(f.)* mouth (15B)
boucherie *(f.)* butcher shop (13B)
boulangerie *(f.)* bakery (13B)
boulangerie-pâtisserie *(f.)* bakery which sells pastries (13S)
bouteille (de) *(f.)* bottle (of) (13B)
bras *(m.)* arm (15B)
Bretagne *(f.)* Brittany (14S/19B)
briller to shine (6S)
brosse à dents *(f.)* toothbrush (15B)
brosser to brush (15B); **se brosser (les cheveux)** to brush (one's hair) (15B)
bruit *(m.)* noise (12B)
brûler to burn (13S)
brun(e) dark-haired (2B); brown (3B)
bureau *(m.)*, **bureaux** *(pl.)* desk, office (3B); **— de tabac** *(m.)* tobacco shop (14S)
bus *(m., fam.)* (city) bus (18S)

C

ça that; — **coûte cher** it's expensive (11B); — **dépend** that depends (1S); — **me fait peur** that scares me (17S); — **va?** how's it going? (1B); — **y est** that's it, done, finished (1S)

cabine téléphonique *(f.)* telephone booth (14B)

cacher to hide (16S)

cadeau *(m.),* **cadeaux** *(pl.)* present, gift (4B)

cadre *(m.)* executive (12B)

café *(m.)* café (6B); coffee (9B); — **au lait** *(m.)* coffee and milk (9S)

cahier *(m.)* notebook (1B)

caissier *(m.),* **caissière** *(f.)* cashier (12S)

calculatrice *(f.)* calculator (3S)

caleçon *(m.)* boxer shorts (10S)

Californie *(f.)* California (18B)

calme calm (5S); *(m.)* calm, peace and quiet (19B)

camarade de chambre *(m. ou f.)* roommate (3B)

camarade de classe *(m. ou f.)* classmate (4B)

Cameroun *(m.)* Cameroon (18B)

camerounais(e) Cameroonian (18S)

caméscope *(m.)* camcorder (18S)

campagne *(f.)* country, countryside (6B)

camping *(m.)* camping (14S)

camion *(m.)* truck (18S)

Canada *(m.)* Canada (18B)

canadien, canadienne Canadian (2B)

canapé *(m.)* couch (11B)

cancer *(m.)* cancer (20S)

car *(m., fam.)* bus (between cities) (18S)

caractère *(m.)* personality (16S)

carotte *(f.)* carrot (9B)

carte *(f.)* card (8S); restaurant menu (13B); map (18B); — **de crédit** *(f.)* credit card (13B); — **postale** *(f.)* postcard (14B)

cassette *(f.)* cassette (3S); — **vidéo** *(f.)* video tape (17S)

cathédrale *(f.)* cathedral (19S)

cauchemar *(m.)* nightmare (20S)

cave *(f.)* basement (11B)

CD *(m.)* a CD ((3S)

ce, cet, cette/ces this, that/these, those (8B)

célèbre famous (8S/17B)

célébrité *(f.)* celebrity (14S)

célibataire unmarried, single (7B)

centime *(m.)* centime ($^1/100$ franc) (11S)

centre *(m.)* center (19B)

centre-ville *(m.)* center of town, downtown (11S/19B)

cependant nevertheless, however (20B)

céréales *(f.pl.)* cereal (9S)

c'est (ce n'est pas) it is, he is, she is (isn't) (4B); — **à qui?** whose is it? (4S/5B); — **bon/mauvais pour la santé** it's healthy/unhealthy (good/bad for your health) (9S); — **quel jour aujourd'hui?** what's the date today? (1S/6B); — **tout** that's all (2S); — **vrai** that's true (4B)

chaîne *(f.)* television station, channel (17B); — **hi-fi** *(f.)* stereo (3B)

chaise *(f.)* chair (3B)

chambre *(f.)* bedroom (3B)

champ *(m.)* field (6S)

Champs-Élysées *(m.pl.)* Champs-Élysées (main street in Paris) (19S)

champagne *(m.)* champagne (9S)

champignon *(m.)* mushroom (9S)

changement *(m.)* change (20S)

changer to change (15S); — **(de train, d'avion)** to change (trains, planes) (18S); **se changer** to change one's clothes (15S)

chanson *(f.)* song (4S/17B)

chanter to sing (4B)

chanteur *(m.),* **chanteuse** *(f.)* singer (17B)

chapeau *(m.)* hat (10B)

chaque each (19S/20B)

charcuterie *(f.)* cold cuts (9S); pork shop, delicatessen (13B)

chasser to hunt (19S)

chat *(m.)* cat (1B)

châtain(e) light brown (hair) (15S)

château *(m.),* **châteaux** *(pl.)* castle, mansion (19B)

chaud(e) warm, hot; **avoir** — to be hot (6B)

chaussette *(f.)* sock (10B)

chaussure *(f.)* shoe (10B)

chauve bald (15S)

chef d'entreprise *(m.)* business owner (12B)

chemin *(m.)* path, way (11S)

chemise *(f.)* shirt (man's) (10B)

chemisier *(m.)* shirt (woman's) (10B)

chèque *(m.)* check (13B); — **de voyage** *(m.)* traveler's check (18S)

chéquier *(m.)* checkbook (13S)

cher, chère expensive (10B); dear (14B)

chercher to look for, search (for) (6B); — **du travail/un travail** to look for work/a job (12B)

cheveu *(m.),* **cheveux** *(pl.)* hair (15S)

chez at the house of (5B)

chien *(m.)* dog (1B)

chiffre *(m.)* number (1S)

Chine *(f.)* China (18B)

chinois(e) Chinese (9S/18B)

chocolat *(m.)* chocolate (9B)

choisir (de + inf.) to choose (10B)

chômage *(m.)* unemployment (20B)

chômeur *(m.),* **chômeuse** *(f.)* unemployed person (12S)

chose *(f.)* thing (8B)

ciel *(m.)* sky (6S)

cigarette *(f.)* cigarette (4S)

cinéma *(m.)* movie theater, the movies (4B)

cinq five (1B)

cité universitaire *(f.)* dormitory (6B)

citron *(m.)* lemon (9S)

clair(e) bright, full of light (3S/11B); light (color) (10B)

clé *(f.)* key (3B)

client *(m.),* **cliente** *(f.)* client, customer (12B)

climat *(m.)* climate (18S)

Coca-Cola *(m.)* Coca-Cola, cola (9S)

coiffer to fix someone's hair (15S); **se coiffer** to fix one's own hair (15S)

coiffeur *(m.),* **coiffeuse** *(f.)* hairdresser (12S)

coin *(m.)* corner (11S)

coin-repas *(m.)* breakfast nook, eating area (11S)

collant *(m.)* tights, pantyhose (15S)

colline *(f.)* hill (19B)

combien (de) how many (of), how much (5B); — **coûte... ?** how much does . . . cost? (10S/11B); — **de fois (par jour)** how many times (a day) (10S/15B); — **est-ce que je vous dois?** how much do I owe you? (13B)

comédie *(f.)* comedy (movie, play) (17B)

comique funny, amusing, comic (17B)

commander to order (13B)

comme like, as (4B)

commencer (à + inf.) to begin (to), start (to) (6B)

comment what, how (6B); **comment?** what did you say? (1S); — **allez-vous?** how are you? *(formal)* (1B); — **ça va?** how's it going? (1B); — **est Jean?** what is Jean like? (2S); — **t'appelles-tu?** *(fam.)* what's your name? (1S/15B); — **vous appelez-vous?** what's your name? (1S/15B)

commentaire *(m.)* comment, remark (19S)

commerçant(e) shopkeeper (12B)

commissariat de police *(m.)* police station (11S)

commode *(f.)* bureau, chest of drawers (3S)

compartiment *(m.)* (train) compartment (18S)

compréhensif, compréhensive understanding (5B)

comprendre to understand (17B)

concerner to concern (20S)

concert *(m.)* concert (4S/17B)
conduire to drive (18B)
confiture *(f.)* jam (9S)
confort *(m.)* comfort (20S)
confortable comfortable (3S/10B)
congélateur *(m.)* freezer (9S)
connaître to know (16B)
conserves *(f.pl.)* canned food (9S)
content(e) glad (5B)
continent *(m.)* continent (18S)
continuer (à + inf.) to continue (11B);
— **jusqu'à** to continue as far as (11B)
contre la montre timed race (19S)
corbeille à papier *(f.)* wastepaper basket (3S)
corps *(m.)* body (15B)
costume *(m.)* suit (man's) (10B)
côte *(f.)* coast (19B)
Côte d'Azur *(f.)* French Riviera (19S)
coucher to put to bed (15B); **se coucher** to go to bed (15B)
couleur *(f.)* color (3S)
couloir *(m.)* hall, corridor (11S)
coup de foudre *(m.)* love at first sight (16S)
couple *(m.)* couple (16B)
coureur (cycliste) *(m.)* racer (bicycle) (19S)
courrier *(m.)* mail, correspondence (14B)
cours *(m.)* course, class (2B)
course *(f.)* errand (7B)
course (cycliste) *(f.)* race (bicycle) (19S)
court(e) short (10S)
cousin *(m.)*, **cousine** *(f.)* cousin (7B)
couteau *(m.)*, **couteaux** *(pl.)* knife (13B)
coûter to cost (10S/11B); — **cher** to be expensive (10S/11B)
couvert *(m.)* silverware, place setting (13S)
couvert (le temps) overcast (14S)
cravate *(f.)* tie (10B)
crayon *(m.)* pencil (3B)
crèche *(f.)* day-care center, nursery (15S)
crevette *(f.)* shrimp (9B)
crime *(m.)* crime (17S)
crise *(f.)* crisis (16S)
critiquer to criticize (20B)
croire (à) (que) to believe (in) (that) (17B); — **au Père Noël** to believe in Santa Claus (17S); — **en Dieu** to believe in God (17S); — **que oui/non** to believe so/not to believe so (17B)
croisière *(f.)* cruise (18S)
croissant *(m.)* croissant (9S)
crudités *(f.pl.)* raw vegetables (9S)
cuillère *(f.)* spoon (13B); — **à soupe** *(f.)* soup spoon, tablespoon (13B)
cuisine *(f.)* cooking, cuisine (4S/9B); kitchen (7B)
cuisinier *(m.)*, **cuisinière** *(f.)* cook (12S)

cuisinière *(f.)* stove (11S)
culturel, culturelle cultural (14S)

D

d'abord first (of all) (11B)
d'accord all right, OK (1B)
dangereux, dangereuse dangerous (12B)
dans in, within (3B)
danser to dance (4B)
danseur *(m.)*, **danseuse** *(f.)* dancer (17S)
date *(f.)* date (1S)
de of, from, about (1B)
de luxe luxurious (18S)
déborder to spill over (13S)
débrouillard(e) resourceful (5B)
début *(m.)* beginning (17B)
décembre *(m.)* December (1B)
décider (de + inf.) to decide (to do something) (12B)
découvrir to discover (18B)
décrire to describe (14B)
déçu(e) disappointed (16S/20B)
déjà already, yet (11B)
déjeuner *(m.)* lunch (9B)
délicieux, délicieuse delicious (9S/13B)
demain tomorrow (6B)
demander to ask (14B); **se demander** to wonder (16B)
déménager to move (house) (12S)
démodé(e) out of fashion (10S)
dent *(f.)* tooth (15B)
dentifrice *(m.)* toothpaste (15S)
dentiste *(m. ou f.)* dentist (5S/12B)
déodorant *(m.)* deodorant (15S)
départ *(m.)* departure (18S/19B)
se dépêcher to hurry (up) (16B)
déprimé(e) depressed (2S/5B)
dernier, dernière last (11B); **dernier étage** *(m.)* top floor (11S)
derrière behind, in back of (5B); *(m.)* rear end (15S)
descendre to go down (11B)
désert *(m.)* desert (18S)
déshabiller to undress (someone else) (15S); **se déshabiller** to get undressed (15S)
dessert *(m.)* dessert (9B)
dessin animé *(m.)* animated cartoon (17B)
dessin humoristique *(m.)* cartoon (14S)
détester to hate (4B)
deux two (1B)
devant in front of (5B)
devenir to become (17B)
devoir to have to, must (8B); to owe (11B)
devoir *(m.)* assignment (2B); **devoirs** *(m.pl.)* homework (2B)

d'habitude usually (15B)
dictionnaire *(m.)* dictionary (3S)
Dieu God (20S)
différent(e) different (8B)
difficile difficult (5B)
dimanche *(m.)* Sunday (1B)
dinde *(f.)* turkey (9S)
dîner *(m.)* dinner (8S/9B)
dire to say, to tell (14B)
directeur *(m.)*, **directrice** *(f.)* manager (12S)
diriger to manage, run (12B)
discuter (de) to discuss (20B)
se disputer (avec) to argue (with) (16B)
disque *(m.)* record, disc (3B); — **compact** *(m.)* CD (3S)
dissertation *(f.)* paper (written for class) (14B)
disquette *(f.)* microdisk (3S)
divers(e) miscellaneous
divorce *(m.)* divorce (16B)
divorcer to divorce (16B)
divorcé(e) divorced (7B)
dix ten (1B); **dix-huit** eighteen (1B); **dix-neuf** nineteen (1B); **dix-sept** seventeen (1B)
documentaire (sur) *(m.)* documentary (on) (17B)
doigt *(m.)* finger (13B)
donc therefore, thus, so (2B)
donner to give (4B); — **sur** to overlook (11S)
dormir to sleep (4S/5B)
dos *(m.)* back (15B)
douane *(f.)* customs (18S)
douanier *(m.)* customs officer (18S)
douche *(f.)* shower (11B)
dramatique dramatic (17B)
drame *(m.)* drama (17B)
drogue *(f.)* drug (illegal) (20S)
drogué(e) drug addict (20S)
se droguer to take (illegal) drugs (20S)
droit *(m.)* law (5S/14B)
dur(e) hard, tough (12B)
durer to last (17B)
dynamique dynamic (12S)

E

eau *(f.)* water (9B); — **minérale** *(f.)* mineral water (9S)
école *(f.)* school (5B); — **maternelle** *(f.)* nursery school, kindergarten (15S); — **primaire** *(f.)* elementary school (11S)
écologie *(f.)* ecology (20S)
écouter to listen to (4B)
écrire to write (4S/14B)
écrivain *(m.)* writer (14B)
efficace efficient (12S)

égalité *(f.)* equality (20S)
église *(f.)* church (6S/11B)
égoïste selfish (2S/5B)
élégant(e) elegant (5S/10B)
embrasser to kiss, to embrace (16B)
émission *(f.)* program (17B); — **de variétés** *(f.)* variety show (17S)
emmener to take (15B)
employé *(m.)*, **employée** *(f.)* employee (12B)
emporter take, carry (away) (18B)
en in (6B); — **bas** downstairs (11B); — **désordre** messy (3S/11B); — **effet** indeed (17S); — **face (de)** across (from) (11S); — **forme** in shape (5S); — **groupe** as a group (18S); — *haut upstairs (11B); — **même temps** at the same time (17S); — **ordre** straight, neat (3S/11B); — **solde** on sale (10S)
enceinte pregnant (16S)
encore still, again (15B)
s'endormir to fall asleep (16B)
endroit *(m.)* place, spot (6S/18B)
énergique energetic (5S)
énervant(e) annoying (15S)
énerver to irritate/annoy (someone) (15B); **s'énerver** to get irritated/annoyed (15B)
enfant *(m. ou f.)* child (4B)
enfin at last, finally (12B)
ennuyer to bore (15B); **s'ennuyer** to be bored (15B)
ennuyeux, ennuyeuse boring (5S/17B)
ensemble together (10B)
ensoleillé(e) sunny (11S/14B)
ensuite then, next (11B)
entendre to hear (11B); **s'entendre (bien/mal) (avec qqn)** to get along (well/badly) (with someone) (16B)
enthousiaste enthusiastic (5S)
entre between (9B)
entrée *(f.)* first course (appetizer) (9S/13B); entranceway (11S)
entreprise *(f.)* firm, business (12B)
entrer to come/go in, to enter (11B)
environnement *(m.)* environment (20B)
enveloppe *(f.)* envelope (14B)
envoyer to send (14B)
épicerie *(f.)* grocery store (13B)
épinards *(m.pl.)* spinach (9S)
équilibré(e) well-adjusted (2S/5B)
équipe *(f.)* team (8S)
escalier *(m.)* staircase, stairs (11B)
Espagne *(f.)* Spain (18B)
espagnol *(m.)* Spanish (language) (4B)
espérer (que) to hope (that) (18B)
essayer (de + inf.) to try (to) (15B)
est *(m.)* east (14S/19B)
et and (1B); — **toi?** what about you? (1B); — **vous?** what about you? (1B)

étage *(m.)* floor (11B); **dernier —** *(m.)* top floor (11S)
étagère *(f.)* bookcase, shelf (3B)
étape *(f.)* step, stage, stop (18S)
état *(m.)* state, nation (12S)
États-Unis *(m.pl.)* United States (11S/18B); **aux —** in the United States (11S/18B)
été *(m.)* summer (1B)
étoile *(f.)* star (19B)
étranger, étrangère foreign (17B); *(m. ou f.)* foreigner, stranger (19B)
être to be (2B); — **à** to belong to (18B); — **à la mode** to be in fashion (10S); — **à l'heure** to be on time (18B); — **au chômage** to be unemployed (12S); — **au courant de** (+ nom) to be informed, know about (14B); — **au régime** to be on a diet (5S/9B); — **(bien/mal) payé** to be paid (well/badly) (12B); — **conscient(e) de** to be aware of (20S); — **contre** to be against (20B); — **debout** to be standing (up) (18B); — **difficile à vivre** to be hard to get along with (17B); — **en avance** to be early (18B); — **en bonne/mauvaise santé** to be in good/bad health (9B); — **en crise** to be in a crisis (16S); — **en forme** to be in shape, to feel good (5S/9B); — **en retard** to be late (18B); — **entouré(e) de** to be surrounded by (19S); — **en train de** (+ inf.) to be in the middle of (14B); — **en vie** to be alive (7S); — **étudiant(e) en (droit, médecine...)** to study (law, medicine...) (14B); — **facile à vivre** to be easy to get along with (17B); — **indiqué(e)** to be indicated (19S); — **membre (de)** to be a member (of) (8S); — **pour** to be for (20B)
études *(f.pl.)* studies (5S)
étudiant(e) student (1B)
étudier to study (4B)
Europe *(f.)* Europe (18B)
européen, européenne European (18S)
événement *(m.)* event (14S)
évidemment obviously, of course (20B)
évier *(m.)* kitchen sink (11S)
examen *(m.)* test, exam (2B)
excellent(e) excellent (9S/13B)
expliquer to explain (12B)

F

fâché(e) angry, mad, disgruntled (5S)
facile easy (5B)
facteur *(m.)* mail carrier (14B)
facultatif, facultative optional

faim *(f.)* hunger; **avoir —** to be hungry (9B)
faire to do, to make (7B); — **attention** to pay attention, to be careful (16B); — **de l'auto-stop** to hitchhike (18S); — **de la marche** to walk (for exercise) (8B); — **de la musique** to make music (8S/20B); — **de la natation** to swim (8B); — **de la peinture** to paint (8S); — **de la photo** to take pictures (photos) (8S); — **de la planche à voile** to windsurf (8S); — **de la plongée sous-marine** to go scuba diving (8S); — **de la politique** to be involved in politics (20S); — **de la voile** to go sailing (8S); — **de l'exercice** to exercise (8B); — **des bêtises** to do dumb things (15S); — **des économies** to save money (18S); — **du bateau (à voile)** to go (sail) boating (8B); — **du bricolage** to do odd jobs around the house (8S/20B); — **du bruit** to make noise (12S); — **du camping** to go camping, camp (14S); — **du cheval** to go horseback riding (19S); — **du dessin** to draw (8S); — **du jardinage** to work in the garden, to garden (8S/20B); — **du jogging** to jog (8B); — **du ski** to ski(8B); — **du sport** to participate in a sport (8B); — **du surf** to go surfing (19S); — **du vélo** to ride a bike, cycle (8B); — **la connaissance de (qqn)** to meet (someone) (18B); — **la cuisine** to cook (7B); — **la lessive** to do the laundry (7S/16B); — **la sieste** to take a nap (15S); — **la vaisselle** to do the dishes (7B); — **le ménage** to do housework (7B); — **les (ses) bagages** to pack (18S); — **les courses** to run errands (7B); — **les lits** to make the beds (7S); — **les magasins** to go shopping (18S); — **les musées** to do the museums (8B); — **le tour du monde** to go around the world (18S); — **peur (à)** to scare (17S); — **une enquête** to hold/run an investigation (17S); — **une promenade** to take a walk (8B); — **une randonnée** to hike (8B); — **un voyage** to take a trip (18B) **il fait beau** it's nice out (7B); **il fait bon** it's pleasant (mild) (7S); **il fait chaud** it's warm, it's hot (7S); **il fait frais** it's cool (7S); **il fait froid** it's cold (7B); **il fait gris** it's overcast (7S); **il fait lourd** it's hot and humid (7S); **il fait mauvais** it's nasty out (7B)
familier, familière familiar, informal
famille *(f.)* family (7B)
fatigant(e) tiring (8B)
fatigué(e) tired (2B)

fauteuil *(m.)* armchair (3S/11B)
faux, fausse false (4S)
féminin(e) feminine (14S)
femme *(f.)* woman (4B); wife (7B); **— au foyer** *(f.)* housewife (12B); **— de ménage** *(f.)* house cleaner (7S)
fenêtre *(f.)* window (3B)
ferme *(f.)* farm (6S/11B)
fermé(e) closed (13B)
fermer to close (13B)
fête *(f.)* holiday, party (2B)
feuilleton *(m.)* soap opera (17S)
février *(m.)* February (1B)
fiancé *(m.)*, **fiancée** *(f.)* fiancé(e) (16S)
se fiancer to get engaged (16S)
fidèle (à) faithful (to) (16S)
fille *(f.)* girl (4B); daughter (7B)
film *(m.)* film, movie (4S/17B); **— d'amour** romantic movie (17B); **— d'aventures** adventure movie (17B); **— d'espionnage** spy movie (17S); **— d'horreur** horror movie (17B); **— de science-fiction** science fiction movie (17B); **— policier** detective/police movie (17B)
fils *(m.)* son (7B)
fin *(f.)* end (16B)
finalement finally (15B)
financier, financière financial (20S)
finir (de + inf.) to finish (10B)
fleur *(f.)* flower (1S/3B)
fleuve *(m.)* river (major) (11S/19B)
Floride *(f.)* Florida (18B)
fois time; **combien de — ?** how many times? (10S, 15B); **une —** one time, once (10B)
foncé(e) dark (10B)
fonctionnaire *(m. ou f.)* civil servant (12S)
fonder une famille to start a family (16S)
football *(m.)* soccer (4S/8B)
football américain *(m.)* football (8S)
forêt *(f.)* forest (19B)
fort(e) strong, heavy (12B)
foule *(f.)* crowd (19B)
fourchette *(f.)* fork (13B)
fraise *(f.)* strawberry (9B)
franc *(m.)* franc (10B)
français *(m.)* French (language) (4B)
français(e) French (2B)
France *(f.)* France (11S/18B)
frère *(m.)* brother (4B)
frisé(e) curly (15S)
frites *(f.pl.)* (French) fries (9B)
froid *(m.)* cold; **avoir —** to be cold (6B)
fromage *(m.)* cheese (9B)
fruit *(m.)* fruit (9B)
fumer to smoke (4B)

G

gagner to earn (12B); to win (8B); **— sa vie** to earn a living (12S); **— X dollars/francs (l'heure, par jour, par semaine, par mois)** to earn X dollars/francs (per hour, per day, per week, per month) (12S)
gant *(m.)* glove (10B); **— de toilette** *(m.)* washcloth (15S)
garage *(m.)* garage (11S)
garagiste *(m.)* garage owner (12S)
garçon *(m.)* boy (4B)
gare *(f.)* train station (6S/11B)
gâteau (au chocolat) *(m.)*, **gâteaux** *(pl.)* cake (chocolate) (9B)
gâté(e) spoiled (5S)
gens *(m.pl.)* people (19B)
gentil, gentille kind, nice (5B)
généreux, généreuse generous (2B)
géographie *(f.)* geography (5S)
gérant *(m.)*, **gérante** *(f.)* manager (hotel, shop, etc.) (12S)
glace *(f.)* ice cream (9B)
golf *(m.)* golf (8S)
gouvernement *(m.)* government (20S)
goût *(m.)* taste (17S)
goûter *(m.)* light afternoon meal (9S)
gramme (de) *(m.)* gram (of) (13S)
grand(e) tall (person) (2B); big (thing) (3B)
grand-mère *(f.)* grandmother (7B)
grand-père *(m.)* grandfather (7B)
grands-parents *(m.pl.)* grandparents (7B)
gratuit(e) free (of charge) (13S)
grave serious (17B)
grenier *(m.)* attic (11S)
gris(e) gray (10B)
gros, grosse big, fat (2B)
grossir to gain weight (10B)
groupe *(m.)* group (19B)
guerre *(f.)* war (20B)
guichet *(m.)* ticket window (18S)
guitare *(f.)* guitar (3S/5B)

H

habillé(e) dressed, dressed up, formal (10B)
habiller to dress (someone else) (15B); **s'habiller** to get dressed (15B)
habitant *(m.)*, **habitante** *(f.)* native, inhabitant (18S/19B)
habiter to live (inhabit) (5B)
*****haricots verts** *(m.pl.)* green beans (9B)
heure *(f.)* hour, time (6B)
heureusement happily (13B)

heureux, heureuse happy (2B)
hier yesterday (10B)
histoire *(f.)* history (5S); story (16B)
historique historical (19S)
hiver *(m.)* winter (1B)
homme *(m.)* man (4B)
honnête honest (12B)
horrible horrible (8S/18B)
hôpital *(m.)* hospital (6S/11B)
hôtel *(m.)* hotel (6B)
hôtesse de l'air *(f.)* flight attendant, stewardess (18S)
*****huit** eight (1B)
humeur *(f.):* **être de (bonne, mauvaise) —** to be in a (good, bad) mood (5S)

I

ici here (8B)
idéaliste idealistic (20B)
idée *(f.)* idea (9B)
il he, it (1B); **— fait beau** it's nice out (7B); **— fait bon** it's pleasant (mild) (7S); **— fait chaud** it's warm, it's hot (7B); **— fait frais** it's cool (7S); **— fait froid** it's cold (7B); **— fait gris** it's overcast (7S); **— fait lourd** it's hot and humid (7S); **— fait mauvais** it's nasty out (7B)
il faudrait (+ inf.) one should (+ inf.) (15S)
il faut (que) it is necessary that (20B); **il faut + nom ou inf.** you have to + infinitive, one needs + noun (9S)
il neige it's snowing (7B)
il n'y a pas de there is no, there are not (3B)
il pleut it's raining (7B)
il/elle s'appelle his/her name is (7S/15B)
île *(f.)* island (18B)
illusion *(f.)* illusion (20S)
il y a there is, there are (3B); **il y a ... ... ago** (12B); **— beaucoup de monde** it's crowded (19S); **— du soleil** it's sunny (7B); **— du vent** it's windy (7B); **— des nuages** it is cloudy (7S)
immeuble *(m.)* apartment house (11B)
immigration *(f.)* immigration (20B)
immigré *(m.)*, **immigrée** *(f.)* immigrant (12S/20B)
imperméable *(m.)* raincoat (10B)
impoli(e) impolite (5S)
important(e) important (3S/8B)
imposer to impose (20S)
impossible impossible (3S)
imprimante *(f.)* printer (3S)
indépendant(e) independent (20B)
indiquer to indicate (19S)
individualiste individualistic (20B)

Lexique: français – anglais

infidèle unfaithful (16S)
infirmier *(m.)*, **infirmière** *(f.)* nurse (12S)
informations *(f.pl.)* news (17B)
ingénieur *(m.)* engineer (12B)
injuste unfair (20B)
injustice *(f.)* injustice (20S)
inquiet, inquiète worried (20B)
inspecteur *(m.)*, **inspectrice** *(f.)* inspector (police) (17S)
instituteur *(m.)*, **institutrice** *(f.)* teacher (grade school) (12B)
intellectuel, intellectuelle intellectual (5S)
intelligent(e) smart, intelligent (2B)
intéressant(e) interesting (12B)
intéresser to interest (20B); **s'intéresser à** to be interested in (20B)
international(e), internationaux *(pl)* international (17S)
interroger to interrogate, to question (17S)
interview *(f.)* interview (17B)
intolérance *(f.)* intolerance (20S)
invité(e) *(m. ou f.)* guest (13B)
inviter to invite (9S/13B)
Israël *(m.)* Israel (18B)
israélien, israélienne Israeli (18S)
Italie *(f.)* Italy (18B)
italien, italienne Italian (9S/18B)

J

jaloux, jalouse jealous (16B)
jamais never (8B); **— de la vie** not on your life (8S)
jambe *(f.)* leg (15B)
jambon *(m.)* ham (9B)
janvier *(m.)* January (1B)
Japon *(m.)* Japan (18B)
japonais(e) Japanese (9S/18B)
jardin *(m.)* garden, yard (11B)
jaune yellow (3B)
jazz *(m.)* jazz (2B)
je m'appelle my name is (1B)
je voudrais (tu voudrais, il/elle voudrait) I would like (you would like, he/she would like) (7B)
jean *(m.)* jeans (pair of) (10B)
jeu électronique *(m.)* electronic game (3S); **— télévisé** *(m.)* game show (17B)
jeudi *(m.)* Thursday (1B)
jeune young (2S/5B); **— fille** *(f.)* girl (5B)
jeunes *(m.pl.)* young people (5B)
joli(e) pretty (5B)
jouer to play (5B); **— au football** to play soccer (8B); **— au golf** to play golf (8S); **— au tennis** to play tennis (8B); **— aux cartes** to play cards (8B); **— de la guitare** to play the guitar (5S/8B); **— du piano** to play the piano (8B); **— du violon** to play the violin (8B)

joueur *(m.)*, **joueuse** *(f.)* player (8S)
jour *(m.)* day (1S/6B)
journal *(m.)*, **journaux** *(pl.)* newspaper (14B); diary, journal (18S); **— (télévisé)** *(m.)* (television) news (17B)
journaliste *(m. ou f.)* journalist, reporter (14B)
journée *(f.)* day (period of time) (6B)
juillet *(m.)* July (1B)
juin *(m.)* June (1B)
jupe *(f.)* skirt (10B)
juriste *(m. ou f.)* attorney (12B)
jus de fruit *(m.)* fruit juice (9B)
jusqu'à as far as, up to, until (11B)
juste fair, just, right (20B)

K

kilo (de) *(m.)* kilogram (of) (13B)
kilomètre *(m.)* kilometer (19S)

L

là there, here (7B)
là-bas over there (18B)
laboratoire *(m.)* laboratory (6S)
lac *(m.)* lake (6B)
laid(e) ugly (2B)
laisser un pourboire to leave a tip (13S)
lait *(m.)* milk (9B)
laitue *(f.)* lettuce (9S)
lampe *(f.)* lamp (3S/11B)
langue étrangère *(f.)* foreign language (5S)
lavabo *(m.)* sink (3B)
lave-linge *(m.)* washing machine (11S)
laver to wash (15B); **se laver** to wash (oneself) (15B)
lave-vaisselle *(m.)* dishwasher (11S)
lecteur CD *(m.)* CD player (3S); **— CD-ROM** *(m.)* CD-ROM player (3S); **— de cassette** *(m.)* cassette player (3S)
léger, légère light (weight) (18B)
légume *(m.)* vegetable (9B)
lendemain *(m.)* day after, next day (18S)
lent(e) slow (18B)
lentement slowly, slow (18B)
lettre *(f.)* letter (4S/14B)
lever to lift, to raise (15B); **se lever** to get up (15B)
liberté *(f.)* freedom (20S)
librairie *(f.)* bookstore (14B)
lieu du crime *(m.)* crime scene (17S)
lire to read (4S/14B)
liste (de) *(f.)* list (of) (13B)
lit *(m.)* bed (3B)
litre (de) *(m.)* liter (of) (13S)
littéraire literary (14S)
littérature *(f.)* literature (5S/14B)

livre *(m.)* book (1B)
loin (de) far (from) (5B)
loisirs *(m.pl.)* leisure activities (20S)
long, longue long (10B)
longtemps a long time (16B)
louer to rent (18B)
Louisiane *(f.)* Louisiana (18B)
lourd(e) heavy (18B)
lundi *(m.)* Monday (1B)
lune de miel *(f.)* honeymoon (16S)
lunettes *(f.pl.)* eyeglasses (10B); **— de soleil** *(f.pl.)* sunglasses (10S)
lycée *(m.)* high school (5B)

M

machine à écrire *(f.)* typewriter (3S)
Madame (Mme) ma'am, Mrs. (1B)
Mademoiselle (Mlle) miss, Miss (1B)
magasin *(m.)* store (6B)
magazine *(m.)* magazine (14B); **— littéraire** *(m.)* literature show (television) (17S); **— d'information** *(m.)* news show (television) (17S)
magnétoscope *(m.)* videocassette recorder (17S)
magnifique magnificent, superb (18S)
mai *(m.)* May (1B)
maigrir to lose weight (10B)
maillot de bain *(m.)* swimsuit, bathing suit (10B)
main *(f.)* hand (13B)
maintenant now (2B)
mairie *(f.)* city hall (11S)
mais but (1B)
maison *(f.)* house (6B)
mal bad, badly (8B); **— élevé(e)** ill-mannered, rude (5S); **— habillé(e)** badly dressed (10S); **— payé** badly paid (12B)
malade sick (2B)
maladie *(f.)* sickness, illness (20B)
malgré in spite of, despite (19S)
malheur *(m.)* misfortune (20B)
malheureusement unfortunately (13B)
malheureux, malheureuse unhappy (2B)
manger to eat (4B)
manquer (un train, un avion) to miss (a train, a plane) (18B)
manteau *(m.)*, **manteaux** *(pl.)* coat (10B)
maquiller to make up (someone else) (15S); **se maquiller** to put makeup on (oneself) (15S)
marche *(f.)* walking (8B)
marché *(m.)* market (13B)
marcher to walk (4B)
mardi *(m.)* Tuesday (1B)
mari *(m.)* husband (7B)
marié(e) married (7B)

se marier (avec) to marry, get married (to) (16B)
Maroc *(m.)* Morocco (16S/18B)
marocain(e) Moroccan (5S/18B)
marron *(adj. invar.)* brown (eyes) (15B)
mars *(m.)* March (1B)
masculin(e) masculine (14S)
match *(m.)* game (4S)
matérialiste materialistic (20B)
matériel, matérielle material (20S)
mathématiques *(f.pl.)* mathematics (4S)
matin *(m.)* morning (6B)
matinal(e) early riser, morning person (15S)
mauvais(e) bad (9B)
mayonnaise *(f.)* mayonnaise (9S)
méchant(e) mean (2S/5B)
médecin *(m.)* doctor, physician (12B)
médecine *(f.)* medecine (studies, science) (5S/14B)
médias *(m.pl.)* media (17S)
médicament *(m.)* medicine (13B)
se méfier de to mistrust, not to trust (20S)
meilleur(e) better (9B)
melon *(m.)* melon (cantaloupe) (9S)
membre *(m.)* member (8S)
même same; even (17B)
ménage *(m.)* housework (4S/7B); household, couple (16S)
menu *(m.)* fixed-price meal (13S)
mer *(f.)* sea (6B)
merci thank you (1B)
mercredi *(m.)* Wednesday (1B)
mère *(f.)* mother (4B)
mère de famille *(f.)* wife and mother (12B)
merveilleux, merveilleuse wonderful, marvelous (8S/18B)
métier *(m.)* profession, trade (12B)
météo *(f.)* weather forecast (7S/14B)
métro *(m.)* subway (18B)
mètre *(m.)* meter (19S)
mettre to put, to put on, to wear (10B); **— la table** to set the table (13S); **— une lettre à la poste** to mail a letter (14S)
meuble *(m.)* piece of furniture (3S/11B); **meubles** *(m.pl.)* furniture (11B)
meurtre *(m.)* murder (17S)
meurtrier *(m.),* **meurtrière** *(f.)* murderer (17S)
Mexique *(m.)* Mexico (18B)
mexicain(e) Mexican (18S)
mieux better (15B)
mignon, mignonne cute (5B)
mince slim, thin (2B)
Minitel *(m.)* Minitel (14S)
miroir *(m.)* mirror (3S)

moderne modern, contemporary (11S)
moi me (1B); **— aussi** me too, so do I (1S/5B); **— non plus** me neither, neither do I (1S/5B)
moins (moins... que) less (less . . . than) (2B)
mois *(m.)* month (1S/6B)
monde *(m.)* world (18B)
monnaie *(f.)* change, coins (13S)
Monsieur *(m.)* sir, Mr. (1B)
montagne *(f.)* mountain(s) (6B)
monter to go up (11B)
monter/descendre en ascenseur to take the elevator up/down (11S)
monter/descendre par l'escalier to take the stairs up/down (11S)
montre *(f.)* wristwatch (10B)
montrer to show (17B)
monument *(m.)* monument (19S)
morceau (de) *(m.),* **morceaux** *(pl.)* piece (of) (13B)
mort *(f.)* death (20B)
mort(e) (en) dead (in) (7B)
moustache *(f.)* moustache (15S)
moutarde *(f.)* mustard (9S)
mouton *(m.)* mutton (9B)
moyen de transport *(m.)* means of transportation (18S)
mur *(m.)* wall (3S/11B)
musée *(m.)* museum (8B)
musicien *(m.),* **musicienne** *(f.)* musician (17S)
musique *(f.)* music (2B); **— classique** *(f.)* classical music (2S)

N

nager to swim (6S/8B)
naïf, naïve naive (2B)
nappe *(f.)* tablecloth (13S)
natation *(f.)* swimming (8B)
national(e), nationaux, nationales national (17S)
né(e) (en) born (in) (7B)
ne... jamais not ever, never (8B)
ne... pas not (2B)
ne... personne not anyone, no one (8B)
ne... personne de (gentil) no one (nice) (17S)
ne... plus not anymore (8B)
ne... rien not anything, nothing (8B)
ne... rien de (comique) nothing (funny) (17S)
neige *(f.)* snow (6B)
neiger to snow (7S)
n'est-ce pas? isn't it?, etc. (4B)
neuf nine (1B)
neveu *(m.)* nephew (7B)
nez *(m.)* nose (15S)

nièce *(f.)* niece (7B)
noir(e) black (3B)
nom *(m.)* name (4B); noun; **— de famille** last name (4S)
non no (1B)
nord *(m.)* north (14S/19B)
normal(e), normaux, normales normal (2S/5B)
Normandie *(f.)* Normandy (19S)
nourriture *(f.)* food (9S)
nouveau (nouvel), nouvelle, nouveaux, nouvelles new (10B)
nouvelle *(f.)* piece of news (14S)
novembre *(m.)* November (1B)
nu(e) naked (15S)
nuage *(m.)* cloud (7S/19B)
nuageux cloudy (14S)
nuit *(f.)* night, darkness (6B)
numéro (de téléphone) *(m.)* (telephone) number (14B)

O

objet *(m.)* object (3S)
occupé(e) busy (2B)
s'occuper (de) to take care (of) (16B)
océan *(m.)* ocean (19S)
octobre *(m.)* October (1B)
œil *(m.),* **yeux** *(pl.)* eye (15B)
œuf *(m.)* egg (9B)
offrir to offer (13B)
oignon *(m.)* onion (9S)
oiseau *(m.),* **oiseaux** *(pl.)* bird (4S)
omelette (au fromage) *(f.)* omelette (cheese) (9S)
on one, they, people (3B); **— verra** we'll see (18B)
oncle *(m.)* uncle (7B)
onze eleven (1B)
opinion *(f.)* opinion (20S)
optimiste optimistic (5S/20B)
orage *(m.)* thunderstorm (19S)
orange *(adj. invar.)* orange (3B)
orange *(f.)* orange (9B)
ordinateur *(m.)* computer (3B)
ordre *(m.)* order (20S)
oreille *(f.)* ear (15B)
oser to dare (20S)
ou or (2B)
où where (2B); **— sont les toilettes?** where's the restroom? (11S)
oublier (de + inf.) to forget (to do something) (12B)
ouest *(m.)* west (14S/19B)
oui yes (1B)
ouvert(e) open (13B)
ouvrier *(m.),* **ouvrière** *(f.)* worker (blue collar) (12B)
ouvrir to open (13B)

P

page *(f.)* page (14B)
pain *(m.)* bread (9B)
paix *(f.)* peace (20B)
pamplemousse *(m.)* grapefruit (9S)
pantalon *(m.)* pants (pair of) (10B)
par by, through (18B); **— exemple** for example (4S); **— terre** on the floor (3S)
parapluie *(m.)* umbrella (10B)
parc *(m.)* park (6B)
parce que because (2B)
pardon excuse me (1B)
parent *(m.)* parent, relative (7B)
paresseux, paresseuse lazy (2B)
parfois sometimes (5B)
parka *(f.)* parka, ski jacket (10S)
parler to talk, to speak (4B)
partager to share (5S/15B)
partir to leave (5B)
partout everywhere (15B)
pas (ne...) not (2B); **— du tout** not at all (1S/13B); **— encore** not yet (11B); **— mal** not bad (1B); **— moi** not me (1S/5B); **— question** no way, out of the question (8B)
passager *(m.)*, **passagère** *(f.)* passenger (18S)
passeport *(m.)* passport (18B)
passé(e) last (day, month, etc.) (14B)
passer to spend (17B); to go by, to stop by, to pass (18B); **— l'aspirateur** to vacuum (7S/16B); **— un examen** to take a test (14S)
passe-temps *(m.)* pastime (8S/20B)
pâté *(m.)* pâté (9S)
pâtes *(f.pl.)* pasta, spaghetti, noodles (9S)
patience *(f.)* patience (16S)
patient(e) patient (16B)
pâtisserie *(f.)* pastry shop, pastry (13B)
patron *(m.)*, **patronne** *(f.)* boss (12B)
pauvre poor (5B)
pauvreté *(f.)* poverty (20S)
payer to pay (13B); **— avec une carte de crédit** to pay by credit card (13S); **— en liquide** to pay cash (13S); **— par chèque** to pay by check (13S)
pays *(m.)* country (18B)
paysage *(m.)* landscape, scenery (19S)
pêche *(f.)* peach (9B)
pêcher to fish (19S)
peigne *(m.)* comb (15S)
peigner to comb (someone else) (15S); **se peigner (les cheveux)** to comb (one's own hair) (15S)
pelouse *(f.)* lawn (11S)
pendant during (6B); **— que** while (16B)
pénible obnoxious (2B)
penser (à/de) to think (about/of) (16B); **— que** to think that (16B)

perdre to lose (11B); **— son travail** to lose one's job (12B)
père *(m.)* father (4B)
permettre (de) to allow, to permit (17B)
permis de conduire *(m.)* driver's license (18S)
personnage *(m.)* character (in play, book) (17S)
personne *(f.)* person (3S/4B); *(m.)* nobody, no one (8B); **— âgée** *(f.)* older person (5B)
personnel, personnelle personal (20S)
pessimiste pessimistic (5S/20B)
petit(e) little, small, short (3B); **petit ami** *(m.)* boyfriend; **petite amie** *(f.)* girlfriend (5B); **petit déjeuner** *(m.)* breakfast (9B); **petite annonce** *(f.)* classified ad (14B); **petite cuillère** *(f.)* teaspoon (13B)
petits pois *(m.pl.)* peas (9B)
petite-fille *(f.)* granddaughter (7B)
petit-fils *(m.)* grandson (7B)
petits-enfants *(m.pl.)* grandchildren (7B)
peu (un) little (a) (4B)
peur *(f.)* fear; **avoir —** to be afraid (17S)
peut-être maybe, perhaps (3B)
pharmacie *(f.)* pharmacy (13B)
pharmacien *(m.)*, **pharmacienne** *(f.)* pharmacist (13B)
photo *(f.)* photograph (3B)
piano *(m.)* piano (8B)
pièce *(f.)* room (general term) (11B); **— (de théâtre)** *(f.)* play (17B)
pied *(m.)* foot (15B)
pilote *(m.)* pilot (18S)
pique-nique *(m.)* picnic (6S)
piscine *(f.)* swimming pool (6B)
pizza *(f.)* pizza (9S)
placard *(m.)* closet (3B)
place *(f.)* square (town) (11B); room, place, seat (18S)
plage *(f.)* beach (6B)
plan *(m.)* (town, city) map (11S)
plante verte *(f.)* houseplant (13B)
plat(e) flat (19B)
plat *(m.)* serving dish, dish of food (13B); **— principal** *(m.)* main dish, main course (9S/13B)
platane *(m.)* plane tree (19S)
plein(e) full, crowded (18S)
pleurer to cry (5S/15B)
pleuvoir to rain (7S)
plongée sous-marine *(f.)* scuba diving (8S)
pluie *(f.)* rain (14B)
plus (plus... que) more (more . . . than) (2B); **le/la — jeune** *(m.ou f.)* youngest (7B); **— ou moins** more or less (2S)
poème *(m.)* poem (14S)
poire *(f.)* pear (9S)

poisson *(m.)* fish (1S/9B)
poivre *(m.)* pepper (9S)
poli(e) polite (5S)
policier *(m.)* police officer (12B)
politique *(f.)* politics (14B)
pollution *(f.)* pollution (20S)
polo *(m.)* tennis (golf) shirt (10S)
pomme *(f.)* apple (9B)
pomme de terre *(f.)* potato (9B)
pompier *(m.)* firefighter (12S)
pont *(m.)* bridge (11S)
porc *(m.)* pork (9B)
port *(m.)* port (19S)
porte *(f.)* door (3B); gate (18S)
porter to carry, to wear (10B)
poser une question (à qqn) to ask a question (of someone) (14B); **se poser des questions** to wonder, to have doubts (20S)
possible possible (3S)
poste *(f.)* post office (6B)
poulet *(m.)* chicken (9B)
pour for, in order to (1B); **— que + subjonctif** so that, in order to (20B)
pourboire *(m.)* tip (13S); **laisser un —** to leave a tip (13S)
pourquoi why (4S/6B)
pourtant however (12S/17B)
pouvoir *(m.)* power (20B)
pouvoir can, to be able to (8B)
pratique practical (3S/10B)
préféré(e) preferred, favorite (6S)
préférer to prefer (6B)
premier first (1B)
prendre to take; to have; to eat; to drink (9B); **— la retraite** to retire (20S); **— (un petit) quelque chose** to have a snack (9B); **— un bain** to take a bath (15S); **— une douche** to take a shower (15B); **— un verre** to have a drink (9S)
prénom *(m.)* first name (4S)
préparer to prepare (13S); **se préparer** to get (oneself) ready (15S)
près (de) near (to) (5B)
préservatif *(m.)* condom (20S)
presque almost (18S)
presse *(f.)* press, (news)papers (14S)
principe *(m.)* principle (20S)
printemps *(m.)* spring (1B)
privé(e) private (20B)
prix *(m.)* price (10B)
probablement probably (20B)
problème *(m.)* problem (5B)
professeur *(m.)* teacher (1B)
profiter de la vie to make the most of life (20S)
programme *(m.)* television/radio schedule (17S)
projet *(m.)* plan, project (8B)
promenade *(f.)* walk (8B)

promener to walk (a dog, for example) (15B); **se promener** to take a walk (15B)

promettre to promise (17B)

propre clean (15S)

propriétaire *(m. ou f.)* owner (12B)

protection *(f.)* protection (20S)

Provence *(f.)* Provence (south of France) (19S)

prune *(f.)* plum (9S)

psychologue *(m. ou f.)* psychologist (4S/12B)

publicité *(f.)* advertising (14B)

puis (et puis) then (and then) (11B)

pull *(m.)* sweater (10B)

pyjama *(m.)* pair of pajamas (10S)

Pyrénées *(f.pl.)* Pyrenees (19S)

Q

quai *(m.)* platform (18S)

quand when (5B); **— même** all the same, even so (17S)

quartier *(m.)* neighborhood (11S/18B)

quatorze fourteen (1B)

quatre four (1B)

que that (16B)

quel, quelle, quels, quelles which, what (6B); **quel âge as-tu (avez-vous)?** how old are you? (5S); **quelle est la date aujourd'hui?** what's the date today? (1S/6B); **quelle heure est-il?** what time is it? (6B); **quelle sorte de... ?** what kind/sort of . . . ? (13B); **quel temps fait-il?** what's the weather like? (7S/14B)

quelque few, some (18S/20B); **— chose** something (9B); **— chose (d'intéressant)** something (interesting) (16B)

quelquefois sometimes (11B)

quelqu'un someone (9B); **— (d'intéressant)** someone (interesting) (16B)

qu'est-ce que... ? what . . . ? (8B); **— c'est?** what is this/that? (3B); **— tu aimes? (il/elle aime)** what do you like? (does he/she like) (4S); **qu'est ce qu'il y a à faire?** what is there to do? (19S)

qu'est-ce qui... ? what . . . ? (18B); **— se passe?** what's happening? (16B) **— s'est passé?** what happened? (18B)

question *(f.)* question (14B)

qui... ? who . . . ? (2S/7B); **qui** who, that *(relative pronoun)* (7S/12B); **— est-ce que?** who/whom? (8B)

quinze fifteen (1B)

quitter to leave (16B)

quoi what (8B)

R

racisme *(m.)* racism (20B)

raconter to tell (a story) (16B)

radio *(f.)* radio (3B); **radio-réveil** *(m.)* clock radio (3S)

raisin *(m.)* grape (9S)

raisonnable reasonable, sensible (2B)

randonnée *(f.)* hike (8B)

ranger to straighten up; to clean up (4B)

rapide fast, rapid (18B)

rare rare (19S)

raser to shave (someone else) (15S); **se raser** to shave (oneself) (15S)

rasoir *(m.)* razor (15S)

réaliste realistic (20B)

réalité *(f.)* reality (20S)

recherche (sur) *(f.)* research (on) (20S)

se réconcilier to make up (16S)

réfléchir (à + qqch.) to think (about), reflect (10B)

réfrigérateur *(m.)* refrigerator (3S/11B)

refuser (de + inf.) to refuse (to) (20B)

regarder to look at (4B); **se regarder** to look at oneself (15B)

régime *(m.)* diet (5S)

région *(f.)* region (19B)

rencontre *(f.)* encounter, meeting (16S)

rencontrer to meet (8B)

rendre visite à to visit (a person) (18B)

renseignement *(m.)* piece of information (14B)

rentrer to go/come home, back (11B)

renverser to knock over (13S)

repas *(m.)* meal (9B)

repasser to iron (7S/16B)

répondeur *(m.)* answering machine (3S)

répondre (à qqn) to answer (someone) (11B)

reportage *(m.)* report, story (television) (17B)

reporter *(m.)* reporter (17S)

se reposer to rest (16B)

réservé(e) reserved, quiet (5S)

réserver to reserve (18S)

respecter to respect (20B)

responsable responsible (12B)

restaurant *(m.)* restaurant (6B); **— universitaire** *(m.)* college cafeteria (6S)

rester to stay (someplace) (8B); **— à la maison** to stay home (4B)

restes *(m.pl.)* leftovers (9S)

retourner to go back, to return (11B)

retraité *(m.)*, **retraitée** *(f.)* retired person (5S/12B)

se retrouver to get together, to meet (again) (16B)

réussir (à + inf.) to succeed (14B); **— (à) un examen** to pass a test (14B)

S

rêve *(m.)* dream (15S/20B)

réveil *(m.)* alarm clock (3B)

réveillé(e) awake (15S)

réveiller to wake (someone up) (15B); **se réveiller** to wake up (oneself) (15B)

revenir to come back (17B)

rêver (de) to dream (about, of) (15B)

revolver *(m.)* revolver, gun (17S)

rez-de-chaussée *(m.)* ground floor (first floor) (11B)

riche rich (5B)

richesse *(f.)* wealth (20S)

rideau *(m.)*, **rideaux** *(pl.)* curtain (3S/11B)

rien *(m.)* nothing (8B)

rire to laugh (4S)

rivière *(f.)* river, stream (19S)

riz *(m.)* rice (9B)

robe *(f.)* dress (10B)

rock *(m.)* rock (music) (2B)

romain(e) Roman (19S)

roman *(m.)* novel (14S); **— policier** *(m.)* murder mystery (17S)

romantique romantic (17S)

rose rose-colored, pink (10B)

rôti *(m.)* roast (9B)

rouge red (3B)

route *(f.)* road (18B)

roux, rousse red (hair) (15B)

rubrique *(f.)* section, column (periodical) (14S)

rue *(f.)* street (11B)

russe Russian (18S)

Russie *(f.)* Russia (18B)

S

sable *(m.)* sand (19B)

sac *(m.)* sack, purse (3B); **— à dos** *(m.)* backpack (18S)

sage well-behaved (5S)

saison *(f.)* season (1S); **— des pluies** *(f.)* rainy season (18S)

salade *(f.)* salad (9B)

salaire *(m.)* salary (12B)

sale dirty (15S)

salé(e) salted, salty (9S)

salle *(f.)* room; **— à manger** *(f.)* dining room (11B); **— de bains** *(f.)* bathroom (11B); **— de classe** *(f.)* classroom (3B); **— de séjour** *(f.)* living room, family room (7B)

salon *(m.)* living room (11B)

salut! hi! bye! (1B)

samedi *(m.)* Saturday (1B)

sandale *(f.)* sandal (10S)

sandwich *(m.)* sandwich (9B)

sans without (8B)

santé *(f.)* health (20B)

satisfait(e) (de) satisfied (with) (20B)
sauce *(f.)* sauce, gravy (13S)
saucisson *(m.)* salami (9S)
sauf except (20B)
saumon *(m.)* salmon (9B)
savoir to know (16B)
savon *(m.)* soap (15S)
sciences *(f.pl.)* sciences (4S); — **économiques** *(f.pl.)* economics (14B)
scientifique scientific (14S)
sécher to dry (someone, something) (15S); **se sécher** to dry off (oneself) (15S)
séchoir (à cheveux) *(m.)* (hair) dryer (15S)
secrétaire *(m. ou f.)* secretary (12B)
sécurité *(f.)* security (20S)
seize sixteen (1B)
sel *(m.)* salt (9B)
semaine *(f.)* week (1S/6B)
Sénégal *(m.)* Senegal (18B)
sénégalais(e) Senegalese (18B)
sentiment *(m.)* feeling (20S)
se séparer to separate, to break up (16S)
sept seven (1B)
septembre *(m.)* September (1B)
série *(f.)* series (17B)
sérieux, sérieuse serious, hardworking (2S/4B)
séropositif, séropositive HIV positive (20S)
serrer qqn dans ses bras to hug somebody (16S)
serveur *(m.)*, **serveuse** *(f.)* waiter, waitress (12B)
service compris tip included (13S)
serviette *(f.)* napkin (13B); — **de bain** *(f.)* bath towel (15S)
seul(e) alone (5B)
seulement only (16B)
sévère strict (5S)
shampooing *(m.)* shampoo (15S)
short *(m.)* pair of shorts (10B)
si yes (on the contrary) (7B); if, so (11B)
sida *(m.)* AIDS (20S)
s'il te plaît *(fam.)* please (6B)
s'il vous plaît *(formal)* please (6B)
siècle *(m.)* century (19S)
sieste *(f.)* nap (15S)
simple simple (20S)
six six (1B)
ski *(m.)* skiing (8B)
skier to ski (6S/8B)
slip *(m.)* brief (men's), panties (women's) (10S)
SMIC *(m.)* minimum wage (12S)
S.N.C.F. *(f.)* French national railway (12S)
sociable sociable, gregarious (2B)
social, sociale, sociaux, sociales social (20B)
société *(f.)* society (20B)

sœur *(f.)* sister (4B)
soif *(f.)* thirst; **avoir —** to be thirsty (9B)
soigner to take care of (15S); **se soigner** to take care of oneself (15S)
soir *(m.)* evening (6B)
soirée *(f.)* party, evening (9S/13B)
soleil *(m.)* sun (6B)
solitude *(f.)* solitude (20B)
sombre dark (3S/11B)
sommaire *(m.)* table of contents (magazine) (14S)
sommeil *(m.)* sleep; **avoir —** to be sleepy (6B)
sonner to ring (12B)
sortie *(f.)* outing, evening/night out (20B)
sortir to go out (4S/5B); — **avec** to go out with, to date (16S); — **ensemble** to go out together, to date (16S)
souci *(m.)* problem, worry (20S)
souffrir to suffer (20S)
soupe (aux tomates) *(f.)* (tomato) soup (9B)
sous under (3B)
sous-sol *(m.)* basement level, underground (11S)
soutien-gorge *(m.)* bra (10S)
souvenir *(m.)* souvenir, memory (18S); **se souvenir de** to remember (16B)
souvent often (5B)
sous-vêtements *(m.pl.)* underwear (10B)
spécialité *(f.)* specialty (19S)
spiritualité *(f.)* spirituality (20S)
sport *(m.)* sport(s) (4B)
sportif, sportive athletic (2B)
station *(f.)* (radio) station (17B); — **de métro** *(f.)* subway station (18S)
steak *(m.)* steak (9B); — **haché** *(m.)* hamburger meat (9S)
steward *(m.)* flight attendant, steward (18S)
stressé(e) stressed (12S)
stylo *(m.)* pen (1B)
sucre *(m.)* sugar (9B)
sucré(e) sweet (9S)
sud *(m.)* south (14S/19B)
Suisse *(f.)* Switzerland (14S/18B)
suisse Swiss (14S/18B)
suivre to follow (17B); — **un cours** to take a class, a course (17B)
supermarché *(m.)* supermarket (6B)
supplémentaire supplementary, extra
sur on, on top of (3B)
sûrement certainly (20B)
surgelé(e) frozen (9S)
surprendre to surprise (17B)
surtout especially (4S/9B)
survêtement *(m.)* sweatsuit (10S)
suspect *(m.)*, **suspecte** *(f.)* suspect (17S)
sympathique nice, congenial, likable (2B)

T

table *(f.)* table (3B); — **de nuit** *(f.)* nightstand, night table (3S)
tableau *(m.)*, **tableaux** *(pl.)* painting (3S/11B)
Tahiti Tahiti (18B)
tahitien, tahitienne Tahitian (18S)
tailleur *(m.)* suit (woman's) (10B)
tante *(f.)* aunt (7B)
taper à la machine to type (12S)
tapis *(m.)* area rug (3B)
tard late (15B)
tarte (aux pommes) *(f.)* pie (apple) (9B)
tasse (de) *(f.)* cup (of) (13B)
taxi *(m.)* taxi (18B)
tee-shirt *(m.)* T-shirt (10S)
télécommande *(f.)* remote control (17S)
télécopieur *(m.)* fax machine (3S)
téléfilm *(m.)* movie made for television (17B)
téléphone *(m.)* telephone (3B); — **mobile** *(m.)* cellular telephone (3S); — **sans fil** *(m.)* portable telephone (3S)
téléphoner (à qqn) to telephone (someone) (6B)
télévision *(f.)* television (3B)
témoin *(m.)* witness (17S)
temps *(m.)* weather; **quel — fait-il?** what's the weather like? (7S/14B)
tennis *(m.)* tennis (4S); *(m.pl.)* sneakers (10S)
terminer to finish, to end (6B)
terrasse *(f.)* patio, terrace (11B)
terre *(f.)* earth, ground (19B)
terrible terrible (19B)
terrorisme *(m.)* terrorism (20S)
tête *(f.)* head (15B)
têtu(e) stubborn (5S/15B)
Texas *(m.)* Texas (18B)
TGV (train à grande vitesse) *(m.)* high-speed French train (18S)
thé *(m.)* tea (9B)
théâtre *(m.)* theater (4S)
thon *(m.)* tuna (9B)
ticket *(m.)* ticket (bus or subway) (18B)
timbre *(m.)* stamp (14B)
timide shy (2B)
tiroir *(m.)* drawer (3S)
titre *(m.)* title (14S)
toilettes *(f.pl.)* toilet, bathroom (10S)
toit *(m.)* roof (11S)
tomate *(f.)* tomato (9B)
tomber to fall (8B); — **amoureux, amoureuse (de)** to fall in love (with) (16B)
tôt early (15B)
toujours always (5B)
tour du monde *(m.)* trip around the world (18S)

touriste *(m. ou f.)* tourist (19B)
tourner to turn (11B)
tous (toutes) les deux both (13B); **tous les jours** every day (13B)
tousser to cough (15S)
tout, tous, toute, toutes all (13B); **tout à coup** all of a sudden (12B); **tout à fait** absolutely, completely (13B); **tout de suite** right away, at once (13B); **tout droit** straight (11B); **tout le monde** everybody, everyone (8B); **tout le temps** all the time (5B); **tout(e) nu(e)** stark naked (15S); **tout(e) seul(e)** all alone, all by oneself (15B)
traditionnel, traditionnelle traditional (20B)
train *(m.)* train (18B)
tranche (de) *(f.)* slice (of) (13B)
travail *(m.)* work, job (12B)
travailler to work (4B); **— dur** to work hard (12B)
travailleur, travailleuse hardworking (2B)
traverser to go across, to cross (11S/18B)
treize thirteen (1B)
trente thirty (1B)
très very (2B); **— bien** fine, good, very good (1B)
triste sad (5B)
trois three (1B)
tromper to fool, to cheat (16S); **se tromper (de)** to be wrong, to make a mistake (16B)
trop too (too much) (2S/4B); **— (de)** too much (of) (13B)
trouver to find (6B); **— du travail/un travail** to find work/a job (12B); **se trouver** to be located (19B)
tuer to kill (17S)
tueur *(m.)*, **tueuse** *(f.)* killer (17S)
typique typical (5S)

U

un(e) one, a (1B)

une fois once (10B)
universitaire *(adj.)* university (6B)
université *(f.)* university, college (2B)
usine *(f.)* factory (11B)
utiliser to use (13B)

V

vacances *(f.pl.)* vacation (2B)
vache *(f.)* cow (6S/19B)
vaisselle *(f.)* dishes (7B)
valise *(f.)* suitcase (10B)
vanille *(f.)* vanilla (9B)
vedette (de la télévision, du cinéma...) *(f.)* (television, movie, etc.) celebrity (17B)
végétarien, végétarienne vegetarian (9S)
veille *(f.)* day before, eve (18S)
vélo *(m.)* bicycle, bike (8B); **vélo tout terrain** *(m.)* (VTT) mountain bike
vendeur *(m.)*, **vendeuse** *(f.)* salesperson (12B)
vendre to sell (11B)
vendredi *(m.)* Friday (1B)
venir to come (13B)
venir de to have just (13B)
vent *(m.)* wind (7B)
ventre *(m.)* stomach, abdomen (15S)
verbe *(m.)* verb
vérifier to verify, to check (17S)
vérité *(f.)* truth (14B)
verre (de) *(m.)* glass (of) (13B)
vert(e) green (3B)
veste *(f.)* jacket, sport coat (10B)
vêtements *(m.pl.)* clothes (10B)
veuf *(m.)*, **veuve** *(f.)* widower, widow (7B)
viande *(f.)* meat (9B)
victime *(f.)* victim (17S)
vide empty (18B)
vie *(f.)* life (5B)
vie quotidienne *(f.)* daily life (20S)
vieux (vieil), vieille, vieux, vieilles old (5B)
village *(m.)* village (rural) (6B)
ville *(f.)* city, town (6B)

vin *(m.)* wine (9B)
vingt *(m.)* twenty (1B)
vinaigrette *(f.)* oil and vinegar dressing (9S)
violence *(f.)* violence (20B)
violent(e) violent (17B)
violet, violette purple (10B)
violon *(m.)* violin (8B)
visage *(m.)* face (15S)
visiter to visit (a place) (18B)
vite fast, rapidly (18B)
vivre to be alive, to live (17B)
voici here is, here are (8B)
voilà there is/are; here is/are (2S/3B)
voir to see (13B)
voiture *(f.)* car (5B)
vol *(m.)* flight (18S)
volets *(m.pl.)* shutters (11S)
votre nom, s'il vous plaît? your name, please? (4B)
vouloir to want, to wish (7B); **— dire** to mean (14B)
voyage *(m.)* trip (10B); **— organisé** *(m.)* tour (package) (18S)
voyager to travel (4B)
vrai(e) true, right (4B)
vraiment really (12B)

W

week-end *(m.)* weekend (1S)
western *(m.)* western (movie) (17B)
W.C. *(m.pl.)* toilet, restroom (11B)

Y

yaourt *(m.)* yogurt (9B)
yeux *(m.pl.)* eyes (15B)

Z

zéro *(m.)* zero (1B)
zoo *(m.)* zoo (19S)

➤ Anglais-Français

A

abandon *(v.)* abandonner
abdomen ventre *(m.)*
about de, à peu près
abroad à l'étranger
absolutely tout à fait
accept *(v.)* accepter (de + inf.)
accident accident *(m.)*
according to d'après; — to you à votre avis
accountant comptable *(m. ou f.)*
acquaintance connaissance *(f.)*
across (from) en face (de)
act *(v.)* agir
active actif, active
activity activité *(f.)*
actor acteur *(m.)*
actress actrice *(f.)*
adapt to *(v.)* (s')adapter à
address adresse *(f.)*
adjective adjectif *(m.)*
adolescent adolescent *(m.)*, adolescente *(f.)*
adorable adorable
adult adulte *(m.)*
adventure movie film d'aventures *(m.)*
advertising, advertisement publicité *(f.)*
Africa Afrique *(f.)*
African africain(e)
after, afterwards après
afternoon après-midi *(m.)*
again encore
agreeable agréable
ago il y a...
AIDS sida *(m.)*
airplane avion *(m.)*
airport aéroport *(m.)*
à la carte à la carte
alarm clock réveil *(m.)*
Algeria Algérie *(f.)*
Algerian algérien, algérienne
alive vivant(e); to be — être en vie
all tout, tous, toute, toutes; — alone, — by oneself tout(e) seul(e); — of a sudden tout à coup; — right d'accord; — the same, even so quand même; — the time tout le temps
allergy allergie *(f.)*
allow *(v.)* permettre (de)
all right d'accord
almost à peu près, presque
alone seul(e)
Alps Alpes *(f.pl.)*
already déjà
also aussi
always toujours

America Amérique *(f.)*
American américain(e)
amuse (someone) *(v.)* amuser
amusing comique
and et
angry fâché(e)
animal animal *(m.)*, animaux *(pl.)*
animated cartoon dessin animé *(m.)*
ankle cheville *(f.)*
announce *(v.)* annoncer
annoy (someone) *(v.)* énerver
annoying énervant(e)
answer (someone) *(v.)* répondre (à qqn)
answering machine répondeur *(m.)*
antique ancien, ancienne
apartment appartement *(m.)*
apartment house/building immeuble *(m.)*
apple pomme *(f.)*
appreciate *(v.)* apprécier
April avril *(m.)*
are you ready to order? vous avez choisi?
argue (with) *(v.)* se disputer (avec)
arm bras *(m.)*
armchair fauteuil *(m.)*
arrival arrivée *(f.)*
arrive (at) *(v.)* arriver (à + inf.)
article article *(m.)*
artist artiste *(m. ou f.)*
as comme; — a group en groupe; — far as jusqu'à; — ... as aussi... que
Asia Asie *(f.)*
Asian asiatique
ask *(v.)* demander; — *(v.)* a question (of someone) poser une question (à qqn)
asparagus asperges *(f.pl.)*
aspirin aspirine *(f.)*
assignment devoir *(m.)*
at à; — ease à l'aise; — last enfin; — ... o'clock à... heure(s); — once tout de suite; — the house of chez; — the same time en même temps; — the side of au bord de; — what time? à quelle heure?
athletic sportif, sportive
attack (of) crise (de) *(f.)*
attic grenier *(m.)*
attorney avocat *(m.)*, avocate *(f.)*; juriste *(m. ou f.)*
August août *(m.)*
aunt tante *(f.)*
Australia Australie *(f.)*
Australian australien, australienne
authority autorité *(f.)*
autumn automne *(m.)*
avenue avenue *(f.)*
awake réveillé(e)

B

baby bébé *(m.)*
baby-sit *(v.)* garder des enfants
back dos *(m.)*
backpack sac à dos *(m.)*
bad mauvais(e)
badly mal; — dressed mal habillé(e); — paid mal payé(e)
bad-mannered mal élevé(e)
bakery boulangerie *(f.)*; — that sells pastries boulangerie-pâtisserie *(f.)*
balcony balcon *(m.)*
bald chauve
banana banane *(f.)*
Band-Aid sparadrap *(m.)*
bandage pansement *(m.)*
bank banque *(f.)*
banker banquier *(m.)*, banquière *(f.)*
basement cave *(f.)*; — level sous-sol *(m.)*
basketball basket-ball *(m.)*
bathing suit maillot de bain *(m.)*
bathroom salle de bains *(f.)*; toilettes *(f.pl.)*
bathtub baignoire *(f.)*
be *(v.)* être; — a member (of) être membre (de); — able to pouvoir; — afraid (of) avoir peur (de); — against être contre; — alive vivre, être vivant(e); — allergic to être allergique à; — aware of être conscient(e) de; — bored s'ennuyer; — careful faire attention; — cold avoir froid; — early être en avance; — easy to get along with avoir bon caractère, être facile à vivre; — expensive coûter cher; — for être pour; — free to être libre de; — good at être fort(e) en; — good at/in être bon/bonne en; — hard to get along with avoir mauvais caractère, être difficile à vivre; — hot avoir chaud; — hungry avoir faim; — in shape être en forme; — in the middle of être en train de (+ inf.); — informed être au courant de (+ nom); — interested in s'intéresser à; — involved in politics faire de la politique; — late être en retard; — located se trouver; — lucky avoir de la chance; — mad at être en colère contre; — named s'appeler; — no good at/in être nul/nulle en; — on a diet être au régime; — on time être à l'heure; — over (a sickness) être remis(e) (de); — paid (well, badly) être (bien, mal) payé(e); — right avoir raison; — sleepy avoir sommeil;

— **standing (up)** être debout; — **thirsty** avoir soif; — **wrong** avoir tort, se tromper (de); — **... years old** avoir... ans

beach plage *(f.)*

beard barbe *(f.)*

beautiful beau (bel), belle, beaux, belles

because parce que

because of à cause de

become *(v.)* devenir

bed lit *(m.)*; **to make one's** — faire son lit

bedroom chambre *(f.)*

beef bœuf *(m.)*

beer bière *(f.)*

before avant, avant de + inf., avant que + subjonctif

begin (to) *(v.)* commencer (à + inf.)

beginning début *(m.)*

behind derrière *(prep.)*; derrière *(m.)*

beige beige

Belgian belge

Belgium Belgique *(f.)*

believe (in) *(v.)* croire (à); **to — in God** croire en Dieu

belong to *(v.)* être à

belongings affaires *(f.pl.)*

bench banc *(m.)*

beside à côté de

better meilleur(e) *(adj.)*, mieux *(adv.)*

between entre

beverage boisson *(f.)*

bicycle vélo *(m.)*

big grand(e); gros, grosse

bill addition *(f.)*

billion un milliard

biology biologie *(f.)*

bird oiseau *(m.)*, oiseaux *(pl.)*

birthday anniversaire *(m.)*

black noir(e)

blond blond(e)

blow coup *(m.)*

blow one's nose *(v.)* se moucher

blue bleu(e)

boat bateau *(m.)*, bateaux *(pl.)*

body corps *(m.)*

book livre *(m.)*

bookcase étagère *(f.)*

bookstore librairie *(f.)*

bore *(v.)* ennuyer

boring ennuyeux, ennuyeuse

born (in) né(e) (en)

boss patron *(m.)*, patronne *(f.)*

both tous (toutes) les deux

bother *(v.)* gêner

bottle (of) bouteille (de) *(f.)*

box (of) boîte (de) *(f.)*

boy garçon *(m.)*

boyfriend petit ami *(m.)*

bra soutien-gorge *(m.)*

bread pain *(m.)*

break (one's arm, leg) *(v.)* se casser (le bras, la jambe); — **up** *(v.)* se séparer

breakfast petit déjeuner *(m.)*; — **nook** coin-repas *(m.)*

bridge pont *(m.)*

briefs slip *(m.)*

bright clair(e)

bring *(v.)* apporter

British anglais(e)

Brittany Bretagne *(f.)*

brother frère *(m.)*

brother-in-law beau-frère *(m.)*

brown brun(e); — **(eyes)** marron *(invar.)*; — **(light, hair)** châtain(e)

bruise bleu *(m.)*

brush *(v.)* brosser; — **(one's hair)** se brosser (les cheveux)

bureau commode *(f.)*

burn *(v.)* brûler; — **oneself** se brûler

bus (between cities) autocar *(m.)*, car *(m., fam.)*

bus (city) autobus *(m.)*, bus *(m., fam.)*

business affaires *(f.pl.)*, entreprise *(f.)*; — **owner** chef d'entreprise *(m.)*; — **is good** les affaires marchent bien

busy occupé(e)

but mais

butcher shop boucherie *(f.)*

butter beurre *(m.)*

buy *(v.)* acheter

by par

by chance par hasard

bye! salut!

C

café café *(m.)*

cake (chocolate) gâteau (au chocolat) *(m.)*, gâteaux *(pl.)*

calculator calculatrice *(f.)*

California Californie *(f.)*

call *(v.)* appeler

calm calme *(m.)*; calme *(adj.)*

camcorder caméscope *(m.)*

camera appareil-photo *(m.)*

Cameroon Cameroun *(m.)*

Cameroonian camerounais(e)

camp *(v.)* faire du camping

camping camping *(m.)*

can *(v.)* pouvoir

can (of) boîte (de) *(f.)*

Canada Canada *(m.)*; **in —** au Canada

Canadian canadien, canadienne

cancer cancer *(m.)*

candy (piece of) bonbon *(m.)*

canned food conserves *(f.pl.)*

car voiture *(f.)*

card carte *(f.)*

careful prudent(e)

carrot carotte *(f.)*

carry *(v.)* porter; — **(away)** emporter

cartoon dessin humoristique *(m.)*

cash argent *(m.)*; **pay —** payer en liquide

cashier caissier *(m.)*, caissière *(f.)*

cassette cassette *(f.)*; — **player** lecteur de cassette *(m.)*

castle château *(m.)*, châteaux *(pl.)*

cat chat *(m.)*

catastrophic catastrophique

catch *(v.)* attraper

cathedral cathédrale *(f.)*

CD disque compact *(m.)*

CD player lecteur CD *(m.)*

CD-ROM player lecteur CD-ROM *(m.)*

celebrate *(v.)* fêter

celebrity célébrité*(f.)*; **(movie, television)** — vedette (du cinéma, de la télévision) *(f.)*

center centre *(m.)*

centime (1/100 franc) centime *(m.)*

century siècle *(m.)*

CEO PDG (président directeur général) *(m.)*

cereal céréales *(f.pl.)*

certainly sûrement

chair chaise *(f.)*

chairman PDG (président directeur général) *(m.)*

champagne champagne *(m.)*

chance *hasard *(m.)*

change *(v.)* changer; — **(trains, planes)** changer (de train, d'avion); — **one's clothes** se changer

change changement *(m.)*

change (currency) monnaie *(f.)*

channel (television) chaîne *(f.)*

character (in play, book) personnage *(m.)*

chat *(v.)* bavarder

cheap bon marché *(invar.)*

cheat (on someone) *(v.)* tromper (qqn)

check *(v.)* vérifier

check chèque *(m.)*; — **(restaurant)** addition *(f.)*

checkbook chéquier *(m.)*

cheese fromage *(m.)*

chemistry chimie *(f.)*

chest of drawers commode *(f.)*

chicken poulet *(m.)*

child enfant *(m. ou f.)*

China Chine *(f.)*

Chinese chinois(e)

chocolate chocolat *(m.)*

choose *(v.)* choisir (de + inf.)

church église *(f.)*

cigarette cigarette *(f.)*

city ville *(f.)*; — **hall** mairie *(f.)*; — **map** plan *(m.)*

civil servant fonctionnaire *(m. ou f.)*

class cours *(m.)*
classical music musique classique *(f.)*
classified ad petite annonce *(f.)*
classmate camarade de classe *(m. ou f.)*
classroom salle de classe *(f.)*
clean propre; *(v.)* — up ranger
cleaning person femme de ménage *(f.)*
client client *(m.)*, cliente *(f.)*
climate climat *(m.)*
clock radio radio-réveil *(m.)*
close *(v.)* fermer
closed fermé(e)
closet placard *(m.)*
clothes vêtements *(m.pl.)*
cloud nuage *(m.)*
cloudy nuageux
coast côte *(f.)*
coat manteau *(m.)*, manteaux *(pl.)*
Coca-Cola Coca-Cola *(m.)*
coffee café *(m.)*; — with milk café au lait *(m.)*
coffeeshop café *(m.)*
cold froid *(m.)*; rhume *(m.)*; to be — avoir froid; to have a — avoir un rhume; it's — (weather) il fait froid
cold cuts charcuterie *(f.)*
college université *(f.)*; — cafeteria restaurant universitaire *(m.)*
color couleur *(f.)*
column (periodical) rubrique *(f.)*
comb (one's own hair) *(v.)* se peigner (les cheveux); — (someone else's hair) peigner
comb peigne *(m.)*
come *(v.)* venir; — back revenir; — in *(v.)* entrer
comedy (movie, play) comédie *(f.)*
comfort confort *(m.)*
comfortable (thing) confortable
comfortable (person) à l'aise
comic comique; — book, — strip bande dessinée *(f.)*
comment commentaire *(m.)*
company société *(f.)*
company head chef d'entreprise *(m.)*
competent compétent(e)
completely tout à fait
computer ordinateur *(m.)*; — specialist informaticien *(m.)*, informaticienne *(f.)*
concern *(v.)* concerner
concert concert *(m.)*
condom préservatif *(m.)*
contagious contagieux, contagieuse
contemporary moderne
content content(e)
continent continent *(m.)*
continue *(v.)* continuer (à + inf.); — as far as continuer jusqu'à
cook *(v.)* faire la cuisine

cook cuisinier *(m.)*, cuisinière *(f.)*
cooking cuisine *(f.)*
corner coin *(m.)*
correspondence courrier *(m.)*
corridor couloir *(m.)*
cost coûter *(v.)*; how much does . . . —? combien coûte... ?
couch canapé *(m.)*
cough *(v.)* tousser
country campagne *(f.)*; pays *(m.)*
countryside campagne *(f.)*
couple couple *(m.)*, ménage *(m.)*
course cours *(m.)*
cousin cousin *(m.)*, cousine *(f.)*
cow vache *(f.)*
credit card carte de crédit *(f.)*
crisis crise *(f.)*; to be in a — être en crise
crime crime *(m.)*
criticize *(v.)* critiquer
croissant croissant *(m.)*
cross *(v.)* traverser
crowd foule *(f.)*
crowded plein(e); it is — il y a beaucoup de monde
cruise croisière *(f.)*
cry *(v.)* pleurer
cuisine cuisine *(f.)*
cultural culturel, culturelle
cup (of) tasse (de) *(f.)*
curly frisé(e)
current actuel, actuelle
curtain rideau *(m.)*, rideaux *(pl.)*
customer client *(m.)*, cliente *(f.)*
customs douane *(f.)*; — officer douanier *(m.)*
cut *(v.)* couper; — oneself se couper
cute mignon, mignonne
cycle *(v.)* faire du vélo
cyclist coureur cycliste *(m.)*

D

daily life vie quotidienne *(f.)*
dance *(v.)* danser
dancer danseur *(m.)*, danseuse *(f.)*
dangerous dangereux, dangereuse
dare *(v.)* oser
dark foncé(e), sombre
dark-haired brun(e)
date *(v.)* sortir avec, sortir ensemble
date date *(f.)*
daughter fille *(f.)*
daughter-in-law belle-fille *(f.)*
day jour *(m.)*, journée *(f.)*; — after le lendemain; — before la veille
day-care center crèche *(f.)*
dead mort(e)
dear cher, chère
death mort *(f.)*

December décembre *(m.)*
decide (to do something) *(v.)* décider (de + inf.)
degree diplôme *(m.)*
delicate délicat(e)
delicatessen, deli meats charcuterie *(f.)*
delicious délicieux, délicieuse
dentist dentiste *(m. ou f.)*
deodorant déodorant *(m.)*
departure départ *(m.)*
depressed déprimé(e)
descend *(v.)* descendre
describe *(v.)* décrire
desert désert *(m.)*
desk bureau *(m.)*, bureaux *(pl.)*
despite malgré
dessert dessert *(m.)*
detective/police movie film policier *(m.)*
diary journal *(m.)*, journaux *(pl.)*
dictionary dictionnaire *(m.)*
diet régime *(m.)*; to be on a — être au régime
different différent(e)
difficult difficile
diploma diplôme *(m.)*
dining room salle à manger *(f.)*
dinner dîner *(m.)*
dirty sale
disappointed déçu(e)
discotheque discothèque *(f.)*
discover *(v.)* découvrir
discuss *(v.)* discuter (de)
disgruntled fâché(e)
dish (of food) plat *(m.)*
dishes vaisselle *(f.)*; to do the — faire la vaisselle
dishwasher lave-vaisselle *(m.)*
divorce *(v.)* divorcer
divorce divorce *(m.)*
divorced divorcé(e)
do *(v.)* faire; — dumb things faire des bêtises; — housework faire le ménage; — the dishes faire la vaisselle; — the museums faire les musées
doctor médecin *(m.)*
documentary (on) documentaire (sur) *(m.)*
dog chien *(m.)*
done! ça y est!
door porte *(f.)*
dormitory cité universitaire *(f.)*
doubt doute *(m.)*; to have —s se poser des questions
downstairs en bas
downtown centre-ville *(m.)*, en ville
drama drame *(m.)*
dramatic dramatique
draw *(v.)* dessiner, (hobby) faire du dessin
drawer tiroir *(m.)*

dream rêve (m.)
dream (about, of) (v.) rêver (de)
dress robe (f.)
dress (someone else) (v.) habiller
dressed habillé(e); **— up** habillé(e); **well — ** bien habillé(e); **badly — ** mal habillé(e); **to get — ** s'habiller
dressing (bandage) pansement (m.)
dressing (oil and vinegar) vinaigrette (f.)
drink (v.) boire, prendre
drink (served before a meal) apéritif (m.)
drive (v.) aller en voiture, conduire
driver's license permis de conduire (m.)
drug (medicine) médicament (m.); **— (illegal)** drogue (f.); **— addict** drogué(e), toxicomane; **to take (illegal) — ** se droguer
dry (someone, something) (v.) sécher; **— off (oneself)** se sécher
dumb bête; **— thing** bêtise (f.)
during pendant
dynamic dynamique

E
---

each chaque
ear oreille (f.)
early tôt
earn (v.) gagner; **— a living** gagner sa vie; **— $X (per hour, per day, per week, per month)** gagner $X (l'heure, par jour, par semaine, par mois)
earth terre (f.)
east est (m.)
easy facile
eat (v.) manger
ecology écologie (f.)
economics sciences économiques (f.pl.)
efficient efficace
egg œuf (m.)
eight *huit
eighteen dix-huit
eighty quatre-vingts; **— -one** quatre-ving-un
elderly âgé(e)
electronic game jeu électronique (m.)
elegant élégant(e)
elementary school école primaire (f.)
elevator ascenseur (m.)
eleven onze
embarrass (v.) gêner
embrace (v.) embrasser
employee employé (m.), employée (f.)
empty vide
encounter rencontre (f.)
end fin (f.); **at the — (of)** au bout (de)
end (v.) terminer
enemy ennemi (m.), ennemie (f.)
energetic énergique

engineer ingénieur (m.)
England Angleterre (f.)
English anglais(e)
enough assez; **— (of)** assez (de)
enter (v.) entrer
enthusiastic enthousiaste
entranceway entrée (f.)
envelope enveloppe (f.)
environment environnement (m.)
equality égalité (f.)
errand course (f.); **to run — ** faire les courses
especially surtout
Europe Europe (f.)
European européen, européenne
eve veille (f.)
even même
evening soir (m.), soirée (f.); **— (night) out** sortie (f.)
event événement (m.)
every chaque; **— day** tous les jours
everybody tout le monde
everyone tout le monde
everywhere partout
exam examen (m.)
example exemple (m.); **for — ** par exemple
excellent excellent(e)
except sauf
excuse me pardon, excusez-moi
executive cadre (m.)
exercise (v.) faire de l'exercice
exist (v.) exister
expensive cher, chère; **to be — ** coûter cher
explain (v.) expliquer
expressway autoroute (f.)
extra supplémentaire
extract passage (m.)
eye œil (m.), yeux (pl.)

F
---

face (v.) donner sur
face visage (m.)
factory usine (f.)
fail (v.) rater
fair juste
faithful (to) fidèle (à)
fall (v.) tomber; **— asleep** s'endormir; **— in love (with)** tomber amoureux, amoureuse (de)
false faux, fausse
familiar familier, familière
family famille (f.); **— room** salle de séjour (f.); **start a — ** fonder une famille
famous célèbre
far (from) loin (de)
farm ferme (f.)

farmer agriculteur (m.), agricultrice (f.)
fashion mode (f.); **to be in — ** être à la mode; **to be out of — ** être démodé
fast (adj.) rapide; (adv.) vite
fat gros, grosse
fate *hasard (m.)
father père (m.)
father-in-law beau-père (m.)
favorite préféré(e)
fax machine télécopieur (m.)
fear peur (f.)
February février (m.)
feel bad (v.) aller mal
feel better (v.) aller mieux
feel good (v.) aller bien; être en forme
feel great (v.) être en forme
feel like (+ inf.) (v.) avoir envie de (+ inf.)
feeling sentiment (m.)
feminine féminin(e)
fever fièvre (f.)
few peu (adv.), quelque (adj.)
fiancé(e) fiancé (m.), fiancée (f.)
field champ (m.)
fifteen quinze
fifty cinquante
film film (m.)
filmmaker cinéaste (m. ou f.)
finally enfin, finalement
financial financier, financière
find (v.) trouver; **— work/a job** trouver du travail/un travail
fine bien
finger doigt (m.)
finish (v.) finir, terminer
finished! ça y est!
firefighter pompier (m.)
firm entreprise (f.)
first premier; **— (of all)** d'abord; **— course (appetizer)** entrée (f.); **— floor** rez-de-chaussée (m.)
fish (v.) pêcher
fish poisson (m.)
five cinq
fix one's own hair (v.) se coiffer; **— someone's hair** coiffer
fixed-price meal menu (m.)
flat plat(e)
flight vol (m.); **— attendant** steward (m.), hôtesse de l'air (f.)
floor étage (m.); **on the first — ** au rez-de-chaussée; **on the second — ** au premier étage
flower fleur (f.)
flu grippe (f.); **to have the — ** avoir la grippe
fly (v.) aller en avion
follow (v.) suivre
food nourriture (f.)
fool (v.) tromper
foot pied (m.)

football football américain *(m.)*; **to play** — jouer au football américain
for pour; — **example** par exemple
foreign étranger, étrangère
foreigner étranger *(m.)*, étrangère *(f.)*
forest forêt *(f.)*
forget (to do something) *(v.)* oublier (de + inf.)
fork fourchette *(f.)*
formal habillé(e)
forty quarante
four quatre
fourteen quatorze
fragile fragile
franc franc *(m.)*
France France *(f.)*
free libre; — **(of charge)** gratuit(e)
freedom liberté *(f.)*
freezer congélateur *(m.)*
French français(e); — **(language)** français *(m.)*
French fries frites *(f.pl.)*
French national railway S.N.C.F. *(f.)*
French Riviera Côte d'Azur *(f.)*
Friday vendredi *(m.)*
friend ami *(m.)*, amie *(f.)*
friendship amitié *(f.)*
from de
frozen surgelé(e)
fruit fruit *(m.)*; — **juice** jus de fruit *(m.)*
full plein(e); — **of light** clair(e)
funny comique
furniture meubles *(m.pl.)*; **piece of** — meuble *(m.)*
future avenir *(m.)*

G

gain weight *(v.)* grossir
game match *(m.)*; — **show** jeu (télévisé) *(m.)*
garage garage *(m.)*; — **owner (mechanic)** garagiste *(m.)*
garden jardin *(m.)*
garden *(v.)* faire du jardinage, jardiner
gate porte *(f.)*
generous généreux, généreuse
German allemand(e)
Germany Allemagne *(f.)*
get *(v.)* recevoir; — **(oneself) ready** se préparer; — **(to)** arriver (à + inf.); — **along (well/badly) (with someone)** s'entendre (bien/mal) (avec qqn); — **annoyed** s'énerver; — **dressed** s'habiller; — **engaged** se fiancer; — **irritated** s'énerver; — **married (to)** se marier (avec); — **sunburned** attraper un coup de soleil; — **together** se retrouver; — **undressed** se déshabiller; — **up** se lever

geography géographie *(f.)*
gift cadeau *(m.)*, cadeaux *(pl.)*
girl fille *(f.)*, jeune fille *(f.)*
girlfriend petite amie *(f.)*
give *(v.)* donner
glad content(e)
glass (of) verre (de) *(m.)*
glasses (eye) lunettes *(f.pl.)*
glove gant *(m.)*
go *(v.)* aller; — **(sail)boating** faire du bateau (à voile); — **across** traverser; — **around the world** faire le tour du monde; — **back** retourner; — **by** passer; — **camping** faire du camping; — **down** descendre; — **horseback riding** faire du cheval; — **in** entrer; — **out** sortir; — **out together** sortir ensemble; — **out with** sortir avec; — **sailing** faire de la voile; — **scuba diving** faire de la plongée sous-marine; — **shopping** faire les magasins; — **surfing** faire du surf; — **to** aller jusqu'à; — **to bed** se coucher; — **to the doctor** aller chez le médecin; — **up** monter; — **home, back** rentrer
God Dieu *(m.)*; **to believe in** — croire en Dieu
golf golf *(m.)*; **to play** — jouer au golf
good bien *(adv.)*; bon, bonne *(adj.)*
goodbye au revoir
government gouvernement *(m.)*
grade note *(f.)*
gram (of) gramme (de) *(m.)*
grandchildren petits-enfants *(m.pl.)*
granddaughter petite-fille *(f.)*
grandfather grand-père *(m.)*
grandmother grand-mère *(f.)*
grandparents grands-parents *(m.pl.)*
grandson petit-fils *(m.)*
grape raisin *(m.)*
grapefruit pamplemousse *(m.)*
gravy sauce *(f.)*
gray gris(e)
green vert(e); — **beans** *haricots verts *(m.pl.)*
grocery store épicerie *(f.)*
ground terre *(f.)*; — **floor** rez-de-chaussée *(m.)*; **on the** — **floor** par terre
group groupe *(m.)*
guest invité *(m.)*, invitée *(f.)*
guilty coupable
guitar guitare *(f.)*
gun revolver *(m.)*

H

hair cheveu *(m.)*, cheveux *(pl.)*
hairdresser coiffeur *(m.)*, coiffeuse *(f.)*; — **dryer** séchoir (à cheveux) *(m.)*
half brother demi-frère *(m.)*

half sister demi-sœur *(f.)*
hall couloir *(m.)*
ham jambon *(m.)*
hamburger steak haché, *hamburger *(m.)*
hand main *(f.)*
handsome beau (bel), belle, beaux, belles
happily heureusement
happiness bonheur *(m.)*
happy heureux, heureuse
hard dur(e)
hardworking sérieux, sérieuse; travailleur, travailleuse
hat chapeau *(m.)*
hate *(v.)* détester
have *(v.)* avoir; — **(some) doubts** avoir des doutes; — **a bruise** avoir un bleu; — **a cold** avoir un rhume; — **a drink** prendre un verre; — **a fever** avoir de la fièvre; — **a good time** s'amuser; — **a grudge against** en vouloir à qqn; — **a nice weekend!** bon week-end!; — **a runny nose** avoir le nez qui coule; — **a snack** prendre (un petit) quelque chose; — **a sunburn** avoir un coup de soleil; — **illusions** avoir des illusions; — **just** venir de; — **responsibilities** avoir des responsabilités; — **the choice** avoir le choix; — **the flu** avoir la/une grippe; — **time off** avoir congé; — **time to (+ inf.)** avoir le temps de (+ inf.); — **to** devoir; — **worries** avoir des soucis
head tête *(f.)*
health santé *(f.)*; **to be in good/bad** — être en bonne/mauvaise santé
healthy (thing, activity) bon (bonne) pour la santé; **(person)** en bonne santé
hear *(v.)* entendre; — **from someone** recevoir des nouvelles de qqn
heavy fort(e), lourd(e)
hello bonjour
help *(v.)* aider (qqn à + inf.)
here ici; — **is,** — **are** voici; **here!** tiens!
hi! salut!
hide *(v.)* cacher
high school lycée *(m.)*; **(French)** — **diploma** baccalauréat *(m.)*
highway autoroute *(f.)*
hike *(v.)* faire une randonnée
hike randonnée *(f.)*
hill colline *(f.)*
historical historique
history histoire *(f.)*
hitchhike *(v.)* faire de l'auto-stop
hitchhiking auto-stop *(m.)*
HIV positive séropositif, séropositive
holiday fête *(f.)*
homework devoirs *(m.pl.)*
honest honnête

honeymoon lune de miel (f.)
hope (that) (v.) espérer (que)
horrible horrible
horror movie film d'horreur (m.)
horse cheval (m.) **go —back riding** faire du cheval
hospital hôpital (m.)
hot chaud(e); **to be** — avoir chaud; **it's — (weather)** il fait chaud
hotel hôtel (m.)
hour heure (f.)
house maison (f.)
household ménage (m.)
houseplant plante verte (f.)
housewife femme au foyer (f.)
housework ménage (m.); **to do** — faire le ménage
how comment; **— are you?** (formal) comment allez-vous?; **— many (of)** combien (de); **— many times (a day)** combien de fois (par jour); **— much** combien (de); **— much do I owe you?** combien est-ce que je vous dois?; **— much does . . . cost?** combien coûte... ?; **— old are you?** quel âge as-tu (avez-vous)?; **—'s it going?** ça va?; comment ça va?
however cependant, pourtant
hundred cent
hug (v.) serrer dans ses bras
hunger faim (f.)
hunt (v.) chasser
hurry (up) (v.) se dépêcher
hurt blessé(e)
hurt (v.) avoir mal; **— oneself** (v.) se faire mal; **— oneself badly** se blesser; **— (someplace)** avoir mal à (la tête, la gorge)
husband mari (m.)

I

I'm going je m'en vais
I'm kidding je plaisante
I'm leaving je m'en vais
I'm paying c'est moi qui invite
I've had enough j'en ai assez
I've had it j'en ai assez
ice cream glace (f.)
idea idée (f.)
idealistic idéaliste
if si
if it were me à ta (votre) place
ill-mannered mal élevé(e)
illness maladie (f.)
illusion illusion (f.)
immigrant immigré, immigrée
immigration immigration (f.)
impolite impoli(e)

important important(e)
impose (v.) imposer
impossible impossible
in à, dans, en; **— back of** derrière; **— front of** devant; **— love (with)** amoureux, amoureuse (de); **— my opinion** à mon avis; **— order to** pour, pour que + subjonctif; **— spite of** malgré; **— the middle (of)** au milieu (de); **— laws** beaux-parents (m.pl.)
including y compris
indeed en effet
independent indépendant(e)
indicate (v.) indiquer
indigestion indigestion (f.)
individualistic individualiste
inexpensive bon marché (invar.)
inhabitant habitant (m.), habitante (f.)
injured blessé(e)
injustice injustice (f.)
innocent innocent(e)
inside (of) à l'intérieur (de)
inspector (police) inspecteur (m.), inspectrice (f.)
intellectual intellectuel, intellectuelle
intelligent intelligent(e)
interest (v.) intéresser
interesting intéressant(e)
international international(e), internationaux, internationales
interrogate (v.) interroger
interview interview (f.)
intolerance intolérance (f.)
investigation enquête (f.)
invite (v.) inviter
iron (v.) repasser
irritate (someone) (v.) énerver (qqn.)
isn't it?/isn't he?/isn't she?, etc. n'est-ce pas?
is there any room? il y a de la place?
island île (f.)
Israel Israël (m.)
Israeli israélien, israélienne
it is necessary that il faut que + subjonctif
it's . . . : — cloudy il y a des nuages, il fait nuageux/couvert; **— cold** il fait froid; **— cool** il fait frais; **— hot and humid** il fait lourd; **— nasty out** il fait mauvais; **— nice out** il fait beau; **— overcast** il fait gris/couvert; **— pleasant (mild)** il fait bon; **— raining** il pleut; **— snowing** il neige; **— sunny** il y a du soleil; **— warm, it's hot** il fait chaud; **— windy** il y a du vent; **— crowded** il y a beaucoup de monde; **— expensive** ça coûte cher; **— my treat** c'est moi qui invite
Italian italien, italienne
Italy Italie (f.)

J

jacket veste (f.); **— (aviator)** blouson (m.)
jam confiture (f.)
January janvier (m.)
Japan Japon (m.)
Japanese japonais(e)
jazz jazz (m.)
jealous jaloux, jalouse
jeans jeans (m.pl.)
jewelry bijou (m.), bijoux (pl.)
job travail (m.)
jog (v.) faire du jogging
journal journal (m.), journaux (pl.)
journalist journaliste (m. ou f.)
July juillet (m.)
June juin (m.)

K

keep (v.) garder
key clé (f.)
kill (v.) tuer
killer tueur (m.), tueuse (f.)
kilogram (of) kilo (de) (m.)
kilometer kilomètre (m.)
kind gentil, gentille
kindergarten école maternelle (f.)
kiss (v.) embrasser
kitchen cuisine (f.)
knee genou (m.), genoux (pl.)
knife couteau (m.), couteaux (pl.)
knock over (v.) renverser
know (v.) connaître, savoir; **— about** être au courant de (+ nom)

L

laboratory laboratoire (m.)
lake lac (m.)
lamp lampe (f.)
landscape paysage (m.)
language langue (f.); **foreign** — langue étrangère (f.)
last (v.) durer
last dernier, dernière; **— (month, year, etc.)** passé(e)
late tard
laugh (v.) rire
laundry lessive (f.); **to do the** — faire la lessive
law droit (m.)
lawn pelouse (f.)
lawyer (court) avocat (m.), avocate (f.)
lazy paresseux, paresseuse
learn (to) (v.) apprendre (à)
leave (v.) laisser, partir, quitter; **— a note for someone** laisser un mot pour qqn; **— a tip** laisser un pourboire

left gauche *(f.)*; **to the —** **(of)** à gauche (de)
leftovers restes *(m.pl.)*
leg jambe *(f.)*
leisure activities loisirs *(m.pl.)*
lemon citron *(m.)*
less (less . . . than) moins (moins... que)
let *(v.)* laisser
let's eat! à table!
letter lettre *(f.)*
lettuce laitue *(f.)*
library bibliothèque *(f.)*
lie *(v.)* mentir
life vie *(f.)*
lift *(v.)* lever
light clair(e), léger, légère
likable sympathique
like *(v.)* aimer **— better (than)** aimer mieux (que)
like comme
list (of) liste (de) *(f.)*
listen to *(v.)* écouter
liter litre *(m.)*
literary littéraire
literature littérature *(f.)*
little petit(e) *(adj.)*; peu *(adv.)*; **a —** un peu
live *(v.)* vivre, habiter
liver foie *(m.)*
living room salle de séjour *(f.)*, salon *(m.)*
long long, longue; **— time** longtemps
look *(v.)* regarder; **— after children** garder des enfants; **— at** regarder; **— at oneself** se regarder; **— for** chercher; **— for work/a job** chercher du travail/un travail; **— healthy** avoir bonne mine; **— like** avoir l'air (+ adj.), avoir l'air (de + inf.); ressembler (à qqn); **— sick** avoir mauvaise mine; **— unwell** avoir mauvaise mine; **— well** avoir bonne mine
lose *(v.)* perdre; **— one's job** perdre son travail; **— weight** maigrir
lot (of) beaucoup de
Louisiana Louisiane *(f.)*
love *(v.)* adorer, aimer
love amour *(m.)*; **— at first sight** coup de foudre *(m.)*
luckily heureusement
luggage bagages *(m.pl.)*
lunch déjeuner *(m.)*
luxurious de luxe

M

ma'am Madame (Mme)
mad fâché(e)
magazine magazine *(m.)*
magnificent magnifique
mail courrier *(m.)*; **— carrier** facteur *(m.)*

mail a letter *(v.)* mettre une lettre à la poste
mailbox boîte aux lettres *(f.)*
main dish plat principal *(m.)*
make *(v.)* faire; **— a mistake** se tromper (de); **— music** faire de la musique; **— the beds** faire les lits; **— the most of life** profiter de la vie; **— up** se réconcilier; **— up (someone else)** maquiller
man homme *(m.)*
manage *(v.)* diriger
manager (business) directeur *(m.)*, directrice *(f.)*
manager (hotel, shop, etc.) gérant *(m.)*, gérante *(f.)*
mansion château *(m.)*, châteaux *(pl.)*
many beaucoup de
map carte *(f.)*; **(town, ciy)** plan *(m.)*
March mars *(m.)*
market marché *(m.)*
married marié(e)
marry *(v.)* se marier (avec)
marvelous merveilleux, merveilleuse
masculine masculin(e)
material matériel, matérielle
materialistic matérialiste
mathematics mathématiques *(f.pl.)*
May mai *(m.)*
maybe peut-être
mayonnaise mayonnaise *(f.)*
me moi; **— neither** moi non plus; **— too** moi aussi; **— not** pas moi
meal repas *(m.)*; **meal's ready!, meal's served!** à table!
mean *(v.)* vouloir dire
mean méchant(e)
means of transportation moyen de transport *(m.)*
meat viande *(f.)*
media médias *(m.pl.)*
medicine médicament *(m.)*; **(studies, science)** médecine *(f.)*
meet *(v.)* rencontrer; **— (again)** se retrouver; **— (someone)** faire la connaissance de (qqn)
meeting rencontre *(f.)*
melon (cantaloupe) melon *(m.)*
member membre *(m.)*
memory souvenir *(m.)*
messy (room) en désordre; **(person)** désordonné(e)
meter mètre *(m.)*
Mexican mexicain(e)
Mexico Mexique *(m.)*
microdisk (computer) disquette *(f.)*
middle (in the —) au milieu (de)
milk lait *(m.)*
million million *(m.)*
mineral water eau minérale *(f.)*
mirror miroir *(m.)*

miscellaneous divers
misfortune malheur *(m.)*
miss (a train, a plane) *(v.)* manquer (un train, un avion)
miss, Miss Mademoiselle (Mlle)
Mister Monsieur (M.)
mistrust *(v.)* se méfier de
modern moderne
Monday lundi *(m.)*
money argent *(m.)*
mononucleosis mononucléose *(f.)*
monster monstre *(m.)*
month mois *(m.)*
monument monument *(m.)*
mood (good, bad) humeur (bonne, mauvaise) *(f.)*; **to be in a good/bad —** être de bonne/mauvaise humeur
more (more . . . than) plus (plus... que)
more or less plus ou moins
morning matin *(m.)*
Moroccan marocain(e)
Morocco Maroc *(m.)*
mother mère *(f.)*
mother-in-law belle-mère *(f.)*
mountain(s) montagne *(f.)*; **— bike** vélo tout terrain (VTT) (m)
moustache moustache *(f.)*
mouth bouche *(f.)*
move (house) *(v.)* déménager
movie film *(m.)*; **— made for television** téléfilm *(m.)*; **— theater** cinéma *(m.)*; **movies** cinéma *(m.)*
Mr. Monsieur (M.)
Mrs. Madame (Mme)
much beaucoup
murder meurtre *(m.)*; **— mystery** roman policier *(m.)*
murderer meurtrier *(m.)*, meurtrière *(f.)*
mushroom champignon *(m.)*
music musique *(f.)*; **to make —** faire de la musique
musician musicien *(m.)*, musicienne *(f.)*
must devoir *(v.)*
mustard moutarde *(f.)*
mutton mouton *(m.)*
my name is je m'appelle

N

naive naïf, naïve
naked nu(e); **stark naked** tout(e) nu(e)
name nom *(m.)*; **first —** prénom *(m.)*; **last —** nom de famille *(m.)*; **my — is** je m'appelle; **your —, please?** votre nom s'il vous plaît?
nap sieste *(f.)*
napkin serviette *(f.)*
nation (state) état *(m.)*
national national(e), nationaux, nationales
native habitant *(m.)*, habitante *(f.)*

near (to) près de
nearly à peu près
neat (thing) en ordre; **(person)** ordonné(e)
need *(v.)* avoir besoin de
need besoin *(m.)*
neighborhood quartier *(m.)*
neither do I moi non plus
nephew neveu *(m.)*
never jamais, ne... jamais
nevertheless cependant
new nouveau (nouvel), nouvelle, nouveaux, nouvelles
news informations *(f. pl.);* — **(from someone)** nouvelles *(f. pl.);* — **(television)** journal (télévisé) *(m.)*
newspaper journal *(m.)*, journaux *(pl.)*
next ensuite; — **day** lendemain *(m.);* — **to** à côté de
nice agréable; gentil, gentille; sympathique
niece nièce *(f.)*
night nuit *(f.)*
nightmare cauchemar *(m.)*
nightstand table de nuit *(f.)*
nine neuf
nineteen dix-neuf
ninety quatre-vingt-dix
no non; — **good in, at** nul, nulle en; — **one** personne, ne... personne; — **one (nice . . .)** ne... personne de (gentil...); — **way** pas question
nobody personne, ne... personne
noise bruit *(m.);* **to make** — faire du bruit
noodles pâtes *(f.pl.)*
normal normal(e), normaux, normales
Normandy Normandie *(f.)*
North America Amérique du Nord *(f.)*
north nord *(m.)*
nose nez *(m.)*
not pas (ne...) ; — **any** aucun(e); — **anymore** ne... plus; — **anyone** ne... personne; — **anything** ne... rien; — **at all** pas du tout; — **bad** pas mal; — **ever** ne... jamais; — **me** pas moi; — **on your life** jamais de la vie; — **one** aucun(e); — **think so** *(v.)* penser que non; — **yet** pas encore
notebook cahier *(m.)*, carnet *(m.)*
nothing ne... rien; rien *(m.);* — **(funny)** ne... rien de (comique)
noun nom *(m.)*
novel roman *(m.)*
November novembre *(m.)*
now maintenant
number chiffre *(m.)*
nurse infirmier *(m.)*, infirmière *(f.)*
nursery crèche *(f.);* — **school** école maternelle *(f.)*

O

object objet *(m.)*

obnoxious pénible *(fam.)*
obvious évident(e)
obviously évidemment
ocean océan *(m.)*
October octobre *(m.)*
odd bizarre
of de; — **course** bien sûr, évidemment; — **which (whom)** dont
offer *(v.)* offrir
office bureau *(m.)*, bureaux *(pl.)*
often souvent
OK d'accord
old âgé(e); ancien, ancienne; vieux (vieil), vieille, vieux, vieilles
older person personne âgée *(f.)*
oldest (person in family) aîné *(m.)*, ainée *(f.)*
omelette (cheese) omelette (au fromage) *(f.)*
on sur; — **foot** à pied; — **purpose** exprès; — **sale** en solde; — **television** à la télévision; — **the contrary** si; — **the first floor** au rez-de-chaussée; — **the floor** par terre; — **the radio** à la radio; — **the second floor** au premier étage; — **top of** sur
once une fois
one on
one, a un(e); — **time** une fois
onion oignon *(m.)*
only seulement
open ouvert(e)
open *(v.)* ouvrir
opinion avis *(m.)*, opinion *(f.)*
optimistic optimiste
optional facultatif, facultative
or ou
orange *(adj.)* orange *(invar.)*
orange orange *(f.)*
order *(v.)* commander
order ordre *(m.)*
other autre
out of fashion démodé(e)
out of the question pas question
outing sortie *(f.)*
outside (of) à l'extérieur (de)
over there là-bas
overcast (weather) couvert
overlook *(v.)* donner sur
owe *(v.)* devoir; **how much do I** — **you?** combien est-ce que je vous dois?
owner propriétaire *(m. ou f.)*

P

pack *(v.)* faire les (ses) bagages
page page *(f.)*
paint *(v.)* faire de la peinture
painting tableau *(m.)*, tableaux *(pl.)*
pale pâle

panties slip *(m.)*
pants (pair of) pantalon *(m.)*
panty hose collant *(m.)*, bas *(m.pl.)*
paper papier *(m.); **paper (written for class)** dissertation *(f.)*
parent parent *(m.)*
parents-in-law beaux-parents *(m.pl.)*
park parc *(m.)*
parka parka *(f.)*, anorak *(m.)*
participate in a sport *(v.)* faire du sport
party fête *(f.)*, soirée *(f.)*
pass *(v.)* passer, réussir (à + inf.)
passage passage *(m.)*
passenger passager *(m.)*, passagère *(f.)*
passport passeport *(m.)*
pasta pâtes *(f.pl.)*
pastime passe-temps *(m.)*
pastry, — shop pâtisserie *(f.)*
pâté pâté *(m.)*
path chemin *(m.)*
patience patience *(f.);* **to have —/to not have** — avoir de la patience/ne pas avoir de patience
patient patient(e)
patio terrasse *(f.)*
pay *(v.)* payer; — **attention** faire attention; — **by check** payer par chèque; — **by credit card** payer avec une carte de crédit; — **cash** payer en liquide
peace paix *(f.);* — **and quiet** calme *(m.)*
peach pêche *(f.)*
pear poire *(f.)*
peas petits pois *(m.pl.)*
pen stylo *(m.)*
pencil crayon *(m.)*
people gens *(m.pl.)*, on
pepper poivre *(m.)*
perhaps peut-être
permit *(v.)* permettre (de)
person personne *(f.)*
personal personnel, personnelle
personality caractère *(m.)*
pessimistic pessimiste
pharmacist pharmacien *(m.)*, pharmacienne *(f.)*
pharmacy pharmacie *(f.)*
philosophy philosophie *(f.)*
photograph photo *(f.)*
physics physique *(f.)*
piano piano *(m.);* **to play the** — jouer du piano
picnic pique-nique *(m.)*
picture photo *(f.);* **to take pictures** prendre des photos; **(hobby)** faire de la photo
pie (apple) tarte (aux pommes) *(f.)*
piece (of) morceau (de) *(m.)*, morceaux *(pl.);* — **of furniture** meuble *(m.);* — **of information** renseignement *(m.);* — **of jewelry** bijou *(m.)*, bijoux *(pl.);* — **of news** nouvelle *(f.)*

pilot pilote *(m.)*
pimple bouton *(m.)*
pink rose
pizza pizza *(f.)*
place endroit *(m.)*, place *(f.)*; — **setting** couvert *(m.)*; **in your** — à ta (votre) place
plan projet *(m.)*
plane (air) avion *(m.)*
plane tree platane *(m.)*
plate (of) assiette (de) *(f.)*
platform quai *(m.)*
play *(v.)* jouer; — **cards** jouer aux cartes; — **soccer** jouer au football; — **tennis** jouer au tennis; — **the guitar** jouer de la guitare; — **music** jouer de la musique; — **the piano** jouer du piano; — **the violin** jouer du violon
play pièce (de théâtre) *(f.)*
player joueur *(m.)*, joueuse *(f.)*
pleasant agréable
please s'il te plaît *(fam.)*
please s'il vous plaît *(formal)*
plum prune *(f.)*
poem poème *(m.)*
poison poison *(m.)*
police officer policier *(m.)*
police station commissariat de police *(m.)*
policeman gendarme *(m.)*
polite poli(e)
political science sciences politiques *(f.pl.)*
politics politique *(f.)*
pollution pollution *(f.)*
poor pauvre
pork porc *(m.)*; — **shop** charcuterie *(f.)*
port port *(m.)*
possible possible
post office poste *(f.)*
postcard carte postale *(f.)*
poster affiche *(f.)*
potato pomme de terre *(f.)*
poverty pauvreté *(f.)*
power pouvoir *(m.)*
practical pratique
prefer *(v.)* aimer mieux (que), préférer
preferred préféré(e)
pregnant enceinte
prepare *(v.)* préparer
present actuel, actuelle
present cadeau *(m.)*, cadeaux *(pl.)*
president président *(m.)*; PDG (président directeur général) *(m.)*
press (newspapers) presse *(f.)*
pretty joli(e)
price prix *(m.)*
principle principe *(m.)*
printer imprimante *(f.)*
private privé(e)
probably probablement

problem problème *(m.)*, souci *(m.)*
profession métier *(m.)*
program émission *(f.)*
project projet *(m.)*
promise *(v.)* promettre
protection protection *(f.)*
Provence (south of France) Provence *(f.)*
psychologist psychologue *(m. ou f.)*
psychology psychologie *(f.)*
purple violet, violette
purse sac *(m.)*
put *(v.)* mettre; — **makeup on (oneself)** se maquiller; — **on** mettre; — **to bed** coucher
pajamas (pair of) pyjama *(m.)*
Pyrenees Pyrénées *(f.pl.)*

Q

Quebec Québec *(m.)*
Québécois québécois(e)
question *(v.)* interroger
question question *(f.)*
quiet réservé(e)
quite assez
quiz interrogation *(f.)*

R

race (bicycle) course (cycliste) *(f.)*
racer (bicycle) coureur (cycliste) *(m.)*
racism racisme *(m.)*
radio radio *(f.)*; — **station** station *(f.)*
rain *(v.)* pleuvoir; *(noun)* pluie *(f.)*
raincoat imperméable *(m.)*
rainy season saison des pluies *(f.)*
raise *(v.)* lever
rapid rapide
rapidly vite
rare rare
raw vegetables crudités *(f.pl.)*
razor rasoir *(m.)*
read *(v.)* lire
real estate agent agent immobilier *(m. ou f.)*
realistic réaliste
reality réalité *(f.)*
really vraiment
rear end derrière *(m.)*
reasonable raisonnable
receive *(v.)* recevoir
record disque *(m.)*
red rouge; — **(hair)** roux, rousse
reflect (on, about) *(v.)* réfléchir (à + qqch.)
refrigerator réfrigérateur *(m.)*
refuse *(v.)* refuser (de + inf.)
region région *(f.)*
relative parent *(m.)*

remark commentaire *(m.)*
remedy remède *(m.)*
remember *(v.)* se souvenir de
remote control télécommande *(f.)*
rent *(v.)* louer
report rapport *(m.)*; **(television)** reportage *(m.)*
reporter reporter *(m.)*
research (on) recherche (sur) *(f.)*
researcher chercheur *(m.)*
resemble *(v.)* **(someone)** ressembler (à qqn)
reserve *(v.)* réserver
reserved réservé(e)
resourceful débrouillard(e)
respect *(v.)* respecter
responsibility responsabilité *(f.)*; **to have responsibilities** avoir des responsabilités
responsible responsable
rest *(v.)* se reposer
restaurant restaurant *(m.)*; — **menu** carte *(f.)*; — **bill** addition *(f.)*
restroom W.C. *(m.pl.)*; toilettes *(f.pl.)*
result résultat *(m.)*
retired person retraité *(m.)*, retraitée *(f.)*
return *(v.)* retourner
return retour *(m.)*
revolver revolver *(m.)*
rice riz *(m.)*
rich riche
ride a bicycle *(v.)* aller en vélo, faire du vélo
right droit(e), vrai(e); **to the** — **(of)** à droite (de); — **away** tout de suite
ring *(v.)* sonner
retire *(v.)* prendre la retraite
river rivière *(f.)*; — **(major)** fleuve *(m.)*
road route *(f.)*
roast rôti *(m.)*
robber voleur *(m.)*, voleuse *(f.)*
rock (music) rock *(m.)*
Roman romaine(e)
romantic romantique
romantic movie film d'amour *(m.)*
roof toit *(m.)*
room salle *(f.)*, place *(f.)*, pièce *(f.)*
roommate camarade de chambre *(m. ou f.)*
rose-colored rose
rude mal élevé(e); grossier, grossière
rug (area) tapis *(m.)*
run *(v.)* courir, diriger; — **errands** faire les courses
Russia Russie *(f.)*
Russian russe

S

sack sac *(m.)*

sad triste
sailboat bateau à voile *(m.)*
salad salade *(f.)*
salami saucisson *(m.)*
salary salaire *(m.)*
sale solde *(f.)* **to be on** — être en solde
salesperson vendeur *(m.)*, vendeuse *(f.)*
salmon saumon *(m.)*
salt sel *(m.)*
salted salé(e)
salty salé(e)
same même
sand sable *(m.)*
sandal sandale *(f.)*
sandwich sandwich *(m.)*
Santa Claus le Père Noël
satisfied (with) satisfait(e) (de)
Saturday samedi *(m.)*
sauce sauce *(f.)*
save money faire des économies
say *(v.)* dire
scar cicatrice *(f.)*
scare *(v.)* faire peur (à)
scary effrayant(e)
scenery paysage *(m.)*
school école *(f.)*
science fiction movie film de science-
    fiction *(m.)*
sciences sciences *(f.pl.)*
scientific scientifique
scientist chercheur *(m.)*
scream *(v.)* crier
scream cri *(m.)*
scuba diving plongée sous-marine *(f.)*
sea mer *(f.)*
search (for) *(v.)* chercher
season saison *(f.)*
seat place *(f.)*
seated assis(e)
secondary school-leaving exam
    baccalauréat *(m.)*
secret secret *(m.)*
secretary secrétaire *(m. ou f.)*
section (newspaper, magazine) rubrique
    (f.)
security sécurité *(f.)*
see *(v.)* voir; — **you soon** à bientôt; —
    you tomorrow à demain
seem *(v.)* avoir l'air (+ adj.), (de + inf.)
selfish égoïste
sell *(v.)* vendre
send *(v.)* envoyer
Senegal Sénégal *(m.)*
Senegalese sénégalais(e)
sensible raisonnable
separate *(v.)* se séparer
September septembre *(m.)*
series série *(f.)*
serious grave; sérieux, sérieuse
serving dish plat *(m.)*

set the table *(v.)* mettre la table
seven sept
seventeen dix-sept
seventy soixante-dix
shampoo shampooing *(m.)*
shape (to be in —) être en forme
share *(v.)* partager
shave (oneself) *(v.)* se raser; — **(someone
    else)** raser
sheet of paper feuille de papier *(f.)*
shelf étagère *(f.)*
shine *(v.)* briller
shirt (man's) chemise *(f.)*, **(woman's)**
    chemisier *(m.)*
shoe chaussure *(f.)*
shoot (someone) *(v.)* tirer (sur qqn)
shopkeeper commerçant *(m.)*,
    commerçante *(f.)*
shopping (to go —) faire les magasins
short court(e), petit(e)
shorts (pair of) short *(m.)*; **boxer** —
    caleçon *(m.)*
shot coup de feu *(m.)*
shout *(v.)* crier
shout cri *(m.)*
show *(v.)* montrer
show (television) émission *(f.)*; **news** —
    magazine d'information *(m.)*
shower douche *(f.)*
shrimp crevette *(f.)*
shutters volets *(m.pl.)*
shy timide
sick malade
sickness maladie *(f.)*
silverware couvert *(m.)*
simple simple
sing *(v.)* chanter
singer chanteur *(m.)*, chanteuse *(f.)*
single célibataire
sink lavabo *(m.)*; **kitchen** — évier *(m.)*
sir Monsieur *(m.)*
sister sœur *(f.)*
sister-in-law belle-sœur *(f.)*
sitting down assis(e)
situation situation *(f.)*
six six
sixteen seize
sixty soixante
ski *(v.)* faire du ski, skier
ski jacket parka *(f.)*, anorak *(m.)*
skiing ski *(m.)*
skin peau *(f.)*
skirt jupe *(f.)*
sky ciel *(m.)*
sleep *(v.)* dormir
sleep sommeil *(m.)*
sleepy (to be —) avoir sommeil
slice (of) tranche (de) *(f.)*
slim mince
slow lent(e)

slowly lentement
small petit(e)
smart intelligent(e)
smile *(v.)* sourire
smoke *(v.)* fumer
snack (afternoon) goûter *(m.)*; **to have a**
    — prendre (un petit) quelque chose
sneakers tennis *(m.pl.)*
sneeze *(v.)* éternuer
snow *(v.)* neiger
snow neige *(f.)*
so alors, si; — **do I** moi aussi; — **that**
    pour que + subjonctif
soap savon *(m.)*; — **opera** feuilleton *(m.)*
soccer football *(m.)*; **to play** — jouer au
    football
sociable sociable
social social, sociale, sociaux, sociales
society société *(f.)*
sociology sociologie *(f.)*
sock chaussette *(f.)*
solitude solitude *(f.)*
some quelque
someone quelqu'un; — **(interesting)**
    quelqu'un (d'intéressant)
something quelque chose; —
    (interesting) quelque chose
    (d'intéressant)
sometimes parfois, quelquefois
son fils *(m.)*
son-in-law beau-fils *(m.)*, gendre *(m.)*
song chanson *(f.)*
soup (tomato) soupe (aux tomates) *(f.)*;
    — **plate** assiette à soupe *(f.)*; — **spoon**
    cuillère à soupe *(f.)*
South America Amérique du Sud *(f.)*
south sud *(m.)*
souvenir souvenir *(m.)*
spaghetti pâtes *(f.pl.)*
Spain Espagne *(f.)*
Spanish espagnol(e)
speak *(v.)* parler
specialty spécialité *(f.)*
spend (money) *(v.)* dépenser; **(time)**
    passer
spill over *(v.)* déborder
spinach épinards *(m.pl.)*
spirituality spiritualité *(f.)*
spoiled (person) gâté(e)
spoon cuillère *(f.)*
sport coat veste *(f.)*
sport(s) sport *(m.)*
spot endroit *(m.)*
sprain *(v.)* se fouler
spring printemps *(m.)*
square (town) place *(f.)*
stage étape *(f.)*
staircase escalier *(m.)*
stairs escalier *(m.)*
stamp timbre *(m.)*

star étoile *(f.)*
start (to) *(v.)* commencer (à + inf.)
state état *(m.)*
stay (someplace) *(v.)* rester; — **home** *(v.)* rester à la maison
steak steak *(m.)*
steal *(v.)* voler
step étape *(f.)*
stepbrother demi-frère *(m.)*
stepdaughter belle-fille *(f.)*
stepfather beau-père *(m.)*
stepmother belle-mère *(f.)*
stepsister demi-sœur *(f.)*
stepson beau-fils *(m.)*
stereo chaîne hi-fi *(f.)*
steward steward *(m.)*
stewardess hôtesse de l'air *(f.)*
still encore
stomach estomac *(m.)*, ventre *(m.)*
stop *(v.)* arrêter; — **by** passer (par); — **oneself** s'arrêter
stop étape *(f.)*
store magasin *(m.)*
story histoire *(f.)*; **(television) to do a story (on)** faire un reportage (sur)
stove cuisinière *(f.)*
straight (tidy) en ordre
straight (ahead) tout droit
straighten up *(v.)* ranger
strange bizarre
stranger étranger, étrangère
strawberry fraise *(f.)*
stream rivière *(f.)*
street rue *(f.)*
stressed stressé(e)
strict sévère
strong fort(e)
stubborn têtu(e)
student étudiant(e); **to be a — in...** être étudiant en...
study *(v.)* étudier
stuff affaires *(f.pl.)*
stupid bête
subway métro *(m.)*; — **station** station de métro *(f.)*
succeed *(v.)* réussir (à + inf.)
suffer *(v.)* souffrir
sugar sucre *(m.)*
suit (man's) costume *(m.)*; — **(woman's)** tailleur *(m.)*
suitcase valise *(f.)*
summary résumé *(m.)*
summer été *(m.)*; — **camp** colonie de vacances *(f.)*
sun soleil *(m.)*
sunburn coup de soleil *(m.)*
Sunday dimanche *(m.)*
sunglasses lunettes de soleil *(f.pl.)*
sunny ensoleillé(e)

suntan oil/lotion huile solaire *(f.)*
supermarket supermarché *(m.)*
supplementary supplémentaire
sure sûr(e)
surfing (to go) faire du surf
surprise *(v.)* surprendre
surrounded (by) entouré(e) (de)
suspect suspect *(m.)*
sweater pull *(m.)*
sweatsuit survêtement *(m.)*
sweet (food) sucré(e)
swim *(v.)* faire de la natation, nager
swimming natation *(f.)*; — **pool** piscine *(f.)*
swimsuit maillot de bain *(m.)*
Swiss suisse
Switzerland Suisse *(f.)*
symptom symptôme *(m.)*

T

T-shirt tee-shirt *(m.)*
table table *(f.)*; — **of contents (magazine)** sommaire *(m.)*
tablecloth nappe *(f.)*
tablespoon cuillère à soupe *(f.)*
Tahiti Tahiti
Tahitian tahitien, tahitienne
take *(v.)* prendre, emmener **(someone somewhere)**, emporter **(something somewhere)**; — **a bath** prendre un bain; — **a course** suivre un cours; — **a nap** faire la sieste; — **a shower** prendre une douche; — **a test** passer un examen; — **a trip** faire un voyage; — **a walk** faire une promenade, se promener; — **care of** s'occuper (de), soigner; — **care of oneself** se soigner; — **the elevator up/down** monter/descendre en ascenseur; — **the stairs up/down** monter/descendre par l'escalier
talk *(v.)* parler
talkative bavard(e)
tall (person) grand(e)
tan *(v.)* bronzer
tan, tanned bronzé(e)
taste goût *(m.)*
taxi taxi *(m.)*
tea thé *(m.)*
teacher professeur *(m.)*; — **(grade school)** instituteur *(m.)*, institutrice *(f.)*
team équipe *(f.)*
teaspoon petite cuillère *(f.)*
teenager adolescent *(m.)*, adolescente *(f.)*
telephone (someone) *(v.)* téléphoner (à qqn)

telephone téléphone *(m.)*; — **book** annuaire (des téléphones) *(m.)*; — **booth** cabine téléphonique *(f.)*; — **number** numéro (de téléphone) *(m.)*; **cellular** — téléphone mobile *(m.)*; **portable** — téléphone sans fil *(m.)*
television télévision *(f.)*; — **station** chaîne *(f.)*; — **/radio schedule** programme *(m.)*
tell *(v.)* dire; — **(a story)** raconter
ten dix
tennis tennis *(m.)*; **to play** — jouer au tennis
tennis (golf) shirt polo *(m.)*
terrace terrasse *(f.)*
terrible terrible
terrorism terrorisme *(m.)*
test examen *(m.)*
Texas Texas *(m.)*
thank you merci
that ça; — **depends** ça dépend; — **hurts** ça fait mal; — **scares me** ça me fait peur; **that's all** c'est tout; **that's it, done** ça y est; **that's true** c'est vrai; **that's (it's) too bad** c'est dommage; **that's for sure** c'est sûr
that que, qui
theater théâtre *(m.)*
then ensuite; — **(and then)** puis (et puis)
there! tiens!
there, here là
there is/are il y a
therefore donc
they on; ils; elles
thief voleur *(m.)*, voleuse *(f.)*
thin mince
thing chose *(f.)*
think (about) *(v.)* réfléchir (à + qqch.), penser (à/de); — **(that)** penser (que); — **so** penser que oui
thirst soif *(f.)*
thirteen treize
thirty trente
this, that / these, those ce, cet, cette / ces
thousand mille
three trois
through par
thunderstorm orage *(m.)*
Thursday jeudi *(m.)*
thus donc
ticket (bus or subway) ticket *(m.)*; — **(round trip, one way)** billet (aller-retour, simple) *(m.)*; — **window** guichet *(m.)*
tie cravate *(f.)*
tights collant *(m.)*
time heure *(f.)*; temps *(m.)*; fois *(f.)*; **how many times (a day, a week...)** combien de fois (par jour, par semaine)...

time off congé *(m.)*
timed race course contre la montre *(f.)*
tip pourboire *(m.);* — included service compris
tired fatigué(e)
tiring fatigant(e)
tissue mouchoir *(m.)* (en papier)
title titre *(m.)*
to à; — /on the left (of) à gauche (de); — /on the right (of) à droite (de)
tobacco shop bureau de tabac *(m.)*
today aujourd'hui
together ensemble
toilet toilettes *(f.pl.),* W. C. *(m.pl.);* — article article de toilette *(m.)*
tomato tomate *(f.)*
tomorrow demain
too (too much) trop
too much (of) trop (de)
tooth dent *(f.)*
toothbrush brosse à dents *(f.)*
toothpaste dentifrice *(m.)*
top floor dernier étage *(m.)*
tough dur(e)
tour (package) voyage organisé *(m.)*
tourist touriste *(m. ou f.)*
towel (bath) serviette de bain *(f.)*
town ville *(f.)*
trade métier *(m.)*
traditional traditionnel, traditionnelle
tragic tragique
train train *(m.);* — compartment compartiment *(m.);* — station gare *(f.)*
travel *(v.)* voyager
traveler's check chèque de voyage *(m.)*
treat *(v.)* (illness) soigner; — oneself (take care of oneself) se soigner
tree arbre *(m.)*
trip voyage *(m.);* — around the world tour du monde *(m.)*
truck camion *(m.)*
true vrai(e)
truth vérité *(f.)*
try (to) *(v.)* essayer (de + inf.)
Tuesday mardi *(m.)*
tuna thon *(m.)*
turkey dinde *(f.)*
turn *(v.)* tourner
twenty vingt *(m.)*
twin jumeau, jumelle, jumeaux, jumelles
two deux
type *(v.)* taper à la machine
typewriter machine à écrire *(f.)*
typical typique

U

ugly laid(e)
umbrella parapluie *(m.)*
uncle oncle *(m.)*

under sous
underground sous-sol *(m.)*
underpants (women's) slip *(m.)*
understand *(v.)* comprendre
understanding compréhensif, compréhensive
underwear sous-vêtements *(m.pl.)*
undress *(v.)* (someone else) déshabiller; — (get undressed) se déshabiller
unemployed person chômeur *(m.),* chômeuse *(f.);* to be — être au chômage
unemployment chômage *(m.)*
unfair injuste
unfaithful infidèle
unfortunately malheureusement
unhappily malheureusement
unhappy malheureux, malheureuse
unhealthy mauvais(e) pour la santé
United States États-Unis *(m.pl.);* in the — aux États-Unis
university (noun) université *(f.)*
university (adj.) universitaire
unluckily malheureusement
unmarried célibataire
until jusqu'à
upstairs en *haut
use *(v.)* utiliser
usually d'habitude

V

vacation vacances *(f.pl.)*
vacuum *(v.)* passer l'aspirateur
vanilla vanille *(f.)*
variety show émission de variétés *(f.)*
vegetable légume *(m.)*
vegetarian végétarien, végétarienne
verb verbe *(m.)*
verify *(v.)* vérifier
very très; — good très bien
victim victime *(f.)*
videocassette recorder magnétoscope *(m.)*
video tape cassette vidéo *(f.)*
village (rural) village *(m.)*
violin violon *(m.);* to play the — jouer du violon
violence violence *(f.)*
violent violent(e)
visit (a person) *(v.)* rendre visite à; — (a place) visiter

W

wage salaire *(m.);* (French) minimum — SMIC *(m.)*
wait (for) *(v.)* attendre
waiter serveur *(m.)*

waitress serveuse *(f.)*
wake (someone up) *(v.)* réveiller
wake up (oneself) *(v.)* se réveiller
walk *(v.)* marcher; — (a dog, for example) promener; — (for exercise) faire de la marche; — to aller à pied à (au, en)
walk promenade *(f.);* to take a — faire une promenade, se promener
walking marche *(f.)*
walkman baladeur *(m.)*
wall mur *(m.)*
want *(v.)* vouloir
war guerre *(f.)*
wardrobe armoire *(f.)*
warm chaud(e); it's — (weather) il fait chaud; to be — avoir chaud
wash *(v.)* laver; — (oneself) se laver
washcloth gant de toilette *(m.)*
washing machine lave-linge *(m.)*
wastepaper basket corbeille à papier *(f.)*
water eau *(f.)*
we'll see on verra
weak fragile
wealth richesse *(f.)*
weapon arme *(f.)*
wear *(v.)* mettre, porter
weather temps *(m.);* — forecast météo *(f.);* what's the — like? quel temps fait-il?
Wednesday mercredi *(m.)*
week semaine *(f.)*
weekend week-end *(m.)*
weird bizarre
well bien; — dressed bien habillé(e); — adjusted équilibré(e); — behaved sage; — mannered bien élevé(e); — paid bien payé(e)
west ouest *(m.)*
western (movie) western *(m.)*
what quel, quelle, quels, quelles, que, quoi; what . . . ? qu'est-ce que... ?; — about you? et toi?, et vous?; — did you say? comment?; — happened? qu'est-ce qui s'est passé?; — is Jean like? comment est Jean?; — is there to do? qu'est-ce qu'il y a à faire?; — is this/that? qu'est-ce que c'est?; — kind/sort of . . . ? quelle sorte de... ?; — time is it? quelle heure est-il?; —'s the weather like? quel temps fait-il? —'s happening? qu'est-ce qui se passe?; —'s the date today? quelle est la date aujourd'hui? —'s the matter with you? qu'est-ce que vous avez?; —'s your name? comment t'appelles-tu? *(fam.);* comment vous appelez-vous?
when quand
where où; — is the restroom? où sont les toilettes?
which quel, quelle, quels, quelles
while pendant que

white blanc, blanche
who qui; **who . . . ?** qui... ?, qui est-ce que?
whom? qui est-ce que?
whose dont; — **is it?** c'est à qui?
why pourquoi
widow veuve *(f.)*
widowed *(adj.)* veuf, veuve
widower veuf *(m.)*
wife femme *(f.);* — **and mother** mère de famille *(f.)*
win *(v.)* gagner
window fenêtre *(f.)*
windsurf *(v.)* faire de la planche à voile
wine vin *(m.)*
winter hiver *(m.)*
wipe one's nose *(v.)* se moucher
wish *(v.)* vouloir
with avec
within dans
without sans

witness témoin *(m.)*
woman femme *(f.)*
wonder *(v.)* se demander
wonderful merveilleux, merveilleuse
work travail *(m.);* **to look for** — chercher du travail
work *(v.)* travailler; — **hard** travailler dur
worker (**blue collar**) ouvrier *(m.),* ouvrière *(f.)*
workshop atelier *(m.)*
world monde *(m.)*
worried inquiet, inquiète
worry souci *(m.)*
wounded blessé(e)
wrist poignet *(m.)*
wristwatch montre *(f.)*
write *(v.)* écrire; — **a note to someone** écrire un mot à qqn
writer écrivain *(m.)*

Y

yard jardin *(m.)*
year an *(m.),* année *(f.)*
yellow jaune
yes oui; (**on the contrary**) si
yesterday hier
yet déjà
yogurt yaourt *(m.)*
you have to + **inf.** il faut + inf.
young jeune; — **people** jeunes *(m.pl.)*
youngest le/la plus jeune

Z

zero zéro *(m.)*
zoo zoo *(m.)*

Index

Index

Credits

Text/Realia Credits

p. 3, *Programmes et Fréquences*, nº 59, 1995, Radio France Internationale / **p. 24,** Dessin "Bonne Fête", *Le Pèlerin*, nº 5280, 12 février 1984, Bayard Presse; "Pour vos futurs [petits-] enfants, quel prénom?" *L'Avenir*, nº 1, juillet-août 1994 / **p. 30,** "Les 50 hommes les plus influents de la planète", *Le Nouvel Observateur*, nº 1574, 5-11 janvier 1995 / **p. 46,** Montage de sondages, *Figaro-Magazine*, 22 oct. 1988 / **p. 50,** La Maison de Valérie, *Catalogue Maison et Loisirs*, automne-hiver 94-95 / **p. 65,** *Catalogue Demain Étudiant*, Université Libre de Bruxelles, janvier 1990 / **p. 67,** Courtesy of Hôtel des Tuileries / **p. 68,** Plan de Paris, Office de tourisme de Paris / **pp. 74-75,** Valberg, Office de tourisme; Photographers: B. Giani; JL. Petit; JC. Fayet; Ch. A. Ginesy; D. Faure; Rossignol: C. Pedrotti, 1995-1996 / **p. 88,** Christophe Lambert: «L'important, c'est la passion» (excerpt), *Marie-Claire*, novembre 1987, p. 350 / **p. 90,** "Du rock, du rap... mais en français", *Clés de l'Actualité Junior*, nº 48, 18-24 janvier 1996. / **pp. 92-93,** "30 Ans de Musiques Africaines pour les 10 ans d'Africa N° 1", *Jeune Afrique Économique*, nº 137, novembre 1990 / **p. 97,** "Festiv d'été", *Les Clés de l'Actualité*, nº 162/163, 6-19 juillet 1995, Milan Presse / **p. 98,** "La fête du travail", Sophie Cindel, *Les Clés de l'Actualité Junior*, nº 16, 27 avril-3 mai 1995, Milan Presse; "Pâques, une fête pour deux religions", *Les Clés de l'Actualité Junior*, nº 15, 20-26 avril 1995, Milan Presse; "La Fête de l'Action de Grâce", texte de Michel Cailloux, illustration de Mohamed Danawi, © *Vidéo-Presse*, vol. XXIV, nº 2, p. 12, octobre 1994, Médiaspaul; "La fête du travail" de Michel Cailloux, © *Vidéo-Presse*, vol. XXIV, nº 1, p. 12, septembre 1994, Médiaspaul / **p. 99,** Le Sénégal, from *Jet Tours*, 1 avril-31 octobre 1995, Air France; "Souleymane Keita, le peintre de Gorée", *Diagonales*, nº 33, février 1995; Page d'écriture, Jacques Prévert, *Paroles*, 1942, © Éditions Gallimard / **p. 103,** *Nouvel Observateur*, nº 1532, 17-23 mars 1994 / **p. 114,** "Plus on est jeune, plus on est grand" in *Francoscopie 1995*, p. 67, © Direction de la communication de Renault / **p. 115,** "Quelles sont les principales qualites / principaux defauts des Francais?", *Figaro-Magazine*, 22 oct. 1988, pp. 172-173 / **p. 123,** "Le difficile passage à la vie adulte", *Les Clés de l'Actualité*, nº 167, 31 août-6 septembre 1995, Milan Presse / **p. 125,** *Guide des Jeunes*, Service d'Information et de diffusion, Premier Ministre, Albin Michel, 1983 / **p. 131** Office de Tourisme de Versailles / **p. 153,** in *Francoscopie 1995*, p. 418, © Madame Figaro/Sofres / **pp. 154-155,** "L'art de vivre ses loisirs", *L'Express*, 4 janvier 1996; photographer: Aldo Soares / **pp. 160-161,** "À qui va-t-il ressembler?", *Famili*, nº 30, août 1995 / **p. 179,** "Trois générations et un budget", *Nouvel Observateur*, 14-20 octobre 1993 / **pp. 180-181,** "La famille wolof", Éditions Karthala, 22-24 boulevard Arago, 75013 Paris, 1985 / **p. 186,** "Une empreinte unique...", *Forces*, nº 88, hiver 1990; carte de Montréal, Saintonge Vision Design, Tourisme Québec / **p. 194,** "Les week-ends des Francais", in *Francoscopie 1995*, p. 419, © Madame Figaro/Sofres / **p. 203,** in *Francoscopie 1995*, p. 412, © Secodip/Openers / **p. 204,** "Qu'est-ce qui vous fait sortir?", *Les Clés de l'Actualité*, nº 149 / **p. 207,** "Monsieur Dubois", *Les Clés de l'Actualité Junior*, nº 39, p. 4, 9-15 novembre 1995, Milan Presse; "Le Québec depuis 1534", Les Clés de l'Actualité Junior, nº 39, p. 3, 9-15 novembre 1995, Milan Presse; "Tout sur la famille", de Francine Gagnon, © *Vidéo-Presse*, vol. XXIV, nº 4, décembre 1994, Médiaspaul / **p. 208,** "La famille? Pas de problème!", *L'Actualité*, juillet 1994, Magazines MacLean Hunter / **p. 209,** Québec, from *Voyages Québec à la carte*, p. 5; "De temps en temps, moi, j'ai les bleus", Angèle Arseneault; "Chanter le français", *Les Clés de l'Actualité Junior*, nº 39, 9-15 novembre 1995, p. 3, Milan Presse / **pp. 212-213,** "Accueil en pays thiernois", Auberge des Quatre Chemins / **p. 221,** "Un an de nourriture", in *Francoscopie 1995*, p. 181, © INSEE / **pp. 232-233,** *Cuisine sénégalaise d'hier et d'aujourd'hui*, Éditions Papeterie WAKHATILENE, 1989 / **p. 238,** Courtesy of Tricotage Toulousain / **p. 248,** "Palmarès 1993 (femmes)" & "Palmarès 1993 (hommes)", in *Francoscopie*

1995, p. 76, © CTCOE / **pp. 256-257,** "Chic et propre pour pas cher", *L'Express*, 4 janvier 1996; photographer: Aldo Soares / **p. 258,** Gérard Mermet, *Francoscopie 1995*, © Larousse 1994, p. 76; illustrations from *Les 3 Suisses–Belgique*, automne-hiver 1987 and *La Redoute*, printemps-été 1994 / **pp. 264-265,** "Les couleurs de la France", © Éditions le Moniteur / **pp. 282 & 283,** "Dessine-moi une maison", *L'Express*, 4 janvier 1996; photographer: Aldo Soares / **p. 285,** Courtesy of Castorama: Author: Dominique Machabert; Photographer: Joël Damase; Title: "Découvrir le Puy-de-Dôme"; Editor: Conjoncture / **pp. 290-291,** Courtesy of Canon France / **p. 298,** Adapté de *Francoscopie 1995*, © Tribune/Sofres / **p. 299,** Reproduit avec permission. Extrait de "Une école pas comme les autres" de Daniel Pérusse, *Sélection*, p. 37, octobre 1987, © 1987, par Périodiques Reader's Digest Limitée, Montréal, Québec / **p. 310,** "La revanche d'un cancre", *Les Clés de l'Actualité*, 17-23 février 1994, Milan Presse / **p. 312,** "Le temps perdu", Jacques Prévert, *Paroles*, 1942, © Éditions Gallimard / **p. 315,** "Quand elles ont obtenu?", *Les Clés de l'Actualité*, nº 144, 2-8 mars 1995, Milan Presse; "Un combat", *Les Clés de l'Actualité*, nº 167, 31 août-6 septembre 1995, Milan Presse; "Ce que les femmes ont acquis en France", *L'Actualité*, nº 95, 3-9 mars 1994, Milan Presse / **p. 316,** "Hommage: une femme au Panthéon", *Les Clés de l'Actualité Junior*, nº 15, 20-26 avril 1995, p. 4, Milan Presse; "Masculin et Féminin au Québec", *Diagonales*, nº 33, p. 11, février 1995; Gazette Officielle du Québec, from Féminin, Guide de Féminisation des titres de fonction et des textes, Direction des Services Linguistiques de l'Office de la Langue Française / **p. 317,** "Zap Mama", *Diagonales*, nº 26, avril 1993, p. 14; 317, "Pour toi mon amour", Jacques Prévert, *Paroles*, 1942, © Éditions Gallimard; "Déjeuner du matin", Jacques Prévert, *Paroles*, 1942, © Éditions Gallimard / **p. 331,** "Menu Hippopotamus", Courtesy of Hippo gestion, Paris / **pp. 338-339,** *T.D.C.*, nº 438, 11 février 1987, CNDP / **p. 348,** postcard of La Baule, Jack Editions d'Art, Louannec / **p. 351,** postcard of La Baule, Jack Editions d'Art, Louannec / **p. 356,** A. *Notre Temps*, nº 308, août 1995, Bayard Presse; B. *Guide Cuisine*, nº 50, août 1995, Prisma Presse; C. *L'auto journal*, numéro spécial 1995; D. *L'Équipe Magazine*, nº 655, 10 sept. 1994; E. *Mieux Vivre Votre Argent*, nº 183, septembre 1995; F. *Géo*, nº 186, août 1994; G. *Le Point*, nº 1217, 13 janv. 1996; H. *Nouvel Observateur*, nº 1633, 22-28 février 1996; I. *Paris Match*, nº 2421, Scoop, service de diffusion d'articles; J. Notre Histoire, nº 124; K. *Femme Actuelle*, nº 566, 31 juillet-6 août 1995; L. *On lines micro!*, nº 1, juillet-août 1995 / **p. 366** Ministère des PTT Direction Générale des Télécommunications, Paris / **pp. 368-369,** Courtesy of France-Télécom / **p. 370,** Courtesy of Hertz France, 1996 / **p. 383,** Gérard Mermet, *Francoscopie 1995*, © Larousse 1994, p. 176 / **pp. 393 & 394,** Œuvres Sociales, Municipalite de Clermont / **p. 395,** "Travailler à temps partiel", *Famili*, nº 30, août 1995 / **p. 396,** Gérard Mermet, *Francoscopie 1995*, © Larousse 1994, and © OCDE / **p. 401,** Coton Chipie / **p. 417,** Gérard Mermet, *Francoscopie 1995*, © Larousse 1994, pp. 138-139 / **p. 423,** "Khalid El Quandili", *Le Nouvel Observateur*, nº 1517, 2-8 décembre 1993; "Près de 100.000", *Les Clés de l'Actualité*, nº 129, 17-23 novembre 1994, Milan Presse; "Djamel, Farouk, Bouzid", *Le Nouvel Observateur*, nº 1517, 2-8 décembre 1993, p. 10 / **p. 424,** "Les Asiatiques d'ici" de LamVan Be, © *Vidéo-Presse*, vol. XXIII, février 1994, pp. 46-49, Médiaspaul / **p. 425,** "Les Vacances de Simon", *Nord Sud, Portraits de Famille*, Angèle Kingué, Tête Bêche, Éditions Hurtebise HMH Ltée, 1993 ; "La maison de Natyk", by Mohammed Dib, from *Feu beau feu*, Éditions du Seuil / **pp. 428-429,** Sempé, "La Grande Panique", © Galerie Martine Gossieaux / **p. 430,** Courtesy of TF1, France 2, France 3, Canal +, Arte, M6 / **p. 437,** *Télé 7 Jours*, nº 1838, 19-25 août 1995 / **pp. 439 & 450-451,** *TV Plus*, vol. 18, nº 1, 31 décembre-6 janvier 1995, Éditions Télémédia / **p. 452,** "Les jeunes préfèrent la radio", *Les Clés de l'Actualité*, nº 90, 27 janvier-2 février 1994, Milan Presse / **p. 458,** *Voyager*

Magazine, FNAC Voyages / **p. 473,** Source SNCF / **pp. 482 & 483,** *L'Actualité,* juillet 1994, Magazines MacLean Hunter / **p. 485,** Gérard Mermet, *Francoscopie 1995,* © Larousse 1994, p. 427 / **pp. 486-487,** "Rev' Vacances", *Voyager Magazine,* nº 57, décembre-janvier 1996, Les Éditions de Demain / **p. 493,** "Premier Salon des Vacances en France", photographer: Aline Perrier; *Détours en France,* nº 25, janvier-février 1996 / **p. 510,** dessin de Jacques Faizant, *Le Figaro Magazine,* p. 243, 22 oct. 1988; "Ce qu'ils visitent le plus chez nous", de Jean Creiser avec illustration de A. Letoct et H. Quenelle, *Le Figaro-Magazine,* pp. 244-245, 22 oct. 1988 /

pp. 512-513, Strasbourg, *Guide Voir France,* © Hachette, 1995 / **pp. 518-519,** "Pourquoi 88% des Français se déclarent heureux", *Le Nouvel Observateur,* nº 1496, 8-14 juillet 1993 / **p. 526,** "Les grandes causes", in *Francoscopie,* p. 159, © Ministère de la Jeunesse et des Sports/Sofres, avril 1993 / **p. 527,** "D'une génération à l'autre", *Le Nouvel Observateur,* nº 1496, 8-14 juillet 1993 / **p. 536,** "Français, comme vous avez changé", *L'Express,* 4 janvier 1996; photographer: Aldo Soares / **p. 538,** "Vie morose, ou vie en rose", *Les Clés de l'Actualité,* nº 175, 26 octobre-1 novembre 1995, Milan Presse

Photo Credits

p. 1, Greg Meadors/Stock, Boston, **p. 4,** (T) © R. Lucas/The Image Works, (MR) Owen Franken, (BL) Owen Franken / **p. 5,** (T) (B) Owen Franken / **p. 8,** (TL) Boccon-Gibod/SIPA Press, (TR) Peter Menzel/Stock, Boston, (BL) Malanca/Sipa Press, (BR) © Alain Evrard/Liaison Int. / **p. 9,** (TL) © John Coletti/The Picture Cube, Inc., (BR) Jonathan Stark, Heinle & Heinle / **p. 13,** (TL) © Ulrike Welsch, (TR) © Beryl Goldberg Photography, (BL) © Ulrike Welsch, (BR) Jonathan Stark, Heinle & Heinle / **p. 16,** (BL) © Beryl Goldberg Photography, (BR) Claude Toussaint Tournier / **p. 23,** Jonathan Stark, Heinle & Heinle / **p. 25,** Isabelle Kaplan / **p. 29,** © Beryl Goldberg Photography / **p. 30,** Courtesy of NASA / **p. 33,** (TL) (TM) The Bettman Archive, Inc., (TR) Archive Photos, (ML) (MCL), Jonathan Stark, Heinle & Heinle, (MCR)© R. Lucas/The Image Works, (MR) © R. Lucas/The Image Works, (BL) Jonathan Stark, Heinle & Heinle, (BML) © Ulrike Welsch, (BMR) © Ulrike Welsch, (BR) Jonathan Stark, Heinle & Heinle / **p. 39,** Owen Franken / **p. 43,** (L) Owen Franken, (M) Jonathan Stark, Heinle & Heinle, (R) Cary Wolinsky/Stock, Boston / **p. 49,** © Ulrike Welsch / **p. 61,** (TL) © Ulrike Welsch, (TR) © Daemmrich/The Image Works, (BL) Creg Meadors/Stock, Boston, (BR) Bob Daemmrich/Stock, Boston / **p. 67,** © Stuart Cohen / **p. 73,** © Ulrike Welsch / **p. 76,** Rhoda Sidney/Stock, Boston / **p. 84,** (TR) Lee Page/© Tony Stone Images / **p. 89,** (B) Clergue/Sipa Press / **p. 90,** (L) M. Rosenstiehl/Sygma, (R) J. Bourguet/Sygma / **p. 98,** (TR) Franco Origlia/Sygma / **p. 99,** (BR) Valérie Brierley / **p. 101,** © Beryl Goldberg Photography / **p. 107,** (M) Charly Nes/Liaison, Int. / **p. 108,** (BM) © Lee Snider/The Image Works / **p. 110,** (T) © R. Lucas/The Image Works, (B) Jonathan Stark, Heinle & Heinle / **p. 114,** (BL), Claude Toussaint Tournier / **p. 115,** (TL) (TR) Claude Toussaint Tournier, (BL) Jonathan Stark, Heinle & Heinle, (BR) © Beryl Goldberg Photography / **p. 119,** (B) © Philippe Gontier/The Image Works / **p. 125,** (TR) © Ermakoff/The Image Works, (MR) Raphael Gaillarde/Gamma Liaison, (BR) David Simson/Stock, Boston, (BL) Jonathan Stark, Heinle & Heinle / **p. 129,** Claude Toussaint Tournier / **p. 134,** (TL) David Simson/Stock, Boston, (TR) © Thierry Prat/Sygma / **p. 136,** (T) © Lee Snider/The Image Works, (M) © Lee Snider/The Image Works, (B) © J. Messerschmidt/The Picture Cube / **p. 140,** Isabelle Kaplan / **p. 141,** Isabelle Kaplan / **p. 142,** Claude Toussaint Tournier / **p. 143,** (TR) Jonathan Stark, Heinle & Heinle, (ML) © Bill Bachmann/Stock Boston / **p. 151,** Jonathan Stark, Heinle & Heinle / **p. 151,** © 1986 Comstock / **p. 153,** (T) David Simson/Stock, Boston, (M) © Frank White/Liaison International (B) Jonathan Stark, Heinle & Heinle Photo Video Specialist / **p. 159,** Jonathan Stark, Heinle & Heinle / **p. 168,** © Apeiron/The Bettmann Archive, Inc. / **p. 170,** (all) Claude Toussaint Tournier / **p. 177,** Greg Meadors/Stock, Boston / **p. 180,** Isabelle Kaplan / **p. 185,** © Ermakoff/The Image Works / **p. 194,** Claude Toussaint Tournier / **p. 203,** (TL) © R. Aschentbrenner/Stock, Boston, (BL) © The Image Works, (TR) © Beryl Goldberg Photography, (BR) Jonathan Stark, Heinle & Heinle / **p. 207** (TL) The Bettmann Archive, (TR) Philippe Letelier/Gamma Liaison, (BR) Steve Liss/Gamma Liaison / **p. 208,** Jonathan Stark, Heinle & Heinle / **p. 209,** (TR) Jonathan Stark, Heinle & Heinle, (BL) E. Scorcelletti/Gamma / **p. 211,** Claude Toussaint Tournier / **p. 216,** Claude Toussaint Tournier / **p. 229,** Claude Toussaint Tournier / **p. 230,** Claude Toussaint Tournier / **p. 231,** (L) © Stuart Cohen/Comstock, (R) © Peter Menzel/Stock, Boston / **p. 234,** (B) Isabelle Kaplan / **p. 237,** © Ulrike Welsch / **p. 247,** (L) Jonathan Stark, Heinle & Heinle, (TM) Owen Franken/Stock Boston, (R) © Stuart Cohen/Comstock, (BM) Jonathan Stark, Heinle & Heinle / **p. 255,** Claude Toussaint Tournier / **p. 263,**

© Stuart Cohen/Comstock / **p. 267,** (T) Claude Toussaint Tournier, (B) © Ulrike Welsch / **p. 268,** Jonathan Stark, Heinle & Heinle / **p. 271,** (all) Claude Toussaint Tournier / **p. 286,** Isabelle Kaplan / **p. 289,** © Catherine Karnow/Woodfin Camp & Assoc. / **p. 298,** (all) Jonathan Stark, Heinle & Heinle / **p. 316,** Marc Tulane/Rapho / **p. 319,** © Ulrike Welsch / **p. 320,** © R. Lucas/The Image Works / **p. 321,** Isabelle Kaplan / **p. 322,** (TL) © Tony Freeman/PhotoEdit, (R) © Erica Lansher/Tony Stone Images, Inc., (BL) © David R. Frazier Photolibrary/Photo Researchers, Inc., (BM) Jonathan Stark, Heinle & Heinle, (BR) © Stuart Cohen / **p. 323,** Claude Toussaint Tournier / **p. 339,** Philippe Plailly / **p. 340,** Brian Seed/© Tony Stone Images, Inc. / **p. 345,** Jonathan Stark, Heinle & Heinle / **p. 346,** © Ulrike Welsch / **p. 347,** (TL) (BR) Claude Toussaint Tournier, (BL) Jonathan Stark, Heinle & Heinle / **p. 348,** (TR) Jonathan Stark, Heinle & Heinle, (TL) Isabelle Kaplan, (BL) Jonathan Stark, Heinle & Heinle, / **p. 349,** (T) Jonathan Stark, Heinle & Heinle, (M) © DeRichemond/The Image Works, (BR) Jonathan Stark, Heinle & Heinle / **p. 350,** Claude Toussaint Tournier / **p. 351,** Jonathan Stark, Heinle & Heinle / **p. 373,** © Ulrike Welsch / **p. 374,** (TR) © Ulrike Welsch, (BL) (BR) Jonathan Stark, Heinle & Heinle / **p. 375,** © Ulrike Welsch / **p. 392,** (T) © Ulrike Welsch, (B) © Richard Frieman/PhotoResearchers, Inc. / **p. 395,** (TL) David Young-Wolff/PhotoEdit, (ML) © Owen Franken, (MR) Jonathan Stark, Heinle & Heinle, (TR) © Robert Fried/Stock, Boston, (BL) © Owen Franken/Stock, Boston, (BR) Claude Toussaint Tournier / **p. 399,** Jonathan Stark, Heinle & Heinle / **p. 402,** (TL) Richard Pasley/Stock, Boston, (BR) Gamma Liaison / **p. 403,** (T) Glen Allison/© Tony Stone Images, (B) © Alexander Tsiaras/Stock, Boston / **p. 412,** Jonathan Stark, Heinle & Heinle / **p. 417,** (TL, TR, MR, B) © Ulrike Welsch, (ML) Gilbert Lan/Sygma / **p. 419,** (all) Jonathan Stark, Heinle & Heinle / **p. 421,** Simone Toussaint-Benoit / **p. 423,** (R) A. Ramey/Woodfin Camp & Assoc. / **p. 424,** (L) Jonathan Nourak/PhotoEdit, (M) Mike Yamashita, Woodfin Camp & Assoc., (R) A. Ramey, Woodfin Camp and Assoc. / **p. 427,** © Peter Menzel/Stock, Boston / **p. 457,** © Ulrike Welsch / **p. 460,** (BL) 1983 Robert Rath/Stock Boston, (BML) © Robert Fried 1995/Stock Boston, (BMR) Jonathan Stark, Heinle & Heinle, (BR) © David Simson/Stock, Boston / **p. 459,** (all) Jonathan Stark, Heinle & Heinle / **p. 461,** (ML) © Ulrike Welsch, (BR) Jonathan Stark, Heinle & Heinle / **p. 462,** (L) © Tony Stone Images, Inc. (BR) Joel Rogers/© Tony Stone Images, Inc. / **p. 463,** (ML) © David R. Austen/Stock Boston, (BR) © Sylvain Grandadam/Photo Researchers, Inc. / **p. 464,** (T) © Frank J. Staub/The Picture Cube, Inc., (M) © Mike McCabe/Tony Stone Images, Inc., (B) Claude Toussaint Tournier / **p. 465,** (ML) Monkmeyer Press/Press, (MR) © George Holton/Photo Researchers, Inc. / **p. 485,** (all) Jonathan Stark, Heinle & Heinle / **p. 491,** Eric Renard/© Tony Stone Images, Inc. / **p. 492,** (BL) © DeRichemonde/The Image Works, (M) Gamma/Figaro Magazine, (R) © Lee Snider/The Image Works / **p. 493,** (all) Aline Perrier / **p. 495,** (TL) (MR) Nicholas Raducanu, (BL) Beryl Goldberg Photography / **p. 496,** (B) © G. Rancinan/Sygma / **p. 497,** (T) © Patrick Forestier/Sygma, (ML) © Snider/The Image Works, (MR) © Snider/The Image Works, (BL) © G. Rancinan/Sygma / **p. 498,** (TL) © G. Rancinan/Sygma, (MR) © Jean Marc Barey/Photo Researchers, Inc., (BR) Mike Mazzaschi/Stock, Boston / **p. 499,** (TL) © G. Rancinan/Sygma, (TR) © David Simson/Stock, Boston, (BL) Jonathan Stark, Heinle & Heinle, (BR) © Gamma / **p. 502,** (L) © Lee Snider/The Image Works, (M) © Eric A. Wessman/Stock, Boston, (R) Jonathan Stark, Heinle & Heinle / **p. 517,** © Ulrike Welsch / **p. 519,** Ken Fisher, © Tony Stone Images, Inc.

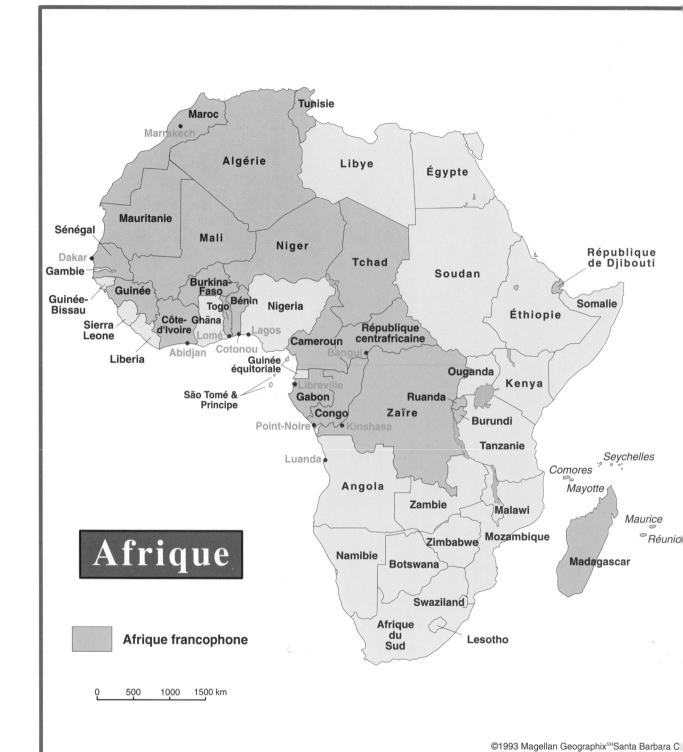

Afrique

Maroc
Marrakech
Algérie
Tunisie
Libye
Égypte
Mauritanie
Sénégal
Dakar
Gambie
Mali
Niger
Tchad
Soudan
République
de Djibouti
Guinée-
Bissau
Guinée
Burkina-
Faso
Togo
Bénin
Nigeria
Somalie
Éthiopie
Sierra
Leone
Côte-
d'Ivoire
Ghāna
Lomé
Lagos
Liberia
Abidjan
Cotonou
Cameroun
République
centrafricaine
Bangui
Ouganda
Kenya
Guinée
équitoriale
Libreville
Gabon
Ruanda
Burundi
São Tomé &
Principe
Congo
Zaïre
Point-Noire
Kinshasa
Tanzanie
Luanda
Seychelles
Comores
Mayotte
Angola
Zambie
Malawi
Maurice
Mozambique
Réunio
Zimbabwe
Madagascar
Namibie
Botswana
Swaziland
Afrique
du
Sud
Lesotho

Afrique francophone

0   500   1000   1500 km